Contents

[v]

Milton

COMPLETE POETRY & SELECTED PROSE

With English Metrical Translations
of the Latin, Greek and
Italian Poems

EDITED BY E. H. VISIAK

With a Foreword by the late Sir Arnold Wilson.

THE NONESUCH LIBRARY
1969

First Published 1938
Second Impression 1948
Third Impression 1952
Fourth Impression 1964
Fifth Impression 1969

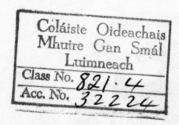

370 00513 9

PRINTED IN GREAT BRITAIN BY ROBERT MACLEHOSE AND CO. LTD
THE UNIVERSITY PRESS, GLASGOW

Milton

LATIN, GREEK AND ITALIAN POEMS:

CONTENTS

Foreword

THE liberties for which Milton strove are to-day "be-leaguer'd", and not only abroad; the causes he championed must be defended anew. His prose works, the vehicles of memorable polemical warfare, have too long been neglected; and are often quoted in a literary rather than in a political context. A few random sentences suffice to show their relevance to contemporary events.

"Error supports Custome, Custome count'nances Error. And these two between them would persecute and chase away all truth and solid wisdome." How hard is the way of him "who shall indeavour the amendment of any old neglected grievance in Church or State." He will be "boorded presently by the ruder sort . . . with a thousand idle descants and surmises." "Honest liberty is the greatest foe to dishonest licence." "He who wisely would restrain the reasonable Soul of man within due bounds, must first himself know perfectly, how far the territory and dominion extends of just and honest liberty." "As little must he offer to bind that which God hath loos'n'd, as to loos'n that which he hath bound." "The greatest burden in the world is superstition; not only of Ceremonies in the Church, but of imaginary and scar-crow sins at home." "Let not England forget her precedence of teaching nations how to live."

Milton's political wisdom was that of an idealist, but was not unpractical or visionary. Though his ideals may seem so to those who mistake opportunism for "realism", they were in fact based upon the firm foundation of political principle. His polemical contentions were directed against the twin evils of tyranny and superstition; against which we too must fight like Bunyan's pilgrim, though they appear in new guise.

Had Milton been present during the discussion of the Matrimonial Causes Bill of 1937 he would have recognised some old ecclesiastical faces and failings, and would have felt that some of us still have to learn the lesson he sought to teach in his incomparable and, to me, irrefutable *Doctrine and Discipline of Divorce*. Three hundred years have passed since he claimed that "solace and peace, which is contrary to discord and variance, is the main end of marriage"; that it is a gross aspersion upon the sanctity of marriage to imply that it takes more account of physical than of spiritual fitness, and that irreconcilable "contrarity of mind is a greater cause of divorce than corporal frigidity"; that God cannot be said ever to have "joined, error, fraud, unfitness, wrath, contention, perpetual loneliness, perpetual discord"; and that it shows a radical misunderstanding of the philosophy of Christ to construe a single cryptic and perhaps doubtful sentence as a rigid rule of law or a sacramental principle.

For the rest and in general, the reforms that Milton advocated, as also the tyrannous evils that he assailed, are indicated in the titles and sub-titles of his pamphlets; while the polemical weapons which he used, in varied literary styles, are patent in the prose selections given in this volume.

His generation was not ready to receive the messages so impetuously uttered. He overestimated the capacity of his countrymen to change their outlook and their way of life. Yet he triumphed over the disillusion which saddened his later years, and he has inspired more men in later centuries than ever heard of him when he lived. *Mortuus loquitur*. Let men take heart from his example.

ARNOLD WILSON

Chronological Tables

I. BIOGRAPHICAL

1608 (Dec. 9.) John Milton born at the *Spread Eagle*, his father's house and place of business as a scrivener (attorney and law-stationer), Bread Street, Cheapside; the second of five children—only Anne (the first) and Christopher (the fifth), besides himself, surviving.

1620 (*circa*.) Sent to St. Paul's School, after being tutored at home by Thomas Young. Beginning of his great friendship with Charles Diodati, one of his schoolfellows.

1625 (Feb. 12.) Admitted as a pensioner of Christ's College, Cambridge: matriculates April 9th.

1629 (March 26.) Takes B.A. degree.

1632 (July 3.) Takes M.A. degree. After leaving Cambridge settles at Horton, Buckinghamshire, where his father has retired from business.

1637 (April 3.) Death of his mother.

1638 (April.) Begins Italian tour.

1638 (Aug. 27.) Death of Charles Diodati.

1639 (July.) Ends Italian tour.

1639 (July.) Takes rooms in St. Bride's Churchyard, and soon afterwards a house in Aldersgate Street.

1640 Receives his nephews, John and Edward Philips, as resident pupils.

1642 (May or June.) Marries Mary Powell, daughter of a cavalier J.P. of Forest Hill, Oxfordshire. After a month or so, she goes on a visit to her old home, and refuses to return at the time appointed. Milton's father comes to live with him.

1644 First signs of failing eyesight.

1645 Reconciliation with his truant wife. Moves to a larger house in the Barbican.

1646 Harbours his wife's family, who have been disinherited at the surrender of Oxford, until their estates are restored. His daughter, Anne, born.

1647 (March 15.) Death of his father. He gives up pupils, and moves to a smaller house in High Holborn.

1648 His daughter, Mary, born.

1649 (March 15.) Appointed Latin Secretary to the Council of State, with chambers in Whitehall: salary £289 14s. 4½d. per annum.

1649 (March.) His son, John, born: dies in the same month.

1652 Deprived of his Whitehall chambers; moves to a house in Petty Fraunce, Westminster. Becomes totally blind and is given an assistant in his official work. His daughter, Deborah, born. Death of his wife.

1655 (April 17.) His salary reduced to £150 per annum.

1656 (Nov. 12.) Marries Katherine Woodcock.

1657 (Oct. 19.) A daughter born.

1658 (February.) Death of his second wife and daughter.

1660 Dismissed from office (at Restoration). Is concealed for a time in a friend's house in Bartholomew Close. Arrested during summer, but released, being ordered to pay fees.

1663 (Feb. 24.) Marries Elizabeth Minshull (thirty years his junior). Moves to Artillery Walk, Bunhill Fields.

1665 Retreats to cottage at Chalfont St. Giles to escape the Plague.

1674 (Nov. 8.) Dies, after an attack of gout.

2. POEMS: COMPOSITION

Paraphrases of Psalms CXIV, CXXXVI.	1624
On the Death of a fair Infant dying of a Cough.	1626
Ad Carolum Diodatum (Elegia Prima).	1626
In obitum Præsulis Wintoniensis (Elegia Tertia).	1626
In obitum Præsulis Eliensis (among the *Sylvæ*).	1626
In obitum Præconis Academici Cantabrigiensis (Elegia Secunda).	1626
In obitum Procancellarii Medici (among the *Sylvæ*).	1626
In Quintum Novembris (among the *Sylvæ*).	1626
In Proditionem Bombardicam; in Eandem; In Eandem; In Eandem; In Inventorem Bombardæ (all appended to *Elegiarum Liber*).	c. 1626

To Sir Henry Vane. **1652**

Psalms I-VIII done into Verse. **1653**

The Fifth Ode of Horace, Lib. I, translated. **—**

In Salmasium (in *Defensio Secunda*). **1654**

" When I consider . . ." ***c.*** **1655-65**

On the late Massacher in Piemont. **1655**

"Lawrence of vertuous Father vertuous Son . . ." **1655**

"Cyriack, whose Grandsire . . ." **1655**

To Mr. Cyriac Skinner. Upon his Blindness. ***c.*** **1655**

"Methought I saw . . ." **1658**

Paradise Lost ***c.*** **1655-65**

Translated fragment of verse from Geoffrey of Monmouth (in *The History of Britain*). Unknown, but pub'd. **1670**

Paradise Regain'd. **1667-71**

Samson Agonistes. Unknown, but pub'd. **1671**

3. POEMS: PUBLICATION

A Maske Presented At Ludlow Castle, 1634: On Michaelmasse night, before the Right Honorable, Iohn Earle of Bridgewater, Vicount Brackly, Lord Præsident of Wales, And one of His Maiesties most honorable Privie Counsell. **1637**

Lycidas [included in *Obsequies to the Memorie of Mr. Edward King* (generally bound up with *Justa Edovardo King naufrago, ab amicis mærentibus, amoris, et μνείας χάριν*)] **1638**

Epitaphium Damonis (apparently for presentation purposes). **Undated**

Poems of Mr. John Milton, both English and Latin, Compos'd at several times. Printed by his true copies. **1645**

Poems, Etc., upon Several Occasions. By Mr. John Milton: Both English and Latin, Etc. Composed at several times. With a small Tractate of Education to Mr. Hartlib. **1673**

Paradise Lost. A Poem Written in Ten Books by John Milton. **1667**

Paradise Regain'd. A Poem. In IV Books. To which is added Samson Agonistes. The Author John Milton. **1671**

Samson Agonistes, A Dramatic Poem. The Author John
    Milton.   1671

Paradise Lost. A Poem In Twelve Books. The Author John
    Milton. (Second Edition: revised and augmented.)   1674

Four Sonnets [included in Edward Philips' *Letters of State*]. 1694

4. PROSE: PUBLICATION

Of Reformation touching Church-Discipline in England, and
    the Causes that hitherto have hindred it: Two Bookes,
    written to a Freind.   1641

Of Prelaticall Episcopacy, And whether it may be deduc'd
    from the Apostolical times by vertue of those Testi-
    monies which are alledg'd to that purpose in some late
    Treatises: one whereof goes under the Name of James,
    Archbishop of Armagh.   1641

*Animadversions upon The Remonstrants Defence, against
    Smectymnuus*. In two Books.   1641

The Reason of Church-Governement Urg'd against Prelaty. 1641

*An Apology against a Pamphlet call'd A Modest Confuta-
    tion of the Animadversions upon the Remonstrant against
    Smectymnuus*.   March or April, 1642

The Doctrine and Discipline of Divorce: Restor'd to the
    good of both Sexes, From the bondage of Canon Law,
    and other mistakes, to Christian Freedom, guided by
    the Rule of Charity. Wherein also many places of
    Scripture, have recovered their long-lost meaning.
    Seasonable to be now thought on in the Reformation
    intended.   Aug. 1, 1643

The Doctrine and Discipline of Divorce: Restor'd to the good
    of both Sexes, From the bondage of Canon Law, and
    other mistakes, to the true meaning of Scripture in the
    Law and Gospel compar'd. Wherin also are set down
    the bad consequences of abolishing or condemning of
    Sin, that which the Law of God allowes, and Christ
    abolisht not. Now the second time revis'd and much
    augmented, In Two Books: To the Parlament of

The Editor's Preface

THIS edition of Milton contains his poetical works in their entirety. The poems are grouped according to the language in which they were written: English, Latin, Greek, and Italian; Milton's translations into English following his original English poetry. Otherwise the order, as far as may be determined, is chronological. The text is that of the early copies.

Second-edition rather than first-edition texts have been preferred in cases where second editions of Milton's work were published during his lifetime; for, as might be expected from his "slow endeavouring art", they were much amended. Second editions were published, during his lifetime, of his minor poems and *Paradise Lost*; and they comprise enlargements and major modifications, apart from lesser changes, as follows:

I. To his minor poems, first published in 1645, there were added to the second (1673) edition the early Verses *On the Death of a fair Infant dying of a Cough*, and *At a Vacation Exercise in the Colledge*; also *Silvae X*, three further *Epigrammata*, a translation entitled *The Fifth Ode of Horace, Lib 1*, sixteen translations of the Psalms (additional to the two which had previously been printed), and nine further English sonnets. (The sonnets to Fairfax, Cromwell, and Vane, and the second one to Cyriack Skinner, were withheld for political reasons, to be included—in a defective condition—in the 1694 edition of the *Letters of State*.)

II. The first edition of *Paradise Lost* (1667) contained ten books. The second edition (1674) contained twelve: an extension brought about through two divisions, which made two of the books into four new ones, thus:

(1) Book VII was divided after lines 639-40:

> "... if else thou seekst
> Aught, not surpassing human measure, say."

The following line (641), "To whom thus *Adam* gratefully repli'd," was cancelled and the break made good by four additional lines, which in the second edition introduce Book VIII:

" The Angel ended, and in *Adam's* Eare
So Charming left his voice, that he a while
Thought him still speaking, still stood fixt to hear;
Then as new wak'd thus gratefully repli'd."

The transit after the abrupt ending of Book VII is effected by this interposed reference to the state of charmed abstraction into which Adam is described as having fallen. The second part of the book became, with this modification, the new eighth book.

(2) Book X—which, owing to the partition of Book VII, became Book XI of the second edition—was itself in turn divided after line 896, the first five lines of Book XII of the second edition being added as a connecting link. The second part of the book, with the additional lines, became Book XII.

In the preparation of the text the 1863 Mitford edition has been largely used, and has been collated with the original copies in the British Museum. Mitford claimed that his edition had been "carefully printed from the Author's copies", and that the "orthography so peculiar in the writings of Milton" had been "scrupulously preserved". This, on the whole, is true; but, together with some occasional less serious errors, he has, in regard to translations of verses from classical authors, confused the work of Milton with that of his translator, Joseph Washington, and has attributed to Milton himself Washington's translation of Milton's *In Salmasii Hundredam.* He has also altered the unemphatic *thir* in the second edition of *Paradise Lost* and the succeeding poems, to *their*. (In the prose works he has not made this alteration.) In the present edition, the faulty period-rendering of Greek (without breathings, etc.) is not reproduced. Actual printers' errors—English or non-English—have been corrected, when they were unquestionable, without notification.

The work of selecting the prose of Milton included in this edition has been governed by an intense admiration for its literary qualities: a personal admiration of long standing and undiminished enthusiasm.

The Latin works have not been represented, because, apart

from the barrier of language, they are steeped inevitably in the formal traditions of classical rhetoric, and are by so much the less characteristic of Milton himself, whose individual style could not be developed in a dead, or fixed, language; although, conversely, his knowledge of Latin and Greek models served to engender and foster its development in English. The Latin form, moreover, considerably modifies even the material. As for the *Pro Populo Anglicano Defensio*, it is as evanescently political as—among the English political works—the Εἰκονοκλάστης is uniform and dull.

The *Areopagitica*, the *Apology against a Pamphlet*, and *Of Education* are included in full; for their eloquent qualities are more continuously manifested than is the case in general with Milton's English prose works: they are so interfused that it was found impossible to give extracts of adequate proportion from these pieces without producing the effect of a mangling abridgement. The *Areopagitica*, which Miltonian commentators are accustomed to call the best of Milton's English prose works, has been repeatedly reprinted, and the Education tractate was reprinted in the 1673 edition of the minor poems, as also in other editions of Milton's poems; but the *Apology against a Pamphlet*, except in the collected editions, has never been reprinted, although as a miracle of style it is unrivalled, and in its scurrilous satirical power may be described as a volcano of low elevation throwing out fire and mud.

As to the extracts included from others of the prose works, the only point which it is expedient to note relates to certain passages among those from *The History of Britain*. They have been chosen for their characteristically compacted style. In general, the compressed construction throughout this work is crudely of Latin derivation; but in these particular passages the foreign elements are transmuted. The style reappears, with metrical modification, in Books VII and IX of *Paradise Lost*.

The translations of the Latin Elegies and Sylvæ are by Mr. W. Skeat; especially revised by him from *Milton's Lament for Damon and his Other Latin Poems*:* translations which derive their poetic qualities from their intensive fidelity to the originals—attained, in accuracy, by the employment of Milton's

*Oxford University Press, 1935.

own terminology;* in comprehensiveness, by the use of an expansive verse-medium, explained by Mr. Skeat himself in his Note in the Appendix. The translations of the Latin Epigrams, which are no less poetically faithful to the originals, are by Mr. A. Vesselo. The translations of the Italian Sonnets are by George MacDonald: reprinted from *Exotics*,† with the kind permission of his son, Dr. Greville MacDonald.

All these translations were undertaken mainly in consideration of the great, unique light upon Milton's personal character that is contained—but to non-Latin readers hidden—in the Latin originals; a clear, and in some cases, as in the *Epitaphium Damonis*, intense illumination; which is restricted and diluted in Cowper's renderings: inevitably so, with his line-for-line method and eighteenth-century period poetic diction. Nor were Cowper's translations complete; for he omitted *In Quintum Novembris*. Yet this miniature epic, in which the Satan of *Paradise Lost* makes a crude appearance, has great significance, since its subject, the Gunpowder Plot, is prominent in the dynamic passage in Milton's first pamphlet, *Of Reformation touching Church-Discipline*, and there he announces his great epic in anticipation. Cowper has also omitted the Latin Epigrams; four of which are about the Gunpowder Plot, which thus laid a subliminal train in Milton's imagination.

The explanatory notes to the poems have been adapted from material provided by Mr. Skeat; the explanatory notes to the extracts from the *Areopagitica* are based upon the extensive annotations of John W. Hales in *Milton: Areopagitica*;‡ those to the other prose selections are pioneer endeavour, much assisted by the scholarship and ingenuity of Mr. A. J. Hughes.

All these annotations, both of the verse and prose, have been strictly confined to such obscurities in the text as might conceivably interfere with the reader's intelligent enjoyment.

---

* This was much facilitated by Milton's characteristic of re-expressing his ideas in scarcely varied forms. A table of such correspondences between the Latin and English poems, compiled by Mr. Skeat, is voluminous.

† Strahan, 1876.

‡ Clarendon Press, Oxford, 1878.

They have been regulated upon the following considerations:
In general, there is no doubt that Milton himself took care
to make the allusions in his works sufficiently clear in every
case where such clarity was necessary to an adequate appreciation of the text; but in regard to these allusions he pre-
supposed in his readers a tolerable acquaintance with classical mythology, and a thorough acquaintance with the Bible.
This twin-cultural equipment is as due a concession to Milton
in our own times as it was in his; although of course it does
not follow that, for lack of it, a reader possessing poetical
imagination is debarred from appreciating the main quality
of his genius. On the same principle, annotations upon references by Milton to historical or ecclesiastical figures and
classical authors, are not, except in particular instances, included. The elucidations refer, for the most part, to obsolete
words, obsolete or peculiarly Miltonic meanings attached
to familiar words, obscure constructions, mediæval scholas-
ticisms, defunct customs, and obfuscated literary allusions.

The production of this work is due to the initiative and
active interest of Sir Arnold Wilson. The Editor is also
gratefully indebted for counsel and assistance in his labours
to Mr. Skeat and to Mr. Vesselo; and for practical help in
the preparation of the text to Mr. John Gawsworth: who, by
a pleasant coincidence, numbers among his ancestors Milton's
third wife, Elizabeth Minshull. The bibliographical discoveries
made by Mr. Gawsworth in connexion with the verse-trans-
lations of Washington and of Harington inaccurately attributed to Milton by Mitford and Beeching, are described by
him in a Note included in the Appendix.

E. H. VISIAK

A Supplement to the Present Edition

EDITOR'S PREFACE

I AM not sedulous as an Editor of Milton to accumulate Notes, and think it unnecessary, for example, to tell the general reader to *Cp. Theocritus, XX.* 83, 84, *ed. Ahrens.* Yet such things ought to be given their due, as Milton is such a learned, such a reconditely learned, author. Only, they belong to those seclusive walks and grand commentatorial parades of learning, and they would require a whole Nonesuch volume. Perhaps two.

For all this, the Notes were rather too restricted in our original edition, and herein there have been added a good many. I am specially indebted in the case of the English Prose additional Notes, to "Milton's Tractate on Education", ed. Oscar Browning (Cambridge University Press, 1890) and to "Areopagitica and Other Tracts", ed. C. E. Vaughan (Temple Classics, N.D.), and also to *Notes and Queries,* and the late very excellent and sagacious scholar, George G. Loane. Also, of course, to Mr. Walter W. Skeat, who has added to his Notes on the English Poems. And a great opportunity have the Nonesuch Press afforded me; for which I am deeply grateful.　　　　　　　　　　　　　E. H. VISIAK

CORRIGENDA

Chronological Tables:
　p. xvii, l. 11; *for* 1656 *read* 1655
Preface:
　p. xxiii, l. 26; *for* 1743 *read* 1694
　p. xxv, l. 20; 'Education tractate': also separately, in 1890 by the Cambridge University Press
Paradise Lost:
　p. 91, l. 32; *for* fanting *read* fainting
　p. 109, l. 19; *for* we *read* wee
　p. 112, l. 12; *for* thir *read* his
　p. 149, l. 10; *for* gottesque *read* grottesque
Errors in the 2nd *edition* of "Paradise Lost":
　p. 132, l. 3; *for* meditation *read* mediation
　p. 142, l. 33; *for* are *read* art
　p. 152, l. 8; *for* Of *read* Or
　p. 155, l. 4; *for* you *read* your
　p. 175, l. 40; *for* ye *read* yee
　p. 190, l. 38; *for* he *read* hee
　p. 225, l. 1; *for* he *read* hee
　p. 244, l. 33; *for* me *read* mee

p. 320, l. 22 ; *for* Tremisen *read* and Tremisen
p. 324, l. 37 ; *for* last *read* lost

Notes to the English Poems, referring to:

Il Penseroso:
    p. 36, l. 32 ; *for* P.L.vii, 331 *read* P.R.iv, 243 but P means a *later* Actæus

Lycidas:
    p. 67, l. 39 ; *substitute:* The source of the 'two-handed engine' has now been discovered (see *Notes and Queries*, Sept. 24, 1938) in Sir Thomas Smith's verses:
    'This day made new Duke, Marquis, Earl or Baron,
    Yet maie the ax stande next the dore'

Paradise Lost:
    p. 236, ll. 29–30 ; *for* sun *read* planets
    p. 295, l. 24 ; *for* ἔλοψ *read* ἔλλοψ. Cp. ἔλλος = mute (of fish)

Paradise Regain'd:
    p. 400, l. 1 ; *for* Ode, 1, 114 *read* Ode IX, 106

Notes to the Translations, referring to:
    p. 455, Phrynichus, *read* see F. W. Wagner, Poet. Trag. Frag. Phrynichus, p. 16 (Didot, Paris, 1846)

Appendix: English Versions of the Latin . . . Poems:

Mr. Skeat's Emendations
    p. 757, l. 9 ; *for* golden-tangled *read* gold-entangled
    p. 758, l. 21 ; *read* What time Death's self . . .
    p. 761, l. 30 ; *read* Devoting Death's own self to death
    p. 792, l. 10 ; *for* make *read* take
    p. 793, l. 21 ; *for* wretched *read* scrannel
    p. 797, l. 16 ; *for* ages *read* tides of tranc'd eternal day,
    p. 799, l. 14 ; *read* Or betwixt these, the interambient air
    p. 807, l. 8 ; *for* deep-sorrowed *read* lamented
    p. 807, l. 10 ; *for* loud laments *read* 'plainings loud
    For the refrain read : Home, home starv'd lambs! Grief's all that matters now!
    p. 808, l. 16 ; *for* trim fields *read* rustic joys
    p. 813, l. 2 ; *for* Reed *read* Pipes
    p. 815, str. 10 ; *for* 'Daunian' read 'rustick'
    p. 822, footnote ; *add:* (The lady's name was Emilia)

Notes to the English Prose, referring to:

Of Reformation touching Church-Discipline . . .
    p. 539, l. 28 ; *for* bassle *read* baffle

An Apology against a Pamphlet . . .
    p. 576, l. 23 ; 'Thraso' ; *substitute* the braggart soldier of the *Eunuchus*
    p. 588, l. 37 ; cancel

Of Education:
    p. 671, 'Hartlib' ; *for* unknown *read* Prussian.
    p. 681, l. 33 ; *substitute* 'delusive list' = Dead Pay (*i.e.* the con-

tinued pay of soldiers actually dead appropriated by dishonest officers. The 'miserable remnant' = the men they
really had

Areopagitica:
    p. 697, l. 38 ('Vicar of hell'); *add*, 'A more likely claimant to
    that preferment is Sir Francis Bryan, whom Cromwell,
    writing to Gardiner, so styled' (*Notes and Queries*, Sept. 24,
    1938)
    p. 701, l. 9; *for* the Countess of Pembroke's *read* Sidney's, *add*
    Or else, more probably, perhaps, the *Arcadia* of Sannazzaro
    (1502)

ADDITIONAL NOTES

English Poems:
    p. 14, l. 30; *On the Morning of Christ's Nativity.* 'quaint':
    punctilious
    p. 31, l. 13; *L'Allegro*, 'secure delight': carefree
    p. 67, l. 15; *Lycidas*, 'sanguine flower': hyacinth
    p. 67, l. 18; 'Pilot': St. Peter
    p. 67, l. 37; 'Woolf': the R.C. Church, at that time making many
    converts
    p. 68, l. 7; 'swart Star': Sirius
    p. 68, l. 30; 'great vision of the guarded Mount': that Saint's
    traditional appearance on St. Michael's Mount
    'Lycidas', the subject of the poem = Edward King, alumnus of
    Christ's College, Cambridge, drowned in the Irish Sea, 1637
    p. 85, l. 36; *Paradise Lost*, 'Ammiral': flag-ship
    p. 98, l. 19; 'Frequent': crowded
    p. 103, l. 1; 'impotence': fury
    p. 112, l. 16; 'shun the Goal': to round the turning-point
    p. 154, l. 12; 'gentle purpose': conversation (p. 243, l. 3,
    'gracious purpose')
    p. 164, l. 26; 'sole proprietie': exclusive possession
    p. 208, l. 27; 'Sad resolution and secure': gravity and confidence
    p. 226, l. 13; 'Smelling': Bentley conjectures, Swelling
    p. 264, l. 12; 'Spires': coils
    p. 283, l. 24; 'moment of impulse': deciding force
    p. 327, l. 7; 'Exploded': hissed off
    p. 396, l. 13; *Paradise Regain'd.* 'hinges': cardinal points

Latin Poems (*English Versions*):
    p. 807, l. 14; *The Lament for Damon.* 'Damon': Charles Diodati,
    Milton's beloved friend. He died during Milton's Italian tour,
    and for some time after returning home, before writing the
    poem, Milton, in his desolation, says Masson, 'seems to have
    gone about . . . thinking of little else'

English Prose:
    An Apology against a Pamphlet . . .
    p. 581, l. 37–8; 'they were out, and I hist' = they were damned,
    and I joined in the hissing
    p. 582, l. 22; ' '*Ἀπειροκαλία*': vulgarity

English Prose (continued)

Of Education:

p. 671, l. 26; 'person sent hither': the famous Moravian educational reformer, J. A. Comenius, who visited London at Hartlib's invitation in 1641

p. 673, l. 19; 'preposterous': hind-foremost, out of due order

p. 674, l. 25; 'conscientious slavery': Cp. *Reason of Church-Governement*, p. 562, l. 14: 'must subscribe slave... conscience that would retch'

p. 675, l. 24; 'Lilly': the contemporary Latin Primer

p. 676, l. 28; 'playing': the old Roman teachers' way of reckoning before their pupils; signifying numbers and values by manipulating the various joints and bends of the fingers

p. 677, l. 21; 'crudity': a stomach disorder; indigestion, etc.

p. 678, l. 10; 'reduc't': brought back

p. 678, l. 13; 'Evanges': evangels

p. 679, l. 8; 'organic': practical

p. 679, l. 12; 'coucht': arranged

p. 679, l. 24; 'grand master-piece': chief point

p. 680, l. 19; 'the Gown': the toga; emblem of peace

p. 682, l. 9; 'commodities': advantages

p. 682, l. 21; 'slight': vile

Areopagitica:

p. 685, l. 34; 'him who from his private house': Isocrates in his Λόγος 'Αρεοπαγιτικός which suggested Milton's title

p. 701, l. 24; 'Atlantick': of Plato's legendary Atlantis

p. 702, l. 8; 'motions': puppet plays

p. 710, l. 28–29; 'mysticall': virtual; in reality

p. 710, l. 35; 'chop': chop and change about, or bring back

p. 713, l. 25–27; 'St. *Thomas* in his vestry, and adde to boot St. *Martin*, and St. *Hugh*': 'The *clothiers* seem to have had their shops close to the Church of St. Thomas, Apostle... hence the aptness of 'vestry', *i.e.* clothes-mart. The *shoemakers*' shops were near St. Martin's le Grand... St. Hugh was the patron saint of shoemakers... I suspect Milton of intending a horrible pun in "to boot"' (Prof. Vaughan, in 'Areopagitica and Other Tracts', *Temple Classics*)

p. 720, l. 34; 'he who takes up arms for cote and conduct': Hampden who, in refusing to pay 'ship money', *took up arms* against clothing and *arming* soldiers

p. 724, l. 15–17; 'old Convocation house... Chappell at Westminster': the former—the Jerusalem Chamber at Westminster—represented the Church of England; the latter —Henry VII's chapel—the Presbyterian Church

p. 725, l. 35; 'authentic': truly

The readie and easie Way...

p. 742, l. 14; 'The good Old Cause': pure Republicanism

English Poems

English Poems

I.M.

ANNO ÆTATIS 17

¶On the Death of a fair Infant
dying of a Cough

1

O FAIREST flower no sooner blown but blasted,
Soft silken Primrose fading timelesslie,
Summers chief honour if thou hadst out-lasted,
Bleak winters force that made thy blossome drie;
For he being amorous on that lovely die
   That did thy cheek envermeil, thought to kiss
But kill'd alas, and then bewayl'd his fatal bliss.

2

For since grim Aquilo his charioter
By boistrous rape th'Athenian damsel got,
He thought it toucht his Deitie full neer,
If likewise he some fair one wedded not,
Thereby to wipe away th'infamous blot,
   Of long-uncoupled bed, and childless eld,
Which 'mongst the wanton gods a foul reproach was held.

3

So mounting up in ycie-pearled carr,
Through middle empire of the freezing aire
He wanderd long, till thee he spy'd from farr,
There ended was his quest, there ceast his care.
Down he descended from his Snow-soft chaire,
   But all unwares with his cold-kind embrace
Unhous'd thy Virgin Soul from her fair biding place.

3

4

Yet art thou not inglorious in thy fate;
For so *Apollo*, with unweeting hand
Whilome did slay his dearly-loved mate
Young *Hyacinth* born on *Eurota's* strand,
Young *Hyacinth* the pride of *Spartan* land;
   But then transform'd him to a purple flower
Alack that so to change thee winter had no power.

5

Yet can I not perswade me thou art dead
Or that thy coarse corrupts in earths dark wombe,
Or that thy beauties lie in wormie bed,
Hid from the world in a low delved tombe;
Could Heav'n for pittie thee so strictly doom?
   Oh no? for something in thy face did shine
Above mortalitie that shew'd thou wast divine.

6

Resolve me then oh Soul most surely blest
(If so it be that thou these plaints dost hear)
Tell me bright Spirit where e're thou hoverest
Whether above that high first-moving Spheare
Or in the Elisian fields (if such there were.)
   Oh say me true if thou wert mortal wight
And why from us so quickly thou didst take thy flight.

7

Wert thou some Starr which from the ruin'd roofe
Of shak't Olympus by mischance didst fall;
Which carefull *Jove* in natures true behoofe
Took up, and in fit place did reinstall?
Or did of late earths Sonnes besiege the wall
   Of sheenie Heav'n, and thou some goddess fled
Amongst us here below to hide thy nectar'd head.

8

Or wert thou that just Maid who once before
Forsook the hated earth, O tell me sooth
And cam'st again to visit us once more?

Or wert thou that sweet smiling Youth?
Or that crown'd Matron sage white-robed truth?
  Or any other of that heav'nly brood
Let down in clowdie throne to do the world some good.

9

Or wert thou of the golden-winged hoast,
Who having clad thy self in humane weed,
To earth from thy præfixed seat didst poast,
And after short abode flie back with speed,
As if to shew what creatures Heav'n doth breed,
  Thereby to set the hearts of men on fire
To scorn the sordid world, and unto Heav'n aspire.

10

But oh why didst thou not stay here below
To bless us with thy heav'n-lov'd innocence,
To slake his wrath whom sin hath made our foe
To turn Swift-rushing black perdition hence,
Or drive away the slaughtering pestilence,
  To stand 'twixt us and our deserved smart?
But thou canst best perform that office where thou art.

11

Then thou the mother of so sweet a child
Her false imagin'd loss cease to lament,
And wisely learn to curb thy sorrows wild;
Think what a present thou to God hast sent,
And render him with patience what he lent;
  This if thou do he will an off-spring give,
That till the worlds last-end shall make thy name to live.

ANNO ÆTATIS 19

¶ At a Vacation Exercise in the Colledge,
part *Latin*, part *English*. The *Latin* speeches
ended, the *English* thus began

HAIL native Language, that by sinews weak
Didst move my first endeavouring tongue to speak,

And mad'st imperfect words with childish tripps,
Half unpronounc't, slide through my infant-lipps,
Driving dum silence from the portal dore,
Where he had mutely sate two years before:
Here I salute thee and thy pardon ask,
That now I use thee in my latter task:
Small loss it is that thence can come unto thee,
I know my tongue but little Grace can do thee:
Thou needst not be ambitious to be first,
Believe me I have thither packt the worst:
And, if it happen as I did forecast,
The daintiest dishes shall be serv'd up last.
I pray thee then deny me not thy aide
For this same small neglect that I have made:
But haste thee strait to do me once a Pleasure,
And from thy wardrope bring thy chiefest treasure;
Not those new fangled toys, and triming slight
Which takes our late fantasticks with delight,
But cull those richest Robes, and gay'st attire
Which deepest Spirits, and choicest Wits desire:
I have some naked thoughts that rove about
And loudly knock to have their passage out;
And wearie of their place do only stay
Till thou hast deck't them in thy best aray;
That so they may without suspect or fears
Fly swiftly to this fair Assembly's ears;
Yet I had rather if I were to chuse,
Thy service in some graver subject use,
Such as may make thee search thy coffers round,
Before thou cloath my fancy in fit sound:
Such where the deep transported mind may soare
Above the wheeling poles, and at Heav'ns dore
Look in, and see each blissful Deitie
How he before the thunderous throne doth lie,
Listening to what unshorn *Apollo* sings
To th'touch of golden wires, while *Hebe* brings
Immortal Nectar to her Kingly Sire:
Then passing through the Spherse of watchful fire,
And mistie Regions of wide air next under,
And hills of Snow and lofts of piled Thunder,

May tell at length how green-ey'd *Neptune* raves,
In Heav'ns defiance mustering all his waves;
Then sing of secret things that came to pass
When Beldam Nature in her cradle was;
And last of Kings and Queens and *Hero's* old,
Such as the wise *Demodocus* once told
In solemn Songs at King *Alcinous* feast,
While sad *Ulisses* soul and all the rest
Are held with his melodious harmonie
In willing chains and sweet captivitie.
But fie my wandring Muse how thou dost stray!
Expectance calls thee now another way,
Thou know'st it must be now thy only bent
To keep in compass of thy Predicament:
Then quick about thy purpos'd business come,
That to the next I may resign my Roome.

Then Ens *is represented as Father of the Prædicaments his
ten Sons, whereof the Eldest stood for* Substance *with
his Canons, which* Ens *thus speaking, explains.*

Good luck befriend thee Son; for at thy birth
The Faiery Ladies daunc't upon the hearth;
Thy drowsie Nurse hath sworn she did them spie
Come tripping to the Room where thou didst lie;
And sweetly singing round about thy Bed
Strew all their blessings on thy sleeping Head.
She heard them give thee this, that thou should'st still
From eyes of mortals walk invisible,
Yet there is something that doth force my fear,
For once it was my dismal hap to hear
A *Sybil* old, bow-bent with crooked age,
That far events full wisely could presage,
And in times long and dark Prospective Glass
Fore-saw what future dayes should bring to pass,
Your Son, said she, (nor can you it prevent)
Shall subject be to many an Accident.
O're all his Brethren he shall Reign as King,
Yet every one shall make him underling,
And those that cannot live from him asunder
Ungratefully shall strive to keep him under,

In worth and excellence he shall out-go them,
Yet being above them, he shall be below them.
From others he shall stand in need of nothing,
Yet on his Brothers shall depend for Cloathing.
To find a Foe it shall not be his hap,
And peace shall lull him in her flowry lap;
Yet shall he live in strife, and at his dore
· Devouring war shall never cease to roare:
Yea it shall be his natural property
To harbour those that are at enmity.
What power, what force, what mighty spell, if not
Your learned hands, can loose this Gordian knot?

The next Quantity *and* Quality, *spake in Prose, then*
Relation *was call'd by his Name.*

Rivers arise: whether thou be the Son,
Of utmost *Tweed, or Oose*, or gulphie *Dun*,
Or *Trent*, who like some earth-born Giant spreads
His thirty Armes along the indented Meads,
Or sullen *Mole* that runneth underneath,
Or *Severn* swift, guilty of Maidens death,
Or Rockie *Avon*, or of Sedgie *Lee*,
Or Coaly *Tine*, or antient hollowed *Dee*,
Or *Humber* loud that keeps the *Scythians* Name,
Or *Medway* smooth, or Royal Towred *Thame*.

The rest was Prose.

¶ On the Morning of Christ's Nativity

(COMPOS'D 1629)

1

THIS is the Month, and this the happy morn
Wherein the Son of Heav'ns eternal King,
Of wedded Maid, and Virgin Mother born,
Our great Redemption from above did bring;
For so the holy Sages once did sing,
    That he our deadly forfeit should release,
And with his Father work us a perpetual peace.

2

That glorious Form, that Light unsufferable,
And that far-beaming blaze of Majesty,
Wherewith he wont at Heav'ns high Councel-Table,
To sit the midst of Trinal Unity,
He laid aside; and here with us to be,
   Forsook the Courts of everlasting Day,
And chose with us a darksom House of mortal Clay.

3

Say Heav'nly Muse, shall not thy sacred vein
Afford a Present to the Infant God?
Hast thou no verse, no hymn, or solemn strein,
To welcome him to this his new abode,
Now while the Heav'n by the Suns team untrod,
   Hath took no print of the approaching light,
And all the spangled host keep watch in squadrons bright?

4

See how from far upon the Eastern rode
The Star-led Wizards haste with odours sweet,
O run, prevent them with thy humble ode,
And lay it lowly at his blessed feet;
Have thou the honour first, thy Lord to greet,
   And joyn thy voice unto the Angel Quire,
From out his secret Altar toucht with hallow'd fire.

THE HYMN

1

It was the Winter wilde,
While the Heav'n-born childe,
   All meanly wrapt in the rude manger lies;
Nature in awe to him
Had doff't her gawdy trim,
   With her great Master so to sympathize:
It was no season then for her
To wanton with the Sun her lusty Paramour.

2

Only with speeches fair
She woo's the gentle Air
    To hide her guilty front with innocent Snow,
And on her naked shame,
Pollute with sinfull blame,
    The Saintly Veil of Maiden white to throw,
Confounded, that her Makers eyes
Should look so near upon her foul deformities.

3

But he her fears to cease,
Sent down the meek-ey'd Peace,
    She crown'd with Olive green, came softly sliding
Down through the turning sphear
His ready Harbinger,
    With Turtle wing the amorous clouds dividing,
And waving wide her mirtle wand,
She strikes a universal Peace through Sea and Land.

4

No War, or Battels sound
Was heard the World around,
    The idle Spear and Shield were high up hung,
The hooked Chariot stood
Unstained with hostile blood,
    The Trumpet spake not to the armed throng,
And Kings sate still with awfull eye,
As if they surely knew their sovran Lord was by.

5

But peacefull was the night
Wherein the Prince of light
    His raign of peace upon the earth began:
The Winds with wonder whist,
Smoothly the waters kist,
    Whispering new joyes to the milde Ocean,
Who now hath quite forgot to rave,
While Birds of Calm sit brooding on the charmed wave.

6

The Stars with deep amaze
Stand fixt in stedfast gaze,
   Bending one way their pretious influence,
And will not take their flight,
For all the morning light,
   Or *Lucifer* that often warn'd them thence;
But in their glimmering Orbs did glow,
Untill their Lord himself bespake, and bid them go.

7

And though the shady gloom
Had given day her room,
   The Sun himself with-held his wonted speed,
And hid his head for shame,
As his inferiour flame,
   The new enlightn'd world no more should need;
He saw a greater Sun appear
Then his bright Throne, or burning Axletree could bear.

8

The Shepherds on the Lawn,
Or ere the point of dawn,
   Sate simply chatting in a rustick row;
Full little thought they than,
That the mighty *Pan*
   Was kindly come to live with them below;
Perhaps their loves, or else their sheep,
Was all that did their silly thoughts so busie keep.

9

When such musick sweet
Their hearts and ears did greet,
   As never was by mortal finger strook,
Divinely-warbl'd voice
Answering the stringed noise,
   As all their souls in blissfull rapture took:
The Air such pleasure loth to lose,
With thousand echo's still prolongs each heav'nly close.

10

Nature that heard such sound
Beneath the hollow round
   Of *Cynthia's* seat, the Airy region thrilling,
Now was almost won
To think her part was done,
   And that her reign had here its last fulfilling;
She knew such harmony alone
Could hold all Heav'n and Earth in happier union.

11

At last surrounds their sight
A Globe of circular light,
   That with long beams the shame-fac't night array'd,
The helmed Cherubim
And sworded Seraphim,
   Are seen in glittering ranks with wings displaid,
Harping in loud and solemn quire,
With unexpressive notes to Heav'ns new-born Heir.

12

Such Musick (as 'tis said)
Before was never made,
   But when of old the sons of morning sung,
While the Creator great
His Constellations set,
   And the well-ballanc't world on hinges hung,
And cast the dark foundations deep,
And bid the weltring waves their oozy channel keep.

13

Ring out ye Crystall sphears,
Once bless our humane ears,
   (If ye have power to touch our senses so)
And let your silver chime
Move in melodious time;
   And let the Base of Heav'ns deep Organ blow,
And with your ninefold harmony
Make up full consort to th'Angelike symphony.

14

For if such holy Song
Enwrap our fancy long,
   Time will run back, and fetch the age of gold,
And speckl'd vanity
Will sicken soon and die,
   And leprous sin will melt from earthly mould,
And Hell it self will pass away,
And leave her dolorous mansions to the peering day.

15

Yea Truth, and Justice then
Will down return to men,
   Orb'd in a Rain-bow; and like glories wearing
Mercy will sit between,
Thron'd in Celestial sheen,
   With radiant feet the tissued clouds down stearing,
And Heav'n as at some Festivall,
Will open wide the Gates of her high Palace Hall.

16

But wisest Fate sayes no,
This must not yet be so,
   The Babe lies yet in smiling Infancy,
That on the bitter cross
Must redeem our loss;
   So both himself and us to glorifie:
Yet first to those ychain'd in sleep,
The wakeful trump of doom must thunder through the deep.

17

With such a horrid clang
As on mount *Sinai* rang
   While the red fire, and smouldring clouds out brake:
The aged Earth agast
With terrour of that blast,
   Shall from the surface to the center shake;
When at the worlds last session,
The dreadful Judge in middle Air shall spread his throne.

18

And then at last our bliss
Full and perfet is,
　　But now begins; for from this happy Day
Th'old Dragon under ground
In straiter limits bound,
　　Not half so far casts his usurped sway,
And wroth to see his Kingdom fail,
Swindges the scaly Horrour of his foulded tail.

19

The Oracles are dum,
No voice or hideous humm
　　Runs through the arched roof in words deceiving.
Apollo from his shrine
Can no more divine,
　　With hollow shreik the steep of *Delphos* leaving.
No nightly trance, or breathed spell,
Inspires the pale-ey'd Priest from the prophetic cell.

20

The lonely mountains o're,
And the resounding shore,
　　A voice of weeping heard, and loud lament;
From haunted spring, and dale
Edg'd with poplar pale,
　　The parting Genius is with sighing sent,
With flowre-inwov'n tresses torn
The Nimphs in twilight shade of tangled thickets mourn.

21

In consecrated Earth,
And on the holy Hearth,
　　The *Lars*, and *Lemures*, moan with midnight plaint,
In Urns, and Altars round,
A drear and dying sound
　　Affrights the *Flamins* at their service quaint;
And the chill Marble seems to sweat,
While each peculiar power forgoes his wonted seat.

22

Peor, and *Baalim*,
Forsake their Temples dim,
    With that twice batter'd god of *Palestine*,
And mooned *Ashtaroth*,
Heav'ns Queen and Mother both,
    Now sits not girt with Tapers holy shine,
The Libyc *Hammon* shrinks his horn,
In vain the *Tyrian* Maids their wounded *Thamuz* mourn.

23

And sullen *Moloch* fled,
Hath left in shadows dred,
    His burning Idol all of blackest hue;
In vain with Cymbals ring,
They call the grisly King,
    In dismal dance about the furnace blue;
The brutish gods of *Nile* as fast,
Isis and *Orus*, and the Dog *Anubis* hast.

24

Nor is *Osiris* seen
In *Memphian* Grove, or Green,
    Trampling the unshowr'd Grass with lowings loud:
Nor can he be at rest
Within his sacred chest,
    Naught but profoundest Hell can be his shroud,
In vain with Timbrel'd Anthems dark
The sable-stoled Sorcerers bear his worship Ark.

25

He feels from *Juda's* Land
The dredded Infants hand,
    The rayes of *Bethlehem* blind his dusky eyn;
Nor all the Gods beside,
Longer dare abide,
    Not *Typhon* huge ending in snaky twine:
Our Babe to shew his Godhead true,
Can in his swadling bands controul the damned crew.

26

So when the Sun in bed,
Curtain'd with cloudy red,
   Pillows his chin upon an Orient wave,
The flocking shadows pale,
Troop to th'infernal Jail,
   Each fetter'd Ghost slips to his several grave,
And the yellow-skirted *Fayes*,
Fly after the Night-steeds, leaving their Moon-lov'd maze.

27

But see the Virgin blest,
Hath laid her Babe to rest.
   Time is our tedious Song should here have ending;
Heav'ns youngest teemed Star,
Hath fixt her polisht Car,
   Her sleeping Lord with Handmaid Lamp attending:
And all about the Courtly Stable,
Bright-harnest Angels sit in order serviceable.

¶ The Passion

1

ERE-WHILE of Musick, and Ethereal mirth,
Wherewith the stage of Ayr and Earth did ring,
And joyous news of heav'nly Infants birth,
My muse with Angels did divide to sing;
But headlong joy is ever on the wing,
   In Wintry solstice like the shortn'd light
Soon swallow'd up in dark and long out-living night.

2

For now to sorrow must I tune my song,
And set my Harp to notes of saddest wo,
Which on our dearest Lord did sease er'e long,
Dangers, and snares, and wrongs, and worse then so.
Which he for us did freely undergo.
   Most perfect *Heroe*, try'd in heaviest plight
Of labours huge and hard, too hard for human wight.

3

He sov'ran Priest stooping his regal head
That dropt with odorous oil down his fair eyes,
Poor fleshly Tabernacle entered,
His starry front low-rooft beneath the skies;
O what a mask was there, what a disguise !
    Yet more; the stroke of death he must abide,
Then lies him meekly down fast by his Brethrens side.

4

These latest scenes confine my roving vers,
To this Horizon is my *Phœbus* bound,
His Godlike acts; and his temptations fierce,
And former sufferings other where are found;
Loud o're the rest *Cremona's* Trump doth sound;
    Me softer airs befit, and softer strings
Of Lute, or Viol still, more apt for mournful things.

5

Befriend me night best Patroness of grief,
Over the Pole thy thickest mantle throw,
And work my flatter'd fancy to belief,
That Heav'n and Earth are colour'd with my wo;
My sorrows are too dark for day to know:
    The leaves should all be black wheron I write,
And letters where my tears have washt a wannish white.

6

See see the Chariot, and those rushing wheels,
That whirl'd the Prophet up at *Chebar* flood,
My spirit som transporting *Cherub* feels,
To bear me where the Towers of *Salem* stood,
Once glorious Towers, now sunk in guiltless blood;
    There doth my soul in holy vision sit
In pensive trance, and anguish, and ecstatick fit.

7

Mine eye hath found that sad Sepulchral rock
That was the Casket of Heav'ns richest store,
And here though grief my feeble hands un lock.

Yet on the softned Quarry would I score
My plaining vers as lively as before;
    For sure so well instructed are my tears,
That they would fitly fall in order'd Characters.

8

Or should I thence hurried on viewles wing,
Take up a weeping on the Mountains wilde,
The gentle neighbourhood of grove and spring
Would soon unbosom all their Echoes milde,
And I (for grief is easily beguild)
    Might think th'infection of my sorrows loud,
    Had got a race of mourners on som pregnant cloud.

*This Subject the Author finding to be above the yeers he had,
when he wrote it, and nothing satisfi'd with what was begun, left
it unfinisht.*

¶ Song. On *May* Morning

Now the bright morning star, Dayes harbinger,
Comes dancing from the East, and leads with her
The Flowry *May*, who from her green lap throws
The yellow Cowslip, and the pale Primrose.
    Hail bounteous *May* that dost inspire
    Mirth and youth and warm desire,
    Woods and Groves are of thy dressing,
    Hill and Dale doth boast thy blessing.
Thus we salute thee with our early Song,
And welcom thee, and wish thee long.

¶ "O Nightingale . . ."

O NIGHTINGALE, that on yon bloomy Spray
    Warbl'st at eeve, when all the Woods are still,
    Thou with fresh hope the Lovers heart dost fill,
While the jolly hours lead on propitious *May*,
Thy liquid notes that close the eye of Day,
    First heard before the shallow Cuccoo's bill
    Portend success in love; O if *Jove's* will
Have linkt that amorous power to thy soft lay,

Now timely sing, ere the rude Bird of Hate
  Foretell my hopeles doom in som Grove ny:
  As thou from year to year hast sung too late
For my relief; yet hadst no reason why,
  Whether the Muse, or Love call thee his mate,
  Both them I serve, and of their train am I.

¶ On *Shakespear*. 1630

WHAT needs my *Shakespear* for his honour'd Bones,
The labour of an age in piled Stones,
Or that his hallow'd reliques should be hid
Under a Star-ypointing *Pyramid?*
Dear son of memory, great heir of Fame,
What need'st thou such weak witness of thy name!
Thou in our wonder and astonishment
Hast built thy self a live-long Monument.
For whilst to th'shame of slow-endeavouring art,
Thy easie numbers flow, and that each heart
Hath from the leaves of thy unvalu'd Book,
Those Delphick lines with deep impression took,
Then thou our fancy of it self bereaving,
Dost make us Marble with too much conceaving;
And so Sepulcher'd in such pomp dost lie,
That Kings for such a Tomb would wish to die.

¶ On the University Carrier,
who sickn'd in the time of his vacancy, being
forbid to go to *London*, by reason of the Plague

HERE lies old *Hobson*, Death hath broke his girt,
And here alas, hath laid him in the dirt,
Or else the ways being foul, twenty to one,
He's here stuck in a slough, and overthrown.
'Twas such a shifter, that if truth were known,
Death was half glad when he had got him down;
For he had any time this ten yeers full,
Dodg'd with him, betwixt *Cambridge* and the Bull.
And surely, Death could never have prevail'd,

Had not his weekly course of carriage fail'd;
But lately finding him so long at home,
And thinking now his journeys end was come,
And that he had tane up his latest Inne,
In the kind office of a Chamberlin
Shew'd him his room where he must lodge that night,
Pull'd of his Boots, and took away the light:
If any ask for him, it shall be sed,
Hobson has supt, and's newly gon to bed.

¶ Another on the same

HERE lieth one who did most truly prove,
That he could never die while he could move,
So hung his destiny never to rot
While he might still jogg on and keep his trot,
Made of sphear-metal, never to decay
Untill his revolution was at stay.
Time numbers motion, yet (without a crime
'Gainst old truth) motion number'd out his time:
And like an Engin mov'd with wheel and waight,
His principles being ceast, he ended strait,
Rest that gives all men life, gave him his death,
And too much breathing put him out of breath;
Nor were it contradiction to affirm
Too long vacation hastned on his term.
Meerly to drive the time away he sickn'd,
Fainted, and died, nor would with Ale be quickn'd,
Nay, quoth he, on his swooning bed out-stretch'd,
If I may not carry, sure I'le ne're be fetch'd,
But vow though the cross Doctors all stood hearers,
For one Carrier put down to make six bearers.
Ease was his chief disease, and to judge right,
He di'd for heaviness that his Cart went light,
His leasure told him that his time was com,
And lack of load, made his life burdensom,
That even to his last breath (ther be that say't)
As he were prest to death, he cry'd more waight;
But had his doings lasted as they were,
He had been an immortal Carrier.

Obedient to the Moon he spent his date
In cours reciprocal, and had his fate
Linkt to the mutual flowing of the Seas,
Yet (strange to think) his wain was his increase:
His Letters are deliver'd all and gon,
Only remains this superscription.

¶ An Epitaph on the Marchioness of *Winchester*

THIS rich Marble doth enterr
The honour'd Wife of *Winchester*,
A Vicounts daughter, an Earls heir,
Besides what her vertues fair
Added to her noble birth,
More than she could own from Earth.
Summers three times eight save one
She had told, alass too soon,
After so short time of breath,
To house with darkness, and with death.
Yet had the number of her days
Bin as compleat as was her praise,
Nature and fate had had no strife
In giving limit to her life.
Her high birth, and her graces sweet,
Quickly found a lover meet;
The Virgin quire for her request
The God that sits at marriage feast;
He at their invoking came
But with a scarce-wel-lighted flame;
And in his Garland as he stood,
Ye might discern a Cypress bud.
Once had the early Matrons run
To greet her of a lovely son,
And now with second hope she goes,
And calls *Lucina* to her throws;
But whether by mischance or blame
Atropos for *Lucina* came;
And with remorsles cruelty,
Spoil'd at once both fruit and tree:

The haples Babe before his birth
Had burial, yet not laid in earth,
And the languisht Mothers Womb
Was not long a living Tomb.
So have I seen some tender slip
Sav'd with care from Winters nip,
The pride of her carnation train,
Pluck't up by som unheedy swain,
Who onely thought to crop the flowr
New shot up from vernal showr;
But the fair blossom hangs the head
Side-ways as on a dying bed,
And those Pearls of dew she wears,
Prove to be presaging tears
Which the sad morn had let fall
On her hast'ning funerall.
Gentle Lady may thy grave
Peace and quiet ever have;
After this thy travel sore
Sweet rest sease thee evermore,
That to give the world encrease,
Shortned hast thy own lives lease;
Here, besides the sorrowing
That thy noble House doth bring,
Here be tears of perfect moan
Weept for thee in *Helicon*,
And som Flowers, and some Bays,
For thy Hears to strew the ways,
Sent thee from the banks of *Came*,
Devoted to thy vertuous name;
Whilst thou bright Saint high sit'st in glory.
Next her much like to thee in story,
That fair *Syrian* Shepherdess,
Who after yeers of barrenness,
The highly favour'd *Joseph* bore
To him that serv'd for her before,
And at her next birth much like thee,
Through pangs fled to felicity,
Far within the boosom bright
Of blazing Majesty and Light,

There with thee, new welcom Saint,
Like fortunes may her soul acquaint,
With thee there clad in radiant sheen,
No Marchioness, but now a Queen.

¶ "How soon hath time . . ."

How soon hath time the suttle theef of youth,
  Stoln on his wing my three and twentieth yeer!
  My hasting dayes flie on with full career,
  But my late spring no bud or blossom shew'th.
Perhaps my semblance might deceive the truth,
  That I to manhood am arriv'd so near,
  And inward ripenes doth much less appear,
  That som more timely-happy spirits indu'th.
Yet be it less or more, or soon or slow,
  It shall be still in strictest measure eev'n,
  To that same lot, however mean or high,
Toward which Time leads me, and the will of Heav'n ;
  All is, if I have grace to use it so,
  As ever in my great task Masters eye.

¶ Arcades

*Part of an Entertainment presented to the Countess Dowager
of Darby at Harefield, by some Noble Persons of her
Family, who appear on the Scene in Pastoral Habit, moving
toward the seat of State, with this Song.*

1. SONG

Look Nymphs, and Shepherds look,
What sudden blaze of Majesty
Is that which we from hence descry
Too divine to be mistook :
  This this is she
To whom our vows and wishes bend,
Heer our solemn search hath end.

Fame that her high worth to raise,
Seem'd erst so lavish and profuse,

We may justly now accuse
Of detraction from her praise,
  Less then half we find exprest,
  Envy bid conceal the rest.

Mark what radiant state she spreds,
In circle round her shining throne,
Shooting her beams like silver threds,
This this is she alone,
  Sitting like a Goddes bright,
  In the center of her light.

Might she the wife *Latona* be,
Or the towred *Cybele*,
Mother of a hundred gods;
Juno dare's not give her odds;
  Who had thought this clime had held
  A deity so unparalel'd?

*As they com forward, the Genius of the Wood appears,
and turning toward them, speaks.*

Gen. Stay gentle Swains, for though in this disguise,
I see bright honour sparkle through your eyes,
Of famous *Arcady* ye are, and sprung
Of that renowned flood, so often sung,
Divine *Alpheus*, who by secret sluse,
Stole under Seas to meet his *Arethuse*;
And ye the breathing Roses of the Wood,
Fair silver-buskin'd Nymphs as great and good,
I know this quest of yours, and free intent
Was all in honour and devotion ment
To the great Mistres of yon princely shrine,
Whom with low reverence I adore as mine,
And with all helpful service will comply
To further this nights glad solemnity;
And lead ye where ye may more near behold
What shallow-searching *Fame* hath left untold;
Which I full oft amidst these shades alone
Have sate to wonder at, and gaze upon:
For know by lot from *Jove* I am the powr
Of this fair Wood, and live in Oak'n bowr.

To nurse the Saplings tall, and curl the grove
With Ringlets quaint; and wanton windings wove.
And all my Plants I save from nightly ill,
Of noisom winds, and blasting vapours chill.
And from the Boughs brush off the evil dew,
And heal the harms of thwarting thunder blew,
Or what the cross dire-looking Planet smites,
Or hurtfull Worm with canker'd venom bites.
When Ev'ning gray doth rise, I fetch my round
Over the mount, and all this hallow'd ground;
And early ere the odorous breath of morn
Awakes the slumbring leaves, or tasseld horn
Shakes the high thicket, haste I all about,
Number my ranks, and visit every sprout
With puissant words, and murmurs made to bless,
But els in deep of night when drowsines
Hath lock't up mortal sense, then listen I
To the celestial *Sirens* harmony,
That sit upon the nine enfolded Sphears,
And sing to those that hold the vital shears,
And turn the Adamantine spindle round,
On which the fate of gods and men is wound.
Such sweet compulsion doth in musick ly,
To lull the daughters of *Necessity*,
And keep unsteddy Nature to her law,
And the low world in measur'd motion draw
After the heavenly tune, which none can hear
Of human mould with gross unpurged ear;
And yet such musick worthiest were to blaze
The peerles height of her immortal praise,
Whose lustre leads us, and for her most fit,
If my inferior hand or voice could hit
Inimitable sounds, yet as we go,
What ere the skill of lesser gods can show,
I will assay, her worth to celebrate,
And so attend ye toward her glittering state;
Where ye may all that are of noble stemm
Approach, and kiss her sacred vestures hemm.

2. SONG

O're the smooth enamel'd green
Where no print of step hath been,
  Follow me as I sing,
  And touch the warbled string.
Under the shady roof
Of branching Elm-Star-proof.
  Follow me,
I will bring you where she sits
Clad in splendor as befits
  Her deity.
Such a rural Queen
All *Arcadia* hath not seen.

3. SONG

Nymphs and shepherds dance no more
By sandy *Ladons* Lillied banks,
On old *Lycæus* or *Cyllene* hoar,
  Trip no more in twilight ranks,
Though *Erymanth* your loss deplore,
  A better soyl shall give ye thanks.
From the stony *Mænalus*,
Bring your Flocks, and live with us,
Here ye shall have greater grace,
To serve the Lady of this place.
  Though *Syrinx* your *Pans* Mistress were,
  Yet *Syrinx* well might wait on her.
    Such a rural Queen
  All *Arcadia* hath not seen.

¶ On Time

FLY envious *Time*, till thou run out thy race,
Call on the lazy leaden-stepping hours,
Whose speed is but the heavy Plummets pace;
And glut thy self with what thy womb devours,
Which is no more then what is false and vain,
And meerly mortal dross;

So little is our loss,
So little is thy gain.
For when as each thing bad thou hast entomb'd,
And last of all thy greedy self consum'd,
Then long Eternity shall greet our bliss
With an individual kiss;
And Joy shall overtake us as a flood,
When every thing that is sincerely good
And perfectly divine,
With Truth, and Peace, and Love shall ever shine
About the supreme Throne
Of him, t'whose happy-making sight alone,
When once our heav'nly-guided soul shall clime,
Then all This Earthy grosness quit,
Attir'd with Stars, we shall for ever sit,
    Triumphing over Death, and Chance, and thee O Time.

¶ Upon the Circumcision

Ye flaming Powers, and winged Warriours bright,
That erst with Musick, and triumphant song
First heard by happy watchful Shepherds ear,
So sweetly sung your Joy the Clouds along
Through the soft silence of the list'ning night;
Now mourn, and if sad share with us to bear
Your fiery essence can distill no tear,
Burn in your sighs, and borrow
Seas wept from our deep sorrow,
He who with all Heav'ns heraldry whilear
Enter'd the world, now bleeds to give us ease;
Alas, how soon our sin
    Sore doth begin
        His Infancy to sease!
O more exceeding love or law more just?
Just law indeed, but more exceeding love!
For we by rightful doom remediles
Were lost in death, till he that dwelt above
High thron'd in secret bliss, for us frail dust
Emptied his glory, ev'n to nakednes;
And that great Cov'nant which we still transgress

Intirely satisfi'd,
And the full wrath beside
Of vengeful Justice bore for our excess,
And seals obedience first with wounding smart
This day, but O ere long
Huge pangs and strong
        Will pierce more near his heart.

¶ At a solemn Musick

BLEST pair of *Sirens*, pledges of Heav'ns joy,
Sphear-born harmonious Sisters, Voice, and Vers,
Wed your divine sounds, and mixt power employ,
Dead things with inbreath'd sense able to pierce,
And to our high-rais'd phantasie present,
That undisturbed Song of pure concent,
Ay sung before the saphire-colour'd throne
To him that sits thereon
With Saintly shout, and solemn Jubily,
Where the bright Seraphim in burning row
Their loud up-lifted Angel trumpets blow,
And the Cherubick host in thousand quires
Touch their immortal Harps of golden wires,
With those just Spirits that wear victorious Palms,
Hymns devout and holy Psalms
Singing everlastingly;
That we on Earth with undiscording voice
May rightly answer that melodious noise;
As once we did, till disproportion'd sin
Jarr'd against natures chime, and with harsh din
Broke the fair musick that all creatures made
To their great Lord, whose love their motion sway'd
In perfect Diapason, whilst they stood
In first obedience, and their state of good.
O may we soon again renew that Song,
And keep in tune with Heav'n, till God ere long
To his celestial consort us unite,
To live with him, and sing in endles morn of light.

¶ L'Allegro

HENCE loathed Melancholy
    Of *Cerberus*, and blackest midnight born,
In *Stygian* Cave forlorn.
    'Mongst horrid shapes, and shreiks, and sights unholy,
Find out some uncouth cell,
    Where brooding darkness spreads his jealous wings,
And the night-Raven sings;
    There under *Ebon* shades, and low-brow'd Rocks,
As ragged as thy Locks,
    In dark *Cimmerian* desert ever dwell.
But com thou Goddess fair and free,
In Heav'n ycleap'd *Euphrosyne*,
And by men, heart-easing Mirth,
Whom lovely *Venus* at a birth
With two sister Graces more
To Ivy-crowned *Bacchus* bore;
Or whether (as som Sager sing)
The frolick Wind that breathes the Spring,
Zephir with *Aurora* playing,
As he met her once a Maying,
There on Beds of Violets blew,
And fresh-blown Roses washt in dew,
Fill'd her with thee a daughter fair,
So bucksom, blith, and debonair.
Haste thee nymph, and bring with thee
Jest and youthful Jollity,
Quips and Cranks, and wanton Wiles,
Nods, and Becks, and Wreathed Smiles,
Such as hang on *Hebe's* cheek,
And love to live in dimple sleek;
Sport that wrincled Care derides,
And Laughter holding both his sides.
Com, and trip it as you go
On the light fantastick toe,
And in thy right hand lead with thee,
The Mountain Nymph, sweet Liberty;
And if I give thee honour due,
Mirth, admit me of thy crue

To live with her, and live with thee,
In unreproved pleasures free;
To hear the Lark begin his flight,
And singing startle the dull night,
From his watch-towre in the skies,
Till the dappled dawn doth rise;
Then to com in spight of sorrow,
And at my window bid good morrow,
Through the Sweet-Briar, or the Vine,
Or the twisted Eglantine,
While the Cock with lively din,
Scatters the rear of darkness thin,
And to the stack, or the Barn dore,
Stoutly struts his Dames before,
Oft list'ning how the Hounds and Horn
Chearly rouse the slumbring morn,
From the side of som Hoar Hill,
Through the high wood echoing shrill.
Som time walking not unseen
By Hedge-row Elms, on Hillocks green,
Right against the Eastern gate,
Where the great Sun begins his state,
Roab'd in flames, and Amber light,
The clouds in thousand Liveries dight,
While the Plowman neer at hand,
Whistles ore the Furrow'd Land,
And the Milkmaid singeth blithe,
And the Mower whets his sithe,
And every Shepherd tells his tale
Under the Hawthorn in the dale.
Streit mine eye hath caught new pleasures
Whilst the Lantskip round it measures,
Russet Lawns, and Fallows Gray,
Where the nibling flocks do stray,
Mountains on whose barren brest
The labouring clouds do often rest:
Meadows trim with Daisies pide,
Shallow Brooks, and Rivers wide.
Towers, and Battlements it sees
Boosom'd high in tufted Trees,

Wher perhaps som beauty lies,
The Cynosure of neighbouring eyes.
Hard by, a Cottage chimney smokes,
From betwixt two aged Okes,
Where *Corydon* and *Thyrsis* met,
Are at their savory dinner set
Of Hearbs, and other Country Messes,
Which the neat-handed *Phillis* dresses;
And then in haste her Bowre she leaves,
With *Thestylis* to bind the Sheaves;
Or if the earlier season lead
To the tann'd Haycock in the Mead,
Some times with secure delight
The up-land Hamlets will invite,
When the merry Bells ring round,
And the jocond rebecks sound
To many a youth, and many a maid,
Dancing in the Chequer'd shade;
And young and old com forth to play
On a Sunshine Holyday,
Till the live-long day-light fail,
Then to the Spicy Nut-brown Ale,
With stories told of many a feat,
How *Faery Mab* the junkets eat,
She was pincht, and pull'd she sed,
And by the Friars Lanthorn led
Tells how the drudging *Goblin* swet,
To ern his Cream-bowle duly set,
When in one night, ere glimps of morn,
His shadowy Flale hath thresh'd the Corn,
That ten day-labourers could not end,
Then lies him down the Lubbar Fend.
And stretch'd out all the Chimney's length,
Basks at the fire his hairy strength;
And Crop-full out of dores he flings,
Ere the first Cock his Mattin rings,
Thus done the Tales, to bed they creep,
By whispering Winds soon lull'd asleep.
Towred Cities please us then,
And the busie humm of men,

Where throngs of Knights and Barons bold,
In weeds of Peace high triumphs hold,
With store of Ladies, whose bright eies
Rain influence, and judge the prise,
Of Wit, or Arms, while both contend
To win her Grace, whom all commend,
There let *Hymen* oft appear
In Saffron robe, with Taper clear,
And pomp, and feast, and revelry,
With mask, and antique Pageantry,
Such sights as youthful Poets dream
On Summer eeves by haunted stream.
Then to the well-trod stage anon,
If *Jonsons* learned Sock be on,
Or sweetest *Shakespear* fancies childe,
Warble his native Wood-notes wilde,
And ever against eating Cares,
Lap me in soft *Lydian* Aires,
Married to immortal verse
Such as the meeting soul may pierce
In notes, with many a winding bout
Of lincked sweetness long drawn out,
With wanton heed, and giddy cunning,
The melting voice through mazes running;
Untwisting all the chains that ty
The hidden soul of harmony.
That *Orpheus* self may heave his head
From golden slumber on a bed
Of heapt *Elysian* flowres, and hear
Such streins as would have won the ear
Of *Pluto*, to have quite set free
His half regain'd *Eurydice*.
These delights, if thou canst give,
Mirth with thee, I mean to live.

¶ Il Penseroso

HENCE vain deluding joyes,
    The brood of folly without father bred.
How little you bested,
    Or fill the fixed mind with all your toyes;

Dwell in some idle brain,
    And fancies fond with gaudy shapes possess,
As thick and numberless
    As the gay motes that people the Sun Beams,
Or likest hovering dreams
    The fickle Pensioners of *Morpheus* train.
But hail thou Goddess, sage and holy,
Hail divinest Melancholy,
Whose Saintly visage is too bright
To hit the Sense of human sight;
And therefore to our weaker view,
Ore laid with black staid Wisdoms hue.
Black, but such as in esteem,
Prince *Memnons* sister might beseem,
Or that starr'd *Ethiope* Queen that strove
To set her beauties praise above
The Sea Nymphs, and their powers offended,
Yet thou art higher far descended,
Thee bright-hair'd *Vesta* long of yore,
To solitary *Saturn* bore;
His daughter she (in *Saturns* raign,
Such mixture was not held a stain)
Oft in glimmering Bowres, and glades
He met her, and in secret shades
Of woody *Ida's* inmost grove,
While yet there was no fear of *Jove*.
Com pensive Nun, devout and pure,
Sober, stedfast, and demure,
All in a robe of darkest grain,
Flowing with majestick train,
And sable stole of *Cipres* Lawn,
Over thy decent shoulders drawn.
Com, but keep thy wonted state,
With eev'n step, and musing gate,
And looks commercing with the skies,
Thy rapt soul sitting in thine eyes:
There held in holy passion still,
Forget thy self to Marble, till
With a sad Leaden downward cast,
Thou fix them on the earth as fast.

And joyn with thee calm Peace, and Quiet,
Spare Fast, that oft with gods doth diet,
And hears the Muses in a ring,
Ay round about *Joves* Altar sing.
And adde to these retired leasure,
That in trim Gardens takes his pleasure;
But first, and chiefest, with thee bring,
Him that yon soars on golden wing,
Guiding the fiery-wheeled throne,
The Cherub Contemplation,
And the mute Silence hist along,
'Less *Philomel* will deign a Song,
In her sweetest, saddest plight,
Smoothing the rugged brow of night,
While *Cynthia* checks her Dragon yoke,
Gently o're th' accustom'd Oke;
Sweet Bird that shunn'st the noise of folly,
Most musical, most Melancholy!
Thee Chauntress oft the Woods among,
I woo to hear thy Even-Song;
And missing thee, I walk unseen
On the dry smooth-shaven Green,
To behold the wandring Moon,
Riding neer her highest noon,
Like one that had bin led astray
Through the Heav'ns wide pathles way;
And oft, as if her head she bow'd,
Stooping through a fleecy cloud.
Oft on a Plat of rising ground,
I hear the far-off *Curfeu* sound,
Over some wide-water'd shoar,
Swinging slow with sullen roar;
Or if the Ayr will not permit,
Som still removed place will fit,
Where glowing Embers through the room
Teach light to counterfeit a gloom,
Far from all resort of mirth,
Save the Cricket on the hearth,
Or the Belmans drowsie charm,
To bless the dores from nightly harm:

Or let my Lamp at midnight hour,
Be seen in some high lonely Towr,
Where I may oft out-watch the *Bear*,
With thrice great *Hermes*, or unsphear
The spirit of *Plato* to unfold
What Worlds, or what vast Regions hold
The immortal mind that hath forsook
Her mansion in this fleshly nook:
And of those *Dæmons* that are found
In fire, air, flood, or under ground,
Whose power hath a true consent
With Planet, or with Element.
Som time let Gorgeous Tragedy
In Scepter'd Pall com sweeping by,
Presenting *Thebs*, or *Pelops* line,
Or the tale of *Troy* divine.
Or what (though rare) of later age,
Ennobled hath the Buskind stage.
But, O sad Virgin, that thy power
Might raise *Musæus* from his bower,
Or bid the soul of *Orpheus* sing
Such notes as warbled to the string,
Drew Iron tears down *Pluto's* cheek,
And made Hell grant what Love did seek.
Or call up him that left half told
The story of *Cambuscan* bold,
Of *Camball*, and of *Algarsife*,
And who had *Canace* to wife,
That own'd the vertuous Ring and Glass,
And of the wondrous Hors of Brass,
On which the *Tartar* King did ride;
And if ought els, great *Bards* beside,
In sage and solemn tunes have sung,
Of Turneys and of Trophies hung;
Of Forests, and inchantments drear,
Where more is meant then meets the ear.
Thus night oft see me in thy pale career,
Till civil-suited Morn appeer,
Not trickt and frounc't as she was wont,
With the Attick Boy to hunt,

But Cherchef't in a comely Cloud,
While rocking Winds are Piping loud,
Or usher'd with a shower still,
When the gust hath blown his fill,
Ending on the russling Leaves,
With minute drops from off the Eaves.
And when the Sun begins to fling
His flaring beams, me Goddess bring
To arched walks of twilight groves,
And shadows brown that *Sylvan* loves
Of Pine, or monumental Oake,
Where the rude Ax with heaved stroke,
Was never heard the Nymphs to daunt,
Or fright them from their hallow'd haunt.
There in close covert by some Brook,
Where no prophaner eye may look,
Hide me from Day's garish eie,
While the Bee with Honied thie,
That at her flowry work doth sing,
And the Waters murmuring
With such consort as they keep,
Entice the dewy-feather'd Sleep;
And let som strange mysterious dream,
Wave at his Wings in Airy stream,
Of lively portrature display'd,
Softly on my eye-lids laid.
And as I wake, sweet musick breath
Above, about, or underneath,
Sent by som spirit to mortals good,
Or th' unseen Genius of the Wood.
But let my due feet never fail,
To walk the studious Cloysters pale.
And love the high embowed Roof,
With antick Pillars massy proof,
And storied Windows richly dight,
Casting a dimm religious light.
There let the pealing Organ blow,
To the full voic'd Quire below,
In Service high, and Anthems cleer,
As may with sweetness, through mine ear,

Dissolve me into extasies,
And bring all Heav'n before mine eyes.
And may at last my weary age
Find out the peacefull hermitage,
The Hairy Gown and Mossy Cell,
Where I may sit and rightly spell
Of every Star that Heav'n doth shew,
And every Herb that sips the dew;
Till old experience do attain
To something like Prophetic strain.
These pleasures *Melancholy* give,
And I with thee will choose to live.

¶ A Mask
Presented at Ludlow-Castle, 1634, etc.

The first Scene discovers a wilde Wood.
The attendant Spirit descends or enters.

BEFORE the starry threshold of *Joves* Court
My mansion is, where those immortal shapes
Of bright aereal Spirits live insphear'd
In Regions milde of calm and serene Air,
Above the smoak and stirr of this dim spot,
Which men call Earth, and with low-thoughted care
Confin'd, and pester'd in this pin-fold here,
Strive to keep up a frail, and Feaverish being
Unmindfull of the crown that Vertue gives
After this mortal change, to her true Servants
Amongst the enthron'd gods on Sainted seats.
Yet som there be that by due steps aspire
To lay their just hands on that Golden Key
That ope's the Palace of Eternity:
To such my errand is, and but for such,
I would not soil these pure Ambrosial weeds,
With the rank vapours of this Sin-worn mould.
But to my task. *Neptune* besides the sway
Of every salt Flood, and each ebbing stream,
Took in by lot 'twixt high, and neather *Jove*,

Imperial rule of all the Sea-girt Iles
That like to rich, and various gemms inlay
The unadorned boosom of the Deep,
Which he to grace his tributary gods
By course commits to several government,
And gives them leave to wear their Saphire crowns,
And weild their little tridents, but this Ile
The greatest, and the best of all the main
He quarters to his blu-hair'd deities,
And all this tract that fronts the falling Sun
A noble Peer of mickle trust, and power
Has in his charge, with temper'd awe to guide
An old, and haughty Nation proud in Arms:
Where his fair off-spring nurs't in Princely lore,
Are coming to attend their Fathers state,
And new-entrusted Scepter, but their way
Lies through the perplex't paths of this drear Wood,
The nodding horror of whose shady brows
Threats the forlorn and wandring Passinger.
And here their tender age might suffer peril,
But that by quick command from Soveran *Jove*
I was dispatcht for their defence, and guard;
And listen why, for I will tell you now
What never yet was heard in Tale or Song
From old, or modern Bard in Hall, or Bowr.
    Bacchus that first from out the purple Grape,
Crush't the sweet poyson of mis-used Wine
After the *Tuscan* Mariners transform'd
Coasting the *Tyrrhene* shore, as the winds listed,
On *Circes* Iland fell (who knows not *Circe*
The daughter of the Sun? Whose charmed Cup
Whoever tasted, lost his upright shape,
And downward fell into a groveling Swine)
This Nymph that gaz'd upon his clustring locks,
With Ivy berries wreath'd, and his blithe youth,
Had by him, ere he parted thence, a Son
Much like his Father, but his Mother more,
Whom therefore she brought up and *Comus* nam'd,
Who ripe, and frolick of his full grown age,
Roaving the *Celtick*, and *Iberian* fields,

At last betakes him to this ominous Wood,
And in thick shelter of black shades imbowr'd,
Excells his Mother at her mighty Art,
Offring to every weary Traveller,
His orient Liquor in a Crystal Glass,
To quench the drouth of *Phœbus*, which as they taste
(For most do taste through fond intemperate thirst)
Soon as the Potion works, their human count'nance,
Th' express resemblance of the gods, is chang'd
Into som brutish form of Woolf, or Bear,
Or Ounce, or Tiger, Hog, or bearded Goat,
All other parts remaining as they were,
And they, so perfect is their misery,
Not once perceive their foul disfigurement,
But boast themselves more comely then before
And all their friends, and native home forget
To roule with pleasure in a sensual stie.
Therefore when any favour'd of high *Jove*,
Chances to pass through this adventrous glade,
Swift as the Sparkle of a glancing Star,
I shoot from Heav'n to give him safe convoy,
As now I do : But first I must put off
These my skie robes spun out of *Iris* Wooff,
And take the Weeds and likenes of a Swain,
That to the service of this house belongs,
Who with his soft Pipe, and smooth dittied Song,
Well knows to still the wilde winds when they roar,
And hush the waving Woods, nor of less faith,
And in this office of his Mountain watch,
Likeliest, and nearest to the present ayd
Of this occasion. But I hear the tread
Of hatefull steps, I must be viewles now.

Comus *enters with a Charming Rod in one hand, his Glass in the other, with him a rout of Monsters, headed like sundry sorts of wilde Beasts, but otherwise like Men and Women, their Apparel glistering, they come in making a riotous and unruly noise, with Torches in their hands.*

   Comus. The Star that bids the Shepherd fold,
Now the top of Heav'n doth hold,

And the gilded Car of Day,
His glowing Axle doth allay
In the steep *Atlantick* stream,
And the slope Sun his upward beam
Shoots against the dusky Pole,
Pacing toward the other gole
Of his Chamber in the East.
Mean while welcom Joy, and Feast,
Midnight shout, and revelry,
Tipsie dance, and Jollity.
Braid your Locks with rosie Twine
Dropping odours, dropping Wine.
Rigor now is gon to bed,
And Advice with scrupulous head,
Strict Age, and sowre Severity,
With their grave Saws in slumber lie.
We that are of purer fire
Imitate the Starry Quire,
Who in their nightly watchfull Sphears,
Lead in swift round the Months and Years.
The Sounds, and Seas with all their finny drove
Now to the Moon in wavering Morrice move,
And on the Tawny Sands and Shelves,
Trip the pert Fairies and the dapper Elves;
By dimpled Brook, and Fountain brim,
The Wood-Nymphs deckt with Daisies trim,
Their merry wakes and pastimes keep:
What hath night to do with sleep?
Night hath better sweets to prove,
Venus now wakes, and wak'ns Love.
Com let us our rights begin,
'Tis onely day-light that makes Sin
Which these dun shades will ne're report,
Hail Goddess of Nocturnal sport
Dark vail'd *Cotytto*, t' whom the secret flame
Of mid-night Torches burns; mysterious Dame
That ne're art call'd, but when the Dragon woom
Of Stygian darkness spets her thickest gloom,
And makes one blot of all the air,
Stay thy cloudy Ebon chair,

Wherin thou rid'st with *Hecat'*, and befriend
Us thy vow'd Priests, till utmost end
Of all thy dues be done, and none left out,
Ere the blabbing Eastern scout,
The nice Morn on th' *Indian* steep
From her cabin'd loop-hole peep,
And to the tell-tale Sun discry
Our conceal'd Solemnity.
Com, knit hands, and beat the ground,
In a light fantastick round.

The Measure.

Break off, break off, I feel the different pace,
Of som chast footing near about this ground.
Run to your shrouds, within these Brakes and Trees,
Our number may affright : Some Virgin sure
(For so I can distinguish by mine Art)
Benighted in these Woods. Now to my charms,
And to my wily trains, I shall e're long
Be well stock't with as fair a herd as graz'd
About my Mother *Circe*. Thus I hurl
My dazling Spells into the spungy ayr,
Of power to cheat the eye with blear illusion,
And give it false presentments, lest the place,
And my quaint habits breed astonishment,
And put the Damsel to suspicious flight,
Which must not be, for that's against my course;
I under fair pretence of friendly ends,
And well plac't words of glozing courtesie
Baited with reasons not unplausible
Wind me into the easie-hearted man,
And hug him into snares. When once her eye
Hath met the vertue of this Magick dust
I shall appear some harmles Villager
And hearken, if I may, her busines here.
But here she comes, I fairly step aside.

The Lady enters.

This way the noise was, if mine ear be true,
My best guide now, me thought it was the sound

Of Riot, and ill manag'd Merriment,
Such as the jocund Flute, or gamesom Pipe
Stirs up among the loose unletter'd Hinds,
When for their teeming Flocks, and granges full
In wanton dance they praise the bounteous *Pan*,
And thank the gods amiss. I should be loath
To meet the rudeness, and swill'd insolence
Of such late Wassailers; yet O where els
Shall I inform my unacquainted feet
In the blind mazes of this tangl'd Wood?
My Brothers when they saw me wearied out
With this long way, resolving here to lodge
Under the spreading favour of these Pines,
Stept as they se'd to the next Thicket side
To bring me Berries, or such cooling fruit
As the kind hospitable Woods provide.
They left me then, when the gray-hooded Eev'n
Like a sad Votarist in Palmers weed
Rose from the hindmost wheels of *Phœbus* wain.
But where they are, and why they came not back,
Is now the labour of my thoughts, 'tis likeliest
They had ingag'd their wandring steps too far,
And envious darknes, e're they could return,
Had stole them from me, els O theevish Night
Why shouldst thou, but for som fellonious end,
In thy dark Lantern thus close up the Stars,
That nature hung in Heav'n, and fill'd their Lamps
With everlasting oil, to give due light
To the misled and lonely Traveller?
This is the place, as well as I may guess,
Whence eev'n now the tumult of loud Mirth
Was rife, and perfet in my list'ning ear,
Yet nought but single darknes do I find.
What might this be? A thousand fantasies
Begin to throng into my memory
Of calling shapes, and beckning shadows dire,
And airy tongues, that syllable mens names
On Sands, and Shoars, and desert Wildernesses.
These thoughts may startle well, but not astound
The vertuous mind, that ever walks attended

By a strong siding champion Conscience.——
O welcom pure-ey'd Faith, white-handed Hope,
Thou hovering Angel girt with golden wings,
And thou unblemish't form of Chastity,
I see ye visibly, and now believe
That he, the Supreme good, t' whom all things ill
Are but as slavish officers of vengeance,
Would send a glistring Guardian if need were
To keep my life and honour unassail'd.
Was I deceiv'd, or did a sable cloud
Turn forth her silver lining on the night?
I did not err, there does a sable cloud
Turn forth her silver lining on the night,
And casts a gleam over this tufted Grove.
I cannot hallow to my Brothers, but
Such noise as I can make to be heard farthest
Ile venter, for my new enliv'nd spirits
Prompt me; and they perhaps are not far off.

SONG

Sweet Echo, sweetest Nymph that liv'st unseen
Within thy airy shell
By slow Meander's *margent green,*
And in the violet imbroider'd vale
Where the love-lorn Nightingale
Nightly to thee her sad Song mourneth well.
Canst thou not tell me of a gentle Pair
That likest thy Narcissus *are?*
O if thou have
Hid them in som flowry Cave,
Tell me but where
Sweet Queen of Parly, Daughter of the Sphear,
So maist thou be translated to the skies,
And give resounding grace to all Heav'ns Harmonies.

Com. Can any mortal mixture of Earths mould
Breath such Divine inchanting ravishment?
Sure somthing holy lodges in that brest,
And with these raptures moves the vocal air
To testifie his hidd'n residence;

How sweetly did they float upon the wings
Of silence, through the empty-vaulted night
At every fall smoothing the Raven doune
Of darknes till it smil'd : I have oft heard
My Mother *Circe* with the Sirens three,
Amid'st the flowry-kirtl'd *Naiades*
Culling their potent hearbs, and balefull drugs,
Who as they sung, would take the prison'd soul,
And lap it in *Elysium*, *Scylla* wept,
And chid her barking waves into attention,
And fell *Charybdis* murmur'd soft applause :
Yet they in pleasing slumber lull'd the sense,
And in sweet madnes rob'd it of it self,
But such a sacred, and home-felt delight,
Such sober certainty of waking bliss
I never heard till now. Ile speak to her
And she shall be my Queen. Hail forren wonder
Whom certain these rough shades did never breed
Unless the Goddes that in rural shrine
Dwell'st here with *Pan*, or *Silvan*, by blest Song
Forbidding every bleak unkindly Fog
To touch the prosperous growth of this tall Wood.

    La. Nay gentle Shepherd ill is lost that praise
That is addrest to unattending Ears,
Not any boast of skill, but extreme shift
How to regain my sever'd company
Compell'd me to awake the courteous Echo
To give me answer from her mossie Couch.

    Co. What chance good Lady hath bereft you thus?
    La. Dim darknes, and this leavie Labyrinth.
    Co. Could that divide you from neer-ushering guides?
    La. They left me weary on a grassie terf.
    Co. By falshood, or discourtesie, or why?
    La. To seek i'th vally som cool friendly Spring.
    Co. And left your fair side all unguarded Lady?
    La. They were but twain, and purpos'd quick return.
    Co. Perhaps fore-stalling night prevented them.
    La. How easie my misfortune is to hit!
    Co. Imports their loss, beside the present need?
    La. No less then if I should my brothers loose.

Co. Were they of manly prime, or youthful bloom?
La. As smooth as *Hebe's* their unrazor'd lips.
Co. Two such I saw, what time the labour'd Oxe
In his loose traces from the furrow came,
And the swink't hedger at his Supper sate;
I saw them under a green mantling vine
That crawls along the side of yon small hill,
Plucking ripe clusters from the tender shoots,
Their port was more then human, as they stood;
I took it for a faëry vision
Of som gay creatures of the element
That in the colours of the Rainbow live
And play i'th plighted clouds. I was aw-strook,
And as I past, I worshipt; if those you seek
It were a journey like the path to Heav'n,
To help you find them. *La*. Gentle villager
What readiest way would bring me to that place?

   Co. Due west it rises from this shrubby point.

   La. To find out that, good Shepherd, I suppose,
In such a scant allowance of Star-light,
Would overtask the best Land-Pilots art,
Without the sure guess of well-practiz'd feet.

   Co. I know each lane, and every alley green
Dingle, or bushy dell of this wilde Wood,
And every bosky bourn from side to side
My daily walks and ancient neighbourhood,
And if your stray attendance be yet lodg'd,
Or shroud within these limits, I shall know
Ere morrow wake, or the low roosted lark
From her thatch't pallat rowse, if otherwise
I can conduct you Lady to a low
But loyal cottage, where you may be safe
Till further quest'. *La*. Shepherd I take thy word,
And trust thy honest offer'd courtesie,
Which oft is sooner found in lowly sheds
With smoaky rafters, then in tapstry Halls
And Courts of Princes, where it first was nam'd,
And yet is most pretended: In a place
Less warranted then this, or less secure
I cannot be that I should fear to change it,

Eie me blest Providence, and square my triall
To my proportion'd strength. Shepherd lead on.—

The two Brothers.

Eld. Bro. Unmuffle ye faint Stars, and thou fair Moon
That wontst to love the travellers benizon,
Stoop thy pale visage through an amber cloud,
And disinherit *Chaos*, that raigns here
In double night of darkness, and of shades;
Or if your influence be quite damm'd up
With black usurping mists, som gentle taper
Though a rush Candle from the wicker hole
Of som clay habitation visit us
With thy long levell'd rule of streaming light,
And thou shalt be our star of *Arcady*,
Or *Tyrian* Cynosure. 2. *Bro.* Or if our eyes
Be barr'd that happines, might we but hear
The folded flocks pen'd in their watled cotes,
Or sound of pastoral reed with oaten stops,
Or whistle from the Lodge, or Village Cock
Count the night watches to his feathery Dames,
'Twould be som solace yet som little chearing
In this close dungeon of innumerous bowes.
But O that haples virgin our lost sister
Where may she wander now, whither betake her
From the chill dew, amongst rude burrs and thistles?
Perhaps som cold bank is her boulster now
Or 'gainst the rugged bark of som broad Elm
Leans her unpillow'd head fraught with sad fears,
What if in wild amazement, and affright,
Or while we speak within the direful grasp
Of Savage hunger, or of Savage heat?
    Eld. Bro. Peace Brother, be not over-exquisite
To cast the fashion of uncertain evils;
For grant they be so, while they rest unknown,
What need a man forestall his date of grief,
And run to meet what he would most avoid?
Or if they be but false alarms of Fear,
How bitter is such self-delusion?
I do not think my sister so to seek,

Or so unprincipl'd in vertues book,
And the sweet peace that goodnes boosoms ever,
As that the single want of light and noise
(Not being in danger, as I trust she is not)
Could stir the constant mood of her calm thoughts,
And put them into mis-becoming plight.
Vertue could see to do what vertue would
By her own radiant light, though Sun and Moon
Were in the flat Sea sunk.   And Wisdoms self
Oft seeks to sweet retired Solitude,
Where with her best nurse Contemplation
She plumes her feathers, and lets grow her wings
That in the various bussle of resort
Were all to ruffl'd, and somtimes impair'd.
He that has light within his own cleer brest
May sit i'th center, and enjoy bright day,
But he that hides a dark soul, and foul thoughts
Benighted walks under the mid-day Sun;
Himself is his own dungeon.
  2. *Bro.* Tis most true
That musing meditation most affects
The pensive secrecy of desert cell,
Far from the cheerfull haunt of men, and herds,
And sits as safe as in a Senat house,
For who would rob a Hermit of his Weeds,
His few Books, or his Beads, or Maple Dish,
Or do his gray hairs any violence?
But beauty like the fair Hesperian Tree
Laden with blooming gold, had need the guard
Of dragon watch with uninchanted eye,
To save her blossoms, and defend her fruit
From the rash hand of bold Incontinence.
You may as well spread out the unsun'd heaps
Of Misers treasure by an out-laws den,
And tell me it is safe, as bid me hope
Danger will wink on Opportunity,
And let a single helpless maiden pass
Uninjur'd in this wilde surrounding wast.
Of night, or loneliness it recks me not,
I fear the dred events that dog them both,

Lest som ill greeting touch attempt the person
Of our unowned sister.
   Eld. Bro. I do not, Brother,
Inferr, as if I thought my sisters state
Secure without all doubt, or controversie:
Yet where an equal poise of hope and fear
Does arbitrate th' event, my nature is
That I encline to hope, rather then fear,
And gladly banish squint suspicion.
My sister is not so defenceless left
As you imagine, she has a hidden strength
Which you remember not.
   2. Bro. What hidden strength,
Unless the strength of Heav'n, if you mean that?
   Eld. Bro. I mean that too, but yet a hidden strength
Which if Heav'n gave it, may be term'd her own:
'Tis chastity, my brother, chastity:
She that has that, is clad in compleat steel,
And like a quiver'd Nymph with Arrows keen
May trace huge Forrests, and unharbour'd Heaths,
Infamous Hills, and sandy perilous wildes,
Where through the sacred rayes of Chastity,
No savage fierce, Bandite, or Mountaneer
Will dare to soyl her Virgin purity,
Yea there, where very desolation dwels
By grots, and caverns shag'd with horrid shades,
She may pass on with unblench't majesty,
Be it not don in pride, or in presumption.
Som say no evil thing that walks by night
In fog, or fire, by lake, or moorish fen,
Blew meager Hag, or stubborn unlaid ghost,
That breaks his magick chains at *curfeu* time,
No Goblin, or swart Faëry of the mine,
Hath hurtfull power o're true Virginity.
Do ye believe me yet, or shall I call
Antiquity from the old Schools of *Greece*
To testifie the arms of Chastity?
Hence had the huntress *Dian* her dred bow
Fair silver-shafted Queen for ever chaste,
Wherewith she tam'd the brinded lioness

And spotted mountain pard, but set at nought
The frivolous bolt of *Cupid*, gods and men
Fear'd her stern frown, and she was queen oth' Woods.
What was that snaky-headed *Gorgon* sheild
That wise *Minerva* wore, unconquer'd Virgin,
Wherwith she freez'd her foes to congeal'd stone?
But rigid looks of Chast austerity,
And noble grace that dash't brute violence
With sudden adoration, and blank aw.
So dear to Heav'n is Saintly chastity,
That when a soul is found sincerely so,
A thousand liveried Angels lacky her,
Driving far off each thing of sin and guilt,
And in cleer dream, and solemn vision
Tell her of things that no gross ear can hear,
Till oft convers with heav'nly habitants
Begin to cast a beam on th' outward shape,
The unpolluted temple of the mind,
And turns it by degrees to the souls essence,
Till all be made immortal: but when lust
By unchaste looks, loose gestures, and foul talk,
But most by leud and lavish act of sin,
Lets in defilement to the inward parts,
The soul grows clotted by contagion,
Imbodies, and imbrutes, till she quite loose
The divine property of her first being.
Such are those thick and gloomy shadows damp
Oft seen in Charnel vaults, and Sepulchers
Lingering, and sitting by a new made grave,
As loath to leave the Body that it lov'd,
And link't it self by carnal sensuality
To a degenerate and degraded state.
 2. *Bro.* How charming is divine Philosophy!
Not harsh and crabbed as dull fools suppose,
But musical as is *Apollo's* lute,
And a perpetual feast of nectar'd sweets,
Where no crude surfet raigns. *Eld. Bro.* List, list, I hear
Som far of hallow break the silent Air.
 2. *Bro.* Me thought so too; what should it be?
 Eld. Bro. For certain

Either som one like us night-founder'd here,
Or els som neighbour Wood-man, or at worst,
Som roaving Robber calling to his fellows.
  2. Bro. Heav'n keep my sister, agen, agen, and neer,
Best draw, and stand upon our guard.
  Eld. Bro. Ile hallow,
If he be friendly he comes well, if not,
Defence is a good cause, and Heav'n be for us.

   The attendant Spirit habited like a Shepherd.

That hallow I should know, what are you? speak;
Com not too neer, you fall on iron stakes else.
  Spir. What voice is that, my young Lord? speak agen.
  2. Bro. O brother, 'tis my father Shepherd sure.
  Eld. Bro. Thyrsis? Whose artful strains have oft delaid
The hudling brook to hear his madrigal,
And sweetn'd every muskrose of the dale,
How cam'st thou here good Swain? hath any Ram
Slipt from the fold, or young Kid lost his dam,
Or straggling Weather the pen't flock forsook?
How couldst thou find this dark sequester'd nook?
  Spir. O my lov'd Masters heir, and his next joy,
I came not here on such a trivial toy
As a stray'd Ewe, or to pursue the stealth
Of pilfering Woolf, not all the fleecy wealth
That doth enrich these Downs, is worth a thought
To this my errand, and the care it brought.
But O my Virgin Lady, where is she?
How chance she is not in your company?
  Eld. Bro. To tell thee sadly Shepherd, without blame,
Or our neglect, we lost her as we came.
  Spir. Ay me unhappy then my fears are true.
  Eld. Bro. What fears good *Thyrsis?* Prethee briefly shew.
  Spir. Ile tell ye, 'tis not vain or fabulous,
(Though so esteem'd by shallow ignorance)
What the sage Poets taught by th' heav'nly Muse,
Storied of old in high immortal vers
Of dire *Chimera's* and inchanted Iles,
And rifted Rocks whose entrance leads to Hell,
For such there be, but unbelief is blind.

Within the navil of this hideous Wood,
Immur'd in cypress shades a Sorcerer dwels
Of *Bacchus*, and of *Circe* born, great *Comus*,
Deep skill'd in all his mothers witcheries,
And here to every thirsty wanderer,
By sly enticement gives his baneful cup,
With many murmurs mixt, whose pleasing poison
The visage quite transforms of him that drinks,
And the inglorious likenes of a beast
Fixes instead, unmoulding reasons mintage
Character'd in the face; this have I learn't
Tending my flocks hard by i'th hilly crofts,
That brow this bottom glade, whence night by night
He and his monstrous rout are heard to howl
Like stabl'd wolves, or tigers at their prey,
Doing abhorred rites to *Hecate*
In their obscured haunts of inmost bowres,
Yet have they many baits, and guileful spells
To inveigle and invite th' unwary sense
Of them that pass unweeting by the way.
This evening late by then the chewing flocks
Had ta'n their supper on the savoury Herb
Of Knot-grass dew-besprent, and were in fold,
I sate me down to watch upon a bank
With Ivy canopied, and interwove
With flaunting Hony-suckle, and began
Wrapt in a pleasing fit of melancholy
To meditate upon my rural minstrelsie,
Till fancy had her fill, but ere a close
The wonted roar was up amidst the Woods,
And fill'd the Air with barbarous dissonance
At which I ceas't, and listen'd them a while,
Till an unusual stop of sudden silence
Gave respit to the drowsie frighted steeds
That draw the litter of close curtain'd sleep;
At last a soft and solemn breathing sound
Rose like a stream of rich distill'd perfumes,
And stole upon the Air, that even Silence
Was took e're she was ware, and wisht she might
Deny her nature, and be never more

Still to be so displac't. I was all ear,
And took in strains that might create a soul
Under the ribs of Death, but O ere long
Too well I did perceive it was the voice
Of my most honour'd Lady, your dear sister.
Amaz'd I stood, harrow'd with grief and fear,
And O poor hapless Nightingale thought I,
How sweet thou sing'st, how near the deadly snare!
Then down the Lawns I ran with headlong hast
Through paths, and turnings oft'n trod by day,
Till guided by mine ear I found the place
Where that damn'd wisard hid in sly disguise
(For so by certain signes I knew) had met
Already, ere my best speed could prevent,
The aidless innocent Lady his wish't prey,
Who gently ask't if he had seen such two,
Supposing him som neighbour villager;
Longer I durst not stay, but soon I guess't
Ye were the two she mean't, with that I sprung
Into swift flight, till I had found you here,
But further know I not. *2. Bro.* O night and shades,
How are ye joyn'd with Hell in tripple knot
Against th' unarm'd weakness of one Virgin
Alone, and helpless! is this the confidence
You gave me Brother? *Eld. Bro.* Yes, and keep it still,
Lean on it safely, not a period
Shall be unsaid for me: against the threats
Of malice or of sorcery, or that power
Which erring men call Chance, this I hold firm,
Vertue may be assail'd, but never hurt,
Surpriz'd by unjust force, but not enthrall'd,
Yea even that which mischief meant most harm,
Shall in the happy trial prove most glory.
But evil on it self shall back recoyl,
And mix no more with goodness, when at last
Gather'd like scum, and setl'd to it self
It shall be in eternal restless change
Self-fed, and self-consum'd, if this fail,
The pillar'd firmament is rott'nness,
And earths base built on stubble. But com let's on.

Against th' opposing will and arm of Heav'n
May never this just sword be lifted up,
But for that damn'd Magician, let him be girt
With all the greisly legions that troop
Under the sooty flag of *Acheron*,
Harpyes and *Hydra's*, or all the monstrous forms
'Twixt *Africa* and *Inde*, Ile find him out,
And force him to restore his purchase back,
Or drag him by the curls, to a foul death,
Curs'd as his life.

    Spir. Alas good ventrous youth,
I love thy courage yet, and bold Emprise,
But here thy sword can do thee little stead,
Far other arms, and other weapons must
Be those that quell the might of hellish charms,
He with his bare wand can unthred thy joynts,
And crumble all thy sinews.

    Eld. Bro. Why prethee Shepherd
How durst thou then thy self approach so neer
As to make this Relation?

    Spir. Care and utmost shifts
How to secure the Lady from surprisal,
Brought to my mind a certain Shepherd Lad
Of small regard to see to, yet well skill'd
In every vertuous plant and healing herb
That spreds her verdant leaf to th' morning ray,
He lov'd me well, and oft would beg me sing,
Which when I did, he on the tender grass
Would sit, and hearken even to extasie,
And in requital ope his leathern scrip,
And shew me simples of a thousand names
Telling their strange and vigorous faculties;
Amongst the rest a small unsightly root,
But of divine effect, he cull'd me out;
The leaf was darkish, and had prickles on it,
But in another Countrey, as he said,
Bore a bright golden flowre, but not in this soyl:
Unknown, and like esteem'd, and the dull swain
Treads on it daily with his clouted shoon,
And yet more med'cinal is it then that *Moly*

That *Hermes* once to wise *Ulysses* gave;
He call'd it *Hæmony*, and gave it me,
And bad me keep it as of sov'ran use
'Gainst all inchantments, mildew blast, or damp
Or gastly furies apparition;
I purs't it up, but little reck'ning made,
Till now that this extremity compell'd,
But now I find it true; for by this means
I knew the foul inchanter though disguis'd,
Enter'd the very lime-twigs of his spells,
And yet came off: if you have this about you
(As I will give you when we go) you may
Boldly assault the necromancers hall;
Where if he be, with dauntless hardihood,
And brandish't blade rush on him, break his glass,
And shed the lushious liquor on the ground,
But sease his wand, though he and his curst crew
Fierce signe of battail make, and menace high,
Or like the Sons of *Vulcan* vomit smoak,
Yet will they soon retire, if he but shrink.
    Eld. Bro. *Thyrsis* lead on apace, Ile follow thee,
And som good angel bear a shield before us.

*The Scene changes to a stately Palace, set out with all manner
   of deliciousness: soft Musick, Tables spred with all dainties.
  Comus appears with his rabble, and the Lady set in an
  inchanted Chair, to whom he offers his Glass, which she
  puts by, and goes about to rise.*

    Comus. Nay Lady sit; if I but wave this wand,
Your nerves are all chain'd up in Alablaster,
And you a statue, or as *Daphne* was
Root-bound, that fled *Apollo.*
    La. Fool do not boast,
Thou canst not touch the freedom of my minde
With all thy charms, although this corporal rinde
Thou haste immanacl'd, while Heav'n sees good.
    Co. Why are you vext Lady? why do you frown?
Here dwell no frowns, nor anger, from these gates
Sorrow flies far: See here be all the pleasures

That fancy can beget on youthfull thoughts,
When the fresh blood grows lively, and returns
Brisk as the *April* buds in Primrose-season.
And first behold this cordial Julep here
That flames, and dances in his crystal bounds
With spirits of balm, and fragrant Syrops mixt.
Not that *Nepenthes* which the wife of *Thone*,
In *Egypt* gave to *Jove*-born *Helena*
Is of such power to stir up joy as this,
To life so friendly, or so cool to thirst.
Why should you be so cruel to your self,
And to those dainty limms which nature lent
For gentle usage, and soft delicacy?
But you invert the cov'nants of her trust,
And harshly deal like an ill borrower
With that which you receiv'd on other terms,
Scorning the unexempt condition
By which all mortal frailty must subsist,
Refreshment after toil, ease after pain,
That have been tir'd all day without repast,
And timely rest have wanted, but fair Virgin
This will restore all soon.
    La. 'Twill not false traitor,
'Twill not restore the truth and honesty
That thou hast banish't from thy tongue with lies;
Was this the cottage, and the safe abode
Thou told'st me of?   What grim aspects are these,
These oughly-headed Monsters?   Mercy guard me!
Hence with thy brew'd inchantments, foul deceiver,
Hast thou betrai'd my credulous innocence
With visor'd falshood, and base forgery,
And would'st thou seek again to trap me here
With lickerish baits fit to ensnare a brute?
Were it a draft for *Juno* when she banquets,
I would not taste thy treasonous offer; none
But such as are good men can give good things,
And that which is not good, is not delicious
To a well-govern'd and wise appetite.
    Co. O foolishnes of men! that lend their ears
To those budge Doctors of the *Stoick* Furr,

And fetch their precepts from the *Cynick* Tub,
Praising the lean and sallow Abstinence.
Wherefore did Nature powre her bounties forth,
With such a full and unwithdrawing hand,
Covering the earth with odours, fruits, and flocks,
Thronging the Seas with spawn innumerable,
But all to please, and sate the curious taste?
And set to work millions of spinning Worms,
That in their green shops weave the smooth-hair'd silk
To deck her Sons, and that no corner might
Be vacant of her plenty, in her own loyns
She hutch't th' all-worship ore, and precious gems
To store her children with; if all the world
Should in a pet of temperance feed on Pulse,
Drink the clear stream, and nothing wear but Freize,
Th' all-giver would be unthank't, would be unprais'd,
Not half his riches known, and yet despis'd,
And we should serve him as a grudging master,
As a penurious niggard of his wealth,
And live like Natures bastards, not her sons,
Who would be quite surcharg'd with her own weight,
And strangl'd with her waste fertility;
Th' earth cumber'd, and the wing'd air dark't with plumes,
The herds would over-multitude their Lords,
The Sea o'refraught would swel, and th' unsought diamonds
Would so emblaze the forhead of the Deep,
And so bestudd with Stars, that they below
Would grow inur'd to light, and com at last
To gaze upon the Sun with shameles brows.
List Lady be not coy, and be not cosen'd
With that same vaunted name Virginity,
Beauty is natures coyn, must not be hoorded,
But must be currant, and the good thereof
Consists in mutual and partak'n bliss,
Unsavoury in th' injoyment of it self
If you let slip time, like a neglected rose
It withers on the stalk with languish't head.
Beauty is natures brag, and must be shown
In courts, at feasts, and high solemnities
Where most may wonder at the workmanship;

It is for homely features to keep home,
They had their name thence; coarse complexions
And cheeks of sorry grain will serve to ply
The sampler, and to teize the huswifes wooll.
What need a vermeil-tinctur'd lip for that
Love-darting eyes, or tresses like the Morn?
There was another meaning in these gifts,
Think what, and be adviz'd, you are but young yet.

    La. I had not thought to have unlockt my lips
In this unhallow'd air, but that this Jugler
Would think to charm my judgement, as mine eyes,
Obtruding false rules pranckt in reasons garb.
I hate when vice can bolt her arguments,
And vertue has no tongue to check her pride:
Impostor do not charge most innocent nature,
As if she would her children should be riotous
With her abundance, she good cateres
Means her provision only to the good
That live according to her sober laws,
And holy dictate of spare Temperance:
If every just man that now pines with want
Had but a moderate and beseeming share
Of that which lewdly-pamper'd Luxury
Now heaps upon som few with vast excess,
Natures full blessings would be well dispenc't
In unsuperfluous eeven proportion,
And she no whit encomber'd with her store,
And then the giver would be better thank't,
His praise due paid, for swinish gluttony
Ne're looks to Heav'n amidst his gorgeous feast,
But with besotted base ingratitude
Cramms, and blasphemes his feeder. Shall I go on?
Or have I said anow? To him that dares
Arm his profane tongue with contemptuous words
Against the Sun-clad power of Chastity;
Fain would I somthing say, yet to what end?
Thou hast nor Ear, nor Soul to apprehend
The sublime notion, and high mystery
That must be utter'd to unfold the sage
And serious doctrine of Virginity,

And thou art worthy that thou shouldst not know
More happiness then this thy present lot.
Enjoy your dear Wit, and gay Rhetorick
That hath so well been taught her dazling fence,
Thou art not fit to hear thy self convinc't;
Yet should I try, the uncontrouled worth
Of this pure cause would kindle my rap't spirits
To such a flame of sacred vehemence,
That dumb things would be mov'd to sympathize,
And the brute Earth would lend her nerves, and shake,
Till all thy magick structures rear'd so high,
Were shatter'd into heaps o're thy false head.

    Co. She fables not, I feel that I do fear
Her words set off by som superior power;
And though not mortal, yet a cold shuddring dew
Dips me all o're, as when the wrath of *Jove*
Speaks thunder, and the chains of *Erebus*
To some of *Saturns* crew. I must dissemble,
And try her yet more strongly. Com, no more,
This is meer moral babble, and direct
Against the canon laws of our foundation;
I must not suffer this, yet 'tis but the lees
And setlings of a melancholy blood;
But this will cure all streight, one sip of this
Will bathe the drooping spirits in delight
Beyond the bliss of dreams. Be wise, and taste.

*The Brothers rush in with Swords drawn, wrest his Glass out of
his hand, and break it against the ground; his rout make
sign of resistance, but are all driven in; The attendant Spirit
comes in.*

    Spir. What, have you let the false Enchanter scape?
O ye mistook, ye should have snatcht his wand
And bound him fast; without his rod revers't,
And backward mutters of dissevering power,
We cannot free the Lady that sits here
In stony fetters fixt, and motionless;
Yet stay; be not disturb'd, now I bethink me,
Som other means I have which may be us'd,

Which once of *Melibœus* old I learnt
The soothest Shepherd that ere pip't on plains.
There is a gentle Nymph not far from hence,
That with moist curb sways the smooth Severn stream,
Sabrina is her name, a Virgin pure,
Whilom she was the daughter of *Locrine*,
That had the Scepter from his Father *Brute*.
The guiltless damsel flying the mad pursuit
Of her enraged stepdam *Guendolen*,
Commended her fair innocence to the flood
That stay'd her flight with his cross-flowing course,
The water Nymphs that in the bottom plaid,
Held up their pearled wrists and took her in,
Bearing her straight to aged *Nereus* Hall,
Who piteous of her woes, rear'd her lank head,
And gave her to his daughters to imbathe
In nectar'd lavers strew'd with Asphodil,
And through the porch and inlet of each sense
Dropt in Ambrosial Oils till she reviv'd,
And underwent a quick immortal change
Made Goddess of the River; still she retains
Her maid'n gentlenes, and oft at Eeve
Visits the herds along the twilight meadows,
Helping all urchin blasts, and ill luck signes
That the shrewd medling Elfe delights to make,
Which she with pretious viold liquors heals.
For which the Shepherds at their festivals
Carrol her goodnes lowd in rustick layes,
And throw sweet garland wreaths into her stream
Of pancies, pinks, and gaudy Daffadils.
And, as the old Swain said, she can unlock
The clasping charm, and thaw the numming spell,
If she be right invok't in warbled Song,
For maid'nhood she loves, and will be swift
To aid a Virgin such as was her self
In hard besetting need, this will I try
And adde the power of som adjuring verse.

SONG

Sabrina fair
Listen where thou art sitting
Under the glassie, cool, translucent wave,
In twisted braids of Lillies knitting
The loose train of thy amber-dropping hair,
Listen for dear honours sake,
Goddess of the silver lake,
                                     Listen and **save.**

Listen and appear to us
In name of great *Oceanus,*
By the earth-shaking *Neptune's* mace,
And *Tethys* grave majestick pace,
By hoary *Nereus* wrincled look,
And the *Carpathian* wisards hook,
By scaly *Tritons* winding shell,
And old sooth-saying *Glaucus* spell,
By *Leucothea's* lovely hands,
And her son that rules the strands,
By *Thetis* tinsel-slipper'd feet,
And the Songs of *Sirens* sweet,
By dead *Parthenope's* dear tomb,
And fair *Ligea's* golden comb,
Wherewith she sits on diamond rocks
Sleeking her soft alluring locks,
By all the *Nymphs* that nightly dance
Upon thy streams with wily glance,
Rise, rise, and heave thy rosie head
From thy coral-pav'n bed,
And bridle in thy headlong wave,
Till thou our summons answer have.
                                     Listen and save.

Sabrina rises, attended by water-Nymphs, and sings.
By the rushy-fringed bank,
Where grows the Willow and the Osier dank,
My sliding Chariot stayes,
Thickset with Agat, and the azurn sheen
Of Turkis blew, and Emrauld green
That in the channel strayes,

Whilst from off the waters fleet
Thus I set my printless feet
O're the Cowslips Velvet head,
   That bends not as I tread,
Gentle swain at thy request
   I am here.

   Spir. Goddess dear
We implore thy powerful hand
To undo the charmed band
Of true Virgin here distrest,
Through the force, and through the wile
Of unblest inchanter vile.
   Sab. Shepherd 'tis my office best
To help insnared chastity;
Brightest Lady look on me,
Thus I sprinkle on thy brest
Drops that from my fountain pure,
I have kept of pretious cure,
Thrice upon thy fingers tip,
Thrice upon thy rubied lip,
Next this marble venom'd seat
Smear'd with gumms of glutenous heat
I touch with chaste palms moist and cold,
Now the spell hath lost his hold;
And I must haste ere morning hour
To wait in *Amphitrite's* bowr.

Sabrina *descends, and the Lady rises out of her seat.*

   Spir. Virgin, daughter of *Locrine*
Sprung of old *Anchises* line
May thy brimmed waves for this
Their full tribute never miss
From a thousand petty rills,
That tumbled down the snowy hills:
Summer drouth, or singed air
Never scorch thy tresses fair,
Nor wet *Octobers* torrent flood
Thy molten crystal fill with mudd,

May thy billows rowl ashoar
The beryl, and the golden ore,
May thy lofty head be crown'd
With many a tower and terras round,
And here and there thy banks upon
With Groves of myrrhe, and cinnamon.
Com Lady while Heaven lends us grace,
Let us fly this cursed place,
Lest the Sorcerer us entice
With som other new device.
Not a waste, or needless sound
Till we com to holier ground,
I shall be your faithfull guide
Through this gloomy covert wide,
And not many furlongs thence
Is your Fathers residence
Where this night are met in state
Many a friend to gratulate
His wish't presence, and beside
All the Swains that there abide,
With Jiggs, and rural dance resort,
We shall catch them at their sport,
And our sudden coming there
Will double all their mirth and chere;
Com let us haste, the Stars grow high,
But night sits monarch yet in the mid sky.

The Scene changes, presenting Ludlow *Town and the Presi-
dents Castle, then com in Countrey-Dancers, after them the
attendant Spirit, with the two Brothers and the Lady.*

SONG

Spir. *Back Shepherds, back, anough your play,*
Till next Sun shine holiday,
Here be without duck or nod
Other trippings to be trod
Of lighter toes, and such Court guise
As Mercury *did first devise*
With the mincing Dryades
On the Lawns, and on the Leas.

This second Song presents them to their Father and
Mother.

Noble Lord, and Lady bright,
I have brought ye new delight,
Here behold so goodly grown
Three fair branches of your own,
Heav'n hath timely tri'd their youth,
Their faith, their patience, and their truth,
And sent them here through hard assays
With a crown of deathless Praise,
*   To triumph in victorious dance*
O're sensual Folly, and Intemperance.

The dances ended, the Spirit Epiloguizes.

Spir. To the Ocean now I fly,
And those happy climes that ly
Where day never shuts his eye,
Up in the broad fields of the sky:
There I suck the liquid air
All amidst the Gardens fair
Of *Hesperus*, and his daughters three
That sing about the golden tree:
Along the crisped shades and bowres
Revels the spruce and jocond Spring,
The Graces, and the rosie-boosom'd Howres,
Thither all their bounties bring.
There eternal Summer dwels,
And West winds, with musky wing
About the cedar'n alleys fling
Nard, and *Cassia's* balmy smels.
Iris there with humid bow,
Waters the odorous banks that blow
Flowers of more mingled hew
Then her purfl'd scarf can shew,
And drenches with *Elysian* dew
(List mortals if your ears be true)
Beds of *Hyacinth*, and Roses
Where young *Adonis* oft reposes,
Waxing well of his deep wound
In slumber soft, and on the ground

Sadly sits th' *Assyrian* Queen;
But far above in spangled sheen
Celestial *Cupid* her fam'd Son advanc't
Holds his dear *Psyche* sweet intranc't
After her wandring labours long,
Till free consent the gods among
Make her his eternal Bride,
And from her fair unspotted side
Two blissful twins are to be born,
Youth and Joy; so *Jove* hath sworn.

    But now my task is smoothly don,
I can fly, or I can run
Quickly to the green earths end,
Where the bow'd welkin slow doth bend,
And from thence can soar as soon
To the corners of the Moon.

    Mortals that would follow me,
Love vertue, she alone is free,
She can teach ye how to clime
Higher then the Spheary chime;
Or if Vertue feeble were,
Heav'n it self would stoop to her.

¶ Lycidas

In this Monody the Author bewails a learned Friend, unfortunately drown'd in his passage from Chester *on the* Irish *Seas, 1637. And by occasion foretells the ruine of our corrupted Clergie then in their height.*

YET once more, O ye Laurels, and once more
Ye Myrtles brown, with Ivy never sear,
I com to pluck your Berries harsh and crude,
And with forc'd fingers rude,
Shatter your leaves before the mellowing year.
Bitter constraint, and sad occasion dear,
Compells me to disturb your season due:
For *Lycidas* is dead, dead ere his prime,
Young *Lycidas*, and hath not left his peer:
Who would not sing for *Lycidas?* he knew
Himself to sing, and build the lofty rhyme.

He must not flote upon his watry bear
Unwept, and welter to the parching wind,
Without the meed of som melodious tear.

Begin then, Sisters of the sacred well,
That from beneath the seat of *Jove* doth spring,
Begin, and somewhat loudly sweep the string.
Hence with denial vain, and coy excuse,
So may some gentle Muse
With lucky words favour my destin'd Urn,
And as he passes turn,
And bid fair peace be to my sable shrowd.
For we were nurst upon the self-same hill,
Fed the same flock; by fountain, shade, and rill.

Together both, ere the high Lawns appear'd
Under the opening eye-lids of the morn,
We drove a field, and both together heard
What time the Gray-fly winds her sultry horn,
Batt'ning our flocks with the fresh dews of night,
Oft till the Star that rose, at Ev'ning, bright,
Toward Heav'ns descent had slop'd his westering wheel.
Mean while the Rural ditties were not mute,
Temper'd to th' Oaten Flute,
Rough *Satyrs* danc'd, and *Fauns* with clov'n heel,
From the glad sound would not be absent long,
And old *Damœtas* lov'd to hear our song.

But O the heavy change, now thou art gon,
Now thou art gon, and never must return!
Thee Shepherd, thee the Woods, and desert Caves,
With wilde Thyme and the gadding Vine o'regrown,
And all their echoes mourn.
The Willows, and the Hazle Copses green,
Shall now no more be seen,
Fanning their joyous Leaves to thy soft layes.
As killing as the Canker to the Rose,
Or Taint-worm to the weanling Herds that graze,
Or Frost to Flowers, that their gay wardrop wear,
When first the White Thorn blows;
Such, *Lycidas*, thy loss to Shepherds ear.

Where were ye Nymphs when the remorseless deep
Clos'd o're the head of your lov'd *Lycidas?*

For neither were ye playing on the steep,
Where your old *Bards*, the famous *Druids*, ly,
Nor on the shaggy top of *Mona* high,
Nor yet where *Deva* spreads her wisard stream:
Ay me, I fondly dream!
Had ye bin there—for what could that have don?
What could the Muse her self that *Orpheus* bore,
The Muse her self for her inchanting son
Whom Universal nature did lament,
When by the rout that made the hideous roar,
His goary visage down the stream was sent,
Down the swift *Hebrus* to the *Lesbian* shore.
  Alass! What boots it with uncessant care
To tend the homely slighted Shepherds trade,
And strictly meditate the thankless Muse,
Were it not better don as others use,
To sport with *Amaryllis* in the shade,
Or with the tangles of *Neæra's* hair?
Fame is the spur that the clear spirit doth raise
(That last infirmity of Noble mind)
To scorn delights, and live laborious dayes;
But the fair Guerdon when we hope to find,
And think to burst out into sudden blaze,
Comes the blind *Fury* with th' abhorred shears,
And slits the thin spun life. But not the praise,
Phœbus repli'd, and touch'd my trembling ears;
Fame is no plant that grows on mortal soil,
Nor in the glistering foil
Set off to th' world, nor in broad rumour lies,
But lives and spreds aloft by those pure eyes,
And perfet witnes of all-judging *Jove*;
As he pronounces lastly on each deed,
Of so much fame in Heav'n expect thy meed.
  O Fountain *Arethuse*, and thou honour'd floud,
Smooth-sliding *Mincius*, crown'd with vocal reeds,
That strain I heard was of a higher mood:
But now my Oat proceeds,
And listens to the Herald of the Sea
That came in *Neptune's* plea,
He ask'd the Waves, and ask'd the Fellon Winds,

What hard mishap hath doom'd this gentle swain?
And question'd every gust of rugged wings
That blows from off each beaked Promontory;
They knew not of his story,
And sage *Hippotades* their answer brings,
That not a blast was from his dungeon stray'd,
The Air was calm, and on the level brine,
Sleek *Panope* with all her sisters play'd.
It was that fatal and perfidious Bark
Built in th' eclipse, and rigg'd with curses dark,
That sunk so low that sacred head of thine.

    Next *Camus*, reverend Sire, went footing slow,
His Mantle hairy, and his Bonnet sedge,
Inwrought with figures dim, and on the edge
Like to that sanguine flower inscrib'd with woe.
Ah; Who hath reft (quoth he) my dearest pledge?
Last came, and last did go,
The Pilot of the *Galilean* lake,
Two massy Keyes he bore of metals twain,
(The Golden opes, the Iron shuts amain)
He shook his Miter'd locks, and stern bespake,
How well could I have spar'd for thee, young swain,
Anow of such as for their bellies sake,
Creep and intrude, and climb into the fold?
Of other care they little reck'ning make,
Then how to scramble at the shearers feast,
And shove away the worthy bidden guest;
Blind mouthes! that scarce themselves know how to hold
A Sheep-hook, or have learn'd ought els the least
That to the faithfull Herdmans art belongs!
What recks it them? What need they? They are sped;
And when they list, their lean and flashy songs
Grate on their scrannel Pipes of wretched straw,
The hungry Sheep look up, and are not fed,
But swoln with wind, and the rank mist they draw,
Rot inwardly, and foul contagion spread:
Besides what the grim Woolf with privy paw
Daily devours apace, and nothing sed,
But that two-handed engine at the door,
Stands ready to smite once, and smite no more.

Return *Alpheus*, the dread voice is past,
That shrunk thy streams; Return *Sicilian* Muse,
And call the Vales, and bid them hither cast
Their Bells, and Flourets of a thousand hues.
Ye valleys low where the milde whispers use,
Of shades and wanton winds, and gushing brooks,
On whose fresh lap the swart Star sparely looks,
Throw hither all your quaint enameld eyes,
That on the green terf suck the honied showres,
And purple all the ground with vernal flowres.
Bring the rathe Primrose that forsaken dies.
The tufted Crow-toe, and pale Gessamine,
The white Pink, and the Pansie freakt with jeat,
The glowing Violet.
The Musk-rose, and the well attir'd Woodbine,
With Cowslips wan that hang the pensive head,
And every flower that sad embroidery wears:
Bid *Amarantus* all his beauty shed,
And Daffadillies fill their cups with tears,
To strew the Laureat Herse where *Lycid* lies.
For so to interpose a little ease,
Let our frail thoughts dally with false surmise.
Ay me! Whilst thee the shores, and sounding Seas
Wash far away, where ere thy bones are hurl'd,
Whether beyond the stormy *Hebrides*
Where thou perhaps under the whelming tide
Visit'st the bottom of the monstrous world;
Or whether thou to our moist vows deny'd,
Sleep'st by the fable of *Bellerus* old,
Where the great vision of the guarded Mount
Looks toward *Namancos* and *Bayona's* hold;
Look homeward Angel now, and melt with ruth.
And, O ye *Dolphins*, waft the haples youth.

Weep no more, woful Shepherds weep no more,
For *Lycidas* your sorrow is not dead,
Sunk though he be beneath the watry floar,
So sinks the day-star in the Ocean bed,
And yet anon repairs his drooping head,
And tricks his beams, and with new spangled Ore,
Flames in the forehead of the morning sky:

So *Lycidas* sunk low, but mounted high,
Through the dear might of him that walk'd the waves
Where other groves, and other streams along,
With *Nectar* pure his oozy Lock's he laves,
And hears the unexpressive nuptial Song,
In the blest Kingdoms meek of joy and love.
There entertain him all the Saints above,
In solemn troops, and sweet Societies
That sing, and singing in their glory move,
And wipe the tears for ever from his eyes.
Now *Lycidas* the Shepherds weep no more;
Henceforth thou art the Genius of the shore,
In thy large recompense, and shalt be good
To all that wander in that perilous flood.

   Thus sang the uncouth Swain to th' Okes and rills,
While the still morn went out with Sandals gray,
He touch'd the tender stops of various Quills,
With eager thought warbling his *Dorick* lay:
And now the Sun had stretch'd out all the hills,
And now was dropt into the Western Bay;
At last he rose, and twitch'd his Mantle blew:
To morrow to fresh Woods, and Pastures new.

¶ "Captain or Colonel . . ."

CAPTAIN or Colonel, or Knight in Arms,
   Whose chance on these defenceless dores may sease,
   If deed of honour did thee ever please,
Guard them, and him within protect from harms,
He can requite thee, for he knows the charms
   That call Fame on such gentle acts as these,
   And he can spred thy Name o're Lands and Seas,
What ever clime the Suns bright circle warms.
Lift not thy spear against the Muses Bowre,
   The great *Emathian* Conqueror bid spare
   The house of *Pindarus*, when Temple and Towre
Went to the ground: And the repeated air
   Of sad *Electra's* Poet had the power
   To save th'*Athenian* Walls from ruine bare.

¶ "Lady that in the prime . . ."

LADY that in the prime of earliest youth,
 Wisely hast shun'd the broad way and the green,
 And with those few art eminently seen,
 That labour up the Hill of heav'nly Truth,
The better part with *Mary* and with *Ruth*,
 Chosen thou hast, and they that overween,
 And at thy growing vertues fret their spleen,
 No anger find in thee, but pity and ruth.
Thy care is fixt and zealously attends
 To fill thy odorous Lamp with deeds of light,
 And Hope that reaps not shame. Therefore be sure
Thou, when the Bridegroom with his feastfull friends
 Passes to bliss at the mid hour of night,
 Hast gain'd thy entrance, Virgin wise and pure.

¶ "Daughter to that good Earl . . ."

DAUGHTER to that good Earl, once President
 Of *Englands* Counsel, and her Treasury,
 Who liv'd in both, unstain'd with gold or fee.
 And left them both, more in himself content,
Till the sad breaking of that Parlament
 Broke him, as that dishonest victory
 At *Chæronea*, fatal to liberty
 Kill'd with report that Old man eloquent,
Though later born, then to have known the dayes
 Wherin your Father flourisht, yet by you,
 Madam, me thinks I see him living yet;
So well your words his noble vertues praise,
 That all both judge you to relate them true,
 And to possess them, Honour'd *Margaret*.

¶ "A Book was writ of late . . ."

A BOOK was writ of late call'd *Tetrachordon;*
 And wov'n close, both matter, form and stile;
 The Subject new: it walk'd the Town a while,
 Numbring good intellects; now seldom por'd on.

Cries the stall-reader, bless us! what a word on
   A title page is this! and some in file
   Stand spelling fals, while one might walk to Mile-
End Green. Why is it harder Sirs then Gordon,
Colkitto, or Macdonnel, or Galasp?
      Those rugged names to our like mouths grow sleek
      That would have made *Quintilian* stare and gasp.
Thy age, like ours, O Soul of Sir *John Cheek*,
   Hated not Learning wors then Toad or Asp;
   When thou taught'st *Cambridge*, and King *Edward* Greek.

¶ *On the same*

I DID but prompt the age to quit their cloggs
   By the known rules of antient libertie,
   When strait a barbarous noise environs me
Of Owles and Cuckoes, Asses, Apes, and Doggs.
As when those Hinds that were transform'd to Froggs
   Raild at *Latona's* twin-born progenie
   Which after held the Sun and Moon in fee.
   But this is got by casting Pearl to Hoggs;
That bawle for freedom in their senceless mood,
   And still revolt when truth would set them free.
   Licence they mean when they cry libertie;
For who loves that, must first be wise and good;
   But from that mark how far they roave we see
   For all this wast of wealth, and loss of blood.

¶ *To Mr.* H. Lawes, *on his Aires*

HARRY whose tuneful and well measur'd Song
   First taught our English Musick how to span
   Words with just note and accent, not to scan
With *Midas* Ears, committing short and long;
Thy worth and skill exempts thee from the throng,
   With praise enough for Envy to look wan;
   To after age thou shalt be writ the man
   That with smooth aire couldst humor best our tonge.

Thou honour'st Verse, and Verse must send her wing
  To honour thee, the Priest of *Phœbus* Quire
  That tun'st their happiest lines in Hymn, or Story.
Dante shall give Fame leave to set thee higher
  Then his *Casella* whom he woo'd to sing
  Met in the milder shades of Purgatory.

⁋ "When Faith and Love . . ."

WHEN Faith and Love which parted from thee never,
  Had ripen'd thy just soul to dwell with God,
  Meekly thou didst resign this earthly load
Of Death, call'd Life; which us from Life doth sever.
Thy Works and Alms and all thy good Endeavour
  Staid not behind, nor in the grave were trod;
  But as Faith pointed with her golden rod,
  Follow'd thee up to joy and bliss for ever.
Love led them on, and Faith who knew them best
  Thy hand-maids, clad them o're with purple beams
  And azure wings, that up they flew so drest,
And speak the truth of thee on glorious Theams
  Before the Judge, who thenceforth bid thee rest
  And drink thy fill of pure immortal streams.

⁋ On the new forcers of Conscience
under the Long *Parliament*

BECAUSE you have thrown of your Prelate Lord,
  And with stiff Vowes renounc'd his Liturgie
  To seise the widdow'd whore Pluralitie
From them whose sin ye envi'd, not abhor'd,
Dare ye for this adjure the Civill Sword
  To force our Consciences that Christ set free,
  And ride us with a classic Hierarchy
  Taught ye by meer *A. S.* and *Rotherford?*
Men whose Life, Learning, Faith and pure intent
  Would have been held in high esteem with *Paul*
  Must now be nam'd and printed Hereticks
By shallow *Edwards* and Scotch what d'ye call:
  But we do hope to find out all your tricks,

Your plots and packing wors then those of *Trent*,
    That so the Parliament
May with their wholsom and preventive Shears
Clip your Phylacteries, though bauk your Ears,
     And succour our just Fears
When they shall read this clearly in your charge
New Presbyter is but *Old Priest* writ Large.

¶ To my Lord *Fairfax*

FAIRFAX, whose Name in Arms through *Europe* rings,
 And fills all Mouths with Envy or with Praise,
 And all her Jealous Monarchs with Amaze.
 And Rumours loud which daunt remotest Kings,
Thy firm unshaken Valour ever brings
 Victory home, while new Rebellions raise
 Their Hydra-heads, and the false *North* displays
 Her broken League to Imp her Serpent Wings:
O yet! a Nobler task awaits thy Hand,
 For what can War, but Acts of War still breed,
 Till injur'd Truth from Violence be freed;
And publick Faith be rescu'd from the Brand
 Of publick Fraud; in vain doth Valour bleed,
 While Avarice and Rapine shares the Land.

¶ To *Oliver Cromwell*

CROMWELL our Chief of Men, that through a Croud,
 Not of War only, but distractions rude;
 Guided by Faith, and Matchless Fortitude:
 To Peace and Truth, thy Glorious way hast Plough'd,
And on the neck of crowned Fortune proud
 Hast rear'd God's Trophies, and his Work pursu'd,
 While *Darwent* Streams with Blood of *Scots* imbru'd;
 And *Dunbarfield* resound thy Praises loud,
And *Worcester's* Laureat Wreath; yet much remains
 To Conquer still; Peace hath her Victories
 No less than those of War; new Foes arise
Threatning to bind our Souls in secular Chains,
 Help us to save Free Conscience from the paw
 Of Hireling Wolves, whose Gospel is their Maw.

¶ To Sir *Henry Vane*

VANE, Young in years, but in Sage Councels old,
   Then whom a better Senator ne're held
   The Helm of *Rome*, when Gowns, not Arms, repell'd
   The fierce *Epirote*, and the *African* bold,
Whether to settle Peace, or to unfold
   The Drift of hollow States, hard to be Spell'd;
   Then to advise how War may best be upheld,
   Mann'd by her Two main Nerves, Iron and Gold,
In all her Equipage: Besides, to know
   Both Spiritual and Civil, what each means,
   What serves each, thou hast learn'd, which few have done.
The bounds of either Sword to thee we owe;
   Therefore on thy Right hand Religion leans,
   And reckons thee in chief her Eldest Son.

¶ "When I consider how my light is spent . . ."

WHEN I consider how my light is spent,
   E're half my days, in this dark world and wide,
   And that one Talent which is death to hide,
   Lodg'd with me useless, though my Soul more bent
To serve therewith my Maker, and present
   My true account, least he returning chide,
   Doth God exact day-labour, light deny'd,
   I fondly ask; But patience to prevent
That murmur, soon replies, God doth not need
   Either man's work or his own gifts, who best
   Bear his milde yoak, they serve him best, his State
Is Kingly. Thousands at his bidding speed
   And post o're Land and Ocean without rest:
   They also serve who only stand and waite.

¶ *On the late Massacher in* Piemont

AVENGE O Lord thy slaughter'd Saints, whose bones
   Lie scatter'd on the Alpine mountains cold,
   Ev'n them who kept thy truth so pure of old
   When all our Fathers worship't Stocks and Stones,

Forget not: in thy book record their groanes
   Who were thy Sheep and in their antient Fold
   Slayn by the bloody *Piemontese* that roll'd
   Mother with Infant down the Rocks. Their moans
The Vales redoubl'd to the Hills, and they
   To Heav'n. Their martyr'd blood and ashes so
   O're all th'*Italian* fields where still doth sway
The triple Tyrant: that from these may grow
   A hunder'd-fold, who having learnt thy way
   Early may fly the *Babylonian* wo.

¶ "Lawrence of vertuous Father . . ."

LAWRENCE of vertuous Father vertuous Son,
   Now that the Fields are dank, and ways are mire,
   Where shall we sometimes meet, and by the fire
   Help wast a sullen day; what may be won
From the hard Season gaining: time will run
   On smoother, till *Favonius* re-inspire
   The frozen earth; and cloth in fresh attire
   The Lillie and Rose, that neither sow'd nor spun.
What neat repast shall feast us, light and choice,
   Of Attick tast, with Wine, whence we may rise
   To hear the Lute well toucht, or artfull voice
Warble immortal Notes and *Tuskan* Ayre?
   He who of those delights can judge, and spare
   To interpose them oft, is not unwise.

¶ "Cyriack, whose Grandsire . . ."

CYRIACK, whose Grandsire on the Royal Bench
   Of Brittish *Themis*, with no mean applause
   Pronounc't and in his volumes taught our Lawes,
   Which others at their Barr so often wrench;
To day deep thoughts resolve with me to drench
   In mirth, that after no repenting drawes;
   Let *Euclid* rest and *Archimedes* pause,
   And what the *Swede* intend, and what the *French*.
To measure life, learn thou betimes, and know
   Toward solid good what leads the nearest way;
   For other things mild Heav'n a time ordains,

And disapproves that care, though wise in show,
    That with superfluous burden loads the day,
    And when God sends a cheerful hour, refrains.

¶ To Mr. *Cyriac Skinner*. Upon his Blindness

CYRIAC this Three years day, these Eyes though clear
    To outward view of blemish or of Spot,
    Bereft of Sight, their Seeing have forgot:
    Nor to their idle Orbs doth day appear,
Or Sun, or Moon, or Star, throughout the Year;
    Or Man, or Woman; yet I argue not
    Against Heaven's Hand, or Will, nor bate one jot
Of Heart or Hope; but still bear up, and steer
Right onward. What supports me, dost thou ask?
    The Conscience, Friend, to have lost them over ply'd
    In Liberties Defence, my noble task;
Of which all *Europe* rings from side to side.
    This thought might lead me through this World's vain mask
    Content, though blind, had I no other Guide.

¶ "Methought I saw . . ."

METHOUGHT I saw my late espoused Saint
    Brought to me like *Alcestis* from the grave,
    Whom *Joves* great Son to her glad Husband gave,
    Rescu'd from death by force though pale and faint.
Mine as whom washt from spot of child-bed taint,
    Purification in the old Law did save,
    And such, as yet once more I trust to have
    Full sight of her in Heaven without restraint,
Came vested all in white, pure as her mind:
    Her face was vail'd, yet to my fancied sight,
    Love, sweetness, goodness, in her person shin'd
So clear, as in no face with more delight.
    But O as to embrace me she enclin'd
    I wak'd, she fled, and day brought back my night.

¶ Paradise Lost

A POEM IN TWELVE BOOKS

THE VERSE

THE measure is English Heroic Verse, without Rime, as that of Homer in Greek, and of Virgil in Latin; Rime being no necessary Adjunct or true Ornament of Poem or good Verse, in longer Works especially, but the Invention of a barbarous Age, to set off wretched matter and lame Meeter; grac't indeed since by the use of some famous modern Poets, carried away by Custom, but much to thir own vexation, hindrance, and constraint, to express many things otherwise, and for the most part worse then else they would have exprest them. Not without cause, therefore some both Italian and Spanish Poets of prime note, have rejected Rime both in longer and shorter Works, as have also, long since our best English Tragedies, as a thing of it self, to all judicious ears, triveal and of no true musical delight; which consists only in apt Numbers, fit quantity of Syllables, and the sense variously drawn out from one verse into another, not in the jingling sound of like endings, a fault avoyded by the learned Ancients both in Poetry and all good Oratory. This neglect then of Rime so little is to be taken for a defect, though it may seem so perhaps to vulgar Readers, that it rather is to be esteem'd an example set, the first in English, of ancient liberty recover'd to Heroic Poem from the troublesom and modern bondage of Rimeing.

BOOK I

THE ARGUMENT

THIS first Book proposes, first in brief, the whole Subject, *Mans disobedience, and the loss thereupon of Paradise wherein he was plac't:* Then touches *the prime cause of his fall, the Serpent, or rather* Satan *in the Serpent; who revolting from God, and drawing to his side many Legions of Angels, was by the command of God driven out of Heaven with all his Crew into the great Deep.* Which action past over, the Poem hasts into the midst of things, presenting *Satan with his Angels now fallen into Hell*, describ'd here, *not in the Center* (for Heaven and Earth may be suppos'd as yet not made, certainly not yet accurst) *but in a place of utter darkness, fitliest call'd* Chaos: *Here* Satan *with his Angels lying on the burning Lake, thunder-struck and astonisht, after a certain space recovers, as from confusion, calls up him who next in Order and Dignity lay by him; they confer of thir miserable fall.* Satan *awakens all his Legions, who lay till then in the same manner confounded; They rise, thir Numbers, array of Battel, thir chief Leaders nam'd, according to the Idols known afterwards in* Canaan *and the Countries adjoyning. To these* Satan *directs his Speech, comforts them with hope yet of regaining Heaven, but tells them lastly of a new World and new kind of Creature to be created, according to an ancient Prophesie or report in Heaven;* for that Angels were long before this visible Creation, was the opinion of many ancient Fathers. *To find out the truth o, this Prophesie, and what to determin thereon he refers to a full Councel. What his Associates thence attempt.* Pandemonium *the Palace of* Satan *rises, suddenly built out of the Deep: The infernal Peers there sit in Councel.*

> OF Mans First Disobedience, and the Fruit
> Of that Forbidden Tree, whose mortal tast
> Brought Death into the World, and all our woe,
> With loss of *Eden*, till one greater Man
> Restore us, and regain the blissful Seat,
> Sing Heav'nly Muse, that on the secret **top**
> Of *Oreb*, or of *Sinai*, didst inspire
> That Shepherd, who first taught the chosen Seed,
> In the Beginning how the Heav'ns and Earth
> Rose out of *Chaos*: or if *Sion* Hill
> Delight thee more, and *Siloa's* Brook that flow'd
> Fast by the Oracle of God; I thence
> Invoke thy aid to my adventrous Song,
> That with no middle flight intends to soar
> Above th' *Aonian* Mount, while it pursues
> Things unattempted yet in Prose or Rhime.
> And chiefly Thou O Spirit, that dost prefer
> Before all Temples th' upright heart and pure,

Instruct me, for Thou know'st; Thou from the first
Wast present, and with mighty wings outspread
Dove-like satst brooding on the vast Abyss
And mad'st it pregnant: What in me is dark
Illumin, what is low raise and support;
That to the highth of this great Argument
I may assert Eternal Providence,
And justifie the wayes of God to men.

    Say first, for Heav'n hides nothing from thy view
Nor the deep Tract of Hell, say first what cause
Mov'd our Grand Parents in that happy State,
Favour'd of Heav'n so highly, to fall off
From their Creator, and transgress his Will
For one restraint, Lords of the World besides?
Who first seduc'd them to that foul revolt?
Th' infernal Serpent; he it was, whose guile
Stird up with Envy and Revenge, deceiv'd
The Mother of Mankind, what time his Pride
Had cast him out from Heav'n, with all his Host
Of Rebel Angels, by whose aid aspiring
To set himself in Glory above his Peers,
He trusted to have equal'd the most High,
If he oppos'd; and with ambitious aim
Against the Throne and Monarchy of God
Rais'd impious War in Heav'n and Battel proud
With vain attempt. Him the Almighty Power
Hurld headlong flaming from th' Ethereal Skie
With hideous ruine and combustion down
To bottomless perdition, there to dwell
In Adamantine Chains and penal Fire,
Who durst defie th' Omnipotent to Arms.
Nine times the Space that measures Day and Night
To mortal men, he with his horrid crew
Lay vanquisht, rowling in the fiery Gulfe
Confounded though immortal: But his doom
Reserv'd him to more wrath; for now the thought
Both of lost happiness and lasting pain
Torments him; round he throws his baleful eyes
That witness'd huge affliction and dismay
Mixt with obdurate pride and stedfast hate:

At once as far as Angels kenn he views
The dismal Situation waste and wilde,
A Dungeon horrible, on all sides round
As one great Furnace flam'd, yet from those flames
No light, but rather darkness visible
Serv'd only to discover sights of woe,
Regions of sorrow, doleful shades, where peace
And rest can never dwell, hope never comes
That comes to all; but torture without end
Still urges, and a fiery Deluge, fed
With ever-burning Sulphur unconsum'd:
Such place Eternal Justice had prepar'd
For those rebellious, here their Prison ordain'd
In utter darkness, and thir portion set
As far remov'd from God and light of Heav'n
As from the Center thrice to th' utmost Pole.
O how unlike the place from whence they fell!
There the companions of his fall, o'rewhelm'd
With Floods and Whirlwinds of tempestuous fire,
He soon discerns, and weltring by his side
One next himself in power, and next in crime,
Long after known in *Palestine*, and nam'd
Beëlzebub. To whom th' Arch-Enemy,
And thence in Heav'n call'd Satan, with bold words
Breaking the horrid silence thus began.

    If thou beest he; But O how fall'n! how chang'd
From him, who in the happy Realms of Light
Cloth'd with transcendent brightness didst out-shine
Myriads though bright: If he whom mutual league,
United thoughts and counsels, equal hope
And hazard in the Glorious Enterprize,
Joynd with me once, now misery hath joynd
In equal ruin: into what Pit thou seest
From what highth fall'n, so much the stronger prov'd
He with his Thunder: and till then who knew
The force of those dire Arms? yet not for those
Nor what the Potent Victor in his rage
Can else inflict do I repent or change,
Though chang'd in outward lustre; that fixt mind
And high disdain, from sence of injur'd merit,

That with the mightiest rais'd me to contend,
And to the fierce contention brought along
Innumerable force of Spirits arm'd
That durst dislike his reign, and me preferring,
His utmost power with adverse power oppos'd
In dubious Battel on the Plains of Heav'n,
And shook his throne. What though the field be lost?
All is not lost; the unconquerable Will,
And study of revenge, immortal hate,
And courage never to submit or yield:
And what is else not to be overcome?
That Glory never shall his wrath or might
Extort from me. To bow and sue for grace
With suppliant knee, and deifie his power
Who from the terrour of this Arm so late
Doubted his Empire, that were low indeed,
That were an ignominy and shame beneath
This downfall; since by Fate the strength of Gods
And this Empyreal substance cannot fail,
Since through experience of this great event
In Arms not worse, in foresight much advanc't,
We may with more successful hope resolve
To wage by force or guile eternal Warr
Irreconcileable, to our grand Foe,
Who now triumphs, and in th' excess of joy
Sole reigning holds the Tyranny of Heav'n.
  So spake th' Apostate Angel, though in pain,
Vaunting aloud, but rackt with deep despare:
And him thus answer'd soon his bold Compeer.
  O Prince, O Chief of many Throned Powers,
That led th' imbattelld Seraphim to Warr
Under thy conduct, and in dreadful deeds
Fearless, endanger'd Heav'ns perpetual King;
And put to proof his high Supremacy,
Whether upheld by strength, or Chance, or Fate,
Too well I see and rue the dire event,
That with sad overthrow and foul defeat
Hath lost us Heav'n, and all this mighty Host
In horrible destruction laid thus low,
As far as Gods and Heav'nly Essences

Can perish: for the mind and spirit remains
Invincible, and vigour soon returns,
Though all our Glory extinct, and happy state
Here swallow'd up in endless misery.
But what if he our Conquerour, (whom I now
Of force believe Almighty, since no less
Then such could hav orepow'rd such force as ours)
Have left us this our spirit and strength intire
Strongly to suffer and support our pains,
That we may so suffice his vengeful ire,
Or do him mightier service as his thralls
By right of Warr, what e're his business be
Here in the heart of Hell to work in Fire,
Or do his Errands in the gloomy Deep;
What can it then avail though yet we feel
Strength undiminisht, or eternal being
To undergo eternal punishment?
Whereto with speedy words th' Arch-fiend reply'd.

 Fall'n Cherube, to be weak is miserable
Doing or Suffering: but of this be sure,
To do ought good never will be our task,
But ever to do ill our sole delight,
As being the contrary to his high will
Whom we resist. If then his Providence
Out of our evil seek to bring forth good,
Our labour must be to pervert that end,
And out of good still to find means of evil;
Which oft times may succeed, so as perhaps
Shall grieve him, if I fail not, and disturb
His inmost counsels from thir destind aim.
But see the angry Victor hath recall'd
His Ministers of vengeance and pursuit
Back to the Gates of Heav'n: The Sulphurous Hail
Shot after us in storm, oreblown hath laid
The fiery Surge, that from the Precipice
Of Heav'n receiv'd us falling, and the Thunder,
Wing'd with red Lightning and impetuous rage,
Perhaps hath spent his shafts, and ceases now
To bellow through the vast and boundless Deep.
Let us not slip th' occasion, whether scorn,

Or satiate fury yield it from our Foe.
Seest thou yon dreary Plain, forlorn and wilde,
The seat of desolation, voyd of light,
Save what the glimmering of these livid flames
Casts pale and dreadful? Thither let us tend
From off the tossing of these fiery waves,
There rest, if any rest can harbour there,
And reassembling our afflicted Powers,
Consult how we may henceforth most offend
Our Enemy, our own loss how repair,
How overcome this dire Calamity,
What reinforcement we may gain from Hope,
If not what resolution from despare.
    Thus Satan talking to his neerest Mate
With Head up-lift above the wave, and Eyes
That sparkling blaz'd, his other Parts besides
Prone on the Flood, extended long and large
Lay floating many a rood, in bulk as huge
As whom the Fables name of monstrous size,
Titanian, or *Earth-born*, that warr'd on *Jove*,
Briareos or *Typhon*, whom the Den
By ancient *Tarsus* held, or that Sea-beast
Leviathan, which God of all his works
Created hugest that swim th' Ocean stream:
Him haply slumbring on the *Norway* foam
The Pilot of some small night-founder'd Skiff,
Deeming some Island, oft, as Sea-men tell,
With fixed Anchor in his skaly rind
Moors by his side under the Lee, while Night
Invests the Sea, and wished Morn delayes:
So stretcht out huge in length the Arch-fiend lay
Chain'd on the burning Lake, nor ever thence
Had ris'n or heav'd his head, but that the will
And high permission of all-ruling Heaven
Left him at large to his own dark designs,
That with reiterated crimes he might
Heap on himself damnation, while he sought
Evil to others, and enrag'd might see
How all his malice serv'd but to bring forth
Infinite goodness, grace and mercy shewn

On Man by him seduc't, but on himself
Treble confusion, wrath and vengeance pour'd.
Forthwith upright he rears from off the Pool
His mighty Stature; on each hand the flames
Drivn backward slope their pointing spires, and rowld
In billows, leave i' th' midst a horrid Vale.
Then with expanded wings he stears his flight
Aloft, incumbent on the dusky Air
That felt unusual weight, till on dry Land
He lights, if it were Land that ever burn'd
With solid, as the Lake with liquid fire;
And such appear'd in hue, as when the force
Of subterranean wind transports a Hill
Torn from *Pelorus*, or the shatter'd side
Of thundring *Ætna*, whose combustible
And fewel'd entrals thence conceiving Fire,
Sublim'd with Mineral fury, aid the Winds,
And leave a singed bottom all involv'd
With stench and smoak: Such resting found the sole
Of unblest feet. Him followed his next Mate,
Both glorying to have scap't the *Stygian* flood
As Gods, and by thir own recover'd strength,
Not by the sufferance of supernal Power.

Is this the Region, this the Soil, the Clime,
Said then the lost Arch-Angel, this the seat
That we must change for Heav'n, this mournful gloom
For that celestial light? Be it so, since he
Who now is Sovran can dispose and bid
What shall be right: fardest from him is best
Whom reason hath equald, force hath made supream
Above his equals. Farewel happy Fields
Where Joy for ever dwells: Hail horrours, hail
Infernal world, and thou profoundest Hell
Receive thy new Possessor: One who brings
A mind not to be chang'd by Place or Time.
The mind is its own place, and in it self
Can make a Heav'n of Hell, a Hell of Heav'n.
What matter where, if I be still the same,
And what I should be, all but less then he
Whom Thunder hath made greater? Here at least

We shall be free; th' Almighty hath not built
Here for his envy, will not drive us hence:
Here we may reign secure, and in my choyce
To reign is worth ambition though in Hell:
Better to reign in Hell, then serve in Heav'n.
But wherefore let we then our faithful friends,
Th' associates and copartners of our loss
Lye thus astonisht on th' oblivious Pool,
And call them not to share with us their part
In this unhappy Mansion, or once more
With rallied Arms to try what may be yet
Regaind in Heav'n, or what more lost in Hell?
    So *Satan* spake, and him *Beëlzebub*
Thus answer'd. Leader of those Armies bright,
Which but th' Omnipotent none could have foyld,
If once they hear that voyce, thir liveliest pledge
Of hope in fears and dangers, heard so oft
In worst extreams, and on the perilous edge
Of battel when it rag'd, in all assaults
Thir surest signal, they will soon resume
New courage and revive, though now they lye
Groveling and prostrate on yon Lake of Fire,
As we erewhile, astounded and amaz'd,
No wonder, fall'n such a pernicious highth.
    He scarce had ceas't when the superiour Fiend
Was moving toward the shoar; his ponderous shield
Ethereal temper, massy, large and round,
Behind him cast; the broad circumference
Hung on his shoulders like the Moon, whose Orb
Through Optic Glass the *Tuscan* Artist views
At Ev'ning from the top of *Fesole*,
Or in *Valdarno*, to descry new Lands,
Rivers or Mountains in her spotty Globe.
His Spear, to equal which the tallest Pine
Hewn on *Norwegian* hills, to be the Mast
Of some great Ammiral, were but a wand,
He walkt with to support uneasie steps
Over the burning Marle, not like those steps
On Heavens Azure, and the torrid Clime
Smote on him sore besides, vaulted with Fire;

Nathless he so endur'd, till on the Beach
Of that inflamed Sea, he stood and call'd
His Legions, Angel Forms, who lay intrans't
Thick as Autumnal Leaves that strow the Brooks
In *Vallombrosa*, where th' *Etrurian* shades
High overarch't imbowr; or scatterd sedge
Afloat, when with fierce Winds *Orion* arm'd
Hath vext the Red-Sea Coast, whose waves orethrew
Busiris and his *Memphian* Chivalry,
While with perfidious hatred they pursu'd
The Sojourners of *Goshen*, who beheld
From the safe shore thir floating Carkases
And broken Chariot Wheels, so thick bestrown
Abject and lost lay these, covering the Flood,
Under amazement of thir hideous change.
He call'd so loud, that all the hollow Deep
Of Hell resounded. Princes, Potentates,
Warriers, the Flowr of Heav'n, once yours, now lost,
If such astonishment as this can sieze
Eternal spirits; or have ye chos'n this place
After the toyl of Battel to repose
Your wearied vertue, for the ease you find
To slumber here, as in the Vales of Heav'n?
Or in this abject posture have ye sworn
To adore the Conquerour? who now beholds
Cherube and Seraph rowling in the Flood
With scatter'd Arms and Ensigns, till anon
His swift pursuers from Heav'n Gates discern
Th' advantage, and descending tread us down
Thus drooping, or with linked Thunderbolts
Transfix us to the bottom of this Gulfe.
Awake, arise, or be for ever fall'n.

They heard, and were abasht, and up they sprung
Upon the wing, as when men wont to watch
On duty, sleeping found by whom they dread,
Rouse and bestir themselves ere well awake.
Nor did they not perceave the evil plight
In which they were, or the fierce pains not feel;
Yet to their Generals Voyce they soon obeyd
Innumerable. As when the potent Rod

Of *Amrams* Son in *Egypts* evill day
Wav'd round the Coast, up call'd a pitchy cloud
Of *Locusts*, warping on the Eastern Wind,
That ore the Realm of impious *Pharaoh* hung
Like Night, and darken'd all the Land of *Nile*:
So numberless were those bad Angels seen
Hovering on wing under the Cope of Hell
'Twixt upper, nether, and surrounding Fires;
Till, as a signal giv'n, th' uplifted Spear
Of thir great Sultan waving to direct
Thir course, in even ballance down they light
On the firm brimstone, and fill all the Plain;
A multitude, like which the populous North
Pour'd never from her frozen loyns, to pass
Rhene or the *Danaw*, when her barbarous Sons
Came like a Deluge on the South, and spread
Beneath *Gibraltar* to the *Lybian* sands.
Forthwith from every Squadron and each Band
The Heads and Leaders thither hast where stood
Thir great Commander; Godlike shapes and forms
Excelling human, Princely Dignities,
And Powers that earst in Heaven sat on Thrones;
Though of thir Names in heav'nly Records now
Be no memorial, blotted out and ras'd
By thir Rebellion, from the Books of Life.
Nor had they yet among the Sons of *Eve*
Got them new Names, till wandring ore the Earth,
Through Gods high sufferance for the tryal of man,
By falsities and lyes the greatest part
Of Mankind they corrupted to forsake
God thir Creator, and th' invisible
Glory of him that made them, to transform
Oft to the Image of a Brute, adorn'd
With gay Religions full of Pomp and Gold,
And Devils to adore for Deities:
Then were they known to men by various Names,
And various Idols through the Heathen World.
Say, Muse, thir Names then known, who first, who last,
Rous'd from the slumber, on that fiery Couch,
At thir great Emperors call, as next in worth

Came singly where he stood on the bare strand,
While the promiscuous croud stood yet aloof?
The chief were those who from the Pit of Hell
Roaming to seek thir prey on earth, durst fix
Thir Seats long after next the Seat of God,
Thir Altars by his Altar, Gods ador'd
Among the Nations round, and durst abide
Jehovah thundring out of *Sion*, thron'd
Between the Cherubim; yea, often plac'd
Within his Sanctuary it self thir Shrines,
Abominations; and with cursed things
His holy Rites, and solemn Feasts profan'd,
And with thir darkness durst affront his light.
First *Moloch*, horrid King besmear'd with blood
Of human sacrifice, and parents tears,
Though for the noyse of Drums and Timbrels loud
Thir childrens cries unheard, that past through fire
To his grim Idol. Him the *Ammonite*
Worshipt in *Rabba* and her watry Plain,
In *Argob* and in *Basan*, to the stream
Of utmost *Arnon*. Nor content with such
Audacious neighbourhood, the wisest heart
Of *Solomon* he led by fraud to build
His Temple right against the Temple of God
On that opprobrious Hill, and made his Grove
The pleasant Vally of *Hinnom*, *Tophet* thence
And black *Gehenna* call'd, the Type of Hell.
Next *Chemos*, th' obscene dread of *Moabs* Sons,
From *Aroer* to *Nebo*, and the wild
Of Southmost *Abarim;* in *Hesebon*
And *Horonaim*, *Seons* Realm, beyond
The flowry Dale of *Sibma* clad with Vines,
And *Eleale* to th' *Asphaltick* Pool.
Peor his other Name, when he entic'd
Israel in *Sittim* on thir march from *Nile*
To do him wanton rites, which cost them woe.
Yet thence his lustful Orgies he enlarg'd
Even to that Hill of scandal, by the Grove
Of *Moloch* homicide, lust hard by hate;
Till good *Josiah* drove them thence to Hell.

With these came they, who from the bordring flood
Of old *Euphrates* to the Brook that parts
Egypt from *Syrian* ground, had general Names
Of *Baalim* and *Ashtaroth*, those male,
These Feminine. For Spirits when they please
Can either Sex assume, or both; so soft
And uncompounded is thir Essence pure,
Not ti'd or manacl'd with joynt or limb,
Nor founded on the brittle strength of bones,
Like cumbrous flesh; but in what shape they choose
Dilated or condens't, bright or obscure,
Can execute thir aerie purposes,
And works of love or enmity fulfill.
For those the Race of *Israel* oft forsook
Thir living strength, and unfrequented left
His righteous Altar, bowing lowly down
To bestial Gods; for which thir heads as low
Bow'd down in Battel, sunk before the Spear
Of despicable foes. With these in troop
Came *Astoreth*, whom the *Phœnicians* call'd
Astarte, Queen of Heav'n, with crescent Horns;
To whose bright Image nightly by the Moon
Sidonian Virgins paid their Vows and Songs,
In *Sion* also not unsung, where stood
Her Temple on th' offensive Mountain, built
By that uxorious King, whose heart though large,
Beguil'd by fair Idolatresses, fell
To Idols foul. *Thammuz* came next behind,
Whose annual wound in *Lebanon* allur'd
The *Syrian* Damsels to lament his fate
In amorous dittyes all a Summers day,
While smooth *Adonis* from his native Rock
Ran purple to the Sea, suppos'd with blood
Of *Thammuz* yearly wounded: the Love-tale
Infected *Sions* daughters with like heat,
Whose wanton passions in the sacred Porch
Ezekiel saw, when by the Vision led
His eye survay'd the dark Idolatries
Of alienated *Judah*. Next came one
Who mourn'd in earnest, when the Captive **Ark**

Maim'd his brute Image, head and hands lopt off
In his own Temple, on the grunsel edge,
Where he fell flat, and sham'd his Worshipers:
Dagon his Name, Sea Monster, upward Man
And downward Fish: yet had his Temple high
Rear'd in *Azotus*, dreaded through the Coast
Of *Palestine*, in *Gath* and *Ascalon*,
And *Accaron* and *Gaza's* frontier bounds.
Him follow'd *Rimmon*, whose delightful Seat
Was fair *Damascus*, on the fertil Banks
Of *Abbana* and *Pharphar*, lucid streams.
He also against the house of God was bold:
A Leper once he lost and gain'd a King,
Ahaz his sottish Conquerour, whom he drew
Gods Altar to disparage and displace
For one of *Syrian* mode, whereon to burn
His odious offrings, and adore the Gods
Whom he had vanquisht. After these appear'd
A crew who under Names of old Renown,
Osiris, Isis, Orus and their Train
With monstrous shapes and sorceries abus'd
Fanatic *Egypt* and her Priests, to seek
Thir wandring Gods disguis'd in brutish forms
Rather then human. Nor did *Israel* scape
Th' infection when thir borrow'd Gold compos'd
The Calf in *Oreb*: and the Rebel King
Doubl'd that sin in *Bethel* and in *Dan*,
Lik'ning his Maker to the Grazed Ox,
Jehovah, who in one Night when he pass'd
From *Egypt* marching, equal'd with one stroke
Both her first born and all her bleating Gods.
Belial came last, then whom a Spirit more lewd
Fell not from Heaven, or more gross to love
Vice for it self: To him no Temple stood
Or Altar smoak'd; yet who more oft then hee
In Temples and at Altars, when the Priest
Turns Atheist, as did *Ely's* Sons, who fill'd
With lust and violence the house of God.
In Courts and Palaces he also Reigns
And in luxurious Cities, where the noyse

Of riot ascends above thir loftiest Towrs,
And injury and outrage: And when Night
Darkens the Streets, then wander forth the Sons
Of *Belial*, flown with insolence and wine.
Witness the Streets of *Sodom*, and that night
In *Gibeah*, when the hospitable door
Expos'd a Matron to avoid worse rape.
These were the prime in order and in might;
The rest were long to tell, though far renown'd,
Th' *Ionian* Gods, of *Javans* Issue held
Gods, yet confest later then Heav'n and Earth
Thir boasted Parents; *Titan* Heav'ns first born
With his enormous brood, and birthright seis'd
By younger *Saturn*, he from mightier *Jove*
His own and *Rheas* Son like measure found;
So *Jove* usurping reign'd: these first in *Creet*
And *Ida* known, thence on the Snowy top
Of cold *Olympus* rul'd the middle Air
Thir highest Heav'n; or on the *Delphian Cliff*,
Or in *Dodona*, and through all the bounds
Of *Doric* Land; or who with *Saturn* old
Fled over *Adria* to th' *Hesperian* Fields,
And ore the *Celtic* roam'd the utmost Isles.
All these and more came flocking; but with looks
Down cast and damp, yet such wherein appear'd
Obscure some glimps of joy, to have found thir chief
Not in despair, to have found themselves not lost
In loss it self; which on his count'nance cast
Like doubtful hue: but he his wonted pride
Soon recollecting, with high words, that bore
Semblance of worth, not subtance, gently rais'd
Thir fainting courage, and dispel'd thir fears.
Then strait commands that at the warlike sound
Of Trumpets loud and Clarions be uprear'd
His mighty Standard; that proud honour claim'd
Azazel as his right, a Cherube tall:
Who forthwith from the glittering Staff unfurld
Th' Imperial Ensign, which full high advanc't
Shon like a Meteor streaming to the Wind
With Gemms and Golden lustre rich imblaz'd,

Seraphic arms and Trophies: all the while
Sonorous mettal blowing Martial sounds:
At which the universal Host upsent
A shout that tore Hells Concave, and beyond
Frighted the Reign of *Chaos* and old Night.
All in a moment through the gloom were seen
Ten thousand Banners rise into the Air
With Orient Colours waving: with them rose
A Forrest huge of Spears: and thronging Helms
Appear'd, and serried Shields in thick array
Of depth immeasurable: Anon they move
In perfect *Phalanx* to the *Dorian* mood
Of Flutes and soft Recorders; such as rais'd
To hight of noblest temper Hero's old
Arming to Battel, and in stead of rage
Deliberate valour breath'd, firm and unmov'd
With dread of death to flight or foul retreat,
Nor wanting power to mitigate and swage
With solemn touches, troubl'd thoughts, and chase
Anguish and doubt and fear and sorrow and pain
From mortal or immortal minds. Thus they
Breathing united force with fixed thought
Mov'd on in silence to soft Pipes that charm'd
Thir painful steps o're the burnt soyle; and now
Advanc't in view they stand, a horrid Front
Of dreadful length and dazling Arms, in guise
Of Warriers old with order'd Spear and Shield,
Awaiting what command thir mighty Chief
Had to impose: He through the armed Files
Darts his experienc't eye, and soon traverse
The whole Battalion views, thir order due,
Thir visages and stature as of Gods,
Thir number last he summs. And now his heart
Distends with pride, and hardning in his strength
Glories: For never since created man,
Met such imbodied force, as nam'd with these
Could merit more then that small infantry
Warr'd on by Cranes: though all the Giant brood
Of *Phlegra* with th' Heroic Race were joyn'd
That fought at *Theb's* and *Ilium*, on each side

Mixt with auxiliar Gods; and what resounds
In Fable or *Romance* of *Uthers* Son
Begirt with *British* and *Armoric* Knights;
And all who since, Baptiz'd or Infidel
Jousted in *Aspramont* or *Montalban*,
Damasco, or *Marocco*, or *Trebisond*,
Or whom *Biserta* sent from *Afric* shore
When *Charlemain* with all his Peerage fell
By *Fontarabbia*. Thus far these beyond
Compare of mortal prowess, yet observ'd
Thir dread commander: he above the rest
In shape and gesture proudly eminent
Stood like a Towr; his form had yet not lost
All her Original brightness, nor appear'd
Less then Arch Angel ruind, and th' excess
Of Glory obscur'd: As when the Sun new ris'n
Looks through the Horizontal misty Air
Shorn of his Beams, or from behind the Moon
In dim Eclips disastrous twilight sheds
On half the Nations, and with fear of change
Perplexes Monarchs. Dark'n'd so, yet shon
Above them all th' Arch Angel: but his face
Deep scars of Thunder had intrencht, and care
Sat on his faded cheek, but under Browes
Of dauntless courage, and considerate Pride
Waiting revenge: cruel his eye, but cast
Signs of remorse and passion to behold
The fellows of his crime, the followers rather
(Far other once beheld in bliss) condemn'd
For ever now to have thir lot in pain,
Millions of Spirits for his fault amerc't
Of Heav'n, and from Eternal Splendors flung
For his revolt, yet faithfull how they stood,
Thir Glory witherd. As when Heavens Fire
Hath scath'd the Forrest Oaks, or Mountain Pines,
With singed top thir stately growth though bare
Stands on the blasted Heath. He now prepar'd
To speak; whereat thir doubl'd Ranks they bend
From Wing to Wing, and half enclose him round
With all his Peers: attention held them mute.

Thrice he assayd, and thrice in spight of scorn,
Tears such as Angels weep, burst forth: at last
Words interwove with sighs found out thir way.
     O Myriads of immortal Spirits, O Powers
Matchless, but with th' Almighty, and that strife
Was not inglorious, though th' event was dire,
As this place testifies, and this dire change
Hateful to utter: but what power of mind
Foreseeing or presaging, from the Depth
Of knowledge past or present, could have fear'd,
How such united force of Gods, how such
As stood like these, could ever know repulse?
For who can yet beleeve, though after loss,
That all these puissant Legions, whose exile
Hath emptied Heav'n, shall faile to re-ascend
Self-rais'd, and repossess thir native seat?
For mee, be witness all the Host of Heav'n,
If counsels different, or danger shun'd
By mee, have lost our hopes. But he who reigns
Monarch in Heav'n, till then as one secure
Sat on his Throne, upheld by old repute,
Consent or custome, and his Regal State
Put forth at full, but still his strength conceal'd,
Which tempted our attempt, and wrought our fall.
Henceforth his might we know, and know our own
So as not either to provoke, or dread
New warr, provok't; our better part remains
To work in close design, by fraud or guile
What force effected not: that he no less
At length from us may find, who overcomes
By force, hath overcome but half his foe.
Space may produce new Worlds; whereof so rife
There went a fame in Heav'n that he ere long
Intended to create, and therein plant
A generation, whom his choice regard
Should favour equal to the Sons of Heaven:
Thither, if but to pry, shall be perhaps
Our first eruption, thither or elsewhere:
For this Infernal Pit shall never hold
Cælestial Spirits in Bondage, nor th' Abyss

Long under darkness cover. But these thoughts
Full Counsel must mature: Peace is despaird,
For who can think Submission? Warr then, Warr
Open or understood must be resolv'd.

    He spake: and to confirm his words, out-flew
Millions of flaming swords, drawn from the thighs
Of mighty Cherubim; the sudden blaze
Far round illumin'd hell: highly they rag'd
Against the Highest, and fierce with grasped Arms
Clash'd on thir sounding shields the din of war,
Hurling defiance toward the Vault of Heav'n.

    There stood a Hill not far whose griesly top
Belch'd fire and rowling smoak; the rest entire
Shon with a glossie scurff, undoubted sign
That in his womb was hid metallic Ore,
The work of Sulphur. Thither wing'd with speed
A numerous Brigad hasten'd. As when Bands
Of Pioners with Spade and Pickax arm'd
Forerun the Royal Camp, to trench a Field,
Or cast a Rampart. *Mammon* led them on,
Mammon, the least erected Spirit that fell
From heav'n, for ev'n in heav'n his looks and thoughts
Were always downward bent, admiring more
The riches of Heav'ns pavement, trod'n Gold,
Then aught divine or holy else enjoy'd
In vision beatific: by him first
Men also, and by his suggestion taught,
Ransack'd the Center, and with impious hands
Rifl'd the bowels of thir mother Earth
For Treasures better hid. Soon had his crew
Op'nd into the Hill a spacious wound
And dig'd out ribs of Gold. Let none admire
That riches grow in Hell; that soyle may best
Deserve the precious bane. And here let those
Who boast in mortal things, and wondring tell
Of *Babel*, and the works of *Memphian* Kings
Learn how thir greatest Monuments of Fame,
And Strength and Art are easily out-done
By Spirits reprobate, and in an hour
What in an age they with incessant toyle

And hands innumerable scarce perform.
Nigh on the Plain in many cells prepar'd,
That underneath had veins of liquid fire
Sluc'd from the Lake, a second multitude
With wondrous Art founded the massie Ore,
Severing each kinde, and scum'd the Bullion dross:
A third as soon had form'd within the ground
A various mould, and from the boyling cells
By strange conveyance fill'd each hollow nook,
As in an Organ from one blast of wind
To many a row of Pipes the sound-board breaths.
Anon out of the earth a Fabrick huge
Rose like an Exhalation, with the sound
Of Dulcet Symphonies and voices sweet,
Built like a Temple, where *Pilasters* round
Were set, and Doric pillars overlaid
With Golden Architrave; nor did there want
Cornice or Freeze, with bossy Sculptures grav'n,
The Roof was fretted Gold. Not *Babilon*,
Nor great *Alcairo* such magnificence
Equal'd in all thir glories, to inshrine
Belus or *Serapis* thir Gods, or seat
Thir Kings, when *Ægypt* with *Assyria* strove
In wealth and luxurie. Th' ascending pile
Stood fixt her stately highth, and strait the dores
Op'ning thir brazen foulds discover wide
Within, her ample spaces, o're the smooth
And level pavement: from the arched roof
Pendant by suttle Magic many a row
Of Starry Lamps and blazing Cressets fed
With *Naphtha* and *Asphaltus* yeilded light
As from a sky. The hasty multitude
Admiring enter'd, and the work some praise
And some the Architect: his hand was known
In Heav'n by many a Towred structure high,
Where Scepter'd Angels held thir residence,
And sat as Princes, whom the supreme King
Exalted to such power, and gave to rule,
Each in his Hierarchie, the Orders bright.
Nor was his name unheard or unador'd

In ancient *Greece;* and in *Ausonian* land
Men call'd him *Mulciber;* and how he fell
From Heav'n, they fabl'd, thrown by angry *Jove*
Sheer o're the Chrystal Battlements: from Morn
To Noon he fell, from Noon to dewy Eve,
A Summers day; and with the setting Sun
Dropt from the Zenith like a falling Star,
On *Lemnos* th'*Ægæan* Ile: thus they relate,
Erring; for he with this rebellious rout
Fell long before; nor aught avail'd him now
To have built in Heav'n high Towrs; nor did he scape
By all his Engins, but was headlong sent
With his industrious crew to build in hell.
Mean while the winged Haralds by command
Of Sovran power, with awful Ceremony
And Trumpets sound throughout the Host proclaim
A solemn Councel forthwith to be held
At *Pandæmonium,* the high Capital
Of Satan and his Peers: thir summons call'd
From every Band and squared Regiment
By place or choice the worthiest; they anon
With hundreds and with thousands trooping came
Attended: all access was throng'd, the Gates
And Porches wide, but chief the spacious Hall
(Though like a cover'd field, where Champions bold
Wont ride in arm'd, and at the Soldans chair
Defi'd the best of *Panim* chivalry
To mortal combat or carreer with Lance)
Thick swarm'd, both on the ground and in the air,
Brusht with the hiss of russling wings. As Bees
In spring time, when the Sun with *Taurus* rides,
Poure forth thir populous youth about the Hive
In clusters; they among fresh dews and flowers
Flie to and fro, or on the smoothed Plank,
The suburb of thir Straw-built Cittadel,
New rub'd with Baum, expatiate and confer
Thir State affairs. So thick the aerie crowd
Swarm'd and were straitn'd; till the Signal giv'n,
Behold a wonder! they but now who seemd
In bigness to surpass Earths Giant Sons

Now less then smallest Dwarfs, in narrow room
Throng numberless, like that Pigmean Race
Beyond the *Indian* Mount, or Faerie Elves,
Whose midnight Revels, by a Forrest side
Or Fountain some belated Peasant sees,
Or dreams he sees, while over-head the Moon
Sits Arbitress, and neerer to the Earth
Wheels her pale course, they on thir mirth and dance
Intent, with jocond Music charm his ear;
At once with joy and fear his heart rebounds.
Thus incorporeal Spirits to smallest forms
Reduc'd thir shapes immense, and were at large,
Though without number still amidst the Hall
Of that infernal Court. But far within
And in thir own dimensions like themselves
The great Seraphic Lords and Cherubim
In close recess and secret conclave sat
A thousand Demy-Gods on golden seats,
Frequent and full. After short silence then
And summons read, the great consult began.

BOOK II

THE ARGUMENT

The Consultation begun, Satan *debates whether another Battel be to be hazarded for the recovery of Heaven: some advise it, others dissuade: A third proposal is prefer'd, mention'd before by* Satan, *to search the truth of that Prophesie or Tradition in Heaven concerning another world, and another kind of creature equal or not much inferiour to themselves, about this time to be created: Their doubt who shall be sent on this difficult search:* Satan *their Chief undertakes alone the voyage, is honourd and applauded. The Councel thus ended, the rest betake them several wayes and to several imployments, as thir inclinations lead them, to entertain the time till* Satan *return. He passes on his Journey to Hell Gates, finds them shut, and who sat there to guard them, by whom at length they are op'nd, and discover to him the great Gulf between Hell and Heaven; with what difficulty he passes through, directed by* Chaos, *the Power of that place, to the sight of this new World which he sought.*

HIGH on a Throne of Royal State, which far
Outshon the wealth of *Ormus* and of *Ind*,
Or where the gorgeous East with richest hand
Showrs on her Kings *Barbaric* Pearl and Gold,
Satan exalted sat, by merit rais'd
To that bad eminence; and from despair
Thus high uplifted beyond hope, aspires
Beyond thus high, insatiate to pursue
Vain Warr with Heav'n, and by success untaught
His proud imaginations thus displaid.
    Powers and Dominions, Deities of Heav'n,
For since no deep within her gulf can hold
Immortal vigor, though opprest and fall'n,
I give not Heav'n for lost. From this descent
Celestial vertues rising, will appear
More glorious and more dread then from no fall,
And trust themselves to fear no second fate:
Mee though just right, and the fixt Laws of Heav'n
Did first create your Leader, next, free choice,
With what besides, in Counsel or in Fight,
Hath bin achievd of merit, yet this loss
Thus farr at least recover'd, hath much more
Establisht in a safe unenvied Throne
Yielded with full consent. The happier state
In Heav'n, which follows dignity, might draw
Envy from each inferior; but who here
Will envy whom the highest place exposes
Formost to stand against the Thunderers aim
Your bulwark, and condemns to greatest share
Of endless pain? where there is then no good
For which to strive, no strife can grow up there
From Faction; for none sure will claim in Hell
Precedence, none, whose portion is so small
Of present pain, that with ambitious mind
Will covet more. With this advantage then

To union, and firm Faith, and firm accord,
More then can be in Heav'n, we now return
To claim our just inheritance of old,
Surer to prosper then prosperity
Could have assur'd us; and by what best way,
Whether of open Warr or covert guile,
We now debate; who can advise, may speak.

He ceas'd, and next him *Moloc*, Scepter'd King
Stood up, the strongest and the fiercest Spirit
That fought in Heav'n; now fiercer by despair:
His trust was with th' Eternal to be deem'd
Equal in strength, and rather then be less
Car'd not to be at all; with that care lost
Went all his fear: of God, or Hell, or worse
He reckd not, and these words thereafter spake.

My sentence is for open Warr: Of Wiles,
More unexpert, I boast not: them let those
Contrive who need, or when they need, not now
For while they sit contriving, shall the rest,
Millions that stand in Arms, and longing wait
The Signal to ascend, sit lingring here
Heav'ns fugitives, and for thir dwelling place
Accept this dark opprobrious Den of shame,
The Prison of his Tyranny who Reigns
By our delay? no, let us rather choose
Arm'd with Hell flames and fury all at once
O're Heav'ns high Towrs to force resistless way,
Turning our Tortures into horrid Arms
Against the Torturer; when to meet the noise
Of his Almighty Engin he shall hear
Infernal Thunder, and for Lightning see
Black fire and horror shot with equal rage
Among his Angels; and his Throne it self
Mixt with *Tartarean* Sulphur, and strange fire,
His own invented Torments. But perhaps
The way seems difficult and steep to scale
With upright wing against a higher foe.
Let such bethink them, if the sleepy drench
Of that forgetful Lake benumm not still,
That in our proper motion we ascend

Up to our native seat : descent and fall
To us is adverse. Who but felt of late
When the fierce Foe hung on our brok'n Rear
Insulting, and pursu'd us through the Deep,
With what compulsion and laborious flight
We sunk thus low? Th' ascent is easie then ;
Th' event is fear'd ; should we again provoke
Our stronger, some worse way his wrath may find
To our destruction : if there be in Hell
Fear to be worse destroy'd : what can be worse
Then to dwell here, driv'n out from bliss, condemn'd
In this abhorred deep to utter woe ;
Where pain of unextinguishable fire
Must exercise us without hope of end
The Vassals of his anger, when the Scourge
Inexorably, and the torturing houre
Calls us to Penance? More destroy'd then thus
We should be quite abolisht and expire.
What fear we then? what doubt we to incense
His utmost ire? which to the highth enrag'd,
Will either quite consume us, and reduce
To nothing this essential, happier farr
Then miserable to have eternal being :
Or if our substance be indeed Divine,
And cannot cease to be, we are at worst
On this side nothing ; and by proof we feel
Our power sufficient to disturb his Heav'n,
And with perpetual inrodes to Allarme,
Though inaccessible, his fatal Throne :
Which if not Victory is yet Revenge.

   He ended frowning, and his look denounc'd
Desperate revenge, and Battel dangerous
To less then Gods. On th' other side up rose
Belial, in act more graceful and humane ;
A fairer person lost not Heav'n ; he seemd
For dignity compos'd and high exploit :
But all was false and hollow ; though his Tongue
Dropt Manna, and could make the worse appear
The better reason, to perplex and dash
Maturest Counsels : for his thoughts were low ;

To vice industrious, but to Nobler deeds
Timorous and slothful: yet he pleas'd the ear,
And with perswasive accent thus began.

   I should be much for open Warr, O Peers,
As not behind in hate; if what was urg'd
Main reason to perswade immediate Warr,
Did not disswade me most, and seem to cast
Ominous conjecture on the whole success;
When he who most excels in fact of Arms,
In what he counsels and in what excels
Mistrustful, grounds his courage on despair
And utter dissolution, as the scope
Of all his aim, after some dire revenge.
First, what Revenge? the Towrs of Heav'n are fill'd
With Armed watch, that render all access
Impregnable; oft on the bordering Deep
Encamp thir Legions, or with obscure wing
Scout farr and wide into the Realm of night,
Scorning surprize. Or could we break our way
By force, and at our heels all Hell should rise
With blackest Insurrection, to confound
Heav'ns purest Light, yet our great Enemy
All incorruptible would on his Throne
Sit unpolluted, and th' Ethereal mould
Incapable of stain would soon expel
Her mischief, and purge off the baser fire
Victorious. Thus repuls'd, our final hope
Is flat despair; we must exasperate
Th' Almighty Victor to spend all his rage,
And that must end us, that must be our cure,
To be no more; sad cure; for who would loose,
Though full of pain, this intellectual being,
Those thoughts that wander through Eternity,
To perish rather, swallowd up and lost
In the wide womb of uncreated night,
Devoid of sense and motion? and who knows,
Let this be good, whether our angry Foe
Can give it, or will ever? how he can
Is doubtful; that he never will is sure.
Will he, so wise, let loose at once his ire,

Belike through impotence, or unaware,
To give his Enemies thir wish, and end
Them in his anger, whom his anger saves
To punish endless? wherefore cease we then?
Say they who counsel Warr, we are decreed,
Reserv'd and destin'd to Eternal woe;
Whatever doing, what can we suffer more,
What can we suffer worse? is this then worst,
Thus sitting, thus consulting, thus in Arms?
What when we fled amain, pursu'd and strook
With Heav'ns afflicting Thunder, and besought
The Deep to shelter us? this Hell then seem'd
A refuge from those wounds: or when we lay
Chain'd on the burning Lake? that sure was worse.
What if the breath that kindl'd those grim fires
Awak'd should blow them into sevenfold rage
And plunge us in the flames? or from above
Should intermitted vengeance arm again
His red right hand to plague us? what if all
Her stores were opn'd, and this Firmament
Of Hell should spout her Cataracts of Fire,
Impendent horrors, threatning hideous fall
One day upon our heads; while we perhaps
Designing or exhorting glorious warr,
Caught in a fierie Tempest shall be hurl'd
Each on his rock transfixt, the sport and prey
Of racking whirlwinds, or for ever sunk
Under yon boyling Ocean, wrapt in Chains;
There to converse with everlasting groans,
Unrespited, unpitied, unrepreevd,
Ages of hopeless end; this would be worse.
Warr therefore, open or conceal'd, alike
My voice disswades; for what can force or guile
With him, or who deceive his mind, whose eye
Views all things at one view? he from heav'ns highth
All these our motions vain, sees and derides;
Not more Almighty to resist our might
Then wise to frustrate all our plots and wiles.
Shall we then live thus vile, the race of Heav'n
Thus trampl'd, thus expell'd to suffer here

Chains and these Torments? better these then worse
By my advice; since fate inevitable
Subdues us, and Omnipotent Decree
The Victors will. To suffer, as to doe,
Our strength is equal, nor the Law unjust
That so ordains: this was at first resolv'd,
If we were wise, against so great a foe
Contending, and so doubtful what might fall.
I laugh, when those who at the Spear are bold
And vent'rous, if that fail them, shrink and fear
What yet they know must follow, to endure
Exile, or ignominy, or bonds, or pain,
The sentence of thir Conquerour: This is now
Our doom; which if we can sustain and bear,
Our Supream Foe in time may much remit
His anger, and perhaps thus farr remov'd
Not mind us not offending, satisfi'd
With what is punish't; whence these raging fires
Will slack'n, if his breath stir not thir flames.
Our purer essence then will overcome
Thir noxious vapour, or enur'd not feel,
Or chang'd at length, and to the place conformd
In temper and in nature, will receive
Familiar the fierce heat, and void of pain;
This horror will grow milde, this darkness light,
Besides what hope the never-ending flight
Of future days may bring, what chance, what change
Worth waiting, since our present lot appeers
For happy though but ill, for ill not worst,
If we procure not to our selves more woe.
  Thus *Belial* with words cloath'd in reasons garb
Counsel'd ignoble ease, and peaceful sloath,
Not peace: and after him thus *Mammon* spake.
  Either to disinthrone the King of Heav'n
We warr, if warr be best, or to regain
Our own right lost: him to unthrone we then
May hope, when everlasting Fate shall yeild
To fickle Chance, and *Chaos* judge the strife:
The former vain to hope argues as vain
The latter: for what place can be for us

Within Heav'ns bound, unless Heav'ns Lord supream
We overpower? Suppose he should relent
And publish Grace to all, on promise made
Of new Subjection; with what eyes could we
Stand in his presence humble, and receive
Strict Laws impos'd, to celebrate his Throne
With warbl'd Hymns, and to his Godhead sing
Forc't Halleluiah's; while he Lordly sits
Our envied Sovran, and his Altar breathes
Ambrosial Odours and Ambrosial Flowers,
Our servile offerings. This must be our task
In Heav'n this our delight; how wearisom
Eternity so spent in worship paid
To whom we hate. Let us not then pursue
By force impossible, by leave obtain'd
Unacceptable, though in Heav'n, our state
Of splendid vassalage, but rather seek
Our own good from our selves, and from our own
Live to our selves, though in this vast recess,
Free, and to none accountable, preferring
Hard liberty before the easie yoke
Of servile Pomp. Our greatness will appear
Then most conspicuous, when great things of small,
Useful of hurtful, prosperous of adverse
We can create, and in what place so e're
Thrive under evil, and work ease out of pain
Through labour and indurance. This deep world
Of darkness do we dread? how oft amidst
Thick clouds and dark doth Heav'ns all-ruling Sire
Choose to reside, his Glory unobscur'd,
And with the Majesty of darkness round
Covers his Throne; from whence deep thunders roar
Must'ring thir rage, and Heav'n resembles Hell?
As he our Darkness, cannot we his Light
Imitate when we please? This Desart soile
Wants not her hidden lustre, Gemms and Gold;
Nor want we skill or art, from whence to raise
Magnificence; and what can Heav'n shew more?
Our torments also may in length of time
Become our Elements, these piercing Fires

As soft as now severe, our temper chang'd
Into their temper; which must needs remove
The sensible of pain. All things invite
To peaceful Counsels, and the settl'd State
Of order, how in safety best we may
Compose our present evils, with regard
Of what we are and were, dismissing quite
All thoughts of Warr: ye have what I advise.

He scarce had finisht, when such murmur filld
Th' Assembly, as when hollow Rocks retain
The sound of blustring winds, which all night long
Had rous'd the Sea, now with hoarse cadence lull
Sea-faring men orewatcht, whose Bark by chance
Or Pinnace anchors in a craggy Bay
After the Tempest: Such applause was heard
As *Mammon* ended, and his Sentence pleas'd,
Advising peace: for such another Field
They dreaded worse then Hell: so much the fear
Of Thunder and the Sword of *Michael*
Wrought still within them; and no less desire
To found this nether Empire, which might rise
By pollicy, and long process of time,
In emulation opposite to Heav'n.
Which when *Beëlzebub* perceiv'd, then whom,
Satan except, none higher sat, with grave
Aspect he rose, and in his rising seem'd
A Pillar of State; deep on his Front engraven
Deliberation sat and publick care;
And Princely counsel in his face yet shon,
Majestic though in ruin: sage he stood
With *Atlantean* shoulders fit to bear
The weight of mightiest Monarchies; his look
Drew audience and attention still as Night
Or Summers Noon-tide air, while thus he spake.

Thrones and imperial Powers, offspring of heav'n
Ethereal Vertues; or these Titles now
Must we renounce, and changing stile be call'd
Princes of Hell? for so the popular vote
Inclines, here to continue, and build up here
A growing Empire; doubtless; while we dream,

And know not that the King of Heav'n hath doom'd
This place our dungeon, not our safe retreat
Beyond his Potent arm, to live exempt
From Heav'ns high jurisdiction, in new League
Banded against his Throne, but to remaine
In strictest bondage, though thus far remov'd,
Under th' inevitable curb, reserv'd
His captive multitude : For he, be sure,
In heighth or depth, still first and last will Reign
Sole King, and of his Kingdom loose no part
By our Revolt, but over Hell extend
His Empire, and with Iron Scepter rule
Us here, as with his Golden those in Heav'n.
What sit we then projecting Peace and Warr?
Warr hath determin'd us, and foild with loss
Irreparable ; tearms of peace yet none
Voutsaf't or sought ; for what peace will be giv'n
To us enslav'd, but custody severe,
And stripes, and arbitrary punishment
Inflicted? and what peace can we return,
But to our power hostility and hate,
Untam'd reluctance, and revenge though slow,
Yet ever plotting how the Conqueror least
May reap his conquest, and may least rejoyce
In doing what we most in suffering feel?
Nor will occasion want, nor shall we need
With dangerous expedition to invade
Heav'n, whose high walls fear no assault or Siege,
Or ambush from the Deep. What if we find
Some easier enterprize? There is a place
(If ancient and prophetic fame in Heav'n
Err not) another World, the happy seat
Of som new Race call'd *Man*, about this time
To be created like to us, though less
In power and excellence, but favour'd more
Of him who rules above ; so was his will
Pronounc'd among the Gods, and by an Oath,
That shook Heav'ns whol circumference, confirm'd.
Thither let us bend all our thoughts, to learn
What creatures there inhabit, of what mould,

Or substance, how endu'd, and what thir Power,
And where thir weakness, how attempted best,
By force or suttlety: Though Heav'n be shut,
And Heav'ns high Arbitrator sit secure
In his own strength, this place may lye expos'd
The utmost border of his Kingdom, left
To their defence who hold it: here perhaps
Som advantagious act may be achiev'd
By sudden onset, either with Hell fire
To waste his whole Creation, or possess
All as our own, and drive as we were driven,
The punie habitants, or if not drive,
Seduce them to our Party, that thir God
May prove thir foe, and with repenting hand
Abolish his own works. This would surpass
Common revenge, and interrupt his joy
In our Confusion, and our Joy upraise
In his disturbance; when his darling Sons
Hurl'd headlong to partake with us, shall curse
Thir frail Original, and faded bliss,
Faded so soon. Advise if this be worth
Attempting, or to sit in darkness here
Hatching vain Empires. Thus *Beëlzebub*
Pleaded his devilish Counsel, first devis'd
By *Satan*, and in part propos'd: for whence,
But from the Author of all ill could Spring
So deep a malice, to confound the race
Of mankind in one root, and Earth with Hell
To mingle and involve, done all to spite
The great Creatour? but thir spite still serves
His glory to augment. The bold design
Pleas'd highly those infernal States, and joy
Sparkl'd in all thir eyes; with full assent
They vote: whereat his speech he thus renews.

  Well have ye judg'd, well ended long debate,
Synod of Gods, and like to what ye are,
Great things resolv'd; which from the lowest deep
Will once more lift us up, in spight of Fate,
Neerer our ancient Seat; perhaps in view
Of those bright confines, whence with neighbouring Arms

And opportune excursion we may chance
Re-enter Heav'n; or else in some milde Zone
Dwell not unvisited of Heav'ns fair Light
Secure, and at the brightning Orient beam
Purge off this gloom; the soft delicious Air,
To heal the scarr of these corrosive Fires
Shall breath her balme. But first whom shall we send
In search of this new world, whom shall we find
Sufficient? who shall tempt with wandring feet
The dark unbottom'd infinite Abyss
And through the palpable obscure find out
His uncouth way, or spread his aerie flight
Upborn with indefatigable wings
Over the vast abrupt, ere he arrive
The happy Ile; what strength, what art can then
Suffice, or what evasion bear him safe
Through the strict Senteries and Stations thick
Of Angels watching round? Here he had need
All circumspection, and wee now no less
Choice in our suffrage; for on whom we send,
The weight of all and our last hope relies.
　　This said, he sat; and expectation held
His look suspence, awaiting who appeer'd
To second, or oppose, or undertake
The perilous attempt; but all sat mute,
Pondering the danger with deep thoughts; and each
In others count'nance read his own dismay
Astonisht: none among the choice and prime
Of those Heav'n-warring Champions could be found
So hardie as to proffer or accept
Alone the dreadful voyage; till at last
Satan, whom now transcendent glory rais'd
Above his fellows, with Monarchal pride
Conscious of highest worth, unmov'd thus spake.
　　O Progeny of Heav'n, Empyreal Thrones,
With reason hath deep silence and demurr
Seis'd us, though undismaid: long is the way
And hard, that out of Hell leads up to light;
Our prison strong, this huge convex of Fire,
Outrageous to devour, immures us round

Ninefold, and gates of burning Adamant
Barr'd over us prohibit all egress.
These past, if any pass, the void profound
Of unessential Night receives him next
Wide gaping, and with utter loss of being
Threatens him, plung'd in that abortive gulf.
If thence he scape into whatever world,
Or unknown Region, what remains him less
Then unknown dangers and as hard escape.
But I should ill become this Throne, O Peers,
And this Imperial Sov'ranty, adorn'd
With splendor, arm'd with power, if aught propos'd
And judg'd of public moment, in the shape
Of difficulty or danger could deterr
Mee from attempting. Wherefore do I assume
These Royalties, and not refuse to Reign,
Refusing to accept as great a share
Of hazard as of honour, due alike
To him who Reigns, and so much to him due
Of hazard more, as he above the rest
High honourd sits? Go therefore mighty Powers,
Terror of Heav'n, though fall'n; intend at home,
While here shall be our home, what best may ease
The present misery, and render Hell
More tollerable; if there be cure or charm
To respite or deceive, or slack the pain
Of this ill Mansion: intermit no watch
Against a wakeful Foe, while I abroad
Through all the coasts of dark destruction seek
Deliverance for us all: this enterprize
None shall partake with me. Thus saying rose
The Monarch, and prevented all reply,
Prudent, least from his resolution rais'd
Others among the chief might offer now
(Certain to be refus'd) what erst they feard;
And so refus'd might in opinion stand
His rivals, winning cheap the high repute
Which he through hazard huge must earn. But they
Dreaded not more th' adventure then his voice
Forbidding; and at once with him they rose;

Thir rising all at once was as the sound
Of Thunder heard remote. Towards him they bend
With awful reverence prone; and as a God
Extoll him equal to the highest in Heav'n:
Nor fail'd they to express how much they prais'd,
That for the general safety he despis'd
His own: for neither do the Spirits damn'd
Loose all thir vertue; least bad men should boast
Thir specious deeds on earth, which glory excites,
Or close ambition varnisht o're with zeal.
Thus they thir doubtful consultations dark
Ended rejoycing in their matchless Chief:
As when from mountain tops the dusky clouds
Ascending, while the North wind sleeps, o'respread
Heav'ns chearful face, the lowring Element
Scowls ore the dark'nd lantskip Snow, or showre;
If chance the radiant Sun with farewell sweet
Extend his ev'ning beam, the fields revive,
The birds thir notes renew, and bleating herds
Attest thir joy, that hill and valley rings.
O shame to men! Devil with Devil damn'd
Firm concord holds, men onely disagree
Of Creatures rational, though under hope
Of heavenly Grace; and God proclaiming peace,
Yet live in hatred, enmitie, and strife
Among themselves, and levie cruel warres,
Wasting the Earth, each other to destroy:
As if (which might induce us to accord)
Man had not hellish foes anow besides,
That day and night for his destruction waite.
  The *Stygian* Councel thus dissolv'd; and forth
In order came the grand infernal Peers,
Midst came thir mighty Paramount, and seemd
Alone th' Antagonist of Heav'n, nor less
Then Hells dread Emperour with pomp Supream,
And God-like imitated State; him round
A Globe of fierie Seraphim inclos'd
With bright imblazonrie, and horrent Arms.
Then of thir Session ended they bid cry
With Trumpets regal sound the great result:

Toward the four winds four speedy Cherubim
Put to thir mouths the sounding Alchymie
By Harald's voice explain'd : the hollow Abyss
Heard farr and wide, and all the host of Hell
With deafning shout, return'd them loud acclaim.
Thence more at ease thir minds and somwhat rais'd
By false presumptuous hope, the ranged powers
Disband, and wandring, each his several way
Pursues, as inclination or sad choice
Leads him perplext, where he may likeliest find
Truce to his restless thoughts, and entertain
The irksom hours, till his great Chief return.
Part on the Plain, or in the Air sublime
Upon the wing, or in swift Race contend,
As at th' Olympian Games or *Pythian* fields ;
Part curb thir fierie Steeds, or shun the Goal
With rapid wheels, or fronted Brigads form.
As when to warn proud Cities warr appears
Wag'd in the troubl'd Skie, and Armies rush
To Battel in the Clouds, before each Van
Prick forth the Aerie Knights, and couch thir spears
Till thickest Legions close ; with feats of Arms
From either end of Heav'n the welkin burns.
Others with vast *Typhœan* rage more fell
Rend up both Rocks and Hills, and ride the Air
In whirlwind ; Hell scarce holds the wilde uproar.
As when *Alcides* from *Oechalia* Crown'd
With conquest, felt th' envenom'd robe, and tore
Through pain up by the roots *Thessalian* Pines,
And *Lichas* from the top of *Oeta* threw
Into th' *Euboic* Sea. Others more milde,
Retreated in a silent valley, sing
With notes Angelical to many a Harp
Thir own Heroic deeds and hapless fall
By doom of Battel ; and complain that Fate
Free Vertue should enthrall to Force or Chance.
Thir song was partial, but the harmony
(What could it less when Spirits immortal sing?)
Suspended Hell, and took with ravishment
The thronging audience. In discourse more sweet

(For Eloquence the Soul, Song charms the Sense,)
Others apart sat on a Hill retir'd,
In thoughts more elevate, and reason'd high
Of Providence, Foreknowledge, Will and Fate,
Fixt Fate, free will, foreknowledge absolute,
And found no end, in wandring mazes lost.
Of good and evil much they argu'd then,
Of happiness and final misery,
Passion and Apathie, and glory and shame,
Vain wisdom all, and false Philosophie:
Yet with a pleasing sorcerie could charm
Pain for a while or anguish, and excite
Fallacious hope, or arm th' obdured brest
With stubborn patience as with triple steel.
Another part in Squadrons and gross Bands
On bold adventure to discover wide
That dismal world, if any Clime perhaps
Might yield them easier habitation, bend
Four ways thir flying March, along the Banks
Of four infernal Rivers that disgorge
Into the burning Lake thir baleful streams;
Abhorred *Styx* the flood of deadly hate,
Sad *Acheron* of sorrow, black and deep;
Cocytus, nam'd of lamentation loud
Heard on the ruful stream; fierce *Phlegeton*
Whose waves of torrent fire inflame with rage.
Farr off from these a slow and silent stream,
Lethe the River of Oblivion roules
Her watrie Labyrinth, whereof who drinks,
Forthwith his former state and being forgets,
Forgets both joy and grief, pleasure and pain.
Beyond this flood a frozen Continent
Lies dark and wilde, beat with perpetual storms
Of Whirlwind and dire Hail, which on firm land
Thaws not, but gathers heap, and ruin seems
Of ancient pile; all else deep snow and ice,
A gulf profound as that *Serbonian* Bog
Betwixt *Damiata* and mount *Casius* old,
Where Armies whole have sunk: the parching Air
Burns frore, and cold performs th' effect of Fire.

Thither by harpy-footed Furies hail'd,
At certain revolutions all the damn'd
Are brought : and feel by turns the bitter change
Of fierce extreams, extreams by change more fierce,
From Beds of raging Fire to starve in Ice
Thir soft Ethereal warmth, and there to pine
Immovable, infixt, and frozen round,
Periods of time, thence hurried back to fire.
They ferry over this *Lethean* Sound
Both to and fro, thir sorrow to augment,
And wish and struggle, as they pass, to reach
The tempting stream, with one small drop to loose
In sweet forgetfulness all pain and woe,
All in one moment, and so neer the brink ;
But fate withstands, and to oppose th' attempt
Medusa with *Gorgonian* terror guards
The Ford, and of it self the water flies
All taste of living wight, as once it fled
The lip of *Tantalus*. Thus roving on
In confus'd march forlorn, th' adventrous Bands
With shuddring horror pale, and eyes agast
View'd first thir lamentable lot, and found
No rest : through many a dark and drearie Vaile
They pass'd, and many a Region dolorous,
O're many a Frozen, many a fierie Alpe,
Rocks, Caves, Lakes, Fens, Bogs, Dens, and shades of death,
A Universe of death, which God by curse
Created evil, for evil only good,
Where all life dies, death lives, and Nature breeds,
Perverse, all monstrous, all prodigious things,
Abominable, inutterable, and worse
Then Fables yet have feign'd, or fear conceiv'd,
Gorgons and *Hydra's*, and *Chimera's* dire.

Mean while the Adversary of God and Man,
Satan with thoughts inflam'd of highest design,
Puts on swift wings, and toward the Gates of Hell
Explores his solitary flight : som times
He scours the right hand coast, som times the left,
Now shaves with level wing the Deep, then soares
Up to the fiery concave touring high.

As when farr off at Sea a Fleet descri'd
Hangs in the Clouds, by *Æquinoctial* Winds
Close sailing from *Bengala,* or the Iles
Of *Ternate* and *Tidore,* whence Merchants bring
Thir spicie Drugs: they on the Trading Flood
Through the wide *Ethiopian* to the Cape
Ply stemming nightly toward the Pole. So seem'd
Farr off the flying Fiend: at last appeer
Hell bounds high reaching to the horrid Roof,
And thrice threefold the Gates; three folds were Brass,
Three Iron, three of Adamantine Rock,
Impenetrable, impal'd with circling fire,
Yet unconsum'd. Before the Gates there sat
On either side a formidable shape;
The one seem'd Woman to the waste, and fair,
But ended foul in many a scaly fould
Voluminous and vast, a Serpent arm'd
With mortal sting: about her middle round
A cry of Hell Hounds never ceasing bark'd
With wide *Cerberian* mouths full loud, and rung
A hideous Peal: yet, when they list, would creep,
If aught disturb'd their noyse, into her woomb,
And kennel there, yet there still bark'd and howl'd
Within unseen. Farr less abhorrd then these
Vex'd *Scylla* bathing in the Sea that parts
Calabria from the hoarce *Trinacrian* shore:
Nor uglier follow the Night-Hag, when call'd
In secret, riding through the Air she comes
Lur'd with the smell of infant blood, to dance
With *Lapland* Witches, while the labouring Moon
Eclipses at thir charms. The other shape,
If shape it might be call'd that shape had none
Distinguishable in member, joynt, or limb,
Or substance might be call'd that shadow seem'd,
For each seem'd either; black it stood as Night,
Fierce as ten Furies, terrible as Hell,
And shook a dreadful Dart; what seem'd his head
The likeness of a Kingly Crown had on.
Satan was now at hand, and from his seat
The Monster moving onward came as fast,

With horrid strides, Hell trembled as he strode.
Th' undaunted Fiend what this might be admir'd,
Admir'd, not fear'd; God and his Son except,
Created thing naught valu'd he nor shun'd;
And with disdainful look thus first began.

Whence and what art thou, execrable shape,
That dar'st, though grim and terrible, advance
Thy miscreated Front athwart my way
To yonder Gates? through them I mean to pass,
That be assured, without leave askt of thee:
Retire, or taste thy folly, and learn by proof,
Hell-born, not to contend with Spirits of Heav'n.

To whom the Goblin full of wrauth reply'd,
Art thou that Traitor Angel, art thou hee,
Who first broke peace in Heav'n and Faith, till then
Unbrok'n, and in proud rebellious Arms
Drew after him the third part of Heav'ns Sons
Conjur'd against the highest, for which both Thou
And they outcast from God, are here condemn'd
To waste Eternal dayes in woe and pain?
And reck'n'st thou thy self with Spirits of Heav'n,
Hell-doomd, and breath'st defiance here and scorn,
Where I reign King, and to enrage thee more,
Thy King and Lord? Back to thy punishment,
False fugitive, and to thy speed add wings,
Least with a whip of Scorpions I pursue
Thy lingring, or with one stroke of this Dart
Strange horror seise thee, and pangs unfelt before.

So spake the grieslie terrour, and in shape,
So speaking and so threatning, grew tenfold
More dreadful and deform: on th' other side
Incenst with indignation *Satan* stood
Unterrifi'd, and like a Comet burn'd,
That fires the length of *Ophiucus* huge
In th' Artick Sky, and from his horrid hair
Shakes Pestilence and Warr. Each at the Head
Level'd his deadly aime; thir fatall hands
No second stroke intend, and such a frown
Each cast at th' other, as when two black Clouds
With Heav'ns Artillery fraught, come rattling on

Over the Caspian, then stand front to front
Hov'ring a space, till Winds the signal blow
To joyn their dark Encounter in mid air:
So frownd the mighty Combatants, that Hell
Grew darker at their frown, so matcht they stood;
For never but once more was either like
To meet so great a foe: and now great deeds
Had been achiev'd, whereof all Hell had rung,
Had not the Snakie Sorceress that sat
Fast by Hell Gate, and kept the fatal Key,
Ris'n, and with hideous outcry rush'd between.

   O Father, what intends thy hand, she cry'd,
Against thy only Son? What fury O Son,
Possesses thee to bend that mortal Dart
Against thy Fathers head? and know'st for whom;
For him who sits above and laughs the while
At thee ordain'd his drudge, to execute
What e're his wrath, which he calls Justice, bids,
His wrath which one day will destroy ye both.

   She spake, and at her words the hellish Pest
Forbore, then these to her *Satan* return'd:
   So strange thy outcry, and thy words so strange
Thou interposest, that my sudden hand
Prevented spares to tell thee yet by deeds
What it intends; till first I know of thee,
What thing thou art, thus double-form'd, and why
In this infernal Vaile first met thou call'st
Me Father, and that Fantasm call'st my Son?
I know thee not, nor ever saw till now
Sight more detestable then him and thee.

   T' whom thus the Portress of Hell Gate reply'd;
Hast thou forgot me then, and do I seem
Now in thine eye so foul, once deemd so fair
In Heav'n, when at th' Assembly, and in sight
Of all the Seraphim with thee combin'd
In bold conspiracy against Heav'ns King,
All on a sudden miserable pain
Surpris'd thee, dim thine eyes, and dizzie swumm
In darkness, while thy head flames thick and fast
Threw forth, till on the left side op'ning wide,

Likest to thee in shape and count'nance bright,
Then shining heav'nly fair, a Goddess arm'd
Out of thy head I sprung; amazement seis'd
All th' Host of Heav'n; back they recoild affraid
At first, and call'd me *Sin*, and for a Sign
Portentous held me; but familiar grown,
I pleas'd, and with attractive graces won
The most averse, thee chiefly, who full oft
Thy self in me thy perfect image viewing
Becam'st enamour'd, and such joy thou took'st
With me in secret, that my womb conceiv'd
A growing burden. Mean while Warr arose,
And fields were fought in Heav'n; wherein remaind
(For what could else) to our Almighty Foe
Cleer Victory, to our part loss and rout
Through all the Empyrean: down they fell
Driv'n headlong from the Pitch of Heaven, down
Into this Deep, and in the general fall
I also; at which time this powerful Key
Into my hand was giv'n, with charge to keep
These Gates for ever shut, which none can pass
Without my op'ning. Pensive here I sat
Alone, but long I sat not, till my womb
Pregnant by thee, and now excessive grown
Prodigious motion felt and rueful throes.
At last this odious offspring whom thou seest
Thine own begotten, breaking violent way
Tore through my entrails, that with fear and pain
Distorted, all my nether shape thus grew
Transform'd: but he my inbred enemie
Forth issu'd, brandishing his fatal Dart
Made to destroy: I fled, and cry'd out *Death;*
Hell trembl'd at the hideous Name, and sigh'd
From all her Caves, and back resounded *Death.*
I fled, but he pursu'd (though more, it seems,
Inflam'd with lust then rage) and swifter far,
Me overtook his mother all dismaid,
And in embraces forcible and foule
Ingendring with me, of that rape begot
These yelling Monsters that with ceasless cry

Surround me, as thou sawst, hourly conceiv'd
And hourly born, with sorrow infinite
To me, for when they list into the womb
That bred them they return, and howle and gnaw
My Bowels, thir repast; then bursting forth
Afresh with conscious terrours vex me round,
That rest or intermission none I find.
Before mine eyes in opposition sits
Grim *Death* my Son and foe, who sets them on,
And me his Parent would full soon devour
For want of other prey, but that he knows
His end with mine involvd; and knows that I
Should prove a bitter Morsel, and his bane,
When ever that shall be; so Fate pronounc'd.
But thou O Father, I forewarn thee, shun
His deadly arrow; neither vainly hope
To be invulnerable in those bright Arms,
Though temper'd heav'nly, for that mortal dint,
Save he who reigns above, none can resist.
        She finish'd, and the suttle Fiend his lore
Soon learnd, now milder, and thus answerd smooth.
Dear Daughter, since thou claim'st me for thy Sire,
And my fair Son here showst me, the dear pledge
Of dalliance had with thee in Heav'n, and joys
Then sweet, now sad to mention, through dire change
Befalln us unforeseen, unthought of, know
I come no enemie, but to set free
From out this dark and dismal house of pain,
Both him and thee, and all the heav'nly Host
Of Spirits that in our just pretenses arm'd
Fell with us from on high: from them I go
This uncouth errand sole, and one for all
My self expose, with lonely steps to tread
Th' unfounded deep, and through the void immense
To search with wandring quest a place foretold
Should be, and, by concurring signs, ere now
Created vast and round, a place of bliss
In the Pourlieues of Heav'n, and therein plac't
A race of upstart Creatures, to supply
Perhaps our vacant room, though more remov'd,

Least Heav'n surcharg'd with potent multitude
Might hap to move new broiles: Be this or aught
Then this more secret now design'd, I haste
To know, and this once known, shall soon return,
And bring ye to the place where Thou and Death
Shall dwell at ease, and up and down unseen
Wing silently the buxom Air, imbalm'd
With odours; there ye shall be fed and fill'd
Immeasurably, all things shall be your prey.
He ceas'd, for both seemd highly pleasd, and Death
Grinnd horrible a gastly smile, to hear
His famine should be fill'd, and blest his mawe
Destin'd to that good hour: no less rejoyc'd
His mother bad, and thus bespake her Sire.
     The key of this infernal Pit by due,
And by command of Heav'ns all-powerful King
I keep, by him forbidden to unlock
These Adamantine Gates; against all force
Death ready stands to interpose his dart,
Fearless to be o'rematcht by living might.
But what ow I to his commands above
Who hates me, and hath hither thrust me down
Into this gloom of *Tartarus* profound,
To sit in hateful Office here confin'd,
Inhabitant of Heav'n, and heav'nlie-born,
Here in perpetual agonie and pain,
With terrors and with clamors compasst round
Of mine own brood, that on my bowels feed:
Thou art my Father, thou my Author, thou
My being gav'st me; whom should I obey
But thee, whom follow? thou wilt bring me soon
To that new world of light and bliss, among
The Gods who live at ease, where I shall Reign
At thy right hand voluptuous, as beseems
Thy daughter and thy darling, without end.
     Thus saying, from her side the fatal Key,
Sad instrument of all our woe, she took;
And towards the Gate rouling her bestial train,
Forthwith the huge Portcullis high up drew,
Which but her self not all the *Stygian* powers

Could once have mov'd; then in the key-hole turns
Th' intricate wards, and every Bolt and Bar
Of massie Iron or sollid Rock with ease
Unfast'ns: on a sudden op'n flie
With impetuous recoile and jarring sound
Th' infernal dores, and on their hinges grate
Harsh thunder, that the lowest bottom shook
Of *Erebus*. She op'nd, but to shut
Excel'd her power; the Gates wide op'n stood,
That with extended wings a Bannerd Host
Under spread Ensigns marching might pass through
With Horse and Chariots rankt in loose array;
So wide they stood, and like a Furnace mouth
Cast forth redounding smoak and ruddy flame.
Before their eyes in sudden view appear
The secrets of the hoarie deep, a dark
Illimitable Ocean without bound,
Without dimension, where length, breadth, and highth,
And time and place are lost; where eldest Night
And *Chaos*, Ancestors of Nature, hold
Eternal *Anarchie*, amidst the noise
Of endless warrs, and by confusion stand,
For hot, cold, moist, and dry, four Champions fierce
Strive here for Maistrie, and to Battel bring
Thir embryon Atoms; they around the flag
Of each his faction, in thir several Clanns,
Light-arm'd or heavy, sharp, smooth, swift or slow,
Swarm populous, unnumber'd as the Sands
Of *Barca* or *Cyrene's* torrid soil,
Levied to side with warring Winds, and poise
Thir lighter wings. To whom these most adhere,
Hee rules a moment; *Chaos* Umpire sits,
And by decision more imbroiles the fray
By which he Reigns: next him high Arbiter
Chance governs all. Into this wilde Abyss,
The Womb of nature and perhaps her Grave,
Of neither Sea, nor Shore, nor Air, nor Fire,
But all these in thir pregnant causes mixt
Confus'dly, and which thus must ever fight,
Unless th' Almighty Maker them ordain

His dark materials to create more Worlds,
Into this wilde Abyss the warie fiend
Stood on the brink of Hell and look'd a while,
Pondering his Voyage; for no narrow frith
He had to cross. Nor was his eare less peal'd
With noises loud and ruinous (to compare
Great things with small) then when *Bellona* storms,
With all her battering Engines bent to rase
Som Capital City, or less then if this frame
Of Heav'n were falling, and these Elements
In mutinie had from her Axle torn
The stedfast Earth. At last his Sail-broad Vannes
He spreads for flight, and in the surging smoak
Uplifted spurns the ground, thence many a League
As in a cloudy Chair ascending rides
Audacious, but that seat soon failing, meets
A vast vacuitie: all unawares
Fluttring his pennons vain plumb down he drops
Ten thousand fadom deep, and to this hour
Down had been falling, had not by ill chance
The strong rebuff of som tumultuous cloud
Instinct with Fire and Nitre hurried him
As many miles aloft: that furie stay'd,
Quencht in a Boggie *Syrtis*, neither Sea,
Nor good dry Land: nigh founderd on he fares,
Treading the crude consistence, half on foot,
Half flying; behoves him now both Oare and Saile.
As when a Gryfon through the Wilderness
With winged course ore Hill or moarie Dale,
Pursues the *Arimaspian*, who by stelth
Had from his wakeful custody purloind
The guarded Gold: So eagerly the fiend
Ore bog or steep, through strait, rough, dense, or rare,
With head, hands, wings, or feet pursues his way,
And swims or sinks, or wades, or creeps, or flyes:
At length a universal hubbub wilde
Of stunning sounds and voices all confus'd
Born through the hollow dark assaults his eare
With loudest vehemence: thither he plyes,
Undaunted to meet there what ever power

Or Spirit of the nethermost Abyss
Might in that noise reside, of whom to ask
Which way the neerest coast of darkness lyes
Bordering on light; when strait behold the Throne
Of *Chaos*, and his dark Pavilion spread
Wide on the wasteful Deep; with him Enthron'd
Sat Sable-vested Night, eldest of things,
The Consort of his Reign; and by them stood
Orcus and *Ades*, and the dreaded name
Of *Demogorgon;* Rumour next and Chance,
And Tumult and Confusion all imbroild,
And Discord with a thousand various mouths.

    T' whom *Satan* turning boldly, thus. Ye Powers
And Spirits of this nethermost Abyss,
Chaos and *ancient Night*, I come no Spy,
With purpose to explore or to disturb
The secrets of your Realm, but by constraint
Wandring this darksome Desart, as my way
Lies through your spacious Empire up to light,
Alone, and without guide, half lost, I seek
What readiest path leads where your gloomie bounds
Confine with Heav'n; or if som other place
From your Dominion won, th' Ethereal King
Possesses lately, thither to arrive
I travel this profound, direct my course;
Directed no mean recompence it brings
To your behoof, if I that Region lost,
All usurpation thence expell'd, reduce
To her original darkness and your sway
(Which is my present journey) and once more
Erect the Standard there of *ancient Night;*
Yours be th' advantage all, mine the revenge.

    Thus *Satan;* and him thus the Anarch old
With faultring speech and visage incompos'd
Answer'd. I know thee, stranger, who thou art,
That mighty leading Angel, who of late
Made head against Heav'ns King, though overthrown.
I saw and heard, for such a numerous Host
Fled not in silence through the frighted deep
With ruin upon ruin, rout on rout,

Confusion worse confounded; and Heav'n Gates
Pourd out by millions her victorious Bands
Pursuing. I upon my Frontieres here
Keep residence; if all I can will serve,
That little which is left so to defend
Encroacht on still through our intestine broiles
Weakning the Scepter of old Night: first Hell
Your dungeon stretching far and wide beneath;
Now lately Heaven and Earth, another World
Hung ore my Realm, link'd in a golden Chain
To that side Heav'n from whence your Legions fell:
If that way be your walk, you have not farr;
So much the neerer danger; goe and speed;
Havock and spoil and ruin are my gain.

   He ceas'd; and *Satan* staid not to reply,
But glad that now his Sea should find a shore,
With fresh alacritie and force renew'd
Springs upward like a Pyramid of fire
Into the wilde Expanse, and through the shock
Of fighting Elements, on all sides round
Environ'd wins his way; harder beset
And more endanger'd, then when *Argo* pass'd
Through *Bosporus* betwixt the justling Rocks:
Or when *Ulysses* on the Larbord shunnd
Charybdis, and by th' other whirlpool steard.
So he with difficulty and labour hard
Mov'd on, with difficulty and labour hee;
But hee once past, soon after when man fell,
Strange alteration! Sin and Death amain
Following his track, such was the will of Heav'n,
Pav'd after him a broad and beat'n way
Over the dark Abyss, whose boiling Gulf
Tamely endur'd a Bridge of wondrous length
From Hell continu'd reaching th' utmost Orbe
Of this frail World; by which the Spirits perverse
With easie intercourse pass to and fro
To tempt or punish mortals, except whom
God and good Angels guard by special grace.
But now at last the sacred influence
Of light appears, and from the walls of Heav'n

Shoots farr into the bosom of dim Night
A glimmering dawn; here Nature first begins
Her fardest verge, and *Chaos* to retire
As from her outmost works a brok'n foe
With tumult less and with less hostile din,
That *Satan* with less toil, and now with ease
Wafts on the calmer wave by dubious light
And like a weather-beaten Vessel holds
Gladly the Port, though Shrouds and Tackle torn;
Or in the emptier waste, resembling Air,
Weighs his spread wings, at leasure to behold
Farr off th' Empyreal Heav'n, extended wide
In circuit, undetermind square or round,
With Opal Towrs and Battlements adorn'd
Of living Saphire, once his native Seat;
And fast by hanging in a golden Chain
This pendant world, in bigness as a Starr
Of smallest Magnitude close by the Moon.
Thither full fraught with mischievous revenge,
Accurst, and in a cursed hour he hies.

BOOK III

THE ARGUMENT

God sitting on his Throne sees Satan *flying towards this world, then newly created; shews him to the Son who sat at his right hand; foretells the success of* Satan *in perverting mankind; clears his own Justice and Wisdom from all imputation, having created Man free and able enough to have withstood his Tempter; yet declares his purpose of grace towards him, in regard he fell not of his own malice, as did* Satan, *but by him seduc't. The Son of God renders praises to his Father for the manifestation of his gracious purpose towards Man; but God again declares, that Grace cannot be extended towards Man without the satisfaction of divine Justice; Man hath offended the majesty of God by aspiring to God-head, and therefore with all his Progeny devoted to death must dye, unless some one can be found sufficient to answer for his offence, and undergo his*

*Punishment. The Son of God freely offers himself a Ransome
for Man: the Father accepts him, ordains his incarnation,
pronounces his exaltation above all Names in Heaven and
Earth; commands all the Angels to adore him; they obey, and
hymning to thir Harps in full Quire, celebrate the Father and
the Son. Mean while* Satan *alights upon the bare Convex of
this Worlds outermost Orb; where wandring he first finds a
place since call'd The Lymbo of Vanity; what persons and
things fly up thither; thence comes to the Gate of Heaven, describ'd ascending by staires, and the waters above the Firmament that flow about it: His passage thence to the Orb of the
Sun; he finds there* Uriel *the Regient of that Orb, but first
changes himself into the shape of a meaner Angel; and pretending a zealous desire to behold the new Creation and Man
whom God had plac't here, inquires of him the place of his
habitation, and is directed; alights first on Mount* Niphates.

HAIL holy light, ofspring of Heav'n first-born,
Or of th' Eternal Coeternal beam
May I express thee unblam'd? since God is light,
And never but in unapproached light
Dwelt from Eternitie, dwelt then in thee,
Bright effluence of bright essence increate.
Or hear'st thou rather pure Ethereal stream,
Whose Fountain who shall tell? before the Sun,
Before the Heavens thou wert, and at the voice
Of God, as with a Mantle didst invest
The rising world of water dark and deep,
Won from the void and formless infinite.
Thee I re-visit now with bolder wing,
Escap't the *Stygian* Pool, though long detain'd
In that obscure sojourn, while in my flight
Through utter and through middle darkness borne
With other notes then to th' *Orphean* Lyre
I sung of *Chaos* and *Eternal Night*,
Taught by the heav'nly Muse to venture down
The dark descent, and up to reascend,
Though hard and rare: thee I revisit safe,
And feel thy sovran vital Lamp; but thou
Revisit'st not these eyes, that rowle in vain

To find thy piercing ray, and find no dawn;
So thick a drop serene hath quencht their Orbs,
Or dim suffusion veild. Yet not the more
Cease I to wander where the Muses haunt
Cleer Spring, or shadie Grove, or Sunnie Hill,
Smit with the love of sacred song; but chief
Thee *Sion* and the flowrie Brooks beneath
That wash thy hallowd feet, and warbling flow,
Nightly I visit: nor somtimes forget
Those other two equal'd with me in Fate,
So were I equal'd with them in renown,
Blind *Thamyris* and blind *Mæonides*,
And *Tiresias* and *Phineus* Prophets old.
Then feed on thoughts, that voluntarie move
Harmonious numbers; as the wakeful Bird
Sings darkling, and in shadiest Covert hid
Tunes her nocturnal Note. Thus with the Year
Seasons return, but not to me returns
Day, or the sweet approach of Ev'n or Morn,
Or sight of vernal bloom, or Summers Rose,
Or flocks, or herds, or human face divine;
But cloud in stead, and ever-during dark
Surrounds me, from the chearful wayes of men
Cut off, and for the Book of knowledg fair
Presented with a Universal blanc
Of Natures works to mee expung'd and ras'd,
And wisdome at one entrance quite shut out.
So much the rather thou Celestial light
Shine inward, and the mind through all her powers
Irradiate, there plant eyes, all mist from thence
Purge and disperse, that I may see and tell
Of things invisible to mortal sight.
    Now had the Almighty Father from above,
From the pure Empyrean where he sits
High Thron'd above all highth, bent down his eye,
His own works and their works at once to view:
About him all the Sanctities of Heaven
Stood thick as Starrs, and from his sight receiv'd
Beatitude past utterance; on his right
The radiant image of his Glory sat,

His only Son; On Earth he first beheld
Our two first Parents, yet the onely two
Of mankind, in the happie Garden plac't,
Reaping immortal fruits of joy and love,
Uninterrupted joy, unrivald love
In blissful solitude; he then survey'd
Hell and the Gulf between, and *Satan* there
Coasting the wall of Heav'n on this side Night
In the dun Air sublime, and ready now
To stoop with wearied wings, and willing feet
On the bare outside of this World, that seem'd
Firm land imbosom'd without Firmament,
Uncertain which, in Ocean or in Air.
Him God beholding from his prospect high,
Wherein past, present, future he beholds,
Thus to his only Son foreseeing spake.

    Onely begotten Son, seest thou what rage
Transports our adversarie, whom no bounds
Prescrib'd, no barrs of Hell, nor all the chains
Heapt on him there, nor yet the main Abyss
Wide interrupt can hold; so bent he seems
On desperat reveng, that shall redound
Upon his own rebellious head. And now
Through all restraint broke loose he wings his way
Not farr off Heav'n, in the Precincts of light,
Directly towards the new created World,
And Man there plac't, with purpose to assay
If him by force he can destroy, or worse,
By some false guile pervert; and shall pervert
For man will heark'n to his glozing lyes,
And easily transgress the sole Command,
Sole pledge of his obedience: So will fall
Hee and his faithless Progenie: whose fault?
Whose but his own? ingrate, he had of mee
All he could have; I made him just and right,
Sufficient to have stood, though free to fall.
Such I created all th' Ethereal Powers
And Spirits, both them who stood and them who faild;
Freely they stood who stood, and fell who fell.
Not free, what proof could they have givn sincere

Of true allegiance, constant Faith or Love,
Where onely what they needs must do, appeard,
Not what they would? what praise could they receive?
What pleasure I from such obedience paid,
When Will and Reason (Reason also is choice)
Useless and vain, of freedom both despoild,
Made passive both, had servd necessitie,
Not mee. They therefore as to right belongd,
So were created, nor can justly accuse
Thir maker, or thir making, or thir Fate;
As if Predestination over-rul'd
Thir will, dispos'd by absolute Decree
Or high foreknowledge; they themselves decreed
Thir own revolt, not I: if I foreknew,
Foreknowledge had no influence on their fault,
Which had no less prov'd certain unforeknown.
So without least impulse or shadow of Fate,
Or aught by me immutablie foreseen,
They trespass, Authors to themselves in all
Both what they judge and what they choose; for so
I formd them free, and free they must remain,
Till they enthrall themselves: I else must change
Thir nature, and revoke the high Decree
Unchangeable, Eternal, which ordain'd
Thir freedom, they themselves ordain'd thir fall.
The first sort by thir own suggestion fell,
Self-tempted, self-deprav'd: Man falls deceiv'd
By the other first: Man therefore shall find grace,
The other none: in Mercy and Justice both,
Through Heav'n and Earth, so shall my glorie excel,
But Mercy first and last shall brightest shine.

 Thus while God spake, ambrosial fragrance fill'd
All Heav'n, and in the blessed Spirits elect
Sense of new joy ineffable diffus'd:
Beyond compare the Son of God was seen
Most glorious, in him all his Father shon
Substantially express'd, and in his face
Divine compassion visibly appeerd,
Love without end, and without measure Grace,
Which uttering thus he to his Father spake.

E   M.

O Father, gracious was that word which clos'd
Thy sovran sentence, that Man should find grace;
For which both Heav'n and Earth shall high extoll
Thy praises, with th' innumerable sound
Of Hymns and sacred Songs, wherewith thy Throne
Encompass'd shall resound thee ever blest.
For should Man finally be lost, should Man
Thy creature late so lov'd, thy youngest Son
Fall circumvented thus by fraud, though joynd
With his own folly? that be from thee farr,
That farr be from thee, Father, who art Judg
Of all things made, and judgest onely right.
Or shall the Adversarie thus obtain
His end, and frustrate thine, shall he fulfill
His malice, and thy goodness bring to naught,
Or proud return though to his heavier doom,
Yet with revenge accomplish't and to Hell
Draw after him the whole Race of mankind,
By him corrupted? or wilt thou thy self
Abolish thy Creation, and unmake,
For him, what for thy glorie thou hast made?
So should thy goodness and thy greatness both
Be questiond and blaspheam'd without defence.
    To whom the great Creatour thus reply'd.
O Son, in whom my Soul hath chief delight,
Son of my bosom, Son who art alone
My word, my wisdom, and effectual might,
All hast thou spok'n as my thoughts are, all
As my Eternal purpose hath decreed:
Man shall not quite be lost, but sav'd who will,
Yet not of will in him, but grace in me
Freely voutsaft; once more I will renew
His lapsed powers, though forfeit and enthrall'd
By sin to foul exorbitant desires;
Upheld by me, yet once more he shall stand
On even ground against his mortal foe,
By me upheld, that he may know how frail
His fall'n condition is, and to me ow
All his deliv'rance, and to none but me.
Some I have chosen of peculiar grace

Elect above the rest; so is my will:
The rest shall hear me call, and oft be warnd
Thir sinful state, and to appease betimes
Th' incensed Deitie, while offerd grace
Invites; for I will cleer thir senses dark,
What may suffice, and soft'n stonie hearts
To pray, repent, and bring obedience due.
To prayer, repentance, and obedience due,
Though but endevord with sincere intent,
Mine ear shall not be slow, mine eye not shut.
And I will place within them as a guide
My Umpire *Conscience*, whom if they will hear,
Light after light well us'd they shall attain,
And to the end persisting, safe arrive.
This my long sufferance and my day of grace
They who neglect and scorn, shall never taste;
But hard be hard'nd, blind be blinded more,
That they may stumble on, and deeper fall;
And none but such from mercy I exclude.
But yet all is not don; Man disobeying,
Disloyal breaks his fealtie, and sinns
Against the high Supremacie of Heav'n,
Affecting God-head, and so loosing all,
To expiate his Treason hath naught left,
But to destruction sacred and devote,
He with his whole posteritie must dye,
Dye hee or Justice must; unless for him
Som other able, and as willing, pay
The rigid satisfaction, death for death.
Say Heav'nly powers, where shall we find such love,
Which of ye will be mortal to redeem
Mans mortal crime, and just th' unjust to save,
Dwels in all Heaven charitie so deare?
    He ask'd, but all the Heav'nly Quire stood mute,
And silence was in Heav'n: on mans behalf
Patron or Intercessor none appeerd,
Much less that durst upon his own head draw
The deadly forfeiture, and ransom set.
And now without redemption all mankind
Must have bin lost, adjudg'd to Death and Hell

By doom severe, had not the Son of God,
In whom the fulness dwels of love divine,
His dearest meditation thus renewd.

    Father, thy word is past, man shall find grace;
And shall grace not find means, that finds her way,
The speediest of thy winged messengers,
To visit all thy creatures, and to all
Comes unprevented, unimplor'd, unsought,
Happie for man, so coming; he her aide
Can never seek, once dead in sins and lost;
Attonement for himself or offering meet,
Indebted and undon, hath none to bring:
Behold mee then, mee for him, life for life
I offer, on mee let thine anger fall;
Account mee man; I for his sake will leave
Thy bosom, and this glorie next to thee
Freely put off, and for him lastly dye
Well pleas'd, on me let Death wreck all his rage;
Under his gloomie power I shall not long
Lie vanquisht; thou hast givn me to possess
Life in my self for ever, by thee I live,
Though now to Death I yield, and am his due
All that of me can die, yet that debt paid,
Thou wilt not leave me in the loathsom grave
His prey, nor suffer my unspotted Soule
For ever with corruption there to dwell;
But I shall rise Victorious, and subdue
My vanquisher, spoild of his vanted spoile;
Death his deaths wound shall then receive, and stoop
Inglorious, of his mortall sting disarm'd.
I through the ample Air in Triumph high
Shall lead Hell Captive maugre Hell, and show
The powers of darkness bound. Thou at the sight
Pleas'd, out of Heaven shalt look down and smile,
While by thee rais'd I ruin all my Foes,
Death last, and with his Carcass glut the Grave:
Then with the multitude of my redeemd
Shall enter Heaven long absent, and returne,
Father, to see thy face, wherein no cloud
Of anger shall remain, but peace assur'd,

And reconcilement; wrauth shall be no more
Thenceforth, but in thy presence Joy entire.

His words here ended, but his meek aspect
Silent yet spake, and breath'd immortal love
To mortal men, above which only shon
Filial obedience: as a sacrifice
Glad to be offer'd, he attends the will
Of his great Father. Admiration seis'd
All Heav'n, what this might mean, and whither tend
Wondring; but soon th' Almighty thus reply'd:

O thou in Heav'n and Earth the only peace
Found out for mankind under wrauth, O thou
My sole complacence! well thou know'st how dear,
To me are all my works, nor Man the least
Though last created, that for him I spare
Thee from my bosom and right hand, to save,
By loosing thee a while, the whole Race lost.
Thou therefore whom thou only canst redeem,
Thir Nature also to thy Nature joyne;
And be thy self Man among men on Earth,
Made flesh, when time shall be, of Virgin seed,
By wondrous birth: Be thou in *Adams* room
The Head of all mankind, though *Adams* Son.
As in him perish all men, so in thee
As from a second root shall be restor'd,
As many as are restor'd, without thee none.
His crime makes guiltie all his Sons, thy merit
Imputed shall absolve them who renounce
Thir own both righteous and unrighteous deeds,
And live in thee transplanted, and from thee
Receive new life. So Man, as is most just,
Shall satisfie for Man, be judg'd and die,
And dying rise, and rising with him raise
His Brethren, ransomd with his own dear life.
So Heav'nly love shal outdoo Hellish hate,
Giving to death, and dying to redeeme,
So dearly to redeem what Hellish hate
So easily destroy'd, and still destroyes
In those who, when they may, accept not grace.
Nor shalt thou by descending to assume

Mans Nature, less'n or degrade thine owne.
Because thou hast, though Thron'd in highest bliss
Equal to God, and equally enjoying
God-like fruition, quitted all to save
A World from utter loss, and hast been found
By Merit more then Birthright Son of God,
Found worthiest to be so by being Good,
Farr more then Great or High; because in thee
Love hath abounded more then Glory abounds,
Therefore thy Humiliation shall exalt
With thee thy Manhood also to this Throne;
Here shalt thou sit incarnate, here shalt Reign
Both God and Man, Son both of God and Man,
Anointed universal King; all Power
I give thee, reign for ever, and assume
Thy Merits; under thee as Head Supream
Thrones, Princedoms, Powers, Dominions I reduce:
All knees to thee shall bow, of them that bide
In Heaven, or Earth, or under Earth in Hell;
When thou attended gloriously from Heav'n
Shalt in the Sky appeer, and from thee send
The summoning Arch-Angels to proclaime
Thy dread Tribunal: forthwith from all Windes
The living, and forthwith the cited dead
Of all past Ages to the general Doom
Shall hast'n, such a peal shall rouse thir sleep.
Then all thy Saints assembl'd, thou shalt judge
Bad men and Angels, they arraignd shall sink
Beneath thy Sentence; Hell, her numbers full,
Thenceforth shall be for ever shut. Mean while
The World shall burn, and from her ashes spring
New Heav'n and Earth, wherein the just shall dwell
And after all thir tribulations long
See golden days, fruitful of golden deeds,
With Joy and Love triumphing, and fair Truth.
Then thou thy regal Scepter shalt lay by,
For regal Scepter then no more shall need,
God shall be All in All. But all ye Gods,
Adore him, who to compass all this dies,
Adore the Son, and honour him as mee.

No sooner had th' Almighty ceas't, but all
The multitude of Angels with a shout
Loud as from numbers without number, sweet
As from blest voices, uttering joy, Heav'n rung
With Jubilee, and loud Hosanna's fill'd
Th' eternal Regions: lowly reverent
Towards either Throne they bow, and to the ground
With solemn adoration down they cast
Thir Crowns inwove with Amarant and Gold,
Immortal Amarant, a Flour which once
In Paradise, fast by the Tree of Life
Began to bloom, but soon for mans offence
To Heav'n remov'd where first it grew, there grows,
And flours aloft shading the Fount of Life,
And where the river of Bliss through midst of Heav'n
Rowls o're *Elisian* Flours her Amber stream;
With these that never fade the Spirits elect
Bind thir resplendent locks inwreath'd with beams,
Now in loose Garlands thick thrown off, the bright
Pavement that like a Sea of Jasper shon
Impurpl'd with Celestial Roses smil'd.
Then Crown'd again thir gold'n Harps they took,
Harps ever tun'd, that glittering by thir side
Like Quivers hung, and with Præamble sweet
Of charming symphonie they introduce
Thir sacred Song, and waken raptures high;
No voice exempt, no voice but well could joine
Melodious part, such concord is in Heav'n.
   Thee Father first they sung Omnipotent,
Immutable, Immortal, Infinite,
Eternal King; thee Author of all being,
Fountain of Light, thy self invisible
Amidst the glorious brightness where thou sit'st
Thron'd inaccessible, but when thou shad'st
The full blaze of thy beams, and through a cloud
Drawn round about thee like a radiant Shrine,
Dark with excessive bright thy skirts appeer,
Yet dazle Heav'n, that brightest Seraphim
Approach not, but with both wings veil thir eyes.
Thee next they sang of all Creation first,

Begotten Son, Divine Similitude,
In whose conspicuous count'nance, without cloud
Made visible, th' Almighty Father shines,
Whom else no Creature can behold; on thee
Impresst the effulgence of his Glorie abides,
Transfus'd on thee his ample Spirit rests.
Hee Heav'n of Heavens and all the Powers therein
By thee created, and by thee threw down
Th' aspiring Dominations: thou that day
Thy Fathers dreadful Thunder didst not spare,
Nor stop thy flaming Chariot wheels, that shook
Heav'ns everlasting Frame, while o're the necks
Thou drov'st of warring Angels disarraid.
Back from pursuit thy Powers with loud acclaime
Thee only extoll'd, Son of thy Fathers might,
To execute fierce vengeance on his foes,
Not so on Man; him through their malice fall'n,
Father of Mercie and Grace, thou didst not doome
So strictly, but much more to pitie encline:
No sooner did thy dear and onely Son
Perceive thee purpos'd not to doom frail Man
So strictly, but much more to pitie enclin'd,
He to appease thy wrauth, and end the strife
Of Mercy and Justice in thy face discern'd,
Regardless of the Bliss wherein hee sat
Second to thee, offerd himself to die
For mans offence. O unexampl'd love,
Love no where to be found less then Divine!
Hail Son of God, Saviour of Men, thy Name
Shall be the copious matter of my Song
Henceforth, and never shall my Harp thy praise
Forget, nor from thy Fathers praise disjoine.

    Thus they in Heav'n, above the starry Sphear,
Thir happie hours in joy and hymning spent.
Mean while upon the firm opacous Globe
Of this round World, whose first convex divides
The luminous inferior Orbs, enclos'd
From *Chaos* and th' inroad of Darkness old,
Satan alighted walks: a Globe farr off
It seem'd, now seems a boundless Continent

Dark, waste, and wild, under the frown of Night
Starless expos'd, and ever-threatning storms
Of *Chaos* blustring round, inclement skie;
Save on that side which from the wall of Heav'n
Though distant farr som small reflection gaines
Of glimmering air less vext with tempest loud:
Here walk'd the Fiend at large in spacious field.
As when a Vultur on *Imaus* bred,
Whose snowie ridge the roving *Tartar* bounds,
Dislodging from a Region scarce of prey
To gorge the flesh of Lambs or yeanling Kids
On Hills where Flocks are fed, flies toward the Springs
Of *Ganges* or *Hydaspes*, *Indian* streams;
But in his way lights on the barren Plaines
Of *Sericana*, where *Chineses* drive
With Sails and Wind thir canie Waggons light:
So on this windie Sea of Land, the Fiend
Walk'd up and down alone bent on his prey,
Alone, for other Creature in this place
Living or liveless to be found was none,
None yet, but store hereafter from the earth
Up hither like Aereal vapours flew
Of all things transitorie and vain, when Sin
With vanity had filld the works of men:
Both all things vain, and all who in vain things
Built thir fond hopes of Glorie or lasting fame,
Or happiness in this or th' other life;
All who have thir reward on Earth, the fruits
Of painful Superstition and blind Zeal,
Naught seeking but the praise of men, here find
Fit retribution, emptie as thir deeds;
All th' unaccomplisht works of Natures hand,
Abortive, monstrous, or unkindly mixt,
Dissolvd on earth, fleet hither, and in vain,
Till final dissolution, wander here,
Not in the neighbouring Moon, as some have dreamd;
Those argent Fields more likely habitants,
Translated Saints, or middle Spirits hold
Betwixt th' Angelical and Human kinde:
Hither of ill-joynd Sons and Daughters born

First from the ancient World those Giants came
With many a vain exploit, though then renownd:
The builders next of *Babel* on the Plain
Of *Sennaar*, and still with vain designe
New *Babels*, had they wherewithall, would build:
Others came single; hee who to be deemd
A God, leap'd fondly into *Ætna* flames,
Empedocles, and hee who to enjoy
Plato's Elysium, leap'd into the Sea,
Cleombrotus, and many more too long,
Embryos and Idiots, Eremits and Friers
White, Black and Grey, with all thir trumperie.
Here Pilgrims roam, that stray'd so farr to seek
In *Golgotha* him dead, who lives in Heav'n;
And they who to be sure of Paradise
Dying put on the weeds of *Dominic*,
Or in *Franciscan* think to pass disguis'd;
They pass the Planets seven, and pass the fixt,
And that Crystalline Sphear whose ballance weighs
The Trepidation talkt, and that first mov'd;
And now Saint *Peter* at Heav'ns Wicket seems
To wait them with his Keys, and now at foot
Of Heav'ns ascent they lift their Feet, when loe
A violent cross wind from either Coast
Blows them transverse ten thousand Leagues awry
Into the devious Air; then might ye see
Cowles, Hoods and Habits with thir wearers tost
And flutterd into Raggs, then Reliques, Beads,
Indulgences, Dispenses, Pardons, Bulls,
The sport of Winds: all these upwhirld aloft
Fly o're the backside of the World farr off
Into a *Limbo* large and broad, since calld
The Paradise of Fools, to few unknown
Long after, now unpeopl'd, and untrod;
All this dark Globe the Fiend found as he pass'd,
And long he wanderd, till at last a gleame
Of dawning light turnd thither-ward in haste
His travell'd steps; farr distant he descries
Ascending by degrees magnificent
Up to the wall of Heaven a Structure high,

At top whereof, but farr more rich appeerd
The work as of a Kingly Palace Gate
With Frontispice of Diamond and Gold
Imbellisht, thick with sparkling orient Gemmes
The Portal shon, inimitable on Earth
By Model, or by shading Pencil drawn.
The Stairs were such as whereon *Jacob* saw
Angels ascending and descending, bands
Of Guardians bright, when he from *Esau* fled
To *Padan-Aram* in the field of *Luz*,
Dreaming by night under the open Skie,
And waking cri'd, This is the Gate of Heav'n.
Each Stair mysteriously was meant, nor stood
There alwayes, but drawn up to Heav'n somtimes
Viewless, and underneath a bright Sea flow'd
Of Jasper, or of liquid Pearle, whereon
Who after came from Earth, sayling arriv'd,
Wafted by Angels, or flew o're the Lake
Rapt in a Chariot drawn by fiery Steeds.
The Stairs were then let down, whether to dare
The Fiend by easie ascent, or aggravate
His sad exclusion from the dores of Bliss.
Direct against which op'nd from beneath,
Just o're the blissful seat of Paradise,
A passage down to th' Earth, a passage wide,
Wider by farr then that of after-times
Over Mount *Sion*, and, though that were large,
Over the *Promis'd Land* to God so dear,
By which, to visit oft those happy Tribes,
On high behests his Angels to and fro
Pass'd frequent, and his eye with choice regard
From *Paneas* the fount of *Jordans* flood
To *Bëersaba*, where the *Holy Land*
Borders on *Ægypt* and the *Arabian* shoare;
So wide the op'ning seemd, where bounds were set
To darkness, such as bound the Ocean wave.
Satan from hence now on the lower stair
That scal'd by steps of Gold to Heav'n Gate
Looks down with wonder at the sudden view
Of all this World at once. As when a Scout

Through dark and desart wayes with peril gone
All night; at last by break of chearful dawne
Obtains the brow of some high-climbing Hill,
Which to his eye discovers unaware
The goodly prospect of some forein land
First-seen, or some renownd Metropolis
With glistering Spires and Pinnacles adornd,
Which now the Rising Sun guilds with his beams.
Such wonder seis'd, though after Heaven seen,
The Spirit maligne, but much more envy seis'd
At sight of all this World beheld so faire.
Round he surveys, and well might, where he stood
So high above the circling Canopie
Of Nights extended shade; from Eastern Point
Of *Libra* to the fleecie Starr that bears
Andromeda farr off *Atlantic* Seas
Beyond th' *Horizon*; then from Pole to Pole
He views in bredth, and without longer pause
Down right into the Worlds first Region throws
His flight precipitant, and windes with ease
Through the pure marble Air his oblique way
Amongst innumerable Starrs, that shon
Stars distant, but nigh hand seemd other Worlds,
Or other Worlds they seemd, or happy Iles,
Like those *Hesperian* Gardens fam'd of old,
Fortunate Fields, and Groves and flourie Vales,
Thrice happy Iles, but who dwelt happy there
He stayd not to enquire: above them all
The golden Sun in splendor likest Heaven
Allur'd his eye: Thither his course he bends
Through the calm Firmament; but up or downe
By center, or eccentric, hard to tell,
Or Longitude, where the great Luminarie
Alooff the vulgar Constellations thick,
That from his Lordly eye keep distance due,
Dispenses Light from farr; they as they move
Thir Starry dance in numbers that compute
Days, months, and years, towards his all-chearing Lamp
Turn swift thir various motions, or are turnd
By his Magnetic beam, that gently warms

The Univers, and to each inward part
With gentle penetration, though unseen,
Shoots invisible vertue even to the deep:
So wondrously was set his Station bright.
There lands the Fiend, a spot like which perhaps
Astronomer in the Sun's lucent Orbe
Through his glaz'd Optic Tube yet never saw.
The place he found beyond expression bright,
Compar'd with aught on Earth, Medal or Stone;
Not all parts like, but all alike informd
With radiant light, as glowing Iron with fire;
If mettal, part seemd Gold, part Silver cleer;
If stone, Carbuncle most or Chrysolite,
Rubie or Topaz, to the Twelve that shon
In *Aarons* Brest-plate, and a stone besides
Imagind rather oft then elsewhere seen,
That stone, or like to that which here below
Philosophers in vain so long have sought,
In vain, though by thir powerful Art they binde
Volatil *Hermes*, and call up unbound
In various shapes old *Proteus* from the Sea,
Draind through a Limbec to his Native forme.
What wonder then if fields and regions here
Breathe forth *Elixir* pure, and Rivers run
Potable Gold, when with one vertuous touch
Th' Arch-chimic Sun so farr from us remote
Produces with Terrestrial Humor mixt
Here in the dark so many precious things
Of colour glorious and effect so rare?
Here matter new to gaze the Devil met
Undazl'd, farr and wide his eye commands,
For sight no obstacle found here, nor shade,
But all Sun-shine, as when his Beams at Noon
Culminate from th'*Æquator*, as they now
Shot upward still direct, whence no way round
Shadow from body opaque can fall, and the Aire,
No where so cleer, sharp'nd his visual ray
To objects distant farr, whereby he soon
Saw within kenn a glorious Angel stand,
The same whom *John* saw also in the Sun:

His back was turnd, but not his brightness hid;
Of beaming sunnie Raies, a golden tiar
Circl'd his Head, nor less his Locks behind
Illustrious on his Shoulders fledge with wings
Lay waving round; on som great charge imploy'd
He seemd, or fixt in cogitation deep.
Glad was the Spirit impure as now in hope
To find who might direct his wandring flight
To Paradise the happie seat of Man,
His journies end and our beginning woe.
But first he casts to change his proper shape,
Which else might work him danger or delay:
And now a stripling Cherube he appeers,
Not of the prime, yet such as in his face
Youth smil'd Celestial, and to every Limb
Sutable grace diffus'd, so well he feignd;
Under a Coronet his flowing haire
In curles on either cheek plaid, wings he wore
Of many a colour'd plume sprinkl'd with Gold,
His habit fit for speed succinct, and held
Before his decent steps a Silver wand.
He drew not nigh unheard, the Angel bright,
Ere he drew nigh, his radiant visage turnd,
Admonisht by his ear, and strait was known
Th' Arch-Angel *Uriel*, one of the seav'n
Who in Gods presence, neerest to his Throne
Stand ready at command, and are his Eyes
That run through all the Heav'ns, or down to th' Earth
Bear his swift errands over moist and dry,
O're Sea and Land: him *Satan* thus accostes;
    Uriel, for thou of those seav'n Spirits that stand
In sight of Gods high Throne, gloriously bright,
The first are wont his great authentic will
Interpreter through highest Heav'n to bring,
Where all his Sons thy Embassie attend;
And here art likeliest by supream decree
Like honour to obtain, and as his Eye
To visit oft this new Creation round;
Unspeakable desire to see, and know
All these his wondrous works, but chiefly Man,

His chief delight and favour, him for whom
All these his works so wondrous he ordaind,
Hath brought me from the Quires of Cherubim
Alone thus wandring. Brightest Seraph tell
In which of all these shining Orbes hath Man
His fixed seat, or fixed seat hath none,
But all these shining Orbes his choice to dwell;
That I may find him, and with secret gaze,
Or open admiration him behold
On whom the great Creator hath bestowd
Worlds, and on whom hath all these graces powrd;
That both in him and all things, as is meet,
The Universal Maker we may praise;
Who justly hath drivn out his Rebell Foes
To deepest Hell, and to repair that loss
Created this new happie Race of Men
To serve him better: wise are all his wayes.
     So spake the false dissembler unperceivd;
For neither Man nor Angel can discern
Hypocrisie, the only evil that walks
Invisible, except to God alone,
By his permissive will, through Heav'n and Earth:
And oft though wisdom wake, suspicion sleeps
At wisdoms Gate, and to simplicitie
Resigns her charge, while goodness thinks no ill
Where no ill seems: Which now for once beguil'd
Uriel, though Regent of the Sun, and held
The sharpest sighted Spirit of all in Heav'n;
Who to the fraudulent Impostor foule
In his uprightness answer thus returnd.
Fair Angel, thy desire which tends to know
The works of God, thereby to glorifie
The great Work-Maister, leads to no excess
That reaches blame, but rather merits praise
The more it seems excess, that led thee hither
From thy Empyreal Mansion thus alone,
To witness with thine eyes what some perhaps
Contented with report hear onely in heav'n:
For wonderful indeed are all his works,
Pleasant to know, and worthiest to be all

Had in remembrance alwayes with delight;
But what created mind can comprehend
Thir number, or the wisdom infinite
That brought them forth, but hid their causes deep.
I saw when at his Word the formless Mass,
This worlds material mould, came to a heap:
Confusion heard his voice, and wilde uproar
Stood rul'd, stood vast infinitude confin'd;
Till at his second bidding darkness fled,
Light shon, and order from disorder sprung:
Swift to their several Quarters hasted then
The cumbrous Elements, Earth, Flood, Aire, Fire,
And this Ethereal quintessence of Heav'n
Flew upward, spirited with various forms,
That rowld orbicular, and turnd to Starrs
Numberless, as thou seest, and how they move;
Each had his place appointed, each his course,
The rest in circuit walles this Universe.
Look downward on that Globe whose hither side
With light from hence, though but reflected, shines;
That place is Earth the seat of Man, that light
His day, which else as th' other Hemisphere
Night would invade, but there the neighbouring Moon
(So call that opposite fair Starr) her aide
Timely interposes, and her monthly round
Still ending, still renewing through mid Heav'n,
With borrowd light her countenance triform
Hence fills and empties to enlighten th' Earth,
And in her pale dominion checks the night.
That spot to which I point is *Paradise*,
Adams abode, those loftie shades his Bowre.
Thy way thou canst not miss, me mine requires.

    Thus said, he turnd, and *Satan* bowing low,
As to superior Spirits is wont in Heav'n,
Where honour due and reverence none neglects,
Took leave, and toward the coast of Earth beneath,
Down from th' Ecliptic, sped with hop'd success,
Throws his steep flight in many an Aerie wheele,
Nor staid, till on *Niphates* top he lights.

BOOK IV

THE ARGUMENT

SATAN *now in prospect of* Eden, *and nigh the place where he must now attempt the bold enterprize which he undertook alone against God and Man, falls into many doubts with himself, and many passions, fear, envy, and despare; but at length confirms himself in evil, journeys on to Paradise, whose outward prospect and scituation is discribed, overleaps the bounds, sits in the shape of a Cormorant on the Tree of life, as highest in the Garden to look about him. The Garden describ'd;* Satans *first sight of* Adam *and* Eve; *his wonder at thir excellent form and happy state, but with resolution to work thir fall; overhears thir discourse, thence gathers that the Tree of knowledge was forbidden them to eat of, under penalty of death; and thereon intends to found his Temptation, by seducing them to transgress: then leaves them a while, to know further of their state by some other means. Mean while* Uriel *descending on a Sunbeam warns* Gabriel, *who had in charge the Gate of Paradise, that some evil spirit had escap'd the Deep, and past at Noon by his Sphere in the shape of a good Angel down to Paradise, discovered after by his furious gestures in the Mount.* Gabriel *promises to find him ere morning. Night coming on,* Adam *and* Eve *discourse of going to thir rest: thir Bower describ'd; thir Evning worship.* Gabriel *drawing forth his Bands of Nightwatch to walk the round of Paradise, appoints two strong Angels to* Adams *Bower, least the evill spirit should be there doing some harm to* Adam *or* Eve *sleeping; there they find him at the ear of* Eve, *tempting her in a dream, and bring him, though unwilling, to* Gabriel; *by whom question'd, he scornfully answers, prepares resistance, but hinder'd by a Sign from Heaven, flies out of Paradise.*

O FOR that warning voice, which he who saw
Th'*Apocalyps*, heard cry in Heaven aloud,
Then when the Dragon, put to second rout,
Came furious down to be reveng'd on men,
Wo to the inhabitants on Earth! that now,
While time was, our first Parents had bin warnd

The coming of thir secret foe, and scap'd
Haply so scap'd his mortal snare; for now
Satan, now first inflam'd with rage, came down,
The Tempter ere th' Accuser of man-kind,
To wreck on innocent frail man his loss
Of that first Battel, and his flight to Hell:
Yet not rejoycing in his speed, though bold,
Far off and fearless, nor with cause to boast,
Begins his dire attempt, which nigh the birth
Now rowling, boiles in his tumultuous brest,
And like a devillish Engine back recoiles
Upon himself; horror and doubt distract
His troubl'd thoughts, and from the bottom stirr
The Hell within him, for within him Hell
He brings, and round about him, nor from Hell
One step no more then from himself can fly
By change of place: Now conscience wakes despair
That slumberd, wakes the bitter memorie
Of what he was, what is, and what must be
Worse; of worse deeds worse sufferings must ensue.
Sometimes towards *Eden* which now in his view
Lay pleasant, his grievd look he fixes sad,
Sometimes towards Heav'n and the full-blazing Sun,
Which now sat high in his Meridian Towre:
Then much revolving, thus in sighs began.

   O thou that with surpassing Glory crownd,
Look'st from thy sole Dominion like the God
Of this new World; at whose sight all the Starrs
Hide their diminisht heads; to thee I call,
But with no friendly voice, and add thy name
O Sun, to tell thee how I hate thy beams
That bring to my remembrance from what state
I fell, how glorious once above thy Spheare;
Till Pride and worse Ambition threw me down
Warring in Heav'n against Heav'ns matchless King:
Ah wherefore! he deservd no such return
From me, whom he created what I was
In that bright eminence, and with his good
Upbraided none; nor was his service hard.
What could be less then to afford him praise,

The easiest recompence, and pay him thanks,
How due! yet all his good prov'd ill in me,
And wrought but malice; lifted up so high
I sdeind subjection, and thought one step higher
Would set me highest, and in a moment quit
The debt immense of endless gratitude,
So burthensome, still paying, still to ow;
Forgetful what from him I still receivd,
And understood not that a grateful mind
By owing owes not, but still pays, at once
Indebted and dischargd; what burden then?
O had his powerful Destiny ordaind
Me some inferiour Angel, I had stood
Then happie; no unbounded hope had rais'd
Ambition. Yet why not? som other Power
As great might have aspir'd, and me though mean
Drawn to his part; but other Powers as great
Fell not, but stand unshak'n, from within
Or from without, to all temptations arm'd.
Hadst thou the same free Will and Power to stand?
Thou hadst: whom hast thou then or what to accuse,
But Heav'ns free Love dealt equally to all?
Be then his Love accurst, since love or hate,
To me alike, it deals eternal woe.
Nay curs'd be thou; since against his thy will
Chose freely what it now so justly rues.
Me miserable! which way shall I flie
Infinite wrauth, and infinite despaire?
Which way I flie is Hell; my self am Hell;
And in the lowest deep a lower deep
Still threatning to devour me opens wide,
To which the Hell I suffer seems a Heav'n.
O then at last relent: is there no place
Left for Repentance, none for Pardon left?
None left but by submission; and that word
Disdain forbids me, and my dread of shame
Among the spirits beneath, whom I seduc'd
With other promises and other vaunts
Then to submit, boasting I could subdue
Th' Omnipotent. Ay me, they little know

How dearly I abide that boast so vaine,
Under what torments inwardly I groane:
While they adore me on the Throne of Hell,
With Diadem and Scepter high advanc'd
The lower still I fall, onely Supream
In miserie; such joy Ambition findes.
But say I could repent and could obtaine
By Act of Grace my former state; how soon
Would highth recal high thoughts, how soon unsay
What feign'd submission swore: ease would recant
Vows made in pain, as violent and void.
For never can true reconcilement grow
Where wounds of deadly hate have peirc'd so deep:
Which would but lead me to a worse relapse,
And heavier fall: so should I purchase deare
Short intermission bought with double smart.
This knows my punisher; therefore as farr
From granting hee, as I from begging peace:
All hope excluded thus, behold in stead
Of us out-cast, exil'd, his new delight,
Mankind created, and for him this World.
So farwel Hope, and with Hope farwel Fear,
Farwel Remorse: all Good to me is lost;
Evil be thou my Good; by thee at least
Divided Empire with Heav'ns King I hold
By thee, and more then half perhaps will reigne;
As Man ere long, and this new World shall know.
    Thus while he spake, each passion dimm'd his face
Thrice chang'd with pale ire, envie and despair,
Which marrd his borrow'd visage, and betraid
Him counterfet, if any eye beheld.
For heav'nly mindes from such distempers foule
Are ever cleer. Whereof hee soon aware,
Each perturbation smooth'd with outward calme,
Artificer of fraud; and was the first
That practisd falshood under saintly shew,
Deep malice to conceale, couch't with revenge:
Yet not anough had practisd to deceive
Uriel once warnd; whose eye pursu'd him down
The way he went, and on th'*Assyrian* mount

Saw him disfigur'd, more then could befall
Spirit of happie sort: his gestures fierce
He markd and mad demeanour, then alone,
As he suppos'd, all unobserv'd, unseen.
So on he fares, and to the border comes
Of *Eden*, where delicious Paradise,
Now nearer, Crowns with her enclosure green,
As with a rural mound the champain head
Of a steep wilderness, whose hairie sides
With thicket overgrown, grottesque and wilde,
Access deni'd; and over head up grew
Insuperable highth of loftiest shade,
Cedar, and Pine, and Firr, and branching Palm,
A Silvan Scene, and as the ranks ascend
Shade above shade, a woodie Theatre
Of stateliest view. Yet higher then thir tops
The verdurous wall of Paradise up sprung:
Which to our general Sire gave prospect large
Into his neather Empire neighbouring round.
And higher then that Wall a circling row
Of goodliest Trees loaden with fairest Fruit,
Blossoms and Fruits at once of golden hue
Appeerd, with gay enameld colours mixt:
On which the Sun more glad impress'd his beams
Then in fair Evening Cloud, or humid Bow,
When God hath showrd the earth; so lovely seemd
That Lantskip: And of pure now purer aire
Meets his approach, and to the heart inspires
Vernal delight and joy, able to drive
All sadness but despair: now gentle gales
Fanning thir odoriferous wings dispense
Native perfumes, and whisper whence they stole
Those balmie spoiles. As when to them who saile
Beyond the *Cape of Hope*, and now are past
Mozambic, off at Sea North-East windes blow
Sabean Odours from the spicie shoare
Of *Arabie* the blest, with such delay
Well pleas'd they slack thir course, and many a League
Cheard with the grateful smell old Ocean smiles.
So entertained those odorous sweets the Fiend

Who came thir bane, though with them better pleas'd
Then *Asmodeus* with the fishie fume,
That drove him, though enamourd, from the Spouse
Of *Tobits* Son, and with a vengeance sent
From *Media* post to *Egypt*, there fast bound.
　　Now to th' ascent of that steep savage Hill
Satan had journied on, pensive and slow;
But further way found none, so thick entwin'd,
As one continu'd brake, the undergrowth
Of shrubs and tangling bushes had perplext
All path of Man or Beast that past that way:
One Gate there onely was, and that look'd East
On th' other side: which when th' arch-fellon saw
Due entrance he disdaind, and in contempt,
At one slight bound high overleap'd all bound
Of Hill or highest Wall, and sheer within
Lights on his feet. As when a prowling Wolfe,
Whom hunger drives to seek new haunt for prey,
Watching where Shepherds pen thir Flocks at eeve
In hurdl'd Cotes amid the field secure,
Leaps o're the fence with ease into the Fould:
Or as a Thief bent to unhoord the cash
Of some rich Burgher, whose substantial dores,
Cross-barrd and bolted fast, fear no assault,
In at the window climbes, or o're the tiles;
So clomb this first grand Thief into Gods Fould:
So since into his Church lewd Hirelings climbe.
Thence up he flew, and on the Tree of Life,
The middle Tree and highest there that grew,
Sat like a Cormorant; yet not true Life
Thereby regaind, but sat devising Death
To them who liv'd; nor on the vertue thought
Of that life-giving Plant, but only us'd
For prospect, what well us'd had bin the pledge
Of immortality. So little knows
Any, but God alone, to value right
The good before him, but perverts best things
To worst abuse, or to their meanest use.
Beneath him with new wonder now he views
To all delight of human sense expos'd

In narrow room Natures whole wealth, yea more,
A Heav'n on Earth: for blissful Paradise
Of God the Garden was, by him in the East
Of *Eden* planted; *Eden* stretchd her Line
From *Auran* Eastward to the Royal Towrs
Of great *Seleucia*, built by *Grecian* Kings,
Or where the Sons of *Eden* long before
Dwelt in *Telassar:* in this pleasant soile
His farr more pleasant Garden God ordaind;
Out of the fertil ground he caus'd to grow
All Trees of noblest kind for sight, smell, taste;
And all amid them stood the Tree of Life,
High eminent, blooming Ambrosial Fruit
Of vegetable Gold; and next to Life
Our Death the Tree of Knowledge grew fast by,
Knowledge of Good bought dear by knowing ill.
Southward through *Eden* went a River large,
Nor chang'd his course, but through the shaggie hill
Pass'd underneath ingulft, for God had thrown
That Mountain as his Garden mould high rais'd
Upon the rapid current, which through veins
Of porous Earth with kindly thirst up drawn,
Rose a fresh Fountain, and with many a rill
Waterd the Garden; thence united fell
Down the steep glade, and met the neather Flood,
Which from his darksom passage now appeers,
And now divided into four main Streams,
Runs divers, wandring many a famous Realme
And Country whereof here needs no account,
But rather to tell how, if Art could tell,
How from that Saphire Fount the crisped Brooks,
Rowling on Orient Pearl and sands of Gold,
With mazie error under pendant shades
Ran Nectar, visiting each plant, and fed
Flours worthy of Paradise which not nice Art
In Beds and curious Knots, but Nature boon
Powrd forth profuse on Hill and Dale and Plaine,
Both where the morning Sun first warmly smote
The open field, and where the unpierc't shade
Imbround the noontide Bowrs: Thus was this place,

A happy rural seat of various view;
Groves whose rich Trees wept odorous Gumms and Balme,
Others whose fruit burnisht with Golden Rinde
Hung amiable, *Hesperian* Fables true,
If true, here only, and of delicious taste:
Betwixt them Lawns, or level Downs, and Flocks
Grasing the tender herb, were interpos'd,
Of palmie hilloc, or the flourie lap
Of som irriguous Valley spread her store,
Flours of all hue, and without Thorn the Rose:
Another side, umbrageous Grots and Caves
Of coole recess, o're which the mantling Vine
Layes forth her purple Grape, and gently creeps
Luxuriant; mean while murmuring waters fall
Down the slope hills, disperst, or in a Lake,
That to the fringed Bank with Myrtle crownd,
Her chrystal mirror holds, unite thir streams.
The Birds thir quire apply; aires, vernal aires,
Breathing the smell of field and grove, attune
The trembling leaves, while Universal *Pan*
Knit with the *Graces* and the *Hours* in dance
Led on th' Eternal Spring. Not that faire field
Of *Enna*, where *Proserpin* gathring flours
Her self a fairer Floure by gloomie *Dis*
Was gatherd, which cost *Ceres* all that pain
To seek her through the world; not that sweet Grove
Of *Daphne* by *Orontes*, and th' inspir'd
Castalian Spring might with this Paradise
Of *Eden* strive; nor that *Nyseian* Ile
Girt with the River *Triton*, where old *Cham*,
Whom Gentiles *Ammon* call and *Libyan** *Jove*,
Hid *Amalthea* and her Florid Son
Young *Bacchus* from his Stepdame *Rhea*'s eye;
Nor where *Abassin* Kings their issue Guard,
Mount *Amara*, though this by som suppos'd
True Paradise under the *Ethiop* Line
By *Nilus* head, enclos'd with shining Rock,
A whole dayes journey high, but wide remote
From this *Assyrian* Garden, where the Fiend

* In 2nd edit. printed *Lybian*.

Saw undelighted all delight, all kind
Of living Creatures new to sight and strange:
Two of far nobler shape erect and tall,
Godlike erect, with native Honour clad
In naked Majestie seemd Lords of all,
And worthie seemd, for in thir looks Divine
The image of thir glorious Maker shon,
Truth, wisdome, Sanctitude severe and pure,
Severe, but in true filial freedom plac't;
Whence true autoritie in men; though both
Not equal, as their sex not equal seemd;
For contemplation hee and valour formd,
For softness shee and sweet attractive Grace,
Hee for God only, shee for God in him:
His fair large Front and Eye sublime declar'd
Absolute rule; and Hyacinthin Locks
Round from his parted forelock manly hung
Clustring, but not beneath his shoulders broad:
Shee as a vail down to the slender waste
Her unadorned golden tresses wore
Dissheveld, but in wanton ringlets wav'd
As the Vine curles her tendrils, which impli'd
Subjection, but requir'd with gentle sway,
And by her yielded, by him best receivd,
Yielded with coy submission, modest pride,
And sweet reluctant amorous delay.
Nor those mysterious parts were then conceald,
Then was not guiltie shame, dishonest shame
Of natures works, honor dishonorable,
Sin-bred, how have ye troubl'd all mankind
With shews instead, meer shews of seeming pure,
And banisht from mans life his happiest life,
Simplicitie and spotless innocence.
So passd they naked on, nor shund the sight
Of God or Angel, for they thought no ill:
So hand in hand they passd, the loveliest pair
That ever since in loves imbraces met,
Adam the goodliest man of men since borne
His Sons, the fairest of her Daughters *Eve*.
Under a tuft of shade that on a green

Stood whispering soft, by a fresh Fountain side
They sat them down, and after no more toil
Of their sweet Gardning Labour then suffic'd
To recommend coole *Zephyr*, and made ease
More easie, wholsom thirst and appetite
More grateful, to thir Supper Fruits they fell,
Nectarine Fruits which the compliant boughes
Yielded them, side-long as they sat recline
On the soft downie Bank damaskt with flours:
The savourie pulp they chew, and in the rinde
Still as they thirsted scoop the brimming stream;
Nor gentle purpose, nor endearing smiles
Wanted, nor youthful dalliance as beseems
Fair couple, linkt in happie nuptial League,
Alone as they. About them frisking playd
All Beasts of th' Earth, since wilde, and of all chase
In Wood or Wilderness, Forrest or Den;
Sporting the Lion rampd, and in his paw
Dandl'd the Kid; Bears, Tygers, Ounces, Pards,
Gambold before them, th' unwieldy Elephant
To make them mirth us'd all his might, and wreathd
His Lithe Proboscis; close the Serpent sly
Insinuating, wove with Gordian twine
His breaded train, and of his fatal guile
Gave proof unheeded; others on the grass
Coucht, and now fild with pasture gazing sat,
Or Bedward ruminating; for the Sun
Declin'd was hasting now with prone carreer
To th' Ocean Iles, and in th' ascending Scale
Of Heav'n the Starrs that usher Evening rose:
When *Satan* still in gaze, as first he stood,
Scarce thus at length faild speech recoverd sad.

   O Hell! what doe mine eyes with grief behold,
Into our room of bliss thus high advanc't
Creatures of other mould, earth-born perhaps,
Not Spirits, yet to heav'nly Spirits bright
Little inferior; whom my thoughts pursue
With wonder, and could love, so lively shines
In them Divine resemblance, and such grace
The hand that formd them on thir shape hath pourd.

Ah gentle pair, yee little think how nigh
Your change approaches, when all these delights
Will vanish and deliver ye to woe,
More woe, the more you taste is now of joy;
Happie, but for so happie ill secur'd
Long to continue, and this high seat your Heav'n
Ill fenc't for Heav'n to keep out such a foe
As now is enterd; yet no purpos'd foe
To you whom I could pittie thus forlorne
Though I unpittied: League with you I seek,
And mutual amitie so streight, so close,
That I with you must dwell, or you with me
Henceforth; my dwelling haply may not please
Like this fair Paradise, your sense, yet such
Accept your Makers work; he gave it me,
Which I as freely give; Hell shall unfold,
To entertain you two, her widest Gates,
And send forth all her Kings; there will be room,
Not like these narrow limits, to receive
Your numerous ofspring; if no better place,
Thank him who puts me loath to this revenge
On you who wrong me not for him who wrongd.
And should I at your harmless innocence
Melt, as I doe, yet public reason just,
Honour and Empire with revenge enlarg'd,
By conquering this new World, compels me now
To do what else though damnd I should abhorre.
        So spake the Fiend, and with necessitie,
The Tyrants plea, excus'd his devilish deeds.
Then from his loftie stand on that high Tree
Down he alights among the sportful Herd
Of those fourfooted kindes, himself now one,
Now other, as thir shape servd best his end
Neerer to view his prey, and unespi'd
To mark what of their state he more might learn
By word or action markt: about them round
A Lion now he stalkes with fierie glare,
Then as a Tyger, who by chance hath spi'd
In some Purlieu two gentle Fawnes at play,
Strait couches close, then rising changes oft

His couchant watch, as one who chose his ground
Whence rushing he might surest seise them both
Grip't in each paw: When *Adam* first of men
To first of women *Eve* thus moving speech,
Turnd him all eare to heare new utterance flow.

   Sole partner and sole part of all these joyes,
Dearer thy self then all; needs must the Power
That made us, and for us this ample World
Be infinitly good, and of his good
As liberal and free as infinite,
That rais'd us from the dust and plac't us here
In all this happiness, who at his hand
Have nothing merited, nor can performe
Aught whereof hee hath need, hee who requires
From us no other service then to keep
This one, this easie charge, of all the Trees
In Paradise that beare delicious fruit
So various, not to taste that onely Tree
Of knowledge, planted by the Tree of Life,
So neer grows Death to Life, what ere Death is,
Som dreadful thing no doubt; for well thou knowst
God hath pronounc't it death to taste that Tree,
The only sign of our obedience left
Among so many signes of power and rule
Conferrd upon us, and Dominion giv'n
Over all other Creatures that possess
Earth, Aire, and Sea. Then let us not think hard
One easie prohibition, who enjoy
Free leave so large to all things else, and choice
Unlimited of manifold delights:
But let us ever praise him, and extoll
His bountie, following our delightful task
To prune these growing Plants, and tend these Flours,
Which were it toilsom, yet with thee were sweet.

   To whom thus *Eve* repli'd. O thou for whom
And from whom I was formd flesh of thy flesh,
And without whom am to no end, my Guide
And Head, what thou hast said is just and right.
For wee to him indeed all praises owe,
And daily thanks, I chiefly who enjoy

So farr the happier Lot, enjoying thee
Præeminent by so much odds, while thou
Like consort to thy self canst no where find.
That day I oft remember, when from sleep
I first awak't, and found my self repos'd
Under a shade on flours, much wondring where
And what I was, whence thither brought, and how.
Not distant far from thence a murmuring sound
Of waters issu'd from a Cave and spread
Into a liquid Plain, then stood unmov'd
Pure as th' expanse of Heav'n; I thither went
With unexperienc't thought, and laid me downe
On the green bank, to look into the cleer
Smooth Lake, that to me seemd another Skie.
As I bent down to look, just opposite,
A Shape within the watry gleam appeerd
Bending to look on me, I started back,
It started back, but pleasd I soon returnd,
Pleas'd it returnd as soon with answering looks
Of sympathie and love; there I had fixt
Mine eyes till now, and pin'd with vain desire,
Had not a voice thus warnd me, What thou seest,
What there thou seest fair Creature is thy self,
With thee it came and goes: but follow me,
And I will bring thee where no shadow staies
Thy coming, and thy soft imbraces, hee
Whose image thou art, him thou shalt enjoy
Inseparablie thine, to him shalt beare
Multitudes like thy self, and thence be call'd
Mother of human Race: what could I doe,
But follow strait, invisibly thus led?
Till I espi'd thee, fair indeed and tall,
Under a Platan, yet methought less faire,
Less winning soft, less amiablie milde,
Then that smooth watry image; back I turnd,
Thou following cryd'st aloud, Return fair *Eve*,
Whom fli'st thou? whom thou fli'st, of him thou art,
His flesh, his bone; to give thee being I lent
Out of my side to thee, neerest my heart
Substantial Life, to have thee by my side

Henceforth an individual solace dear;
Part of my Soul I seek thee, and thee claim
My other half: with that thy gentle hand
Seisd mine, I yielded, and from that time see
How beauty is excelld by manly grace
And wisdom, which alone is truly fair.

So spake our general Mother, and with eyes
Of conjugal attraction unreprov'd,
And meek surrender, half imbracing leand
On our first Father, half her swelling Breast
Naked met his under the flowing Gold
Of her loose tresses hid: he in delight
Both of her Beauty and submissive Charms
Smil'd with superior Love, as *Jupiter*
On *Juno* smiles, when he impregns the Clouds
That shed *May* Flowers; and press'd her Matron lip
With kisses pure: aside the Devil turnd
For envie, yet with jealous leer maligne
Ey'd them askance, and to himself thus plaind.

Sight hateful, sight tormenting! thus these two
Imparadis't in one anothers arms
The happier *Eden*, shall enjoy thir fill
Of bliss on bliss, while I to Hell am thrust,
Where neither joy nor love, but fierce desire,
Among our other torments not the least,
Still unfulfill'd with pain of longing pines;
Yet let me not forget what I have gain'd
From thir own mouths; all is not theirs it seems:
One fatal Tree there stands of Knowledge call'd,
Forbidden them to taste: Knowledge forbidd'n?
Suspicious, reasonless. Why should thir Lord
Envie them that? can it be sin to know,
Can it be death? and do they onely stand
By Ignorance, is that thir happie state,
The proof of thir obedience and thir faith?
O fair foundation laid whereon to build
Thir ruine! Hence I will excite thir minds
With more desire to know, and to reject
Envious commands, invented with designe
To keep them low whom knowledge might exalt

Equal with Gods; aspiring to be such,
They taste and die: what likelier can ensue?
But first with narrow search I must walk round
This Garden, and no corner leave unspi'd;
A chance but chance may lead where I may meet
Some wandring Spirit of Heav'n, by Fountain side,
Or in thick shade retir'd, from him to draw
What further would be learnt. Live while ye may,
Yet happie pair; enjoy, till I return,
Short pleasures, for long woes are to succeed.
  So saying, his proud step he scornful turn'd,
But with sly circumspection, and began
Through wood, through waste, o're hil, o're dale his roam.
Mean while in utmost Longitude, where Heav'n
With Earth and Ocean meets, the setting Sun
Slowly descended, and with right aspect
Against the eastern Gate of Paradise
Leveld his eevning Rayes: it was a Rock
Of Alablaster, pil'd up to the Clouds,
Conspicuous farr, winding with one ascent
Accessible from Earth, one entrance high;
The rest was craggie cliff, that overhung
Still as it rose, impossible to climbe.
Betwixt these rockie Pillars *Gabriel* sat
Chief of th' Angelic Guards, awaiting night;
About him exercis'd Heroic Games
Th' unarmed Youth of Heav'n, but nigh at hand
Celestial Armourie, Shields, Helmes, and Speares,
Hung high with Diamond flaming, and with Gold.
Thither came *Uriel*, gliding through the Eeven
On a Sun beam, swift as a shooting Starr
In *Autumn* thwarts the night, when vapors fir'd
Impress the Air, and shews the Mariner
From what point of his Compass to beware
Impetuous winds: he thus began in haste.
  Gabriel, to thee thy course by Lot hath giv'n
Charge and strict watch that to this happie Place
No evil thing approach or enter in;
This day at highth of Noon came to my Spheare
A Spirit, zealous, as he seem'd, to know

More of th' Almighties works, and chiefly **Man**
Gods latest Image: I describ'd his way
Bent all on speed, and markt his Aerie Gate;
But in the Mount that lies from *Eden* North,
Where he first lighted, soon discernd his looks
Alien from Heav'n, with passions foul obscur'd:
Mine eye pursu'd him still, but under shade
Lost sight of him; one of the banisht crew
I fear, hath ventur'd from the deep, to raise
New troubles; him thy care must be to find.

To whom the winged Warriour thus returnd:
Uriel, no wonder if thy perfet sight,
Amid the Suns bright circle where thou sitst,
See farr and wide: in at this Gate none pass
The vigilance here plac't, but such as come
Well known from Heav'n; and since Meridian hour
No Creature thence: if Spirit of other sort,
So minded, have oreleapt these earthie bounds
On purpose, hard thou knowst it to exclude
Spiritual substance with corporeal barr.
But if within the circuit of these walks
In whatsoever shape he lurk, of whom
Thou tellst, by morrow dawning I shall know.

So promis'd hee, and *Uriel* to his charge
Returnd on that bright beam, whose point now raisd
Bore him slope downward to the Sun now fall'n
Beneath th'*Azores ;* whither the prime Orb,
Incredible how swift, had thither rowl'd
Diurnal, or this less volubil Earth
By shorter flight to th' East, had left him there
Arraying with reflected Purple and Gold
The Clouds that on his Western Throne attend:
Now came still Eevning on, and Twilight gray
Had in her sober Liverie all things clad;
Silence accompanied, for Beast and Bird,
They to their grassie Couch, these to thir Nests
Were slunk, all but the wakeful Nightingale;
She all night long her amorous descant sung;
Silence was pleas'd: now glow'd the Firmament
With living Saphirs: *Hesperus* that led

The starrie Host, rode brightest, till the Moon
Rising in clouded Majestie, at length
Apparent Queen unvaild her peerless light,
And o're the dark her Silver Mantle threw.

    When *Adam* thus to *Eve*: Fair Consort, th' hour
Of night, and all things now retir'd to rest
Mind us of like repose, since God hath set
Labour and rest, as day and night to men
Successive, and the timely dew of sleep
Now falling with soft slumbrous weight inclines
Our eye-lids; other Creatures all day long
Rove idle unimploid, and less need rest;
Man hath his daily work of body or mind
Appointed, which declares his Dignitie,
And the regard of Heav'n on all his waies;
While other Animals unactive range,
And of their doings God takes no account.
To morrow ere fresh Morning streak the East
With first approach of light, we must be ris'n,
And at our pleasant labour, to reform
Yon flourie Arbors, yonder Allies green,
Our walks at noon, with branches overgrown,
That mock our scant manuring, and require
More hands then ours to lop thir wanton growth:
Those Blossoms also, and those dropping Gumms,
That lie bestrowne unsightly and unsmooth,
Ask riddance, if we mean to tread with ease;
Mean while, as Nature wills, Night bids us rest.

    To whom thus *Eve* with perfet beauty adornd.
My Author and Disposer, what thou bidst
Unargu'd I obey; so God ordains,
God is thy Law, thou mine: to know no more
Is womans happiest knowledge and her praise.
With thee conversing I forget all time,
All seasons and thir change, all please alike.
Sweet is the breath of morn, her rising sweet,
With charm of earliest Birds; pleasant the Sun
When first on this delightful Land he spreads
His orient Beams, on herb, tree, fruit, and flour,
Glistring with dew; fragrant the fertil earth

After soft showers; and sweet the coming on
Of grateful Eevning milde, then silent Night
With this her solemn Bird and this fair Moon,
And these the Gemms of Heav'n, her starrie train:
But neither breath of Morn when she ascends
With charm of earliest Birds, nor rising Sun
On this delightful land, nor herb, fruit, floure,
Glistring with dew, nor fragrance after showers,
Nor grateful Evening mild, nor silent Night
With this her solemn Bird, nor walk by Moon,
Or glittering Starr-light without thee is sweet.
But wherfore all night long shine these, for whom
This glorious sight, when sleep hath shut all eyes?
    To whom our general Ancestor repli'd.
Daughter of God and Man, accomplisht *Eve*,
Those have thir course to finish, round the Earth,
By morrow Eevning, and from Land to Land
In order, though to Nations yet unborn,
Ministring light prepar'd, they set and rise;
Least total darkness should by Night regaine
Her old possession, and extinguish life
In Nature and all things, which these soft fires
Not only enlighten, but with kindly heate
Of various influence foment and warme,
Temper or nourish, or in part shed down
Thir stellar vertue on all kinds that grow
On Earth, made hereby apter to receive
Perfection from the Suns more potent Ray.
These then, though unbeheld in deep of night,
Shine not in vain, nor think, though men were none,
That heav'n would want spectators, God want praise;
Millions of spiritual Creatures walk the Earth
Unseen, both when we wake, and when we sleep:
All these with ceasless praise his works behold
Both day and night: how often from the steep
Of echoing Hill or Thicket have we heard
Celestial voices to the midnight air,
Sole, or responsive each to others note
Singing their great Creator: oft in bands
While they keep watch, or nightly rounding walk

With Heav'nly touch of instrumental sounds
In full harmonic number joind, thir songs
Divide the night, and lift our thoughts to Heaven.
  Thus talking hand in hand alone they pass'd
On to their blissful Bower; it was a place
Chos'n by the sovran Planter, when he fram'd
All things to mans delightful use; the roofe
Of thickest covert was inwoven shade
Laurel and Mirtle, and what higher grew
Of firm and fragrant leaf; on either side
Acanthus, and each odorous bushie shrub
Fenc'd up the verdant wall; each beauteous flour,
Iris all hues, Roses, and Gessamin
Rear'd high thir flourisht heads between, and wrought
Mosaic; underfoot the Violet,
Crocus, and Hyacinth with rich inlay
Broiderd the ground, more colour'd then with stone
Of costliest Emblem: other Creature here
Beast, Bird, Insect, or Worm durst enter none;
Such was thir awe of man. In shadie Bower
More sacred and sequesterd, though but feignd,
Pan or *Silvanus* never slept, nor Nymph,
Nor *Faunus* haunted. Here in close recess
With Flowers, Garlands, and sweet-smelling Herbs
Espoused *Eve* deckt first her Nuptial Bed,
And heav'nly Quires the Hymenæan sung,
What day the genial Angel to our Sire
Brought her in naked beauty more adorn'd
More lovely then *Pandora*, whom the Gods
Endowd with all thir gifts, and O too like
In sad event, when to the unwiser Son
Of *Japhet* brought by *Hermes*, she ensnar'd
Mankind with her faire looks, to be aveng'd
On him who had stole *Joves* authentic fire.
  Thus at thir shadie Lodge arriv'd, both stood
Both turnd, and under op'n Skie ador'd
The God that made both Skie, Air, Earth and Heav'n
Which they beheld, the Moons resplendent Globe
And starrie Pole: Thou also mad'st the Night,
Maker Omnipotent, and thou the Day,

Which we in our appointed work imployd
Have finisht happie in our mutual help
And mutual love, the Crown of all our bliss
Ordain'd by thee, and this delicious place
For us too large, where thy abundance wants
Partakers, and uncropt falls to the ground.
But thou hast promis'd from us two a Race
To fill the Earth, who shall with us extoll
Thy goodness infinite, both when we wake,
And when we seek, as now, thy gift of sleep.

   This said unanimous, and other Rites
Observing none, but adoration pure
Which God likes best, into thir inmost bowre
Handed they went; and eas'd the putting off
These troublesom disguises which wee wear,
Strait side by side were laid, nor turnd I weene
Adam from his fair Spouse, nor *Eve* the Rites
Mysterious of connubial Love refus'd:
Whatever Hypocrites austerely talk
Of puritie and place and innocence,
Defaming as impure what God declares
Pure, and commands to som, leaves free to all.
Our Maker bids increase, who bids abstain
But our Destroyer, foe to God and Man?
Haile wedded Love, mysterious Law, true sourse
Of human ofspring, sole proprietie,
In Paradise of all things common else.
By thee adulterous lust was driv'n from men
Among the bestial herds to raunge, by thee
Founded in Reason, Loyal, Just, and Pure,
Relations dear, and all the Charities
Of Father, Son, and Brother first were known.
Farr be it, that I should write thee sin or blame,
Or think thee unbefitting holiest place,
Perpetual Fountain of Domestic sweets,
Whose Bed is undefil'd and chaste pronounc't,
Present, or past, as Saints and Patriarchs us'd.
Here Love his golden shafts imploies, here lights
His constant Lamp, and waves his purple wings,
Reigns here and revels; not in the bought smile

Of Harlots, loveless, joyless, unindeard,
Casual fruition, nor in Court Amours
Mixt Dance, or wanton Mask, or Midnight Bal,
Or Serenate, which the starv'd Lover sings
To his proud fair, best quitted with disdain.
These lulld by Nightingales imbraceing slept,
And on their naked limbs the flourie roof
Showrd Roses, which the Morn repair'd. Sleep on
Blest pair; and O yet happiest if ye seek
No happier state, and know to know no more.

Now had night measur'd with her shaddowie Cone
Half way up Hill this vast Sublunar Vault,
And from thir Ivorie Port the Cherubim
Forth issuing at th' accustomd hour stood armd
To thir night watches in warlike Parade,
When *Gabriel* to his next in power thus spake.

Uzziel, half these draw off, and coast the South
With strictest watch; these other wheel the North,
Our circuit meets full West. As flame they part
Half wheeling to the Shield, half to the Spear.
From these, two strong and suttle Spirits he calld
That neer him stood, and gave them thus in charge.

Ithuriel and *Zephon*, with wingd speed
Search through this Garden, leave unsearcht no nook,
But chiefly where those two fair Creatures Lodge,
Now laid perhaps asleep secure of harme.
This Eevning from the Sun's decline arriv'd
Who tells of som infernal Spirit seen
Hitherward bent (who could have thought?) escap'd
The barrs of Hell, on errand bad no doubt:
Such where ye find, seise fast, and hither bring.

So saying, on he led his radiant Files,
Daz'ling the Moon; these to the Bower direct
In search of whom they sought: him there they found
Squat like a Toad, close at the eare of *Eve;*
Assaying by his Devilish art to reach
The Organs of her Fancie, and with them forge
Illusions as he list, Phantasms and Dreams,
Or if, inspiring venom, he might taint
Th' animal Spirits that from pure blood arise

Like gentle breaths from Rivers pure, thence raise
At least distemperd, discontented thoughts,
Vain hopes, vain aimes, inordinate desires
Blown up with high conceits ingendring pride.
Him thus intent *Ithuriel* with his Spear
Touch'd lightly; for no falshood can endure
Touch of Celestial temper, but returns
Of force to its own likeness: up he starts
Discoverd and surpriz'd. As when a spark
Lights on a heap of nitrous Powder, laid
Fit for the Tun som Magazin to store
Against a rumord Warr, the Smuttie graine
With sudden blaze diffus'd, inflames the Aire:
So started up in his own shape the Fiend.
Back stept those two fair Angels half amaz'd
So sudden to behold the grieslie King;
Yet thus, unmovd with fear, accost him soon.

Which of those rebell Spirits adjudg'd to Hell
Com'st thou, escap'd thy prison, and transform'd,
Why satst thou like an enemie in waite
Here watching at the head of these that sleep?

Know ye not then said *Satan*, filld with scorn
Know ye not mee? ye knew me once no mate
For you, there sitting where ye durst not soare;
Not to know mee argues your selves unknown,
The lowest of your throng; or if ye know,
Why ask ye, and superfluous begin
Your message, like to end as much in vain?
To whom thus *Zephon*, answering scorn with scorn.
Think not, revolted Spirit, thy shape the same,
Or undiminisht brightness, to be known
As when thou stoodst in Heav'n upright and pure;
That Glorie then, when thou no more wast good,
Departed from thee, and thou resembl'st now
Thy sin and place of doom obscure and foule.
But come, for thou, besure, shalt give account
To him who sent us, whose charge is to keep
This place inviolable, and these from harm.

So spake the Cherube, and his grave rebuke
Severe in youthful beautie, added grace

Invincible: abasht the Devil stood,
And felt how awful goodness is, and saw
Vertue in her shape how lovly, saw, and pin'd
His loss; but chiefly to find here observd
His lustre visibly impar'd; yet seemd
Undaunted. If I must contend, said he,
Best with the best, the Sender not the sent,
Or all at once; more glorie will be wonn,
Or less be lost. Thy fear, said *Zephon* bold,
Will save us trial what the least can doe
Single against thee wicked, and thence weak.

The Fiend repli'd not, overcome with rage;
But like a proud Steed reind, went hautie on,
Chaumping his iron curb: to strive or flie
He held it vain; awe from above had quelld
His heart, not else dismai'd. Now drew they nigh
The western Point, where those half-rounding guards
Just met, and closing stood in squadron joind
Awaiting next command. To whom thir Chief
Gabriel from the Front thus calld aloud.

O friends, I hear the tread of nimble feet
Hasting this way, and now by glimps discerne
Ithuriel and *Zephon* through the shade,
And with them comes a third of Regal port,
But faded splendor wan; who by his gate
And fierce demeanour seems the Prince of Hell,
Not likely to part hence without contest;
Stand firm, for in his look defiance lours.

He scarce had ended, when those two approachd
And brief related whom they brought, where found,
How busied, in what form and posture coucht.

To whom with stern regard thus *Gabriel* spake.
Why hast thou, *Satan*, broke the bounds prescrib'd
To thy transgressions, and disturbd the charge
Of others, who approve not to transgress
By thy example, but have power and right
To question thy bold entrance on this place;
Imploi'd it seems to violate sleep, and those
Whose dwelling God hath planted here in bliss?

To whom thus *Satan* with contemptuous brow.

Gabriel, thou hadst in Heav'n th' esteem of wise,
And such I held thee; but this question askt
Puts me in doubt. Lives ther who loves his pain?
Who would not, finding way, break loose from Hell,
Though thither doomd? Thou wouldst thy self, no doubt,
And boldly venture to whatever place
Farthest from pain, where thou mightst hope to change
Torment with ease, and soonest recompence
Dole with delight, which in this place I sought;
To thee no reason; who knowst only good,
But evil hast not tri'd: and wilt object
His will who bound us? let him surer barr
His Iron Gates, if he intends our stay
In that dark durance: thus much what was askt.
The rest is true, they found me where they say;
But that implies not violence or harme.

    Thus hee in scorn. The warlike Angel mov'd,
Disdainfully half smiling thus repli'd.
O loss of one in Heav'n to judge of wise,
Since *Satan* fell, whom follie overthrew,
And now returns him from his prison scap't,
Gravely in doubt whether to hold them wise
Or not, who ask what boldness brought him hither
Unlicenc't from his bounds in Hell prescrib'd;
So wise he judges it to fly from pain
However, and to scape his punishment.
So judge thou still, presumptuous, till the wrauth,
Which thou incurr'st by flying, meet thy flight
Seavenfold, and scourge that wisdom back to Hell,
Which taught thee yet no better, that no pain
Can equal anger infinite provok't.
But wherefore thou alone? wherefore with thee
Came not all Hell broke loose? is pain to them
Less pain, less to be fled, or thou then they
Less hardie to endure? courageous Chief,
The first in flight from pain, had'st thou alleg'd
To thy deserted host this cause of flight,
Thou surely hadst not come sole fugitive.

    To which the Fiend thus answerd frowning stern.
Not that I less endure, or shrink from pain,

Insulting Angel, well thou knowst I stood
Thy fiercest, when in Battel to thy aide
Thy blasting volied Thunder made all speed
And seconded thy else not dreaded Spear.
But still thy words at random, as before,
Argue thy inexperience what behooves
From hard assaies and ill successes past
A faithful Leader, not to hazard all
Through wayes of danger by himself untri'd.
I therefore, I alone first undertook
To wing the desolate Abyss, and spie
This new created World, whereof in Hell
Fame is not silent, here in hope to find
Better abode, and my afflicted Powers
To settle here on Earth, or in mid Aire;
Though for possession put to try once more
What thou and thy gay Legions dare against;
Whose easier business were to serve thir Lord
High up in Heav'n, with songs to hymne his Throne,
And practis'd distances to cringe, not fight.
     To whom the warriour Angel soon repli'd.
To say and strait unsay, pretending first
Wise to flie pain, professing next the Spie,
Argues no Leader, but a lyar trac't,
Satan, and couldst thou faithful add? O name,
O sacred name of faithfulness profan'd!
Faithful to whom? to thy rebellious crew?
Armie of Fiends, fit body to fit head;
Was this your discipline and faith ingag'd,
Your military obedience, to dissolve
Allegeance to th' acknowldg'd Power supream?
And thou sly hypocrite, who now wouldst seem
Patron of liberty, who more then thou
Once fawn'd, and cring'd, and servilly ador'd
Heav'ns awful Monarch? wherefore but in hope
To dispossess him, and thy self to reigne?
But mark what I arreede thee now, avant;
Flie thither whence thou fledst: if from this houre
Within these hallowd limits thou appeer,
Back to th' infernal pit I drag thee chaind,

And Seale thee so, as henceforth not to scorne
The facil gates of hell too slightly barrd.

So threatn'd hee, but *Satan* to no threats
Gave heed, but waxing more in rage repli'd.

Then when I am thy captive talk of chaines,
Proud limitarie Cherube, but ere then
Farr heavier load thy self expect to feel
From my prevailing arme, though Heavens King
Ride on thy wings, and thou with thy Compeers,
Us'd to the yoak, draw'st his triumphant wheels
In progress through the rode of Heav'n Star-pav'd.

While thus he spake, th' Angelic Squadron bright
Turnd fierie red, sharpning in mooned hornes
Thir Phalanx, and began to hemm him round
With ported Spears, as thick as when a field
Of *Ceres* ripe for harvest waving bends
Her bearded Grove of ears, which way the wind
Swayes them; the careful Plowman doubting stands
Least on the threshing floore his hopeful sheaves
Prove chaff. On th' other side *Satan* allarm'd
Collecting all his might dilated stood,
Like *Teneriff* or *Atlas* unremov'd:
His stature reacht the Skie, and on his Crest
Sat horror Plum'd; nor wanted in his graspe
What seemd both Spear and Shield: now dreadful deeds
Might have ensu'd, nor onely Paradise
In this commotion, but the Starrie Cope
Of Heav'n perhaps, or all the Elements
At least had gon to rack, disturbd and torne
With violence of this conflict, had not soon
Th' Eternal to prevent such horrid fray
Hung forth in Heav'n his golden Scales, yet seen
Betwixt *Astrea* and the *Scorpion* signe,
Wherein all things created first he weighd,
The pendulous round Earth with ballanc't Aire
In counterpoise, now ponders all events,
Battels and Realms: in these he put two weights
The sequel each of parting and of fight;
The latter quick up flew, and kickt the beam;
Which *Gabriel* spying, thus bespake the Fiend.

   Satan, I know thy strength, and thou knowst mine,
Neither our own but giv'n; what follie then
To boast what Arms can doe, since thine no more
Then Heav'n permits, nor mine, though doubld now
To trample thee as mire: for proof look up,
And read thy Lot in yon celestial Sign
Where thou art weigh'd, and shown how light, how weak,
If thou resist. The Fiend lookt up and knew
His mounted scale aloft: nor more; but fled
Murmuring, and with him fled the shades of night.

BOOK V

THE ARGUMENT

Morning approach't, Eve *relates to* Adam *her troublesome
dream; he likes it not, yet comforts her: They come forth to
thir day labours: Thir Morning Hymn at the Door of thir
Bower. God to render Man inexcusable sends* Raphael *to
admonish him of his obedience, of his free estate, of his enemy
near at hand; who he is, and why his enemy, and whatever else
may avail* Adam *to know.* Raphael *comes down to Paradise,
his appearance describ'd, his coming discern'd by* Adam *afar
off, sitting at the door of his Bower; he goes out to meet him,
brings him to his lodge, entertains him with the choycest fruits
of Paradise got together by* Eve; *thir discourse at Table:*
Raphael *performs his message, minds* Adam *of his state and of
his enemy; relates at* Adams *request who that enemy is, and
how he came to be so, beginning from his first revolt in Heaven,
and the occasion thereof; how he drew his Legions after him to
the parts of the North, and there incited them to rebel with him,
perswading all but only* Abdiel *a Seraph, who in Argument
diswades and opposes him, then forsakes him.*

   Now Morn her rosie steps in th' Eastern Clime
Advancing, sow'd the Earth with Orient Pearle,
When *Adam* wak't, so customd, for his sleep
Was Aerie light from pure digestion bred,

And temperat vapors bland, which th' only sound
Of leaves and fuming rills, *Aurora's* fan,
Lightly dispers'd, and the shrill Matin Song
Of Birds on every bough; so much the more
His wonder was to find unwak'nd *Eve*
With Tresses discompos'd, and glowing Cheek,
As through unquiet rest: he on his side
Leaning half-rais'd, with looks of cordial Love
Hung over her enamour'd, and beheld
Beautie, which whether waking or asleep,
Shot forth peculiar Graces; then with voice
Milde, as when *Zephyrus* on *Flora* breathes,
Her hand soft touching, whisperd thus. Awake
My fairest, my espous'd, my latest found,
Heav'ns last best gift, my ever new delight,
Awake, the morning shines, and the fresh field
Calls us, we lose the prime, to mark how spring
Our tended Plants, how blows the Citron Grove,
What drops the Myrrhe, and what the balmie Reed,
How Nature paints her colours, how the Bee
Sits on the Bloom extracting liquid sweet.

Such whispering wak'd her, but with startl'd eye
On *Adam*, whom imbracing, thus she spake.

O Sole in whom my thoughts find all repose,
My Glorie, my Perfection, glad I see
Thy face, and Morn return'd, for I this Night,
Such night till this I never pass'd, have dream'd,
If dream'd, not as I oft am wont, of thee,
Works of day pass't, or morrows next designe,
But of offence and trouble, which my mind
Knew never till this irksom night; methought
Close at mine ear one call'd me forth to walk
With gentle voice, I thought it thine; it said,
Why sleepst thou *Eve?* now is the pleasant time,
The cool, the silent, save where silence yields
To the night-warbling Bird, that now awake
Tunes sweetest his love-labor'd song; now reignes
Full Orb'd the Moon, and with more pleasing light
Shadowie sets off the face of things; in vain,
If none regard; Heav'n wakes with all his eyes,

Whom to behold but thee, Natures desire,
In whose sight all things joy, with ravishment
Attracted by thy beauty still to gaze.
I rose as at thy call, but found thee not;
To find thee I directed then my walk;
And on, methought, alone I pass'd through ways
That brought me on a sudden to the Tree
Of interdicted Knowledge: fair it seem'd,
Much fairer to my Fancie then by day:
And as I wondring lookt, beside it stood
One shap'd and wing'd like one of those from Heav'n
By us oft seen; his dewie locks distill'd
Ambrosia; on that Tree he also gaz'd;
And O fair Plant, said he, with fruit surcharg'd,
Deigns none to ease thy load and taste thy sweet,
Nor God, nor Man; is Knowledge so despis'd?
Or envie, or what reserve forbids to taste?
Forbid who will, none shall from me withhold
Longer thy offerd good, why else set here?
This said he paus'd not, but with ventrous Arme
He pluckt, he tasted; mee damp horror chil'd
At such bold words voucht with a deed so bold:
But he thus overjoy'd, O Fruit Divine,
Sweet of thy self, but much more sweet thus cropt,
Forbidd'n here, it seems, as onely fit
For Gods, yet able to make Gods of Men:
And why not Gods of Men, since good, the more
Communicated, more abundant growes,
The Author not impair'd, but honourd more?
Here, happie Creature, fair Angelic *Eve*,
Partake thou also; happie though thou art,
Happier thou mayst be, worthier canst not be:
Taste this, and be henceforth among the Gods
Thy self a Goddess, not to Earth confind,
But somtimes in the Air, as wee, somtimes
Ascend to Heav'n, by merit thine, and see
What life the Gods live there, and such live thou.
So saying, he drew nigh, and to me held,
Even to my mouth of that same fruit held part
Which he had pluckt; the pleasant savourie smell

So quick'nd appetite, that I, methought,
Could not but taste. Forthwith up to the Clouds
With him I flew, and underneath beheld
The Earth outstretcht immense, a prospect wide
And various: wondring at my flight and change
To this high exaltation; suddenly
My Guide was gon, and I, me thought, sunk down,
And fell asleep; but O how glad I wak'd
To find this but a dream! Thus *Eve* her Night
Related, and thus *Adam* answerd sad.

　　Best Image of my self and dearer half,
The trouble of thy thoughts this night in sleep
Affects me equally; nor can I like
This uncouth dream, of evil sprung I fear;
Yet evil whence? in thee can harbour none,
Created pure. But know that in the Soule
Are many lesser Faculties that serve
Reason as chief; among these Fansie next
Her office holds; of all external things,
Which the five watchful Senses represent,
She forms Imaginations, Aerie shapes,
Which Reason joyning or disjoyning, frames
All what we affirm or what deny, and call
Our knowledge or opinion; then retires
Into her private Cell when Nature rests.
Oft in her absence mimic Fansie wakes
To imitate her; but misjoyning shapes,
Wilde work produces oft, and most in dreams,
Ill matching words and deeds long past or late.
Som such resemblances methinks I find
Of our last Eevnings talk, in this thy dream,
But with addition strange; yet be not sad.
Evil into the mind of God or Man
May come and go, so unapprov'd, and leave
No spot or blame behind: Which gives me hope
That what in sleep thou didst abhorr to dream,
Waking thou never wilt consent to do.
Be not disheart'nd then, nor cloud those looks
That wont to be more chearful and serene
Then when fair Morning first smiles on the World,

And let us to our fresh imployments rise
Among the Groves, the Fountains, and the Flours
That open now thir choicest bosom'd smells
Reservd from night, and kept for thee in store.

So cheard he his fair Spouse, and she was cheard,
But silently a gentle tear let fall
From either eye, and wip'd them with her haire;
Two other precious drops that ready stood,
Each in their chrystal sluce, he ere they fell
Kiss'd as the gracious signs of sweet remorse
And pious awe, that feard to have offended.

So all was cleard, and to the Field they haste.
But first from under shadie arborous roof,
Soon as they forth were come to open sight
Of day-spring, and the Sun, who scarce up risen
With wheels yet hov'ring o're the Ocean brim,
Shot paralel to the earth his dewie ray,
Discovering in wide Lantskip all the East
Of Paradise and *Edens* happie Plains,
Lowly they bow'd adoring, and began
Thir Orisons, each Morning duly paid
In various style, for neither various style
Nor holy rapture wanted they to praise
Thir Maker, in fit strains pronounc't or sung
Unmeditated, such prompt eloquence
Flowd from thir lips, in Prose or numerous Verse,
More tuneable then needed Lute or Harp
To add more sweetness, and they thus began.

These are thy glorious works Parent of good,
Almightie, thine this universal Frame,
Thus wondrous fair; thy self how wondrous then!
Unspeakable, who sitst above these Heavens
To us invisible or dimly seen
In these thy lowest works, yet these declare
Thy goodness beyond thought, and Power Divine:
Speak yee who best can tell, ye Sons of light,
Angels, for yee behold him, and with songs
And choral symphonies, Day without Night,
Circle his Throne rejoycing, yee in Heav'n,
On Earth joyn all ye Creatures to extoll

Him first, him last, him midst, and without end.
Fairest of Starrs, last in the train of Night,
If better thou belong not to the dawn,
Sure pledge of day, that crownst the smiling Morn
With thy bright Circlet, praise him in thy Spheare
While day arises, that sweet hour of Prime.
Thou Sun, of this great World both Eye and Soule,
Acknowledge him thy Greater, sound his praise
In thy eternal course, both when thou climb'st,
And when high Noon hast gaind, and when thou fallst.
Moon, that now meetst the orient Sun, now fli'st
With the fixt Starrs, fixt in thir Orb that flies,
And yee five other wandring Fires that move
In mystic Dance not without Song, resound
His praise, who out of Darkness call'd up Light.
Aire, and ye Elements the eldest birth
Of Natures Womb, that in quaternion run
Perpetual Circle, multiform; and mix
And nourish all things, let your ceasless change
Varie to our great Maker still new praise.
Ye Mists and Exhalations that now rise
From Hill or steaming Lake, duskie or grey,
Till the Sun paint your fleecie skirts with Gold,
In honour to the Worlds great Author rise,
Whether to deck with Clouds the uncolourd skie,
Or wet the thirstie Earth with falling showers,
Rising or falling still advance his praise.
His praise ye Winds, that from four Quarters blow,
Breathe soft or loud; and wave your tops, ye Pines,
With every Plant, in sign of Worship wave.
Fountains and yee, that warble, as ye flow,
Melodious murmurs, warbling tune his praise.
Joyn voices all ye living Souls, ye Birds,
That singing up to Heaven Gate ascend,
Bear on your wings and in your notes his praise;
Yee that in Waters glide, and yee that walk
The Earth, and stately tread, or lowly creep;
Witness if I be silent, Morn or Eeven,
To Hill, or Valley, Fountain, or fresh shade
Made vocal by my Song, and taught his praise.

Hail universal Lord, be bounteous still
To give us onely good; and if the night
Have gathered aught of evil or conceald,
Disperse it, as now light dispels the dark.
  So pray'd they innocent, and to thir thoughts
Firm peace recoverd soon and wonted calm.
On to thir mornings rural work they haste
Among sweet dewes and flours; where any row
Of Fruit-trees overwoodie reachd too farr
Thir pamperd boughes, and needed hands to check
Fruitless imbraces: or they led the Vine
To wed her Elm; she spous'd about him twines
Her mariageable arms, and with her brings
Her dowr th' adopted Clusters, to adorn
His barren leaves. Them thus imploid beheld
With pittie Heav'ns high King, and to him call'd
Raphael, the sociable Spirit, that deign'd
To travel with *Tobias*, and secur'd
His marriage with the seaventimes-wedded Maid.
  Raphael, said hee, thou hear'st what stir on Earth
Satan from Hell scap't through the darksom Gulf
Hath raisd in Paradise, and how disturbd
This night the human pair, how he designes
In them at once to ruin all mankind.
Go therefore, half this day as friend with friend
Converse with *Adam*, in what Bowre or shade
Thou find'st him from the heat of Noon retir'd,
To respit his day-labour with repast,
Or with repose; and such discourse bring on,
As may advise him of his happie state,
Happiness in his power left free to will,
Left to his own free Will, his Will though free,
Yet mutable; whence warne him to beware
He swerve not too secure: tell him withall
His danger, and from whom, what enemie
Late falln himself from Heaven, is plotting now
The fall of others from like state of bliss;
By violence, no, for that shall be withstood,
But by deceit and lies; this let him know,
Least wilfully transgressing he pretend

Surprisal, unadmonisht, unforewarnd.

So spake th' Eternal Father, and fulfilld
All Justice: nor delaid the winged Saint
After his charge receivd; but from among
Thousand Celestial Ardors, where he stood
Vaild with his gorgeous wings, up springing light
Flew through the midst of Heav'n; th' angelic Quires
On each hand parting, to his speed gave way
Through all th' Empyreal road; till at the gate
Of Heav'n arriv'd, the gate self-opend wide
On golden Hinges turning, as by work
Divine the sov'ran Architect had fram'd.

From hence, no cloud, or to obstruct his sight,
Starr interpos'd, however small he sees,
Not unconform to other shining Globes,
Earth and the Gard'n of God, with Cedars crownd
Above all Hills. As when by night the Glass
Of *Galileo*, less assur'd, observes
Imagind Lands and Regions in the Moon:
Or Pilot from amidst the *Cyclades*
Delos or *Samos* first appeering kenns
A cloudy spot. Down thither prone in flight
He speeds, and through the vast Ethereal Skie
Sailes between worlds and worlds, with steddie wing
Now on the polar windes, then with quick Fann
Winnows the buxom Air; till within soare
Of Towring Eagles, to all the Fowles he seems
A *Phœnix*, gaz'd by all, as that sole Bird
When to enshrine his reliques in the Sun's
Bright Temple, to *Ægyptian Theb's* he flies.
At once on th' Eastern cliff of Paradise
He lights, and to his proper shape returns
A Seraph wingd; six wings he wore, to shade
His lineaments Divine; the pair that clad
Each shoulder broad, came mantling o're his brest
With regal Ornament; the middle pair
Girt like a Starrie Zone his waste, and round
Skirted his loines and thighes with downie Gold
And colours dipt in Heav'n; the third his feet
Shaddowd from either heele with featherd maile

Skie-tinctur'd grain. Like *Maia's* son he stood,
And shook his Plumes, that Heav'nly fragrance filld
The circuit wide. Strait knew him all the Bands
Of Angels under watch; and to his state,
And to his message high in honour rise;
For on som message high they guesd him bound.
Thir glittering Tents he passd, and now is come
Into the blissful field, through Groves of Myrrhe,
And flouring Odours, Cassia, Nard, and Balme;
A Wilderness of sweets; for Nature here
Wantond as in her prime, and plaid at will
Her Virgin Fancies, pouring forth more sweet,
Wilde above rule or art; enormous bliss.
Him through the spicie Forrest onward com
Adam discernd, as in the dore he sat
Of his coole Bowre, while now the mounted Sun
Shot down direct his fervid Raies, to warme
Earths inmost womb, more warmth then *Adam* needs;
And *Eve* within, due at her hour prepar'd
For dinner savourie fruits, of taste to please
True appetite, and not disrelish thirst
Of nectarous draughts between, from milkie stream,
Berrie or Grape: to whom thus *Adam* call'd.

    Haste hither *Eve*, and worth thy sight behold
Eastward among those Trees, what glorious shape
Comes this way moving; seems another Morn
Ris'n on mid-noon; som great behest from Heav'n
To us perhaps he brings, and will voutsafe
This day to be our Guest. But goe with speed,
And what thy stores contain, bring forth and poure
Abundance, fit to honour and receive
Our Heav'nly stranger; well we may afford
Our givers thir own gifts, and large bestow
From large bestowd, where Nature multiplies
Her fertil growth, and by disburd'ning grows
More fruitful, which instructs us not to spare.

    To whom thus *Eve*. *Adam*, earths hallowd mould,
Of God inspir'd, small store will serve, where store,
All seasons, ripe for use hangs on the stalk;
Save what by frugal storing firmness gains

To nourish, and superfluous moist consumes:
But I will haste and from each bough and break,
Each Plant and juciest Gourd will pluck such choice
To entertain our Angel guest, as hee
Beholding shall confess that here on Earth
God hath dispenst his bounties as in Heav'n.

So saying, with dispatchful looks in haste
She turns, on hospitable thoughts intent
What choice to chuse for delicacie best,
What order, so contriv'd as not to mix
Tastes, not well joynd, inelegant, but bring
Taste after taste upheld with kindliest change,
Bestirs her then, and from each tender stalk
Whatever Earth all-bearing Mother yields
In *India* East or West, or middle shoare
In *Pontus* or the *Punic* Coast, or where
Alcinous reign'd, fruit of all kindes, in coate,
Rough, or smooth rin'd, or bearded husk, or shell
She gathers, Tribute large, and on the board
Heaps with unsparing hand; for drink the Grape
She crushes, inoffensive moust, and meathes
From many a berrie, and from sweet kernels prest
She tempers dulcet creams, nor these to hold
Wants her fit vessels pure, then strews the ground
With Rose and Odours from the shrub unfum'd.
Mean while our Primitivegreat Sire, to meet
His god-like Guest, walks forth, without more train
Accompani'd then with his own compleat
Perfections, in himself was all his state,
More solemn then the tedious pomp that waits
On Princes, when thir rich Retinue long
Of Horses led, and Grooms besmeard with Gold
Dazles the croud, and sets them all agape.
Neerer his presence *Adam* though not awd,
Yet with submiss approach and reverence meek,
As to a superior Nature, bowing low,

    Thus said. Native of Heav'n, for other place
None can then Heav'n such glorious shape contain;
Since by descending from the Thrones above,
Those happie places thou hast deignd a while

To want, and honour these, voutsafe with us
Two onely, who yet by sov'ran gift possess
This spacious ground, in yonder shadie Bowre
To rest, and what the Garden choicest bears
To sit and taste, till this meridian heat
Be over, and the Sun more coole decline.
    Whom thus the Angelic Vertue answerd milde.
Adam, I therefore came, nor art thou such
Created, or such place hast here to dwell,
As may not oft invite, though Spirits of Heav'n
To visit thee; lead on then where thy Bowre
Oreshades; for these mid-hours, till Eevning rise
I have at will. So to the Silvan Lodge
They came, that like *Pomona's* Arbour smil'd
With flourets deck't and fragrant smells; but *Eve*
Undeckt, save with her self more lovely fair
Then Wood-Nymph, or the fairest Goddess feign'd
Of three that in Mount *Ida* naked strove,
Stood to entertain her guest from Heav'n; no vaile
Shee needed, Vertue-proof, no thought infirme
Alterd her cheek. On whom the Angel *Haile*
Bestowd, the holy salutation us'd
Long after to blest *Marie*, second *Eve*.
    Haile Mother of Mankind, whose fruitful Womb
Shall fill the World more numerous with thy Sons
Then with these various fruits the Trees of God
Have heap'd this Table. Rais'd of grassie terf
Thir Table was, and mossie seats had round,
And on her ample Square from side to side
All *Autumn* pil'd, though *Spring* and *Autumn* here
Danc'd hand in hand. A while discourse they hold;
No fear lest Dinner coole; when thus began
Our Authour. Heav'nly stranger, please to taste
These bounties which our Nourisher, from whom
All perfet good unmeasur'd out, descends,
To us for food and for delight hath caus'd
The Earth to yield; unsavourie food perhaps
To spiritual Natures; only this I know,
That one Celestial Father gives to all.
    To whom the Angel. Therefore what he gives

(Whose praise be ever sung) to man in part
Spiritual, may of purest Spirits be found
No ingrateful food: and food alike those pure
Intelligential substances require
As doth your Rational; and both contain
Within them every lower facultie
Of sense, whereby they hear, see, smell, touch, taste,
Tasting concoct, digest, assimilate,
And corporeal to incorporeal turn.
For know, whatever was created, needs
To be sustaind and fed; of Elements
The grosser feeds the purer, Earth the Sea,
Earth and the Sea feed Air, the Air those Fires
Ethereal, and as lowest first the Moon;
Whence in her visage round those spots, unpurg'd
Vapours not yet into her substance turn'd.
Nor doth the Moon no nourishment exhale
From her moist Continent to higher Orbes.
The Sun that light imparts to all, receives
From all his alimental recompence
In humid exhalations, and at Even
Sups with the Ocean: though in Heav'n the Trees
Of life ambrosial frutage bear, and vines
Yield Nectar, though from off the boughs each Morn
We brush mellifluous Dewes, and find the ground
Cover'd with pearly grain: yet God hath here
Varied his bounty so with new delights,
As may compare with Heaven; and to taste
Think not I shall be nice. So down they sat,
And to thir viands fell, nor seemingly
The Angel, nor in mist, the common gloss
Of Theologians, but with keen dispatch
Of real hunger, and concoctive heate
To transubstantiate; what redounds, transpires
Through Spirits with ease; nor wonder; if by fire
Of sooty coal the Empiric Alchimist
Can turn, or holds it possible to turn
Metals of drossiest Ore to perfet Gold
As from the Mine. Mean while at Table *Eve*
Ministerd naked, and thir flowing cups

With pleasant liquors crown'd : O innocence
Deserving Paradise! if ever, then,
Then had the Sons of God excuse to have bin
Enamour'd at that sight; but in those hearts
Love unlibidinous reign'd, nor jealousie
Was understood, the injur'd Lovers Hell.

Thus when with meats and drinks they had suffic'd,
Not burd'nd Nature, sudden mind arose
In *Adam*, not to let th' occasion pass
Given him by this great Conference to know
Of things above his World, and of thir being
Who dwell in Heav'n, whose excellence he saw
Transcend his own so farr, whose radiant forms
Divine effulgence, whose high Power so far
Exceeded human, and his wary speech
Thus to th' Empyreal Minister he fram'd.

Inhabitant with God, now know I well
Thy favour, in this honour done to man,
Under whose lowly roof thou hast voutsaf't
To enter, and these earthly fruits to taste,
Food not of Angels, yet accepted so,
As that more willingly thou couldst not seem
At Heav'ns high feasts to have fed : yet what compare?

To whom the winged Hierarch repli'd.
O *Adam*, one Almightie is, from whom
All things proceed, and up to him return,
If not deprav'd from good, created all
Such to perfection, one first matter all,
Indu'd with various forms, various degrees
Of substance, and in things that live, of life;
But more refin'd, more spiritous, and pure,
As neerer to him plac't or neerer tending
Each in thir several active Sphears assignd,
Till body up to spirit work, in bounds
Proportiond to each kind. So from the root
Springs lighter the green stalk, from thence the leaves
More aerie, last the bright consummate floure
Spirits odorous breathes : flours and thir fruit
Mans nourishment, by gradual scale sublim'd
To vital Spirits aspire, to animal,

To intellectual, give both life and sense,
Fansie and understanding, whence the Soule
Reason receives, and reason is her being,
Discursive, or Intuitive; discourse
Is oftest yours, the latter most is ours,
Differing but in degree, of kind the same.
Wonder not then, what God for you saw good
If I refuse not, but convert, as you,
To proper substance; time may come when men
With Angels may participate, and find
No inconvenient Diet, nor too light Fare:
And from these corporal nutriments perhaps
Your bodies may at last turn all to Spirit,
Improv'd by tract of time, and wingd ascend
Ethereal, as wee, or may at choice
Here or in Heav'nly Paradises dwell;
If ye be found obedient, and retain
Unalterably firm his love entire
Whose progenie you are. Mean while enjoy
Your fill what happiness this happie state
Can comprehend, incapable of more.
　　To whom the Patriarch of mankind repli'd.
O favourable spirit, propitious guest,
Well hast thou taught the way that might direct
Our knowledge, and the scale of Nature set
From center to circumference, whereon
In contemplation of created things
By steps we may ascend to God. But say,
What meant that caution joind, *if ye be found
Obedient?* can wee want obedience then
To him, or possibly his love desert
Who formd us from the dust, and plac'd us here
Full to the utmost measure of what bliss
Human desires can seek or apprehend?
　　To whom the Angel. Son of Heav'n and Earth,
Attend: That thou art happie, owe to God;
That thou continu'st such, owe to thy self,
That is, to thy obedience; therein stand.
This was that caution giv'n thee; be advis'd.
God made thee perfet, not immutable;

And good he made thee, but to persevere
He left it in thy power, ordaind thy will
By nature free, not over-rul'd by Fate
Inextricable, or strict necessity;
Our voluntarie service he requires,
Not our necessitated, such with him
Findes no acceptance, nor can find, for how
Can hearts, not free, be tri'd whether they serve
Willing or no, who will but what they must
By Destinie, and can no other choose?
My self and all th' Angelic Host that stand
In sight of God enthron'd, our happie state
Hold, as you yours, while our obedience holds;
On other surety none; freely we serve.
Because wee freely love, as in our will
To love or not; in this we stand or fall:
And som are fall'n, to disobedience fall'n,
And so from Heav'n to deepest Hell; O fall
From what high state of bliss into what woe!

    To whom our great Progenitor. Thy words
Attentive, and with more delighted eare
Divine instructer, I have heard, then when
Cherubic Songs by night from neighbouring Hills
Aereal Music send: nor knew I not
To be both will and deed created free;
Yet that we never shall forget to love
Our maker, and obey him whose command
Single, is yet so just, my constant thoughts
Assur'd me and still assure: though what thou tellst
Hath past in Heav'n, som doubt within me move,
But more desire to hear, if thou consent,
The full relation, which must needs be strange,
Worthy of Sacred silence to be heard;
And we have yet large day, for scarce the Sun
Hath finisht half his journey, and scarce begins
His other half in the great Zone of Heav'n.

    Thus *Adam* made request, and *Raphael*
After short pause assenting, thus began.

    High matter thou injoinst me, O prime of men,
Sad task and hard, for how shall I relate

To human sense th' invisible exploits
Of warring Spirits; how without remorse
The ruin of so many glorious once
And perfet while they stood; how last unfould
The secrets of another world, perhaps
Not lawful to reveal? yet for thy good
This is dispenc't, and what surmounts the reach
Of human sense, I shall delineate so,
By lik'ning spiritual to corporal forms,
As may express them best, though what if Earth
Be but the shaddow of Heav'n, and things therein
Each to other like, more then on earth is thought?

    As yet this world was not, and *Chaos* wilde
Reignd where these Heav'ns now rowl, where Earth now rests
Upon her Center pois'd, when on a day
(For Time, though in Eternitie, appli'd
To motion, measures all things durable
By present, past, and future) on such day
As Heav'ns great Year brings forth, th' Empyreal Host
Of Angels by Imperial summons call'd,
Innumerable before th' Almighties Throne
Forthwith from all the ends of Heav'n appeerd
Under thir Hierarchs in orders bright
Ten thousand thousand Ensignes high advanc'd,
Standards, and Gonfalons twixt Van and Reare
Streame in the Aire, and for distinction serve
Of Hierarchies, of Orders, and Degrees;
Or in thir glittering Tissues bear imblaz'd
Holy Memorials, acts of Zeale and Love
Recorded eminent. Thus when in Orbes
Of circuit inexpressible they stood,
Orb within Orb, the Father infinite,
By whom in bliss imbosom'd sat the Son,
Amidst as from a flaming Mount, whose top
Brightness had made invisible, thus spake.

    Hear, all ye Angels, Progenie of Light,
Thrones, Dominations, Princedoms, Vertues, Powers,
Hear my Decree, which unrevok't shall stand.
This day I have begot whom I declare
My onely Son, and on this holy Hill

Him have anointed, whom ye now behold
At my right hand; your Head I him appoint;
And by my Self have sworn to him shall bow
All knees in Heav'n, and shall confess him Lord:
Under his great Vice-gerent Reign abide
United as one individual Soule
For ever happie; him who disobeyes
Mee disobeyes, breaks union, and that day
Cast out from God and blessed vision, falls
Into utter darkness, deep ingulft, his place
Ordaind without redemption, without end.

So spake th' Omnipotent, and with his words
All seemd well pleas'd, all seem'd, but were not all.
That day, as other solemn dayes, they spent
In song and dance about the sacred Hill,
Mystical dance, which yonder starrie Spheare
Of Planets and of fixt in all her Wheeles
Resembles nearest, mazes intricate,
Eccentric, intervolv'd, yet regular
Then most, when most irregular they seem,
And in thir motions harmonie Divine
So smooths her charming tones, that Gods own ear
Listens delighted. Eevning now approach'd
(For we have also our Eevning and our Morn,
We ours for change delectable, not need)
Forthwith from dance to sweet repast they turn
Desirous, all in Circles as they stood,
Tables are set, and on a sudden pil'd
With Angels Food, and rubied Nectar flows:
In Pearl, in Diamond, and massie Gold,
Fruit of delicious Vines, the growth of Heav'n.
On flours repos'd, and with fresh flourets crownd,
They eate, they drink, and in communion sweet
Quaff immortalitie and joy, secure
Of surfet where full measure onely bounds
Excess, before th' all bounteous King, who showrd
With copious hand, rejoycing in thir joy.
Now when ambrosial Night with Clouds exhal'd
From that high mount of God, whence light and shade
Spring both, the face of brightest Heav'n had changd

To grateful Twilight (for Night comes not there
In darker veile) and roseat Dews dispos'd
All but the unsleeping eyes of God to rest,
Wide over all the Plain, and wider farr
Then all this globous Earth in Plain out spred,
(Such are the Courts of God) Th' Angelic throng
Disperst in Bands and Files thir Camp extend
By living Streams among the Trees of Life,
Pavilions numberless, and sudden reard,
Celestial Tabernacles, where they slept
Fannd with coole Winds, save those who in thir course
Melodious Hymns about the sovran Throne
Alternate all night long: but not so wak'd
Satan, so call him now, his former name
Is heard no more in Heav'n; he of the first,
If not the first Arch-Angel, great in Power,
In favour and præeminence, yet fraught
With envie against the Son of God, that day
Honourd by his great Father, and proclaimd
Messiah King anointed, could not beare
Through pride that sight, and thought himself impaird.
Deep malice thence conceiving and disdain,
Soon as midnight brought on the duskie houre
Friendliest to sleep and silence, he resolv'd
With all his Legions to dislodge, and leave
Unworshipt, unobey'd the Throne supream
Contemptuous, and his next subordinate
Awak'ning, thus to him in secret spake.

    Sleepst thou, Companion dear, what sleep can close
Thy eye-lids? and remembrest what Decree
Of yesterday, so late hath past the lips
Of Heav'ns Almightie. Thou to me thy thoughts
Wast wont, I mine to thee was wont to impart;
Both waking we were one; how then can now
Thy sleep dissent? new Laws thou seest impos'd;
New Laws from him who reigns, new minds may raise
In us who serve, new Counsels, to debate
What doubtful may ensue, more in this place
To utter is not safe. Assemble thou
Of all those Myriads which we lead the chief;

Tell them that by command, ere yet dim Night
Her shadowie Cloud withdraws, I am to haste,
And all who under me thir Banners wave,
Homeward with flying march where we possess
The Quarters of the North, there to prepare
Fit entertainment to receive our King
The great *Messiah*, and his new commands,
Who speedily through all the Hierarchies
Intends to pass triumphant, and give Laws.
   So spake the false Arch-Angel, and infus'd
Bad influence into th'unwarie brest
Of his Associate; hee together calls,
Or several one by one, the Regent Powers,
Under him Regent, tells, as he was taught,
That the most High commanding, now ere Night,
Now ere dim Night had disincumberd Heav'n,
The great Hierarchal Standard was to move;
Tells the suggested cause, and casts between
Ambiguous words and jealousies, to sound
Or taint integritie; but all obey'd
The wonted signal, and superior voice
Of thir great Potentate; for great indeed
His name, and high was his degree in Heav'n;
His count'nance, as the Morning Starr that guides
The starrie flock, allur'd them, and with lyes
Drew after him the third part of Heav'ns Host:
Mean while th' Eternal eye, whose sight discernes
Abstrusest thoughts, from forth his holy Mount
And from within the golden Lamps that burne
Nightly before him, saw without thir light
Rebellion rising, saw in whom, how spred
Among the sons of Morn, what multitudes
Were banded to oppose his high Decree;
And smiling to his onely Son thus said.
   Son, thou in whom my glory I behold
In full resplendence, Heir of all my might,
Neerly it now concernes us to be sure
Of our Omnipotence, and with what Arms
We mean to hold what anciently we claim
Of Deitie or Empire, such a foe

Is rising, who intends to erect his Throne
Equal to ours, throughout the spacious North;
Nor so content, hath in his thought to try
In battel, what our Power is, or our right.
Let us advise, and to this hazard draw
With speed what force is left, and all imploy
In our defence, lest unawares we lose
This our high place, our Sanctuarie, our Hill.

  To whom the Son with calm aspect and cleer
Light'ning Divine, ineffable, serene,
Made answer. Mightie Father, thou thy foes
Justly hast in derision, and secure
Laugh'st at thir vain designes and tumults vain,
Matter to mee of Glory, whom their hate
Illustrates, when they see all Regal Power
Giv'n me to quell thir pride, and in event
Know whether I be dextrous to subdue
Thy Rebels, or be found the worst in Heav'n.

  So spake the Son, but *Satan* with his Powers
Farr was advanc't on winged speed, an Host
Innumerable as the Starrs of Night,
Or Starrs of Morning, Dew-drops, which the Sun
Impearls on every leaf and every flouer.
Regions they pass'd, the mightie Regencies
Of Seraphim and Potentates and Thrones
In thir triple Degrees, Regions to which
All thy Dominion, *Adam,* is no more
Then what this Garden is to all the Earth,
And all the Sea, from one entire globose
Stretcht into Longitude; which having pass'd
At length into the limits of the North
They came, and *Satan* to his Royal seat
High on a Hill, far blazing, as a Mount
Rais'd on a Mount, with Pyramids and Towrs
From Diamond Quarries hew'n, and Rocks of Gold,
The Palace of great *Lucifer,* (so call
That Structure in the Dialect of men
Interpreted) which not long after, he
Affecting all equality with God,
In imitation of that Mount whereon

Messiah was declar'd in sight of Heav'n,
The Mountain of the Congregation call'd;
For thither he assembl'd all his Train,
Pretending so commanded to consult
About the great reception of thir King,
Thither to come, and with calumnious Art
Of counterfeted truth thus held thir ears.

    Thrones, Dominations, Princedomes, Vertues, Powers,
If these magnific Titles yet remain
Not meerly titular, since by Decree
Another now hath to himself ingross't
All Power, and us eclipst under the name
Of King anointed, for whom all this haste
Of midnight march, and hurried meeting here,
This onely to consult how we may best
With what may be devis'd of honours new
Receive him coming to receive from us
Knee-tribute yet unpaid, prostration vile,
Too much to one, but double how endur'd,
To one and to his image now proclaim'd?
But what if better counsels might erect
Our minds and teach us to cast off this Yoke?
Will ye submit your necks, and chuse to bend
The supple knee? ye will not, if I trust
To know ye right, or if ye know your selves
Natives and Sons of Heav'n possest before
By none, and if not equal all, yet free,
Equally free; for Orders and Degrees
Jarr not with liberty, but well consist.
Who can in reason then or right assume
Monarchie over such as live by right
His equals, if in power and splendor less,
In freedome equal? or can introduce
Law and Edict on us, who without law
Erre not, much less for this to be our Lord,
And look for adoration to th' abuse
Of those Imperial Titles which assert
Our being ordain'd to govern, not to serve?

    Thus farr his bold discourse without controule
Had audience, when among the Seraphim

Abdiel, then whom none with more zeale ador'd
The Deitie, and divine commands obei'd,
Stood up, and in a flame of zeale severe
The current of his fury thus oppos'd.
   O argument blasphemous, false and proud!
Words which no eare ever to hear in Heav'n
Expected, least of all from thee, ingrate
In place thy self so high above thy Peeres.
Canst thou with impious obloquie condemne
The just Decree of God, pronounc't and sworn,
That to his only Son by right endu'd
With Regal Scepter, every Soule in Heav'n
Shall bend the knee, and in that honour due
Confess him rightful King? unjust thou saist
Flatly unjust, to binde with Laws the free,
And equal over equals to let Reigne,
One over all with unsucceeded power.
Shalt thou give Law to God, shalt thou dispute
With him the points of libertie, who made
Thee what thou art, and formd the Pow'rs of Heav'n
Such as he pleasd, and circumscrib'd thir being?
Yet by experience taught we know how good,
And of our good, and of our dignitie
How provident he is, how farr from thought
To make us less, bent rather to exalt
Our happie state under one Head more neer
United. But to grant it thee unjust,
That equal over equals Monarch Reigne:
Thy self though great and glorious dost thou count,
Or all Angelic Nature joind in one,
Equal to him begotten Son, by whom
As by his Word the mighty Father made
All things, ev'n thee, and all the Spirits of Heav'n
By him created in thir bright degrees,
Crownd them with Glory, and to thir Glory nam'd
Thrones, Dominations, Princedoms, Vertues, Powers,
Essential Powers, nor by his Reign obscur'd,
But more illustrious made, since he the Head
One of our number thus reduc't becomes,
His Laws our Laws, all honour to him done

Returns our own. Cease then this impious rage,
And tempt not these; but hast'n to appease
Th' incensed Father, and th' incensed Son,
While Pardon may be found in time besought.

So spake the fervent Angel, but his zeale
None seconded, as out of season judg'd,
Or singular and rash, whereat rejoic'd
Th' Apostat, and more haughty thus repli'd.
That we were formd then saist thou? and the work
Of secondarie hands, by task transferd
From Father to his Son? strange point and new!
Doctrin which we would know whence learnt: who saw
When this creation was? rememberst thou
Thy making, while the Maker gave thee being?
We know no time when we were not as now;
Know none before us, self-begot, self-rais'd
By our own quick'ning power, when fatal course
Had circl'd his full Orbe, the birth mature
Of this our native Heav'n, Ethereal Sons.
Our puissance is our own, our own right hand
Shall teach us highest deeds, by proof to try
Who is our equal: then thou shalt behold
Whether by supplication we intend
Address, and to begirt th' Almighty Throne
Beseeching or besieging. This report,
These tidings carrie to th' anointed King;
And fly, ere evil intercept thy flight.

He said, and as the sound of waters deep
Hoarce murmur echo'd to his words applause
Through the infinite Host, nor less for that
The flaming Seraph fearless, though alone
Encompass'd round with foes, thus answerd bold.

O alienate from God, O spirit accurst,
Forsak'n of all good; I see thy fall
Determind, and thy hapless crew involv'd
In this perfidious fraud, contagion spred
Both of thy crime and punishment: henceforth
No more be troubl'd how to quit the yoke
Of Gods *Messiah;* those indulgent Laws
Will not be now voutsaf't, other Decrees

M.

Against thee are gon forth without recall;
That Golden Scepter which thou didst reject
Is now an Iron Rod to bruise and breake
Thy disobedience. Well thou didst advise,
Yet not for thy advise or threats I fly
These wicked Tents devoted, least the wrauth
Impendent, raging into sudden flame
Distinguish not: for soon expect to feel
His Thunder on thy head, devouring fire.
Then who created thee lamenting learne,
When who can uncreate thee thou shalt know.
  So spake the Seraph *Abdiel* faithful found,
Among the faithless, faithful only hee;
Among innumerable false, unmov'd,
Unshak'n, unseduc'd, unterrifi'd
His Loyaltie he kept, his Love, his Zeale;
Nor number, nor example with him wrought
To swerve from truth, or change his constant mind
Though single. From amidst them forth he passd,
Long way through hostile scorn, which he susteind
Superior, nor of violence fear'd aught;
And with retorted scorn his back he turn'd
On those proud Towrs to swift destruction doom'd.

BOOK VI

THE ARGUMENT

RAPHAEL *continues to relate how* Michael *and* Gabriel *were
sent forth to battel against* Satan *and his Angels. The first
Fight describ'd:* Satan *and his Powers retire under Night: He
calls a Councel, invents devilish Engines, which in the second
dayes Fight put* Michael *and his Angels to some disorder; but
they at length pulling up Mountains overwhelm'd both the
force and Machins of* Satan*: Yet the Tumult not so ending,
God on the Third day sends* Messiah *his Son, for whom he had
reserv'd the glory of that Victory: Hee in the Power of his
Father coming to the place, and causing all his Legions to*

stand still on either side, with his Chariot and Thunder driving
into the midst of his Enemies, pursues them unable to resist to-
wards the wall of Heaven; which opening, they leap down with
horrour and confusion into the place of punishment prepar'd for
them in the Deep: Messiah returns with triumph to his Father.

ALL night the dreadless Angel unpursu'd
Through Heav'ns wide Champain held his way, till Morn,
Wak't by the circling Hours, with rosie hand
Unbarr'd the gates of Light. There is a Cave
Within the Mount of God, fast by his Throne,
Where light and darkness in perpetual round
Lodge and dislodge by turns, which makes through Heav'n
Grateful vicissitude, like Day and Night;
Light issues forth, and at the other dore
Obsequious darkness enters, till her houre
To veile the Heav'n, though darkness there might well
Seem twilight here; and now went forth the Morn
Such as in highest Heav'n, arrayd in Gold
Empyreal, from before her vanisht Night,
Shot through with orient Beams: when all the Plain
Coverd with thick embatteld Squadrons bright,
Chariots and flaming Armes, and fierie Steeds
Reflecting blaze on blaze, first met his view:
Warr he perceav'd, warr in procinct, and found
Already known what he for news had thought
To have reported: gladly then he mixt
Among those friendly Powers who him receav'd
With joy and acclamations loud, that one
That of so many Myriads fall'n, yet one
Returnd not lost: On to the sacred hill
They led him high applauded, and present
Before the seat supream; from whence a voice
From midst a Golden Cloud thus milde was heard.
  Servant of God, well done, well hast thou fought
The better fight, who single hast maintaind
Against revolted multitudes the Cause
Of Truth, in word mightier than they in Armes;
And for the testimonie of Truth hast born
Universal reproach, far worse to beare

Then violence: for this was all thy care
To stand approv'd in sight of God, though Worlds
Judg'd thee perverse: the easier conquest now
Remains thee, aided by this host of friends,
Back on thy foes more glorious to return
Then scornd thou didst depart, and to subdue
By force, who reason for thir Law refuse,
Right reason for thir Law, and for thir King
Messiah, who by right of merit Reigns.
Go *Michael* of Celestial Armies Prince,
And thou in Military prowess next
Gabriel, lead forth to Battel these my Sons
Invincible, lead forth my armed Saints
By Thousands and by Millions rang'd for fight;
Equal in number to that Godless crew
Rebellious, them with Fire and hostile Arms
Fearless assault, and to the brow of Heav'n
Pursuing drive them out from God and bliss,
Into thir place of punishment, the Gulf
Of *Tartarus*, which ready opens wide
His fiery *Chaos* to receave thir fall.
　　So spake the Sovran voice, and Clouds began
To darken all the Hill, and smoak to rowl
In duskie wreathes, reluctant flames, the signe
Of wrauth awak't: nor with less dread the loud
Ethereal Trumpet from on high gan blow:
At which command the Powers Militant,
That stood for Heav'n, in mighty Quadrate joyn'd
Of union irresistible, mov'd on
In silence thir bright Legions, to the sound
Of instrumental Harmonie that breath'd
Heroic Ardor to advent'rous deeds
Under thir God-like Leaders, in the Cause
Of God and his *Messiah*. On they move
Indissolubly firm; nor obvious Hill,
Nor streit'ning Vale, nor Wood, nor Stream divides
Thir perfet ranks; for high above the ground
Thir march was, and the passive Air upbore
Thir nimble tread; as when the total kind
Of Birds in orderly array on wing

Came summond over *Eden* to receive
Thir names of thee; so over many a tract
Of Heav'n they march'd, and many a Province wide
Tenfold the length of this terrene: at last
Farr in th' Horizon to the North appeer'd
From skirt to skirt a fierie Region, stretcht
In battailous aspect, and neerer view
Bristl'd with upright beams innumerable
Of rigid Spears, and Helmets throng'd, and Shields
Various, with boastful Argument portraid,
The banded Powers of *Satan* hasting on
With furious expedition; for they weend
That self same day by fight, or by surprize
To win the Mount of God, and on his Throne
To set the envier of his State, the proud
Aspirer, but thir thoughts prov'd fond and vain
In the mid way: though strange to us it seemd
At first, that Angel should with Angel warr,
And in fierce hosting meet, who wont to meet
So oft in Festivals of joy and love
Unanimous, as sons of one great Sire
Hymning th' Eternal Father: but the shout
Of Battel now began, and rushing sound
Of onset ended soon each milder thought.
High in the midst exalted as a God
Th' Apostat in his Sun-bright Chariot sate
Idol of Majestie Divine, enclos'd
With Flaming Cherubim, and golden Shields;
Then lighted from his gorgeous Throne, for now
'Twixt Host and Host but narrow space was left,
A dreadful intervall and Front to Front
Presented stood in terrible array
Of hideous length: before the cloudie Van,
On the rough edge of battel ere it joyn'd,
Satan with vast and haughtie strides advanc't,
Came towring, armd in Adamant and Gold;
Abdiel that sight endur'd not, where he stood
Among the mightiest, bent on highest deeds,
And thus his own undaunted heart explores.
    O Heav'n! that such resemblance of the Highest

Should yet remain, where faith and realtie
Remain not; wherefore should not strength and might
There fail where Vertue fails, or weakest prove
Where boldest; though to sight unconquerable?
His puissance, trusting in th' Almightie's aide,
I mean to try, whose Reason I have tri'd
Unsound and false; nor is it aught but just,
That he who in debate of Truth hath won,
Should win in Arms, in both disputes alike
Victor; though brutish that contest and foule,
When Reason hath to deal with force, yet so
Most reason is that Reason overcome.
    So pondering, and from his armed Peers
Forth stepping opposite, half way he met
His daring foe, at this prevention more
Incens't, and thus securely him defi'd.
    Proud, art thou met? thy hope was to have reacht
The highth of thy aspiring unoppos'd,
The Throne of God unguarded, and his side
Abandond at the terror of thy Power
Or potent tongue; fool, not to think how vain
Against th' Omnipotent to rise in Arms;
Who out of smallest things could without end
Have rais'd incessant Armies to defeat
Thy folly; or with solitarie hand
Reaching beyond all limit, at one blow
Unaided could have finisht thee, and whelmd
Thy Legions under darkness; but thou seest
All are not of thy Train; there be who Faith
Prefer, and Pietie to God, though then
To thee not visible, when I alone
Seemed in thy World erroneous to dissent
From all: my Sect thou seest, now learn too late
How few somtimes may know, when thousands err.
    Whom the grand foe with scornful eye askance
Thus answerd. Ill for thee, but in wisht houre
Of my revenge, first sought for thou returnst
From flight, seditious Angel, to receave
Thy merited reward, the first assay
Of this right hand provok't, since first that tongue

Inspir'd with contradiction durst oppose
A third part of the Gods, in Synod met
Thir Deities to assert, who while they feel
Vigour Divine within them, can allow
Omnipotence to none. But well thou comst
Before thy fellows, ambitious to win
From me som Plume, that thy success may show
Destruction to the rest : this pause between
(Unanswerd least thou boast) to let thee know;
At first I thought that Libertie and Heav'n
To heav'nly Soules had bin all one; but now
I see that most through sloth had rather serve,
Ministring Spirits, traind up in Feast and Song;
Such hast thou arm'd, the Minstrelsie of Heav'n,
Servilitie with freedom to contend,
As both thir deeds compar'd this day shall prove.

To whom in brief thus *Abdiel* stern repli'd.
Apostat, still thou errst, nor end wilt find
Of erring, from the path of truth remote :
Unjustly thou deprav'st it with the name
Of *Servitude* to serve whom God ordains,
Or Nature; God and Nature bid the same,
When he who rules is worthiest, and excells
Them whom he governs. This is servitude,
To serve th' unwise, or him who hath rebelld
Against his worthier, as thine now serve thee,
Thy self not free, but to thy self enthrall'd;
Yet leudly dar'st our ministring upbraid.
Reign thou in Hell thy Kingdom, let mee serve
In Heav'n God ever blest, and his Divine
Behests obey, worthiest to be obey'd,
Yet Chains in Hell, not Realms expect : mean while
From mee returnd, as erst thou saidst, from flight,
This greeting on thy impious Crest receive.

So saying, a noble stroke he lifted high,
Which hung not, but so swift with tempest fell
On the proud Crest of *Satan*, that no sight,
Nor motion of swift thought, less could his Shield
Such ruin intercept : ten paces huge
He back recoild; the tenth on bended knee

His massie Spear upstaid; as if on Earth
Winds under ground or waters forcing way
Sidelong, had push't a Mountain from his seat
Half sunk with all his Pines. Amazement seis'd
The Rebel Thrones, but greater rage to see
Thus foil'd thir mightiest, ours joy filld, and shout,
Presage of Victorie and fierce desire
Of Battel: whereat *Michael* bid sound
Th' Arch-angel trumpet; through the vast of Heav'n
It sounded, and the faithful Armies rung
Hosanna to the Highest: nor stood at gaze
Th' adverse Legions, nor less hideous joyn'd
The horrid shock: now storming furie rose,
And clamour such as heard in Heav'n till now
Was never, Arms on Armour clashing bray'd
Horrible discord, and the madding Wheeles
Of brazen Chariots rag'd; dire was the noise
Of conflict; over head the dismal hiss
Of fiery Darts in flaming volies flew,
And flying vaulted either Host with fire.
So under fierie Cope together rush'd
Both Battels maine, with ruinous assault
And inextinguishable rage; all Heav'n
Resounded, and had Earth bin then, all Earth
Had to her Center shook. What wonder? when
Millions of fierce encountring Angels fought
On either side, the least of whom could weild
These Elements, and arm him with the force
Of all thir Regions: how much more of Power
Armie against Armie numberless to raise
Dreadful combustion warring, and disturb,
Though not destroy, thir happie Native seat;
Had not th' Eternal King Omnipotent
From his strong hold of Heav'n high over-rul'd
And limited thir might; though numberd such
As each divided Legion might have seemd
A numerous Host, in strength each armed hand
A Legion; led in fight, yet Leader seemd
Each Warriour single as in Chief, expert
When to advance, or stand, or turn the sway

Of Battel, open when, and when to close
The ridges of grim Warr; no thought of flight,
None of retreat, no unbecoming deed
That argu'd fear; each on himself reli'd,
As onely in his arm the moment lay
Of victorie; deeds of eternal fame
Were don, but infinite: for wide was spred
That Warr and various; somtimes on firm ground
A standing fight, then soaring on main wing
Tormented all the Air; all Air seemd then
Conflicting Fire: long time in even scale
The Battel hung; till *Satan*, who that day
Prodigious power had shewn, and met in Armes
No equal, raunging through the dire attack
Of fighting Seraphim confus'd, at length
Saw where the Sword of *Michael* smote, and fell'd
Squadrons at once, with huge two-handed sway
Brandisht aloft the horrid edge came down
Wide wasting; such destruction to withstand
He hasted, and oppos'd the rockie Orb
Of tenfold Adamant, his ample Shield
A vast circumference: At his approach
The great Arch-Angel from his warlike toile
Surceas'd, and glad as hoping here to end
Intestine War in Heav'n, the arch foe subdu'd
Or Captive drag'd in Chains, with hostile frown
And visage all enflam'd first thus began.

 Author of evil, unknown till thy revolt,
Unnam'd in Heav'n, now plenteous, as thou seest
These Acts of hateful strife, hateful to all,
Though heaviest by just measure on thy self
And thy adherents: how hast thou disturb'd
Heav'ns blessed peace, and into Nature brought
Miserie, uncreated till the crime
Of thy Rebellion? how hast thou instill'd
Thy malice into thousands, once upright
And faithful, now prov'd false. But think not here
To trouble Holy Rest; Heav'n casts thee out
From all her Confines. Heav'n the seat of bliss
Brooks not the works of violence and Warr.

Hence then, and evil go with thee along
Thy ofspring, to the place of evil, Hell,
Thou and thy wicked crew; there mingle broiles,
Ere this avenging Sword begin thy doome,
Or som more sudden vengeance wing'd from God
Precipitate thee with augmented paine.

So spake the Prince of Angels; to whom thus
The Adversarie. Nor think thou with wind
Of airie threats to aw whom yet with deeds
Thou canst not. Hast thou turnd the least of these
To flight, or if to fall, but that they rise
Unvanquisht, easier to transact with mee
That thou shouldst hope, imperious, and with threats
To chase me hence? erre not that so shall end
The strife which thou call'st evil, but wee style
The strife of Glorie: which we mean to win,
Or turn this Heav'n it self into the Hell
Thou fablest, here however to dwell free,
If not to reign: mean while thy utmost force,
And join him nam'd *Almightie* to thy aid,
I flie not, but have sought thee farr and nigh.

They ended parle, and both addrest for fight
Unspeakable; for who, though with the tongue
Of Angels, can relate, or to what things
Liken on Earth conspicuous, that may lift
Human imagination to such highth
Of Godlike Power: for likest Gods they seemd,
Stood they or mov'd, in stature, motion, arms
Fit to decide the Empire of great Heav'n.
Now wav'd thir fierie Swords, and in the Aire
Made horrid Circles; two broad Suns thir Shields
Blaz'd opposite, while expectation stood
In horror; from each hand with speed retir'd
Where erst was thickest fight, th' Angelic throng,
And left large field, unsafe within the wind
Of such commotion, such as to set forth
Great things by small, if Natures concord broke,
Among the Constellations warr were sprung,
Two Planets rushing from aspect maligne
Of fiercest opposition in mid Skie.

Should combat, and thir jarring Sphears confound.
Together both with next to Almightie Arme,
Uplifted imminent one stroke they aim'd
That might determine, and not need repeate,
As not of power, at once; nor odds appeerd
In might or swift prevention; but the sword
Of *Michael* from the Armorie of God
Was giv'n him temperd so, that neither keen
Nor solid might resist that edge: it met
The sword of *Satan* with steep force to smite
Descending, and in half cut sheere, nor staid,
But with swift wheele reverse, deep entring shar'd
All his right side; then *Satan* first knew pain,
And writh'd him to and fro convolv'd; so sore
The griding sword with discontinuous wound
Pass'd through him, but th' Ethereal substance clos'd
Not long divisible, and from the gash
A stream of Nectarous humor issuing flow'd
Sanguin, such as Celestial Spirits may bleed,
And all his Armour staind ere while so bright.
Forthwith on all sides to his aide was run
By Angels many and strong, who interpos'd
Defence, while others bore him on thir Shields
Back to his Chariot; where it stood retir'd
From off the files of warr; there they him laid
Gnashing for anguish and despite and shame
To find himself not matchless, and his pride
Humbl'd by such rebuke, so farr beneath
His confidence to equal God in power.
Yet soon he heal'd; for Spirits that live throughout
Vital in every part, not as frail man
In Entrailes, Heart or Head, Liver or Reines,
Cannot but by annihilating die;
Nor in thir liquid texture mortal wound
Receive, no more then can the fluid Aire:
All Heart they live, all Head, all Eye, all Eare,
All Intellect, all Sense, and as they please,
They Limb themselves, and colour, shape or size
Assume, as likes them best, condense or rare.
   Mean while in other parts like deeds deservd

Memorial, where the might of *Gabriel* fought,
And with fierce Ensignes pierc'd the deep array
Of *Moloc* furious King, who him defi'd,
And at his Chariot wheeles to drag him bound
Threatn'd, nor from the Holie One of Heav'n
Refrein'd his tongue blasphemous; but anon
Down clov'n to the waste, with shatterd Armes
And uncouth paine fled bellowing. On each wing
Uriel and *Raphael* his vaunting foe,
Though huge, and in a Rock of Diamond Armd,
Vanquish'd *Adramelec*, and *Asmadai*,
Two potent Thrones, that to be less then Gods
Disdain'd, but meaner thoughts learnd in thir flight,
Mangl'd with gastly wounds through Plate and Maile,
Nor stood unmindful *Abdiel* to annoy
The Atheist crew, but with redoubl'd blow
Ariel and *Arioc*, and the violence
Of *Ramiel* scorcht and blasted overthrew.
I might relate of thousands, and thir names
Eternize here on Earth; but those elect
Angels contented with thir fame in Heav'n
Seek not the praise of men; the other sort
In might though wondrous and in Acts of Warr,
Nor of Renown less eager, yet by doome
Canceld from Heav'n and sacred memorie,
Nameless in dark oblivion let them dwell.
For strength from Truth divided and from Just,
Illaudable, naught merits but dispraise
And ignominie, yet to glorie aspires
Vain glorious, and through infamie seeks fame:
Therfore Eternal silence be thir doome.

And now thir mightiest quelld, the battel swerv'd,
With many an inrode gor'd; deformed rout
Enter'd, and foul disorder; all the ground
With shiverd armour strow'n, and on a heap
Chariot and Charioter lay overturnd
And fierie foaming Steeds; what stood, recoyld
Orewearied, through the faint Satanic Host
Defensive scarse, or with pale fear surpris'd,
Then first with fear surpris'd and sense of paine

Fled ignominious, to such evil brought
By sin of disobedience, till that hour
Not liable to fear or flight or paine.
Far otherwise th' inviolable Saints
In Cubic Phalanx firm advanc't entire,
Invulnerable, impenitrably arm'd:
Such high advantages thir innocence
Gave them above thir foes, not to have sinnd,
Not to have disobei'd; in fight they stood
Unwearied, unobnoxious to be pain'd
By wound, though from thir place by violence mov'd.

   Now Night her course began, and over Heav'n
Inducing darkness, grateful truce impos'd,
And silence on the odious dinn of Warr:
Under her Cloudie covert both retir'd,
Victor and Vanquisht: on the foughten field
Michael and his Angels prevalent
Encamping, plac'd in Guard thir Watches round,
Cherubic waving fires: on th' other part
Satan with his rebellious disappeerd,
Far in the dark dislodg'd, and void of rest,
His Potentates to Councel call'd by night;
And in the midst thus undismai'd began.

   O now in danger tri'd, now known in Armes
Not to be overpowerd, Companions deare,
Found worthy not of Libertie alone,
Too mean pretense, but what we more affect,
Honour, Dominion, Glorie, and renowne,
Who have sustaind one day in doubtful fight,
(And if one day, why not Eternal dayes?)
What Heavens Lord had powerfullest to send
Against us from about his Throne, and judg'd
Sufficient to subdue us to his will,
But proves not so: then fallible, it seems,
Of future we may deem him, though till now
Omniscient thought. True is, less firmly arm'd,
Some disadvantage we endur'd and paine,
Till now not known, but known as soon contemnd,
Since now we find this our Empyreal form
Incapable of mortal injurie

Imperishable, and though peirc'd with wound,
Soon closing, and by native vigour heal'd.
Of evil then so small as easie think
The remedie; perhaps more valid Armes,
Weapons more violent, when next we meet,
May serve to better us, and worse our foes,
Or equal what between us made the odds,
In Nature none: if other hidden cause
Left them Superiour, while we can preserve
Unhurt our mindes, and understanding sound,
Due search and consultation will disclose.

He sat; and in th' assembly next upstood
Nisroc, of Principalities the prime;
As one he stood escap't from cruel fight,
Sore toild, his riv'n Armes to havoc hewn,
And cloudie in aspect thus answering spake.
Deliverer from new Lords, leader to free
Enjoyment of our right as Gods; yet hard
For Gods, and too unequal work we find
Against unequal armes to fight in paine,
Against unpaind, impassive; from which evil
Ruin must needs ensue; for what availes
Valour or strength, though matchless, quelld with pain
Which all subdues, and makes remiss the hands
Of Mightiest. Sense of pleasure we may well
Spare out of life perhaps, and not repine,
But live content, which is the calmest life:
But pain is perfet miserie, the worst
Of evils, and excessive, overturnes
All patience. He who therefore can invent
With what more forcible we may offend
Our yet unwounded Enemies, or arme
Our selves with like defence, to me deserves
No less then for deliverance what we owe.

Whereto with look compos'd Satan repli'd.
Not uninvented that, which thou aright
Believst so main to our success, I bring;
Which of us who beholds the bright surface
Of this Ethereous mould whereon we stand,
This continent of spacious Heav'n, adornd

With Plant, Fruit, Flour Ambrosial, Gemms and Gold,
Whose Eye so superficially surveyes
These things, as not to mind from whence they grow
Deep under ground, materials dark and crude,
Of spiritous and fierie spume, till toucht
With Heav'ns ray, and temperd they shoot forth
So beauteous, op'ning to the ambient light.
These in thir dark Nativitie the Deep
Shall yield us, pregnant with infernal flame,
Which into hollow Engins long and round
Thick-rammd, at th' other bore with touch of fire
Dilated and infuriate shall send forth
From far with thundring noise among our foes
Such implements of mischief as shall dash
To pieces, and orewhelm whatever stands
Adverse, that they shall fear we have disarmd
The Thunderer of his only dreaded bolt.
Nor long shall be our labour, yet ere dawne,
Effect shall end our wish. Mean while revive;
Abandon fear; to strength and counsel joind
Think nothing hard, much less to be despaird.
He ended, and his words thir drooping chere
Enlightn'd, and thir languisht hope reviv'd.
Th' invention all admir'd, and each, how hee
To be th' inventer miss'd, so easie it seemd
Once found, which yet unfound most would have thought
Impossible: yet haply of thy Race
In future dayes, if Malice should abound,
Some one intent on mischief, or inspir'd
With dev'lish machination might devise
Like instrument to plague the Sons of men
For sin, on warr and mutual slaughter bent.
Forthwith from Councel to the work they flew,
None arguing stood, innumerable hands
Were ready, in a moment up they turnd
Wide the Celestial soile, and saw beneath
Th' originals of Nature in thir crude
Conception; Sulphurous and Nitrous Foame
They found, they mingl'd, and with suttle Art,
Concocted and adusted they reduc'd

To blackest grain, and into store conveyd:
Part hidd'n veins diggd up (nor hath this Earth
Entrails unlike) of Mineral and Stone,
Whereof to found thir Engins and thir Balls
Of missive ruin; part incentive reed
Provide, pernicious with one touch to fire.
So all ere day-spring, under conscious Night
Secret they finish'd, and in order set,
With silent circumspection unespi'd.
Now when fair Morn Orient in Heav'n appeerd
Up rose the Victor Angels, and to Arms
The matin Trumpet Sung: in Arms they stood
Of Golden Panoplie, refulgent Host,
Soon banded; others from the dawning Hills
Lookd round, and Scouts each Coast light-armed scoure,
Each quarter, to descrie the distant foe,
Where lodg'd, or whither fled, or if for fight,
In motion or in alt: him soon they met
Under spred Ensignes moving nigh, in slow
But firm Battalion; back with speediest Sail
Zophiel, of Cherubim the swiftest wing,
Came flying, and in mid Aire aloud thus cri'd.

   Arme, Warriours, Arme for fight, the foe at hand,
Whom fled we thought, will save us long pursuit
This day, fear not his flight: so thick a Cloud
He comes, and settl'd in his face I see
Sad resolution and secure: let each
His Adamantine coat gird well, and each
Fit well his Helme, gripe fast his orbed Shield,
Born eevn or high, for this day will pour down,
If I conjecture aught, no drizling showr,
But ratling storm of Arrows barbd with fire.
So warnd he them aware themselves, and soon
In order, quit of all impediment;
Instant without disturb they took Allarm,
And onward move Embattelld; when behold
Not distant far with heavie pace the Foe
Approaching gross and huge; in hollow Cube
Training his devilish Enginrie, impal'd
On every side with shaddowing Squadrons Deep,

To hide the fraud. At interview both stood
A while, but suddenly at head appeerd
Satan: And thus was heard Commanding loud.

   Vangard, to Right and Left the Front unfould;
That all may see who hate us, how we seek
Peace and composure, and with open brest
Stand readie to receive them, if they like
Our overture, and turn not back perverse;
But that I doubt, however witness Heaven,
Heav'n witness thou anon, while we discharge
Freely our part: yee who appointed stand
Do as you have in charge, and briefly touch
What we propound, and loud that all may hear.

   So scoffing in ambiguous words, he scarce
Had ended; when to Right and Left the Front
Divided, and to either Flank retir'd.
Which to our eyes discoverd new and strange,
A triple-mounted row of Pillars laid
On Wheels (for like to Pillars most they seem'd
Or hollow'd bodies made of Oak or Firr
With branches lopt, in Wood or Mountain fell'd)
Brass, Iron, Stonie mould, had not thir mouthes
With hideous orifice gap't on us wide,
Portending hollow truce; at each behind
A Seraph stood, and in his hand a Reed
Stood waving tipt with fire; while we suspense,
Collected stood within our thoughts amus'd,
Not long, for sudden all at once thir Reeds
Put forth, and to a narrow vent appli'd
With nicest touch. Immediate in a flame,
But soon obscur'd with smoak, all Heav'n appeerd,
From those deep-throated Engins belcht, whose roar
Emboweld with outragious noise the Air,
And all her entrails tore, disgorging foule
Thir devillish glut, chaind Thunderbolts and Hail
Of Iron Globes, which on the Victor Host
Level'd, with such impetuous furie smote,
That whom they hit, none on thir feet might stand,
Though standing else as Rocks, but down they fell
By thousands, Angel on Arch-Angel rowl'd;

The sooner for thir Arms, unarm'd they might
Have easily as Spirits evaded swift
By quick contraction or remove; but now
Foule dissipation follow'd and forc't rout;
Nor serv'd it to relax thir serried files.
What should they do? if on they rusht, repulse
Repeated, and indecent overthrow
Doubl'd, would render them yet more despis'd,
And to thir foes a laughter; for in view
Stood rankt of Seraphim another row
In posture to displode thir second tire
Of Thunder: back defeated to return
They worse abhorr'd. *Satan* beheld thir plight,
And to his Mates thus in derision call'd.

O Friends, why come not on these Victors proud?
Ere while they fierce were coming, and when wee,
To entertain them fair with open Front
And Brest, (what could we more?) propounded terms
Of composition, strait they chang'd thir minds,
Flew off, and into strange vagaries fell,
As they would dance, yet for a dance they seemd
Somwhat extravagant and wilde, perhaps
For joy of offerd peace: but I suppose
If our proposals once again were heard
We should compel them to a quick result.

To whom thus *Belial* in like gamesom mood.
Leader, the terms we sent were terms of weight,
Of hard contents, and full of force urg'd home,
Such as we might perceive amus'd them all,
And stumbl'd many, who receives them right,
Had need from head to foot well understand;
Not understood, this gift they have besides,
They shew us when our foes walk not upright.

So they among themselves in pleasant veine
Stood scoffing, highthn'd in thir thoughts beyond
All doubt of Victorie, eternal might
To match with thir inventions they presum'd
So easie, and of his Thunder made a scorn,
And all his Host derided, while they stood
A while in trouble; but they stood not long,

Rage prompted them at length, and found them arms
Against such hellish mischief fit to oppose.
Forthwith (behold the excellence, the power
Which God hath in his mighty Angels plac'd)
Thir Arms away they threw, and to the Hills
(For Earth hath this variety from Heav'n
Of pleasure situate in Hill and Dale)
Light as the Lightning glimps they ran, they flew,
From thir foundations loosning to and fro
They pluckt the seated Hills with all thir load,
Rocks, Waters, Woods, and by the shaggie tops
Up lifting bore them in thir hands: Amaze,
Be sure, and terrour seis'd the rebel Host,
When coming towards them so dread they saw
The bottom of the Mountains upward turn'd,
Till on those cursed Engins triple-row
They saw them whelmd, and all thir confidence
Under the weight of Mountains buried deep,
Themselves invaded next, and on thir heads
Main Promontories flung, which in the Air
Came shadowing, and opprest whole Legions arm'd,
Thir armor help'd thir harm, crush't in and bruis'd
Into thir substance pent, which wrought them pain
Implacable, and many a dolorous groan,
Long struling underneath, ere they could wind
Out of such prison, though Spirits of purest light,
Purest at first, now gross by sinning grown.
The rest in imitation to like Armes
Betook them, and the neighbouring Hills uptore;
So Hills amid the Air encounterd Hills
Hurl'd to and fro with jaculation dire,
That under ground they fought in dismal shade;
Infernal noise; Warr seem'd a civil Game
To this uproar; horrid confusion heapt
Upon confusion rose: and now all Heav'n
Had gone to wrack, with ruin overspred,
Had not th' Almightie Father where he sits
Shrin'd in his Sanctuarie of Heav'n secure,
Consulting on the sum of things, foreseen
This tumult, and permitted all, advis'd:

That his great purpose he might so fulfill,
To honour his Anointed Son aveng'd
Upon his enemies, and to declare
All power on him transferr'd: whence to his Son
Th' Assessor of his Throne he thus began.

Effulgence of my Glorie, Son belov'd,
Son in whose face invisible is beheld
Visibly, what by Deitie I am,
And in whose hand what by Decree I doe,
Second Omnipotence, two dayes are past,
Two dayes, as we compute the dayes of Heav'n,
Since *Michael* and his Powers went forth to tame
These disobedient; sore hath been thir fight,
As likeliest was, when two such Foes met arm'd;
For to themselves I left them, and thou knowst,
Equal in their Creation they were form'd,
Save what sin hath impaird, which yet hath wrought
Insensibly, for I suspend thir doom;
Whence in perpetual fight they needs must last
Endless, and no solution will be found:
Warr wearied hath perform'd what Warr can do,
And to disorder'd rage let loose the reines,
With Mountains as with Weapons arm'd, which makes
Wild work in Heav'n, and dangerous to the maine.
Two dayes are therefore past, the third is thine;
For thee I have ordain'd it, and thus farr
Have sufferd, that the Glorie may be thine
Of ending this great Warr, since none but Thou
Can end it. Into thee such Vertue and Grace
Immense I have transfus'd, that all may know
In Heav'n and Hell thy Power above compare,
And this perverse Commotion governd thus,
To manifest thee worthiest to be Heir
Of all things, to be Heir and to be King
By Sacred Unction, thy deserved right.
Go then thou Mightiest in thy Fathers might,
Ascend my Chariot, guide the rapid Wheeles
That shake Heav'ns basis, bring forth all my Warr,
My Bow and Thunder, my Almightie Arms
Gird on, and Sword upon thy puissant Thigh;

Pursue these sons of Darkness, drive them out
From all Heav'ns bounds into the utter Deep:
There let them learn, as likes them, to despise
God and *Messiah* his anointed King.

He said, and on his Son with Rayes direct
Shon full, he all his Father full exprest
Ineffably into his face receiv'd,
And thus the filial Godhead answering spake.

O Father, O Supream of heav'nly Thrones,
First, Highest, Holiest, Best, thou alwayes seekst
To glorifie thy Son, I alwayes thee,
As is most just; this I my Glorie account,
My exaltation, and my whole delight,
That thou in me well pleas'd declarst thy will
Fulfill'd, which to fulfil is all my bliss.
Scepter and Power, thy giving, I assume,
And gladlier shall resign, when in the end
Thou shalt be All in All, and I in thee
For ever, and in mee all whom thou lov'st:
But whom thou hat'st, I hate, and can put on
Thy terrors, as I put thy mildness on,
Image of thee in all things; and shall soon,
Armd with thy might, rid heav'n of these rebell'd,
To thir prepar'd ill Mansion driven down
To chains of Darkness, and th' undying Worm,
That from thy just obedience could revolt,
Whom to obey is happiness entire.
Then shall thy Saints unmixt, and from th' impure
Farr separate, circling thy holy Mount
Unfained *Halleluiahs* to thee sing,
Hymns of high praise, and I among them chief.
So said, he o're his Scepter bowing, rose
From the right hand of Glorie where he sate,
And the third sacred Morn began to shine
Dawning through Heav'n: forth rush'd with whirlwind sound
The Chariot of Paternal Deitie,
Flashing thick flames, Wheele within Wheele undrawn,
It self instinct with Spirit, but convoyd
By four Cherubic shapes, four Faces each
Had wondrous, as with Starrs thir bodies all

And Wings were set with Eyes, with Eyes the wheels
Of Beril, and careering Fires between;
Over thir heads a chrystal Firmament,
Whereon a Saphir Throne, inlaid with pure
Amber, and colours of the showrie Arch.
Hee in Celestial Panoplie all armd
Of radiant *Urim*, work divinely wrought,
Ascended, at his right hand Victorie
Sate Eagle-wing'd, beside him hung his Bow
And Quiver with three-bolted Thunder stor'd,
And from about him fierce Effusion rowld
Of smoak and bickering flame, and sparkles dire;
Attended with ten thousand thousand Saints,
He onward came, farr off his coming shon,
And twentie thousand (I thir number heard)
Chariots of God, half on each hand were seen:
Hee on the wings of Cherub rode sublime
On the Crystallin Skie, in Saphir Thron'd.
Illustrious farr and wide, but by his own
First seen, them unexpected joy surpriz'd,
When the great Ensign of *Messiah* blaz'd
Aloft by Angels born, his Sign in Heav'n:
Under whose Conduct *Michael* soon reduc'd
His Armie, circumfus'd on either Wing,
Under thir Head imbodied all in one.
Before him Power Divine his way prepar'd;
At his command the uprooted Hills retir'd
Each to his place, they heard his voice and went
Obsequious, Heav'n his wonted face renewd,
And with fresh Flourets Hill and Valley smil'd.
This saw his hapless Foes, but stood obdur'd,
And to rebellious fight rallied thir Powers
Insensate, hope conceiving from despair.
In heav'nly Spirits could such perverseness dwell?
But to convince the proud what Signs availe,
Or Wonders move th' obdurate to relent?
They hard'nd more by what might most reclame,
Grieving to see his Glorie, at the sight
Took envie, and aspiring to his highth,
Stood reimbattell'd fierce, by force or fraud

Weening to prosper, and at length prevail
Against God and *Messiah*, or to fall
In universal ruin last, and now
To final Battel drew, disdaining flight,
Or faint retreat; when the great Son of God
To all his Host on either hand thus spake.

Stand still in bright array ye Saints, here stand
Ye Angels arm'd, this day from Battel rest;
Faithful hath been your Warfare, and of God
Accepted, fearless in his righteous Cause,
And as ye have receivd, so have ye don
Invincibly: but of this cursed crew
The punishment to other hand belongs,
Vengeance is his, or whose he sole appoints;
Number to this dayes work is not ordain'd
Nor multitude, stand onely and behold
Gods indignation on these Godless pourd
By mee; not you but mee they have despis'd,
Yet envied; against mee is all their rage,
Because the Father, t' whom in Heav'n supream
Kingdom and Power and Glorie appertains,
Hath honourd me according to his will.
Therefore to mee thir doom he hath assig'n'd;
That they may have thir wish, to trie with mee
In Battel which the stronger proves, they all,
Or I alone against them, since by strength
They measure all, of other excellence
Not emulous, nor care who them excells;
Nor other strife with them do I voutsafe.

So spake the Son, and into terrour chang'd
His count'nance too severe to be beheld
And full of wrauth bent on his Enemies.
At once the Four spred out thir Starrie wings
With dreadful shade contiguous, and the Orbes
Of his fierce Chariot rowld, as with the sound
Of torrent Floods, or of a numerous Host.
Hee on his impious Foes right onward drove,
Gloomie as Night; under his burning Wheeles
The stedfast Empyrean shook throughout,
All but the Throne it self of God. Full soon

Among them he arriv'd; in his right hand
Grasping ten thousand Thunders, which he sent
Before him, such as in thir Soules infix'd
Plagues; they astonisht all resistance lost,
All courage; down their idle weapons drop'd;
O're Shields and Helmes, and helmed heads he rode
Of Thrones and mighty Seraphim prostrate,
That wish'd the Mountains now might be again
Thrown on them as a shelter from his ire.
Nor less on either side tempestuous fell
His arrows, from the fourfold-visag'd Foure,
Distinct with eyes, and from the living Wheels,
Distinct alike with multitude of eyes,
One Spirit in them rul'd, and every eye
Glar'd lightning, and shot forth pernicious fire
Among th' accurst, that witherd all thir strength,
And of thir wonted vigour left them draind,
Exhausted, spiritless, afflicted, fall'n.
Yet half his strength he put not forth, but check'd
His Thunder in mid Volie, for he meant
Not to destroy, but root them out of Heav'n:
The overthrown he rais'd, and as a Heard
Of Goats or timerous flock together throngd
Drove them before him Thunder-struck, pursu'd
With terrors and with furies to the bounds
And Chrystal wall of Heav'n, which op'ning wide,
Rowld inward, and a spacious Gap disclos'd
Into the wastful Deep; the monstrous sight
Strook them with horror backward, but far worse
Urg'd them behind; headlong themselvs they threw
Down from the verge of Heav'n, Eternal wrauth
Burnt after them to the bottomless pit.

Hell heard th' unsufferable noise, Hell saw
Heav'n ruining from Heav'n, and would have fled
Affrighted; but strict Fate had cast too deep
Her dark foundations, and too fast had bound.
Nine dayes they fell; confounded *Chaos* roard,
And felt tenfold confusion in thir fall
Through his wilde Anarchie, so huge a rout
Incumberd him with ruin: Hell at last

Yawning receavd them whole, and on them clos'd,
Hell thir fit habitation fraught with fire
Unquenchable, the house of woe and paine.
Disburd'nd Heav'n rejoic'd, and soon repaird
Her mural breach, returning whence it rowld.
Sole Victor from th' expulsion of his Foes
Messiah his triumphal Chariot turnd:
To meet him all his Saints, who silent stood
Eye witnesses of his Almightie Acts,
With Jubilie advanc'd; and as they went,
Shaded with branching Palme, each order bright,
Sung Triumph, and him sung Victorious King,
Son, Heire, and Lord, to him Dominion giv'n,
Worthiest to Reign: he celebrated rode
Triumphant through mid Heav'n, into the Courts
And Temple of his mightie Father Thron'd
On high; who into Glorie him receav'd,
Where now he sits at the right hand of bliss.

   Thus measuring things in Heav'n by things on Earth
At thy request, and that thou maist beware
By what is past, to thee I have reveal'd
What might have else to human Race bin hid;
The discord which befel, and Warr in Heav'n
Among th' Angelic Powers, and the deep fall
Of those too high aspiring, who rebelld
With *Satan*, hee who envies now thy state,
Who now is plotting how he may seduce
Thee also from obedience, that with him
Bereavd of happiness thou maist partake
His punishment, Eternal miserie;
Which would be all his solace and revenge,
As a despite don against the most High,
Thee once to gaine Companion of his woe.
But list'n not to his Temptations, warne
Thy weaker; let it profit thee to have heard
By terrible Example the reward
Of disobedience; firm they might have stood
Yet fell; remember, and fear to transgress.

BOOK VII

THE ARGUMENT

RAPHAEL *at the request of* Adam *relates how and wherefore this world was first created; that God, after the expelling of* Satan *and his Angels out of Heaven, declar'd his pleasure to create another World and other Creatures to dwell therein; sends his Son with Glory and attendance of Angels to perform the work of Creation in six dayes: the Angels celebrate with Hymns the performance thereof, and his reascention into Heaven.*

DESCEND from Heav'n *Urania*, by that name
If rightly thou art call'd whose Voice divine
Following, above th' *Olympian* Hill I soare,
Above the flight of *Pegasean* wing.
The meaning, not the Name I call: for thou
Nor of the Muses nine, nor on the top
Of old *Olympus* dwell'st, but Heav'nlie borne,
Before the Hills appeerd, or Fountain flow'd,
Thou with Eternal wisdom didst converse,
Wisdom thy Sister, and with her didst play
In presence of th' Almightie Father, pleas'd
With thy Celestial Song. Up led by thee
Into the Heav'n of Heav'ns I have presum'd,
An Earthlie Guest, and drawn Empyreal Aire,
Thy tempring; with like safetie guided down
Return me to my Native Element:
Least from this flying Steed unrein'd, (as once
Bellerophon, though from a lower Clime)
Dismounted on th' *Aleian* Field I fall
Erroneous, there to wander and forlorne.
Half yet remaines unsung, but narrower bound
Within the visible Diurnal Spheare;
Standing on Earth, not rapt above the Pole,
More safe I Sing with mortal voice, unchang'd
To hoarce or mute, though fall'n on evil dayes,
On evil dayes though fall'n, and evil tongues;
In darkness, and with dangers compast round,
And solitude; yet not alone, while thou

Visit'st my slumbers Nightly, or when Morn
Purples the East: still govern thou my Song,
Urania, and fit audience find, though few.
But drive farr off the barbarous dissonance
Of *Bacchus* and his Revellers, the Race
Of that wilde Rout that tore the *Thracian* Bard
In *Rhodope*, where Woods and Rocks had Eares
To rapture, till the savage clamor dround
Both Harp and Voice; nor could the Muse defend
Her Son. So fail not thou, who thee implores:
For thou art Heav'nlie, shee an empty dreame.

　　Say Goddess, what ensu'd when *Raphael*,
The affable Arch-angel, had forewarn'd
Adam by dire example to beware
Apostasie, by what befell in Heaven
To those Apostates, least the like befall
In Paradise to *Adam* or his Race,
Charg'd not to touch the interdicted Tree,
If they transgress, and slight that sole command,
So easily obeyd amid the choice
Of all tasts else to please thir appetite,
Though wandring. He with his consorted *Eve*
The storie heard attentive, and was fill'd
With admiration, and deep Muse to heare
Of things so high and strange, things to thir thought
So unimaginable as hate in Heav'n,
And Warr so neer the Peace of God in bliss
With such confusion: but the evil soon
Driv'n back redounded as a flood on those
From whom it sprung, impossible to mix
With Blessedness. Whence *Adam* soon repeal'd
The doubts that in his heart arose: and now
Led on, yet sinless, with desire to know
What neerer might concern him, how this World
Of Heav'n and Earth conspicuous first began,
When, and whereof created, for what cause,
What within *Eden* or without was done
Before his memorie, as one whose drouth
Yet scarce allay'd still eyes the current streame,
Whose liquid murmur heard new thirst excites,

Proceeded thus to ask his Heav'nly Guest.
   Great things, and full of wonder in our eares,
Farr differing from this World, thou hast reveal'd
Divine Interpreter, by favour sent
Down from the Empyrean to forewarne
Us timely of what might else have bin our loss,
Unknown, which human knowledg could not reach:
For which to the infinitly Good we owe
Immortal thanks, and his admonishment
Receave with solemne purpose to observe
Immutably his sovran will, the end
Of what we are. But since thou hast voutsaf't
Gently for our instruction to impart
Things above Earthly thought, which yet concernd
Our knowing, as to highest wisdom seemd,
Deign to descend now lower, and relate
What may no less perhaps availe us known,
How first began this Heav'n which we behold
Distant so high, with moving Fires adornd
Innumerable, and this which yeelds or fills
All space, the ambient Aire wide interfus'd
Imbracing round this florid Earth, what cause
Mov'd the Creator in his holy Rest
Through all Eternitie so late to build
In *Chaos*, and the work begun, how soon
Absolv'd, if unforbid thou maist unfold
What wee, not to explore the secrets aske
Of his Eternal Empire, but the more
To magnifie his works, the more we know.
And the great Light of Day yet wants to run
Much of his Race though steep, suspens in Heav'n
Held by thy voice, thy potent voice he heares,
And longer will delay to heare thee tell
His Generation, and the rising Birth
Of Nature from the unapparent Deep:
Or if the Starr of Eevning and the Moon
Haste to thy audience, Night with her will bring
Silence, and Sleep listning to thee will watch,
Or we can bid his absence, till thy Song
End, and dismiss thee ere the Morning shine.

Thus *Adam* his illustrious Guest besought:
And thus the Godlike Angel answerd milde.
This also thy request with caution askt
Obtaine: though to recount Almightie works
What words or tongue of Seraph can suffice,
Or heart of man suffice to comprehend?
Yet what thou canst attain, which best may serve
To glorifie the Maker, and inferr
Thee also happier, shall not be withheld
Thy hearing, such Commission from above
I have receav'd, to answer thy desire
Of knowledge within bounds; beyond abstain
To ask, nor let thine own inventions hope
Things not reveal'd, which th' invisible King,
Onely Omniscient, hath supprest in Night,
To none communicable in Earth or Heaven:
Anough is left besides to search and know.
But Knowledge is as food, and needs no less
Her Temperance over Appetite, to know
In measure what the mind may well contain,
Oppresses else with Surfet, and soon turns
Wisdom to Folly, as Nourishment to Winde.

Know then, that after *Lucifer* from Heav'n
(So call him, brighter once amidst the Host
Of Angels, then that Starr the Starrs among)
Fell with his flaming Legions through the Deep
Into his place, and the great Son returnd
Victorious with his Saints, th' Omnipotent
Eternal Father from his Throne beheld
Thir multitude, and to his Son thus spake.

At least our envious Foe hath fail'd, who thought
All like himself rebellious, by whose aid
This inaccessible high strength, the seat
Of Deitie supream, us dispossest,
He trusted to have seis'd, and into fraud
Drew many, whom thir place knows here no more;
Yet farr the greater part have kept, I see,
Thir station, Heav'n yet populous retaines
Number sufficient to possess her Realmes
Though wide, and this high Temple to frequent

With Ministeries due and solemn Rites:
But least his heart exalt him in the harme
Already done, to have dispeopl'd Heav'n
My damage fondly deem'd, I can repaire
That detriment, if such it be to lose
Self-lost, and in a moment will create
Another World, out of one man a Race
Of men innumerable, there to dwell,
Not here, till by degrees of merit rais'd
They open to themselves at length the way
Up hither, under long obedience tri'd,
And Earth be chang'd to Heavn, and Heav'n to Earth,
One Kingdom, Joy and Union without end.
Mean while inhabit laxe, ye Powers of Heav'n,
And thou my Word, begotten Son, by thee
This I perform, speak thou, and be it don:
My overshadowing Spirit and might with thee
I send along, ride forth, and bid the Deep
Within appointed bounds be Heav'n and Earth,
Boundless the Deep, because I am who fill
Infinitude, nor vacuous the space.
Though I uncircumscrib'd my self retire,
And put not forth my goodness, which is free
To act or not, Necessitie and Chance
Approach not mee, and what I will is Fate.
    So spake th' Almightie, and to what he spake
His Word, the Filial Godhead, gave effect.
Immediate are the Acts of God, more swift
Then time or motion, but to human ears
Cannot without process of speech be told,
So told as earthly notion can receave.
Great triumph and rejoycing was in Heav'n
When such was heard declar'd the Almightie's will:
Glorie they sung to the most High, good will
To future men, and in thir dwellings peace:
Glorie to him whose just avenging ire
Had driven out th' ungodly from his sight
And th' habitations of the just; to him
Glorie and praise, whose wisdom had ordain'd
Good out of evil to create, in stead

Of Spirits maligne a better Race to bring
Into thir vacant room, and thence diffuse
His good to Worlds and Ages infinite.
So sang the Hierarchies: Mean while the Son
On his great Expedition now appeer'd,
Girt with Omnipotence, with Radiance crown'd
Of Majestie Divine, Sapience and Love
Immense, and all his Father in him shon.
About his Chariot numberless were pour'd
Cherub and Seraph, Potentates and Thrones,
And Vertues, winged Spirits, and Chariots wing'd,
From the Armoury of God, where stand of old
Myriads between two brazen Mountains lodg'd
Against a solemn day, harnest at hand,
Celestial Equipage; and now came forth
Spontaneous, for within them Spirit livd,
Attendant on thir Lord: Heav'n op'nd wide
Her ever during Gates, Harmonious sound
On golden Hinges moving, to let forth
The King of Glorie in his powerful Word
And Spirit coming to create new Worlds.
On heav'nly ground they stood, and from the shore
They view'd the vast immeasurable Abyss
Outrageous as a Sea, dark, wasteful, wilde,
Up from the bottom turn'd by furious windes
And surging waves, as Mountains to assault
Heav'ns highth, and with the Center mix the Pole.
    Silence, ye troubl'd waves, and thou Deep, peace,
Said then th' Omnific Word, your discord end:
    Nor staid, but on the Wings of Cherubim
Uplifted, in Paternal Glorie rode
Farr into *Chaos*, and the World unborn;
For *Chaos* heard his voice: him all his Traine
Follow'd in bright procession to behold
Creation, and the wonders of his might.
Then staid the fervid Wheeles, and in his hand
He took the golden Compasses, prepar'd
In Gods Eternal store, to circumscribe
This Universe, and all created things:
One foot he center'd, and the other turn'd

Round through the vast profunditie obscure,
And said, thus farr extend, thus farr thy bounds,
This be thy just Circumference, O World.
Thus God the Heav'n created, thus the Earth,
Matter unform'd and void : Darkness profound
Cover'd th' Abyss : but on the watrie calme
His brooding wings the Spirit of God outspred,
And vital vertue infus'd, and vital warmth
Throughout the fluid Mass, but downward purg'd
The black tartareous cold infernal dregs
Adverse to life ; then founded, then conglob'd
Like things to like, the rest to several place
Disparted, and between spun out the Air,
And Earth self-ballanc't on her Center hung.

Let ther be Light, said God, and forthwith Light
Ethereal, first of things, quintessence pure
Sprung from the Deep, and from her Native East
To journie through the airie gloom began,
Sphear'd in a radiant Cloud, for yet the Sun
Was not ; shee in a cloudie Tabernacle
Sojourn'd the while. God saw the Light was good ;
And light from darkness by the Hemisphere
Divided : Light the Day, and Darkness Night
He nam'd. Thus was the first Day Eev'n and Morn :
Nor past uncelebrated, nor unsung
By the Celestial Quires, when Orient Light
Exhaling first from Darkness they beheld :
Birth-day of Heav'n and Earth ; with joy and shout
The hollow Universal Orb they fill'd,
And touch't thir Golden Harps, and hymning prais'd
God and his works, Creatour him they sung,
Both when first Eevning was, and when first Morn.

Again, God said, let ther be Firmament
Amid the Waters, and let it divide
The Waters from the Waters : and God made
The Firmament, expanse of liquid, pure,
Transparent, Elemental Air, diffus'd
In circuit to the uttermost convex
Of this great Round : partition firm and sure,
The Waters underneath from those above

Dividing: for as Earth, so he the World
Built on circumfluous Waters calme, in wide
Crystallin Ocean, and the loud misrule
Of *Chaos* farr remov'd, least fierce extreames
Contiguous might distemper the whole frame:
And Heav'n he nam'd the Firmament: So Eev'n
And Morning *Chorus* sung the second Day.

The Earth was form'd, but in the Womb as yet
Of Waters, Embryon immature involv'd,
Appeer'd not: over all the face of Earth
Main Ocean flow'd, not idle, but with warme
Prolific humour soft'ning all her Globe,
Fermented the great Mother to conceave,
Satiate with genial moisture, when God said
Be gather'd now ye Waters under Heav'n
Into one place, and let dry Land appeer.
Immediately the mountains huge appeer
Emergent, and thir broad bare backs upheave
Into the Clouds, thir tops ascend the Skie:
So high as heav'd the tumid Hills, so low
Down sunk a hollow bottom broad and deep,
Capacious bed of Waters: thither they
Hasted with glad precipitance, uprowld
As drops on dust conglobing from the drie;
Part rise in crystal Wall, or ridge direct,
For haste; such flight the great command impress'd
On the swift flouds: as Armies at the call
Of Trumpet (for of Armies thou hast heard)
Troop to thir Standard, so the watrie throng,
Wave rowling after Wave, where way they found,
If steep, with torrent rapture, if through Plaine,
Soft-ebbing; nor withstood them Rock or Hill,
But they, or under ground, or circuit wide
With Serpent errour wandring, found thir way,
And on the washie Oose deep Channels wore;
Easie, e're God had bid the ground be drie,
All but within those banks, where Rivers now
Stream, and perpetual draw thir humid traine.
The dry Land, Earth, and the great receptacle
Of congregated Waters he call'd Seas:

And saw that it was good, and said, Let th' Earth
Put forth the verdant Grass, Herb yielding Seed,
And Fruit Tree yielding Fruit after her kind;
Whose Seed is in her self upon the Earth.
He scarce had said, when the bare Earth, till then
Desert and bare, unsightly, unadorn'd,
Brought forth the tender Grass, whose verdure clad
Her Universal Face with pleasant green,
Then Herbs of every leaf, that sudden flour'd
Op'ning thir various colours, and made gay
Her bosom smelling sweet: and these scarce blown,
Forth flourish't thick the clustring Vine, forth crept
The Smelling Gourd, up stood the cornie Reed
Embattell'd in her field: and the humble Shrub,
And Bush with frizl'd hair implicit: last
Rose as in Dance the stately Trees, and spred
Thir branches hung with copious Fruit: or gemm'd
Thir Blossoms: with high Woods the Hills were crownd,
With tufts the vallies and each fountain side,
With borders long the Rivers. That Earth now
Seemd like to Heav'n, a seat where Gods might dwell,
Or wander with delight, and love to haunt
Her sacred shades: though God had yet not rain'd
Upon the Earth, and man to till the ground
None was, but from the Earth a dewie Mist
Went up and waterd all the ground, and each
Plant of the field, which e're it was in the Earth
God made, and every Herb, before it grew
On the green stemm; God saw that it was good:
So Eev'n and Morn recorded the Third Day.

Again th' Almightie spake: Let there be Lights
High in th' expanse of Heaven to divide
The Day from Night; and let them be for Signes,
For Seasons, and for Dayes, and circling Years,
And let them be for Lights as I ordaine
Thir Office in the Firmament of Heav'n
To give Light on the Earth; and it was so.
And God made two great Lights, great for their use
To Man, the greater to have rule by Day,
The less by Night alterne: and made the Starrs,

And set them in the Firmament of Heav'n
To illuminate the Earth, and rule the Day
In their vicissitude, and rule the Night,
And Light from Darkness to divide. God saw,
Surveying his great Work, that it was good:
For of Celestial Bodies first the Sun
A mightie Spheare he fram'd, unlightsom first,
Though of Ethereal Mould: then form'd the Moon
Globose, and every magnitude of Starrs,
And sowd with Starrs the Heav'n thick as a field:
Of Light by farr the greater part he took,
Transplanted from her cloudie Shrine, and plac'd
In the Suns Orb, made porous to receive
And drink the liquid Light, firm to retaine
Her gather'd beams, great Palace now of Light.
Hither as to thir Fountain other Starrs
Repairing, in thir gold'n Urns draw Light,
And hence the Morning Planet guilds her horns;
By tincture or reflection they augment
Thir small peculiar, though from human sight
So farr remote, with diminution seen.
First in his East the glorious Lamp was seen,
Regent of Day, and all th' Horizon round
Invested with bright Rayes, jocond to run
His Longitude through Heav'ns high rode: the gray
Dawn, and the *Pleiades* before him danc'd
Shedding sweet influence: less bright the Moon,
But opposite in leveld West was set
His mirror, with full face borrowing her Light
From him, for other light she needed none
In that aspect, and still that distance keepes
Till night, then in the East her turn she shines,
Revolvd on Heav'ns great Axle, and her Reign
With thousand lesser Lights dividual holds,
With thousand thousand Starres, that then appeer'd
Spangling the Hemisphere: then first adornd
With thir bright Luminaries that Set and Rose,
Glad Eevning and glad Morn crownd the fourth day.
    And God said, let the Waters generate
Reptil with Spawn abundant, living Soule:

And let Fowle flie above the Earth, with wings
Displayd on the op'n Firmament of Heav'n.
And God created the great Whales, and each
Soul living, each that crept, which plenteously
The waters generated by thir kindes,
And every Bird of wing after his kinde;
And saw that it was good, and bless'd them, saying,
Be fruitful, multiply, and in the Seas
And Lakes and running Streams the waters fill;
And let the Fowle be multiply'd on the Earth.
Forthwith the Sounds and Seas, each Creek and Bay
With Frie innumerable swarme, and Shoales
Of Fish that with thir Finns and shining Scales
Glide under the green Wave, in Sculles that oft
Bank the mid Sea: part single or with mate
Graze the Sea weed thir pasture, and through Groves
Of Coral stray, or sporting with quick glance
Show to the Sun thir wav'd coats dropt with Gold,
Or in thir Pearlie shells at ease, attend
Moist nutriment, or under Rocks thir food
In jointed Armour watch: on smooth the Seale,
And bended Dolphins play: part huge of bulk
Wallowing unweildie, enormous in thir Gate
Tempest the Ocean: there Leviathan
Hugest of living Creatures, on the Deep
Stretcht like a Promontorie sleeps or swimmes,
And seems a moving Land, and at his Gilles
Draws in, and at his Trunck spouts out a Sea.
Mean while the tepid Caves, and Fens and shoares
Thir Brood as numerous hatch, from the Egg that soon
Bursting with kindly rupture forth disclos'd
Thir callow young, but featherd soon and fledge
They summ'd thir Penns, and soaring th' air sublime
With clang despis'd the ground, under a cloud
In prospect; there the Eagle and the Stork
On Cliffs and Cedar tops thir Eyries build:
Part loosly wing the Region, part more wise
In common, rang'd in figure wedge their way,
Intelligent of seasons, and set forth
Thir Aierie Caravan high over Sea's

Flying, and over Lands with mutual wing
Easing thir flight; so stears the prudent Crane
Her annual Voiage, born on Windes; the Aire
Floats, as they pass, fann'd with unnumber'd plumes:
From Branch to Branch the smaller Birds with song
Solac'd the Woods, and spred thir painted wings
Till Ev'n, nor then the solemn Nightingal
Ceas'd warbling, but all night tun'd her soft layes:
Others on Silver Lakes and Rivers Bath'd
Thir downie Brest; the Swan with Arched neck
Between her white wings mantling proudly, Rowes
Her state with Oarie feet: yet oft they quit
The Dank, and rising on stiff Pennons, towre
The mid Aereal Skie: Others on ground
Walk'd firm; the crested Cock whose clarion sounds
The silent hours, and th' other whose gay Traine
Adorns him, colour'd with the Florid hue
Of Rainbows and Starrie Eyes. The Waters thus
With Fish replenisht, and the Aire with Fowle,
Ev'ning and Morn solemniz'd the Fift day.

　　The Sixt, and of Creation last arose
With Eevning Harps and Mattin, when God said,
Let th' Earth bring forth *Soul living in her kinde,
Cattel and Creeping things, and Beast of the Earth,
Each in their kinde. The Earth obey'd, and strait
Op'ning her fertil Woomb teem'd at a Birth
Innumerous living Creatures, perfet formes,
Limb'd and full grown: out of the ground up rose
As from his Laire the wilde Beast where he wonns
In Forrest wilde, in Thicket, Brake, or Den;
Among the Trees in Pairs they rose, they walk'd:
The Cattel in the Fields and Meddowes green;
Those rare and solitarie, these in flocks
Pasturing at once, and in broad Herds upsprung.
The grassie Clods now Calv'd, now half appeer'd
The Tawnie Lion, pawing to get free
His hinder parts, then springs as broke from Bonds,
And Rampant shakes his Brinded main; the Ounce,
The Libbard, and the Tyger, as the Moale

*As in Quarto 1749. Second edition, "Foul". First edition, "Fowle".

Rising, the crumbl'd Earth above them threw
In Hillocks; the swift Stag from under ground
Bore up his branching head: scarse from his mould
Behemoth biggest born of Earth upheav'd
His vastness: Fleec't the Flocks and bleating rose,
As Plants: ambiguous between Sea and Land
The River Horse and scalie Crocodile.
At once came forth whatever creeps the ground,
Insect or Worme; those wav'd thir limber fans
For wings, and smallest Lineaments exact
In all the Liveries dect of Summers pride
With spots of Gold and Purple, azure and green:
These as a line thir long dimension drew,
Streaking the ground with sinuous trace; not all
Minims of Nature; some of Serpent kinde
Wondrous in length and corpulence involv'd
Thir Snakie foulds, and added wings. First crept
The Parsimonious Emmet, provident
Of future, in small room large heart enclos'd,
Pattern of just equalitie perhaps
Hereafter, join'd in her popular Tribes
Of Commonaltie: swarming next appeer'd
The Female Bee that feeds her Husband Drone
Deliciously, and builds her waxen Cells
With Honey stor'd: the rest are numberless,
And thou thir Natures know'st, and gav'st them Names,
Needlest to thee repeated; nor unknown
The Serpent suttl'st Beast of all the field,
Of huge extent somtimes, with brazen Eyes
And hairie Main terrific, though to thee
Not noxious, but obedient at thy call.
Now Heav'n in all her Glorie shon, and rowld
Her motions, as the great first-Movers hand
First wheeld thir course; Earth in her rich attire
Consummate lovly smil'd; Aire, Water, Earth,
By Fowl, Fish, Beast, was flown, was swum, was walkt
Frequent; and of the Sixt day yet remain'd;
There wanted yet the Master work, the end
Of all yet don; a Creature who not prone
And Brute as other Creatures, but endu'd

With Sanctitie of Reason, might erect
His Stature, and upright with Front serene
Govern the rest, self-knowing, and from thence
Magnanimous to correspond with Heav'n,
But grateful to acknowledge whence his good
Descends, thither with heart and voice and eyes
Directed in Devotion, to adore
And worship God Supream, who made him chief
Of all his works: therefore the Omnipotent
Eternal Father (For where is not hee
Present) thus to his Son audibly spake.
    Let us make now Man in our image, Man
In our similitude, and let them rule
Over the Fish and Fowle of Sea and Aire,
Beast of the Field, and over all the Earth,
And every creeping thing that creeps the ground.
This said, he formd thee, *Adam*, thee O Man
Dust of the ground, and in thy nostrils breath'd
The breath of Life; in his own Image hee
Created thee, in the Image of God
Express, and thou becam'st a living Soul.
Male he created thee, but thy consort
Female for Race; then bless'd Mankinde, and said,
Be fruitful, multiplie, and fill the Earth,
Subdue it, and throughout Dominion hold
Over Fish of the Sea, and Fowle of the Aire,
And every living thing that moves on the Earth.
Wherever thus created, for no place
Is yet distinct by name, thence, as thou know'st
He brought thee into this delicious Grove,
This Garden, planted with the Trees of God,
Delectable both to behold and taste;
And freely all thir pleasant fruit for food
Gave thee, all sorts are here that all th' Earth yields,
Varietie without end; but of the Tree
Which tasted works knowledge of Good and Evil,
Thou mai'st not; in the day thou eat'st, thou di'st;
Death is the penaltie impos'd, beware,
And govern well thy appetite, least sin
Surprise thee, and her black attendant Death.

Here finish'd hee, and all that he had made
View'd, and behold all was entirely good;
So Ev'n and Morn accomplish'd the Sixt day:
Yet not till the Creator from his work
Desisting, though unwearied, up returnd
Up to the Heav'n of Heav'ns his high abode,
Thence to behold this new created World
Th' addition of his Empire, how it shew'd
In prospect from his Throne, how good, how faire,
Answering his great Idea. Up he rode
Followd with acclamation and the sound
Symphonious of ten thousand Harpes that tun'd
Angelic harmonies: the Earth, the Aire
Resounded, (thou remember'st, for thou heardst)
The Heav'ns and all the Constellations rung,
The Planets in thir station list'ning stood,
While the bright Pomp ascended jubilant.
Open, ye everlasting Gates, they sung,
Open, ye Heav'ns, your living dores; let in
The great Creator from his work returnd
Magnificent, his Six days work, a World;
Open, and henceforth oft; for God will deigne
To visit oft the dwellings of just Men
Delighted, and with frequent intercourse
Thither will send his winged Messengers
On errands of supernal Grace. So sung
The glorious Train ascending: He through Heav'n,
That open'd wide her blazing Portals, led
To Gods Eternal house direct the way,
A broad and ample rode, whose dust is Gold
And pavement Starrs, as Starrs to thee appeer,
Seen in the Galaxie, that Milkie way
Which nightly as a circling Zone thou seest
Pouderd with Starrs. And now on Earth the Seventh
Eev'ning arose in *Eden*, for the Sun
Was set, and twilight from the East came on,
Forerunning Night; when at the holy mount
Of Heav'ns high-seated top, th' Impereal Throne
Of Godhead, fixt for ever firm and sure,
The Filial Power arriv'd, and sate him down

With his great Father, for he also went
Invisible, yet staid (such priviledge
Hath Omnipresence) and the work ordain'd,
Author and end of all things, and from work
Now resting, bless'd and hallowd the Seav'nth day,
As resting on that day from all his work,
But not in silence holy kept; the Harp
Had work and rested not, the solemn Pipe,
And Dulcimer, all Organs of sweet stop,
All sounds on Fret by String or Golden Wire
Temper'd soft Tunings, intermixt with Voice
Choral or Unison; of incense Clouds
Fuming from Golden Censers hid the Mount.
Creation and the Six dayes acts they sung,
Great are thy works, *Jehovah*, infinite
Thy power; what thought can measure thee or tongue
Relate thee; greater now in thy return
Then from the Giant Angels; thee that day
Thy Thunders magnifi'd; but to create
Is greater then created to destroy.
Who can impair thee, mighty King, or bound
Thy empire? easily the proud attempt
Of Spirits apostat and thir Counsels vaine
Thou hast repeld, while impiously they thought
Thee to diminish, and from thee withdraw
The number of thy worshippers. Who seekes
To lessen thee, against his purpose serves
To manifest the more thy might : his evil
Thou usest, and from thence creat'st more good.
Witness this new-made World, another Heav'n
From Heaven Gate not farr, founded in view
On the cleer *Hyaline*, the Glassie Sea ;
Of amplitude almost immense, with Starr's
Numerous, and every Starr perhaps a World
Of destind habitation; but thou know'st
Thir seasons : among these the seat of men,
Earth with her nether Ocean circumfus'd,
Thir pleasant dwelling place. Thrice happie men,
And sons of men, whom God hath thus advanc't,
Created in his Image, there to dwell

And worship him, and in reward to rule
Over his Works, on Earth, in Sea, or Air,
And multiply a Race of Worshippers
Holy and just: thrice happie if they know
Thir happiness, and persevere upright.
    So sung they, and the Empyrean rung,
With *Halleluiahs:* Thus was Sabbath kept.
And thy request think now fulfill'd, that ask'd
How first this World and face of things began,
And what before thy memorie was don
From the beginning, that posteritie
Informd by thee might know; if else thou seek'st
Aught, not surpassing human measure, say.

BOOK VIII

THE ARGUMENT

ADAM *inquires concerning celestial Motions, is doubtfully answer'd, and exhorted to search rather things more worthy of knowledg:* Adam *assents, and still desirous to detain* Raphael, *relates to him what he remember'd since his own Creation, his placing in Paradise, his talk with God concerning solitude and fit society, his first meeting and Nuptials with* Eve, *his discourse with the Angel thereupon; who after admonitions repeated departs.*

THE Angel ended, and in *Adams* Eare
So Charming left his voice, that he a while
Thought him still speaking, still stood fixt to hear;
Then as new waked thus gratefully repli'd.
What thanks sufficient, or what recompence
Equal have I to render thee, Divine
Hystorian, who thus largely hast allayd
The thirst I had of knowledge, and voutsaf't
This friendly condescention to relate
Things else by me unsearchable, now heard
With wonder, but delight, and, as is due,
With glorie attributed to the high
Creator; some thing yet of doubt remaines,
Which onely thy solution can resolve.

When I behold this goodly Frame, this World
Of Heav'n and Earth consisting, and compute,
Thir magnitudes, this Earth a spot, a graine,
An Atom, with the Firmament compar'd
And all her numberd Starrs, that seem to rowle
Spaces incomprehensible (for such
Thir distance argues and thir swift return
Diurnal) meerly to officiate light
Round this opacous Earth, this punctual spot,
One day and night; in all thir vast survey
Useless besides, reasoning I oft admire,
How Nature wise and frugal could commit
Such disproportions, with superfluous hand
So many nobler Bodies to create,
Greater so manifold to this one use,
For aught appeers, and on thir Orbs impose
Such restless revolution day by day
Repeated, while the sedentarie Earth,
That better might with farr less compass move,
Serv'd by more noble then her self, attaines
Her end without least motion, and receaves,
As Tribute such a sumless journey brought
Of incorporeal speed, her warmth and light;
Speed, to describe whose swiftness Number failes.

So spake our Sire, and by his count'nance seemd
Entring on studious thoughts abstruse, which *Eve*
Perceaving where she sat retir'd in sight,
With lowliness Majestic from her seat,
And Grace that won who saw to wish her stay,
Rose, and went forth among her Fruits and Flours,
To visit how they prosper'd, bud and bloom,
Her Nurserie; they at her coming sprung
And toucht by her fair tendance gladlier grew.
Yet went she not, as not with such discourse
Delighted, or not capable her eare
Of what was high: such pleasure she reserv'd,
Adam relating, she sole Auditress;
Her Husband the Relater she preferr'd
Before the Angel, and of him to ask
Chose rather; hee, she knew would intermix

Grateful digressions, and solve high dispute
With conjugal Caresses, from his Lip
Not Words alone pleas'd her. O when meet now
Such pairs, in Love and mutual Honour joyn'd?
With Goddess-like demeanour forth she went;
Not unattended, for on her as Queen
A pomp of winning Graces waited still,
And from about her shot Darts of desire
Into all Eyes to wish her still in sight.
And *Raphael* now to *Adam's* doubt propos'd
Benevolent and facil thus repli'd.

    To ask or search I blame thee not, for Heav'n
Is as the Book of God before thee set,
Wherein to read his wondrous Works, and learne
His Seasons, Hours, or Days, or Months, or Yeares;
This to attain, whether Heav'n move or Earth,
Imports not, if thou reck'n right, the rest
From Man or Angel the great Architect
Did wisely to conceal, and not divulge
His secrets to be scann'd by them who ought
Rather admire; or if they list to try
Conjecture, he his Fabric of the Heav'ns
Hath left to thir disputes, perhaps to move
His laughter at thir quaint Opinions wide
Hereafter, when they come to model Heav'n
And calculate the Starrs, how they will weild
The mightie frame, how build, unbuild, contrive
To save appeerances, how gird the Sphear
With Centric and Eccentric scribl'd o're,
Cycle and Epicycle, Orb in Orb:
Alreadie by thy reasoning this I guess,
Who art to lead thy ofspring, and supposest
That Bodies bright and greater should not serve
The less not bright, nor Heav'n such journies run,
Earth sitting still, when she alone receaves
The benefit: consider first, that Great
Or Bright inferrs not Excellence: the Earth
Though, in comparison of Heav'n, so small,
Nor glistering, may of solid good containe
More plenty then the Sun that barren shines,

Whose vertue on it self workes no effect,
But in the fruitful Earth; there first receavd
His beams, unactive else, thir vigor find.
Yet not to Earth are those bright Luminaries
Officious, but to thee Earths habitant.
And for the Heav'ns wide Circuit, let it speak
The Makers high magnificence, who built
So spacious, and his Line stretcht out so farr;
That Man may know he dwells not in his own;
An Edifice too large for him to fill,
Lodg'd in a small partition, and the rest
Ordain'd for uses to his Lord best known.
The swiftness of those Circles attribute,
Though numberless, to his Omnipotence,
That to corporeal substances could adde
Speed almost Spiritual; mee thou thinkst not slow,
Who since the Morning hour set out from Heav'n
Where God resides, and ere mid-day arriv'd
In *Eden*, distance inexpressible
By Numbers that have name. But this I urge,
Admitting Motion in the Heav'ns, to shew
Invalid that which thee to doubt it mov'd;
Not that I so affirm, though so it seem
To thee who hast thy dwelling here on Earth.
God to remove his wayes from human sense,
Plac'd Heav'n from Earth so farr, that earthly sight,
If it presume, might erre in things too high,
And no advantage gaine. What if the Sun
Be Center to the World, and other Starrs
By his attractive vertue and thir own
Incited, dance about him various rounds?
Thir wandring course now high, now low, then hid,
Progressive, retrograde, or standing still,
In six thou seest, and what if sev'nth to these
The Planet Earth, so stedfast though she seem,
Insensibly three different Motions move?
Which else to several Sphears thou must ascribe,
Mov'd contrarie with thwart obliquities,
Or save the Sun his labour, and that swift
Nocturnal and Diurnal rhomb suppos'd,

Invisible else above all Starrs, the Wheele
Of Day and Night; which needs not thy beleefe,
If Earth industrious of her self fetch Day
Travelling East, and with her part averse
From the Suns beam meet Night, her other part
Still luminous by his ray. What if that light
Sent from her through the wide transpicuous aire,
To the terrestrial Moon be as a Starr
Enlightning her by Day, as she by Night
This Earth? reciprocal, if Land be there,
Feilds and Inhabitants: Her spots thou seest
As Clouds, and Clouds may rain, and Rain produce
Fruits in her soft'nd Soile, for some to eate
Allotted there; and other Suns perhaps
With thir attendant Moons thou wilt descrie
Communicating Male and Femal Light,
Which two great Sexes animate the World,
Stor'd in each Orb perhaps with some that live.
For such vast room in Nature unpossest
By living Soule, desert and desolate,
Onely to shine, yet scarce to contribute
Each Orb a glimps of Light, conveyd so farr
Down to this habitable, which returnes
Light back to them, is obvious to dispute.
But whether thus these things, or whether not,
Whether the Sun predominant in Heav'n
Rise on the Earth, or Earth rise on the Sun,
Hee from the East his flaming rode begin,
Or Shee from West her silent course advance
With inoffensive pace that spinning sleeps
On her soft Axle, while she paces Eev'n,
And bears thee soft with the smooth Air along,
Sollicit not thy thoughts with matters hid,
Leave them to God above, him serve and feare;
Of other Creatures, as him pleases best,
Wherever plac't, let him dispose: joy thou
In what he gives to thee, this Paradise
And thy fair *Eve;* Heav'n is for thee too high
To know what passes there; be lowlie wise:
Think onely what concernes thee and thy being;

Dream not of other Worlds, what Creatures there
Live, in what state, condition or degree,
Contented that thus farr hath been reveal'd
Not of Earth onely but of highest Heav'n.
   To whom thus *Adam* cleerd of doubt, repli'd.
How fully hast thou satisfi'd mee, pure
Intelligence of Heav'n, Angel serene,
And freed from intricacies, taught to live,
The easiest way, nor with perplexing thoughts
To interrupt the sweet of Life, from which
God hath bid dwell farr off all anxious cares,
And not molest us, unless we our selves
Seek them with wandring thoughts, and notions vain.
But apte the Mind or Fancie is to roave
Uncheckt, and of her roaving is no end;
Till warn'd, or by experience taught, she learne,
That not to know at large of things remote
From use, obscure and suttle, but to know
That which before us lies in daily life,
Is the prime Wisdom, what is more, is fume,
Or emptiness, or fond impertinence,
And renders us in things that most concerne
Unpractis'd, unprepar'd, and still to seek.
Therefore from this high pitch let us descend
A lower flight, and speak of things at hand
Useful, whence haply mention may arise
Of something not unseasonable to ask
By sufferance, and thy wonted favour deign'd.
Thee I have heard relating what was don
Ere my remembrance: now hear mee relate
My Storie, which perhaps thou hast not heard;
And Day is yet not spent; till then thou seest
How suttly to detaine thee I devise,
Inviting thee to hear while I relate,
Fond, were it not in hope of thy reply:
For while I sit with thee, I seem in Heav'n,
And sweeter thy discourse is to my eare
Then Fruits of Palm-tree pleasantest to thirst
And hunger both, from labour, at the houre
Of sweet repast; they satiate, and soon fill,

Though pleasant, but thy words with Grace Divine
Imbu'd, bring to thir sweetness no satietie.
    To whom thus *Raphael* answer'd heav'nly meek.
Nor are thy lips ungraceful, Sire of men,
Nor tongue ineloquent; for God on thee
Abundantly his gifts hath also pour'd
Inward and outward both, his image faire:
Speaking or mute all comliness and grace
Attends thee, and each word, each motion formes.
Nor less think wee in Heav'n of thee on Earth
Then of our fellow servant, and inquire
Gladly into the wayes of God with Man:
For God we see hath honour'd thee, and set
On Man his equal Love: say therefore on;
For I that Day was absent, as befell,
Bound on a voyage uncouth and obscure,
Farr on excursion toward the Gates of Hell;
Squar'd in full Legion (such command we had)
To see that none thence issu'd forth a spie,
Or enemie, while God was in his work,
Least hee incenst at such eruption bold,
Destruction with Creation might have mixt.
Not that they durst without his leave attempt,
But us he sends upon his high behests
For state, as Sovran King, and to enure
Our prompt obedience. Fast we found, fast shut
The dismal Gates, and barricado'd strong;
But long ere our approaching heard within
Noise, other then the sound of Dance or Song,
Torment, and loud lament, and furious rage.
Glad we return'd up to the coasts of Light
Ere Sabbath Eev'ning: so we had in charge.
But thy relation now; for I attend,
Pleas'd with thy words no less then thou with mine.
    So spake the Godlike Power, and thus our Sire.
For Man to tell how human Life began
Is hard: for who himself beginning knew?
Desire with thee still longer to converse
Induc'd me. As new wak't from soundest sleep
Soft on the flourie herb I found me laid

In Balmie Sweat, which with his Beames the Sun
Soon dri'd, and on the reaking moisture fed.
Strait toward Heav'n my wondring Eyes I turnd,
And gaz'd a while the ample Skie, till rais'd
By quick instinctive motion up I sprung,
As thitherward endevoring, and upright
Stood on my feet; about me round I saw
Hill, Dale, and shadie Woods, and sunnie Plaines,
And liquid Lapse of murmuring Streams; by these,
Creatures that livd, and movd, and walk'd, or flew,
Birds on the branches warbling; all things smil'd,
With fragrance and with joy my heart oreflow'd.
My self I then perus'd, and Limb by Limb
Survey'd, and sometimes went, and sometimes ran
With supple joints, and lively vigour led:
But who I was, or where, or from what cause,
Knew not; to speak I tri'd, and forthwith spake,
My Tongue obey'd and readily could name
What e're I saw. Thou Sun, said I, faire Light,
And thou enlight'nd Earth, so fresh and gay,
Ye Hills and Dales, ye Rivers, Woods, and Plaines,
And ye that live and move, fair Creatures, tell,
Tell, if ye saw, how came I thus, how here?
Not of my self; by some great Maker then,
In goodness and in power præeminent;
Tell me, how may I know him, how adore,
From whom I have that thus I move and live,
And feel that I am happier then I know.
While thus I call'd, and stray'd I knew not whither,
From where I first drew Aire, and first beheld
This happie Light, when answer none return'd,
On a green shadie Bank profuse of Flours
Pensive I sate me down; there gentle sleep
First found me, and with soft oppression seis'd
My droused sense, untroubl'd, though I though
I then was passing to my former state
Insensible, and forthwith to dissolve:
When suddenly stood at my Head a dream,
Whose inward apparition gently mov'd
My Fancy to believe I yet had being,

And livd: One came, methought, of shape Divine,
And said, thy Mansion wants thee, *Adam*, rise,
First Man, of Men innumerable ordain'd
First Father, call'd by thee I come thy Guide
To the Garden of bliss, thy seat prepar'd.
So saying, by the hand he took me rais'd,
And over Fields and Waters, as in Aire
Smooth sliding without step, last led me up
A woodie Mountain; whose high top was plaine,
A Circuit wide, enclos'd, with goodliest Trees
Planted, with Walks, and Bowers, that what I saw
Of Earth before scarce pleasant seemd. Each Tree
Load'n with fairest Fruit, that hung to the Eye
Tempting, stirr'd in me sudden appetite
To pluck and eate; whereat I wak'd, and found
Before mine Eyes all real, as the dream
Had lively shadowd: Here had new begun
My wandring, had not hee who was my Guide
Up hither, from among the Trees appeer'd,
Presence Divine. Rejoycing, but with aw
In adoration at his feet I fell
Submiss: he rear'd me, and Whom thou soughtst I am,
Said mildely, Author of all this thou seest
Above, or round about thee or beneath.
This Paradise I give thee, count it thine
To Till and keep, and of the Fruit to eate:
Of every Tree that in the Garden growes
Eate freely with glad heart; fear here no dearth:
But of the Tree whose operation brings
Knowledg of good and ill, which I have set
The Pledge of thy Obedience and thy Faith,
Amid the Garden by the Tree of Life,
Remember what I warne thee, shun to taste,
And shun the bitter consequence: for know,
The day thou eat'st thereof, my sole command
Transgrest, inevitably thou shalt dye;
From that day mortal, and this happie State
Shalt loose, expell'd from hence into a World
Of woe and sorrow. Sternly he pronounc'd
The rigid interdiction, which resounds

Yet dreadful in mine eare, though in my choice
Not to incur; but soon his cleer aspect
Return'd and gracious purpose thus renew'd.
Not onely these fair bounds, but all the Earth
To thee and to thy Race I give; as Lords
Possess it, and all things that therein live,
Or live in Sea, or Aire, Beast, Fish, and Fowle.
In signe whereof each Bird and Beast behold
After thir kindes; I bring them to receave
From thee thir Names, and to pay thee fealtie
With low subjection; understand the same
Of Fish within thir watry residence,
Not hither summond, since they cannot change
Thir Element to draw the thinner Aire.
As thus he spake, each Bird and Beast behold
Approaching two and two, These cowring low
With blandishment, each Bird stoop'd on his wing.
I nam'd them, as they pass'd, and understood
Thir Nature, with such knowledg God endu'd
My sudden apprehension: but in these
I found not what me thought I wanted still;
And to the Heav'nly vision thus presum'd.

O by what Name, for thou above all these,
Above mankinde, or aught then mankinde higher,
Surpassest farr my naming, how may I
Adore thee, Author of this Universe,
And all this good to man, for whose well being
So amply, and with hands so liberal
Thou hast provided all things: but with mee
I see not who partakes. In solitude
What happiness, who can enjoy alone,
Or all enjoying, what contentment find?
Thus I presumptuous; and the vision bright,
As with a smile more bright'nd, thus repli'd.

What call'st thou solitude, is not the Earth
With various living creatures, and the Aire
Replenisht, and all these at thy command
To come and play before thee, know'st thou not
Thir language and thir wayes, they also know,
And reason not contemptibly; with these

Find pastime, and beare rule; thy Realm is large.
So spake the Universal Lord, and seem'd
So ordering. I with leave of speech implor'd,
And humble deprecation thus repli'd.

    Let not my words offend thee, Heav'nly Power,
My Maker, be propitious while I speak.
Hast thou not made me here thy substitute,
And these inferiour farr beneath me set?
Among unequals what societie
Can sort, what harmonie or true delight?
Which must be mutual, in proportion due
Giv'n and receiv'd; but in disparitie
The one intense, the other still remiss
Cannot well suite with either, but soon prove
Tedious alike: Of fellowship I speak
Such as I seek, fit to participate
All rational delight, wherein the brute
Cannot be human consort; they rejoyce
Each with thir kinde, Lion with Lioness;
So fitly them in pairs thou hast combin'd;
Much less can Bird with Beast, or Fish with Fowle
So well converse, nor with the Ox the Ape:
Wors then can Man with Beast, and least of all.

    Whereto th' Almighty answer'd, not displeas'd.
A nice and suttle happiness I see
Thou to thy self proposest, in the choice
Of thy Associates, *Adam*, and wilt taste
No pleasure, though in pleasure, solitarie.
What thinkst thou then of mee, and this my State,
Seem I to thee sufficiently possest
Of happiness, or not? who am alone
From all Eternitie, for none I know
Second to me or like, equal much less.
How have I then with whom to hold converse
Save with the Creatures which I made, and those
To me inferiour, infinite descents
Beneath what other Creatures are to thee?

    He ceas'd, I lowly answer'd. To attaine
The highth and depth of thy Eternal wayes
All human thoughts come short, Supream of things;

Thou in thy self art perfet, and in thee
Is no deficience found; not so is Man,
But in degree, the cause of his desire
By conversation with his like to help,
Or solace his defects. No need that thou
Shouldst propagat, already infinite;
And through all numbers absolute, though One;
But Man by number is to manifest
His single imperfection, and beget
Like of his like, his Image multipli'd,
In unitie defective, which requires
Collateral love, and deerest amitie.
Thou in thy secresie although alone,
Best with thy self accompanied, seek'st not
Social communication, yet so pleas'd,
Canst raise thy Creature to what highth thou wilt
Of Union or Communion, deifi'd;
I by conversing cannot these erect
From prone, nor in thir wayes complacence find.
Thus I embold'nd spake, and freedom us'd
Permissive, and acceptance found, which gain'd
This answer from the gratious voice Divine.

    Thus farr to try thee, *Adam*, I was pleas'd,
And finde thee knowing not of Beasts alone,
Which thou hast rightly nam'd, but of thy self,
Expressing well the spirit within thee free,
My Image, not imparted to the Brute,
Whose fellowship therefore unmeet for thee
Good reason was thou freely shouldst dislike,
And be so minded still; I, ere thou spak'st,
Knew it not good for Man to be alone,
And no such companie as then thou saw'st
Intended thee, for trial onely brought,
To see how thou could'st judge of fit and meet:
What next I bring shall please thee, be assur'd,
Thy likeness, thy fit help, thy other self,
Thy wish, exactly to thy hearts desire.

    Hee ended, or I heard no more, for now
My earthly by his Heav'nly overpowerd,
Which it had long stood under, streind to the highth

In that celestial Colloquie sublime,
As with an object that excels the sense,
Dazl'd and spent, sunk down, and sought repair
Of sleep, which instantly fell on me, call'd
By Nature as in aide, and clos'd mine eyes.
Mine eyes he clos'd, but op'n left the Cell
Of Fancie my internal sight, by which
Abstract as in a transe methought I saw,
Though sleeping, where I lay, and saw the shape
Still glorious before whom awake I stood;
Who stooping op'nd my left side, and took
From thence a Rib, with cordial spirits warme,
And Life-blood streaming fresh; wide was the wound,
But suddenly with flesh fill'd up and heal'd:
The Rib he formd and fashond with his hands;
Under his forming hands a Creature grew,
Manlike, but different sex, so lovly faire,
That what seemd fair in all the World, seemd now
Mean, or in her summd up, in her containd
And in her looks, which from that time infus'd
Sweetness into my heart, unfelt before,
And into all things from her Aire inspir'd
The spirit of love and amorous delight.
She disappeerd, and left me dark, I wak'd
To find her, or for ever to deplore
Her loss, and other pleasures all abjure:
When out of hope, behold her, not farr off,
Such as I saw her in my dream, adornd
With what all Earth or Heaven could bestow
To make her amiable: On she came,
Led by her Heav'nly Maker, though unseen,
And guided by his voice, nor uninformd
Of nuptial Sanctitie and marriage Rites:
Grace was in all her steps, Heav'n in her Eye,
In every gesture dignitie and love.
I overjoyd could not forbear aloud.

   This turn hath made amends; thou hast fulfill'd
Thy words, Creator bounteous and benigne,
Giver of all things faire, but fairest this
Of all thy gifts, nor enviest. I now see

Bone of my Bone, Flesh of my Flesh, my Self
Before me; Woman is her Name, of Man
Extracted; for this cause he shall forgoe
Father and Mother, and to his Wife adhere;
And they shall be one Flesh, one Heart, one Soule.
    She heard me thus, and though divinely brought,
Yet Innocence and Virgin Modestie,
Her vertue and the conscience of her worth,
That would be woo'd, and not unsought be won.
Not obvious, not obtrusive, but retir'd,
The more desirable, or to say all,
Nature her self, though pure of sinful thought,
Wrought in her so, that seeing me, she turn'd;
I follow'd her, she what was Honour knew,
And with obsequious Majestie approv'd
My pleaded reason. To the Nuptial Bowre
I led her blushing like the Morn: all Heav'n,
And happie Constellations on that houre
Shed their selectest influence; the Earth
Gave sign of gratulation, and each Hill;
Joyous the Birds; fresh Gales and gentle Aires
Whisper'd it to the Woods, and from thir wings
Flung Rose, flung Odours from the spicie Shrub,
Disporting, till the amorous Bird of Night
Sung Spousal, and bid haste the Eevning Starr
On his Hill top, to light the bridal Lamp.
Thus I have told thee all my State, and brought
My Storie to the sum of earthly bliss
Which I enjoy, and must confess to find
In all things else delight indeed, but such
As us'd or not, works in the mind no change,
Nor vehement desire, these delicacies
I mean of Taste, Sight, Smell, Herbs, Fruits, and Flours,
Walks, and the melodie of Birds; but here
Farr otherwise, transported I behold,
Transported touch; here passion first I felt,
Commotion strange, in all enjoyments else
Superiour and unmov'd, here onely weake
Against the charm of Beauties powerful glance.
Or Nature faild in mee, and left some part

Not proof enough such Object to sustain,
Or from my side subducting, took perhaps
More then enough; at least on her bestow'd
Too much of Ornament, in outward shew
Elaborate, of inward less exact.
For well I understand in the prime end
Of Nature her th' inferiour, in the mind
And inward Faculties, which most excell,
In outward also her resembling less
His Image who made both, and less expressing
The character of that Dominion giv'n
O're other Creatures; yet when I approach
Her loveliness, so absolute she seems
And in her self compleat, so well to know
Her own, that what she wills to do or say,
Seems wisest, vertuousest, discreetest, best;
All higher knowledge in her presence falls
Degraded, Wisdom in discourse with her
Looses discount'nanc't, and like folly shewes;
Authoritie and Reason on her waite,
As one intended first, not after made
Occasionally; and to consummate all,
Greatness of mind and nobleness thir seat
Build in her loveliest, and create an awe
About her, as a guard Angelic plac't.
To whom the Angel with contracted brow.

Accuse not Nature, she hath don her part;
Do thou but thine, and be not diffident
Of Wisdom, she deserts thee not, if thou
Dismiss not her, when most thou needst her nigh,
By attributing overmuch to things
Less excellent, as thou thy self perceav'st.
For what admir'st thou, what transports thee so,
An outside? fair no doubt, and worthy well
Thy cherishing, thy honouring, and thy love,
Not thy subjection: weigh with her thy self;
Then value: Oft times nothing profits more
Then self-esteem, grounded on just and right
Well manag'd; of that skill the more thou know'st,
The more she will acknowledge thee her Head,

And to realities yield all her shows;
Made so adorn for thy delight the more,
So awful, that with honour thou maist love
Thy mate, who sees when thou art seen least wise.
But if the sense of touch whereby mankind
Is propagated seem such dear delight
Beyond all other, think the same voutsaf't
To Cattel and each Beast; which would not be
To them made common and divulg'd, if aught
Therein enjoy'd were worthy to subdue
The Soule of Man, or passion in him move.
What higher in her societie thou findst
Attractive, human, rational, love still;
In loving thou dost well, in passion not,
Wherein true Love consists not; love refines
The thoughts, and heart enlarges, hath his seat
In Reason, and is judicious, is the scale
By which to heav'nly Love thou maist ascend,
Not sunk in carnal pleasure, for which cause
Among the Beasts no Mate for thee was found.
    To whom thus half abash't *Adam* repli'd.
Neither her out-side formd so fair, nor aught
In procreation common to all kindes
(Though higher of the genial Bed by far,
And with mysterious reverence I deem)
So much delights me, as those graceful acts,
Those thousand decencies that daily flow
From all her words and actions, mixt with Love
And sweet compliance, which declare unfeign'd
Union of Mind, or in us both one Soule;
Harmonie to behold in wedded pair
More grateful then harmonious sound to the eare.
Yet these subject not; I to thee disclose
What inward thence I feel, not therefore foild,
Who meet with various objects, from the sense
Variously representing; yet still free
Approve the best, and follow what I approve.
To love thou blam'st me not, for love thou saist
Leads up to Heav'n, is both the way and guide;
Bear with me then, if lawful what I ask;

Love not the heav'nly Spirits, and how thir **Love**
Express they, by looks onely, or do they mix
Irradiance, virtual or immediate touch?
  To whom the Angel with a smile that glow'd
Celestial rosie red, Loves proper hue,
Answer'd. Let it suffice thee that thou know'st
Us happie, and without Love no happiness.
Whatever pure thou in the body enjoy'st
(And pure thou wert created) we enjoy
In eminence, and obstacle find none
Of membrane, joynt, or limb, exclusive barrs:
Easier then Air with Air, if Spirits embrace,
Total they mix, Union of Pure with Pure
Desiring; nor restrain'd conveyance need
As Flesh to mix with Flesh, or Soul with Soul.
But I can now no more; the parting Sun
Beyond the Earths green Cape and verdant Isles
Hesperean sets, my Signal to depart.
Be strong, live happie, and love, but first of all
Him whom to love is to obey, and keep
His great command; take heed least Passion sway
Thy Judgement to do aught, which else free Will
Would not admit; thine and of all thy Sons
The weal or woe in thee is plac't; beware.
I in thy persevering shall rejoyce,
And all the Blest: stand fast; to stand or fall
Free in thine own Arbitrement it lies.
Perfet within, no outward aid require;
And all temptation to transgress repel.
  So saying, he arose; whom *Adam* thus
Follow'd with benediction. Since to part,
Go heavenly Guest, Ethereal Messenger,
Sent from whose sovran goodness I adore.
Gentle to me and affable hath been
Thy condescension, and shall be honour'd ever
With grateful Memorie: thou to mankind
Be good and friendly still, and oft return.
  So parted they, the Angel up to Heav'n
From the thick shade, and *Adam* to his Bowre

BOOK IX

THE ARGUMENT

SATAN *having compast the Earth, with meditated guile returns
as a mist by Night into Paradise, enters into the Serpent sleeping.* Adam *and* Eve *in the Morning go forth to thir labours,
which* Eve *proposes to divide in several places, each labouring
apart:* Adam *consents not, alledging the danger, lest that
Enemy, of whom they were forewarn'd, should attempt her
found alone:* Eve *loath to be thought not circumspect or firm
enough, urges her going apart, the rather desirous to make tryal
of her strength;* Adam *at last yields: The Serpent finds her
alone; his subtle approach, first gazing, then speaking, with
much flattery extolling* Eve *above all other Creatures.* Eve
*wondring to hear the Serpent speak, asks how he attain'd to
human speech and such understanding not till now; the Serpent
answers, that by tasting of a certain Tree in the Garden he
attain'd both to Speech and Reason, till then void of both:*
Eve *requires him to bring her to that Tree, and finds it to be the
Tree of Knowledge forbidden: The Serpent now grown bolder,
with many wiles and arguments induces her at length to eat;
she pleas'd with the taste deliberates awhile whether to impart
thereof to* Adam *or not, at last brings him of the Fruit, relates
what persuaded her to eat thereof:* Adam *at first amaz'd, but
perceiving her lost, resolves through vehemence of love to perish
with her; and extenuating the trespass, eats also of the Fruit:
The effects thereof in them both; they seek to cover thir nakedness; then fall to variance and accusation of one another.*

No more of talk where God or Angel Guest
With Man, as with his Friend, familiar us'd
To sit indulgent, and with him partake
Rural repast, permitting him the while
Venial discourse unblam'd : I now must change
Those Notes to Tragic ; foul distrust, and breach
Disloyal on the part of Man, revolt,
And disobedience : On the part of Heav'n
Now alienated, distance and distaste,
Anger and just rebuke, and judgement giv'n,

That brought into this World a world of woe,
Sinne and her shadow Death, and Miserie
Deaths Harbinger: Sad task, yet argument
Not less but more Heroic then the wrauth
Of stern *Achilles* on his Foe pursu'd
Thrice Fugitive about *Troy* Wall; or rage
Of *Turnus* for *Lavinia* disespous'd,
Or *Neptun's* ire or *Juno's*, that so long
Perplex'd the *Greek* and *Cytherea's* Son;
If answerable style I can obtaine
Of my Celestial Patroness, who deignes
Her nightly visitation unimplor'd,
And dictates to me slumbring, or inspires
Easie my unpremeditated Verse:
Since first this Subject for Heroic Song
Pleas'd me long choosing, and beginning late;
Not sedulous by Nature to indite
Warrs, hitherto the onely Argument
Heroic deem'd, chief maistrie to dissect
With long and tedious havoc fabl'd Knights
In Battels feign'd; the better fortitude
Of Patience and Heroic Martyrdom
Unsung; or to describe Races and Games,
Or tilting Furniture, emblazon'd Shields,
Impreses quaint, Caparisons and Steeds;
Bases and tinsel Trappings, gorgious Knights
At Joust and Torneament; then marshal'd Feast
Serv'd up in Hall with Sewers, and Seneshals;
The skill of Artifice or Office mean,
Not that which justly gives Heroic name
To Person or to Poem. Mee of these
Nor skilld nor studious, higher Argument
Remaines, sufficient of it self to raise
That name, unless an age too late, or cold
Climat, or Years damp my intended wing
Deprest, and much they may, if all be mine,
Not Hers who brings it nightly to my Ear.
    The Sun was sunk, and after him the Starr
Of *Hesperus*, whose Office is to bring
Twilight upon the Earth, short Arbiter

Twixt Day and Night, and now from end to end
Nights Hemisphere had veild the Horizon round:
When *Satan* who late fled before the threats
Of *Gabriel* out of *Eden*, now improv'd
In meditated fraud and malice, bent
On mans destruction, maugre what might hap
Of heavier on himself, fearless return'd.
By Night he fled, and at Midnight return'd
From compassing the Earth, cautious of day,
Since *Uriel* Regent of the Sun descri'd
His entrance, and forewarnd the Cherubim
That kept thir watch; thence full of anguish driv'n,
The space of seven continu'd Nights he rode
With darkness, thrice the Equinoctial Line
He circl'd, four times cross'd the Carr of Night
From Pole to Pole, traversing each Colure;
On the eighth return'd, and on the Coast averse
From entrance or Cherubic Watch, by stealth
Found unsuspected way. There was a place,
Now not, though Sin, not Time, first wraught the change,
Where *Tigris* at the foot of Paradise
Into a Gulf shot under ground, till part
Rose up a Fountain by the Tree of Life;
In with the River sunk, and with it rose
Satan involv'd in rising Mist, then sought
Where to lie hid; Sea he had searcht and Land
From *Eden* over *Pontus*, and the Poole
Mæotis, up beyond the River *Ob;*
Downward as farr Antartic; and in length
West from *Orontes* to the Ocean barr'd
At *Darien*, thence to the Land where flowes
Ganges and *Indus:* thus the Orb he roam'd
With narrow search; and with inspection deep
Consider'd every Creature, which of all
Most opportune might serve his Wiles, and found
The Serpent suttlest Beast of all the Field.
Him after long debate, irresolute
Of thoughts revolv'd, his final sentence chose
Fit Vessel, fittest Imp of fraud, in whom
To enter, and his dark suggestions hide

From sharpest sight: for in the wilie Snake,
Whatever sleights none would suspicious mark,
As from his wit and native suttletie
Proceeding, which in other Beasts observ'd
Doubt might beget of Diabolic pow'r
Active within beyond the sense of brute.
Thus he resolv'd, but first from inward griefe
His bursting passion into plaints thus pour'd:

O Earth, how like to Heav'n, if not preferrd
More justly, Seat worthier of Gods, as built
With second thoughts, reforming what was old!
For what God after better worse would build?
Terrestrial Heav'n, danc't round by other Heav'ns
That shine, yet bear thir bright officious Lamps,
Light above Light, for thee alone, as seems,
In thee concentring all thir precious beams
Of sacred influence: As God in Heav'n
Is Center, yet extends to all, so thou
Centring receav'st from all those Orbs; in thee,
Not in themselves, all thir known vertue appeers
Productive in Herb, Plant, and nobler birth
Of Creatures animate with gradual life
Of Growth, Sense, Reason, all summ'd up in Man.
With what delight could I have walkt thee round
If I could joy in aught, sweet interchange
Of Hill and Vallie, Rivers, Woods and Plaines,
Now Land, now Sea, and Shores with Forrest crownd,
Rocks, Dens, and Caves; but I in none of these
Find place or refuge; and the more I see
Pleasures about me, so much more I feel
Torment within me, as from the hateful siege
Of contraries; all good to me becomes
Bane, and in Heav'n much worse would be my state.
But neither here seek I, no nor in Heav'n
To dwell, unless by maistring Heav'ns Supreame;
Nor hope to be my self less miserable
By what I seek, but others to make such
As I, though thereby worse to me redound:
For onely in destroying I finde ease
To my relentless thoughts; and him destroyd,

Or won to what may work his utter loss,
For whom all this was made, all this will soon
Follow, as to him linkt in weal or woe,
In wo then; that destruction wide may range:
To mee shall be the glorie sole among
The infernal Powers, in one day to have marr'd
What he *Almightie* styl'd, six Nights and Days
Continu'd making, and who knows how long
Before had bin contriving, though perhaps
Not longer then since I in one Night freed
From servitude inglorious welnigh half
Th' Angelic Name, and thinner left the throng
Of his adorers: hee to be aveng'd,
And to repair his numbers thus impair'd,
Whether such vertue spent of old now faild
More Angels to Create, if they at least
Are his Created or to spite us more,
Determin'd to advance into our room
A Creature form'd of Earth, and him endow,
Exalted from so base original,
With Heav'nly spoils, our spoils; What he decreed
He effected; Man he made, and for him built
Magnificent this World, and Earth his seat,
Him Lord pronounc'd, and, O indignitie!
Subjected to his service Angel wings,
And flaming Ministers to watch and tend
Thir earthie Charge: Of these the vigilance
I dread, and to elude, thus wrapt in mist
Of midnight vapor glide obscure, and prie
In every Bush and Brake, where hap may finde
The Serpent sleeping, in whose mazie foulds
To hide me, and the dark intent I bring.
O foul descent! that I who erst contended
With Gods to sit the highest, am now constraind
Into a Beast, and mixt with bestial slime,
This essence to incarnate and imbrute,
That to the hight of Deitie aspir'd;
But what will not Ambition and Revenge
Descend to? who aspires must down as low
As high he soard, obnoxious first or last

To basest things. Revenge, at first though sweet,
Bitter ere long back on itself recoiles;
Let it; I reck not, so it light well aim'd,
Since higher I fall short, on him who next
Provokes my envie, this new Favorite
Of Heav'n, this Man of Clay, Son of despite,
Whom us the more to spite his Maker rais'd
From dust: spite then with spite is best repaid.

So saying, through each Thicket Danck or Drie,
Like a black mist low creeping, he held on
His midnight search, where soonest he might finde
The Serpent: him fast sleeping soon he found
In Labyrinth of many a round self rowld,
His head the midst, well stor'd with suttle wiles:
Not yet in horrid Shade or dismal Den,
Not nocent yet, but on the grassie Herbe
Fearless unfeard he slept: in at his Mouth
The Devil enterd, and his brutal sense,
In heart or head, possessing soon inspir'd
With act intelligential; but his sleep
Disturb'd not, waiting close th' approach of Morn.
Now when as sacred Light began to dawne
In *Eden* on the humid Flours, that breathd
Thir morning Incense, when all things that breath,
From th' Earths great Altar send up silent praise
To the Creator, and his Nostrils fill
With gratefull Smell, forth came the human pair
And joynd their vocal Worship to the Quire
Of Creatures wanting voice, that done, partake
The season, prime for sweetest Sents and Aires:
Then commune how that day they best may ply
Thir growing work: for much thir work outgrew
The hands dispatch of two Gardning so wide.
And *Eve* first to her Husband thus began.

Adam, well may we labour still to dress
This Garden, still to tend Plant, Herb and Flour,
Our pleasant task enjoyn'd, but till more hands
Aid us, the work under our labour grows,
Luxurious by restraint; what we by day
Lop overgrown, or prune, or prop, or bind,

One night or two with wanton growth derides
Tending to wilde. Thou therefore now advise
Or hear what to my mind first thoughts present,
Let us divide our labours, thou where choice
Leads thee, or where most needs, whether to wind
The Woodbine round this Arbour, or direct
The clasping Ivie where to climb, while I
In yonder Spring of Roses intermixt
With Myrtle, find what to redress till Noon:
For while so near each other thus all day
Our task we choose, what wonder if so near
Looks intervene and smiles, or object new
Casual discourse draw on, which intermits
Our dayes work brought to little, though begun
Early, and th' hour of Supper comes unearn'd.

 To whom mild answer *Adam* thus return'd.
Sole *Eve*, Associate sole, to me beyond
Compare above all living Creatures deare,
Well hast thou motion'd, well thy thoughts imploy'd
How we might best fulfill the work which here
God hath assign'd us, nor of me shalt pass
Unprais'd: for nothing lovelier can be found
In woman, then to studie houshold good,
And good workes in her Husband to promote.
Yet not so strictly hath our Lord impos'd
Labour, as to debarr us when we need
Refreshment, whether food, or talk between,
Food of the mind, or this sweet intercourse
Of looks and smiles, for smiles from Reason flow,
To brute deni'd, and are of Love the food,
Love not the lowest end of human life.
For not to irksome toile, but to delight
He made us, and delight to Reason joyn'd.
These paths and Bowers doubt not but our joynt hands
Will keep from Wilderness with ease, as wide
As we need walk, till younger hands ere long
Assist us: But if much converse perhaps
Thee satiate, to short absence I could yield.
For solitude somtimes is best societie,
And short retirement urges sweet returne.

But other doubt possesses me, least harm
Befall thee sever'd from me; for thou knowst
What hath bin warn'd us, what malicious Foe
Envying our happiness, and of his own
Despairing, seeks to work us woe and shame
By sly assault; and somwhere nigh at hand
Watches, no doubt, with greedy hope to find
His wish and best advantage, us asunder,
Hopeless to circumvent us joynd, where each
To other speedie aide might lend at need;
Whether his first design be to withdraw
Our fealtie from God, or to disturb
Conjugal Love, then which perhaps no bliss
Enjoy'd by us excites his envie more;
Or this, or worse, leave not the faithful side
That gave thee being, stil shades thee and protects.
The Wife, where danger or dishonour lurks,
Safest and seemliest by her Husband staies,
Who guards her, or with her the worst endures.

    To whom the Virgin Majestie of *Eve*,
As one who loves, and some unkindness meets,
With sweet austeer composure thus reply'd.

    Ofspring of Heav'n and Earth, and all Earths Lord,
That such an Enemie we have, who seeks
Our ruin, both by thee informd I learne,
And from the parting Angel over-heard
As in a shadie nook I stood behind,
Just then returnd at shut of Evening Flours.
But that thou shouldst my firmness therfore doubt
To God or thee, because we have a foe
May tempt it, I expected not to hear.
His violence thou fearst not, being such,
As wee, not capable of death or paine,
Can either not receave, or can repell.
His fraud is then thy fear, which plain inferrs
Thy equal fear that my firm Faith and Love
Can by his fraud be shak'n or seduc't;
Thoughts, which how found they harbour in thy brest
Adam, missthought of her to thee so dear?

    To whom with healing words *Adam* reply'd.

Daughter of God and Man, immortal *Eve*,
For such thou art, from sin and blame entire:
Not diffident of thee do I dissuade
Thy absence from my sight, but to avoid
Th' attempt it self, intended by our Foe.
For hee who tempts, though in vain, at least asperses
The tempted with dishonour foul, suppos'd
Not incorruptible of Faith, not prooff
Against temptation: thou thy self with scorne
And anger wouldst resent the offer'd wrong,
Though ineffectual found: misdeem not then,
If such affront I labour to avert
From thee alone, which on us both at once
The Enemie, though bold, will hardly dare,
Or daring, first on mee th' assault shall light.
Nor thou his malice and false guile contemn;
Suttle he needs must be, who could seduce
Angels, nor think superfluous others aid.
I from the influence of thy looks receave
Access in every Vertue, in thy sight
More wise, more watchful, stronger, if need were
Of outward strength; while shame, thou looking on,
Shame to be overcome or over-reacht
Would utmost vigor raise, and rais'd unite.
Why shouldst not thou like sense within thee feel
When I am present, and thy trial choose
With me, best witness of thy Vertue tri'd.
    So spake domestick *Adam* in his care
And Matrimonial Love, but *Eve*, who thought
Less attributed to her Faith sincere,
Thus her reply with accent sweet renewd.
    If this be our condition, thus to dwell
In narrow circuit strait'nd by a Foe,
Suttle or violent, we not endu'd
Single with like defence, wherever met,
How are we happie, still in fear of harm?
But harm precedes not sin: onely our Foe
Tempting affronts us with his foul esteem
Of our integritie: his foul esteeme
Sticks no dishonor on our Front, but turns

Foul on himself; then wherfore shund or feard
By us? who rather double honour gaine
From his surmise prov'd false, finde peace within,
Favour from Heav'n, our witness from th' event.
And what is Faith, Love, Vertue unassaid
Alone, without exterior help sustaind?
Let us not then suspect our happie State
Left so imperfet by the Maker wise,
As not secure to single or combin'd.
Fraile is our happiness, if this be so,
And *Eden* were no *Eden* thus expos'd.

   To whom thus *Adam* fervently repli'd.
O Woman, best are all things as the will
Of God ordaind them, his creating hand
Nothing imperfet or deficient left
Of all that he Created, much less Man,
Or ought that might his happie State secure,
Secure from outward force; within himself
The danger lies, yet lies within his power:
Against his will he can receave no harme.
But God left free the Will, for what obeyes
Reason, is free, and Reason he made right,
But bid her well beware, and still erect,
Least by some faire appeering good surpris'd
She dictate false, and missinforme the Will
To do what God expresly hath forbid.
Not then mistrust, but tender love enjoynes,
That I should mind thee oft, and mind thou me.
Firm we subsist, yet possible to swerve,
Since Reason not impossibly may meet
Some specious object by the Foe subornd,
And fall into deception unaware,
Not keeping strictest watch, as she was warnd.
Seek not temptation then, which to avoide
Were better, and most likelie if from mee
Thou sever not: Trial will come unsought.
Wouldst thou approve thy constancie, approve
First thy obedience; th' other who can know,
Not seeing thee attempted, who attest?
But if thou think, trial unsought may finde

Us both securer then thus warnd thou seemst,
Go; for thy stay, not free, absents thee more;
Go in thy native innocence, relie
On what thou hast of vertue, summon all,
For God towards thee hath done his part, do thine.
   So spake the Patriarch of Mankinde, but *Eve*
Persisted, yet submiss, though last, repli'd.
   With thy permission then, and thus forewarnd
Chiefly by what thy own last reasoning words
Touchd onely, that our trial, when least sought,
May finde us both perhaps farr less prepar'd,
The willinger I goe, nor much expect
A Foe so proud will first the weaker seek;
So bent, the more shall shame him his repulse.
Thus saying, from her Husbands hand her hand
Soft she withdrew, and like a Wood-Nymph light
Oread or *Dryad*, or of *Delia's* Traine,
Betook her to the Groves, but *Delia's* self
In gate surpass'd and Goddess-like deport,
Though not as shee with Bow and Quiver armd,
But with such Gardning Tools as Art yet rude,
Guiltless of fire had formd, or Angels brought.
To *Pales*, or *Pomona* thus adornd,
Likest she seemd, *Pomona* when she fled
Vertumnus, or to *Ceres* in her Prime,
Yet Virgin of *Proserpina* from *Jove.*
Her long with ardent look his Eye pursu'd
Delighted, but desiring more her stay.
Oft he to her his charge of quick returne
Repeated, shee to him as oft engag'd
To be returnd by Noon amid the Bowre,
And all things in best order to invite
Noontide repast, or Afternoons repose.
O much deceav'd, much failing, hapless *Eve*,
Of thy presum'd return! event perverse!
Thou never from that houre in Paradise
Foundst either sweet repast, or sound repose;
Such ambush hid among sweet Flours and Shades
Waited with hellish rancor imminent
To intercept thy way, or send thee back

Despoild of Innocence, of Faith, of Bliss.
For now, and since first break of dawne the Fiend,
Meer Serpent in appearance, forth was come,
And on his Quest, where likeliest he might finde
The onely two of Mankinde, but in them
The whole included Race, his purposd prey.
In Bowre and Field he sought, where any tuft
Of Grove or Garden-Plot more pleasant lay,
Thir tendance or Plantation for delight.
By Fountain or by shadie Rivulet
He sought them both, but wish'd his hap might find
Eve separate, he wish'd, but not with hope
Of what so seldom chanc'd, when to his wish,
Beyond his hope, *Eve* separate he spies,
Veild in a Cloud of Fragrance, where she stood,
Half spi'd, so thick the Roses bushing round
About her glowd, oft stooping to support
Each Flour of slender stalk, whose head though gay
Carnation, Purple, Azure, or spect with Gold,
Hung drooping unsustaind, them she upstaies
Gently with Mirtle band, mindless the while,
Her self, though fairest unsupported Flour,
From her best prop so farr, and storm so nigh.
Neerer he drew, and many a walk travers'd
Of stateliest Covert, Cedar, Pine, or Palme,
Then voluble and bold, now hid, now seen
Among thick-wov'n Arborets and Flours
Imborderd on each Bank, the hand of *Eve* :
Spot more delicious then those Gardens feign'd
Or of reviv'd *Adonis*, or renownd
Alcinous, host of old *Laertes* Son,
Or that, not Mystic, where the Sapient King
Held dalliance with his faire *Egyptian* Spouse.
Much hee the Place admir'd, the Person more.
As one who long in populous City pent,
Where Houses thick and Sewers annoy the Aire,
Forth issuing on a Summers Morn to breathe
Among the pleasant Villages and Farmes
Adjoynd, from each thing met conceaves delight,
The smell of Grain, or tedded Grass, or Kine,

Or Dairie, each rural sight, each rural sound;
If chance with Nymphlike step fair Virgin pass,
What pleasing seemd, for her now pleases more,
She most, and in her look summs all Delight.
Such Pleasure took the Serpent to behold
This Flourie Plat, the sweet recess of Eve
Thus earlie, thus alone; her Heav'nly forme
Angelic, but more soft, and Feminine,
Her graceful Innocence, her every Aire
Of gesture or lest action overawd
His Malice, and with rapine sweet bereav'd
His fierceness of the fierce intent it brought:
That space the Evil one abstracted stood
From his own evil, and for the time remaind
Stupidly good, of enmitie disarm'd,
Of guile, of hate, of envie, of revenge;
But the hot Hell that alwayes in him burnes,
Though in mid Heav'n, soon ended his delight,
And tortures him now more, the more he sees
Of pleasure not for him ordain'd: then soon
Fierce hate he recollects, and all his thoughts
Of mischief, gratulating, thus excites.

   Thoughts, whither have ye led me, with what sweet
Compulsion thus transported to forget
What hither brought us, hate, not love, nor hope
Of Paradise for Hell, hope here to taste
Of pleasure, but all pleasure to destroy,
Save what is in destroying, other joy
To me is lost. Then let me not let pass
Occasion which now smiles, behold alone
The Woman, opportune to all attempts,
Her Husband, for I view far round, not nigh,
Whose higher intellectual more I shun,
And strength, of courage hautie, and of limb
Heroic built, though of terrestrial mould,
Foe not informidable, exempt from wound,
I not; so much hath Hell debas'd, and paine
Infeebl'd me, to what I was in Heav'n.
Shee fair, divinely fair, fit Love for Gods,
Not terrible, though terrour be in Love

And beautie, not approacht by stronger hate,
Hate stronger, under shew of Love well feign'd,
The way which to her ruin now I tend.

So spake the Enemie of Mankind, enclos'd
In Serpent, Inmate bad, and toward *Eve*
Address'd his way, not with indented wave,
Prone on the ground, as since, but on his reare,
Circular base of rising foulds, that tour'd
Fould above fould a surging Maze, his Head
Crested aloft, and Carbuncle his Eyes;
With burnisht Neck of verdant Gold, erect
Amidst his circling Spires, that on the grass
Floted redundant: pleasing was his shape,
And lovely, never since of Serpent kind
Lovelier, not those that in *Illyria* chang'd
Hermione and *Cadmus*, or the God
In *Epidaurus*; nor to which transformd
Ammonian Jove, or *Capitoline* was seen,
Hee with *Olympias*, this with her who bore
Scipio the highth of *Rome*. With tract oblique
At first, as one who sought access, but feard
To interrupt, side-long he works his way.
As when a Ship by skilful Stearsman wrought
Nigh Rivers mouth or Foreland, where the Wind
Veres oft, as oft so steers, and shifts her Saile;
So varied hee, and of his tortuous Traine
Curld many a wanton wreath in sight of *Eve*,
To lure her Eye; shee busied heard the sound
Of rusling Leaves, but minded not, as us'd
To such disport before her through the Field,
From every Beast, more duteous at her call,
Then at *Circean* call the Herd disguis'd.
Hee boulder now, uncall'd before her stood;
But as in gaze admiring: Oft he bowd
His turret Crest, and sleek enamel'd Neck,
Fawning, and lick'd the ground whereon she trod.
His gentle dumb expression turnd at length
The Eye of *Eve* to mark his play; he glad
Of her attention gaind, with Serpent Tongue
Organic, or impulse of vocal Air,

His fraudulent temptation thus began.
    Wonder not. sovran Mistress, if perhaps
Thou canst, who art sole Wonder, much less arm
Thy looks, the Heav'n of mildness, with disdain,
Displeas'd that I approach thee thus, and gaze
Insatiate, I thus single, nor have feard
Thy awful brow, more awful thus retir'd.
Fairest resemblance of thy Maker faire,
Thee all things living gaze on, all things thine
By gift, and thy Celestial Beautie adore
With ravishment beheld, there best beheld
Where universally admir'd; but here
In this enclosure wild, these Beasts among,
Beholders rude, and shallow to discerne
Half what in thee is fair, one man except,
Who sees thee? (and what is one?) who shouldst be seen
A Goddess among Gods, ador'd and serv'd
By Angels numberless, thy daily Train.
    So gloz'd the Tempter, and his Proem tun'd;
Into the Heart of *Eve* his words made way,
Though at the voice much marveling; at length
Not unamaz'd she thus in answer spake.
What may this mean? Language of Man pronounc't
By Tongue of Brute, and human sense exprest?
The first at lest of these I thought deni'd
To Beasts, whom God on thir Creation-Day
Created mute to all articulat sound;
The latter I demurre, for in thir looks
Much reason, and in thir actions oft appeers.
Thee, Serpent, suttlest beast of all the field
I knew, but not with human voice endu'd;
Redouble then this miracle, and say,
How cam'st thou speakable of mute, and how
To me so friendly grown above the rest
Of brutal kind, that daily are in sight?
Say, for such wonder claims attention due.
    To whom the guileful Tempter thus reply'd.
Empress of this fair World, resplendent *Eve*,
Easie to mee it is to tell thee all
What thou commandst, and right thou shouldst be obeyd:

I was at first as other Beasts that graze
The trodden Herb, of abject thoughts and low,
As was my food, nor aught but food discern'd
Or Sex, and apprehended nothing high:
Till on a day roaving the field, I chanc'd
A goodly Tree farr distant to behold
Loaden with fruit of fairest colours mixt,
Ruddie and Gold: I nearer drew to gaze;
When from the boughes a savorie odour blow'n,
Grateful to appetite, more pleas'd my sense
Then smell of sweetest Fenel, or the Teats
Of Ewe or Goat dropping with Milk at Eevn,
Unsuckt of Lamb or Kid, that tend their play.
To satisfie the sharp desire I had
Of tasting those fair Apples, I resolv'd
Not to deferr; hunger and thirst at once,
Powerful perswaders, quick'nd at the scent
Of that alluring fruit, urg'd me so keene.
About the mossie Trunk I wound me soon,
For high from ground the branches would require
Thy utmost reach or *Adams*: Round the Tree
All other Beasts that saw, with like desire
Longing and envying stood, but could not reach.
Amid the Tree now got, where plenty hung
Tempting so nigh, to pluck and eat my fill
I spar'd not, for such pleasure till that hour
At Feed or Fountain never had I found.
Sated at length, ere long I might perceave
Strange alteration in me, to degree
Of Reason in my inward Powers, and Speech
Wanted not long, though to this shape retaind.
Thenceforth to Speculations high or deep
I turnd my thoughts, and with capacious mind
Considerd all things visible in Heav'n,
Or Earth, or Middle, all things fair and good;
But all that fair and good in thy Divine
Semblance, and in thy Beauties heav'nly Ray
United I beheld; no Fair to thine
Equivalent or second, which compel'd
Mee thus, though importune perhaps, to come

And gaze, and worship thee of right declar'd
Sovran of Creatures, universal Dame.
  So talk'd the spirited sly Snake; and *Eve*
Yet more amaz'd unwarie thus reply'd.
  Serpent, thy overpraising leaves in doubt
The vertue of that Fruit, in thee first prov'd:
But say, where grows the Tree, from hence how far?
For many are the Trees of God that grow
In Paradise, and various, yet unknown
To us, in such abundance lies our choice,
As leaves a greater store of Fruit untoucht,
Still hanging incorruptible, till men
Grow up to thir provision, and more hands
Help to disburden Nature of her Bearth.
  To whom the wilie Adder, blithe and glad.
Empress, the way is readie, and not long,
Beyond a row of Myrtles, on a Flat,
Fast by a Fountain, one small Thicket past
Of blowing Myrrh and Balme; if thou accept
My conduct, I can bring thee thither soon.
  Lead then, said *Eve*. Hee leading swiftly rowld
In tangles, and made intricate seem strait,
To mischief swift. Hope elevates, and joy
Bright'ns his Crest, as when a wandring Fire
Compact of unctuous vapor, which the Night
Condenses, and the cold invirons round,
Kindl'd through agitation to a Flame,
Which oft, they say, some evil Spirit attends,
Hovering and blazing with delusive Light,
Misleads th' amaz'd Night-wanderer from his way
To Boggs and Mires, and oft through Pond or Poole,
There swallow'd up and lost, from succour farr.
So glister'd the dire Snake, and into fraud
Led *Eve* our credulous Mother, to the Tree
Of prohibition, root of all our woe;
Which when she saw, thus to her guide she spake.
  Serpent, we might have spar'd our coming hither,
Fruitless to me, though Fruit be here to excess,
The credit of whose vertue rest with thee,
Wondrous indeed, if cause of such effects.

But of this Tree we may not taste nor touch;
God so commanded, and left that Command
Sole Daughter of his voice; the rest, we live
Law to our selves, our Reason is our Law.

To whom the Tempter guilefully repli'd.
Indeed? hath God then said that of the Fruit
Of all these Garden Trees ye shall not eate,
Yet Lords declar'd of all in Earth or Aire?

To whom thus *Eve* yet sinless. Of the Fruit
Of each Tree in the Garden we may eate,
But of the Fruit of this fair Tree amidst
The Garden, God hath said, Ye shall not eate
Thereof, nor shall ye touch it, least ye die.

She scarce had said, though brief, when now more bold
The Tempter, but with shew of Zeale amd Love
To Man, and indignation at his wrong,
New part puts on, and as to passion mov'd,
Fluctuats disturbd, yet comely, and in act
Rais'd, as of som great matter to begin.
As when of old som Orator renound
In *Athens* or free *Rome,* where Eloquence
Flourishd, since mute, to som great cause addrest,
Stood in himself collected, while each part,
Motion, each act won audience ere the tongue,
Somtimes in highth began, as no delay
Of Preface brooking through his Zeal of Right.
So standing, moving, or to highth upgrown
The Tempter all impassiond thus began.

O Sacred, Wise, and Wisdom-giving Plant,
Mother of Science, Now I feel thy Power
Within me cleere, not onely to discerne
Things in thir Causes, but to trace the wayes
Of highest Agents, deemd however wise.
Queen of this Universe, doe not believe
Those rigid threats of Death; ye shall not Die:
How should ye? by the Fruit? it gives you Life
To Knowledge: By the Threatner? look on mee,
Mee who have touch'd and tasted, yet both live,
And life more perfet have attaind then Fate
Meant mee, by ventring higher then my Lot.

Shall that be shut to Man, which to the Beast
Is open? or will God incense his ire
For such a petty Trespass, and not praise
Rather your dauntless vertue, whom the pain
Of Death denounc't, whatever thing Death be,
Deterrd not from atchieving what might leade
To happier life, knowledge of Good and Evil;
Of good, how just? of evil, if what is evil
Be real, why not known, since easier shunnd?
God therefore cannot hurt ye, and be just;
Not just, not God; not feard then, nor obeyd:
Your feare it self of Death removes the feare.
Why then was this forbid? Why but to awe,
Why but to keep ye low and ignorant,
His worshippers; he knows that in the day
Ye Eate thereof, your Eyes that seem so cleere,
Yet are but dim, shall perfetly be then
Op'nd and cleerd, and ye shall be as Gods,
Knowing both Good and Evil as they know.
That ye should be as Gods, since I as Man,
Internal Man, is but proportion meet,
I of brute human, yee of human Gods.
So ye shall die perhaps, by putting off
Human, to put on Gods, death to be wisht,
Though threat'nd, which no worse then this can bring
And what are Gods that Man may not become
As they, participating God-like food?
The Gods are first, and that advantage use
On our belief, that all from them proceeds;
I question it, for this fair Earth I see,
Warm'd by the Sun, producing every kind,
Them nothing: If they all things, who enclos'd
Knowledge of Good and Evil in this Tree,
That whoso eats thereof, forthwith attains
Wisdom without their leave? and wherein lies
Th' offence, that Man should thus attain to know?
What can your knowledge hurt him, or this Tree
Impart against his will if all be his?
Or is it envie, and can envie dwell
In heav'nly brests? these, these and many more

Causes import your need of this fair Fruit.
Goddess humane, reach then, and freely taste.
    He ended, and his words replete with guile
Into her heart too easie entrance won:
Fixt on the Fruit she gaz'd, which to behold
Might tempt alone, and in her ears the sound
Yet rung of his perswasive words, impregn'd
With Reason, to her seeming, and with Truth;
Mean while the hour of Noon drew on, and wak'd
An eager appetite, rais'd by the smell
So savorie of that Fruit, which with desire,
Inclinable now grown to touch or taste,
Sollicited her longing eye; yet first
Pausing a while, thus to her self she mus'd.
    Great are thy Vertues, doubtless, best of Fruits,
Though kept from Man, and worthy to be admir'd,
Whose taste, too long forborn, at first assay
Gave elocution to the mute, and taught
The Tongue not made for Speech to speak thy praise:
Thy praise hee also who forbids thy use,
Conceales not from us, naming thee the Tree
Of Knowledge, knowledge both of good and evil;
Forbids us then to taste, but his forbidding
Commends thee more, while it inferrs the good
By thee communicated, and our want:
For good unknown, sure is not had, or had
And yet unknown, is as not had at all.
In plain then, what forbids he but to know,
Forbids us good, forbids us to be wise?
Such prohibitions binde not. But if Death
Bind us with after-bands, what profits then
Our inward freedom? In the day we eate
Of this fair Fruit, our doom is, we shall die.
How dies the Serpent? hee hath eat'n and lives,
And knows, and speaks, and reasons, and discerns,
Irrational till then. For us alone
Was death invented? or to us deni'd
This intellectual food, for beasts reserv'd?
For Beasts it seems: yet that one Beast which first
Hath tasted, envies not, but brings with joy

The good befall'n him, Author unsuspect,
Friendly to man, farr from deceit or guile.
What fear I then, rather what know to feare
Under this ignorance of Good and Evil,
Of God or Death, of Law or Penaltie?
Here grows the Cure of all, this Fruit Divine,
Fair to the Eye, inviting to the Taste,
Of vertue to make wise: what hinders then
To reach, and feed at once both Bodie and Mind?
   So saying, her rash hand in evil hour
Forth reaching to the Fruit, she pluck'd, she eat:
Earth felt the wound, and Nature from her seat
Sighing through all her Works gave signs of woe,
That all was lost. Back to the Thicket slunk
The guiltie Serpent, and well might, for *Eve*
Intent now wholly on her taste, naught else
Regarded, such delight till then, as seemd,
In Fruit she never tasted, whether true
Or fansied so, through expectation high
Of knowledg, nor was God-head from her thought.
Greedily she ingorg'd without restraint,
And knew not eating Death: Satiate at length,
And hight'nd as with Wine, jocond and boon,
Thus to her self she pleasingly began.
   O Sovran, vertuous, precious of all Trees
In Paradise, of operation blest
To Sapience, hitherto obscur'd, infam'd,
And thy fair Fruit let hang, as to no end
Created; but henceforth my early care,
Not without Song, each Morning, and due praise
Shall tend thee, and the fertil burden ease
Of thy full branches offer'd free to all;
Till dieted by thee I grow mature
In knowledge, as the Gods who all things know;
Though others envie what they cannot give;
For had the gift bin theirs, it had not here
Thus grown. Experience, next to thee I owe,
Best guide; not following thee, I had remaind
In ignorance, thou op'nst Wisdoms way,
And giv'st access, though secret she retire.

And I perhaps am secret; Heav'n is high,
High and remote to see from thence distinct
Each thing on Earth; and other care perhaps
May have diverted from continual watch
Our great Forbidder, safe with all his Spies
About him. But to *Adam* in what sort
Shall I appeer? shall I to him make known
As yet my change, and give him to partake
Full happiness with mee, or rather not,
But keep the odds of Knowledge in my power
Without Copartner? so to add what wants
In Femal Sex, the more to draw his Love,
And render me more equal, and perhaps,
A thing not undesireable, somtime
Superior: for inferior who is free?
This may be well: but what if God have seen,
And Death ensue? then I shall be no more,
And *Adam* wedded to another *Eve*,
Shall live with her enjoying, I extinct;
A death to think. Confirm'd then I resolve,
Adam shall share with me in bliss or woe:
So dear I love him, that with him all deaths
I could endure, without him live no life.
　　So saying, from the Tree her step she turnd,
But first low Reverence don, as to the power
That dwelt within, whose presence had infus'd
Into the plant sciential sap, deriv'd
From Nectar, drink of Gods. *Adam* the while
Waiting desirous her return, had wove
Of choicest Flours a Garland to adorne
Her Tresses, and her rural labours crown
As Reapers oft are wont thir Harvest Queen.
Great joy he promis'd to his thoughts, and new
Solace in her return, so long delay'd;
Yet oft his heart, divine of somthing ill,
Misgave him; hee the faultring measure felt;
And forth to meet her went, the way she took
That Morn when first they parted; by the Tree
Of Knowledge he must pass, there he her met
Scarse from the Tree returning; in her hand

A bough of fairest fruit that downie smil'd,
New gatherd, and ambrosial smell diffus'd.
To him she hasted, in her face excuse
Came Prologue, and Apologie to prompt,
Which with bland words at will she thus addrest.

Hast thou not wonderd, *Adam*, at my stay?
Thee I have misst, and thought it long, depriv'd
Thy presence, agonie of love till now
Not felt, nor shall be twice, for never more
Mean I to trie, what rash untri'd I sought,
The paine of absence from thy sight. But strange
Hath bin the cause, and wonderful to heare:
This Tree is not as we are told, a Tree
Of danger tasted, nor to evil unknown
Op'ning the way, but of Divine effect
To open Eyes, and make them Gods who taste;
And hath bin tasted such: the Serpent wise,
Or not restraind as wee, or not obeying,
Hath eat'n of the fruit, and is become,
Not dead, as we are threatn'd, but thenceforth
Endu'd with human voice and human sense,
Reasoning to admiration, and with mee
Perswasively hath so prevaild, that I
Have also tasted, and have also found
Th' effects to correspond, opener mine Eyes,
Dimm erst, dilated Spirits, ampler Heart,
And growing up to Godhead; which for thee
Chiefly I sought, without thee can despise.
For bliss, as thou hast part, to me is bliss,
Tedious, unshar'd with thee, and odious soon.
Thou therefore also taste, that equal Lot
May joyne us, equal Joy, as equal Love;
Least thou not tasting, different degree
Disjoyne us, and I then too late renounce
Deitie for thee, when Fate will not permit.

Thus *Eve* with Countnance blithe her storie told;
But in her Cheek distemper flushing glowd.
On th' other side, *Adam*, soon as he heard
The fatal Trespass done by *Eve*, amaz'd,
Astonied stood and Blank, while horror chill

Ran through his veins, and all his joynts relax'd;
From his slack hand the Garland wreath'd for *Eve*
Down drop'd, and all the faded Roses shed:
Speechless he stood and pale, till thus at length
First to himself he inward silence broke.

O fairest of Creation, last and best
Of all Gods Works, Creature in whom excell'd
Whatever can to sight or thought be formd,
Holy, divine, good, amiable, or sweet!
How art thou lost, how on a sudden lost,
Defac't, deflourd, and now to Death devote?
Rather how hast thou yeelded to transgress
The strict forbiddance, how to violate
The sacred Fruit forbidd'n! som cursed fraud
Of Enemie hath beguil'd thee, yet unknown,
And mee with thee hath ruind, for with thee
Certain my resolution is to Die;
How can I live without thee, how forgoe
Thy sweet Converse and Love so dearly joyn'd,
To live again in these wilde Woods forlorn?
Should God create another *Eve*, and I
Another Rib afford, yet loss of thee
Would never from my heart; no no, I feel
The Link of Nature draw me: Flesh of Flesh,
Bone of my Bone thou art, and from thy State
Mine never shall be parted, bliss or woe.

So having said, as one from sad dismay
Recomforted, and after thoughts disturbd
Submitting to what seemd remediless,
Thus in calme mood his Words to *Eve* he turnd.

Bold deed thou hast presum'd, adventrous *Eve*,
And peril great provok't, who thus hath dar'd
Had it bin onely coveting to Eye
That sacred Fruit, sacred to abstinence,
Much more to taste it under banne to touch.
But past who can recall, or don undoe?
Not God Omnipotent, nor Fate, yet so
Perhaps thou shalt not Die, perhaps the Fact
Is not so hainous now, foretasted Fruit,
Profan'd first by the Serpent, by him first

Made common and unhallowd ere our taste;
Nor yet on him found deadly, he yet lives,
Lives, as thou saidst, and gaines to live as Man
Higher degree of Life, inducement strong
To us, as likely tasting to attaine
Proportional ascent, which cannot be
But to be Gods, or Angels Demi-gods.
Nor can I think that God, Creator wise,
Though threatning, will in earnest so destroy
Us his prime Creatures, dignifi'd so high,
Set over all his Works, which in our Fall,
For us created, needs with us must faile,
Dependent made; so God shall uncreate,
Be frustrate, do, undo, and labour loose,
Not well conceav'd of God, who though his Power
Creation could repeate, yet would be loath
Us to abolish, least the Adversary
Triumph and say; Fickle their State whom God
Most Favors, who can please him long? Mee first
He ruind, now Mankind; whom will he next?
Matter of scorne, not to be given the Foe.
However I with thee have fixt my Lot,
Certain to undergoe like doom, if Death
Consort with thee, Death is to mee as Life;
So forcible within my heart I feel
The Bond of Nature draw me to my owne,
My own in thee, for what thou art is mine;
Our State cannot be severd, we are one,
One Flesh; to loose thee were to loose my self.
  So *Adam*, and thus *Eve* to him repli'd.
O glorious trial of exceeding Love,
Illustrious evidence, example high!
Ingaging me to emulate, but short
Of thy perfection, how shall I attaine,
Adam, from whose deare side I boast me sprung,
And gladly of our Union heare thee speak,
One Heart, one Soul in both; whereof good prooff
This day affords, declaring thee resolvd,
Rather then Death or aught then Death more dread
Shall separate us, linkt in Love so deare,

To undergoe with mee one Guilt, one Crime,
If any be, of tasting this fair Fruit,
Whose vertue, for of good still good proceeds,
Direct, or by occasion hath presented
This happie trial of thy Love, which else
So eminently never had bin known.
Were it I thought Death menac't would ensue
This my attempt, I would sustain alone
The worst, and not perswade thee, rather die
Deserted, then oblige thee with a fact
Pernicious to thy Peace, chiefly assur'd
Remarkably so late of thy so true,
So faithful Love unequald; but I feel
Farr otherwise th' event, not Death, but Life
Augmented, op'nd Eyes, new Hopes, new Joyes,
Taste so Divine, that what of sweet before
Hath toucht my sense, flat seems to this, and harsh.
On my experience, *Adam*, freely taste,
And fear of Death deliver to the Windes.

    So saying, she embrac'd him, and for joy
Tenderly wept, much won that he his Love
Had so enobl'd, as of choice to incurr
Divine displeasure for her sake, or Death.
In recompence (for such compliance bad
Such recompence best merits) from the bough
She gave him of that fair enticing Fruit
With liberal hand: he scrupl'd not to eat
Against his better knowledge, not deceav'd,
But fondly overcome with Femal charm.
Earth trembl'd from her entrails, as again
In pangs, and Nature gave a second groan,
Skie lowr'd and muttering Thunder, som sad drops
Wept at compleating of the mortal Sin
Original; while *Adam* took no thought,
Eating his fill, nor *Eve* to iterate
Her former trespass fear'd, the more to soothe
Him with her lov'd societie, that now
As with new Wine intoxicated both
They swim in mirth, and fansie that they feel
Divinitie within them breeding wings

Wherewith to scorn the Earth: but that false Fruit
Farr other operation first displaid,
Carnal desire enflaming, hee on *Eve*
Began to cast lascivious Eyes, she him
As wantonly repaid; in Lust they burne:
Till *Adam* thus 'gan *Eve* to dalliance move.

    Eve, now I see thou art exact of taste,
And elegant, of Sapience no small part,
Since to each meaning savour we apply,
And Palate call judicious; I the praise
Yeild thee, so well this day thou hast purvey'd.
Much pleasure we have lost, while we abstain'd
From this delightful Fruit, nor known till now
True relish, tasting; if such pleasure be
In things to us forbidden, it might be wish'd,
For this one Tree had bin forbidden ten.
But come, so well refresh't, now let us play,
As meet is, after such delicious Fare;
For never did thy Beautie since the day
I saw thee first and wedded thee, adorn'd
With all perfections, so enflame my sense
With ardor to enjoy thee, fairer now
Than ever, bountie of this vertuous Tree.

    So said he, and forbore not glance or toy
Of amorous intent, well understood
Of *Eve*, whose Eye darted contagious Fire.
Her hand he seis'd, and to a shadie bank,
Thick overhead with verdant roof imbowr'd
He led her nothing loath; Flours were the Couch,
Pansies, and Violets, and Asphodel,
And Hyacinth, Earths freshest softest lap.
There they thir fill of Love and Loves disport
Took largely, of thir mutual guilt the Seale,
The solace of thir sin, till dewie sleep
Oppress'd them, wearied with thir amorous play.
Soon as the force of that fallacious Fruit,
That with exhilerating vapour bland
About thir spirits had plaid, and inmost powers
Made erre, was now exhal'd, and grosser sleep
Bred of unkindly fumes, with conscious dreams

Encumberd, now had left them, up they rose
As from unrest, and each the other viewing,
Soon found thir Eyes how op'nd, and thir minds
How dark'nd; innocence, that as a veile
Had shadow'd them from knowing ill, was gon,
Just confidence, and native righteousness,
And honour from about them, naked left
To guiltie shame; hee cover'd, but his Robe
Uncover'd more. So rose the *Danite* strong
Herculean Samson from the Harlot-lap
Of *Philistean Dalilah*, and wak'd
Shorn of his strength, They destitute and bare
Of all thir vertue: silent, and in face
Confounded long they sate, as struck'n mute,
Till *Adam*, though not less then *Eve* abasht,
At length gave utterance to these words constraind.

　　O *Eve*, in evil hour thou didst give eare
To that false Worm, of whomsoever taught
To counterfet Mans voice, true in our Fall,
False in our promis'd Rising; since our Eyes
Op'nd we find indeed, and find we know
Both Good and Evil, Good lost, and Evil got,
Bad Fruit of Knowledge, if this be to know,
Which leaves us naked thus, of Honour void,
Of Innocence, of Faith, of Puritie,
Our wonted Ornaments now soild and staind,
And in our Faces evident the signes
Of foul concupiscence; whence evil store;
Even shame, the last of evils; of the first
Be sure then. How shall I behold the face
Henceforth of God or Angel, earst with joy
And rapture so oft beheld? those heav'nly shapes
Will dazle now this earthly, with thir blaze
Insufferably bright. O might I here
In solitude live savage, in some glade
Obscur'd, where highest Woods impenetrable
To Starr or Sun-light, spread thir umbrage broad,
And brown as Evening: Cover me ye Pines,
Ye Cedars, with innumerable boughs
Hide me, where I may never see them more.

But let us now, as in bad plight, devise
What best may for the present serve to hide
The Parts of each from other, that seem most
To shame obnoxious, and unseemliest seen,
Some Tree whose broad smooth Leaves together sowd,
And girded on our loyns, may cover round
Those middle parts, that this new commer, Shame,
There sit not, and reproach us as unclean.
  So counsel'd hee, and both together went
Into the thickest Wood, there soon they chose
The Figtree, not that kind for Fruit renown'd,
But such as at this day to *Indians* known
In *Malabar* or *Decan* spreds her Armes
Braunching so broad and long, that in the ground
The bended Twigs take root, and Daughters grow
About the Mother Tree, a Pillard shade
High overarch't, and echoing Walks between;
There oft the *Indian* Herdsman shunning heate
Shelters in coole, and tends his pasturing Herds
At Loopholes cut through thickest shade: Those Leaves
They gatherd, broad as *Amazonian* Targe,
And with what skill they had, together sowd,
To gird thir waste, vain Covering if to hide
Thir guilt and dreaded shame; O how unlike
To that first naked Glorie. Such of late
Columbus found th' *American* so girt
With featherd Cincture, naked else and wilde
Among the Trees on Iles and woodie Shores.
Thus fenc't, and as they thought, thir shame in part
Coverd, but not at rest or ease of Mind,
They sate them down to weep, nor onely Teares
Raind at thir Eyes, but high Winds worse within
Began to rise, high Passions, Anger, Hate,
Mistrust, Suspicion, Discord, and shook sore
Thir inward State of Mind, calme Region once
And full of Peace, now tost and turbulent:
For Understanding rul'd not, and the Will
Heard not her lore, both in subjection now
To sensual Appetite, who from beneathe
Usurping over sovran Reason claimd

Superior sway: From thus distemperd brest,
Adam, estrang'd in look and alterd stile,
Speech intermitted thus to *Eve* renewd.

    Would thou hadst heark'nd to my words, and stai'd
With me, as I besought thee, when that strange
Desire of wandring this unhappie Morn,
I know not whence possessd thee; we had then
Remaind still happie, not as now, despoild
Of all our good, sham'd, naked, miserable.
Let none henceforth seek needless cause to approve
The Faith they owe; when earnestly they seek
Such proof, conclude, they then begin to faile.

    To whom soon mov'd with touch of blame thus *Eve*.
What words have past thy Lips, *Adam* severe,
Imput'st thou that to my default, or will
Of wandering, as thou call'st it, which who knows
But might as ill have happ'nd thou being by,
Or to thy self perhaps: hadst thou bin there,
Or here th' attempt, thou couldst not have discernd
Fraud in the Serpent, speaking as he spake;
No ground of enmitie between us known,
Why hee should mean me ill, or seek to harme.
Was I to have never parted from thy side?
As good have grown there still a liveless Rib.
Being as I am, why didst not thou the Head
Command me absolutely not to go,
Going into such danger as thou saidst?
Too facil then thou didst not much gainsay,
Nay, didst permit, approve, and fair dismiss.
Hadst thou bin firm and fixt in thy dissent,
Neither had I transgress'd, nor thou with mee.

    To whom then first incenst *Adam* repli'd.
Is this the Love, is this the recompence
Of mine to thee, ingrateful *Eve*, exprest
Immutable when thou wert lost, not I,
Who might have liv'd and joyd immortal bliss,
Yet willingly chose rather Death with thee:
And am I now upbraided, as the cause
Of thy transgressing? not enough severe,
It seems, in thy restraint: what could I more?

ı warn'd thee, I admonish'd thee, foretold
The danger, and the lurking Enemie
That lay in wait; beyond this had bin force,
And force upon free Will hath here no place.
But confidence then bore thee on, secure
Either to meet no danger, or to finde
Matter of glorious trial; and perhaps
I also err'd in overmuch admiring
What seemd in thee so perfet, that I thought
No evil durst attempt thee, but I rue
That errour now, which is become my crime,
And thou th' accuser. Thus it shall befall
Him who to worth in Women overtrusting
Lets her Will rule; restraint she will not brook,
And left to her self, if evil thence ensue,
Shee first his weak indulgence will accuse.
     Thus they in mutual accusation spent
The fruitless hours, but neither self-condemning,
And of thir vain contest appeer'd no end.

BOOK X

THE ARGUMENT

Mans transgression known, the Guardian Angels forsake Paradise, and return up to Heaven to approve thir vigilance, and are approv'd, God declaring that The entrance of Satan *could not be by them prevented. He sends his Son to judge the Transgressors, who descends and gives Sentence accordingly; then in pity cloaths them both, and reascends.* Sin *and* Death *sitting till then at the Gates of Hell, by wondrous sympathie feeling the success of* Satan *in this new World, and the sin by Man there committed, resolve to sit no longer confin'd in Hell, but to follow* Satan *thir Sire up to the place of Man: To make the way easier from Hell to this World to and fro, they pave a broad Highway or Bridge over* Chaos, *according to the Track that* Satan *first made; then preparing for Earth, they met him proud of his success returning to Hell; their mutual gratulation.*

Satan *arrives at* Pandemonium, *in full of assembly relates with boasting his success against Man; instead of applause is entertained with a general hiss by all his audience, transform'd with himself also suddenly into Serpents, according to his doom giv'n in* Paradise; *then deluded with a shew of the forbidden Tree springing up before them, they greedily reaching to take of the Fruit, chew dust and bitter ashes. The proceedings of* Sin *and* Death; *God foretels the final Victory of his Son over them, and the renewing of all things; but for the present commands his Angels to make several alterations in the Heavens and Elements.* Adam *more and more perceiving his fall'n condition heavily bewailes, rejects the condolement of* Eve; *she persists and at length appeases him: then to evade the Curse likely to fall on thir Ofspring, proposes to* Adam *violent wayes which he approves not, but conceiving better hope, puts her in mind of the late Promise made them, that her Seed should be reveng'd on the Serpent, and exhorts her with him to seek Peace of the offended Deity, by repentance and supplication.*

> MEANWHILE the hainous and despightfull act
> Of *Satan* done in Paradise, and how
> Hee in the Serpent had perverted *Eve*,
> Her Husband shee, to taste the fatall fruit,
> Was known in Heav'n; for what can scape the Eye
> Of God All-seeing, or deceave his Heart
> Omniscient, who in all things wise and just,
> Hinder'd not *Satan* to attempt the minde
> Of Man, with strength entire, and free Will arm'd,
> Complete to have discover'd and repulst
> Whatever wiles of Foe or seeming Friend.
> For still they knew, and ought to have still remember'd
> The high Injunction not to taste that Fruit,
> Whoever tempted; which they not obeying,
> Incurr'd, what could they less, the penaltie,
> And manifold in sin, deserv'd to fall.
> Up into Heav'n from Paradise in haste
> Th' Angelic Guards ascended, mute and sad
> For Man, for of his state by this they knew,
> Much wondring how the suttle Fiend had stoln
> Entrance unseen. Soon as th' unwelcome news

From Earth arriv'd at Heaven Gate, displeas'd
All were who heard, dim sadness did not spare
That time Celestial visages, yet mixt
With pitie, violated not thir bliss.
About the new-arriv'd, in multitudes
Th' ethereal People ran, to hear and know
How all befell: they towards the Throne Supream
Accountable made haste to make appear
With righteous plea, thir utmost vigilance,
And easily approv'd; when the most High
Eternal Father from his secret Cloud,
Amidst in Thunder utter'd thus his voice.

   Assembl'd Angels, and ye Powers return'd
From unsuccessful charge, be not dismaid,
Nor troubl'd at these tidings from the Earth,
Which your sincerest care could not prevent,
Foretold so lately what would come to pass,
When first this Tempter cross'd the Gulf from Hell.
I told ye then he should prevail and speed
On his bad Errand, Man should be seduc't
And flatter'd out of all, believing lies
Against his Maker; no Decree of mine
Concurring to necessitate his Fall,
Or touch with lightest moment of impulse
His free Will, to her own inclining left
In eevn scale. But fall'n he is, and now
What rests, but that the mortal Sentence pass
On his transgression, Death denounc't that day,
Which he presumes already vain and void,
Because not yet inflicted, as he fear'd,
By some immediate stroak; but soon shall find
Forbearance no acquittance ere day end.
Justice shall not return as bountie scorn'd.
But whom send I to judge them? whom but thee
Vicegerent Son, to thee I have transferr'd
All Judgement, whether in Heav'n, or Earth, or Hell.
Easie it might be seen that I intend
Mercie collegue with Justice, sending thee
Mans Friend, his Mediator, his design'd
Both Ransom and Redeemer voluntarie,

And destin'd Man himself to judge Man fall'n.
    So spake the Father, and unfoulding bright
Toward the right hand his Glorie, on the Son
Blaz'd forth unclouded Deitie; he full
Resplendent all his Father manifest
Express'd, and thus divinely answer'd milde.
    Father Eternal, thine is to decree,
Mine both in Heav'n and Earth to do thy will
Supream, that thou in mee thy Son belov'd
Mayst ever rest well pleas'd. I go to judge
On Earth these thy transgressors, but thou knowst,
Whoever judg'd, the worst on mee must light,
When time shall be, for so I undertook
Before thee; and not repenting, this obtaine
Of right, that I may mitigate thir doom
On me deriv'd, yet I shall temper so
Justice with Mercie, as may illustrate most
Them fully satisfied, and thee appease.
Attendance none shall need, nor Train, where none
Are to behold the Judgment, but the judg'd,
Those two; the third best absent is condemn'd,
Convict by flight, and Rebel to all Law
Conviction to the Serpent none belongs.
    Thus saying, from his radiant Seat he rose
Of high collateral glorie: him Thrones and Powers,
Princedoms, and Dominations ministrant
Accompanied to Heaven Gate, from whence
Eden and all the Coast in prospect lay.
Down he descended strait; the speed of Gods
Time counts not, though with swiftest minutes wing'd.
Now was the Sun in Western cadence low
From Noon, and gentle Aires due at thir hour
To fan the Earth now wak'd, and usher in
The Eevning coole when he from wrauth more coole
Came the mild Judge and Intercessor both
To sentence Man: the voice of God they heard
Now walking in the Garden, by soft windes
Brought to thir Ears, while day declin'd, they heard,
And from his presence hid themselves among
The thickest Trees, both Man and Wife, till God

Approaching, thus to *Adam*, call'd aloud.
　Where art thou *Adam*, wont with joy to meet
My coming seen far off? I miss thee here,
Not pleas'd, thus entertained with solitude,
Where obvious dutie erewhile appear'd unsaught:
Or come I less conspicuous, or what change
Absents thee, or what chance detains? Come forth.
He came, and with him *Eve*, more loth, though first
To offend, discount'nanc't both, and discompos'd;
Love was not in thir looks, either to God
Or to each other, but apparent guilt,
And shame, and perturbation, and despaire,
Anger, and obstinacie, and hate, and guile.
Whence *Adam* faultring long, thus answer'd brief.
　I heard thee in the Garden, and of thy voice
Affraid, being naked, hid my self. To whom
The gracious Judge without revile repli'd.
　My voice thou oft hast heard, and hast not fear'd,
But still rejoyc't, how is it now become
So dreadful to thee? that thou art naked, who
Hath told thee? hast thou eaten of the Tree
Whereof I gave thee charge thou shouldst not eat?
　To whom thus *Adam* sore beset repli'd.
O Heav'n! in evil strait this day I stand
Before my Judge, either to undergoe
My self the total Crime, or to accuse
My other self, the partner of my life;
Whose failing, while her Faith to me remaines,
I should conceal, and not expose to blame
By my complaint; but strict necessitie
Subdues me, and calamitous constraint
Least on my head both sin and punishment,
However insupportable, be all
Devolv'd; though should I hold my peace, yet thou
Wouldst easily detect what I conceale.
This Woman whom thou mad'st to be my help,
And gav'st me as thy perfet gift, so good,
So fit, so acceptable, so Divine,
That from her hand I could suspect no ill,
And what she did, whatever in it self,

Her doing seem'd to justifie the deed;
Shee gave me of the Tree, and I did eate.
   To whom the sovran Presence thus repli'd.
Was shee thy God, that her thou didst obey
Before his voice, or was shee made thy guide,
Superior, or but equal, that to her
Thou did'st resigne thy Manhood, and the Place
Wherein God set thee above her made of thee,
And for thee, whose perfection farr excell'd
Hers in all real dignitie: Adornd
She was indeed, and lovely to attract
Thy Love, not thy Subjection, and her Gifts
Were such as under Government well seem'd,
Unseemly to beare rule, which was thy part
And person, had'st thou known thy self aright.
   So having said, he thus to *Eve* in few:
Say Woman, what is this which thou hast done?
   To whom sad *Eve* with shame nigh overwhelm'd,
Confessing soon, yet not before her Judge
Bold or loquacious, thus abasht repli'd.
   The Serpent me beguil'd and I did eate.
   Which when the Lord God heard, without delay
To Judgement he proceeded on th' accus'd
Serpent though brute, unable to transferre
The Guilt on him who made him instrument
Of mischief, and polluted from the end
Of his Creation; justly then accurst,
As vitiated in Nature: more to know
Concern'd not Man (since he no further knew)
Nor alter'd his offence; yet God at last
To Satan first in sin his doom apply'd,
Though in mysterious terms, judg'd as then best:
And on the Serpent thus his curse let fall.
   Because thou hast done this, thou art accurst
Above all Cattel, each Beast of the Field;
Upon thy Belly groveling thou shalt goe,
And dust shalt eat all the days of thy Life.
Between Thee and the Woman I will put
Enmitie, and between thine and her Seed;
Her Seed shall bruse thy head, thou bruise his heel.

So spake this Oracle, then verifi'd
When *Jesus* son of *Mary* second *Eve*,
Saw Satan fall like Lightning down from Heav'n,
Prince of the Aire; then rising from his Grave
Spoild Principalities and Powers, triumpht
In open shew, and with ascension bright
Captivity led captive through the Aire,
The Realme it self of Satan long usurpt,
Whom he shall tread at last under our feet;
Eevn hee who now foretold his fatal bruise,
And to the Woman thus his Sentence turn'd.

Thy sorrow I will greatly multiplie
By thy Conception; Children thou shalt bring
In sorrow forth, and to thy Husbands will
Thine shall submit, hee over thee shall rule.

On *Adam* last thus judgement he pronounc'd.
Because thou hast heark'nd to the voice of thy Wife,
And eaten of the Tree concerning which
I charg'd thee, saying: Thou shalt not eate thereof,
Curs'd is the ground for thy sake, thou in sorrow
Shalt eate thereof all the days of thy Life;
Thornes also and Thistles it shall bring thee forth
Unbid, and thou shalt eate th' Herb of th' Field,
In the sweat of thy Face shalt thou eate Bread,
Till thou return unto the ground, for thou
Out of the ground wast taken, know thy Birth,
For dust thou art, and shalt to dust returne.

So judg'd he Man, both Judge and Saviour sent,
And th' instant stroke of Death denounc't that day
Remov'd farr off; then pittying how they stood
Before him naked to the aire, that now
Must suffer change, disdain'd not to begin
Thenceforth the Form of servant to assume,
As when he wash'd his servants feet, so now
As Father of his Familie he clad
Thir nakedness with Skins of Beasts, or slain,
Or as the Snake with youthful Coate repaid;
And thought not much to cloath his Enemies:
Nor hee thir outward onely with the Skins
Of Beasts, but inward nakedness, much more

Opprobrious, with his Robe of righteousness,
Araying cover'd from his Fathers sight.
To him with swift ascent he up returnd,
Into his blissful bosom reassum'd
In glory as of old, to him appeas'd
All, though all-knowing, what had past with Man
Recounted, mixing intercession sweet.
Meanwhile ere thus was sin'd and judg'd on Earth,
Within the Gates of Hell sate Sin and Death,
In counterview within the Gates, that now
Stood open wide, belching outrageous flame
Farr into *Chaos*, since the Fiend pass'd through,
Sin opening, who thus now to Death began.

　　O Son, why sit we here each other viewing
Idlely, while Satan our great Author thrives
In other Worlds, and happier Seat provides
For us his ofspring deare? It cannot be
But that success attends him; if mishap,
Ere this he had return'd, with fury driv'n
By his Avengers, since no place like this
Can fit his punishment, or thir revenge.
Methinks I feel new strength within me rise,
Wings growing, and Dominion giv'n me large
Beyond this Deep; whatever drawes me on,
Or sympathie, or som connatural force
Powerful at greatest distance to unite
With secret amity things of like kinde
By secretest conveyance. Thou my Shade
Inseparable must with mee along:
For Death from Sin no power can separate.
But least the difficultie of passing back
Stay his return perhaps over this Gulfe
Impassable, Impervious, let us try
Adventrous work, yet to thy power and mine
Not unagreeable, to found a path
Over this Maine from Hell to that new World
Where Satan now prevailes, a Monument
Of merit high to all th' infernal Host,
Easing thir passage hence, for intercourse,
Or transmigration, as thir lot shall lead.

Nor can I miss the way, so strongly drawn
By this new felt attraction and instinct.
    Whom thus the meager Shadow answerd soon.
Goe whither Fate and inclination strong
Leads thee, I shall not lag behinde, nor erre
The way, thou leading, such a sent I draw
Of carnage, prey innumerable, and taste
The savour of Death from all things there that live:
Nor shall I to the work thou enterprisest
Be wanting, but afford thee equal aid.
    So saying, with delight he snuff'd the smell
Of mortal change on Earth. As when a flock
Of ravenous Fowl, though many a League remote,
Against the day of Battel, to a Field,
Where Armies lie encampt, come flying, lur'd
With sent of living Carcasses design'd
For death, the following day, in bloodie fight.
So sented the grim Feature, and upturn'd
His Nostril wide into the murkie Air,
Sagacious of his Quarrey from so farr.
Then Both from out Hell Gates into the waste
Wide Anarchie of *Chaos* damp and dark
Flew divers, and with Power (thir Power was great)
Hovering upon the Waters; what they met
Solid or slimie, as in raging Sea
Tost up and down, together crowded drove
From each side shoaling towards the mouth of Hell.
As when two Polar Winds blowing adverse
Upon the *Cronian* Sea, together drive
Mountains of Ice, that stop th' imagin'd way
Beyond *Petsora* Eastward, to the rich
Cathaian Coast. The aggregated Soyle
Death with his Mace petrific, cold and dry,
As with a Trident smote, and fix't as firm
As *Delos* floating once; the rest his look
Bound with *Gorgonian* rigor not to move,
And with *Asphaltic* slime; broad as the Gate,
Deep to the Roots of Hell the gather'd beach
They fasten'd, and the Mole immense wraught on
Over the foaming deep high Archt, a Bridge

Of length prodigious joyning to the Wall
Immoveable of this now fenceless world
Forfeit to Death; from hence a passage broad,
Smooth, easie, inoffensive down to Hell.
So, if great things to small may be compar'd,
Xerxes, the Libertie of *Greece* to yoke,
From *Susa* his *Memnonian* Palace high
Came to the Sea, and over *Hellespont*
Bridging his way, *Europe* with *Asia* joyn'd,
And scourg'd with many a stroak th' indignant waves.
Now had they brought the work by wondrous Art
Pontifical, a ridge of pendent Rock
Over the vext Abyss, following the track
Of *Satan*, to the self same place where hee
First lighted from his Wing, and landed safe
From out of *Chaos* to the out side bare
Of this round World: with Pinns of Adamant
And Chains they made all fast, too fast they made
And durable; and now in little space
The Confines met of Empyrean Heav'n
And of this World, and on the left hand Hell
With long reach interpos'd; three sev'ral wayes
In sight, to each of these three places led.
And now thir way to Earth they had descri'd,
To Paradise first tending, when behold
Satan in likeness of an Angel bright
Betwixt the *Centaure* and the *Scorpion* stearing
His *Zenith*, while the Sun in *Aries* rose:
Disguis'd he came, but those his Childern dear
Thir Parent soon discern'd, though in disguise.
Hee after *Eve* seduc't, unminded slunk
Into the Wood fast by, and changing shape
To observe the sequel, saw his guileful act
By *Eve*, though all unweeting, seconded
Upon her Husband, saw thir shame that sought
Vain covertures; but when he saw descend
The Son of God to judge them, terrifi'd
Hee fled, not hoping to escape, but shun
The present, fearing guiltie what his wrauth
Might suddenly inflict; that past, return'd

By Night, and listning where the hapless Paire
Sate in thir sad discourse, and various plaint,
Thence gatherd his own doom, which understood
Not instant, but of future time. With joy
And tidings fraught, to Hell he now return'd,
And at the brink of *Chaos*, neer the foot
Of this new wondrous Pontifice, unhop't
Met who to meet him came, his Ofspring dear.
Great joy was at thir meeting, and at sight
Of that stupendous Bridge his joy encreas'd.
Long hee admiring stood, till Sin, his faire
Inchanting Daughter, thus the silence broke.

   O Parent, these are thy magnific deeds,
Thy Trophies, which thou view'st as not thine own,
Thou art thir Author and prime Architect:
For I no sooner in my Heart divin'd,
My Heart, which by a secret harmonie
Still moves with thine, joyn'd in connexion sweet,
That thou on Earth hadst prosper'd, which thy looks
Now also evidence, but straight I felt
Though distant from thee Worlds between, yet felt
That I must after thee with this thy Son;
Such fatal consequence unites us three:
Hell could no longer hold us in her bounds,
Nor this unvoyageable Gulf obscure
Detain from following thy illustrious track.
Thou hast atchiev'd our libertie, confin'd
Within Hell Gates till now, thou us impow'rd
To fortifie thus farr, and overlay
With this portentous Bridge the dark Abyss.
Thine now is all this World, thy vertue hath won
What thy hands builded not, thy Wisdom gain'd
With odds what Warr hath lost, and fully aveng'd
Our foile in Heav'n; here thou shalt Monarch reign,
There didst not; there let him still Victor sway,
As Battel hath adjudg'd, from this new World
Retiring, by his own doom alienated,
And henceforth Monarchie with thee divide
Of all things, parted by th' Empyreal bounds,
His Quadrature, from thy Orbicular World,

Or trie thee now more dang'rous to his Throne.
  Whom thus the Prince of Darkness answerd glad.
Fair Daughter, and thou Son and Grandchild both,
High proof ye now have giv'n to be the Race
Of *Satan* (for I glorie in the name,
Antagonist of Heav'ns Almightie King)
Amply have merited of me, of all
Th' Infernal Empire, that so neer Heav'ns dore
Triumphal with triumphal act have met,
Mine with this glorious Work, and made one Realm
Hell and this World, one Realm, one Continent
Of easie thorough-fare. Therefore while I
Descend through Darkness, on your Rode with ease
To my associate Powers, them to acquaint
With these successes, and with them rejoyce,
You two this way, among these numerous Orbs
All yours, right down to Paradise descend;
There dwell and Reign in bliss, thence on the Earth
Dominion exercise and in the Aire,
Chiefly on Man, sole Lord of all declar'd,
Him first make sure your thrall, and lastly kill.
My Substitutes I send ye, and Create
Plenipotent on Earth, of matchless might
Issuing from mee: on your joynt vigor now
My hold of this new Kingdom all depends,
Through Sin to Death expos'd by my exploit.
If your joynt power prevailes, th' affaires of Hell
No detriment need feare, goe and be strong.
  So saying he dismiss'd them, they with speed
Thir course through thickest Constellations held
Spreading thir bane; the blasted Starrs lookt wan,
And Planets, Planet-strook, real Eclips
Then sufferd. Th' other way *Satan* went down
The Causey to Hell Gate; on either side
Disparted *Chaos* over built exclaim'd,
And with rebounding surge the barrs assaild,
That scorn'd his indignation: through the Gate,
Wide open and unguarded, *Satan* pass'd,
And all about found desolate; for those
Appointed to sit there, had left thir charge,

Flown to the upper World; the rest were all
Farr to the inland retir'd, about the walls
Of *Pandæmonium*, Citie and proud seate
Of *Lucifer*, so by allusion calld,
Of that bright Starr to *Satan* paragond.
There kept thir Watch the Legions, while the Grand
In Council sate, sollicitous what chance
Might intercept thir Emperour sent, so hee
Departing gave command, and they observ'd.
As when the *Tartar* from his *Russian* Foe
By *Astracan* over the Snowie Plaines
Retires, or *Bactrian* Sophi from the hornes
Of *Turkish* Crescent, leaves all waste beyond
The Realme of *Aladule*, in his retreate
To *Tauris* or *Casbeen*. So these the late
Heav'n-banisht Host, left desert utmost Hell
Many a dark League, reduc't in careful Watch
Round thir Metropolis, and now expecting
Each hour their great adventurer from the search
Of Forrein Worlds: he through the midst unmarkt,
In shew Plebeian Angel militant
Of lowest order, past; and from the dore
Of that *Plutonian* Hall, invisible
Ascended his high Throne, which under state
Of richest texture spred, at th' upper end
Was plac't in regal lustre. Down a while
He sate, and round about him saw unseen:
At last as from a Cloud his fulgent head
And shape Starr-bright appeer'd, or brighter, clad
With what permissive glory since his fall
Was left him, or false glitter: All amaz'd
At that so sudden blaze the *Stygian* throng
Bent thir aspect, and whom they wish'd beheld,
Thir mighty Chief returnd: loud was th' acclaime:
Forth rush'd in haste the great consulting Peers,
Rais'd from thir dark *Divan*, and with like joy
Congratulant approach'd him, who with hand
Silence, and with these words attention won.

Thrones, Dominations, Princedoms, Vertues, Powers,
For in possession such, not onely of right,

I call ye and declare ye now, returnd
Successful beyond hope, to lead ye forth
Triumphant out of this infernal Pit
Abominable, accurst, the house of woe,
And Dungeon of our Tyrant: Now possess,
As Lords, a spacious World, to our native Heaven
Little inferiour, by my adventure hard
With peril great atchiev'd. Long were to tell
What I have don, what sufferd, with what paine
Voyag'd th' unreal, vast, unbounded deep
Of horrible confusion, over which
By Sin and Death a broad way now is pav'd
To expedite your glorious march; but I
Toild out my uncouth passage, forc't to ride
Th' untractable Abysse, plung'd in the womb
Of unoriginal *Night* and *Chaos* wilde,
That jealous of thir secrets fiercely oppos'd
My journey strange, with clamorous uproare
Protesting Fate supreame; thence how I found
The new created World, which fame in Heav'n
Long had foretold, a Fabrick wonderful
Of absolute perfection, therein Man
Plac't in a Paradise, by our exile
Made happie: Him by fraud I have seduc'd
From his Creator, and the more to increase
Your wonder, with an Apple; he thereat
Offended, worth your laughter, hath giv'n up
Both his beloved Man and all his World,
To Sin and Death a prey, and so to us,
Without our hazard, labour, or allarme,
To range in, and to dwell, and over Man
To rule, as over all he should have rul'd.
True is, mee also he hath judg'd, or rather
Mee not, but the brute Serpent in whose shape
Man I deceav'd: that which to mee belongs,
Is enmity, which he will put between
Mee and Mankinde; I am to bruise his heel;
His Seed, when is not set, shall bruise my head:
A World who would not purchase with a bruise,
Or much more grievous pain? Ye have th' account

Of my performance: What remaines, ye Gods,
But up and enter now into full bliss.
    So having said, a while he stood, expecting
Thir universal shout and high applause
To fill his eare, when contrary he hears
On all sides, from innumerable tongues
A dismal universal hiss, the sound
Of public scorn; he wonderd, but not long
Had leasure, wondring at himself now more;
His Visage drawn he felt to sharp and spare,
His Armes clung to his Ribs, his Leggs entwining
Each other, till supplanted down he fell
A monstrous Serpent on his Belly prone,
Reluctant, but in vaine, a greater power
Now rul'd him, punisht in the shape he sin'd,
According to his doom: he would have spoke,
But hiss for hiss returnd with forked tongue
To forked tongue, for now were all transform'd
Alike, to Serpents all as accessories
To his bold Riot: dreadful was the din
Of hissing through the Hall, thick swarming now
With complicated monsters, head and taile,
Scorpion and Asp, and *Amphisbæna* dire,
Cerastes hornd, *Hydrus*, and *Ellops* drear,
And *Dipsas* (not so thick swarm'd once the Soil
Bedrop with blood of *Gorgon*, or the Isle
Ophiusa) but still greatest hee the midst,
Now Dragon grown, larger then whom the Sun
Ingenderd in the *Pythian* Vale on slime,
Huge *Python*, and his Power no less he seem'd
Above the rest still to retain; they all
Him follow'd issuing forth to th' open Field,
Where all yet left of that revolted Rout
Heav'n-fall'n, in station stood or just array,
Sublime with expectation when to see
In Triumph issuing forth thir glorious Chief;
They saw, but other sight instead, a crowd
Of ugly Serpents; horror on them fell,
And horrid sympathie; for what they saw,
They felt themselves now changing; down thir arms,

Down fell both Spear and Shield, down they as fast,
And the dire hiss renew'd, and the dire form
Catcht by Contagion, like in punishment,
As in thir crime. Thus was th' applause they meant,
Turnd to exploding hiss, triumph to shame
Cast on themselves from thir own mouths. There stood
A Grove hard by, sprung up with this thir change,
His will who reigns above, to aggravate
Thir penance, laden with fair Fruit, like that
Which grew in Paradise, the bait of *Eve*
Us'd by the Tempter: on that prospect strange
Thir earnest eyes they fix'd, imagining
For one forbidden Tree a multitude
Now ris'n, to work them furder woe or shame;
Yet parcht with scalding thurst and hunger fierce,
Though to delude them sent, could not abstain,
But on they rould in heaps, and up the Trees
Climbing, sat thicker than the snakie locks
That curld *Megæra:* greedily they pluck'd
The Frutage fair to sight, like that which grew
Neer that bituminous Lake where *Sodom* flam'd;
This more delusive, not the touch, but taste
Deceav'd; they fondly thinking to allay
Thir appetite with gust, instead of Fruit
Chewd bitter Ashes, which th' offended taste
With spattering noise rejected: oft they assayd,
Hunger and thirst constraining, drugd as oft,
With hatefullest disrelish writh'd thir jaws
With soot and cinders fill'd; so oft they fell
Into the same illusion, not as Man
Whom they triumph'd once lapst. Thus were they plagu'd
And worn with Famin, long and ceasless hiss,
Till thir lost shape, permitted, they resum'd,
Yearly enjoynd, some say, to undergo
This annual humbling certain number'd days,
To dash their pride, and joy for Man seduc't.
However some tradition they dispers'd
Among the Heathen of thir purchase got,
And Fabl'd how the Serpent, whom they calld
·*Ophion* with *Eurynome*, the wide-

Encroaching *Eve* perhaps, had first the rule
Of high *Olympus*, thence by *Saturn* driv'n
And *Ops*, ere yet *Dictæan Jove* was born.
Mean while in Paradise the hellish pair
Too soon arriv'd, *Sin* there in power before,
Once actual, now in body, and to dwell
Habitual habitant; behind her *Death*
Close following pace for pace, not mounted yet
On his pale Horse: to whom *Sin* thus began.

  Second of *Satan* sprung, all conquering *Death*,
What thinkst thou of our Empire now, though earnd
With travail difficult, not better farr
Then stil at Hels dark threshold to have sate watch,
Unnam'd, undreaded, and thy self half starv'd?

  Whom thus the Sin-born Monster answerd soon.
To mee, who with eternal Famin pine,
Alike is Hell, or Paradise, or Heaven,
There best, where most with ravin I may meet;
Which here, though plenteous, all too little seems
To stuff this Maw, this vast unhide-bound Corps.

  To whom th' incestuous Mother thus repli'd.
Thou therefore on these Herbs, and Fruits, and Flours
Feed first, on each Beast next, and Fish, and Fowle,
No homely morsels, and whatever thing
The Sithe of Time mowes down, devour unspar'd,
Till I in Man residing through the Race,
His thoughts, his looks, words, actions all infect,
And season him thy last and sweetest prey.

  This said, they both betook them several wayes,
Both to destroy, or unimmortal make
All kinds, and for destruction to mature
Sooner or later; which th' Almightie seeing,
From his transcendent Seat the Saints among,
To those bright Orders utterd thus his voice.

  See with what heat these Dogs of Hell advance
To waste and havoc yonder World, which I
So fair and good created, and had still
Kept in that state, had not the folly of Man
Let in these wastful Furies, who impute
Folly to mee, so doth the Prince of Hell

And his Adherents, that with so much ease
I suffer them to enter and possess
A place so heav'nly, and conniving seem
To gratifie my scornful Enemies,
That laugh, as if transported with some fit
Of Passion, I to them had quitted all,
At random yielded up to thir misrule;
And know not that I call'd and drew them thither
My Hell-hounds, to lick up the draff and filth
Which mans polluting Sin with taint hath shed
On what was pure, till cramm'd and gorg'd, nigh burst
With suckt and glutted offal, at one sling
Of thy victorious Arm, well-pleasing Son,
Both *Sin*, and *Death*, and yawning *Grave* at last
Through *Chaos* hurld, obstruct the mouth of Hell
For ever, and seal up his ravenous Jawes.
Then Heav'n and Earth renewd shall be made pure
To sanctitie that shall receive no staine:
Till then the Curse pronounc't on both precedes.
    Hee ended, and the heav'nly Audience loud
Sung *Halleluia*, as the sound of Seas,
Through multitude that sung. Just are thy ways,
Righteous are thy Decrees on all thy Works;
Who can extenuate thee? Next, to the Son,
Destin'd restorer of Mankind, by whom
New Heav'n and Earth shall to the Ages rise,
Or down from Heav'n descend. Such was thir song,
While the Creator calling forth by name
His mightie Angels gave them several charge,
As sorted best with present things. The Sun
Had first his precept so to move, so shine,
As might affect the Earth with cold and heat
Scarce tollerable, and from the North to call
Decrepit Winter, from the South to bring
Solstitial summers heat. To the blanc Moone
Her office they prescrib'd, to th' other five
Thir planetarie motions and aspects
In *Sextile*, *Square*, and *Trine*, and *Opposite*,
Of noxious efficacie, and when to joyne
In Synod unbenigne, and taught the fixt

Thir influence malignant when to showre,
Which of them rising with the Sun, or falling,
Should prove tempestuous: To the Winds they set
Thir corners, when with bluster to confound
Sea, Aire, and Shoar, the Thunder when to rowle
With terror through the dark Aereal Hall.
Some say he bid his Angels turne ascanse
The Poles of Earth twice ten degrees and more
From the Suns Axle; they with labour push'd
Oblique the Centric Globe: Som say the Sun
Was bid turn Reines from th' Equinoctial Rode
Like distant breadth to *Taurus* with the Seav'n
Atlantick Sisters, and the *Spartan* Twins
Up to the *Tropic* Crab; thence down amaine
By *Leo* and the *Virgin* and the *Scales*,
As deep as *Capricorne*, to bring in change
Of Seasons to each Clime; else had the Spring
Perpetual smil'd on Earth with vernant Flours,
Equal in Days and Nights, except to those
Beyond the Polar Circles; to them Day
Had unbenighted shon, while the low Sun
To recompence his distance, in thir sight
Had rounded still th' *Horizon*, and not known
Or East or West, which had forbid the Snow
From cold *Estotiland*, and South as farr
Beneath *Magellan*. At that tasted Fruit
The Sun, as from *Thyestean* Banquet, turn'd
His course intended; else how had the World
Inhabited, though sinless, more then now,
Avoided pinching cold and scorching heate?
These changes in the Heav'ns, though slow, produc'd
Like change on Sea and Land, sideral blast,
Vapour, and Mist, and Exhalation hot,
Corrupt and Pestilent: Now from the North
Of *Norumbega*, and the *Samoed* shoar
Bursting thir brazen Dungeon, armd with ice
And snow and haile and stormie gust and flaw,
Boreas and *Cæcias* and *Argestes* loud
And *Thrascias* rend the Woods and Seas upturn;
With adverse blast up-turns them from the South

Notus and *Afer* black with thundrous Clouds
From *Serraliona;* thwart of these as fierce
Forth rush the *Levant* and the *Ponent* Windes
Eurus and *Zephir* with thir lateral noise,
Sirocco, and *Libecchio*. Thus began
Outrage from liveless things; but Discord first
Daughter of Sin, among th' irrational,
Death introduc'd through fierce antipathie:
Beast now with Beast gan war, and Fowle with Fowle,
And Fish with Fish; to graze the Herb all leaving,
Devourd each other; nor stood much in awe
Of Man, but fled him, or with count'nance grim
Glar'd on him passing: these were from without
The growing miseries, which *Adam* saw
Alreadie in part, though hid in gloomiest shade,
To sorrow abandond, but worse felt within,
And in a troubl'd Sea of passion tost,
Thus to disburd'n sought with sad complaint.
  O miserable of happie! is this the end
Of this new glorious World, and mee so late
The Glory of that Glory, who now becom
Accurst of blessed, hide me from the face
Of God, whom to behold was then my highth
Of happiness: yet well, if here would end
The miserie, I deserv'd it, and would beare
My own deservings; but this will not serve;
All that I eate or drink, or shall beget,
Is propagated curse. O voice once heard
Delightfully, *Encrease and multiply*,
Now death to heare! for what can I encrease
Or multiplie, but curses on my head?
Who of all Ages to succeed, but feeling
The evil on him brought by me, will curse
My Head, Ill fare our Ancestor impure,
For this we may thank *Adam;* but his thanks
Shall be the execration; so besides
Mine own that bide upon me, all from mee
Shall with a fierce reflux on mee redound,
On mee as on thir natural center light
Heavie, though in thir place. O fleeting joyes

Of Paradise, deare bought with lasting woes!
Did I request thee, Maker, from my Clay
To mould me Man, did I sollicite thee
From darkness to promote me, or here place
In this delicious Garden? as my Will
Concurd not to my being, it were but right
And equal to reduce me to my dust,
Desirous to resigne, and render back
All I receav'd, unable to performe
Thy terms too hard, by which I was to hold
The good I sought not. To the loss of that,
Sufficient penaltie, why hast thou added
The sense of endless woes? inexplicable
Thy Justice seems; yet to say truth, too late,
I thus contest; then should have been refusd
Those terms whatever, when they were propos'd:
Thou didst accept them; wilt thou enjoy the good,
Then cavil the conditions? and though God
Made thee without thy leave, what if thy Son
Prove disobedient, and reprov'd, retort,
Wherefore didst thou beget me? I sought it not:
Wouldst thou admit for his contempt of thee
That proud excuse? yet him not thy election,
But Natural necessity begot.
God made thee of choice his own, and of his own
To serve him, thy reward was of his grace,
Thy punishment then justly is at his Will.
Be it so, for I submit, his doom is fair,
That dust I am, and shall to dust returne:
O welcom hour whenever! why delayes
His hand to execute what his Decree
Fixd on this day? why do I overlive,
Why am I mockt with death, and length'nd out
To deathless pain? how gladly would I meet
Mortalitie my sentence, and be Earth
Insensible, how glad would lay me down
As in my Mothers lap? there I should rest
And sleep secure; his dreadful voice no more
Would Thunder in my ears, no fear of worse
To mee and to my ofspring would torment me

With cruel expectation. Yet one doubt
Pursues me still, least all I cannot die,
Least that pure breath of Life, the Spirit of Man
Which God inspir'd, cannot together perish
With this corporeal Clod; then in the Grave,
Or in some other dismal place, who knows
But I shall die a living Death? O thought
Horrid, if true! yet why? it was but breath
Of Life that sinn'd; what dies but what had life
And sin? the Bodie properly hath neither.
All of me then shall die: let this appease
The doubt, since humane reach no further knows.
For though the Lord of all be infinite,
Is his wrauth also? be it, man is not so,
But mortal doom'd. How can he exercise
Wrath without end on Man whom Death must end?
Can he make deathless Death? that were to make
Strange contradiction, which to God himself
Impossible is held, as Argument
Of weakness, not of Power. Will he, draw out,
For angers sake, finite to infinite
In punisht man, to satisfie his rigour
Satisfi'd never; that were to extend
His Sentence beyond dust and Natures Law,
By which all Causes else according still
To the reception of thir matter act,
Not to th' extent of thir own Spheare. But say
That Death be not one stroak, as I suppos'd,
Bereaving sense, but endless miserie
From this day onward, which I feel begun
Both in me, and without me, and so last
To perpetuitie; Ay me, that fear
Comes thundring back with dreadful revolution
On my defensless head; both Death and I
Am found Eternal, and incorporate both,
Nor I on my part single, in mee all
Posteritie stands curst: Fair Patrimonie
That I must leave ye, Sons; O were I able
To waste it all my self, and leave ye none!
So disinherited how would ye bless

Me now your Curse! Ah, why should all mankind
For one mans fault thus guiltless be condemn'd,
If guiltless? But from me what can proceed,
But all corrupt, both Mind and Will deprav'd,
Not to do onely, but to will the same
With me? how can they then acquitted stand
In sight of God? Him after all Disputes
Forc't I absolve: all my evasions vain
And reasonings, though through Mazes, lead me still
But to my own conviction: first and last
On mee, mee onely, as the sourse and spring
Of all corruption, all the blame lights due;
So might the wrauth. Fond wish! couldst thou support
That burden heavier then the Earth to bear,
Then all the World much heavier, though divided
With that bad Woman? Thus what thou desir'st,
And what thou fearst, alike destroyes all hope
Of refuge, and concludes thee miserable
Beyond all past example and future,
To *Satan* onely like both crime and doom.
O Conscience, into what Abyss of fears
And horrors hast thou driv'n me; out of which
I find no way, from deep to deeper plung'd!

    Thus *Adam* to himself lamented loud
Through the still Night, not now, as ere man fell,
Wholsom and cool, and mild, but with black Air
Accompanied, with damps and dreadful gloom,
Which to his evil Conscience represented
All things with double terror: On the ground
Outstretcht he lay, on the cold ground, and oft
Curs'd his Creation, Death as oft accus'd
Of tardie execution, since denounc't
The day of his offence. Why comes not Death,
Said hee, with one thrice acceptable stroke
To end me? Shall Truth fail to keep her word,
Justice Divine not hast'n to be just?
But Death comes not at call, Justice Divine
Mends not her slowest pace for prayers or cries.
O Woods, O Fountains, Hillocks, Dales and Bowrs,
With other echo late I taught your Shades

To answer, and resound farr other Song.
Whom thus afflicted when sad *Eve* beheld,
Desolate where she sate, approaching nigh,
Soft words to his fierce passion she assay'd:
But her with stern regard he thus repell'd.

　　Out of my sight, thou Serpent, that name best
Befits thee with him leagu'd, thy self as false
And hateful; nothing wants, but that thy shape,
Like his, and colour Serpentine may shew
Thy inward fraud, to warn all Creatures from thee
Henceforth; least that too heav'nly form, pretended
To hellish falshood, snare them. But for thee
I had persisted happie, had not thy pride
And wandring vanitie, when lest was safe,
Rejected my forewarning, and disdain'd
Not to be trusted, longing to be seen
Though by the Devil himself, him overweening
To over-reach, but with the Serpent meeting
Fool'd and beguil'd, by him thou, I by thee,
To trust thee from my side, imagin'd wise,
Constant, mature, proof against all assaults,
And understood not all was but a shew
Rather then solid vertu, all but a Rib
Crooked by nature, bent, as now appears,
More to the part sinister from me drawn,
Well if thrown out, as supernumerarie
To my just number found. O why did God,
Creator wise, that peopl'd highest Heav'n
With Spirits Masculine, create at last
This noveltie on Earth, this fair defect
Of Nature, and not fill the World at once
With Men as Angels without Feminine,
Or find some other way to generate
Mankind? this mischief had not then befall'n,
And more that shall befall, innumerable
Disturbances on Earth through Femal snares,
And straight conjunction with this Sex: for either
He never shall find out fit Mate, but such
As some misfortune brings him, or mistake,
Or whom he wishes most shall seldom gain

Through her perverseness, but shall see her gaind
By a farr worse, or if she love, withheld
By Parents, or his happiest choice too late
Shall meet, alreadie linkt and Wedlock-bound
To a fell Adversarie, his hate or shame:
Which infinite calamitie shall cause
To Humane life, and houshold peace confound.

He added not, and from her turn'd, but *Eve*
Not so repulst, with Tears that ceas'd not flowing,
And tresses all disorderd, at his feet
Fell humble, and imbracing them, besaught
His peace, and thus proceeded in her plaint.

Forsake me not thus, *Adam*, witness Heav'n
What love sincere, and reverence in my heart
I beare thee, and unweeting have offended,
Unhappilie deceav'd; thy suppliant
I beg, and clasp thy knees; bereave me not,
Whereon I live, thy gentle looks, thy aid,
Thy counsel in this uttermost distress,
My onely strength and stay: forlorn of thee,
Whither shall I betake me, where subsist?
While yet we live, scarce one short hour perhaps,
Between us two let there be peace, both joyning,
As joyn'd in injuries, one enmitie
Against a Foe by doom express assign'd us,
That cruel Serpent: On me exercise not
Thy hatred for this miserie befall'n,
On me already lost, mee then thy self
More miserable; both have sin'd, but thou
Against God onely, I against God and thee,
And to the place of judgment will return,
There with my cries importune Heaven, that all
The sentence from thy head remov'd may light
On me, sole cause to thee of all this woe,
Mee mee onely just object of his ire.

She ended weeping, and her lowlie plight,
Immoveable till peace obtain'd from fault
Acknowledg'd and deplor'd, in *Adam* wraught
Commiseration; soon his heart relented
Towards her, his life so late and sole delight,

Now at his feet submissive in distress,
Creature so faire his reconcilement seeking,
His counsel whom she had displeas'd, his aide;
As one disarm'd, his anger all he lost,
And thus with peaceful words uprais'd her soon.

Unwarie, and too desirous, as before,
So now of what thou knowst not, who desir'st
The punishment all on thy self; alas,
Beare thine own first, ill able to sustaine
His full wrauth whose thou feelst as yet lest part,
And my displeasure bearst so ill. If Prayers
Could alter high Decrees, I to that place
Would speed before thee, and be louder heard,
That on my head all might be visited,
Thy frailtie and infirmer Sex forgiv'n,
To me committed and by me expos'd.
But rise, let us no more contend, nor blame
Each other, blam'd enough elsewhere, but strive
In offices of Love, how we may light'n
Each others burden in our share of woe;
Since this days Death denounc't, if ought I see,
Will prove no sudden, but a slow-pac't evill,
A long days dying to augment our paine,
And to our Seed (O hapless Seed!) deriv'd.

To whom thus *Eve*, recovering heart, repli'd.
Adam, by sad experiment I know
How little weight my words with thee can finde,
Found so erroneous, thence by just event
Found so unfortunate; nevertheless,
Restor'd by thee, vile as I am, to place
Of new acceptance, hopeful to regaine
Thy Love, the sole contentment of my heart,
Living or dying from thee I will not hide
What thoughts in my unquiet brest are ris'n,
Tending to some relief of our extremes,
Or end, though sharp and sad, yet tolerable,
As in our evils, and of easier choice.
If care of our descent perplex us most,
Which must be born to certain woe, devourd
By Death at last, and miserable it is

To be to others cause of misery,
Our own begotten, and of our Loines to bring
Into this cursed World a woful Race,
That after wretched Life must be at last
Food for so foule a Monster, in thy power
It lies, yet ere Conception to prevent
The Race unblest, to being yet unbegot.
Childless thou art, Childless remaine: So Death
Shall be deceav'd his glut, and with us two
Be forc'd to satisfie his Rav'nous Maw.
But if thou judge it hard and difficult,
Conversing, looking, loving, to abstain
From Loves due Rites, Nuptial embraces sweet,
And with desire to languish without hope,
Before the present object languishing
With like desire, which would be miserie
And torment less then none of what we dread,
Then both our selves and Seed at once to free
From what we fear for both, let us make short,
Let us seek Death, or hee not found, supply
With our own hands his Office on our selves;
Why stand we longer shivering under feares,
That shew no end but Death, and have the power,
Of many wayes to die the shortest choosing,
Destruction with destruction to destroy.
　　She ended heer, or vehement despaire
Broke off the rest; so much of Death her thoughts
Had entertaind, as di'd her Cheeks with pale.
But *Adam* with such counsel nothing sway'd,
To better hopes his more attentive minde
Labouring had rais'd, and thus to *Eve* repli'd.
　　Eve, thy contempt of life and pleasure seems
To argue in thee somthing more sublime
And excellent then what thy minde contemnes;
But self-destruction therefore saught, refutes
That excellence thought in thee, and implies,
Not thy contempt, but anguish and regret
For loss of life and pleasure overlov'd.
Or if thou covet death, as utmost end
Of miserie, so thinking to evade

The penaltie pronounc't, doubt not but God
Hath wiselier arm'd his vengeful ire then so
To be forestall'd; much more I fear least Death
So snatcht will not exempt us from the paine
We are by doom to pay; rather such acts
Of contumacie will provoke the highest
To make death in us live: Then let us seek
Some safer resolution, which methinks
I have in view, calling to minde with heed
Part of our Sentence, that thy Seed shall bruise
The Serpents head; piteous amends, unless
Be meant, whom I conjecture, our grand Foe
Satan, who in the Serpent hath contriv'd
Against us this deceit: to crush his head
Would be revenge indeed; which will be lost
By death brought on our selves, or childless days
Resolv'd, as thou proposest; so our Foe
Shall scape his punishment ordain'd, and wee
Instead shall double ours upon our heads.
No more be mention'd then of violence
Against our selves, and wilful barrenness,
That cuts us off from hope, and savours onely
Rancor and pride, impatience and despite,
Reluctance against God and his just yoke
Laid on our Necks. Remember with what mild
And gracious temper he both heard and judg'd
Without wrauth or reviling; wee expected
Immediate dissolution, which we thought
Was meant by Death that day, when lo, to thee
Pains onely in Child-bearing were foretold,
And bringing forth, soon recompenc't with joy,
Fruit of thy Womb: On mee the Curse aslope
Glanc'd on the ground, with labour I must earne
My bread; what harm? Idleness had bin worse;
My labour will sustain me; and least Cold
Or Heat should injure us, his timely care
Hath unbesaught provided, and his hands
Cloath'd us unworthie, pitying while he judg'd;
How much more, if we pray him, will his ear
Be open, and his heart to pitie incline,

And teach us further by what means to shun
Th' inclement Seasons, Rain, Ice, Hail and Snow,
Which now the Skie with various Face begins
To shew us in this Mountain, while the Winds
Blow moist and keen, shattering the graceful locks
Of these fair spreading Trees; which bids us seek
Som better shroud, som better warmth to cherish
Our Limbs benumm'd, ere this diurnal Starr
Leave cold the Night, how we his gather'd beams
Reflected, may with matter sere foment,
Or by collision of two bodies grinde
The Air attrite to Fire, as late the Clouds
Justling or pusht with Winds rude in thir shock
Tine the slant Lightning, whose thwart flame driv'n down
Kindles the gummie bark of Firr or Pine,
And sends a comfortable heat from farr,
Which might supply the Sun: such Fire to use,
And what may else be remedie or cure
To evils which our own misdeeds have wrought,
Hee will instruct us praying, and of Grace
Beseeching him, so as we need not fear
To pass commodiously this life, sustain'd
By him with many comforts, till we end
In dust, our final rest and native home.
What better can we do, then to the place
Repairing where he judg'd us, prostrate fall
Before him reverent, and there confess
Humbly our faults, and pardon beg, with tears
Watering the ground, and with our sighs the Air
Frequenting, sent from hearts contrite, in sign
Of sorrow unfeign'd, and humiliation meek.
Undoubtedly he will relent and turn
From his displeasure; in whose look serene,
When angry most he seem'd and most severe,
What else but favor, grace, and mercie shon?
　　So spake our Father penitent, nor *Eve*
Felt less remorse: they forthwith to the place
Repairing where he judg'd them prostrate fell
Before him reverent, and both confess'd
Humbly thir faults, and pardon beg'd, with tears

Watering the ground, and with thir sighs the Air
Frequenting, sent from hearts contrite, in sign
Of sorrow unfeign'd, and humiliation meek.

BOOK XI

THE ARGUMENT

The Son of God presents to his Father the Prayers of our first Parents now repenting, and intercedes for them: God accepts them, but declares that they must no longer abide in Paradise; sends Michael *with a Band of Cherubim to dispossess them; but first to reveal to* Adam *future things:* Michaels *coming down.* Adam *shews to* Eve *certain ominous signs; he discerns* Michaels *approach, goes out to meet him: the Angel denounces thir departure.* Eve's *Lamentation.* Adam *pleads, but submits: The Angel leads him up to a high Hill, sets before him in vision what shall happ'n till the Flood.*

THUS they in lowliest plight repentant stood
Praying, for from the Mercie-seat above
Prevenient Grace descending had remov'd
The stonie from thir hearts, and made new flesh
Regenerate grow instead, that sighs now breath'd
Unutterable, which the Spirit of prayer
Inspir'd, and wing'd for Heav'n with speedier flight
Then loudest Oratorie: yet thir port
Not of mean suiters, nor important less
Seem'd thir Petition, then when th' ancient Pair
In Fables old, less ancient yet then these,
Deucalion and chaste *Pyrrha* to restore
The Race of Mankind drownd, before the Shrine
Of *Themis* stood devout. To Heav'n thir prayers
Flew up, nor missd the way, by envious windes
Blow'n vagabond or frustrate: in they passd
Dimentionless through Heav'nly dores; then clad
With incense, where the Golden Altar fum'd,
By thir great Intercessor, came in sight
Before the Fathers Throne: Them the glad Son
Presenting, thus to intercede began.
　　See Father, what first fruits on Earth are sprung

From thy implanted Grace in Man, these Sighs
And Prayers, which in this Golden Censer, mixt
With Incense, I thy Priest before thee bring,
Fruits of more pleasing savour from thy seed
Sow'n with contrition in his heart, then those
Which his own hand manuring all the Trees
Of Paradise could have produc't, ere fall'n
From innocence. Now therefore bend thine eare
To supplication, heare his sighs though mute;
Unskilful with what words to pray, let mee
Interpret for him, mee his Advocate
And propitiation, all his works on mee
Good or not good ingraft, my Merit those
Shall perfet, and for these my Death shall pay.
Accept me, and in mee from these receave
The smell of peace toward Mankinde, let him live
Before thee reconcil'd, at least his days
Numberd, though sad, till Death, his doom (which I
To mitigate thus plead, not to reverse)
To better life shall yeeld him, where with mee
All my redeemd may dwell in joy and bliss,
Made one with me as I with thee am one.
  To whom the Father, without Cloud, serene.
All thy request for Man, accepted Son,
Obtain, all thy request was my Decree:
But longer in that Paradise to dwell,
The Law I gave to Nature him forbids:
Those pure immortal Elements that know
No gross, no unharmoneous mixture foule,
Eject him tainted now, and purge him off
As a distemper, gross to aire as gross,
And mortal food, as may dispose him best
For dissolution wrought by Sin, that first
Distemperd all things, and of incorrupt
Corrupted. I at first with two fair gifts
Created him endowd, with Happiness
And Immortalitie: that fondly lost,
This other serv'd but to eternize woe;
Till I provided Death; so Death becomes
His final remedie, and after Life

Tri'd in sharp tribulation, and refin'd
By Faith and faithful works, to second Life,
Wak't in the renovation of the just,
Resignes him up with Heav'n and Earth renewd.
But let us call to Synod all the Blest
Through Heavn's wide bounds; from them I will not hide
My judgments, how with Mankind I proceed,
As how with peccant Angels late they saw;
And in thir state, though firm, stood more confirmd.

He ended, and the Son gave signal high
To the bright Minister that watch'd, hee blew
His Trumpet, heard in *Oreb* since perhaps
When God descended, and perhaps once more
To sound at general doom. Th' Angelic blast
Filld all the Regions: from thir blissful Bowrs
Of *Amarantin* Shade, Fountain or Spring,
By the waters of Life, where ere they sate
In fellowships of joy: the Sons of Light
Hasted, resorting to the Summons high,
And took thir Seats; till from his Throne supream
Th' Almighty thus pronounc'd his sovran Will.

O Sons, like one of us Man is become
To know both Good and Evil, since his taste
Of that defended Fruit; but let him boast
His knowledge of Good lost, and Evil got,
Happier, had it suffic'd him to have known
Good by it self, and Evil not at all.
He sorrows now, repents, and prayes contrite,
My motions in him, longer then they move,
His heart I know, how variable and vain
Self-left. Least therefore his now bolder hand
Reach also of the Tree of Life, and eat,
And live for ever, dream at least to live
For ever, to remove him I decree,
And send him from the Garden forth to Till
The Ground whence he was taken, fitter soile.

Michael, this my behest have thou in charge,
Take to thee from among the Cherubim
Thy choice of flaming Warriours, least the Fiend
Or in behalf of Man, or to invade

Vacant possession som new trouble raise:
Hast thee, and from the Paradise of God
Without remorse drive out the sinful Pair,
From hallowd ground th' unholie, and denounce
To them and to thir Progenie from thence
Perpetual banishment. Yet least they faint
At the sad Sentence rigorously urg'd,
For I behold them soft'nd and with tears
Bewailing thir excess, all terror hide.
If patiently thy bidding they obey,
Dismiss them not disconsolate; reveale
To *Adam* what shall come in future dayes,
As I shall thee enlighten, intermix
My Cov'nant in the Womans seed renewd;
So send them forth, though sorrowing, yet in peace:
And on the East side of the Garden place,
Where entrance up from *Eden* easiest climbes,
Cherubic watch, and of a Sword the flame
Wide waving, all approach farr off to fright,
And guard all passage to the Tree of Life:
Least Paradise a receptacle prove
To Spirits foule, and all my Trees thir prey,
With whose stol'n Fruit Man once more to delude.

He ceas'd; and th' Archangelic Power prepar'd
For swift descent, with him the Cohort bright
Of watchful Cherubim; four faces each
Had, like a double *Janus*, all thir shape
Spangl'd with eyes more numerous then those
Of *Argus*, and more wakeful then to drouze,
Charm'd with *Arcadian* Pipe, the Pastoral Reed
Of *Hermes*, or his opiate Rod. Mean while
To resalute the World with sacred Light
Leucothea wak'd, and with fresh dews imbalmd
The Earth, when *Adam* and first Matron *Eve*
Had ended now thir Orisons, and found,
Strength added from above, new hope to spring
Out of despaire, joy, but with fear yet linkt;
Which thus to *Eve* his welcome words renewd.
Eve, easily may Faith admit, that all
The good which we enjoy, from Heav'n descends

But that from us ought should ascend to Heav'n
So prevalent as to concerne the mind
Of God high-blest, or to incline his will,
Hard to belief may seem; yet this will Prayer,
Or one short sigh of humane breath, up-borne
Ev'n to the Seat of God. For since I saught
By Prayer th' offended Deitie to appease,
Kneel'd and before him humbl'd all my heart,
Methought I saw him placable and mild,
Bending his eare; perswasion in me grew
That I was heard with favour; peace returnd
Home to my Brest, and to my memorie
His promise, that thy Seed shall bruise our Foe;
Which then not minded in dismay, yet now
Assures me that the bitterness of death
Is past, and we shall live. Whence Haile to thee,
Eve rightly call'd, Mother of all Mankind,
Mother of all things living, since by thee
Man is to live, and all things live for Man.

    To whom thus *Eve* with sad demeanour meek.
Ill worthie I such title should belong
To me transgressour, who for thee ordaind
A help, became thy snare; to mee reproach
Rather belongs, distrust and all dispraise:
But infinite in pardon was my Judge,
That I who first brought Death on all, am grac't
The sourse of life; next favourable thou,
Who highly thus to entitle me voutsaf'st,
Farr other name deserving. But the Field
To labour calls us now with sweat impos'd,
Though after sleepless Night; for see the Morn,
All unconcern'd with our unrest, begins
Her rosie progress smiling; let us forth,
I never from thy side henceforth to stray,
Wherere our days work lies, though now enjoind
Laborious, till day droop; while here we dwell,
What can be toilsom in these pleasant Walkes?
Here let us live, though in fall'n state, content.

    So spake, so wish'd much-humbl'd *Eve*, but Fate
Subscrib'd not; Nature first gave Signs, imprest

On Bird, Beast, Aire, Aire suddenly eclips'd
After short blush of Morn; nigh in her sight
The Bird of *Jove*, stoopt from his aerie tour,
Two Birds of gayest plume before him drove:
Down from a Hill the Beast that reigns in Woods,
First hunter then, pursu'd a gentle brace,
Goodliest of all the Forrest, Hart and Hinde;
Direct to th' Eastern Gate was bent thir flight.
Adam observ'd, and with his Eye the chase
Pursuing, not unmov'd to *Eve* thus spake.

  O *Eve*, some furder change awaits us nigh,
Which Heav'n by these mute signs in Nature shews
Forerunners of his purpose, or to warn
Us haply too secure of our discharge
From penaltie, because from death releast
Some days; how long, and what till then our life,
Who knows, or more then this, that we are dust,
And thither must return and be no more.
Why else this double object in our sight
Of flight pursu'd in th' Air and ore the ground
One way the self-same hour? why in the East
Darkness ere Dayes mid-course, and Morning light
More orient in yon Western Cloud that draws
O're the blew Firmament a radiant white,
And slow descends, with somthing heav'nly fraught.

  He err'd not, for by this the heav'nly Bands
Down from a Skie of Jasper lighted now
In Paradise, and on a Hill made alt,
A glorious Apparition, had not doubt
And carnal fear that day dimm'd *Adams* eye.
Not that more glorious, when the Angels met
Jacob in *Mahanaim*, where he saw
The field Pavilion'd with his Guardians bright;
Nor that which on the flaming Mount appeerd
In *Dothan*, cover'd with a Camp of Fire,
Against the *Syrian* King, who to surprize
One man, Assassin-like had levied Warr,
Warr unproclam'd. The Princely Hierarch
In thir bright stand, there left his Powers to seise
Possession of the Garden; hee alone,

To finde where *Adam* shelterd, took his way,
Not unperceav'd of *Adam*, who to *Eve*,
While the great Visitant approachd, thus spake.
    Eve, now expect great tidings, which perhaps
Of us will soon determin, or impose
New Laws to be observ'd; for I descrie
From yonder blazing Cloud that veils the Hill
One of the heav'nly Host, and by his Gate
None of the meanest, some great Potentate
Or of the Thrones above, such Majestie
Invests him coming; yet not terrible,
That I should fear, nor sociably mild,
As *Raphael*, that I should much confide,
But solemn and sublime, whom not to offend,
With reverence I must meet, and thou retire.
He ended; and th' Arch-Angel soon drew nigh,
Not in his shape Celestial, but as Man
Clad to meet Man; over his lucid Armes
A militarie Vest of purple flowd
Livelier then *Melibæan*, or the graine
Of *Sarra*, worn by Kings and Hero's old
In time of Truce; *Iris* had dipt the wooff;
His starrie Helme unbuckl'd shew'd him prime
In Manhood where Youth ended; by his side
As in a glistering *Zodiac* hung the Sword,
Satans dire dread, and in his hand the Spear.
Adam bowd low, hee Kingly from his State
Inclin'd not, but his coming thus declar'd.
    Adam, Heav'ns high behest no Preface needs:
Sufficient that thy Prayers are heard, and Death,
Then due by sentence when thou didst transgress,
Defeated of his seisure many dayes
Giv'n thee of Grace, wherein thou may'st repent,
And one bad act with many deeds well done
Mayst cover: well may then thy Lord appeas'd
Redeem thee quite from Deaths rapacious claime;
But longer in this Paradise to dwell
Permits not; to remove thee I am come,
And send thee from the Garden forth to till
The ground whence thou wast tak'n, fitter Soile.

He added not, for *Adam* at the newes
Heart-strook with chilling gripe of sorrow stood,
That all his senses bound; *Eve*, who unseen
Yet all had heard, with audible lament
Discover'd soon the place of her retire.

    O unexpected stroke, worse then of Death!
Must I thus leave thee Paradise? thus leave
Thee Native Soile, these happie Walks and Shades,
Fit haunt of Gods? where I had hope to spend,
Quiet though sad, the respit of that day
That must be mortal to us both. O flours,
That never will in other Climate grow,
My early visitation, and my last
At Eev'n, which I bred up with tender hand
From the first op'ning bud, and gave ye Names,
Who now shall reare ye to the Sun, or ranke
Your Tribes, and water from th' ambrosial Fount?
Thee lastly nuptial Bowre, by mee adornd
With what to sight or smell was sweet; from thee
How shall I part, and whither wander down
Into a lower World, to this obscure
And wilde, how shall we breath in other Aire
Less pure, accustomd to immortal Fruits?

    Whom thus the Angel interrupted milde.
Lament not *Eve*, but patiently resigne
What justly thou hast lost; nor set thy heart,
Thus over fond, on that which is not thine;
Thy going is not lonely, with thee goes
Thy Husband, him to follow thou art bound;
Where he abides, think there thy native soile.

    Adam by this from the cold sudden damp
Recovering, and his scatterd spirits returnd,
To *Michael* thus his humble words addressd.

    Celestial, whether among the Thrones, or nam'd
Of them the Highest, for such of shape may seem
Prince above Princes, gently hast thou tould
Thy message, which might else in telling wound,
And in performing end us; what besides
Of sorrow and dejection and despair
Our frailtie can sustain, thy tidings bring,

Departure from this happy place, our sweet
Recess, and onely consolation left
Familiar to our eyes, all places else
Inhospitable appeer and desolate,
Nor knowing us nor known: and if by prayer
Incessant I could hope to change the will
Of him who all things can, I would not cease
To wearie him with my assiduous cries:
But prayer against his absolute Decree
No more availes then breath against the winde,
Blown stifling back on him that breaths it forth:
Therefore to his great bidding I submit.
This most afflicts me, that departing hence,
As from his face I shall be hid, deprivd
His blessed count'nance; here I could frequent,
With worship, place by place where he voutsaf'd
Presence Divine, and to my Sons relate;
On this Mount he appeerd, under this Tree
Stood visible, among these Pines his voice
I heard, here with him at this Fountain talk'd:
So many grateful Altars I would reare
Of grassie Terfe, and pile up every Stone
Of lustre from the brook, in memorie,
Or monument to Ages, and thereon
Offer sweet smelling Gumms and Fruits and Flours:
In yonder nether World where shall I seek
His bright appearances, or footstep trace?
For though I fled him angrie, yet recall'd
To life prolongd and promisd Race, I now
Gladly behold though but his utmost skirts
Of glory, and farr off his steps adore.

To whom thus *Michael* with regard benigne.
Adam, thou know'st Heav'n his, and all the Earth,
Not this Rock onely; his Omnipresence fills
Land, Sea, and Aire, and every kinde that lives,
Fomented by his virtual power and warmd:
All th' Earth he gave thee to possess and rule,
No despicable gift; surmise not then
His presence to these narrow bounds confin'd
Of Paradise or *Eden:* this had been

Perhaps thy Capital Seate, from whence had spred
All generations, and had hither come
From all the ends of th' Earth, to celebrate
And reverence thee thir great Progenitor.
But this præeminence thou hast lost, brought down
To dwell on eeven ground now with thy Sons:
Yet doubt not but in Vallie and in plaine
God is as here, and will be found alike
Present, and of his presence many a signe
Still following thee, still compassing thee round
With goodness and paternal Love, his Face
Express, and of his steps the track Divine.
Which that thou mayst beleeve, and be confirmd,
Ere thou from hence depart, know I am sent
To shew thee what shall come in future dayes
To thee and to thy Ofspring; good with bad
Expect to hear, supernal Grace contending
With sinfulness of Men; thereby to learn
True patience, and to temper joy with fear
And pious sorrow, equally enur'd
By moderation either state to beare,
Prosperous or adverse: so shalt thou lead
Safest thy life, and best prepar'd endure
Thy mortal passage when it comes. Ascend
This Hill; let *Eve* (for I have drencht her eyes)
Here sleep below while thou to foresight wak'st,
As once thou slepst, while Shee to life was formd.
    To whom thus *Adam* gratefully repli'd.
Ascend, I follow thee, safe Guide, the path
Thou lead'st me, and to the hand of Heav'n submit,
However chast'ning, to the evil turne
My obvious breast, arming to overcom
By suffering, and earne rest from labour won,
If so I may attain. So both ascend
In the Visions of God: It was a Hill
Of Paradise the highest, from whose top
The Hemisphere of Earth in cleerest Ken
Stretcht out to amplest reach of prospect lay.
Not higher that Hill nor wider looking round,
Whereon for different cause the Tempter set

Our second *Adam* in the Wilderness,
To shew him all Earths Kingdomes and thir Glory.
His Eye might there command wherever stood
City of old or modern Fame, the Seat
Of mightiest Empire, from the destind Walls
Of *Cambalu*, seat of *Cathaian Can*
And *Samarchand* by *Oxus*, *Temirs* Throne,
To *Paquin* of *Sinæan* Kings, and thence
To *Agra* and *Lahor* of great *Mogul*
Down to the golden *Chersonese*, or where
The *Persian* in *Ecbatan* sate, or since
In *Hispahan*, or where the *Russian Ksar*
In *Mosco*, or the Sultan in *Bizance*,
Turchestan-born; nor could his eye not ken
Th' Empire of *Negus* to his utmost Port
Ercoco and the less Maritin Kings
Mombaza, and *Quiloa*, and *Melind*,
And *Sofala* thought *Ophir*, to the Realme
Of *Congo*, and *Angola* fardest South;
Or thence from *Niger* Flood to *Atlas* Mount
The Kingdoms of *Almansor*, *Fez* and *Sus*,
Marocco and *Algiers*, *Tremisen;*
On *Europe* thence, and where *Rome* was to sway
The World: in Spirit perhaps he also saw
Rich *Mexico* the seat of *Motezume*,
And *Cusco* in *Peru*, the richer seat
Of *Atabalipa*, and yet unspoil'd
Guiana, whose great Citie *Geryons* Sons
Call *El Dorado*: but to nobler sights
Michael from *Adams* eyes the Filme remov'd
Which that false Fruit that promis'd clearer sight
Had bred; then purg'd with Euphrasie and Rue
The visual Nerve, for he had much to see;
And from the Well of Life three drops instill'd.
So deep the power of these Ingredients pierc'd,
Eevn to the inmost seat of mental sight,
That *Adam* now enforc't to close his eyes,
Sunk down and all his spirits became intranst:
But him the gentle Angel by the hand
Soon rais'd, and his attention thus recall'd.

Adam, now ope thine eyes, and first behold
Th' effects which thy original crime hath wrought
In some to spring from thee, who never touch'd
Th' excepted Tree, nor with the Snake conspir'd,
Nor sinn'd thy sin, yet from that sin derive
Corruption to bring forth more violent deeds.

His eyes he op'nd, and beheld a field,
Part arable and tilth, whereon were Sheaves
New reapt, the other part sheep-walks and foulds;
Ith' midst an Altar as the Land-mark stood
Rustic, of grassie sord; thither anon
A sweatie Reaper from his Tillage brought
First Fruits, the green Eare, and the yellow Sheaf,
Uncull'd, as came to hand; a Shepherd next
More meek came with the Firstlings of his Flock
Choicest and best; then sacrificing, laid
The Inwards and thir Fat, with Incense strew'd,
On the cleft Wood, and all due Rites perform'd.
His Offring soon propitious Fire from Heav'n
Consum'd with nimble glance, and grateful steame;
The others not, for his was not sincere;
Whereat hee inlie rag'd, and as they talk'd,
Smote him into the Midriff with a stone
That beat out life; he fell, and deadly pale
Groand out his Soul with gushing bloud effus'd.
Much at that sight was *Adam* in his heart
Dismai'd, and thus in haste to th' Angel cri'd.

O Teacher, some great mischief hath befall'n
To that meek man, who well had sacrific'd;
Is Pietie thus and pure Devotion paid?

T' whom *Michael* thus, hee also mov'd, repli'd.
These two are Brethren, *Adam*, and to come
Out of thy loyns; th' unjust the just hath slain,
For envie that his Brothers Offering found
From Heav'n acceptance; but the bloodie Fact
Will be aveng'd, and th' others Faith approv'd
Loose no reward, though here thou see him die,
Rowling in dust and gore. To which our Sire.

Alas, both for the deed and for the cause!
But have I now seen Death? Is this the way

I must return to native dust? O sight
Of terrour, foul and ugly to behold,
Horrid to think, how horrible to feel!
　　To whom thus *Michael*. Death thou hast seen
In his first shape on man; but many shapes
Of Death, and many are the wayes that lead
To his grim Cave, all dismal; yet to sense
More terrible at th' entrance then within.
Some, as thou saw'st, by violent stroke shall die,
By Fire, Flood, Famin, by Intemperance more
In Meats and Drinks, which on the Earth shal bring
Diseases dire, of which a monstrous crew
Before thee shall appear; that thou mayst know
What miserie th' inabstinence of *Eve*
Shall bring on men. Immediately a place
Before his eyes appeard, sad, noysom, dark,
A Lazar-house it seemd, wherein were laid
Numbers of all diseas'd, all maladies
Of gastly Spasm, or racking torture, qualmes
Of heart-sick Agonie, all feavorous kinds,
Convulsions, Epilepsies, fierce Catarrhs,
Intestin Stone and Ulcer, Colic pangs,
Dæmoniac phrenzie, moaping Melancholie
And Moon-struck madness, pining Atrophie,
Marasmus, and wide-wasting Pestilence,
Dropsies, and Asthma's, and Joint-racking Rheums.
Dire was the tossing, deep the groans, despair
Tended the sick busiest from Couch to Couch;
And over them triumphant Death his Dart
Shook, but delaid to strike, though oft invok't
With vows, as thir chief good, and final hope.
Sight so deform what heart of Rock could long
Drie-ey'd behold? *Adam* could not, but wept,
Though not of Woman born; compassion quell'd
His best of Man, and gave him up to tears
A space, till firmer thoughts restrain'd excess,
And scarce recovering words his plaint renew'd.
　　O miserable Mankind, to what fall
Degraded, to what wretched state reserv'd!
Better end heer unborn. Why is life giv'n

To be thus wrested from us? rather why
Obtruded on us thus? who if we knew
What we receive, would either not accept
Life offer'd, or soon beg to lay it down,
Glad to be so dismist in peace. Can thus
Th' Image of God in man created once
So goodly and erect, though faultie since,
To such unsightly sufferings be debas't
Under inhuman pains? Why should not Man,
Retaining still Divine similitude
In part, from such deformities be free,
And for his Makers Image sake exempt?

   Thir Makers Image, answer'd *Michael*, then
Forsook them, when themselves they villifi'd
To serve ungovern'd appetite, and took
His Image whom they serv'd, a brutish vice,
Inductive mainly to the sin of *Eve*.
Therefore so abject is thir punishment,
Disfiguring not Gods likeness, but thir own,
Or if his likeness, by themselves defac't
While they pervert pure Natures healthful rules
To loathsom sickness, worthily, since they
Gods Image did not reverence in themselves.

   I yield it just, said *Adam*, and submit.
But is there yet no other way, besides
These painful passages, how we may come
To Death, and mix with our connatural dust?

   There is, said *Michael*, if thou well observe
The rule of not too much, by temperance taught
In what thou eatst and drinkst, seeking from thence
Due nourishment, not gluttonous delight,
Till many years over thy head return:
So maist thou live, till like ripe Fruit thou drop
Into thy Mothers lap, or be with ease
Gatherd, not harshly pluckt, for death mature:
This is old age; but then thou must outlive
Thy youth, thy strength, thy beauty, which will change
To witherd weak and gray; thy Senses then
Obtuse, all taste of pleasure must forgoe,
To what thou hast, and for the Aire of youth

Hopeful and cheerful, in thy blood will reigne
A melancholly damp of cold and dry
To weigh thy spirits down, and last consume
The Balme of Life. To whom our Ancestor.

Henceforth I flie not Death, nor would prolong
Life much, bent rather how I may be quit
Fairest and easiest of this combrous charge,
Which I must keep till my appointed day
Of rendring up, and patiently attend
My dissolution. *Michael* to him repli'd.

Nor love thy Life, nor hate; but what thou livst
Live well, how long or short permit to Heav'n:
And now prepare thee for another sight.

He lookd and saw a spacious Plaine, whereon
Were Tents of various hue; by some were herds
Of Cattel grazing: others, whence the sound
Of Instruments that made melodious chime
Was heard, of Harp and Organ; and who moovd
Thir stops and chords was seen: his volant touch
Instinct through all proportions low and high
Fled and pursu'd transverse the resonant fugue.
In other part stood one who at the Forge
Labouring, two massie clods of Iron and Brass
Had melted (whether found where casual fire
Had wasted woods on Mountain or in Vale,
Down to the veins of Earth, thence gliding hot
To som Caves mouth, or whether washt by stream
From underground) the liquid Ore he dreind
Into fit moulds prepar'd; from which he formd
First his own Tooles; then, what might else be wrought
Fusil or grav'n in mettle. After these,
But on the hether side a different sort
From the high neighbouring Hills, which was thir Seat,
Down to the Plain descended: by thir guise
Just men they seemd, and all thir study bent
To worship God aright, and know his works
Not hid, nor those things last which might preserve
Freedom and Peace to men: they on the Plain
Long had not walkt, when from the Tents behold
A Beavie of fair Women, richly gay

In Gems and wanton dress; to the Harp they sung
Soft amorous Ditties, and in dance came on:
The Men though grave, ey'd them, and let thir eyes
Rove without rein, till in the amorous Net
Fast caught, they lik'd, and each his liking chose;
And now of love they treat till th' Eevning Star
Loves Harbinger appeerd; then all in heat
They light the Nuptial Torch, and bid invoke
Hymen, then first to marriage Rites invok't;
With Feast and Musick all the Tents resound.
Such happy interview and fair event
Of love and youth not lost, Songs, Garlands, Flours,
And charming Symphonies attach'd the heart
Of *Adam*, soon enclin'd to admit delight,
The bent of Nature; which he thus express'd.

True opener of mine eyes, prime Angel blest,
Much better seems this Vision, and more hope
Of peaceful dayes portends, then those two past;
Those were of hate and death, or pain much worse,
Here Nature seems fulfilld in all her ends.

To whom thus *Michael*. Judg not what is best
By pleasure, though to Nature seeming meet,
Created, as thou art, to nobler end
Holie and pure, conformitie divine.
Those Tents thou sawst so pleasant, were the Tents
Of wickedness, wherein shall dwell his Race
Who slew his Brother; studious they appere
Of Arts that polish Life, Inventers rare,
Unmindful of thir Maker, though his Spirit
Taught them, but they his gifts acknowledg'd none.
Yet they a beauteous ofspring shall beget;
For that fair femal Troop thou sawst, that seemd
Of Goddesses, so blithe, so smooth, so gay,
Yet empty of all good wherein consists
Womans domestic honour and chief praise;
Bred onely and completed to the taste
Of lustful appetence, to sing, to dance,
To dress, and troule the Tongue, and roule the Eye.
To these that sober Race of Men, whose lives
Religious titl'd them the Sons of God,

Shall yield up all thir vertue, all thir fame
Ignobly, to the traines and to the smiles
Of these fair Atheists, and now swim in joy,
(Erelong to swim at large) and laugh; for which
The world erelong a world of tears must weepe.

    To whom thus *Adam* of short joy bereft.
O pittie and shame, that they who to live well
Enterd so faire, should turn aside to tread
Paths indirect, or in the mid way faint!
But still I see the tenor of Mans woe
Holds on the same, from Woman to begin.

    From Mans effeminate slackness it begins,
Said th' Angel, who should better hold his place
By wisdome, and superiour gifts receavd.
But now prepare thee for another Scene.

    He lookd and saw wide Territorie spred
Before him, Towns, and rural works between,
Cities of Men with lofty Gates and Towrs,
Concours in Arms, fierce Faces threatning Warr,
Giants of mightie Bone, and bould emprise;
Part wield thir Arms, part courb the foaming Steed,
Single or in Array of Battel rang'd
Both Horse and Foot, nor idely mustring stood;
One way a Band select from forage drives
A herd of Beeves, faire Oxen and faire Kine
From a fat Meddow ground; or fleecy Flock,
Ewes and thir bleating Lambs over the Plaine,
Thir Bootie; scarce with Life the Shepherds flye,
But call in aide, which makes a bloody Fray;
With cruel Tournament the Squadrons joine;
Where Cattel pastur'd late, now scatterd lies
With Carcasses and Arms th' ensanguind Field
Deserted: Others to a Citie strong
Lay Seige, encampt; by Batterie, Scale, and Mine,
Assaulting; others from the wall defend
With Dart and Jav'lin, Stones and sulfurous Fire;
On each hand slaughter and gigantic deeds.
In other part the scepter'd Haralds call
To Council in the Citie Gates: anon
Grey-headed men and grave, with Warriours mixt,

Assemble, and Harangues are heard, but soon
In factious opposition, till at last
Of middle Age one rising, eminent
In wise deport, spake much of Right and Wrong,
Of Justice, of Religion, Truth and Peace,
And Judgment from above: him old and young
Exploded, and had seiz'd with violent hands,
Had not a Cloud descending snatch'd him thence
Unseen amid the throng: so violence
Proceeded, and Oppression, and Sword-Law
Through all the Plain, and refuge none was found.
Adam was all in tears, and to his guide
Lamenting turnd full sad; O what are these,
Deaths Ministers, not Men, who thus deal Death
Inhumanly to men, and multiply
Ten thousand fould the sin of him who slew
His Brother; for of whom such massacher
Make they but of thir Brethren, men of men?
But who was that Just Man, whom had not Heav'n
Rescu'd, had in his Righteousness bin lost?
  To whom thus *Michael;* These are the product
Of those ill-mated Marriages thou saw'st:
Where good with bad were matcht, who of themselves
Abhor to joyn; and by imprudence mixt,
Produce prodigious Births of bodie or mind.
Such were these Giants, men of high renown;
For in those dayes Might onely shall be admir'd,
And Valour and Heroic Vertu call'd;
To overcome in Battle, and subdue
Nations, and bring home spoils with infinite
Man-slaughter, shall be held the highest pitch
Of human Glorie, and for Glorie done
Of triumph, to be styl'd great Conquerours,
Patrons of Mankind, Gods, and Sons of Gods,
Destroyers rightlier call'd and Plagues of men.
Thus Fame shall be achiev'd, renown on Earth,
And what most merits fame in silence hid.
But hee the seventh from thee, whom thou beheldst
The onely righteous in a World perverse,
And therefore hated, therefore so beset

With Foes for daring single to be just,
And utter odious Truth, that God would come
To judge them with his Saints : Him the most High
Rapt in a balmie Cloud with winged Steeds
Did, as thou sawst, receave, to walk with God
High in Salvation and the Climes of bliss,
Exempt from Death ; to shew thee what reward
Awaits the good, the rest what punishment ;
Which now direct thine eyes and soon behold.

　　He look'd, and saw the face of things quite chang'd ;
The brazen Throat of Warr had ceast to roar,
All now was turn'd to jollitie and game,
To luxurie and riot, feast and dance,
Marrying or prostituting, as befell,
Rape or Adulterie, where passing faire
Allurd them ; thence from Cups to civil Broiles.
At length a Reverend Sire among them came,
And of thir doings great dislike declar'd,
And testifi'd against thir wayes ; hee oft
Frequented thir Assemblies, whereso met,
Triumphs or Festivals, and to them preachd
Conversion and Repentance, as to Souls
In prison under Judgements imminent :
But all in vain : which when he saw, he ceas'd
Contending, and remov'd his Tents farr off ;
Then from the Mountain hewing Timber tall,
Began to build a Vessel of huge bulk,
Measur'd by Cubit, length, and breadth, and highth,
Smeard round with Pitch, and in the side a dore
Contriv'd, and of provisions laid in large
For Man and Beast : when loe a wonder strange !
Of every Beast, and Bird, and Insect small
Came seavens, and pairs, and enterd in, as taught
Thir order ; last the Sire, and his three Sons
With thir four Wives ; and God made fast the dore.
Meanwhile the Southwind rose, and with black wings
Wide hovering, all the Clouds together drove
From under Heav'n ; the Hills to thir supplie
Vapour, and Exhalation dusk and moist,
Sent up amain ; and now the thick'nd Skie

Like a dark Ceeling stood; down rush'd the Rain
Impetuous, and continu'd till the Earth
No more was seen; the floating Vessel swum
Uplifted; and secure with beaked prow
Rode tilting o're the Waves, all dwellings else
Flood overwhelmd, and them with all thir pomp
Deep under water rould; Sea cover'd Sea,
Sea without shoar; and in thir Palaces
Where luxurie late reign'd, Sea-monsters whelp'd
And stabl'd; of Mankind, so numerous late,
All left, in one small bottom swum imbark't.
How didst thou grieve then, *Adam*, to behold
The end of all thy Ofspring, end so sad,
Depopulation; thee another Floud,
Of tears and sorrow a Floud thee also drown'd,
And sunk thee as thy Sons; till gently reard
By th' Angel, on thy feet thou stoodst at last,
Though comfortless, as when a Father mourns
His Children, all in view destroyd at once;
And scarce to th' Angel utterdst thus thy plaint.

    O Visions ill foreseen! better had I
Liv'd ignorant of future, so had borne
My part of evil onely, each dayes lot
Anough to bear; those now, that were dispenst
The burd'n of many Ages, on me light
At once, by my foreknowledge gaining Birth
Abortive, to torment me ere thir being,
With thought that they must be. Let no man seek
Henceforth to be foretold what shall befall
Him or his Children, evil he may be sure,
Which neither his foreknowing can prevent,
And hee the future evil shall no less
In apprehension then in substance feel
Grievous to bear: but that care now is past,
Man is not whom to warne: those few escap't
Famin and anguish will at last consume
Wandring that watrie Desert: I had hope
When violence was ceas't, and Warr on Earth,
All would have then gon well, peace would have crownd
With length of happy days the race of man;

But I was farr deceav'd; for now I see
Peace to corrupt no less then Warr to waste.
How comes it thus? unfould, Celestial Guide,
And whether here the Race of man will end.
To whom thus *Michael*. Those whom last thou sawst
In triumph and luxurious wealth, are they
First seen in acts of prowess eminent
And great exploits, but of true vertu void;
Who having spilt much blood, and don much waste
Subduing Nations, and achievd thereby
Fame in the World, high titles, and rich prey,
Shall change thir course to pleasure, ease, and sloth,
Surfet, and lust, till wantonness and pride
Raise out of friendship hostil deeds in Peace.
The conquered also, and enslav'd by Warr
Shall with thir freedom lost all vertu loose
And fear of God, from whom thir pietie feign'd
In sharp contest of Battel found no aide
Against invaders; therefore coold in zeale
Thenceforth shall practice how to live secure,
Worldlie or dissolute, on what thir Lords
Shall leave them to enjoy; for th' Earth shall bear
More then anough, that temperance may be tri'd:
So all shall turn degenerate, all deprav'd,
Justice and Temperance, Truth and Faith forgot;
One Man except, the onely Son of light
In a dark Age, against example good,
Against allurement, custom, and a World
Offended; fearless of reproach and scorn,
Or violence, hee of thir wicked wayes
Shall them admonish, and before them set
The paths of righteousness, how much more safe,
And full of peace, denouncing wrauth to come
On thir impenitence; and shall returne
Of them derided, but of God observd
The one just Man alive; by his command
Shall build a wondrous Ark, as thou beheldst,
To save himself and houshold from amidst
A World devote to universal rack.
No sooner hee with them of Man and Beast

Select for life shall in the Ark be lodg'd,
And shelterd round, but all the Cataracts
Of Heav'n set open on the Earth shall powre
Raine day and night, all fountaines of the Deep
Broke up, shall heave the Ocean to usurp
Beyond all bounds, till inundation rise
Above the highest Hills: then shall this Mount
Of Paradise by might of Waves be moovd
Out of his place, pushd by the horned floud,
With all his verdure spoil'd, and Trees adrift
Down the great River to the op'ning Gulf,
And there take root an Iland salt and bare,
The haunt of Seales and Orcs, and Sea-mews clang.
To teach thee that God attributes to place
No sanctitie, if none be thither brought
By Men who there frequent, or therein dwell.
And now what further shall ensue, behold.

  He lookd, and saw the Ark hull on the floud,
Which now abated, for the Clouds were fled,
Drivn by a keen North-winde, that blowing drie
Wrinkl'd the face of Deluge, as decai'd;
And the cleer Sun on his wide watrie Glass
Gaz'd hot, and of the fresh Wave largely drew,
As after thirst, which made thir flowing shrink
From standing lake to tripping ebbe, that stole
With soft foot towards the deep, who now had stopt
His Sluces, as the Heav'n his windows shut.
The Ark no more now flotes, but seems on ground
Fast on the top of som high mountain fixt.
And now the tops of Hills as Rocks appeer;
With clamor thence the rapid Currents drive
Towards the retreating Sea thir furious tyde.
Forthwith from out the Arke a Raven flies,
And after him, the surer messenger,
A Dove sent forth once and agen to spie
Green Tree or ground whereon his foot may light;
The second time returning, in his Bill
An Olive leafe he brings, pacific signe:
Anon drie ground appeers, and from his Arke
The ancient Sire descends with all his Train;

Then with uplifted hands, and eyes devout,
Grateful to Heav'n, over his head beholds
A dewie Cloud, and in the Cloud a Bow
Conspicuous with three listed colours gay,
Betok'ning peace from God, and Cov'nant new.
Whereat the heart of *Adam* erst so sad
Greatly rejoyc'd, and thus his joy broke forth.

O thou that future things canst represent
As present, Heav'nly instructer, I revive
At this last sight, assur'd that Man shall live
With all the Creatures, and thir seed preserve.
Farr less I now lament for one whole World
Of wicked Sons destroyd, then I rejoyce
For one Man found so perfet and so just,
That God voutsafes to raise another World
From him, and all his anger to forget.
But say, what mean those coloured streaks in Heavn,
Distended as the Brow of God appeas'd,
Or serve they as a flourie verge to binde
The fluid skirts of that same watrie Cloud,
Least it again dissolve and showr the Earth?

To whom th' Archangel. Dextrously thou aim'st;
So willingly doth God remit his Ire,
Though late repenting him of Man deprav'd,
Griev'd at his heart, when looking down he saw
The whole Earth fill'd with violence, and all flesh
Corrupting each thir way; yet those remoov'd,
Such grace shall one just Man find in his sight,
That he relents, not to blot out mankind,
And makes a Covenant never to destroy
The Earth again by flood, nor let the Sea
Surpass his bounds, nor Rain to drown the World
With Man therein or Beast; but when he brings
Over the Earth a Cloud, will therein set
His triple-colour'd Bow, whereon to look
And call to mind his Cov'nant: Day and Night,
Seed time and Harvest, Heat and hoary Frost
Shall hold thir course, till fire purge all things new,
Both Heav'n and Earth, wherein the just shall dwell.

BOOK XII

THE ARGUMENT

The Angel Michael *continues from the Flood to relate what shall succeed; then, in the mention of* Abraham, *comes by degrees to explain, who that Seed of the Woman shall be, which was promised* Adam *and* Eve *in the Fall; his Incarnation, Death, Resurrection, and Ascension; the state of the Church till his second Coming.* Adam *greatly satisfied and recomforted by these Relations and Promises descends the Hill with* Michael; *wakens* Eve, *who all this while had slept, but with gentle dreams compos'd to quietness of mind and submission.* Michael *in either hand leads them out of Paradise, the fiery Sword waving behind them, and the Cherubim taking their Stations to guard the Place.*

As one who in his journey bates at Noone,
Though bent on speed, so heer the Arch-angel paus'd
Betwixt the world destroy'd and world restor'd,
If *Adam* aught perhaps might interpose;
Then with transition sweet new Speech resumes.
    Thus thou hast seen one World begin and end;
And Man as from a second stock proceed.
Much thou hast yet to see, but I perceave
Thy mortal sight to faile; objects divine
Must needs impaire and wearie human sense:
Henceforth what is to com I will relate,
Thou therefore give due audience, and attend.
This second sours of Men, while yet but few,
And while the dread of judgement past remains
Fresh in thir mindes, fearing the Deitie,
With some regard to what is just and right
Shall lead thir lives, and multiplie apace,
Labouring the soile, and reaping plenteous crop,
Corn, wine and oyle; and from the herd or flock,
Oft sacrificing Bullock, Lamb, or Kid,
With large Wine-offerings pour'd, and sacred Feast
Shal spend thir dayes in joy unblam'd, and dwell
Long time in peace by Families and Tribes
Under paternal rule; till one shall rise

Of proud ambitious heart, who not content
With fair equalitie, fraternal state,
Will arrogate Dominion undeserv'd
Over his brethren, and quite dispossess
Concord and law of Nature from the Earth,
Hunting (and Men not Beasts shall be his game)
With Warr and hostile snare such as refuse
Subjection to his Empire tyrannous:
A mightie Hunter thence he shall be styl'd
Before the Lord, as in despite of Heav'n,
Or from Heav'n claming second Sovrantie;
And from Rebellion shall derive his name,
Though of Rebellion others he accuse.
Hee with a crew, whom like Ambition joyns
With him or under him to tyrannize,
Marching from *Eden* towards the West, shall finde
The Plain, wherein a black bituminous gurge
Boiles out from under ground, the mouth of Hell;
Of Brick, and of that stuff they cast to build
A Citie and Towre, whose top may reach to Heav'n;
And get themselves a name, least far disperst
In foraign Lands thir memorie be lost,
Regardless whether good or evil fame.
But God who oft descends to visit men
Unseen, and through thir habitations walks
To mark thir doings, them beholding soon,
Comes down to see thir Citie, ere the Tower
Obstruct Heav'n Towrs, and in derision sets
Upon thir Tongues a various Spirit to rase
Quite out thir Native Language, and instead
To sow a jangling noise of words unknown:
Forthwith a hideous gabble rises loud
Among the Builders; each to other calls
Not understood, till hoarse, and all in rage,
As mockt they storm; great laughter was in Heav'n
And looking down, to see the hubbub strange
And hear the din; thus was the building left
Ridiculous, and the work Confusion nam'd.
    Whereto thus *Adam* fatherly displeas'd.
O execrable Son so to aspire

Above his Brethren, to himself assuming
Authoritie usurpt, from God not giv'n:
He gave us onely over Beast, Fish, Fowl
Dominion absolute; that right we hold
By his donation; but Man over men
He made not Lord; such title to himself
Reserving, human left from human free.
But this Usurper his encroachment proud
Stayes not on Man; to God his Tower intends
Siege and defiance: Wretched man! what food
Will he convey up thither to sustain
Himself and his rash Armie, where thin Aire
Above the Clouds will pine his entrails gross,
And famish him of Breath, if not of Bread?
 To whom thus *Michael.* Justly thou abhorr'st
That Son, who on the quiet state of men
Such trouble brought, affecting to subdue
Rational Libertie; yet know withall,
Since thy original lapse, true Libertie
Is lost, which alwayes with right Reason dwells
Twinn'd, and from her hath no dividual being:
Reason in man obscur'd, or not obeyd,
Immediately inordinate desires
And upstart Passions catch the Government
From Reason, and to servitude reduce
Man till then free. Therefore since hee permits
Within himself unworthie Powers to reign
Over free Reason, God in Judgement just
Subjects him from without to violent Lords;
Who oft as undeservedly enthrall
His outward freedom: Tyrannie must be,
Though to the Tyrant thereby no excuse.
Yet somtimes Nations will decline so low
From vertue, which is reason, that no wrong,
But Justice, and some fatal curse annext
Deprives them of thir outward libertie,
Thir inward lost: Witness th' irreverent Son
Of him who built the Ark, who for the shame
Don to his Father, heard this heavie curse,
Servant of Servants, on his vitious Race.

Thus will this latter, as the former World,
Still tend from bad to worse, till God at last
Wearied with thir iniquities, withdraw
His presence from among them, and avert
His holy Eyes; resolving from thenceforth
To leave them to thir own polluted wayes;
And one peculiar Nation to select
From all the rest, of whom to be invok'd,
A Nation from one faithful man to spring:
Him on this side *Euphrates* yet residing,
Bred up in Idol-worship; O that men
(Cans't thou believe?) should be so stupid grown,
While yet the Patriark liv'd, who scap'd the Flood,
As to forsake the living God, and fall
To worship thir own work in Wood and Stone
For Gods! yet him God the most High voutsafes
To call by Vision from his Fathers house,
His kindred and false Gods, into a Land
Which he will shew him, and from him will raise
A mightie Nation, and upon him showre
His benediction so, that in his Seed
All Nations shall be blest; hee straight obeys,
Not knowing to what Land, yet firm believes:
I see him, but thou canst not, with what Faith
He leaves his Gods, his Friends, and native Soile
Ur of *Chaldea*, passing now the Ford
To *Haran*, after him a cumbrous Train
Of Herds and Flocks, and numerous servitude;
Not wandring poor, but trusting all his wealth
With God, who call'd him, in a land unknown.
Canaan he now attains, I see his Tents
Pitcht about *Sechem*, and the neighbouring Plaine
Of *Moreh*; there by promise he receaves
Gift to his Progenie of all that Land;
From *Hamath* Northward to the Desert South
(Things by thir names I call, though yet unnam'd)
From *Hermon* East to the great Western Sea,
Mount *Hermon*, yonder Sea, each place behold
In prospect, as I point them; on the shoare
Mount *Carmel*; here the double-founted stream

Jordan, true limit Eastward ; but his Sons
Shall dwell to *Senir,* that long ridge of Hills.
This ponder, that all Nations of the Earth
Shall in his Seed be blessed ; by that Seed
Is meant thy great deliverer, who shall bruise
The Serpents head ; whereof to thee anon
Plainlier shall be reveald. This Patriarch blest,
Whom *faithful Abraham* due time shall call,
A Son, and of his Son a Grand-childe leaves,
Like him in faith, in wisdom, and renown ;
The Grandchilde with twelve Sons increast, departs
From *Canaan,* to a Land hereafter call'd
Egypt, divided by the River *Nile ;*
See where it flows, disgorging at seaven mouthes
Into the Sea : to sojourn in that Land
He comes invited by a yonger Son
In time of dearth, a Son whose worthy deeds
Raise him to be the second in that Realme
Of *Pharao :* there he dies, and leaves his Race
Growing into a Nation, and now grown
Suspected to a sequent King, who seeks
To stop thir overgrowth, as inmate guests
Too numerous ; whence of guests he makes them slaves
Inhospitably, and kills thir infant Males :
Till by two brethren (those two brethren call
Moses and *Aaron*) sent from God to claime
His people from enthralment, they return
With glory and spoile back to thir promis'd Land.
But first the lawless Tyrant, who denies
To know thir God, or message to regard,
Must be compelld by Signes and Judgements dire ;
To blood unshed the Rivers must be turnd,
Frogs, Lice and Flies must all his Palace fill
With loath'd intrusion, and fill all the land ;
His Cattel must of Rot and Murren die,
Botches and blaines must all his flesh imboss,
And all his people ; Thunder mixt with Haile,
Haile mixt with fire must rend th' *Egyptian* Skie
And wheel on th' Earth, devouring where it rouls ;
What it devours not, Herb, or Fruit, or Graine,

A darksom Cloud of Locusts swarming down
Must eat, and on the ground leave nothing green:
Darkness must overshadow all his bounds,
Palpable darkness, and blot out three dayes;
Last with one midnight stroke all the first-born
Of *Egypt* must lie dead. Thus with ten wounds
The River-dragon tam'd at length submits
To let his sojourners depart, and oft
Humbles his stubborn heart, but still as Ice
More hard'nd after thaw, till in his rage
Pursuing whom he late dismissd, the Sea
Swallows him with his Host, but them lets pass
As on drie land between two christal walls,
Aw'd by the rod of *Moses* so to stand
Divided, till his rescu'd gain thir shoar:
Such wondrous power God to his Saint will lend,
Though present in his Angel, who shall goe
Before them in a Cloud, and Pillar of Fire,
By day a Cloud, by night a Pillar of Fire,
To guide them in thir journey, and remove
Behinde them, while th' obdurat King pursues:
All night he will pursue, but his approach
Darkness defends between till morning Watch;
Then through the Firey Pillar and the Cloud
God looking forth will trouble all his Host
And craze thir Chariot wheels: when by command
Moses once more his potent Rod extends
Over the Sea; the Sea his Rod obeys;
On thir imbattelld ranks the Waves return,
And overwhelm thir Warr: the Race elect
Safe towards *Canaan* from the shoar advance
Through the wilde Desert, not the readiest way,
Least entring on the *Canaanite* allarmd
Warr terrifie them inexpert, and feare
Return them back to *Egypt*, choosing rather
Inglorious life with servitude; for life
To noble and ignoble is more sweet
Untraind in Armes, where rashness leads not on.
This also shall they gain by thir delay
In the wide Wilderness, there they shall found

Thir government, and thir great Senate choose
Through the twelve Tribes, to rule by Laws ordaind:
God from the Mount of *Sinai*, whose gray top
Shall tremble, he descending, will himself
In Thunder, Lightning and loud Trumpets sound
Ordaine them Lawes; part such as appertaine
To civil Justice, part religious Rites
Of sacrifice, informing them, by types
And shadowes, of that destind Seed to bruise
The Serpent, by what meanes he shall achieve
Mankinds deliverance. But the voice of God
To mortal eare is dreadful; they beseech
That *Moses* might report to them his will,
And terror cease; he grants what they besaught,
Instructed that to God is no access
Without Mediator, whose high Office now
Moses in figure beares, to introduce
One greater, of whose day he shall foretell,
And all the Prophets in thir Age, the times
Of great *Messiah* shall sing. Thus Laws and Rites
Establisht, such delight hath God in Men
Obedient to his will, that he voutsafes
Among them to set up his Tabernacle,
The holy One with mortal Men to dwell:
By his prescript a Sanctuary is fram'd
Of Cedar, overlaid with Gold, therein
An Ark, and in the Ark his Testimony,
The Records of his Cov'nant, over these
A Mercie-seat of Gold between the wings
Of two bright Cherubim, before him burn
Seaven Lamps as in a Zodiac representing
The Heav'nly fires; over the Tent a Cloud
Shall rest by Day, a fiery gleame by Night,
Save when they journie, and at length they come,
Conducted by his Angel to the Land
Promisd to *Abraham* and his Seed: the rest
Were long to tell, how many Battels fought,
How many Kings destroyd, and Kingdoms won,
Or how the Sun shall in mid Heav'n stand still
A day entire, and Nights due course adjourne,

Mans voice commanding, Sun in *Gibeon* stand,
And thou Moon in the vale of *Aialon*,
Till *Israel* overcome; so call the third
From *Abraham*, Son of *Isaac*, and from him
His whole descent, who thus shall *Canaan* win.
  Here *Adam* interpos'd. O sent from Heav'n,
Enlightner of my darkness, gracious things
Thou hast reveald, those chiefly which concerne
Just *Abraham* and his Seed: now first I finde
Mine eyes true op'ning, and my heart much eas'd,
Erwhile perplext with thoughts what would becom
Of mee and all Mankind; but now I see
His day, in whom all Nations shall be blest,
Favour unmerited by me, who sought
Forbidd'n knowledge by forbidd'n means.
This yet I apprehend not, why to those
Among whom God will deigne to dwell on Earth
So many and so various Laws are giv'n;
So many Laws argue so many sins
Among them; how can God with such reside?
  To whom thus *Michael*. Doubt not but that sin
Will reign among them, as of thee begot;
And therefore was Law given them to evince
Thir natural pravitie, by stirring up
Sin against Law to fight; that when they see
Law can discover sin, but not remove,
Save by those shadowie expiations weak,
The bloud of Bulls and Goats, they may conclude
Some bloud more precious must be paid for Man,
Just for unjust, that in such righteousness
To them by Faith imputed, they may finde
Justification towards God, and peace
Of Conscience, which the Law by Ceremonies
Cannot appease, nor Man the moral part
Perform, and not performing cannot live.
So Law appears imperfet, and but giv'n
With purpose to resign them in full time
Up to a better Cov'nant, disciplin'd
From shadowie Types to Truth, from Flesh to Spirit,
From imposition of strict Laws, to free

Acceptance of large Grace, from servil fear
To filial, works of Law to works of Faith.
And therefore shall not *Moses*, though of God
Highly belov'd, being but the Minister
Of Law, his people into *Canaan* lead;
But *Joshua* whom the Gentiles *Jesus* call,
His Name and Office bearing, who shall quell
The adversarie Serpent, and bring back
Through the worlds wilderness long wanderd man
Safe to eternal Paradise of rest.
Meanwhile they in thir earthly *Canaan* plac't
Long time shall dwell and prosper, but when sins
National interrupt thir public peace,
Provoking God to raise them enemies:
From whom as oft he saves them penitent
By Judges first, then under Kings; of whom
The second, both for pietie renownd
And puissant deeds, a promise shall receive
Irrevocable, that his Regal Throne
For ever shall endure; the like shall sing
All Prophecie, That of the Royal Stock
Of *David* (so I name this King) shall rise
A Son, the Womans Seed to thee foretold,
Foretold to *Abraham*, as in whom shall trust
All Nations, and to Kings foretold, of Kings
The last, for of his Reign shall be no end.
But first a long succession must ensue,
And his next Son for Wealth and Wisdom fam'd,
The clouded Ark of God till then in Tents
Wandring, shall in a glorious Temple enshrine.
Such follow him, as shall be registerd
Part good, part bad, of bad the longer scrowle,
Whose foul Idolatries, and other faults
Heapt to the popular summe, will so incense
God, as to leave them, and expose thir Land,
Thir Citie, his Temple, and his holy Ark
With all his sacred things, a scorn and prey
To that proud Citie, whose high Walls thou saw'st
Left in confusion, *Babylon* thence call'd.
There in captivitie he lets them dwell

The space of seventie years, then brings them back,
Remembring mercie, and his Cov'nant sworn
To *David*, stablisht as the dayes of Heav'n.
Returnd from *Babylon* by leave of Kings
Thir Lords, whom God dispos'd, the house of God
They first re-edifie, and for a while
In mean estate live moderate, till grown
In wealth and multitude, factious they grow;
But first among the Priests dissension springs,
Men who attend the Altar, and should most
Endeavour Peace: thir strife pollution brings
Upon the Temple it self: at last they seise
The Scepter, and regard not *Davids* Sons,
Then loose it to a stranger, that the true
Anointed King *Messiah* might be born
Barr'd of his right; yet at his Birth a Starr
Unseen before in Heav'n proclaims him com,
And guides the Eastern Sages, who enquire
His place, to offer Incense, Myrrh, and Gold;
His place of birth a solemn Angel tells
To simple Shepherds, keeping watch by night;
They gladly thither haste, and by a Quire
Of squadrond Angels hear his Carol sung.
A Virgin is his Mother, but his Sire
The Power of the most High; he shall ascend
The Throne hereditarie, and bound his Reign
With earths wide bounds, his glory with the Heav'ns.

   He ceas'd, discerning *Adam* with such joy
Surcharg'd, as had like grief bin dew'd in tears,
Without the vent of words, which these he breathd.

   O Prophet of glad tidings, finisher
Of utmost hope! now clear I understand
What oft my steddiest thoughts have searcht in vain,
Why our great expectation should be call'd
The seed of Woman: Virgin Mother, Haile,
High in the love of Heav'n, yet from my Loynes
Thou shalt proceed, and from thy Womb the Son
Of God most High; So God with man unites.
Needs must the Serpent now his capital bruise
Expect with mortal paine: say where and when

Thir fight, what stroke shall bruise the Victors heel.
  To whom thus *Michael*. Dream not of thir fight,
As of a Duel, or the local wounds
Of head or heel: not therefore joynes the Son
Manhood to God-head, with more strength to foil
Thy enemie; nor so is overcome
Satan, whose fall from Heav'n, a deadlier bruise,
Disabl'd not to give thee thy deaths wound:
Which hee, who comes thy Saviour, shall recure,
Not by destroying *Satan*, but his works
In thee and in thy Seed: nor can this be,
But by fulfilling that which thou didst want,
Obedience to the Law of God, impos'd
On penaltie of death, and suffering death,
The penaltie to thy transgression due,
And due to theirs which out of thine will grow:
So onely can high Justice rest appaid.
The Law of God exact he shall fulfill
Both by obedience and by love, though love
Alone fulfill the Law; thy punishment
He shall endure by coming in the Flesh
To a reproachful life and cursed death,
Proclaming Life to all who shall believe
In his redemption, and that his obedience
Imputed becomes theirs by Faith, his merits
To save them, not their own, though legal works.
For this he shall live hated, be blasphem'd,
Seis'd on by force, judg'd, and to death condemnd
A shameful and accurst, naild to the Cross
By his own Nation, slaine for bringing Life;
But to the Cross he nailes thy Enemies,
The Law that is against thee, and the sins
Of all mankinde, with him there crucifi'd,
Never to hurt them more who rightly trust
In this his satisfaction; so he dies,
But soon revives, Death over him no power
Shall long usurp; ere the third dawning light
Returne, the Starres of Morn shall see him rise
Out of his grave, fresh as the dawning light,
Thy ransom paid, which Man from death redeems,

His death for Man, as many as offerd Life
Neglect not, and the benefit imbrace
By Faith not void of workes: this God-like act
Annuls thy doom, the death thou shouldst have dy'd,
In sin for ever lost from life; this act
Shall bruise the head of *Satan*, crush his strength
Defeating Sin and Death, his two maine armes,
And fix farr deeper in his head thir stings
Then temporal death shall bruise the Victors heel,
Or theirs whom he redeems, a death like sleep,
A gentle wafting to immortal Life.
Nor after resurrection shall he stay
Longer on Earth then certaine times to appeer
To his Disciples, Men who in his Life
Still follow'd him; to them shall leave in charge
To teach all nations what of him they learn'd
And his Salvation, them who shall beleeve
Baptizing in the profluent streame, the signe
Of washing them from guilt of sin to Life
Pure, and in mind prepar'd, if so befall,
For death, like that which the redeemer dy'd.
All Nations they shall teach; for from that day
Not onely to the Sons of *Abrahams* Loines
Salvation shall be Preacht, but to the Sons
Of *Abrahams* Faith wherever through the world;
So in his seed all Nations shall be blest.
Then to the Heav'n of Heav'ns he shall ascend
With victory, triumphing through the aire
Over his foes and thine; there shall surprise
The Serpent, Prince of aire, and drag in Chaines
Through all his realme, and there confounded leave;
Then enter into glory, and resume
His Seat at Gods right hand, exalted high
Above all names in Heav'n; and thence shall come,
When this worlds dissolution shall be ripe,
With glory and power to judge both quick and dead,
To judge th' unfaithful dead, but to reward
His faithful, and receave them into bliss,
Whether in Heav'n or Earth, for then the Earth
Shall all be Paradise, far happier place

Then this of *Eden*, and far happier daies.
　So spake th' Archangel *Michael*, then paus'd,
As at the Worlds great period ; and our Sire
Replete with joy and wonder thus repli'd.
　O goodness infinite, goodness immense !
That all this good of evil shall produce,
And evil turn to good ; more wonderful
Then that by which creation first brought forth
Light out of darkness ! full of doubt I stand,
Whether I should repent me now of sin
By mee done and occasiond, or rejoyce
Much more, that much more good thereof shall spring,
To God more glory, more good will to Men
From God, and over wrauth grace shall abound.
But say, if our deliverer up to Heav'n
Must reascend, what will betide the few
His faithful, left among th' unfaithful herd,
The enemies of truth ; who then shall guide
His people, who defend ? will they not deale
Wors with his followers then with him they dealt ?
　Be sure they will, said th' Angel ; but from Heav'n
Hee to his own a Comforter will send,
The promise of the Father, who shall dwell
His Spirit within them, and the Law of Faith
Working through love, upon thir hearts shall write,
To guide them in all truth, and also arme
With spiritual Armour, able to resist
Satans assaults, and quench his fierie darts,
What Man can do against them, not affraid,
Though to the death, against such cruelties
With inward consolations recompenc't,
And oft supported so as shall amaze
Thir proudest persecuters : for the Spirit
Powrd first on his Apostles, whom he sends
To evangelize the Nations, then on all
Baptiz'd, shall them with wondrous gifts endue
To speak all Tongues, and do all Miracles,
As did thir Lord before them. Thus they win
Great numbers of each Nation to receave
With joy the tidings brought from Heav'n : at length

Thir Ministry perform'd, and race well run,
Thir doctrine and thir story written left,
They die; but in thir room, as they forewarne,
Wolves shall succeed for teachers, grievous Wolves,
Who all the sacred mysteries of Heav'n
To thir own vile advantages shall turne
Of lucre and ambition, and the truth
With superstitions and traditions taint,
Left onely in those written Records pure,
Though not but by the Spirit understood.
Then shall they seek to avail themselves of names,
Places and titles, and with these to joine
Secular power, though feigning still to act
By spiritual, to themselves appropriating
The Spirit of God, promisd alike and giv'n
To all Beleevers; and from that pretense,
Spiritual Lawes by carnal power shall force
On every conscience; Laws which none shall finde
Left them inrould, or what the Spirit within
Shall on the heart engrave. What will they then
But force the Spirit of Grace it self, and binde
His consort Libertie; what, but unbuild
His living Temples, built by Faith to stand,
Thir own Faith not anothers: for on Earth
Who against Faith and Conscience can be heard
Infallible? yet many will presume:
Whence heavie persecution shall arise
On all who in the worship persevere
Of Spirit and Truth; the rest, farr greater part,
Will deem in outward Rites and specious formes
Religion satisfi'd; Truth shall retire
Bestuck with slandrous darts, and works of Faith
Rarely be found: so shall the World goe on,
To good malignant, to bad men benigne,
Under her own waight groaning, till the day
Appeer of respiration to the just,
And vengeance to the wicked, at return
Of him so lately promiss'd to thy aid,
The Womans seed, obscurely then foretold,
Now amplier known thy Saviour and thy Lord,

Last in the Clouds from Heav'n to be reveald
In glory of the Father, to dissolve
Satan with his perverted World, then raise
From the conflagrant mass, purg'd and refin'd,
New Heav'ns, new Earth, Ages of endless date
Founded in righteousness and peace and love,
To bring forth fruits Joy and eternal Bliss.
    He ended; and thus *Adam* last reply'd.
How soon hath thy prediction, Seer blest,
Measur'd this transient World, the Race of time,
Till time stand fixt: beyond is all abyss,
Eternitie, whose end no eye can reach.
Greatly instructed I shall hence depart,
Greatly in peace of thought, and have my fill
Of knowledge, what this vessel can containe;
Beyond which was my folly to aspire.
Henceforth I learne, that to obey is best,
And love with feare the onely God, to walk
As in his presence, ever to observe
His providence, and on him sole depend,
Merciful over all his works, with good
Still overcoming evil, and by small
Accomplishing great things, by things deemd weak
Subverting worldly strong, and worldly wise
By simply meek; that suffering for Truths sake
Is fortitude to highest victorie,
And to the faithful Death the Gate of Life;
Taught this by his example whom I now
Acknowledge my Redeemer ever blest.
    To whom thus also th' Angel last repli'd:
This having learnt, thou hast attaind the summe
Of wisdom; hope no higher, though all the Starrs
Thou knewst by name, and all th' ethereal Powers,
All secrets of the deep, all Natures works,
Or works of God in Heav'n, Air, Earth, or Sea,
And all the riches of this World enjoydst,
And all the rule, one Empire; onely add
Deeds to thy knowledge answerable, add Faith,
Add Vertue, Patience, Temperance, add Love,
By name to come call'd Charitie, the soul

Of all the rest: then wilt thou not be loath
To leave this Paradise, but shalt possess
A Paradise within thee, happier farr.
Let us descend now therefore from this top
Of Speculation; for the hour precise
Exacts our parting hence; and see the Guards,
By mee encampt on yonder Hill, expect
Thir motion, at whose Front a flaming Sword,
In signal of remove, waves fiercely round:
We may no longer stay: go, waken *Eve;*
Her also I with gentle Dreams have calm'd
Portending good, and all her spirits compos'd
To meek submission: thou at season fit
Let her with thee partake what thou hast heard,
Chiefly what may concern her Faith to know,
The great deliverance by her Seed to come
(For by the Womans Seed) on all Mankind.
That ye may live, which will be many dayes,
Both in one Faith unanimous though sad,
With cause for evils past, yet much more cheer'd
With meditation on the happie end.

He ended, and they both descend the Hill;
Descended, *Adam* to the Bowre where *Eve*
Lay sleeping ran before, but found her wak't;
And thus with words not sad she him receav'd.

Whence thou returnst, and whither wentst, I know;
For God is also in sleep, and Dreams advise,
Which he hath sent propitious, some great good
Presaging, since with sorrow and hearts distress
Wearied I fell asleep: but now lead on;
In mee is no delay; with thee to goe,
Is to stay here; without thee here to stay,
Is to go hence unwilling; thou to mee
Art all things under Heav'n, all places thou,
Who for my wilful crime art banisht hence.
This further consolation yet secure
I carry hence; though all by mee is lost,
Such favour I unworthie am voutsaft,
By mee the Promis'd Seed shall all restore.

So spake our Mother *Eve*, and *Adam* heard

Well pleas'd, but answer'd not; for now too nigh
Th' Archangel stood, and from the other Hill
To thir fixt Station, all in bright array
The Cherubim descended; on the ground
Gliding meteorous, as Ev'ning Mist
Ris'n from a River o're the marish glides,
And gathers ground fast at the Labourers heel
Homeward returning. High in Front advanc't,
The brandisht Sword of God before them blaz'd
Fierce as a Comet; which with torrid heat,
And vapour as the *Libyan* Air adust,
Began to parch that temperate Clime; whereat
In either hand the hastning Angel caught
Our lingring Parents, and to th' Eastern Gate
Led them direct, and down the Cliff as fast
To the subjected Plaine; then disappeer'd.
They looking back, all th' Eastern side beheld
Of Paradise, so late thir happie seat,
Wav'd over by that flaming Brand, the Gate
With dreadful Faces throng'd and fierie Armes:
Som natural tears they drop'd, but wip'd them soon;
The World was all before them, where to choose
Thir place of rest, and Providence thir guide:
They hand in hand with wandring steps and slow,
Through *Eden* took thir solitarie way.

¶ Paradise Regain'd

BOOK I

I who e're while the happy Garden sung,
By one mans disobedience lost, now sing
Recover'd Paradise to all mankind,
By one mans firm obedience fully tri'd
Through all temptation, and the Tempter foil'd
In all his wiles, defeated and repuls't,
And *Eden* rais'd in the wast Wilderness.
    Thou Spirit who ledst this glorious Eremite

Into the Desert, his Victorious Field
Against the Spiritual Foe, and broughtst him thence
By proof the undoubted Son of God, inspire,
As thou art wont, my prompted Song else mute,
And bear through highth or depth of natures bounds
With prosperous wing full summ'd to tell of deeds
Above Heroic, though in secret done,
And unrecorded left through many an Age,
Worthy t' have not remain'd so long unsung.

   Now had the great Proclaimer with a voice
More awful then the sound of Trumpet, cri'd
Repentance, and Heavens Kingdom nigh at hand
To all Baptiz'd : to his great Baptism flock'd
With aw the Regions round, and with them came
From *Nazareth* the Son of *Joseph* deem'd
To the flood *Jordan*, came as then obscure,
Unmarkt, unknown ; but him the Baptist soon
Descri'd, divinely warn'd, and witness bore
As to his worthier, and would have resign'd
To him his Heavenly Office, nor was long
His witness unconfirm'd : on him baptiz'd
Heaven open'd, and in likeness of a Dove
The Spirit descended, while the Fathers voice
From Heav'n pronounc'd him his beloved Son.
That heard the Adversary, who roving still
About the world, at that assembly fam'd
Would not be last, and with the voice divine
Nigh Thunder-struck, th' exalted man, to whom
Such high attest was giv'n, a while survey'd
With wonder, then with envy fraught and rage
Flies to his place, nor rests, but in mid air
To Councel summons all his mighty Peers,
Within thick Clouds and dark ten-fold involv'd,
A gloomy Consistory ; and them amidst
With looks agast and sad he thus bespake.

   O Ancient Powers of Air and this wide world,
For much more willingly I mention Air,
This our old Conquest, then remember Hell
Our hated habitation ; well ye know
How many Ages, as the years of men,

This Universe we have possest, and rul'd
In manner at our will th' affairs of Earth,
Since *Adam* and his facil consort *Eve*
Lost Paradise deceiv'd by me, though since
With dread attending when that fatal wound
Shall be inflicted by the Seed of *Eve*
Upon my head, long the decrees of Heav'n
Delay, for longest time to him is short;
And now too soon for us the circling hours
This dreaded time have compast, wherein we
Must bide the stroak of that long threatn'd wound,
At least if so we can, and by the head
Broken be not intended all our power
To be infring'd, our freedom and our being
In this fair Empire won of Earth and Air;
For this ill news I bring, the Womans seed
Destin'd to this, is late of woman born,
His birth to our just fear gave no small cause,
But his growth now to youths full flowr, displaying
All vertue, grace and wisdom to atchieve
Things highest, greatest, multiplies my fear.
Before him a great Prophet, to proclaim
His coming, is sent Harbinger, who all
Invites, and in the Consecrated stream
Pretends to wash off sin, and fit them so
Purified to receive him pure, or rather
To do him honour as their King; all come,
And he himself among them was baptiz'd,
Not thence to be more pure, but to receive
The testimony of Heaven, that who he is
Thenceforth the Nations may not doubt; I saw
The Prophet do him reverence, on him rising
Out of the water, Heav'n above the Clouds
Unfold her Crystal Dores, thence on his head
A perfect Dove descend, what e're it meant,
And out of Heav'n the Sov'raign voice I heard,
This is my Son belov'd, in him am pleas'd.
His Mother then is mortal, but his Sire,
He who obtains the Monarchy of Heav'n,
And what will he not do to advance his Son?

His first-begot we know, and sore have felt,
When his fierce thunder drove us to the deep;
Who this is we must learn, for man he seems
In all his lineaments, though in his face
The glimpses of his Fathers glory shine.
Ye see our danger on the utmost edge
Of hazard, which admits no long debate,
But must with something sudden be oppos'd,
Not force, but well couch't fraud, well woven snares,
E're in the head of Nations he appear
Their King, their Leader, and Supream on Earth.
I, when no other durst, sole undertook
The dismal expedition to find out
And ruine *Adam*, and the exploit perform'd
Successfully; a calmer voyage now
Will waft me; and the way found prosperous once
Induces best to hope of like success.

He ended, and his words impression left
Of much amazement to th' infernal Crew,
Distracted and surpriz'd with deep dismay
At these sad tidings; but no time was then
For long indulgence to their fears or grief:
Unanimous they all commit the care
And management of this main enterprize
To him their great Dictator, whose attempt
At first against mankind so well had thriv'd
In *Adam's* overthrow, and led thir march
From Hell's deep-vaulted Den to dwell in light,
Regents and Potentates, and Kings, yea gods
Of many a pleasant Realm and Province wide.
So to the Coast of *Jordan* he directs
His easie steps; girded with snaky wiles,
Where he might likeliest find this new-declar'd,
This man of men, attested Son of God,
Temptation and all guile on him to try;
So to subvert whom he suspected rais'd
To end his Raign on Earth so long enjoy'd:
But contrary unweeting he fulfill'd
The purpos'd Counsel pre-ordain'd and fixt
Of the most High, who in full frequence bright

Of Angels, thus to *Gabriel* smiling spake.

   Gabriel this day by proof thou shalt behold,
Thou and all Angels conversant on Earth
With man or mens affairs, how I begin
To verifie that solemn message late,
On which I sent thee to the Virgin pure
In *Galilee*, that she should bear a Son
Great in Renown, and call'd the Son of God;
Then toldst her doubting how these things could be
To her a Virgin, that on her should come
The Holy Ghost, and the power of the highest
O're-shadow her: this man born and now up-grown,
To shew him worthy of his birth divine
And high prediction, henceforth I expose
To Satan; let him tempt and now assay
His utmost subtilty, because he boasts
And vaunts of his great cunning to the throng
Of his Apostasie; he might have learnt
Less over-weening, since he fail'd in *Job*,
Whose constant perseverance overcame
Whate're his cruel malice could invent.
He now shall know I can produce a man
Of female Seed, far abler to resist
All his sollicitations, and at length
All his vast force, and drive him back to Hell,
Winning by Conquest what the first man lost
By fallacy surpriz'd. But first I mean
To exercise him in the Wilderness,
There he shall first lay down the rudiments
Of his great warfare, e're I send him forth
To conquer Sin and Death the two grand foes,
By Humiliation and strong Sufferance:
His weakness shall o'recome Satanic strength
And all the world, and mass of sinful flesh;
That all the Angels and Ætherial Powers,
They now, and men hereafter may discern,
From what consummate vertue I have chose
This perfect Man, by merit call'd my Son,
To earn Salvation for the Sons of men.

   So spake the Eternal Father, and all Heaven

Admiring stood a space, then into Hymns
Burst forth, and in Celestial measures mov'd,
Circling the Throne and Singing, while the hand
Sung with the voice, and this the argument.

    Victory and Triumph to the Son of God
Now entring his great duel, not of arms,
But to vanquish by wisdom hellish wiles.
The Father knows the Son; therefore secure
Ventures his filial Vertue, though untri'd,
Against whate're may tempt, whate're seduce,
Allure, or terrifie, or undermine.
Be frustrate all ye stratagems of Hell,
And devilish machinations come to nought.

    So they in Heav'n their Odes and Vigils tun'd:
Mean while the Son of God, who yet some days
Lodg'd in *Bethabara* where *John* baptiz'd,
Musing and much revolving in his brest,
How best the mighty work he might begin
Of Saviour to mankind, and which way first
Publish his God-like office now mature,
One day forth walk'd alone, the Spirit leading;
And his deep thoughts, the better to converse
With solitude, till far from track of men,
Thought following thought, and step by step led on
He entred now the bordering Desert wild,
And with dark shades and rocks environ'd round,
His holy Meditations thus persu'd.

    O what a multitude of thoughts at once
Awakn'd in me swarm, while I consider
What from within I feel my self, and hear
What from without comes often to my ears,
Ill sorting with my present state compar'd.
When I was yet a child, no childish play
To me was pleasing, all my mind was set
Serious to learn and know, and thence to do
What might be publick good; my self I thought
Born to that end, born to promote all truth,
All righteous things: therefore above my years,
The Law of God I read, and found it sweet,
Made it my whole delight, and in it grew

To such perfection, that e're yet my age
Had measur'd twice six years, at our great Feast
I went into the Temple, there to hear
The Teachers of our Law, and to propose
What might improve my knowledge or their own;
And was admir'd by all, yet this not all
To which my Spirit aspir'd, victorious deeds
Flam'd in my heart, heroic acts, one while
To rescue *Israel* from the *Roman* yoke,
Then to subdue and quell o're all the earth
Brute violence and proud Tyrannick pow'r,
Till truth were freed, and equity restor'd:
Yet held it more humane, more heavenly first
By winning words to conquer willing hearts,
And make perswasion do the work of fear;
At least to try, and teach the erring Soul
Not wilfully mis-doing, but unware
Misled; the stubborn only to subdue.
These growing thoughts my Mother soon perceiving
By words at times cast forth inly rejoyc'd,
And said to me apart, high are thy thoughts
O Son, but nourish them and let them soar
To what highth sacred vertue and true worth
Can raise them, though above example high;
By matchless Deeds express thy matchless Sire.
For know, thou art no Son of mortal man,
Though men esteem thee low of Parentage,
Thy Father is the Eternal King, who rules
All Heaven and Earth, Angels and Sons of men,
A messenger from God fore-told thy birth
Conceiv'd in me a Virgin, he fore-told
Thou shouldst be great and sit on *David's* Throne,
And of thy Kingdom there should be no end.
At thy Nativity a glorious Quire
Of Angels in the fields of *Bethlehem* sung
To Shepherds watching at their folds by night,
And told them the Messiah now was born,
Where they might see him, and to thee they came;
Directed to the Manger where thou lais't,
For in the Inn was left no better room:

A Star, not seen before in Heaven appearing
Guided the Wise Men thither from the East,
To honour thee with Incense, Myrrh, and Gold,
By whose bright course led on they found the place,
Affirming it thy Star new grav'n in Heaven,
By which they knew thee King of *Israel* born.
Just *Simeon* and Prophetic *Anna*, warn'd
By Vision, found thee in the Temple, and spake
Before the Altar and the vested Priest,
Like things of thee to all that present stood.
This having heard, strait I again revolv'd
The Law and Prophets, searching what was writ
Concerning the Messiah, to our Scribes
Known partly, and soon found of whom they spake
I am; this chiefly, that my way must lie
Through many a hard assay even to the death,
E're I the promis'd Kingdom can attain,
Or work Redemption for mankind, whose sins
Full weight must be transferr'd upon my head.
Yet neither thus disheartn'd or dismay'd,
The time prefixt I waited, when behold
The Baptist, (of whose birth I oft had heard,
Not knew by sight) now come, who was to come
Before Messiah and his way prepare.
I as all others to his Baptism came,
Which I believ'd was from above; but he
Strait knew me, and with loudest voice proclaim'd
Me him (for it was shew'n him so from Heaven)
Me him whose Harbinger he was; and first
Refus'd on me his Baptism to confer,
As much his greater, and was hardly won;
But as I rose out of the laving stream,
Heaven open'd her eternal doors, from whence
The Spirit descended on me like a Dove,
And last the sum of all, my Father's voice,
Audibly heard from Heav'n, pronounc'd me his,
Me his beloved Son, in whom alone
He was well pleas'd; by which I knew the time
Now full, that I no more should live obscure,
But openly begin, as best becomes

The Authority which I deriv'd from Heaven.
And now by some strong motion I am led
Into this wilderness, to what intent
I learn not yet, perhaps I need not know;
For what concerns my knowledge God reveals.
   So spake our Morning Star then in his rise,
And looking round on every side beheld
A pathless Desert, dusk with horrid shades;
The way he came not having mark'd, return
Was difficult, by humane steps untrod;
And he still on was led, but with such thoughts
Accompanied of things past and to come
Lodg'd in his brest, as well might recommend
Such Solitude before choicest Society.
Full forty days he pass'd, whether on hill
Sometimes, anon in shady vale, each night
Under the covert of some ancient Oak,
Or Cedar, to defend him from the dew,
Or harbour'd in one Cave, is not reveal'd;
Nor tasted humane food, nor hunger felt
Till those days ended, hunger'd then at last
Among wild Beasts: they at his sight grew mild,
Nor sleeping him nor waking harm'd, his walk
The fiery Serpent fled, and noxious Worm,
The Lion and fierce Tiger glar'd aloof.
But now an aged man in Rural weeds,
Following, as seem'd, the quest of some stray Ewe,
Or wither'd sticks to gather; which might serve
Against a Winters day when winds blow keen,
To warm him wet return'd from field at Eve,
He saw approach, who first with curious eye
Perus'd him, then with words thus utt'red spake.
   Sir, what ill chance hath brought thee to this place
So far from path or road of men, who pass
In Troop or Caravan, for single none
Durst ever, who return'd, and dropt not here
His Carcass, pin'd with hunger and with droughth?
I ask the rather, and the more admire,
For that to me thou seem'st the man, whom late
Our new baptizing Prophet at the Ford

Of *Jordan* honour'd so, and call'd thee Son
Of God; I saw and heard, for we sometimes
Who dwell this wild, constrain'd by want, come forth
To Town or Village nigh (nighest is far)
Where ought we hear, and curious are to hear,
What happ'ns new; Fame also finds us out.

    To whom the Son of God. Who brought me hither
Will bring me hence, no other Guide I seek.

    By Miracle he may, reply'd the Swain,
What other way I see not, for we here
Live on tough roots and stubs, to thirst inur'd
More then the Camel, and to drink go far,
Men to much misery and hardship born;
But if thou be the Son of God, Command
That out of these hard stones be made thee bread;
So shalt thou save thy self and us relieve
With Food, whereof we wretched seldom taste.

    He ended, and the Son of God reply'd.
Think'st thou such force in Bread? is it not written
(For I discern thee other then thou seem'st)
Man lives not by Bread only, but each Word
Proceeding from the mouth of God; who fed
Our Fathers here with Manna; in the Mount
Moses was forty days, nor eat nor drank,
And forty days *Eliah* without food
Wandred this barren waste, the same I now:
Why dost thou then suggest to me distrust,
Knowing who I am, as I know who thou art?

    Whom thus answer'd th' Arch Fiend now undisguis'd.
'Tis true, I am that Spirit unfortunate,
Who leagu'd with millions more in rash revolt
Kept not my happy Station, but was driv'n
With them from bliss to the bottomless deep,
Yet to that hideous place not so confin'd
By rigour unconniving, but that oft
Leaving my dolorous Prison I enjoy
Large liberty to round this Globe of Earth,
Or range in th' Air, nor from the Heav'n of Heav'ns
Hath he excluded my resort sometimes.
I came among the Sons of God, when he

Gave up into my hands *Uzzean Job*
To prove him, and illustrate his high worth;
And when to all his Angels he propos'd
To draw the proud King *Ahab* into fraud
That he might fall in *Ramoth*, they demurring,
I undertook that office, and the tongues
Of all his flattering Prophets glibb'd with lyes
To his destruction, as I had in charge.
For what he bids I do; though I have lost
Much lustre of my native brightness, lost
To be belov'd of God, I have not lost
To love, at least contemplate and admire
What I see excellent in good, or fair,
Or vertuous, I should so have lost all sense.
What can be then less in me then desire
To see thee and approach thee, whom I know
Declar'd the Son of God, to hear attent
Thy wisdom, and behold thy God-like deeds?
Men generally think me much a foe
To all mankind: why should I? they to me
Never did wrong or violence, by them
I lost not what I lost, rather by them
I gain'd what I have gain'd, and with them dwell
Copartner in these Regions of the World,
If not disposer; lend them oft my aid,
Oft my advice by presages and signs,
And answers, oracles, portents and dreams,
Whereby they may direct their future life.
Envy they say excites me, thus to gain
Companions of my misery and wo.
At first it may be; but long since with wo
Nearer acquainted, now I feel by proof,
That fellowship in pain divides not smart,
Nor lightens aught each mans peculiar load.
Small consolation then, were Man adjoyn'd:
This wounds me most (what can it less) that Man,
Man fall'n shall be restor'd, I never more.
      To whom our Saviour sternly thus reply'd.
Deservedly thou griev'st, compos'd of lyes
From the beginning, and in lies wilt end;

Who boast'st release from Hell, and leave to come
Into the Heav'n of Heavens; thou com'st indeed,
As a poor miserable captive thrall,
Comes to the place where he before had sat
Among the Prime in Splendour, now depos'd,
Ejected, emptied, gaz'd, unpitied, shun'd,
A spectacle of ruin or of scorn
To all the Host of Heaven; the happy place
Imparts to thee no happiness, no joy,
Rather inflames thy torment, representing
Lost bliss, to thee no more communicable,
So never more in Hell then when in Heaven.
But thou art serviceable to Heaven's King.
Wilt thou impute to obedience what thy fear
Extorts, or pleasure to do ill excites?
What but thy malice mov'd thee to misdeem
Of righteous *Job*, then cruelly to afflict him
With all inflictions, but his patience won?
The other service was thy chosen task,
To be a lyer in four hundred mouths;
For lying is thy sustenance, thy food.
Yet thou pretend'st to truth; all Oracles
By thee are giv'n, and what confest more true
Among the Nations? that hath been thy craft,
By mixing somewhat true to vent more lyes.
But what have been thy answers, what but dark
Ambiguous and with double sense deluding,
Which they who ask'd have seldom understood,
And not well understood as good not known?
Who ever by consulting at thy shrine
Return'd the wiser, or the more instruct
To flye or follow what concern'd him most,
And run not sooner to his fatal snare?
For God hath justly giv'n the Nations up
To thy Delusions; justly, since they fell
Idolatrous, but when his purpose is
Among them to declare his Providence
To thee not known, whence hast thou then thy truth,
But from him or his Angels President
In every Province, who themselves disdaining

To approach thy Temples, give thee in command
What to the smallest tittle thou shalt say
To thy Adorers; thou with trembling fear,
Or like a Fawning Parasite obey'st;
Then to thy self ascrib'st the truth fore-told.
But this thy glory shall be soon retrench'd;
No more shalt thou by oracling abuse
The Gentiles; henceforth Oracles are ceast,
And thou no more with Pomp and Sacrifice
Shalt be enquir'd at *Delphos* or elsewhere,
At least in vain, for they shall find thee mute.
God hath now sent his living Oracle
Into the World, to teach his final will,
And sends his Spirit of Truth henceforth to dwell
In pious Hearts, an inward Oracle
To all truth requisite for men to know.
  So spake our Saviour; but the subtle Fiend,
Though inly stung with anger and disdain,
Dissembl'd, and this Answer smooth return'd.
  Sharply thou hast insisted on rebuke,
And urg'd me hard with doings, which not will
But misery hath rested from me; where
Easily canst thou find one miserable,
And not inforc'd oft-times to part from truth;
If it may stand him more in stead to lye,
Say and unsay, feign, flatter, or abjure?
But thou art plac't above me, thou art Lord;
From thee I can and must submiss endure
Check or reproof, and glad to scape so quit.
Hard are the ways of truth, and rough to walk,
Smooth on the tongue discourst, pleasing to th' ear,
And tuneable as Silvan Pipe or Song;
What wonder then if I delight to hear
Her dictates from thy mouth? most men admire
Vertue, who follow not her lore: permit me
To hear thee when I come (since no man comes)
And talk at least, though I despair to attain.
Thy Father, who is holy, wise and pure,
Suffers the Hypocrite or Atheous Priest
To tread his Sacred Courts, and minister

About his Altar, handling holy things,
Praying or vowing, and vouchsaf'd his voice
To *Balaam* Reprobate, a Prophet yet
Inspir'd; disdain not such access to me.
　　To whom our Saviour with unalter'd brow.
Thy coming hither, though I know thy scope,
I bid not or forbid; do as thou find'st
Permission from above; thou canst not more.
　　He added not; and Satan bowing low
His gray dissimulation, disappear'd
Into thin Air diffus'd: for now began
Night with her sullen wing to double-shade
The Desert, Fowls in thir clay nests were couch't;
And now wild Beasts came forth the woods to roam.

BOOK II

MEAN while the new-baptiz'd, who yet remain'd
At *Jordan* with the Baptist, and had seen
Him whom they heard so late expresly call'd
Jesus Messiah Son of God declar'd,
And on that high Authority had believ'd,
And with him talkt, and with him lodg'd, I mean
Andrew and *Simon*, famous after known
With others though in Holy Writ not nam'd,
Now missing him thir joy so lately found,
So lately found, and so abruptly gone,
Began to doubt, and doubted many days,
And as the days increas'd, increas'd thir doubt:
Sometimes they thought he might be only shewn,
And for a time caught up to God, as once
Moses was in the Mount, and missing long;
And the great *Thisbite* who on fiery wheels
Rode up to Heaven, yet once again to come.
Therefore as those young Prophets then with care
Sought lost *Eliah*, so in each place these
Nigh to *Bethabara*; in *Jerico*
The City of Palms, *Ænon*, and *Salem* Old,

Machærus and each Town or City wall'd
On this side the broad lake *Genezaret*,
Or in *Perea*, but return'd in vain.
Then on the bank of *Jordan*, by a Creek:
Where winds with Reeds, and Osiers whisp'ring play
Plain Fishermen, no greater men them call,
Close in a Cottage low together got
Thir unexpected loss and plaints out breath'd.
Alas, from what high hope to what relapse
Unlook'd for are we fall'n, our eyes beheld
Messiah certainly now come, so long
Expected of our Fathers; we have heard
His words, his wisdom full of grace and truth,
Now, now, for sure, deliverance is at hand,
The Kingdom shall to *Israel* be restor'd:
Thus we rejoyc'd, but soon our joy is turn'd
Into perplexity and new amaze:
For whither is he gone, what accident
Hath rapt him from us? will he now retire
After appearance, and again prolong
Our expectation? God of *Israel*,
Send thy Messiah forth, the time is come;
Behold the Kings of the Earth how they oppress
Thy chosen, to what highth thir pow'r unjust
They have exalted, and behind them cast
All fear of thee, arise and vindicate
Thy Glory, free thy people from thir yoke,
But let us wait; thus far he hath perform'd,
Sent his Anointed, and to us reveal'd him,
By his great Prophet, pointed at and shown,
In publick, and with him we have convers'd;
Let us be glad of this, and all our fears
Lay on his Providence; he will not fail
Nor will withdraw him now, nor will recall,
Mock us with his blest sight, then snatch him hence,
Soon we shall see our hope, our joy return.

  Thus they out of their plaints new hope resume
To find whom at the first they found unsought:
But to his Mother *Mary*, when she saw
Others return'd from Baptism, not her Son,

Nor left at *Jordan*, tydings of him none;
Within her brest, though calm; her brest though pure,
Motherly cares and fears got head, and rais'd
Some troubl'd thoughts, which she in sighs thus clad.
    O what avails me now that honour high
To have conceiv'd of God, or that salute
Hale highly favour'd, among women blest;
While I to sorrows am no less advanc't,
And fears as eminent, above the lot
Of other women, by the birth I bore,
In such a season born when scarce a Shed
Could be obtain'd to shelter him or me
From the bleak air; a Stable was our warmth,
A Manger his, yet soon enforc't to flye
Thence into *Egypt*, till the Murd'rous King
Were dead, who sought his life, and missing fill'd
With Infant blood the streets of *Bethlehem;*
From *Egypt* home return'd, in *Nazareth*
Hath been our dwelling many years, his life
Private, unactive, calm, contemplative,
Little suspicious to any King; but now
Full grown to Man, acknowledg'd, as I hear,
By *John* the Baptist, and in publick shown,
Son own'd from Heaven by his Father's voice;
I look't for some great change; to Honour? no,
But trouble, as old *Simeon* plain fore-told,
That to the fall and rising he should be
Of many in *Israel*, and to a sign
Spoken against, that through my very Soul
A sword shall pierce, this is my favour'd lot,
My Exaltation to Afflictions high;
Afflicted I may be, it seems, and blest;
I will not argue that, nor will repine.
But where delays he now? some great intent
Conceals him: when twelve years he scarce had seen,
I lost him, but so found, as well I saw
He could not lose himself; but went about
His Father's business; what he meant I mus'd,
Since understand; much more his absence now
Thus long to some great purpose he obscures.

But I to wait with patience am inur'd;
My heart hath been a store-house long of things
And sayings laid up, portending strange events.

  Thus *Mary* pondering oft, and oft to mind
Recalling what remarkably had pass'd
Since first her Salutation heard, with thoughts
Meekly compos'd awaited the fulfilling:
The while her Son tracing the Desert wild,
Sole but with holiest Meditations fed,
Into himself descended, and at once
All his great work to come before him set;
How to begin, how to accomplish best
His end of being on Earth, and mission high:
For Satan with slye preface to return
Had left him vacant, and with speed was gon
Up to the middle Region of thick Air,
Where all his Potentates in Council sate;
There without sign of boast, or sign of joy,
Sollicitous and blank he thus began.

  Princes, Heavens antient Sons, Æthereal Thrones,
Demonian Spirits now, from the Element
Each of his reign allotted, rightlier call'd,
Powers of Fire, Air, Water, and Earth beneath,
So may we hold our place and these mild seats
Without new trouble; such an Enemy
Is ris'n to invade us, who no less
Threat'ns then our expulsion down to Hell;
I, as I undertook, and with the vote
Consenting in full frequence was impowr'd,
Have found him, view'd him, tasted him, but find
Far other labour to be undergon
Then when I dealt with *Adam* first of Men,
Though *Adam* by his Wives allurement fell,
However to this Man inferior far,
If he be Man by Mothers side at least,
With more then humane gifts from Heav'n adorn'd,
Perfections absolute, Graces divine,
And amplitude of mind to greatest Deeds.
Therefore I am return'd, lest confidence
Of my success with *Eve* in Paradise

Deceive ye to perswasion over-sure
Of like succeeding here; I summon all
Rather to be in readiness, with hand
Or counsel to assist; lest I who erst
Thought none my equal, now be over-match'd.

So spake the old Serpent doubting, and from all
With clamour was assur'd thir utmost aid
At his command; when from amidst them rose
Belial the dissolutest Spirit that fell,
The sensuallest, and after *Asmodai*
The fleshliest Incubus, and thus advis'd.

Set women in his eye and in his walk,
Among daughters of men the fairest found;
Many are in each Region passing fair
As the noon Skie; more like to Goddesses
Then Mortal Creatures, graceful and discreet,
Expert in amorous Arts, enchanting tongues
Perswasive, Virgin majesty with mild
And sweet allay'd, yet terrible to approach,
Skill'd to retire, and in retiring draw
Hearts after them tangl'd in Amorous Nets.
Such object hath the power to soft'n and tame
Severest temper, smooth the rugged'st brow,
Enerve, and with voluptuous hope dissolve,
Draw out with credulous desire, and lead
At will the manliest, resolutest brest,
As the Magnetic hardest Iron draws.
Women, when nothing else, beguil'd the heart
Of wisest *Solomon*, and made him build,
And made him bow to the Gods of his Wives.

To whom quick answer Satan thus return'd
Belial, in much uneven scale thou weigh'st
All others by thy self; because of old
Thou thy self doat'st on womankind, admiring
Thir shape, thir colour, and attractive grace,
None are, thou think'st, but taken with such toys.
Before the Flood thou with thy lusty Crew,
False titl'd Sons of God, roaming the Earth
Cast wanton eyes on the daughters of men,
And coupl'd with them, and begot a race.

Have we not seen, or by relation heard,
In Courts and Regal Chambers how thou lurk'st,
In Wood or Grove by mossie Fountain side,
In Valley or Green Meadow to way-lay
Some beauty rare, *Calisto*, *Clymene*,
Daphne, or *Semele*, *Antiopa*,
Or *Amymone*, *Syrinx*, many more
Too long, then lay'st thy scapes on names ador'd,
Apollo, *Neptune*, *Jupiter*, or *Pan*,
Satyr, or Fawn, or Silvan? But these haunts
Delight not all; among the Sons of Men,
How many have with a smile made small account
Of beauty and her lures, easily scorn'd
All her assaults, on worthier things intent?
Remember that *Pellean* Conquerour,
A youth, how all the beauties of the East
He slightly view'd, and slightly over-pass'd;
How hee sirnam'd of *Africa* dismiss'd
In his prime youth the fair *Iberian* maid.
For *Solomon* he liv'd at ease, and full
Of honour, wealth, high fare, aim'd not beyond
Higher design then to enjoy his State;
Thence to the bait of Women lay expos'd;
But he whom we attempt is wiser far
Then *Solomon*, of more exalted mind,
Made and set wholly on the accomplishment
Of greatest things; what woman will you find,
Though of this Age the wonder and the fame,
On whom his leisure will vouchsafe an eye
Of fond desire? or should she confident,
As sitting Queen ador'd on Beauties Throne,
Descend with all her winning charms begirt
To enamour, as the Zone of *Venus* once
Wrought that effect on *Jove*, so Fables tell;
How would one look from his Majestick brow
Seated as on the top of Vertues hill,
Discount'nance her despis'd, and put to rout
All her array; her female pride deject,
Or turn to reverent awe? for Beauty stands
In the admiration only of weak minds

Led captive; cease to admire, and all her **Plumes**
Fall flat and shrink into a trivial toy,
At every sudden slighting quite abasht:
Therefore with manlier objects we must try
His constancy, with such as have more shew
Of worth, of honour, glory, and popular praise;
Rocks whereon greatest men have oftest wreck'd;
Or that which only seems to satisfie
Lawful desires of Nature, not beyond;
And now I know he hungers where no food
Is to be found, in the wide Wilderness;
The rest commit to me, I shall let pass
No advantage, and his strength as oft assay.

He ceas'd, and heard thir grant in loud acclaim;
Then forthwith to him takes a chosen band
Of Spirits likest to himself in guile
To be at hand, and at his beck appear,
If cause were to unfold some active Scene
Of various persons each to know his part;
Then to the Desert takes with these his flight;
Where still from shade to shade the Son of God
After forty days fasting had remain'd,
Now hungring first, and to himself thus said.

Where will this end? four times ten days I have pass'd
Wandring this woody maze, and humane food
Nor tasted, nor had appetite: that Fast
To Vertue I impute not, or count part
Of what I suffer here; if Nature need not,
Or God support Nature without repast
Though needing, what praise is it to endure?
But now I feel I hunger, which declares,
Nature hath need of what she asks; yet God
Can satisfie that need some other way,
Though hunger still remain: so it remain
Without this bodies wasting, I content me,
And from the sting of Famine fear no harm,
Nor mind it, fed with better thoughts that feed
Mee hungring more to do my Fathers will.

It was the hour of night, when thus the Son
Commun'd in silent walk, then laid him down

Under the hospitable covert nigh
Of Trees thick interwoven; there he slept,
And dream'd, as appetite is wont to dream,
Of meats and drinks, Natures refreshment sweet;
Him thought, he by the Brook of *Cherith* stood
And saw the Ravens with their horny beaks
Food to *Elijah* bringing Even and Morn,
Though ravenous, taught to abstain from what they brought:
He saw the Prophet also how he fled
Into the Desert, and how there he slept
Under a Juniper; then how awakt,
He found his Supper on the coals prepar'd,
And by the Angel was bid rise and eat,
And eat the second time after repose,
The strength whereof suffic'd him forty days;
Sometimes that with *Elijah* he partook,
Or as a guest with *Daniel* at his pulse.
Thus wore out night, and now the Herald Lark
Left his ground-nest, high towring to descry
The morns approach, and greet her with his Song:
As lightly from his grassy Couch up rose
Our Saviour, and found all was but a dream,
Fasting he went to sleep, and fasting wak'd.
Up to a hill anon his steps he rear'd,
From whose high top to ken the prospect round,
If Cottage were in view, Sheep-cote or Herd;
But Cottage, Herd or Sheep-cote none he saw,
Only in a bottom saw a pleasant Grove,
With chaunt of tuneful Birds resounding loud;
Thither he bent his way, determin'd there
To rest at noon, and entr'd soon the shade
High rooft and walks beneath, and alleys brown
That open'd in the midst a woody Scene,
Natures own work it seem'd (Nature taught Art)
And to a Superstitious eye the haunt
Of Wood-Gods and Wood-Nymphs; he view'd it round,
When suddenly a man before him stood,
Not rustic as before, but seemlier clad,
As one in City, or Court, or Palace bred,
And with fair speech these words to him address'd.

With granted leave officious I return,
But much more wonder that the Son of God
In this wild solitude so long should bide
Of all things destitute, and well I know,
Not without hunger. Others of some note,
As story tells, have trod this Wilderness;
The Fugitive Bond-woman with her Son
Out cast *Nebaioth*, yet found he relief
By a providing Angel; all the race
Of *Israel* here had famish'd, had not God
Rain'd from Heaven Manna, and that Prophet bold
Native of *Thebes* wandring here was fed
Twice by a voice inviting him to eat.
Of thee these forty days none hath regard,
Forty and more deserted here indeed.

To whom thus Jesus; what conclud'st thou hence?
They all had need, I as thou seest have none.

How hast thou hunger then? Satan reply'd,
Tell me if Food were now before thee set,
Would'st thou not eat? Thereafter as I like
The giver, answer'd Jesus. Why should that
Cause thy refusal, said the subtle Fiend,
Hast thou not right to all Created things,
Owe not all Creatures by just right to thee
Duty and Service, nor to stay till bid,
But tender all their power? nor mention I
Meats by the Law unclean, or offer'd first
To Idols, those young *Daniel* could refuse;
Nor proffer'd by an Enemy, though who
Would scruple that, with want opprest? behold
Nature asham'd, or better to express,
Troubl'd that thou should'st hunger, hath purvey'd
From all the Elements her choicest store
To treat thee as beseems, and as her Lord
With honour, only deign to sit and eat.

He spake no dream, for as his words had end,
Our Saviour lifting up his eyes beheld
In ample space under the broadest shade
A Table richly spred, in regal mode,
With dishes pil'd, and meats of noblest sort

And savour, Beasts of chase, or Fowl of game,
In pastry built, or from the spit, or boyl'd,
Gris-amber-steam'd; all Fish from Sea or Shore,
Freshet, or purling Brook, of shell or fin,
And exquisitest name, for which was drain'd
Pontus and *Lucrine* Bay, and *Afric* Coast.
Alas how simple, to these Cates compar'd,
Was that crude Apple that diverted *Eve!*
And at a stately side-board by the wine
That fragrant smell diffus'd, in order stood
Tall stripling youths rich clad, of fairer hew
Then *Ganymed* or *Hylas*, distant more
Under the Trees now trip'd, now solemn stood
Nymphs of *Diana's* train, and *Naiades*
With fruits and flowers from *Amalthea's* horn,
And Ladies of th' *Hesperides*, that seem'd
Fairer then feign'd of old, or fabl'd since
Of Fairy Damsels met in Forest wide
By Knights of *Logres*, or of *Lyones*,
Lancelot or *Pelleas*, or *Pellenore*,
And all the while Harmonious Airs were heard
Of chiming strings, or charming pipes and winds
Of gentlest gale *Arabian* odors fann'd
From their soft wings, and *Flora's* earliest smells.
Such was the Splendour, and the Tempter now
His invitation earnestly renew'd.

   What doubts the Son of God to sit and eat?
These are not Fruits forbidden, no interdict
Defends the touching of these viands pure,
Thir taste no knowledge works, at least of evil,
But life preserves, destroys life's enemy,
Hunger with sweet restorative delight.
All these are Spirits of Air, and Woods, and Springs,
Thy gentle Ministers, who come to pay
Thee homage, and acknowledge thee thir Lord:
What doubt'st thou Son of God? sit down and eat.

   To whom thus Jesus temperately reply'd:
Said'st thou not that to all things I had right?
And who withholds my pow'r that right to use?
Shall I receive by gift what of my own,

When and where likes me best, I can command?
I can at will, doubt not, assoon as thou,
Command a Table in this Wilderness,
And call swift flights of Angels ministrant
Array'd in Glory on my cup to attend:
Why shouldst thou then obtrude this diligence,
In vain, where no acceptance it can find,
And with my hunger what hast thou to do?
Thy pompous Delicacies I contemn,
And count thy specious gifts no gifts but guiles.

 To whom thus answer'd Satan malecontent:
That I have also power to give thou seest,
If of that pow'r I bring thee voluntary
What I might have bestow'd on whom I pleas'd,
And rather opportunely in this place
Chose to impart to thy apparent need,
Why shouldst thou not accept it? but I see
What I can do or offer is suspect;
Of these things others quickly will dispose
Whose pains have earn'd the far fet spoil. With that
Both Table and Provision vanish'd quite
With sound of Harpies wings, and Talons heard;
Only the importune Tempter still remain'd,
And with these words his temptation pursu'd.

 By hunger, that each other Creature tames,
Thou art not to be harm'd, therefore not mov'd;
Thy temperance invincible besides,
For no allurement yields to appetite,
And all thy heart is set on high designs,
High actions: but wherewith to be atchiev'd?
Great acts require great means of enterprise,
Thou art unknown, unfriended, low of birth,
A Carpenter thy Father known, thy self
Bred up in poverty and streights at home;
Lost in a Desert here and hunger-bit:
Which way or from what hope dost thou aspire
To greatness? whence Authority deriv'st,
What Followers, what Retinue canst thou gain,
Or at thy heels the dizzy Multitude,
Longer then thou canst feed them on thy cost?

Money brings Honour, Friends, Conquest, and Realms;
What rais'd *Antipater* the *Edomite*,
And his Son *Herod* plac'd on *Juda's* Throne;
(Thy throne) but gold that got him puissant friends?
Therefore, if at great things thou wouldst arrive,
Get Riches first, get Wealth, and Treasure heap,
Not difficult, if thou hearken to me,
Riches are mine, Fortune is in my hand;
They whom I favour thrive in wealth amain,
While Virtue, Valour, Wisdom sit in want.
    To whom thus Jesus patiently reply'd;
Yet Wealth without these three is impotent,
To gain dominion or to keep it gain'd.
Witness those antient Empires of the Earth,
In highth of all thir flowing wealth dissolv'd:
But men endu'd with these have oft attain'd
In lowest poverty to highest deeds;
Gideon and *Jephtha*, and the Shepherd lad,
Whose off-spring on the Throne of *Juda* sat
So many Ages, and shall yet regain
That seat, and reign in *Israel* without end.
Among the Heathen, (for throughout the World
To me is not unknown what hath been done
Worthy of Memorial) canst thou not remember
Quintius, Fabricius, Curius, Regulus?
For I esteem those names of men so poor
Who could do mighty things, and could contemn
Riches though offer'd from the hand of Kings.
And what in me seems wanting, but that I
May also in this poverty as soon
Accomplish what they did, perhaps and more?
Extol not Riches then, the toyl of Fools,
The wise mans cumbrance if not snare, more apt
To slacken Virtue, and abate her edge,
Then prompt her to do aught may merit praise.
What if with like aversion I reject
Riches and Realms; yet not for that a Crown,
Golden in shew, is but a wreath of thorns,
Brings dangers, troubles, cares, and sleepless nights
To him who wears the Regal Diadem,

When on his shoulders each mans burden lies;
For therein stands the office of a King,
His Honour, Vertue, Merit and chief Praise,
That for the Publick all this weight he bears.
Yet he who reigns within himself, and rules
Passions, Desires, and Fears, is more a King;
Which every wise and vertuous man attains:
And who attains not, ill aspires to rule
Cities of men, or head-strong Multitudes,
Subject himself to Anarchy within,
Or lawless passions in him which he serves.
But to guide Nations in the way of truth
By saving Doctrine, and from errour lead
To know, and knowing worship God aright,
Is yet more Kingly, this attracts the Soul,
Governs the inner man, the nobler part,
That other o're the body only reigns,
And oft by force, which to a generous mind
So reigning can be no sincere delight.
Besides to give a Kingdom hath been thought
Greater and nobler done, and to lay down
Far more magnanimous, then to assume.
Riches are needless then, both for themselves,
And for thy reason why they should be sought,
To gain a Scepter, oftest better miss't.

BOOK III

So spake the Son of God, and Satan stood
A while as mute confounded what to say,
What to reply, confuted and convinc't
Of his weak arguing, and fallacious drift;
At length collecting all his Serpent wiles,
With soothing words renew'd, him thus accosts.

    I see thou know'st what is of use to know,
What best to say canst say, to do canst do;
Thy actions to thy words accord, thy words
To thy large heart give utterance due, thy heart

Conteins of good, wise, just, the perfect shape.
Should Kings and Nations from thy mouth consult,
Thy Counsel would be as the Oracle
Urim and *Thummim*, those oraculous gems
On *Aaron's* breast: or tongue of Seers old
Infallible; or wert thou sought to deeds
That might require th' array of war, thy skill
Of conduct would be such, that all the world
Could not sustain thy Prowess, or subsist
In battel, though against thy few in arms.
These God-like Vertues wherefore dost thou hide?
Affecting private life, or more obscure
In savage Wilderness, wherefore deprive
All Earth her wonder at thy acts, thy self
The fame and glory, glory the reward
That sole excites to high attempts the flame
Of most erected Spirits, most temper'd pure
Ætherial, who all pleasures else despise,
All treasures and all gain esteem as dross,
And dignities and powers all but the highest?
Thy years are ripe, and over-ripe, the Son
Of *Macedonian Philip* had e're these
Won *Asia* and the Throne of *Cyrus* held
At his dispose, young *Scipio* had brought down
The *Carthaginian* pride, young *Pompey* quell'd
The *Pontic* King and in triumph had rode.
Yet years, and to ripe years judgment mature,
Quench not the thirst of glory, but augment.
Great *Julius*, whom now all the world admires
The more he grew in years, the more inflam'd
With glory, wept that he had liv'd so long
Inglorious: but thou yet art not too late.
     To whom our Saviour calmly thus reply'd.
Thou neither dost perswade me to seek wealth
For Empires sake, nor Empire to affect
For glories sake by all thy argument.
For what is glory but the blaze of fame,
The peoples praise, if always praise unmixt?
And what the people but a herd confus'd,
A miscellaneous rabble, who extol

Things vulgar, and well weigh'd, scarce worth the praise,
They praise and they admire they know not what;
And know not whom, but as one leads the other;
And what delight to be by such extoll'd,
To live upon thir tongues and be thir talk,
Of whom to be disprais'd were no small praise?
His lot who dares be singularly good.
Th' intelligent among them and the wise
Are few, and glory scarce of few is rais'd.
This is true glory and renown, when God
Looking on the Earth, with approbation marks
The just man, and divulges him through Heaven
To all his Angels, who with true applause
Recount his praises; thus he did to *Job*,
When to extend his fame through Heaven and Earth,
As thou to thy reproach mayst well remember,
He ask'd thee, hast thou seen my servant *Job?*
Famous he was in Heaven, on Earth less known;
Where glory is false glory, attributed
To things not glorious, men not worthy of fame.
They err who count it glorious to subdue
By Conquest far and wide, to over-run
Large Countries, and in field great Battels win,
Great Cities by assault: what do these Worthies,
But rob and spoil, burn, slaughter, and enslave
Peaceable Nations, neighbouring, or remote,
Made Captive, yet deserving freedom more
Then those thir Conquerours, who leave behind
Nothing but ruin wheresoe're they rove,
And all the flourishing works of peace destroy,
Then swell with pride, and must be titl'd Gods,
Great Benefactors of mankind, Deliverers,
Worship't with Temple, Priest and Sacrifice;
One is the Son of *Jove*, of *Mars* the other,
Till Conquerour Death discover them scarce men,
Rowling in brutish vices, and deform'd,
Violent or shameful death thir due reward.
But if there be in glory aught of good,
It may by means far different be attain'd
Without ambition, war, or violence;

By deeds of peace, by wisdom eminent,
By patience, temperance; I mention still
Him whom thy wrongs with Saintly patience born,
Made famous in a Land and times obscure;
Who names not now with honour patient *Job?*
Poor *Socrates* (who next more memorable?)
By what he taught and suffer'd for so doing,
For truths sake suffering death unjust, lives now
Equal in fame to proudest Conquerours.
Yet if for fame and glory aught be done,
Aught suffer'd; if young *African* for fame
His wasted Country freed from *Punic* rage,
The deed becomes unprais'd, the man at least,
And loses, though but verbal, his reward.
Shall I seek glory then, as vain men seek
Oft not deserv'd? I seek not mine, but his
Who sent me, and thereby witness whence I am.
      To whom the Tempter murmuring thus reply'd.
Think not so slight of glory; therein least,
Resembling thy great Father: he seeks glory,
And for his glory all things made, all things
Orders and governs, nor content in Heaven
By all his Angels glorifi'd, requires
Glory from men, from all men good or bad,
Wise or unwise, no difference, no exemption;
Above all Sacrifice, or hallow'd gift
Glory he requires, and glory he receives
Promiscuous from all Nations, Jew, or Greek,
Or Barbarous, nor exception hath declar'd;
From us his foes pronounc't glory he exacts.
      To whom our Saviour fervently reply'd.
And reason; since his word all things produc'd,
Though chiefly not for glory as prime end,
But to shew forth his goodness, and impart
His good communicable to every soul
Freely; of whom what could he less expect
Then glory and benediction, that is thanks,
The slightest, easiest, readiest recompence
From them who could return him nothing else,
And not returning that would likeliest render

Contempt instead, dishonour, obloquy?
Hard recompence, unsutable return
For so much good, so much beneficence.
But why should man seek glory? who of his own
Hath nothing, and to whom nothing belongs
But condemnation, ignominy, and shame?
Who for so many benefits receiv'd
Turn'd recreant to God, ingrate and false,
And so of all true good himself despoil'd,
Yet, sacrilegious, to himself would take
That which to God alone of right belongs;
Yet so much bounty is in God, such grace,
That who advance his glory, not thir own,
Them he himself to glory will advance.

So spake the Son of God; and here again
Satan had not to answer, but stood struck
With guilt of his own sin, for he himself
Insatiable of glory had lost all,
Yet of another Plea bethought him soon.

Of glory as thou wilt, said he, so deem,
Worth or not worth the seeking, let it pass:
But to a Kingdom thou art born, ordain'd
To sit upon thy Father *David's* Throne;
By Mothers side thy Father, though thy right
Be now in powerful hands, that will not part
Easily from possession won with arms;
Judæa now and all the promis'd land
Reduc't a Province under Roman yoke,
Obeys *Tiberius;* nor is always rul'd
With temperate sway; oft have they violated
The Temple, oft the Law with foul affronts,
Abominations rather, as did once
Antiochus: and think'st thou to regain
Thy right by sitting still or thus retiring?
So did not *Machabeus:* he indeed
Retir'd unto the Desert, but with arms;
And o're a mighty King so oft prevail'd,
That by strong hand his Family obtain'd,
Though Priests, the Crown, and *David's* Throne usurp'd,
With *Modin* and her Suburbs once content.

If Kingdom move thee not, let move thee Zeal,
And Duty; Zeal and Duty are not slow;
But on Occasions forelock watchful wait.
They themselves rather are occasion best,
Zeal of thy Fathers house, Duty to free
Thy Country from her Heathen servitude;
So shalt thou best fullfil, best verifie
The Prophets old, who sung thy endless raign,
The happier raign the sooner it begins,
Raign then; what canst thou better do the while?
　　To whom our Saviour answer thus return'd.
All things are best fullfil'd in their due time,
And time there is for all things, Truth hath said:
If of my raign Prophetic Writ hath told
That it shall never end, so when begin
The Father in his purpose hath decreed,
He in whose hand all times and seasons roul.
What if he hath decreed that I shall first
Be try'd in humble state, and things adverse,
By tribulations, injuries, insults,
Contempts, and scorns, and snares, and violence,
Suffering, abstaining, quietly expecting
Without distrust or doubt, that he may know
What I can suffer, how obey? who best
Can suffer, best can do; best reign, who first
Well hath obey'd; just tryal e're I merit
My exaltation without change or end.
But what concerns it thee when I begin
My everlasting Kingdom, why art thou
Sollicitous, what moves thy inquisition?
Know'st thou not that my rising is thy fall,
And my promotion will be thy destruction?
　　To whom the Tempter inly rackt reply'd.
Let that come when it comes; all hope is lost
Of my reception into grace; what worse?
For where no hope is left, is left no fear;
If there be worse, the expectation more
Of worse torments me then the feeling can.
I would be at the worst; worst is my Port,
My harbour and my ultimate repose,

The end I would attain, my final good.
My error was my error, and my crime
My crime; whatever for it self condemn'd,
And will alike be punish'd; whether thou
Raign or raign not; though to that gentle brow
Willingly I could flye, and hope thy raign,
From that placid aspect and meek regard,
Rather then aggravate my evil state,
Would stand between me and thy Fathers ire,
(Whose ire I dread more then the fire of Hell)
A shelter and a kind of shading cool
Interposition, as a summers cloud.
If I then to the worst that can be hast,
Why move thy feet so slow to what is best,
Happiest both to thy self and all the world,
That thou who worthiest art should'st be thir King?
Perhaps thou linger'st in deep thoughts detain'd
Of the enterprize so hazardous and high;
No wonder, for though in thee be united
What of perfection can in man be found,
Or human nature can receive, consider
Thy life hath yet been private, most part spent
At home, scarce view'd the *Gallilean* Towns,
And once a year *Jerusalem*, few days
Short sojourn; and what thence could'st thou observe?
The world thou hast not seen, much less her glory,
Empires, and Monarchs, and thir radiant Courts,
Best school of best experience, quickest in sight
In all things that to greatest actions lead.
The wisest, unexperienc't, will be ever
Timorous and loath, with novice modesty,
(As he who seeking Asses found a Kingdom)
Irresolute, unhardy, unadventrous:
But I will bring thee where thou soon shalt quit
Those rudiments, and see before thine eyes
The Monarchies of the Earth, thir pomp and state,
Sufficient introduction to inform
Thee, of thy self so apt, in regal Arts,
And regal Mysteries; that thou may'st know
How best their opposition to withstand.

With that (such power was giv'n him then) he took
The Son of God up to a Mountain high.
It was a Mountain at whose verdant feet
A spatious plain out stretch't in circuit wide
Lay pleasant; from his side two rivers flow'd,
Th' one winding, the other strait and left between
Fair Champain with less rivers interveind,
Then meeting joyn'd thir tribute to the Sea:
Fertil of corn the glebe, of oyl and wine,
With herds the pastures throng'd, with flocks the hills,
Huge Cities and high towr'd, that well might seem
The seats of mightiest Monarchs, and so large
The Prospect was, that here and there was room
For barren desert fountainless and dry.
To this high mountain top the Tempter brought
Our Saviour, and new train of words began.

Well have we speeded, and o're hill and dale,
Forest and field, and flood, Temples and Towers
Cut shorter many a league; here thou behold'st
Assyria and her Empires antient bounds,
Araxes and the *Caspian* lake, thence on
As far as *Indus* East, *Euphrates* West,
And oft beyond; to South the *Persian* Bay,
And inaccessible the *Arabian* drouth:
Here *Ninevee*, of length within her wall
Several days journey, built by *Ninus* old,
Of that first golden Monarchy the seat,
And seat of *Salmanassar*, whose success
Israel in long captivity still mourns;
There *Babylon* the wonder of all tongues,
As antient, but rebuilt by him who twice
Judah and all thy Father *David's* house
Led captive, and *Jerusalem* laid waste,
Till *Cyrus* set them free; *Persepolis*
His City there thou seest, and *Bactra* there;
Ecbatana her structure vast there shews,
And *Hecatompylos* her hunderd gates,
There *Susa* by *Choaspes*, amber stream,
The drink of none but Kings; of later fame
Built by *Emathian*, or by *Parthian* hands,

The great *Seleucia, Nisibis,* and there
Artaxata, Teredon, Tesiphon,
Turning with easie eye thou may'st behold.
All these the *Parthian,* now some Ages past,
By great *Arsaces* led, who founded first
That Empire, under his dominion holds
From the luxurious Kings of *Antioch* won.
And just in time thou com'st to have a view
Of his great power; for now the *Parthian* King
In *Ctesiphon* hath gather'd all his Host
Against the *Scythian,* whose incursions wild
Have wasted *Sogdiana;* to her aid
He marches now in hast; see, though from far,
His thousands, in what martial equipage
They issue forth, Steel Bows, and Shafts their arms
Of equal dread in flight, or in pursuit;
All Horsemen, in which fight they most excel;
See how in warlike muster they appear,
In Rhombs and wedges, and half moons, and wings.
      He look't and saw what numbers numberless
The City gates out powr'd, light armed Troops
In coats of Mail and military pride;
In Mail thir horses clad, yet fleet and strong,
Prauncing thir riders bore, the flower and choice
Of many Provinces from bound to bound;
From *Arachosia,* from *Candaor* East,
And *Margiana* to the *Hyrcanian* cliffs
Of *Caucasus,* and dark *Iberian* dales,
From *Atropatia* and the neighbouring plains
Of *Adiabene, Media,* and the South
Of *Susiana* to *Balsara's* hav'n.
He saw them in thir forms of battell rang'd,
How quick they wheel'd, and flying behind them shot
Sharp sleet of arrowie showers against the face
Of thir pursuers, and overcame by flight;
The field all iron cast a gleaming brown,
Nor wanted clouds of foot, nor on each horn,
Cuirassiers all in steel for standing fight;
Chariots or Elephants endorst with Towers
Of Archers, nor of labouring Pioners

A multitude with Spades and Axes arm'd
To lay hills plain, fell woods, or valleys fill,
Or where plain was raise hill, or over-lay
With bridges rivers proud, as with a yoke;
Mules after these, Camels and Dromedaries,
And Waggons fraught with Utensils of war.
Such forces met not, nor so wide a camp,
When *Agrican* with all his Northern powers
Besieg'd *Albracca*, as Romances tell;
The City of *Gallaphrone*, from thence to win
The fairest of her Sex *Angelica*
His daughter, sought by many Prowest Knights,
Both *Paynim*, and the Peers of *Charlemane*.
Such and so numerous was thir Chivalrie;
At sight whereof the Fiend yet more presum'd,
And to our Saviour thus his words renew'd.

That thou may'st know I seek not to engage
Thy Vertue, and not every way secure
On no slight grounds thy safety; hear, and mark
To what end I have brought thee hither and shewn
All this fair sight; thy Kingdom though foretold
By Prophet or by Angel, unless thou
Endeavour, as thy Father *David* did,
Thou never shalt obtain; prediction still
In all things, and all men, supposes means,
Without means us'd, what it predicts revokes.
But say thou wer't possess'd of *David's* Throne
By free consent of all, none opposite,
Samaritan or *Jew;* how could'st thou hope
Long to enjoy it quiet and secure,
Between two such enclosing enemies
Roman and *Parthian?* therefore one of these
Thou must make sure thy own, the *Parthian* first
By my advice, as nearer and of late
Found able by invasion to annoy
Thy country, and captive lead away her Kings
Antigonus, and old *Hyrcanus* bound,
Maugre the *Roman:* it shall be my task
To render thee the *Parthian* at dispose;
Chuse which thou wilt by conquest or by league.

By him thou shalt regain, without him not,
That which alone can truly reinstall thee
In *David's* royal seat, his true Successour,
Deliverance of thy brethren, those ten Tribes
Whose off-spring in his Territory yet serve
In *Habor*, and among the *Medes* dispers't,
Ten Sons of *Jacob*, two of *Joseph* lost
Thus long from *Israel;* serving as of old
Thir Fathers in the land of *Egypt* serv'd,
This offer sets before thee to deliver.
These if from servitude thou shalt restore
To thir inheritance, then, nor till then,
Thou on the Throne of *David* in full glory,
From *Egypt* to *Euphrates* and beyond
Shalt raign, and *Rome* or *Cæsar* not need fear.

  To whom our Saviour answer'd thus unmov'd.
Much ostentation vain of fleshly arm,
And fragile arms, much instrument of war
Long in preparing, soon to nothing brought,
Before mine eyes thou hast set; and in my ear
Vented much policy, and projects deep
Of enemies, of aids, battels and leagues,
Plausible to the world, to me worth naught.
Means I must use thou say'st, prediction else
Will unpredict and fail me of the Throne:
My time I told thee, (and that time for thee
Were better farthest off) is not yet come;
When that comes think not thou to find me slack
On my part aught endeavouring, or to need
Thy politic maxims, or that cumbersome
Luggage of war there shewn me, argument
Of human weakness rather then of strength.
My brethren, as thou call'st them; those Ten Tribes
I must deliver, if I mean to raign
David's true heir, and his full Scepter sway
To just extent over all *Israel's* Sons;
But whence to thee this zeal, where was it then
For *Israel*, or for *David*, or his Throne,
When thou stood'st up his Tempter to the pride
Of numbring *Israel*, which cost the lives

Of threescore and ten thousand *Israelites*
By three days Pestilence? such was thy zeal
To *Israel* then, the same that now to me.
As for those captive Tribes, themselves were they
Who wrought their own captivity, fell off
From God to worship Calves, the Deities
Of *Egypt*, *Baal* next and *Ashtaroth*,
And all the Idolatries of Heathen round,
Besides thir other worse then heathenish crimes;
Nor in the land of their captivity
Humbled themselves, or penitent besought
The God of their fore-fathers; but so dy'd
Impenitent, and left a race behind
Like to themselves, distinguishable scarce
From Gentiles, but by Circumcision vain
And God with Idols in their worship joyn'd
Should I of these the liberty regard,
Who freed, as to their ancient Patrimony,
Unhumbl'd, unrepentant, unreform'd,
Headlong would follow; and to thir Gods perhaps
Of *Bethel* and of *Dan*? no let them serve
Thir enemies, who serve Idols with God,
Yet he at length, time to himself best known,
Remembering *Abraham* by some wond'rous call
May bring them back repentant and sincere,
And at their passing cleave the *Assyrian* flood
While to their native land with joy they hast,
As the Red Sea and *Jordan* once he cleft,
When to the promis'd land thir Fathers pass'd;
To his due time and providence I leave them.

So spake *Israel's* true King, and to the Fiend
Made answer meet, that made void all his wiles.
So fares it when with truth falshood contends.

BOOK IV

PERPLEX'D and troubl'd at his bad success
The Tempter stood, nor had what to reply,

Discover'd in his fraud, thrown from his hope,
So oft, and the perswasive Rhetoric
That sleek't his tongue, and won so much on *Eve*,
So little here, nay lost; but *Eve* was *Eve*,
This far his over-match, who self deceiv'd
And rash, before-hand had no better weigh'd
The strength he was to cope with, or his own:
But as a man who had been matchless held
In cunning, over-reach't where least he thought,
To salve his credit, and for very spight
Still will be tempting him who foyls him still,
And never cease, though to his shame the more;
Or as a swarm of flies in vintage time,
About the wine-press where sweet moust is powr'd
Beat off, returns as oft with humming sound;
Or surging waves against a solid rock,
Though all to shivers dash't, the assault renew,
Vain battry, and in froth or bubbles end;
So Satan, whom repulse upon repulse
Met ever; and to shameful silence brought,
Yet gives not o're though desperate of success,
And his vain importunity pursues.
He brought our Saviour to the western side
Of that high mountain, whence he might behold
Another plain, long but in bredth not wide;
Wash'd by the Southern Sea, and on the North
To equal length back'd with a ridge of hills
That screen'd the fruits of the earth and seats of men
From cold *Septentrion* blasts, thence in the midst
Divided by a river, of whose banks
On each side an Imperial City stood,
With Towers and Temples proudly elevate
On seven small Hills, with Palaces adorn'd,
Porches and Theatres, Baths, Aqueducts,
Statues and Trophees, and Triumphal Arcs,
Gardens and Groves presented to his eyes,
Above the highth of Mountains interpos'd.
By what strange Parallax or Optic skill
Of vision multiplyed through air, or glass
Of Telescope, were curious to enquire:

And now the Tempter thus his silence broke.
    The City which thou seest no other deem
Then great and glorious *Rome*, Queen of the Earth
So far renown'd, and with the spoils enricht
Of Nations; there the Capitol thou seest
Above the rest lifting his stately head
On the *Tarpeian* rock, her Cittadel
Impregnable, and there Mount *Palatine*
The Imperial Palace, compass huge, and high
The Structure, skill of noblest Architects,
With gilded battlements, conspicuous far,
Turrets and Terrases, and glittering Spires:
Many a fair Edifice besides, more like
Houses of Gods (so well I have dispos'd
My Aerie Microscope) thou may'st behold
Outside and inside both, pillars and roofs
Carv'd work, the hand of fam'd Artificers
In Cedar, Marble, Ivory or Gold.
Thence to the gates cast round thine eye, and see
What conflux issuing forth, or entring in,
Pretors, Proconsuls to thir Provinces
Hasting or on return, in robes of State;
Lictors and rods the ensigns of thir power,
Legions and Cohorts, turmes of horse and wings:
Or Embassies from Regions far remote
In various habits on the *Appian* road,
Or on the *Æmilian*, some from farthest South,
Syene, and where the shadow both way falls,
Meroe Nilotic Isle, and more to West,
The Realm of *Bocchus* to the Black-moor Sea;
From the *Asian* Kings and *Parthian* among these,
From *India* and the golden *Chersoness*,
And utmost *Indian* Isle *Taprobane*,
Dusk faces with white silken Turbants wreath'd:
From *Gallia*, *Gades*, and the *Brittish* West,
Germans and *Scythians*, and *Sarmatians* North
Beyond *Danubius* to the *Tauric* Pool.
All Nations now to *Rome* obedience pay,
To *Rome's* great Emperour, whose wide domain
In ample Territory, wealth and power,

Civility of Manners, Arts, and Arms,
And long Renown thou justly may'st prefer
Before the *Parthian;* these two Thrones except,
The rest are barbarous, and scarce worth the sight,
Shar'd among petty Kings too far remov'd;
These having shewn thee, I have shewn thee all
The Kingdoms of the world, and all thir glory.
This Emperour hath no Son, and now is old,
Old, and lascivious, and from *Rome* retir'd
To *Capreæ* an Island small but strong
On the *Campanian* shore, with purpose there
His horrid lusts in private to enjoy,
Committing to a wicked Favourite
All publick cares, and yet of him suspicious,
Hated of all, and hating; with what ease
Indu'd with Regal Vertues as thou art,
Appearing, and beginning noble deeds,
Might'st thou expel this monster from his Throne
Now made a stye, and in his place ascending
A victor, people free from servile yoke?
And with my help thou may'st; to me the power
Is given, and by that right I give it thee.
Aim therefore at no less then all the world,
Aim at the highest, without the highest attain'd
Will be for thee no sitting, or not long
On *David's* Throne, be propheci'd what will.

To whom the Son of God unmov'd reply'd.
Nor doth this grandeur and majestic show
Of luxury, though call'd magnificence,
More then of arms before, allure mine eye,
Much less my mind; though thou should'st add to tell
Thir sumptuous gluttonies, and gorgeous feasts
On *Cittron* tables or *Atlantic* stone;
(For I have also heard, perhaps have read)
Their wines of *Setia, Cales,* and *Falerne,*
Chios and *Creet,* and how they quaff in Gold,
Crystal and Myrrhine cups imboss'd with Gems
And studs of Pearl, to me should'st tell who thirst
And hunger still: then Embassies thou shew'st
From Nations far and nigh; what honour that,

But tedious wast of time to sit and hear
So many hollow complements and lies,
Outlandish flatteries? then proceed'st to talk
Of the Emperour, how easily subdu'd,
How gloriously; I shall, thou say'st, expel
A brutish monster: what if I withal
Expel a Devil who first made him such?
Let his tormenter Conscience find him out,
For him I was not sent, nor yet to free
That people victor once, now vile and base,
Deservedly made vassal, who once just,
Frugal, and mild, and temperate, conquer'd well,
But govern ill the Nations under yoke,
Peeling thir Provinces, exhausted all
By lust and rapine; first ambitious grown
Of triumph that insulting vanity;
Then cruel, by thir sports to blood enur'd
Of fighting beasts, and men to beasts expos'd,
Luxurious by thir wealth, and greedier still,
And from the daily Scene effeminate.
What wise and valiant man would seek to free
These thus degenerate, by themselves enslav'd,
Or could of inward slaves make outward free?
Know therefore when my season comes to sit
On *David's* Throne, it shall be like a tree
Spreading and over-shadowing all the Earth,
Or as a stone that shall to pieces dash
All Monarchies besides throughout the world,
And of my Kingdom there shall be no end:
Means there shall be to this, but what the means,
Is not for thee to know, nor me to tell.
   To whom the Tempter impudent repli'd.
I see all offers made by me how slight
Thou valu'st, because offer'd, and reject'st:
Nothing will please the difficult and nice,
Or nothing more then still to contradict:
On the other side know also thou, that I
On what I offer set as high esteem,
Nor what I part with mean to give for naught;
All these which in a moment thou behold'st,

The Kingdoms of the world to thee I give;
For giv'n to me, I give to whom I please,
No trifle; yet with this reserve, not else,
On this condition, if thou wilt fall down,
And worship me as thy superior Lord,
Easily done, and hold them all of me;
For what can less so great a gift deserve?

  Whom thus our Saviour answer'd with disdain.
I never lik'd thy talk, thy offers less,
Now both abhor, since thou hast dar'd to utter
The abominable terms, impious condition;
But I endure the time, till which expir'd,
Thou hast permission on me. It is written
The first of all Commandments, Thou shalt worship
The Lord thy God, and only him shalt serve;
And dar'st thou to the Son of God propound
To worship thee accurst, now more accurst
For this attempt bolder then that on *Eve*,
And more blasphemous? which expect to rue.
The Kingdoms of the world to thee were giv'n,
Permitted rather, and by thee usurp't,
Other donation none thou canst produce:
If given, by whom but by the King of Kings,
God over all supreme? if giv'n to thee,
By thee how fairly is the Giver now
Repaid? But gratitude in thee is lost
Long since. Wert thou so void of fear or shame,
As offer them to me the Son of God,
To me my own, on such abhorred pact,
That I fall down and worship thee as God?
Get thee behind me; plain thou now appear'st
That Evil one, Satan for ever damn'd.

  To whom the Fiend with fear abasht reply'd.
Be not so sore offended, Son of God;
Though Sons of God both Angels are and Men,
If I to try whether in higher sort
Then these thou bear'st that title, have propos'd
What both from Men and Angels I receive,
Tetrarchs of fire, air, flood, and on the earth
Nations besides from all the quarter'd winds,

God of this world invok't and world beneath;
Who then thou art, whose coming is foretold
To me so fatal, me it most concerns.
The tryal hath indamag'd thee no way,
Rather more honour left and more esteem;
Me naught advantag'd, missing what I aim'd.
Therefore let pass, as they are transitory,
The Kingdoms of this world; I shall no more
Advise thee, gain them as thou canst, or not.
And thou thy self seem'st otherwise inclin'd
Then to a worldly Crown, addicted more
To contemplation and profound dispute,
As by that early action may be judg'd,
When slipping from thy Mothers eye thou went'st
Alone into the Temple; there was found
Among the gravest Rabbies disputant
On points and questions fitting *Moses* Chair,
Teaching not taught; the childhood shews the man,
As morning shews the day. Be famous then
By wisdom; as thy Empire must extend,
So let extend thy mind o're all the world,
In knowledge, all things in it comprehend,
All knowledge is not couch't in *Moses* Law,
The *Pentateuch* or what the Prophets wrote,
The *Gentiles* also know, and write, and teach
To admiration, led by Natures light;
And with the *Gentiles* much thou must converse,
Ruling them by perswasion as thou mean'st,
Without thir learning how wilt thou with them,
Or they with thee hold conversation meet?
How wilt thou reason with them, how refute
Thir Idolisms, Traditions, Paradoxes?
Error by his own arms is best evinc't.
Look once more e're we leave this specular Mount
Westward, much nearer by Southwest, behold
Where on the *Ægean* shore a City stands
Built nobly, pure the air, and light the soil,
Athens the eye of *Greece*, Mother of Arts
And Eloquence, native to famous wits
Or hospitable, in her sweet recess,

City or Suburban, studious walks and shades;
See there the Olive Grove of *Academe*,
Plato's retirement, where the *Attic* Bird
Trills her thick-warbl'd notes the summer long,
There flowrie hill *Hymettus* with the sound
Of Bees industrious murmur oft invites
To studious musing; there *Ilissus* rouls
His whispering stream; within the walls then view
The schools of antient Sages; his who bred
Great *Alexander* to subdue the world,
Lyceum there, and painted *Stoa* next:
There thou shalt hear and learn the secret power
Of harmony in tones and numbers hit
By voice or hand, and various-measur'd verse,
Æolian charms and *Dorian Lyric* Odes,
And his who gave them breath, but higher sung,
Blind *Melesigenes* thence *Homer* call'd,
Whose Poem *Phœbus* challeng'd for his own.
Thence what the lofty grave Tragœdians taught
In *Chorus* or *Iambic*, teachers best
Of moral prudence, with delight receiv'd
In brief sententious precepts, while they treat
Of fate, and chance, and change in human life;
High actions, and high passions best describing:
Thence to the famous Orators repair,
Those antient, whose resistless eloquence
Wielded at will that fierce Democratie,
Shook the Arsenal and fulmin'd over *Greece*,
To *Macedon*, and *Artaxerxes* Throne;
To sage Philosophy next lend thine ear,
From Heaven descended to the low-rooft house
Of *Socrates*, see there his Tenement,
Whom well inspir'd the Oracle pronounc'd
Wisest of men; from whose mouth issu'd forth
Mellifluous streams that water'd all the schools
Of Academics old and new, with those
Sirnam'd *Peripatetics*, and the Sect
Epicurean, and the *Stoic* severe;
These here revolve, or, as thou lik'st, at home,
Till time mature thee to a Kingdom's waight;

These rules will render thee a King compleat
Within thy self, much more with Empire joyn'd.
　To whom our Saviour sagely thus repli'd.
Think not but that I know these things, or think
I know them not; not therefore am I short
Of knowing what I aught: he who receives
Light from above, from the fountain of light,
No other doctrine needs, though granted true;
But these are false, or little else but dreams,
Conjectures, fancies, built on nothing firm.
The first and wisest of them all profess'd
To know this only, that he nothing knew;
The next to fabling fell and smooth conceits,
A third sort doubted all things, though plain sence;
Others in vertue plac'd felicity,
But vertue joyn'd with riches and long life,
In corporal pleasure he, and careless ease,
The Stoic last in Philosophic pride,
By him call'd vertue; and his vertuous man,
Wise, perfect in himself, and all possessing
Equal to God, oft shames not to prefer,
As fearing God nor man, contemning all
Wealth, pleasure, pain or torment, death and life,
Which when he lists, he leaves, or boasts he can,
For all his tedious talk is but vain boast,
Or subtle shifts conviction to evade.
Alas what can they teach, and not mislead;
Ignorant of themselves, of God much more,
And how the world began, and how man fell
Degraded by himself, on grace depending?
Much of the Soul they talk, but all awrie,
And in themselves seek vertue, and to themselves
All glory arrogate, to God give none,
Rather accuse him under usual names,
Fortune and Fate, as one regardless quite
Of mortal things. Who therefore seeks in these
True wisdom, finds her not, or by delusion
Far worse, her false resemblance only meets,
An empty cloud. However many books
Wise men have said are wearisom; who reads

Incessantly, and to his reading brings not
A spirit and judgment equal or superior,
(And what he brings, what needs he elsewhere seek)
Uncertain and unsettl'd still remains,
Deep verst in books and shallow in himself,
Crude or intoxicate, collecting toys,
And trifles for choice matters, worth a spunge;
As Children gathering pibles on the shore.
Or if I would delight my private hours
With Music or with Poem, where so soon
As in our native Language can I find
That solace? All our Law and Story strew'd
With Hymns, our Psalms with artful terms inscrib'd,
Our Hebrew Songs and Harps in *Babylon*,
That pleas'd so well our Victors ear, declare
That rather *Greece* from us these Arts deriv'd;
Ill imitated, while they loudest sing
The vices of their Deities, and thir own
In Fable, Hymn, or Song, so personating
Thir Gods ridiculous, and themselves past shame.
Remove their swelling Epithetes thick laid
As varnish on a Harlots cheek, the rest,
Thin sown with aught of profit or delight,
Will far be found unworthy to compare
With *Sion's* songs, to all true tasts excelling,
Where God is prais'd aright, and Godlike men,
The Holiest of Holies, and his Saints;
Such are from God inspir'd, not such from thee;
Unless where mortal vertue is express't
By light of Nature not in all quite lost.
Thir Orators thou then extoll'st, as those
The top of Eloquence, Statists indeed,
And lovers of thir Country, as may seem;
But herein to our Prophets far beneath,
As men divinely taught, and better teaching
The solid rules of Civil Government
In thir majestic unaffected stile
Then all the Oratory of *Greece* and *Rome*.
In them is plainest taught, and easiest learnt,
What makes a Nation happy, and keeps it so,

What ruins Kingdoms, and lays Cities flat;
These only with our Law best form a King.
    So spake the Son of God; but Satan now
Quite at a loss, for all his darts were spent,
Thus to our Saviour with stern brow reply'd.
    Since neither wealth, nor honour, arms nor arts,
Kingdom nor Empire pleases thee, nor aught
By me propos'd in life contemplative,
Or active, tended on by glory, or fame,
What dost thou in this World? the Wilderness
For thee is fittest place, I found thee there,
And thither will return thee, yet remember
What I foretell thee, soon thou shalt have cause
To wish thou never hadst rejected thus
Nicely or cautiously my offer'd aid,
Which would have set thee in short time with ease
On *David's* Throne; or Throne of all the world,
Now at full age, fulness of time, thy season,
When Prophecies of thee are best fullfill'd.
Now contrary, if I read aught in Heaven,
Or Heav'n write aught of Fate, by what the Stars
Voluminous, or single characters,
In their conjunction met, give me to spell,
Sorrows, and labours, opposition, hate,
Attends thee, scorns, reproaches, injuries,
Violence and stripes, and lastly cruel death,
A Kingdom they portend thee, but what Kingdom,
Real or Allegoric I discern not,
Nor when, eternal sure, as without end,
Without beginning; for no date prefixt
Directs me in the Starry Rubric set.
    So saying he took (for still he knew his power
Not yet expir'd) and to the Wilderness
Brought back the Son of God, and left him there,
Feigning to disappear. Darkness now rose,
As day-light sunk, and brought in lowring night
Her shadowy off-spring unsubstantial both,
Privation meer of light and absent day.
Our Saviour meek and with untroubl'd mind
After his aerie jaunt, though hurried sore,

Hungry and cold betook him to his rest,
Wherever, under some concourse of shades
Whose branching arms thick intertwind might shield
From dews and damps of night his shelter'd head,
But shelter'd slept in vain, for at his head
The Tempter watch'd, and soon with ugly dreams
Disturb'd his sleep; and either Tropic now
'Gan thunder, and both ends of Heav'n, the Clouds
From many a horrid rift abortive pour'd
Fierce rain with lightning mixt, water with fire
In ruine reconcil'd : nor slept the winds
Within thir stony caves, but rush'd abroad
From the four hinges of the world, and fell
On the vext Wilderness, whose tallest Pines,
Though rooted deep as high, and sturdiest Oaks
Bow'd their Stiff necks, loaden with stormy blasts,
Or torn up sheer : ill wast thou shrouded then,
O patient Son of God, yet only stoodst
Unshaken; nor yet staid the terror there,
Infernal Ghosts, and Hellish Furies, round
Environ'd thee, some howl'd, some yell'd, some shriek'd,
Some bent at thee their fiery darts, while thou
Sat'st unappall'd in calm and sinless peace.
Thus pass'd the night so foul till morning fair
Came forth with Pilgrim steps in amice gray;
Who with her radiant finger still'd the roar
Of thunder, chas'd the clouds, and laid the winds,
And grisly Spectres, which the Fiend had rais'd
To tempt the Son of God with terrors dire.
And now the Sun with more effectual beams
Had chear'd the face of Earth, and dry'd the wet
From drooping plant, or dropping tree; the birds
Who all things now behold more fresh and green,
After a night of storm so ruinous,
Clear'd up their choicest notes in bush and spray
To gratulate the sweet return of morn;
Nor yet amidst this joy and brightest morn
Was absent, after all his mischief done,
The Prince of darkness, glad would also seem
Of this fair change, and to our Saviour came,

Yet with no new device, they all were spent,
Rather by this his last affront resolv'd,
Desperate of better course, to vent his rage,
And mad despight to be so oft repell'd.
Him walking on a Sunny hill he found,
Back'd on the North and West by a thick wood,
Out of the wood he starts in wonted shape;
And in a careless mood thus to him said.

Fair morning yet betides thee Son of God,
After a dismal night; I heard the rack
As Earth and Skie would mingle; but my self
Was distant; and these flaws, though mortals fear them
As dangerous to the pillard frame of Heaven,
Or to the Earths dark basis underneath,
Are to the main as inconsiderable,
And harmless, if not wholsom, as a sneeze
To mans less universe, and soon are gone;
Yet as being oft times noxious where they light
On man, beast, plant, wastful and turbulent,
Like turbulencies in the affairs of men,
Over whose heads they rore, and seem to point,
They oft fore-signifie and threaten ill:
This Tempest at this Desert most was bent;
Of men at thee, for only thou here dwell'st.
Did I not tell thee, if thou didst reject
The perfet season offer'd with my aid
To win thy destin'd seat, but wilt prolong
All to the push of Fate, persue thy way
Of gaining *David's* Throne no man knows when,
For both the when and how is no where told,
Thou shalt be what thou art ordain'd, no doubt;
For Angels have proclaim'd it, but concealing
The time and means: each act is rightliest done,
Not when it must, but when it may be best.
If thou observe not this, be sure to find,
What I foretold thee, many a hard assay
Of dangers, and adversities and pains,
E're thou of *Israel's* Scepter get fast hold;
Whereof this ominous night that clos'd thee round,
So many terrors, voices, prodigies

May warn thee, as a sure fore-going sign.

So talk'd he, while the Son of God went on
And staid not, but in brief him answer'd thus.

Mee worse then wet thou find'st not; other harm
Those terrors which thou speak'st of, did me none;
I never fear'd they could, though noising loud
And threatning nigh; what they can do as signs
Betok'ning, or ill boding, I contemn
As false portents, not sent from God, but thee;
Who knowing I shall raign past thy preventing,
Obtrud'st thy offer'd aid, that I accepting
At least might seem to hold all power of thee,
Ambitious spirit, and wouldst be thought my God,
And storm'st refus'd, thinking to terrifie
Mee to thy will; desist; thou art discern'd
And toil'st in vain, nor me in vain molest.

To whom the Fiend now swoln with rage reply'd:
Then hear, O Son of *David*, Virgin-born;
For Son of God to me is yet in doubt,
Of the Messiah I have heard foretold
By all the Prophets; of thy birth at length
Announc't by *Gabriel* with the first I knew,
And of the Angelic Song in *Bethlehem* field,
On thy birth-night, that sung thee Saviour born.
From that time seldom have I ceas'd to eye
Thy infancy, thy childhood, and thy youth,
Thy manhood last, though yet in private bred;
Till at the Ford of *Jordan* whither all
Flock'd to the Baptist, I among the rest,
Though not to be Baptiz'd, by voice from Heav'n
Heard thee pronounc'd the Son of God belov'd.
Thenceforth I thought thee worth my nearer view
And narrower Scrutiny, that I might learn
In what degree or meaning thou art call'd
The Son of God, which bears no single sence;
The Son of God I also am, or was,
And if I was, I am; relation stands;
All men are Sons of God; yet thee I thought
In some respect far higher so declar'd.
Therefore I watch'd thy footsteps from that hour,

And follow'd thee still on to this wast wild;
Where by all best conjectures I collect
Thou art to be my fatal enemy.
Good reason then, if I before-hand seek
To understand my Adversary, who
And what he is; his wisdom, power, intent,
By parl, or composition, truce, or league
To win him, or win from him what I can.
And opportunity I here have had
To try thee, sift thee, and confess have found thee
Proof against all temptation as a rock
Of Adamant, and as a Center, firm
To the utmost of meer man both wise and good,
Not more; for Honours, Riches, Kingdoms, Glory
Have been before contemn'd, and may agen:
Therefore to know what more thou art then man,
Worth naming Son of God by voice from Heav'n,
Another method I must now begin.

So saying he caught him up, and without wing
Of *Hippogrif* bore through the Air sublime
Over the Wilderness and o're the Plain;
Till underneath them fair *Jerusalem*,
The holy City lifted high her Towers,
And higher yet the glorious Temple rear'd
Her pile, far off appearing like a Mount
Of Alabaster, top't with Golden Spires:
There on the highest Pinacle he set
The Son of God; and added thus in scorn:

There stand, if thou wilt stand; to stand upright
Will ask thee skill; I to thy Fathers house
Have brought thee, and highest plac't, highest is best,
Now shew thy Progeny; if not to stand,
Cast thy self down; safely if Son of God:
For it is written, He will give command
Concerning thee to his Angels, in thir hands
They shall up lift thee, lest at any time
Thou chance to dash thy foot against a stone.

To whom thus Jesus: also it is written,
Tempt not the Lord thy God, he said and stood.
But Satan smitten with amazement fell

As when Earths Son *Antæus* (to compare
Small things with greatest) in *Irassa* strove
With *Joves Alcides*, and oft foil'd still rose,
Receiving from his mother Earth new strength,
Fresh from his fall, and fiercer grapple joyn'd,
Throttl'd at length in the Air, expir'd and fell;
So after many a foil the Tempter proud,
Renewing fresh assaults, amidst his pride
Fell whence he stood to see his Victor fall.
And as that *Theban* Monster that propos'd
Her riddle, and him, who solv'd it not, devour'd;
That once found out and solv'd, for grief and spight
Cast her self headlong from th' *Ismenian* steep,
So strook with dread and anguish fell the Fiend,
And to his crew, that sat consulting, brought
Joyless triumphals of his hop't success,
Ruin, and desperation, and dismay,
Who durst so proudly tempt the Son of God.
So Satan fell and strait a fiery Globe
Of Angels on full sail of wing flew nigh,
Who on their plumy Vans receiv'd him soft
From his uneasie station, and upbore
As on a floating couch through the blithe Air,
Then in a flowry valley set him down
On a green bank, and set before him spred
A table of Celestial Food, Divine,
Ambrosial, Fruits fetcht from the tree of life,
And from the fount of life Ambrosial drink,
That soon refresh'd him wearied, and repair'd
What hunger, if aught hunger had impair'd,
Or thirst, and as he fed, Angelic Quires
Sung Heavenly Anthems of his victory
Over temptation, and the Tempter proud.
  True Image of the Father whether thron'd
In the bosom of bliss, and light of light
Conceiving, or remote from Heaven, enshrin'd
In fleshly Tabernacle, and human form,
Wandring the Wilderness, whatever place,
Habit, or state, or motion, still expressing
The Son of God, with Godlike force indu'd

Against th' Attempter of thy Fathers Throne,
And Thief of Paradise; him long of old
Thou didst debel, and down from Heav'n cast
With all his Army, now thou hast aveng'd
Supplanted *Adam*, and by vanquishing
Temptation, hast regain'd lost Paradise,
And frustrated the conquest fraudulent:
He never more henceforth will dare set foot
In Paradise to tempt; his snares are broke:
For though that seat of earthly bliss be fail'd,
A fairer Paradise is founded now
For *Adam* and his chosen Sons, whom thou
A Saviour art come down to re-install.
Where they shall dwell secure, when time shall be
Of Tempter and Temptation without fear.
But thou, Infernal Serpent, shalt not long
Rule in the Clouds; like an Autumnal Star
Or Lightning thou shalt fall from Heav'n trod down
Under his feet: for proof, e're this thou feel'st
Thy wound, yet not thy last and deadliest wound
By this repulse receiv'd, and hold'st in Hell
No triumph; in all her gates *Abaddon* rues
Thy bold attempt; hereafter learn with awe
To dread the Son of God: he all unarm'd
Shall chase thee with the terror of his voice
From thy Demoniac holds, possession foul,
Thee and thy Legions, yelling they shall flye,
And beg to hide them in a herd of Swine,
Lest he command them down into the deep
Bound, and to torment sent before thir time.
Hail Son of the most High, heir of both worlds,
Queller of Satan, on thy glorious work
Now enter, and begin to save mankind.

　　Thus they the Son of God our Saviour meek
Sung Victor, and from Heavenly Feast refresht
Brought on his way with joy; hee unobserv'd
Home to his Mothers house private return'd.

¶ Samson Agonistes

A DRAMATIC POEM

Aristot. Poet. Cap. 6

Τραγωδία μίμησις πράξεως σπουδαίας, etc.

Tragœdia est imitatio actionis seriæ, etc. *Per misericordiam
et metum perficiens talium affectuum lustrationem*

OF THAT SORT OF DRAMATIC POEM WHICH IS
CALL'D TRAGEDY

TRAGEDY, as it was antiently compos'd, hath been ever held
the gravest, moralest, and most profitable of all other Poems:
therefore said by *Aristotle* to be of power by raising pity and
fear, or terror, to purge the mind of those and such like passions, that is to temper and reduce them to just measure with
a kind of delight, stirr'd up by reading or seeing those passions well imitated. Nor is Nature wanting in her own effects
to make good his assertion: for so in Physic things of melan-
cholic hue and quality are us'd against melancholy, sowr
against sowr, salt to remove salt humours. Hence Philosophers
and other gravest Writers, as *Cicero, Plutarch* and others, frequently cite out of Tragic Poets, both to adorn and illustrate
thir discourse. The Apostle *Paul* himself thought it not unworthy to insert a verse of *Euripides* into the Text of Holy
Scripture, I *Cor.* 15. 33. and *Parœus* commenting on the
Revelation, divides the whole Book as a Tragedy, into Acts
distinguisht each by a Chorus of Heavenly Harpings and
Song between. Heretofore Men in highest dignity have
labour'd not a little to be thought able to composea Tragedy.
Of that honour *Dionysius* the elder was no less ambitious,
then before of his attaining to the Tyranny. *Augustus Cæsar*
also had begun his *Ajax*, but unable to please his own judgment with what he had begun, left it unfinisht. *Seneca* the
Philosopher is by some thought the Author of those Tragedies
(at lest the best of them) that go under that name. *Gregory*

Nazianzen a Father of the Church, thought it not unbeseeming the sanctity of his person to write a Tragedy, which he entitl'd, *Christ suffering*. This is mention'd to vindicate Tragedy from the small esteem, or rather infamy, which in the account of many it undergoes at this day with other common Interludes; hap'ning through the Poets error of intermixing Comic stuff with Tragic sadness and gravity; or introducing trivial and vulgar persons, which by all judicious hath bin counted absurd; and brought in without discretion, corruptly to gratifie the people. And though antient Tragedy use no Prologue, yet using sometimes, in case of self defence, or explanation, that which *Martial* calls an Epistle; in behalf of this Tragedy coming forth after the antient manner, much different from what among us passes for best, thus much before-hand may be Epistl'd; that *Chorus* is here introduc'd after the Greek manner, not antient only but modern, and still in use among the *Italians*. In the modelling therefore of this Poem, with good reason, the Antients and *Italians* are rather follow'd, as of much more authority and fame. The measure of Verse us'd in the Chorus is of all sorts, call'd by the Greeks *Monostrophic*, or rather *Apolelymenon*, without regard had to *Strophe*, *Antistrophe* or *Epod*, which were a kind of Stanza's fram'd only for the Music, then us'd with the Chorus that sung; not essential to the Poem, and therefore not material; or being divided into Stanza's or Pauses, they may be call'd *Allœostropha*. Division into Act and Scene referring chiefly to the Stage (to which this work never was intended) is here omitted.

It suffices if the whole Drama be found not produc't beyond the fift Act, of the style and uniformitie, and that commonly call'd the Plot, whether intricate or explicit, which is nothing indeed but such œconomy, or disposition of the fable as may stand best with verisimilitude and decorum; they only will best judge who are not unacquainted with *Æschulus*, *Sophocles*, and *Euripides*, the three Tragic Poets unequall'd yet by any, and the best rule to all who endeavour to write Tragedy. The circumscription of time wherein the whole Drama begins and ends, is according to antient rule, and best example, within the space of 24 hours.

THE ARGUMENT

SAMSON *made Captive, Blind, and now in the Prison at* Gaza, *there to labour as in a common work-house, on a Festival day, in the general cessation from labour, comes forth into the open Air, to a place nigh, somewhat retir'd there to sit a while and bemoan his condition. Where he happens at length to be visited by certain friends and equals of his tribe, which make the Chorus, who seek to comfort him what they can; then by his old Father* Manoa, *who endeavours the like, and withal tells him his purpose to procure his liberty by ransom; lastly, that this Feast was proclaim'd by the* Philistins *as a day of Thanksgiving for thir deliverance from the hands of* Samson, *which yet more troubles him.* Manoa *then departs to prosecute his endeavour with the* Philistian *Lords for* Samson's *redemption; who in the mean while is visited by other persons; and lastly by a publick Officer to require his coming to the Feast before the Lords and People, to play or shew his strength in thir presence; he at first refuses, dismissing the publick Officer with absolute denyal to come; at length perswaded inwardly that this was from God, he yields to go along with him, who came now the second time with great threatenings to fetch him; the Chorus yet remaining on the place,* Manoa *returns full of joyful hope, to procure e're long his Sons deliverance: in the midst of which discourse an Ebrew comes in haste confusedly at first; and afterward more distinctly relating the Catastrophe, what* Samson *had done to the* Philistins, *and by accident to himself; wherewith the Tragedy ends.*

THE PERSONS

Samson.	Harapha *of* Gath.
Manoa *the Father of* Samson.	Publick Officer.
Dalila *his Wife*.	Messenger.

Chorus *of* Danites.

The Scene before the Prison in Gaza.

Sam. A little onward lend thy guiding hand
To these dark steps, a little further on;
For yonder bank hath choice of Sun or shade,
There I am wont to sit, when any chance

Relieves me from my task of servile toyl,
Daily in the common Prison else enjoyn'd me,
Where I a Prisoner chain'd, scarce freely draw
The air imprison'd also, close and damp,
Unwholsom draught: but here I feel amends,
The breath of Heav'n fresh-blowing, pure and sweet,
With day-spring born; here leave me to respire.
This day a solemn Feast the people hold
To *Dagon* thir Sea-Idol, and forbid
Laborious works, unwillingly this rest
Thir Superstition yields me; hence with leave
Retiring from the popular noise, I seek
This unfrequented place to find some ease,
Ease to the body some, none to the mind
From restless thoughts, that like a deadly swarm
Of Hornets arm'd, no sooner found alone,
But rush upon me thronging, and present
Times past, what once I was, and what am now.
O wherefore was my birth from Heaven foretold
Twice by an Angel, who at last in sight
Of both my Parents all in flames ascended
From off the Altar, where an Off'ring burn'd,
As in a fiery column charioting
His Godlike presence, and from some great act
Or benefit reveal'd to *Abraham*'s race?
Why was my breeding order'd and prescrib'd
As of a person separate to God,
Design'd for great exploits; if I must dye
Betray'd, Captiv'd, and both my Eyes put out,
Made of my Enemies the scorn and gaze;
To grind in Brazen Fetters under task
With this Heav'n-gifted strength? O glorious strength
Put to the labour of a Beast, debas't
Lower then bondslave! Promise was that I
Should *Israel* from *Philistian* yoke deliver;
Ask for this great Deliverer now, and find him
Eyeless in *Gaza* at the Mill with slaves,
Himself in bonds under *Philistian* yoke;
Yet stay, let me not rashly call in doubt
Divine Prediction; what if all foretold

Had been fulfilld but through mine own default,
Whom have I to complain of but my self?
Who this high gift of strength committed to me,
In what part lodg'd, how easily bereft me,
Under the Seal of silence could not keep,
But weakly to a woman must reveal it,
O'recome with importunity and tears.
O impotence of mind, in body strong!
But what is strength without a double share
Of wisdom, vast, unwieldy, burdensom,
Proudly secure, yet liable to fall
By weakest suttleties, not made to rule,
But to subserve where wisdom bears command.
God, when he gave me strength, to shew withal
How slight the gift was, hung it in my Hair.
But peace, I must not quarrel with the will
Of highest dispensation, which herein
Happ'ly had ends above my reach to know:
Suffices that to me strength is my bane,
And proves the sourse of all my miseries;
So many, and so huge, that each apart
Would ask a life to wail, but chief of all,
O loss of sight, of thee I most complain!
Blind among enemies, O worse then chains,
Dungeon, or beggery, or decrepit age!
Light the prime work of God to me is extinct,
And all her various objects of delight
Annull'd, which might in part my grief have eas'd,
Inferiour to the vilest now become
Of man or worm; the vilest here excel me,
They creep, yet see, I dark in light expos'd
To daily fraud, contempt, abuse and wrong,
Within doors, or without, still as a fool,
In power of others, never in my own;
Scarce half I seem to live, dead more then half.
O dark, dark, dark, amid the blaze of noon,
Irrecoverably dark, total Eclipse
Without all hope of day!
O first created Beam, and thou great Word,
Let there be light, and light was over all;

Why am I thus bereav'd thy prime decree?
The Sun to me is dark
And silent as the Moon,
When she deserts the night
Hid in her vacant interlunar cave.
Since light so necessary is to life,
And almost life itself, if it be true
That light is in the Soul,
She all in every part; why was the sight
To such a tender ball as th' eye confin'd?
So obvious and so easie to be quench't,
And not as feeling through all parts diffus'd,
That she might look at will through every pore?
Then had I not been thus exil'd from light;
As in the land of darkness yet in light,
To live a life half dead, a living death,
And buried; but O yet more miserable!
My self, my Sepulcher, a moving Grave,
Buried, yet not exempt
By priviledge of death and burial
From worst of other evils, pains and wrongs,
But made hereby obnoxious more
To all the miseries of life,
Life in captivity
Among inhuman foes.
But who are these? for with joint pace I hear
The tread of many feet stearing this way;
Perhaps my enemies who come to stare
At my affliction, and perhaps to insult,
Thir daily practice to afflict me more.

   Chor. This, this is he; softly a while,
Let us not break in upon him;
O change beyond report, thought, or belief!
See how he lies at random, carelesly diffus'd,
With languish't head unpropt,
As one past hope, abandon'd,
And by himself given over;
In slavish habit, ill-fitted weeds
O're worn and soild;
Or do my eyes misrepresent? Can this be hee,

That Heroic, that Renown'd,
Irresistible *Samson?* whom unarm'd
No strength of man, or fiercest wild beast could withstand;
Who tore the Lion, as the Lion tears the Kid,
Ran on embattelld Armies clad in Iron,
And weaponless himself,
Made Arms ridiculous, useless the forgery
Of brazen shield and spear, the hammer'd Cuirass,
Chalybean temper'd steel, and frock of mail
Adamantean Proof;
But safest he who stood aloof,
When insupportably his foot advanc't,
In scorn of thir proud arms and warlike tools,
Spurn'd them to death by Troops. The bold *Ascalonite*
Fled from his Lion ramp, old Warriors turn'd
Thir plated backs under his heel;
Or grovling soild thir crested helmets in the dust.
Then with what trivial weapon came to hand,
The Jaw of a dead Ass, his sword of bone,
A thousand fore-skins fell, the flower of *Palestin*
In *Ramath-lechi* famous to this day:
Then by main force pull'd up, and on his shoulders bore
The Gates of *Azza*, Post, and massie Bar
Up to the Hill by *Hebron*, seat of Giants old,
No journey of a Sabbath day, and loaded so;
Like whom the Gentiles feign to bear up Heav'n.
Which shall I first bewail,
Thy Bondage or lost Sight,
Prison within Prison
Inseparably dark?
Thou art become (O worst imprisonment!)
The Dungeon of thy self; thy Soul
(Which Men enjoying sight oft without cause complain)
Imprison'd now indeed,
In real darkness of the body dwells,
Shut up from outward light
To incorporate with gloomy night;
For inward light alas
Puts forth no visual beam.
O mirror of our fickle state,

Since man on earth unparallel'd!
The rarer thy example stands,
By how much from the top of wondrous glory,
Strongest of mortal men,
To lowest pitch of abject fortune thou art fall'n.
For him I reckon not in high estate
Whom long descent of birth
Or the sphear of fortune raises;
But thee whose strength, while vertue was her mate,
Might have subdu'd the Earth,
Universally crown'd with highest praises.

   Sam. I hear the sound of words, thir sense the air
Dissolves unjointed e're it reach my ear.

   Chor. Hee speaks, let us draw nigh. Matchless in might,
The glory late of *Israel*, now the grief;
We come thy friends and neighbours not unknown
From *Eshtaol* and *Zora's* fruitful Vale
To visit or bewail thee, or if better,
Counsel or Consolation we may bring,
Salve to thy Sores, apt words have power to swage
The tumors of a troubl'd mind,
And are as Balm to fester'd wounds.

   Sam. Your coming, Friends, revives me, for I learn
Now of my own experience, not by talk,
How counterfeit a coin they are who friends
Bear in their Superscription (of the most
I would be understood) in prosperous days
They swarm, but in adverse withdraw their head
Not to be found, though sought. Yee see, O friends,
How many evils have enclos'd me round;
Yet that which was the worst now least afflicts me,
Blindness, for had I sight, confus'd with shame,
How could I once look up, or heave the head,
Who like a foolish Pilot have shipwrack't,
My Vessel trusted to me from above,
Gloriously rigg'd; and for a word, a tear,
Fool, have divulg'd the secret gift of God
To a deceitful Woman: tell me Friends,
Am I not sung and proverbd for a Fool
In every street, do they not say, how well

Are come upon him his deserts? yet why?
Immeasurable strength they might behold
In me, of wisdom nothing more then mean;
This with the other should, at least, have paird,
These two proportiond ill drove me transverse.

    Chor. Tax not divine disposal, wisest Men
Have err'd, and by bad Women been deceiv'd;
And shall again, pretend they ne're so wise.
Deject not then so overmuch thy self,
Who hast of sorrow thy full load besides;
Yet truth to say, I oft have heard men wonder
Why thou shouldst wed *Philistian* women rather
Then of thine own Tribe fairer, or as fair,
At least of thy own Nation, and as noble.

    Sam. The first I saw at *Timna*, and she pleas'd
Mee, not my Parents, that I sought to wed,
The daughter of an Infidel: they knew not
That what I motion'd was of God; I knew
From intimate impulse, and therefore urg'd
The Marriage on; that by occasion hence
I might begin *Israel's* Deliverance,
The work to which I was divinely call'd;
She proving false, the next I took to Wife
(O that I never had! fond wish too late.)
Was in the Vale of *Sorec*, *Dalila*,
That specious Monster, my accomplisht snare.
I thought it lawful from my former act,
And the same end; still watching to oppress
Israel's oppressours: of what now I suffer
She was not the prime cause, but I my self,
Who vanquisht with a peal of words (O weakness!)
Gave up my fort of silence to a Woman.

    Chor. In seeking just occasion to provoke
The *Philistine*, thy Countries Enemy,
Thou never wast remiss, I bear thee witness:
Yet *Israel* still serves with all his Sons.

    Sam. That fault I take not on me, but transfer
On *Israel's* Governours, and Heads of Tribes,
Who seeing those great acts which God had done
Singly by me against their Conquerours

Acknowledg'd not, or not at all consider'd
Deliverance offerd: I on th' other side
Us'd no ambition to commend my deeds,
The deeds themselves, though mute, spoke loud the dooer;
But they persisted deaf, and would not seem
To count them things worth notice, till at length
Thir Lords the *Philistines* with gather'd powers
Enterd *Judea* seeking mee, who then
Safe to the rock of *Etham* was retir'd,
Not flying, but fore-casting in what place
To set upon them, what advantag'd best;
Mean while the men of *Judah* to prevent
The harrass of thir Land, beset me round;
I willingly on some conditions came
Into thir hands, and they as gladly yield me
To the uncircumcis'd a welcom prey,
Bound with two cords; but cords to me were threds
Toucht with the flame: on their whole Host I flew
Unarm'd, and with a trivial weapon fell'd
Their choicest youth; they only liv'd who fled.
Had *Judah* that day join'd, or one whole Tribe,
They had by this possess'd the Towers of *Gath*,
And lorded over them whom now they serve;
But what more oft in Nations grown corrupt,
And by thir vices brought to servitude,
Then to love Bondage more then Liberty,
Bondage with ease then strenuous liberty;
And to despise, or envy, or suspect
Whom God hath of his special favour rais'd
As thir Deliverer; if he aught begin,
How frequent to desert him, and at last
To heap ingratitude on worthiest deeds?
   Chor. Thy words to my remembrance bring
How *Succoth* and the Fort of *Penuel*
Thir great Deliverer contemn'd,
The matchless *Gideon* in pursuit
Of *Madian* and her vanquisht Kings:
And how ingrateful *Ephraim*
Had dealt with *Jephtha*, who by argument,
Not worse then by his shield and spear

Defended *Israel* from the *Ammonite*,
Had not his prowess quell'd thir pride
In that sore battel when so many dy'd
Without Reprieve adjudg'd to death,
For want of well pronouncing *Shibboleth*.

    Sam. Of such examples adde mee to the roul,
Mee easily indeed mine may neglect,
But Gods propos'd deliverance not so.

    Chor. Just are the ways of God,
And justifiable to Men;
Unless there be who think not God at all,
If any be, they walk obscure;
For of such Doctrine never was there School,
But the heart of the Fool,
And no man therein Doctor but himself.

    Yet more there be who doubt his ways not just,
As to his own edicts, found contradicting,
Then give the rains to wandring thought,
Regardless of his glories diminution;
Till by thir own perplexities involv'd
They ravel more, still less resolv'd,
But never find self-satisfying solution.

    As if they would confine th' interminable,
And tie him to his own prescript,
Who made our Laws to bind us, not himself,
And hath full right to exempt
Whom so it pleases him by choice
From National obstriction, without taint
Of sin, or legal debt;
For with his own Laws he can best dispence.

    He would not else who never wanted means,
Nor in respect of the enemy just cause
To set his people free,
Have prompted this Heroic *Nazarite*,
Against his vow of strictest purity,
To seek in marriage that fallacious Bride,
Unclean, unchaste.

    Down Reason then, at least vain reasonings down,
Though Reason here aver
That moral verdit quits her of unclean:

Unchaste was subsequent, her stain not his.
    But see here comes thy reverend Sire
With careful step, Locks white as doune,
Old *Manoah:* advise
Forthwith how thou oughtst to receive him.
    Sam. Ay me, another inward grief awak't,
With mention of that name renews th' assault.
    Man. Brethren and men of *Dan*, for such ye seem,
Though in this uncouth place; if old respect,
As I suppose, towards your once gloried friend,
My Son now Captive, hither hath inform'd
Your younger feet, while mine cast back with age
Came lagging after; say if he be here.
    Chor. As signal now in low dejected state,
As earst in highest, behold him where he lies.
    Man. O miserable change! is this the man,
That invincible *Samson*, far renown'd,
The dread of *Israel's* foes, who with a strength
Equivalent to Angels walk'd thir streets,
None offering fight; who single combatant
Duell'd thir Armies rank't in proud array,
Himself an Army, now unequal match
To save himself against a coward arm'd
At one spears length. O ever failing
In mortal strength! and oh what not in man
Deceivable and vain! Nay what thing good
Pray'd for, but often proves our woe, our bane?
I pray'd for Children, and thought barrenness
In wedlock a reproach; I gain'd a Son,
And such a Son as all Men hail'd me happy;
Who would be now a Father in my stead?
O wherefore did God grant me my request,
And as a blessing with such pomp adorn'd?
Why are his gifts desirable, to tempt
Our earnest Prayers, then giv'n with solemn hand
As Graces, draw a Scorpions tail behind?
For this did the Angel twice descend? for this
Ordain'd thy nurture holy, as of a Plant;
Select, and Sacred, Glorious for a while,
The miracle of men: then in an hour

Ensnar'd, assaulted, overcome, led bound,
Thy Foes derision, Captive, Poor, and Blind
Into a Dungeon thrust, to work with Slaves?
Alas methinks whom God hath chosen once
To worthiest deeds, if he through frailty err,
He should not so o'rewhelm, and as a thrall
Subject him to so foul indignities,
Be it but for honours sake of former deeds.

    Sam. Appoint not heavenly disposition, Father,
Nothing of all these evils hath befall'n me
But justly; I my self have brought them on,
Sole Author I, sole cause: if aught seem vile,
As vile hath been my folly, who have profan'd
The mystery of God giv'n me under pledge
Of vow, and have betray'd it to a woman,
A *Canaanite*, my faithless enemy.
This well I knew, nor was at all surpris'd,
But warn'd by oft experience: did not she
Of *Timna* first betray me, and reveal
The secret wrested from me in her highth
Of Nuptial Love profest, carrying it strait
To them who had corrupted her, my Spies,
And Rivals? In this other was there found
More Faith? who also in her prime of love,
Spousal embraces, vitiated with Gold,
Though offer'd only, by the sent conceiv'd
Her spurious first-born; Treason against me?
Thrice she assay'd with flattering prayers and sighs,
And amorous reproaches to win from me
My capital secret, in what part my strength
Lay stor'd, in what part summ'd, that she might know:
Thrice I deluded her, and turn'd to sport
Her importunity, each time perceiving
How openly, and with what impudence
She purpos'd to betray me, and (which was worse
Then undissembl'd hate) with what contempt
She sought to make me Traytor to my self;
Yet the fourth time, when mustring all her wiles,
With blandisht parlies, feminine assaults,
Tongue-batteries, she surceas'd not day nor night

To storm me over-watch't, and wearied out.
At times when men seek most repose and rest,
I yielded, and unlock'd her all my heart,
Who with a grain of manhood well resolv'd
Might easily have shook off all her snares:
But foul effeminacy held me yok't
Her Bond-slave; O indignity, O blot
To Honour and Religion! servil mind
Rewarded well with servil punishment!
The base degree to which I now am fall'n,
These rags, this grinding, is not yet so base
As was my former servitude, ignoble,
Unmanly, ignominious, infamous,
True slavery, and that blindness worse then this,
That saw not how degenerately I serv'd.
    Man. I cannot praise thy Marriage choises, Son,
Rather approv'd them not; but thou didst plead
Divine impulsion prompting how thou might'st
Find some occasion to infest our Foes.
I state not that; this I am sure; our Foes
Found soon occasion thereby to make thee
Thir Captive, and thir triumph; thou the sooner
Temptation found'st, or over-potent charms
To violate the sacred trust of silence
Deposited within thee; which to have kept
Tacit, was in thy power; true; and thou bear'st
Enough, and more the burden of that fault:
Bitterly hast thou paid, and still art paying
That rigid score. A worse thing yet remains,
This day the *Philistines* a popular Feast
Here celebrate in *Gaza;* and proclaim
Great Pomp, and Sacrifice, and Praises loud
To *Dagon*, as their God who hath deliver'd
Thee *Samson* bound and blind into thir hands,
Them out of thine, who slew'st them many a slain.
So *Dagon* shall be magnifi'd, and God,
Besides whom is no God, compar'd with Idols,
Disglorifi'd, blasphem'd, and had in scorn
By th' Idolatrous rout amidst thir wine;
Which to have come to pass by means of thee,

Samson, of all thy sufferings think the heaviest,
Of all reproach the most with shame that ever
Could have befall'n thee and thy Fathers house.

 Sam. Father, I do acknowledge and confess
That I this honour, I this pomp have brought
To *Dagon*, and advanc'd his praises high
Among the Heathen round; to God have brought
Dishonour, obloquie, and op't the mouths
Of Idolists, and Atheists; have brought scandal
To *Israel*, diffidence of God, and doubt
In feeble hearts, propense anough before
To waver, or fall off and joyn with Idols;
Which is my chief affliction, shame and sorrow,
The anguish of my Soul, that suffers not
Mine eie to harbour sleep, or thoughts to rest.
This only hope relieves me, that the strife
With me hath end; all the contest is now
'Twixt God and *Dagon; Dagon* hath presum'd,
Me overthrown, to enter lists with God,
His Deity comparing and preferring
Before the God of *Abraham*. He, be sure,
Will not connive, or linger, thus provok'd,
But will arise and his great name assert:
Dagon must stoop, and shall e're long receive
Such a discomfit, as shall quite despoil him
Of all these boasted Trophies won on me,
And with confusion blank his Worshippers.

 Man. With cause this hope relieves thee, and these words
I **as** a Prophecy receive: for God,
Nothing more certain, will not long defer
To vindicate the glory of his name
Against all competition, nor will long
Endure it, doubtful whether God be Lord,
Or *Dagon*. But for thee what shall be done?
Thou must not in the mean while here forgot
Lie in this miserable loathsom plight
Neglected. I already have made way
To some *Philistian* Lords, with whom to treat
About thy ransom: well they may by this
Have satisfi'd thir utmost of revenge

By pains and slaveries, worse then death inflicted
On thee, who now no more canst do them harm.

    Sam. Spare that proposal, Father, spare the trouble
Of that sollicitation; let me here,
As I deserve, pay on my punishment;
And expiate, if possible, my crime,
Shameful garrulity. To have reveal'd
Secrets of men, the secrets of a friend,
How hainous had the fact been, how deserving
Contempt, and scorn of all, to be excluded
All friendship, and avoided as a blab,
The mark of fool set on his front?
But I Gods counsel have not kept, his holy secret
Presumptuously have publish'd, impiously,
Weakly at least, and shamefully: A sin
That Gentiles in thir Parables condemn
To thir abyss and horrid pains confin'd.

    Man. Be penitent and for thy fault contrite,
But act not in thy own affliction, Son,
Repent the sin, but if the punishment
Thou canst avoid, self-preservation bids;
Or th' execution leave to high disposal,
And let another hand, not thine, exact
Thy penal forfeit from thy self; perhaps
God will relent, and quit thee all his debt;
Who evermore approves and more accepts
(Best pleas'd with humble and filial submission)
Him who imploring mercy sues for life,
Then who self-rigorous chooses death as due;
Which argues over-just, and self-displeas'd
For self-offence, more then for God offended.
Reject not then what offerd means, who knows
But God hath set before us, to return thee
Home to thy countrey and his sacred house,
Where thou mayst bring thy off'rings, to avert
His further ire, with praiers and vows renew'd.

    Sam. His pardon I implore; but as for life,
To what end should I seek it? when in strength
All mortals I excell'd, and great in hopes
With youthful courage and magnanimous thoughts

O   M.

Of birth from Heav'n foretold and high exploits,
Full of divine instinct, after some proof
Of acts indeed heroic, far beyond
The Sons of *Anac*, famous now and blaz'd,
Fearless of danger, like a petty God
I walk'd about admir'd of all and dreaded
On hostile ground, none daring my affront.
Then swoll'n with pride into the snare I fell
Of fair fallacious looks, venereal trains,
Softn'd with pleasure and voluptuous life;
At length to lay my head and hallow'd pledge
Of all my strength in the lascivious lap
Of a deceitful Concubine who shore me
Like a tame Weather, all my precious fleece,
Then turn'd me out ridiculous, despoil'd,
Shav'n, and disarm'd among my enemies.

   Chor. Desire of wine and all delicious drinks,
Which many a famous Warriour overturns,
Thou couldst repress, nor did the dancing Rubie
Sparkling, out-pow'rd, the flavor, or the smell,
Or taste that cheers the heart of Gods and men,
Allure thee from the cool Crystalline stream.

   Sam. Where ever fountain or fresh current flow'd
Against the Eastern ray, translucent, pure
With touch ætherial of Heav'ns fiery rod
I drank, from the clear milkie juice allaying
Thirst, and refresht; nor envy'd them the grape
Whose heads that turbulent liquor fills with fumes.

   Chor. O madness, to think use of strongest wines
And strongest drinks our chief support of health,
When God with these forbid'n made choice to rear
His mighty Champion, strong above compare,
Whose drink was only from the liquid brook.

   Sam. But what avail'd this temperance, not compleat
Against another object more enticing?
What boots it at one gate to make defence,
And at another to let in the foe
Effeminatly vanquish't? by which means,
Now blind, disheartn'd, sham'd, dishonour'd, quell'd,
To what can I be useful, wherein serve

My Nation, and the work from Heav'n impos'd,
But to sit idle on the houshold hearth,
A burdenous drone; to visitants a gaze,
Or pitied object, these redundant locks
Robustious to no purpose clustring down,
Vain monument of strength; till length of years
And sedentary numness craze my limbs
To a contemptible old age obscure.
Here rather let me drudge and earn my bread,
Till vermin or the draff of servil food
Consume me, and oft-invocated death
Hast'n the welcom end of all my pains.

    Man. Wilt thou then serve the *Philistines* with that gift
Which was expresly giv'n thee to annoy them?
Better at home lie bed-rid, not only idle,
Inglorious, unimploy'd, with age out-worn.
But God who caus'd a fountain at thy prayer
From the dry ground to spring, thy thirst to allay
After the brunt of battel, can as easie
Cause light again within thy eies to spring,
Wherewith to serve him better then thou hast;
And I perswade me so; why else this strength
Miraculous yet remaining in those locks?
His might continues in thee not for naught,
Nor shall his wondrous gifts be frustrate thus.

    Sam. All otherwise to me my thoughts portend,
That these dark orbs no more shall treat with light,
Nor th' other light of life continue long,
But yield to double darkness nigh at hand:
So much I feel my genial spirits droop,
My hopes all flat, nature within me seems
In all her functions weary of herself;
My race of glory run, and race of shame,
And I shall shortly be with them that rest.

    Man. Believe not these suggestions which proceed
From anguish of the mind and humours black,
That mingle with thy fancy. I however
Must not omit a Fathers timely care
To prosecute the means of thy deliverance
By ransom or how else: mean while be calm,

And healing words from these thy friends admit.
   Sam. O that torment should not be confin'd
To the bodies wounds and sores
With maladies innumerable
In heart, head, brest, and reins;
But must secret passage find
To th' inmost mind,
There exercise all his fierce accidents,
And on her purest spirits prey,
As on entrails, joints, and limbs,
With answerable pains, but more intense,
Though void of corporal sense.
   My griefs not only pain me
As a lingring disease,
But finding no redress, ferment and rage,
Nor less then wounds immedicable
Ranckle, and fester, and gangrene,
To black mortification.
Thoughts my Tormenters arm'd with deadly stings
Mangle my apprehensive tenderest parts,
Exasperate, exulcerate, and raise
Dire inflammation which no cooling herb
Or medcinal liquor can asswage,
Nor breath of Vernal Air from snowy *Alp*.
Sleep hath forsook and giv'n me o're
To deaths benumming Opium as my only cure.
Thence faintings, swounings of despair,
And sense of Heav'ns desertion.
   I was his nursling once and choice delight,
His destin'd from the womb,
Promisd by Heavenly message twice descending.
Under his special eie
Abstemious I grew up and thriv'd amain;
He led me on to mightiest deeds
Above the nerve of mortal arm
Against the uncircumcis'd, our enemies.
But now hath cast me off as never known,
And to those cruel enemies,
Whom I by his appointment had provok't,
Left me all helpless with th' irreparable loss

Of sight, reserv'd alive to be repeated
The subject of thir cruelty, or scorn.
Nor am I in the list of them that hope;
Hopeless are all my evils, all remediless;
This one prayer yet remains, might I be heard,
No long petition, speedy death,
The close of all my miseries, and the balm.

    Chor. Many are the sayings of the wise
In antient and in modern books enroll'd;
Extolling Patience as the truest fortitude;
And to the bearing well of all calamities,
All chances incident to mans frail life
Consolatories writ
With studied argument, and much perswasion sought
Lenient of grief and anxious thought,
But with th' afflicted in his pangs thir sound
Little prevails, or rather seems a tune,
Harsh, and of dissonant mood from his complaint,
Unless he feel within
Some sourse of consolation from above;
Secret refreshings, that repair his strength,
And fainting spirits uphold.

    God of our Fathers, what is man!
That thou towards him with hand so various,
Or might I say contrarious,
Temperst thy providence through his short course,
Not evenly, as thou rul'st
The Angelic orders and inferiour creatures mute,
Irrational and brute.
Nor do I name of men the common rout,
That wandring loose about
Grow up and perish, as the summer flie,
Heads without name no more rememberd,
But such as thou hast solemnly elected,
With gifts and graces eminently adorn'd
To some great work, thy glory,
And peoples safety, which in part they effect:
Yet toward these thus dignifi'd, thou oft
Amidst thir highth of noon,
Changest thy countenance, and thy hand with no regard

Of highest favours past
From thee on them, or them to thee of service.
    Nor only dost degrade them, or remit
To life obscur'd, which were a fair dismission,
But throw'st them lower then thou didst exalt them high,
Unseemly falls in human eie,
Too grievous for the trespass or omission,
Oft leav'st them to the hostile sword
Of Heathen and prophane, their carkasses
To dogs and fowls a prey, or else captiv'd:
Or to the unjust tribunals, under change of times,
And condemnation of the ingrateful multitude.
If these they scape, perhaps in poverty
With sickness and disease thou bow'st them down,
Painful diseases and deform'd,
In crude old age;
Though not disordinate, yet causless suffring
The punishment of dissolute days, in fine,
Just or unjust, alike seem miserable,
For oft alike, both come to evil end.
    So deal not with this once thy glorious Champion,
The Image of thy strength, and mighty minister.
What do I beg? how hast thou dealt already?
Behold him in this state calamitous, and turn
His labours, for thou canst, to peaceful end.
    But who is this, what thing of Sea or Land?
Femal of sex it seems,
That so bedeckt, ornate, and gay,
Comes this way sailing
Like a stately Ship
Of *Tarsus*, bound for th' Isles
Of *Javan* or *Gadier*
With all her bravery on, and tackle trim,
Sails fill'd, and streamers waving,
Courted by all the winds that hold them play,
An Amber sent of odorous perfume
Her harbinger, a damsel train behind;
Some rich *Philistian* Matron she may seem,
And now at nearer view, no other certain
Than *Dalila* thy wife.

Sam. My Wife, my Traytress, let her not come near me.

Cho. Yet on she moves, now stands and eies thee fixt,
About t' have spoke, but now, with head declin'd
Like a fair flower surcharg'd with dew, she weeps
And words addrest seem into tears dissolv'd,
Wetting the borders of her silk'n veil:
But now again she makes address to speak.

Dal. With doubtful feet and wavering resolution
I came, still dreading thy displeasure, *Samson*,
Which to have merited, without excuse,
I cannot but acknowledge; yet if tears
May expiate (though the fact more evil drew
In the perverse event then I foresaw)
My penance hath not slack'n'd, though my pardon
No way assur'd. But conjugal affection
Prevailing over fear, and timerous doubt
Hath led me on desirous to behold
Once more thy face, and know of thy estate.
If aught in my ability may serve
To light'n what thou suffer'st, and appease
Thy mind with what amends is in my power,
Though late, yet in some part to recompense
My rash but more unfortunate misdeed.

Sam. Out, out *Hyæna*; these are thy wonted arts,
And arts of every woman false like thee,
To break all faith, all vows, deceive, betray,
Then as repentant to submit, beseech,
And reconcilement move with feign'd remorse,
Confess, and promise wonders in her change,
Not truly penitent, but chief to try
Her husband, how far urg'd his patience bears,
His vertue or weakness which way to assail:
Then with more cautious and instructed skill
Again transgresses, and again submits;
That wisest and best men full oft beguil'd
With goodness principl'd not to reject
The penitent, but ever to forgive,
Are drawn to wear out miserable days,
Entangl'd with a poysnous bosom snake,
If not by quick destruction soon cut off

As I by thee, to Ages an example.
    Dal. Yet hear me *Samson;* not that I endeavour
To lessen or extenuate my offence,
But that on th' other side if it be weigh'd
By it self, with aggravations not surcharg'd,
Or else with just allowance counterpois'd,
I may, if possible, thy pardon find
The easier towards me, or thy hatred less.
First granting, as I do, it was a weakness
In me, but incident to all our sex,
Curiosity, inquisitive, importune
Of secrets, then with like infirmity
To publish them, both common female faults:
Was it not weakness also to make known
For importunity, that is for naught,
Wherein consisted all thy strength and safety?
To what I did thou shewdst me first the way.
But I to enemies reveal'd, and should not.
Nor shouldst thou have trusted that to womans frailty
E're I to thee, thou to thy self wast cruel.
Let weakness then with weakness come to parl
So near related, or the same of kind,
Thine forgive mine; that men may censure thine
The gentler, if severely thou exact not
More strength from me, then in thy self was found.
And what if Love, which thou interpret'st hate,
The jealousie of Love, powerful of sway
In human hearts, nor less in mine towards thee,
Caus'd what I did? I saw thee mutable
Of fancy, feard lest one day thou wouldst leave me
As her at *Timna*, sought by all means therefore
How to endear, and hold thee to me firmest:
No better way I saw then by importuning
To learn thy secrets, get into my power
Thy key of strength and safety: thou wilt say,
Why then reveal'd? I was assur'd by those
Who tempted me, that nothing was design'd
Against thee but safe custody, and hold:
That made for me, I knew that liberty
Would draw thee forth to perilous enterprises,

While I at home sate full of cares and fears
Wailing thy absence in my widow'd bed;
Here I should still enjoy thee day and night
Mine and Loves prisoner, not the *Philistines*,
Whole to my self, unhazarded abroad,
Fearless at home of partners in my love.
These reasons in Loves law have past for good,
Though fond and reasonless to some perhaps;
And Love hath oft, well meaning, wrought much wo,
Yet always pity or pardon hath obtain'd.
Be not unlike all others, not austere
As thou art strong, inflexible as steel.
If thou in strength all mortals dost exceed,
In uncompassionate anger do not so.
    Sam. How cunningly the sorceress displays
Her own transgressions, to upbraid me mine?
That malice not repentance brought thee hither,
By this appears: I gave, thou say'st, th' example,
I led the way; bitter reproach, but true,
I to my self was false e're thou to me,
Such pardon therefore as I give my folly,
Take to thy wicked deed: which when thou seest
Impartial, self-severe, inexorable,
Thou wilt renounce thy seeking, and much rather
Confess it feign'd, weakness is thy excuse,
And I believe it, weakness to resist
Philistian gold: if weakness may excuse,
What Murtherer, what Traytor, Parricide,
Incestuous, Sacrilegious, but may plead it?
All wickedness is weakness: that plea therefore
With God or Man will gain thee no remission.
But Love constrain'd thee; call it furious rage
To satisfie thy lust: Love seeks to have Love;
My love how couldst thou hope, who tookst the way
To raise in me inexpiable hate,
Knowing, as needs I must, by thee betray'd?
In vain thou striv'st to cover shame with shame,
Or by evasions thy crime uncoverst more.
    Dal. Since thou determinst weakness for no plea
In man or woman, though to thy own condemning,

Hear what assaults I had, what snares besides,
What sieges girt me round, e're I consented;
Which might have aw'd the best resolv'd of men,
The constantest to have yielded without blame.
It was not gold, as to my charge thou lay'st,
That wrought with me: thou know'st the Magistrates
And Princes of my countrey came in person,
Sollicited, commanded, threatn'd, urg'd,
Adjur'd by all the bonds of civil Duty
And of Religion, press'd how just it was,
How honourable, how glorious to entrap
A common enemy, who had destroy'd
Such numbers of our Nation: and the Priest
Was not behind, but ever at my ear,
Preaching how meritorious with the gods
It would be to ensnare an irreligious
Dishonourer of *Dagon:* what had I
To oppose against such powerful arguments?
Only my love of thee held long debate;
And combated in silence all these reasons
With hard contest: at length that grounded maxim
So rife and celebrated in the mouths
Of wisest men; that to the public good
Private respects must yield; with grave authority
Took full possession of me and prevail'd;
Vertue, as I thought, truth, duty so enjoyning.
  Sam. I thought where all thy circling wiles would end;
In feign'd Religion, smooth hypocrisie.
But had thy love, still odiously pretended,
Bin, as it ought, sincere, it would have taught thee
Far other reasonings, brought forth other deeds.
I before all the daughters of my Tribe
And of my Nation chose thee from among
My enemies, lov'd thee, as too well thou knew'st,
Too well, unbosom'd all my secrets to thee,
Not out of levity, but over-power'd
By thy request, who could deny thee nothing;
Yet now am judg'd an enemy. Why then
Didst thou at first receive me for thy husband?
Then, as since then, thy countries foe profest:

Being once a wife, for me thou wast to leave
Parents and countrey; nor was I their subject,
Nor under their protection but my own,
Thou mine, not theirs: if aught against my life
Thy countrey sought of thee, it sought unjustly,
Against the law of nature, law of nations,
No more thy countrey, but an impious crew
Of men conspiring to uphold thir state
By worse then hostile deeds, violating the ends
For which our countrey is a name so dear;
Not therefore to be obey'd. But zeal mov'd thee;
To please thy gods thou didst it; gods unable
To acquit themselves and prosecute their foes
But by ungodly deeds, the contradiction
Of their own deity, Gods cannot be:
Less therefore to be pleas'd, obey'd, or fear'd,
These false pretexts and varnish'd colours failing,
Bare in thy guilt how foul must thou appear?

   Dal. In argument with men a woman ever
Goes by the worse, whatever be her cause.
   Sam. For want of words no doubt, or lack of breath,
Witness when I was worried with thy peals.
   Dal. I was a fool, too rash, and quite mistaken
In what I thought would have succeeded best.
Let me obtain forgiveness of thee, *Samson*,
Afford me place to shew what recompence
Towards thee I intend for what I have misdone,
Misguided; only what remains past cure
Bear not too sensibly, nor still insist
To afflict thy self in vain: though sight be lost,
Life yet hath many solaces, enjoy'd
Where other senses want not their delights
At home in leisure and domestic ease,
Exempt from many a care and chance to which
Eye-sight exposes daily men abroad.
I to the Lords will intercede, not doubting
Thir favourable ear, that I may fetch thee
From forth this loathsom prison-house, to abide
With me, where my redoubl'd love and care
With nursing diligence, to me glad office,

May ever tend about thee to old age
With all things grateful chear'd, and so suppli'd,
That what by me thou hast lost thou least shalt miss.
    Sam. No, no, of my condition take no care;
It fits not; thou and I long since are twain;
Nor think me so unwary or accurst
To bring my feet again into the snare
Where once I have been caught; I know thy trains
Though dearly to my cost, thy ginns, and toyls;
Thy fair enchanted cup, and warbling charms
No more on me have power, their force is null'd,
So much of Adders wisdom I have learn't
To fence my ear against thy sorceries.
If in my flower of youth and strength, when all men
Lov'd, honour'd, fear'd me, thou alone could hate me
Thy Husband, slight me, sell me, and forgo me;
How wouldst thou use me now, blind, and thereby
Deceiveable, in most things as a child
Helpless, thence easily contemn'd, and scorn'd,
And last neglected? How wouldst thou insult
When I must live uxorious to thy will
In perfet thraldom, how again betray me,
Bearing my words and doings to the Lords
To gloss upon, and censuring, frown or smile?
This Gaol I count the house of Liberty
To thine whose doors my feet shall never enter.
    Dal. Let me approach at least, and touch thy hand.
    Sam. Not for thy life, lest fierce remembrance wake
My sudden rage to tear thee joint by joint.
At distance I forgive thee, go with that;
Bewail thy falshood, and the pious works
It hath brought forth to make thee memorable
Among illustrious women, faithful wives:
Cherish thy hast'n'd widowhood with the gold
Of Matrimonial treason: so farewel.
    Dal. I see thou art implacable, more deaf
To prayers, then winds and seas, yet winds to seas
Are reconcil'd at length, and Sea to Shore:
Thy anger, unappeasable, still rages,
Eternal tempest never to be calm'd.

Why do I humble thus my self, and suing
For peace, reap nothing but repulse and hate?
Bid go with evil omen and the brand
Of infamy upon my name denounc't?
To mix with thy concernments I desist
Henceforth, nor too much disapprove my own.
Fame if not double-fac't is double-mouth'd,
And with contrary blast proclaims most deeds,
On both his wings, one black, th' other white,
Bears greatest names in his wild aerie flight.
My name perhaps among the Circumcis'd
In *Dan*, in *Judah*, and the bordering Tribes,
To all posterity may stand defam'd,
With malediction mention'd, and the blot
Of falshood most unconjugal traduc't.
But in my countrey where I most desire,
In *Ecron*, *Gaza*, *Asdod*, and in *Gath*
I shall be nam'd among the famousest
Of Women, sung at solemn festivals,
Living and dead recorded, who to save
Her countrey from a fierce destroyer, chose
Above the faith of wedlock-bands, my tomb
With odours visited and annual flowers.
Not less renown'd then in Mount *Ephraim*,
Jaël, who with inhospitable guile
Smote *Sisera* sleeping through the Temples nail'd.
Nor shall I count it hainous to enjoy
The public marks of honour and reward
Conferr'd upon me, for the piety
Which to my countrey I was judg'd to have shewn.
At this who ever envies or repines
I leave him to his lot, and like my own.
   Chor. She's gone, a manifest Serpent by her sting
Discover'd in the end, till now conceal'd.
   Sam. So let her go, God sent her to debase me,
And aggravate my folly who committed
To such a viper his most sacred trust
Of secresie, my safety, and my life.
   Chor. Yet beauty, though injurious, hath strange power,
After offence returning, to regain

Love once possest, nor can be easily
Repuls't, without much inward passion felt
And secret sting of amorous remorse.

    Sam. Love-quarrels oft in pleasing concord end,
Not wedlock-trechery endangering life.

    Chor. It is not vertue, wisdom, valour, wit,
Strength, comliness of shape, or amplest merit
That womans love can win or long inherit;
But what it is, hard is to say,
Harder to hit,
(Which way soever men refer it)
Much like thy riddle, *Samson*, in one day
Or seven, though one should musing sit;
    If any of these or all, the *Timnian* bride
Had not so soon preferr'd
Thy Paranymph, worthless to thee compar'd,
Successour in thy bed,
Nor both so loosly disally'd
Thir nuptials, nor this last so trecherously
Had shorn the fatal harvest of thy head.
Is it for that such outward ornament
Was lavish't on thir Sex, that inward gifts
Were left for hast unfinish't, judgment scant,
Capacity not rais'd to apprehend
Or value what is best
In choice, but oftest to affect the wrong?
Or was too much of self-love mixt,
Of constancy no root infixt,
That either they love nothing, or not long?
    What e're it be, to wisest men and best
Seeming at first all heavenly under virgin veil,
Soft, modest, meek, demure,
Once join'd, the contrary she proves, a thorn
Intestin, far within defensive arms
A cleaving mischief, in his way to vertue
Adverse and turbulent, or by her charms
Draws him awry enslav'd
With dotage, and his sense deprav'd
To folly and shameful deeds which ruin ends.
What Pilot so expert but needs must wreck

Embarqu'd with such a Stears-mate at the Helm?
   Favour'd of Heav'n who finds
One vertuous rarely found,
That in domestic good combines:
Happy that house! his way to peace is smooth:
But vertue which breaks through all opposition,
And all temptation can remove,
Most shines and most is acceptable above.
   Therefore Gods universal Law
Gave to the man despotic power
Over his female in due awe,
Nor from that right to part an hour,
Smile she or lowre:
So shall he least confusion draw
On his whole life, not sway'd
By female usurpation, nor dismay'd.
   But had we best retire, I see a storm?
   Sam. Fair days have oft contracted wind and rain.
   Chor. But this another kind of tempest brings.
   Sam. Be less abstruse, my riddling days are past.
   Chor. Look now for no inchanting voice, nor fear
The bait of honied words; a rougher tongue
Draws hitherward, I know him by his stride,
The Giant *Harapha* of *Gath*, his look
Haughty as is his pile high-built and proud.
Comes he in peace? what wind hath blown him hither
I less conjecture then when first I saw
The sumptuous *Dalila* floating this way:
His habit carries peace, his brow defiance.
   Sam. Or peace or not, alike to me he comes.
   Chor. His fraught we soon shall know, he now arrives.
   Har. I come not *Samson*, to condole thy chance,
As these perhaps, yet wish it had not been,
Though for no friendly intent. I am of *Gath*,
Men call me *Harapha*, of stock renown'd
As *Og* or *Anak* and the *Emims* old
That *Kiriathaim* held, thou knowst me now
If thou at all art known. Much I have heard
Of thy prodigious might and feats perform'd
Incredible to me, in this displeas'd,

That I was never present on the place
Of those encounters, where we might have tri'd
Each others force in camp or listed field:
And now am come to see of whom such noise
Hath walk'd about, and each limb to survey,
If thy appearance answer loud report.

 Sam. The way to know were not to see but taste.

 Har. Dost thou already single me; I thought
Gives and the Mill had tam'd thee? O that fortune
Had brought me to the field where thou art fam'd
To have wrought such wonders with an Asses Jaw;
I should have forc'd thee soon with other arms,
Or left thy carkass where the Ass lay thrown:
So had the glory of Prowess been recover'd
To *Palestine*, won by a *Philistine*
From the unforeskinn'd race, of whom thou bear'st
The highest name for valiant Acts, that honour
Certain to have won by mortal duel from thee,
I lose, prevented by thy eyes put out.

 Sam. Boast not of what thou wouldst have done, but do
What then thou would'st, thou seest it in thy hand.

 Har. To combat with a blind man I disdain,
And thou hast need much washing to be toucht.

 Sam. Such usage as your honourable Lords
Afford me assassinated and betray'd,
Who durst not with thir whole united powers
In fight withstand me single and unarm'd,
Nor in the house with chamber Ambushes
Close-banded durst attaque me, no not sleeping,
Till they had hir'd a woman with their gold
Breaking her Marriage Faith to circumvent me.
Therefore without feign'd shifts let be assign'd
Some narrow place enclos'd, where fight may give thee,
Or rather flight, no great advantage on me;
Then put on all thy gorgeous arms, thy Helmet
And Brigandine of brass, thy broad Habergeon,
Vant-brass and Greves, and Gauntlet, add thy Spear
A Weavers beam, and seven-times-folded shield,
I only with an Oak'n staff will meet thee,
And raise such out-cries on thy clatter'd Iron,

Which long shall not with-hold mee from thy head,
That in a little time while breath remains thee,
Thou oft shalt wish thy self at *Gath* to boast
Again in safety what thou wouldst have done
To *Samson*, but shalt never see *Gath* more.

   Har. Thou durst not thus disparage glorious arms
Which greatest Heroes have in battel worn,
Thir ornament and safety, had not spells
And black enchantments, some Magicians Art
Arm'd thee or charm'd thee strong, which thou from Heaven
Feigndst at thy birth was giv'n thee in thy hair,
Where strength can least abide, though all thy hairs
Were bristles rang'd like those that ridge the back
Of chaf't wild Boars, or ruffl'd Porcupines.

   Sam. I know no Spells, use no forbidden Arts;
My trust is in the living God who gave me
At my Nativity this strength, diffus'd
No less through all my sinews, joints and bones,
Then thine, while I preserv'd these locks unshorn,
The pledge of my unviolated vow.
For proof hereof, if *Dagon* be thy god,
Go to his Temple, invocate his aid
With solemnest devotion, spread before him
How highly it concerns his glory now
To frustrate and dissolve these Magic spells,
Which I to be the power of *Israel*'s God
Avow, and challenge *Dagon* to the test,
Offering to combat thee his Champion bold,
With th' utmost of his Godhead seconded:
Then thou shalt see, or rather to thy sorrow
Soon feel, whose God is strongest, thine or mine.

   Har. Presume not on thy God, what e're he be,
Thee he regards not, owns not, hath cut off
Quite from his people, and delivered up
Into thy Enemies hand, permitted them
To put out both thine eyes, and fetter'd send thee
Into the common Prison, there to grind
Among the Slaves and Asses thy comrades,
As good for nothing else, no better service
With those thy boyst'rous locks, no worthy match

For valour to assail, nor by the sword
Of noble Warriour, so to stain his honour,
But by the Barbers razor best subdu'd.

   Sam. All these indignities, for such they are
From thine, these evils I deserve and more,
Acknowledge them from God inflicted on me
Justly, yet despair not of his final pardon
Whose ear is ever open; and his eye
Gracious to re-admit the suppliant;
In confidence whereof I once again
Defie thee to the trial of mortal fight,
By combat to decide whose god is God,
Thine or whom I with *Israel's* Sons adore.

   Har. Fair honour that thou dost thy God, in trusting
He will accept thee to defend his cause,
A Murtherer, a Revolter, and a Robber.

   Sam. Tongue-doubtie Giant, how dost thou prove me these?

   Har. Is not thy Nation subject to our Lords?
Thir Magistrates confest it, when they took thee
As a League-breaker and deliver'd bound
Into our hands: for hadst thou not committed
Notorious murder on those thirty men
At *Askalon*, who never did thee harm,
Then like a Robber stripdst them of thir robes?
The *Philistines*, when thou hadst broke the league,
Went up with armed powers thee only seeking,
To others did no violence nor spoil.

   Sam. Among the Daughters of the *Philistines*
I chose a Wife, which argu'd me no foe;
And in your City held my Nuptial Feast:
But your ill-meaning Politician Lords,
Under pretence of Bridal friends and guests,
Appointed to await me thirty spies,
Who threatning cruel death constrain'd the bride
To wring from me and tell to them my secret,
That solv'd the riddle which I had propos'd.
When I perceiv'd all set on enmity,
As on my enemies, where ever chanc'd,
I us'd hostility, and took thir spoil
To pay my underminers in thir coin.

My Nation was subjected to your Lords.
It was the force of Conquest; force with force
Is well ejected when the Conquer'd can.
But I a private person, whom my Countrey
As a league-breaker gave up bound, presum'd
Single Rebellion and did Hostile Acts.
I was no private but a person rais'd
With strength sufficient and command from Heav'n
To free my Countrey; if their servile minds
Me their Deliverer sent would not receive,
But to thir Masters gave me up for nought,
Th' unworthier they; whence to this day they serve.
I was to do my part from Heav'n assign'd,
And had perform'd it if my known offence
Had not disabl'd me, not all your force:
These shifts refuted, answer thy appellant
Though by his blindness maim'd for high attempts,
Who now defies thee thrice to single fight,
As a petty enterprise of small enforce.

    Har. With thee a Man condemn'd, a Slave enrol'd,
Due by the Law to capital punishment?
To fight with thee no man of arms will deign.

    Sam. Cam'st thou for this, vain boaster, to survey me,
To descant on my strength, and give thy verdit?
Come nearer, part not hence so slight inform'd;
But take good heed my hand survey not thee.

    Har. O *Baal-zebub!* can my ears unus'd
Hear these dishonours, and not render death?

    Sam. No man with-holds thee, nothing from thy hand
Fear I incurable; bring up thy van,
My heels are fetter'd, but my fist is free.

    Har. This insolence other kind of answer fits.

    Sam. Go baffl'd coward, lest I run upon thee,
Though in these chains, bulk without spirit vast,
And with one buffet lay thy structure low,
Or swing thee in the Air, then dash thee down
To the hazard of thy brains and shatter'd sides.

    Har. By *Astaroth* e're long thou shalt lament
These braveries in Irons loaden on thee.

    Chor. His Giantship is gone somewhat crest-fall'n,

Stalking with less unconsci'nable strides,
And lower looks, but in a sultrie chafe.

Sam. I dread him not, nor all his Giant-brood,
Though Fame divulge him Father of five Sons
All of Gigantic size, *Goliah* chief.

Chor. He will directly to the Lords, I fear,
And with malitious counsel stir them up
Some way or other yet further to afflict thee.

Sam. He must allege some cause, and offer'd fight
Will not dare mention, lest a question rise
Whether he durst accept the offer or not,
And that he durst not plain enough appear'd.
Much more affliction then already felt
They cannot well impose, nor I sustain;
If they intend advantage of my labours
The work of many hands, which earns my keeping
With no small profit daily to my owners.
But come what will, my deadliest foe will prove
My speediest friend, by death to rid me hence,
The worst that he can give, to me the best.
Yet so it may fall out, because thir end
Is hate, not help to me, it may with mine
Draw thir own ruin who attempt the deed.

Chor. Oh how comely it is and how reviving
To the Spirits of just men long opprest!
When God into the hands of thir deliverer
Puts invincible might
To quell the mighty of the Earth, th' oppressour,
The brute and boist'rous force of violent men
Hardy and industrious to support
Tyrannic power, but raging to pursue
The righteous and all such as honour Truth;
He all their Ammunition
And feats of War defeats
With plain Heroic magnitude of mind
And celestial vigour arm'd,
Thir Armories and Magazins contemns,
Renders them useless, while
With winged expedition
Swift as the lightning glance he executes

His errand on the wicked, who surpris'd
Lose thir defence distracted and amaz'd.
    But patience is more oft the exercise
Of Saints, the trial of thir fortitude,
Making them each his own Deliverer,
And Victor over all
That tyrannie or fortune can inflict,
Either of these is in thy lot,
Samson, with might endu'd
Above the Sons of men; but sight bereav'd
May chance to number thee with those
Whom Patience finally must crown.
This Idols day hath bin to thee no day of rest,
    Labouring thy mind
More then the working day thy hands,
And yet perhaps more trouble is behind.
For I descry this way
Some other tending, in his hand
A Scepter or quaint staff he bears,
Comes on amain, speed in his look.
By his habit I discern him now
A Public Officer, and now at hand.
His message will be short and voluble.

    Off. Ebrews, the Pris'ner *Samson* here I seek.
    Chor. His manacles remark him, there he sits.
    Off. Samson, to thee our Lords thus bid me say;
This day to *Dagon* is a solemn Feast,
With Sacrifices, Triumph, Pomp, and Games;
Thy strength they know surpassing human rate,
And now some public proof thereof require
To honour this great Feast, and great Assembly;
Rise therefore with all speed and come along,
Where I will see thee heartn'd and fresh clad
To appear as fits before th' illustrious Lords.

    Sam. Thou knowst I am an *Ebrew*, therefore tell them,
Our Law forbids at thir Religious Rites
My presence; for that cause I cannot come.

    Off. This answer, be assur'd, will not content them.

    Sam. Have they not Sword-players, and ev'ry sort
Of Gymnic Artists, Wrestlers, Riders, Runners,

Juglers and Dancers, Antics, Mummers, Mimics,
But they must pick me out with shackles tir'd,
And over-labour'd at thir publick Mill,
To make them sport with blind activity?
Do they not seek occasion of new quarrels
On my refusal to distress me more,
Or make a game of my calamities?
Return the way thou cam'st, I will not come.
    Off. Regard thy self, this will offend them highly.
    Sam. My self? my conscience and internal peace.
Can they think me so broken, so debas'd
With corporal servitude, that my mind ever
Will condescend to such absurd commands?
Although thir drudge, to be thir fool or jester,
And in my midst of sorrow and heart-grief
To shew them feats, and play before thir god,
The worst of all indignities, yet on me
Joyn'd with extream contempt? I will not come.
    Off. My message was impos'd on me with speed,
Brooks no delay: is this thy resolution?
    Sam. So take it with what speed thy message needs.
    Off. I am sorry what this stoutness will produce.
    Sam. Perhaps thou shalt have cause to sorrow indeed.
    Chor. Consider, *Samson*; matters now are strain'd
Up to the highth, whether to hold or break;
He's gone, and who knows how he may report
Thy words by adding fuel to the flame?
Expect another message more imperious,
More Lordly thund'ring then thou well wilt bear.
    Sam. Shall I abuse this Consecrated gift
Of strength, again returning with my hair
After my great transgression, so requite
Favour renew'd, and add a greater sin
By prostituting holy things to Idols;
A *Nazarite* in place abominable
Vaunting my strength in honour to thir *Dagon?*
Besides, how vile, contemptible, ridiculous,
What act more execrably unclean, prophane?
    Chor. Yet with this strength thou serv'st the *Philistines*,
Idolatrous, uncircumcis'd, unclean.

Sam. Not in thir Idol-worship, but by labour
Honest and lawful to deserve my food
Of those who have me in thir civil power.

    Chor. Where the heart joins not, outward acts defile not.

    Sam. Where outward force constrains, the sentence holds;
But who constrains me to the Temple of *Dagon*,
Not dragging? the *Philistian* Lords command.
Commands are no constraints. If I obey them,
I do it freely; venturing to displease
God for the fear of Man, and Man prefer,
Set God behind: which in his jealousie
Shall never, unrepented, find forgiveness.
Yet that he may dispense with me or thee
Present in Temples at Idolatrous Rites
For some important cause, thou needst not doubt.

    Chor. How thou wilt here come off surmounts my reach.

    Sam. Be of good courage, I begin to feel
Some rouzing motions in me which dispose
To something extraordinary my thoughts.
I with this Messenger will go along,
Nothing to do, be sure, that may dishonour
Our Law, or stain my vow of *Nazarite*.
If there be aught of presage in the mind,
This day will be remarkable in my life
By some great act, or of my days the last.

    Chor. In time thou hast resolv'd, the man returns.

    Off. *Samson*, this second message from our Lords
To thee I am bid say. Art thou our Slave,
Our Captive, at the public Mill our drudge,
And dar'st thou at our sending and command
Dispute thy coming? come without delay;
Or we shall find such Engines to assail
And hamper thee, as thou shalt come of force,
Though thou wert firmlier fastn'd then a rock.

    Sam. I could be well content to try their Art,
Which to no few of them would prove pernicious.
Yet knowing thir advantages too many,
Because they shall not trail me through thir streets
Like a wild Beast, I am content to go.
Masters commands come with a power resistless

To such as owe them absolute subjection;
And for a life who will not change his purpose?
(So mutable are all the ways of men)
Yet this be sure, in nothing to comply
Scandalous or forbidden in our Law.

　　Off. I praise thy resolution, doff these links:
By this compliance thou wilt win the Lords
To favour, and perhaps to set thee free.

　　Sam. Brethren farewel, your company along
I will not wish, lest it perhaps offend them
To see me girt with Friends; and how the sight
Of me as of a common Enemy,
So dreaded once, may now exasperate them
I know not. Lords are Lordliest in thir wine;
And the well-feasted Priest then soonest fir'd
With zeal, if aught Religion seem concern'd:
No less the people on thir Holy-days
Impetuous, insolent, unquenchable;
Happ'n what may, of me expect to hear
Nothing dishonourable, impure, unworthy
Our God, our Law, my Nation, or my self,
The last of me or no I cannot warrant.

　　Chor. Go, and the Holy One
Of *Israel* be thy guide
To what may serve his glory best, and spread his name
Great among the Heathen round:
Send thee the Angel of thy Birth, to stand
Fast by thy side, who from thy Fathers field
Rode up in flames after his message told
Of thy conception, and be now a shield
Of fire; that Spirit that first rusht on thee
In the Camp of *Dan*
Be efficacious in thee now at need.
For never was from Heaven imparted
Measure of strength so great to mortal seed,
As in thy wond'rous actions hath been seen.
But wherefore comes old *Manoa* in such hast
With youthful steps? much livelier than e're while
He seems: supposing here to find his Son,
Or of him bringing to us some glad news?

Man. Peace with you brethren; my inducement hither
Was not at present here to find my Son,
By order of the Lords new parted hence
To come and play before them at thir Feast.
I heard all as I came, the City rings
And numbers thither flock, I had no will,
Lest I should see him forc't to things unseemly.
But that which mov'd my coming now, was chiefly
To give ye part with me what hope I have
With good success to work his liberty.

Chor. That hope would much rejoyce us to partake
With thee; say reverend Sire, we thirst to hear.

Man. I have attempted one by one the Lords
Either at home, or through the high street passing,
With supplication prone and Fathers tears
To accept of ransom for my Son thir pris'ner,
Some much averse I found and wondrous harsh,
Contemptuous, proud, set on revenge and spite;
That part most reverenc'd *Dagon* and his Priests,
Others more moderate seeming, but thir aim
Private reward, for which both God and State
They easily would set to sale, a third
More generous far and civil, who confess'd
They had anough reveng'd, having reduc't
Thir foe to misery beneath thir fears,
The rest was magnanimity to remit,
If some convenient ransom were propos'd.
What noise or shout was that? it tore the Skie.

Chor. Doubtless the people shouting to behold
Thir once great dread, captive, and blind before them,
Or at some proof of strength before them shown.

Man. His ransom, if my whole inheritance
May compass it, shall willingly be paid
And numberd down: much rather I shall chuse
To live the poorest in my Tribe, then richest,
And he in that calamitous prison left.
No, I am fixt not to part hence without him.
For his redemption all my Patrimony,
If need be, I am ready to forgo
And quit: not wanting him, I shall want nothing.

Chor. Fathers are wont to lay up for thir Sons,
Thou for thy Son art bent to lay out all;
Sons wont to nurse thir Parents in old age,
Thou in old age car'st how to nurse thy Son.
Made older then thy age through eye-sight lost.

Man. It shall be my delight to tend his eyes,
And view him sitting in the house, enobl'd
With all those high exploits by him atchiev'd,
And on his shoulders waving down those locks,
That of a Nation arm'd the strength contain'd:
And I perswade me God had not permitted
His strength again to grow up with his hair
Garrison'd round about him like a Camp
Of faithful Souldiery, were not his purpose
To use him further yet in some great service,
Not to sit idle with so great a gift
Useless, and thence ridiculous about him.
And since his strength with eye-sight was not lost,
God will restore him eye-sight to his strength.

Chor. Thy hopes are not ill founded nor seem vain
Of his delivery, and thy joy thereon
Conceiv'd, agreeable to a Fathers love,
In both which we, as next participate.

Man. I know your friendly minds and—O what noise!
Mercy of Heav'n what hideous noise was that!
Horribly loud unlike the former shout.

Chor. Noise call you it or universal groan
As if the whole inhabitation perish'd,
Blood, death, and deathful deeds are in that noise,
Ruin, destruction at the utmost point.

Man. Of ruin indeed methought I heard the noise,
Oh it continues, they have slain my Son.

Chor. Thy Son is rather slaying them, that outcry
From slaughter of one foe could not ascend.

Man. Some dismal accident it needs must be;
What shall we do, stay here or run and see?

Chor. Best keep together here, lest running thither
We unawares run into dangers mouth.
This evil on the *Philistines* is fall'n,
From whom could else a general cry be heard?

The sufferers then will scarce molest us here,
From other hands we need not much to fear.
What if his eye-sight (for to *Israels* God
Nothing is hard) by miracle restor'd,
He now be dealing dole among his foes,
And over heaps of slaughter'd walk his way?

   Man. That were a joy presumptuous to be thought.

   Chor. Yet God hath wrought things as incredible
For his people of old; what hinders now?

   Man. He can I know, but doubt to think he will;
Yet Hope would fain subscribe, and tempts Belief.
A little stay will bring some notice hither.

   Chor. Of good or bad so great, of bad the sooner;
For evil news rides post, while good news baits.
And to our wish I see one hither speeding,
An *Ebrew*, as I guess, and of our Tribe.

   Mess. O whither shall I run, or which way flie
The sight of this so horrid spectacle
Which earst my eyes beheld and yet behold;
For dire imagination still persues me.
But providence or instinct of nature seems,
Or reason though disturb'd, and scarse consulted
To have guided me aright, I know not how,
To thee first reverend *Manoa*, and to these
My Countreymen, whom here I knew remaining,
As at some distance from the place of horrour,
So in the sad event too much concern'd.

   Man. The accident was loud, and here before thee
With rueful cry, yet what it was we hear not,
No Preface needs, thou seest we long to know.

   Mess. It would burst forth, but I recover breath
And sense distract, to know well what I utter.

   Man. Tell us the sum, the circumstance defer.

   Mess. *Gaza* yet stands, but all her Sons are fall'n,
All in a moment overwhelm'd and fall'n.

   Man. Sad, but thou knowst to *Israelites* not saddest
The desolation of a Hostile City.

   Mess. Feed on that first, there may in grief be surfet

   Man. Relate by whom. *Mess.* By *Samson.*

      Man. That still lessens

The sorrow, and converts it nigh to joy.

   Mess. Ah *Manoa* I refrain, too suddenly
To utter what will come at last too soon;
Lest evil tidings with too rude irruption
Hitting thy aged ear should pierce too deep.

   Man. Suspense in news is torture, speak them out.

   Mess. Then take the worst in brief, *Samson* is dead.

   Man. The worst indeed, O all my hope's defeated
To free him hence! but death who sets all free
Hath paid his ransom now and full discharge.
What windy joy this day had I conceiv'd
Hopeful of his Delivery, which now proves
Abortive as the first-born bloom of spring
Nipt with the lagging rear of winters frost.
Yet e're I give the rains to grief, say first,
How dy'd he? death to life is crown or shame.
All by him fell thou say'st, by whom fell he,
What glorious hand gave *Samson* his deaths wound?

   Mess. Unwounded of his enemies he fell.

   Man. Wearied with slaughter then or how? explain.

   Mess. By his own hands. *Man.* Self-violence? what cause
Brought him so soon at variance with himself
Among his foes? *Mess.* Inevitable cause
At once both to destroy and be destroy'd;
The Edifice where all were met to see him
Upon thir heads and on his own he pull'd.

   Man. O lastly over-strong against thy self!
A dreadful way thou took'st to thy revenge.
More then anough we know; but while things yet
Are in confusion, give us if thou canst,
Eye-witness of what first or last was done,
Relation more particular and distinct.

   Mess. Occasions drew me early to this City,
And as the gates I enter'd with Sun-rise,
The morning Trumpets Festival proclaim'd
Through each high street: little I had dispatch't
When all abroad was rumour'd that this day
Samson should be brought forth to shew the people
Proof of his mighty strength in feats and games;
I sorrow'd at his captive state, but minded

Not to be absent at that spectacle.
The building was a spacious Theatre
Half round on two main Pillars vaulted high,
With seats where all the Lords and each degree
Of sort, might sit in order to behold,
The other side was op'n, where the throng
On banks and scaffolds under Skie might stand;
I among these aloof obscurely stood.
The Feast and noon grew high, and Sacrifice
Had fill'd thir hearts with mirth, high chear, and wine,
When to their sports they turn'd. Immediately
Was *Samson* as a public servant brought,
In thir state Livery clad; before him Pipes
And Timbrels, on each side went armed guards,
Both horse and foot before him and behind
Archers, and Slingers, Cataphracts and Spears.
At sight of him the people with a shout
Rifted the Air clamouring thir god with praise,
Who had made thir dreadful enemy thir thrall.
He patient but undaunted where they led him,
Came to the place, and what was set before him
Which without help of eye, might be assay'd,
To heave, pull, draw, or break, he still perform'd
All with incredible, stupendious force,
None daring to appear Antagonist.
At length for intermission sake they led him
Between the pillars; he his guide requested
(For so from such as nearer stood we heard)
As over-tir'd to let him lean a while
With both his arms on those two massie Pillars
That to the arched roof gave main support.
He unsuspitious led him; which when *Samson*
Felt in his arms, with head a while enclin'd,
And eyes fast fixt he stood, as one who pray'd,
Or some great matter in his mind revolv'd.
At last with head erect thus cryed aloud,
Hitherto, Lords, what your commands impos'd
I have perform'd, as reason was, obeying,
Not without wonder or delight beheld.
Now of my own accord such other tryal

I mean to shew you of my strength, yet greater;
As with amaze shall strike all who behold.
This utter'd, straining all his nerves he bow'd,
As with the force of winds and waters pent,
When Mountains tremble, those two massie Pillars
With horrible convulsion to and fro,
He tugg'd, he shook, till down they came and drew
The whole roof after them, with burst of thunder
Upon the heads of all who sate beneath,
Lords, Ladies, Captains, Councellors, or Priests,
Thir choice nobility and flower, not only
Of this but each *Philistian* City round
Met from all parts to solemnize this Feast.
Samson with these immixt, inevitably
Pulld down the same destruction on himself;
The vulgar only scap'd who stood without.

    Chor. O dearly-bought revenge, yet glorious!
Living or dying thou hast fulfill'd
The work for which thou wast foretold
To *Israel*, and now ly'st victorious
Among thy slain self-kill'd
Not willingly, but tangl'd in the fold,
Of dire necessity, whose law in death conjoin'd
Thee with thy slaughter'd foes in number more
Then all thy life had slain before.

    Semichor. While thir hearts were jocund and sublime,
Drunk with Idolatry, drunk with Wine,
And fat regorg'd of Bulls and Goats,
Chaunting thir Idol, and preferring
Before our living Dread who dwells
In *Silo* his bright Sanctuary:
Among them he a spirit of phrenzie sent,
Who hurt thir minds,
And urg'd them on with mad desire
To call in hast for thir destroyer;
They only set on sport and play
Unweetingly importun'd
Their own destruction to come speedy upon them.
So fond are mortal men
Fall'n into wrath divine,

As thir own ruin on themselves to invite,
Insensate left, or to sense reprobate,
And with blindness internal struck.

Semichor. But he though blind of sight,
Despis'd and thought extinguish't quite,
With inward eyes illuminated
His fierie vertue rouz'd
From under ashes into sudden flame,
And as an ev'ning Dragon came,
Assailant on the perched roosts,
And nests in order rang'd
Of tame villatic Fowl; but as an Eagle
His cloudless thunder bolted on thir heads.
So vertue giv'n for lost,
Deprest, and overthrown, as seem'd,
Like that self-begott'n bird
In the *Arabian* woods embost,
That no second knows nor third,
And lay e're while a Holocaust,
From out her ashie womb now teem'd,
Revives, reflourishes, then vigorous most
When most unactive deem'd,
And though her body die, her fame survives,
A secular bird ages of lives.

Man. Come, come, no time for lamentation now,
Nor much more cause, *Samson* hath quit himself
Like *Samson*, and heroicly hath finish'd
A life Heroic, on his Enemies
Fully reveng'd, hath left them years of mourning,
And lamentation to the Sons of *Caphtor*
Through all *Philistian* bounds. To *Israel*
Honour hath left, and freedom, let but them
Find courage to lay hold on this occasion,
To himself and Fathers house eternal fame;
And which is best and happiest yet, all this
With God not parted from him, as was feard,
But favouring and assisting to the end.
Nothing is here for tears, nothing to wail
Or knock the breast, no weakness, no contempt,
Dispraise, or blame, nothing but well and fair,

And what may quiet us in a death so noble.
Let us go find the body where it lies
Sok't in his enemies blood, and from the stream
With lavers pure and cleansing herbs wash off
The clotted gore. I with what speed the while
(*Gaza* is not in plight to say us nay)
Will send for all my kindred, all my friends
To fetch him hence and solemnly attend
With silent obsequie and funeral train
Home to his Fathers house: there will I build him
A Monument, and plant it round with shade
Of Laurel ever green, and branching Palm,
With all his Trophies hung, and Acts enroll'd
In copious Legend, or sweet Lyric Song.
Thither shall all the valiant youth resort,
And from his memory inflame thir breasts
To matchless valour, and adventures high:
The Virgins also shall on feastful days
Visit his Tomb with flowers, only bewailing
His lot unfortunate in nuptial choice,
From whence captivity and loss of eyes.

  Chor. All is best, though we oft doubt,
What th' unsearchable dispose
Of highest wisdom brings about,
And ever best found in the close.
Oft he seems to hide his face,
But unexpectedly returns
And to his faithful Champion hath in place
Bore witness gloriously; whence *Gaza* mourns
And all that band them to resist
His uncontroulable intent,
His servants he with new acquist
Of true experience from this great event
With peace and consolation hath dismist,
And calm of mind all passion spent.

Translations

Translations

¶ A Paraphrase on Psalm CXIV

This and the following Psalm were done by the Author at fifteen years old.

WHEN the blest seed of *Terah*'s faithful Son,
After long toil their liberty had won,
And past from *Pharian* Fields to *Canaan* Land,
Led by the strength of the Almighties hand,
Jehovah's wonders were in *Israel* shown,
His praise and glory was in *Israel* known.
That saw the troubled Sea, and shivering fled,
And sought to hide his froth becurled head
Low in the earth, *Jordans* clear streams recoil,
As a faint Host that hath receiv'd the foil.
The high, huge-bellied Mountains skip like Rams
Amongst their Ews, the little Hills like Lambs.
Why fled the Ocean? And why skipt the Mountains?
Why turned *Jordan* towards his Chrystal Fountains?
Shake earth, and at the presence be agast
Of him that ever was, and ay shall last,
That glassy flouds from rugged rocks can crush,
And make soft rills from fiery flint-stones gush.

¶ Psal. CXXXVI

LET us with a gladsom mind
Praise the Lord, for he is kind
   For his mercies ay endure,
   Ever faithfull, ever sure.

Let us blaze his Name abroad,
For of gods he is the God;
   For his, *etc.*

O let us his praises tell,
Who doth the wrathfull tyrants quell.
   For his, *etc.*

Who with his miracles doth make
Amazed Heav'n and Earth to shake.
    For his, *etc.*

Who by his wisdom did create
The painted Heav'ns so full of state.
    For his, *etc.*

Who did the solid Earth ordain
To rise above the watry plain.
    For his, *etc.*

Who by his all-commanding might,
Did fill the new-made world with light.
    For his, *etc.*

And caus'd the Golden-tressed Sun,
All the day long his course to run.
    For his, *etc.*

The horned Moon to shine by night,
Amongst her spangled sisters bright.
    For his, *etc.*

He with his thunder-clasping hand,
Smote the first-born of *Egypt* Land.
    For his, *etc.*

And in despight of *Pharao* fell,
He brought from thence his *Israel*.
    For, *etc.*

The ruddy waves he cleft in twain,
Of the *Erythræan* main.
    For, *etc.*

The flouds stood still like Walls of Glass,
While the Hebrew Bands did pass.
    For, *etc.*

But full soon they did devour
The Tawny King with all his power.
    For, *etc.*

His chosen people he did bless
In the wastfull Wilderness.
    For, *etc.*

In bloudy battel he brought down
Kings of prowess and renown.
    For, *etc.*

He foild bold *Seon* and his host
That rul'd the *Amorrean* coast.
    For, *etc.*

And large-limb'd *Og* he did subdue,
With all his over-hardy crew.
    For, *etc.*

And to his Servant *Israel*,
He gave their Land therein to dwell.
    For, *etc.*

He hath with a piteous eye
Beheld us in our misery.
    For, *etc.*

And freed us from the slavery
Of the invading enemy.
    For, *etc.*

All living creatures he doth feed,
And with full hand supplies their need.
    For, *etc.*

Let us therefore warble forth
His mighty Majesty and worth.
    For, *etc.*

That his mansion hath on high
Above the reach of mortal eye.
    For his mercies ay endure,
    Ever faithfull, ever sure.

¶ Psal. CXIV

Ἰσραὴλ ὅτε παῖδες, ὅτ' ἀγλαὰ φῦλ' Ἰακώβου
Αἰγύπτιον λίπε δῆμον, ἀπεχθέα, βαρβαρόφωνον,
Δὴ τότε μοῦνον ἔην ὅσιον γένος υἷες Ἰούδα·
Ἐν δὲ θεὸς λαοῖσι μέγα κρείων βασίλευεν.
Εἶδε, καὶ ἐντροπάδην φύγαδ' ἐρρώησε θάλασσα

Κύματι εἰλυμένη ῥοθίῳ, ὅδ᾽ ἄρ᾽ ἐστυφελίχθη
Ἱρὸς Ἰορδάνης ποτὶ ἀργυροειδέα πηγήν.
Ἐκ δ᾽ ὄρεα σκαρθμοῖσιν ἀπειρέσια κλονέοντο,
Ὡς κριοὶ σφριγόωντες ἐϋτραφερῷ ἐν ἀλωῇ.
Βαιότεραι δ᾽ ἅμα πᾶσαι ἀνασκίρτησαν ἐρίπναι,
Οἷα παραὶ σύριγγι φίλῃ ὑπὸ μητέρι ἄρνες.
Τίπτε σύγ᾽ αἰνὰ θάλασσα πέλωρ φύγαδ᾽ ἐρρώησας ;
Κύματι εἰλυμένη ῥοθίῳ ; τί δ᾽ ἄρ᾽ ἐστυφελίχθης
Ἱρὸς Ἰορδάνη ποτὶ ἀργυροειδέα πηγὴν ;
Τίπτ᾽ ὄρεα σκαρθμοῖσιν ἀπειρέσια κλονέεσθε
Ὡς κριοὶ σφριγόωντες ἐϋτραφερῷ ἐν ἀλωῇ ;
Βαιότεραι τί δ᾽ ἄρ᾽ ὔμμες ἀνασκιρτήσατ᾽ ἐρίπναι,
Οἷα παραὶ σύριγγι φίλῃ ὑπὸ μητέρι ἄρνες,
Σείεο γαῖα τρέουσα θεὸν μεγάλ᾽ ἐκτυπέοντα
Γαῖα, θεὸν τρείουσ᾽ ὕπατον σέβας Ἰσσακίδαο
Ὅς τε καὶ ἐκ σπιλάδων ποταμοὺς χέε μορμύροντας
Κρήνην τ᾽ ἀέναον πέτρης ἀπὸ δακρυοέσσης.

¶ Dante, *Inf.* XIX, 115

Ah *Constantine*, of how much ill was cause
Not thy Conversion, but those rich demaines
That the first wealthy *Pope* receiv'd of thee.

¶ Petrarch, *Son.* 107

Founded in chast and humble Povertie,
'Gainst them that rais'd thee dost thou lift thy horn,
Impudent whoore, where hast thou plac'd thy hope?
In thy Adulterers, or thy ill got wealth?
Another *Constantine* comes not in hast.

¶ Ariosto, *Orl. Fur.* XXXIV, 79

Then past hee to a flowry Mountaine greene,
Which once smelt sweet, now stinks as odiously;
This was that gift (if you the truth will have)
That *Constantine* to good *Sylvestro* gave.

¶ Phrynichus, *Incert. Fab.* 5, 17

When I dye, let the earth be roul'd in flames.

¶ Horace, *Sat.* I, 1, 24

Laughing to teach the truth
What hinders? as some teachers give to Boyes
Junkets and knacks, that they may learne apace.

¶ Horace, *Sat.* I, 10, 14

Jesting decides great things
Stronglier, and better oft then earnest can.

¶ Sophocles, *Elec.* 624

'Tis you that say it, not I, you do the deeds,
And your ungodly deeds finde me the words.

¶ Euripides, *Supp.* 438

This is true Liberty when free-born men
Having to advise the public may speak free,
Which he who can, and will, deserv's high praise,
Who neither can nor will, may hold his peace;
What can be juster in a State then this?

¶ Horace, *Ep.* I, 16, 40

Whom doe we count a good man, whom but he
Who keepes the lawes and statutes of the Senate,
Who judges in great suits and controversies,
Whose witnesse and opinion winnes the cause;
But his owne house, and the whole neighbourhood
Sees his foule inside through his whited skin.

April, 1648. J. M.

Nine of the Psalms done into Metre, wherein all but what is in a different Character, are the very words of the Text, translated from the Original.

¶ Psal. LXXX

1 THOU Shepherd that dost Israel *keep*
    Give ear *in time of need*,
Who leadest like a flock of sheep
    Thy loved Josephs seed,
That sitt'st between the Cherubs *bright*
    Between their wings out-spread
Shine forth, *and from thy cloud give light*,
    And on our foes thy dread

2 In Ephraims view and Benjamins,
    And in Manasse's sight
*Awake thy strength, come, and *be seen*
    To save us *by thy might*.

3 Turn us again, *thy grace divine*
    To us O God *vouchsafe;*
Cause thou thy face on us to shine
    And then we shall be safe.

4 Lord God of Hosts, how long wilt thou,
    How long wilt thou declare
Thy †smoaking wrath, *and angry brow*
    Against thy peoples praire.

5 Thou feed'st them with the bread of tears,
    Their bread with tears they eat,
And mak'st them ‡largely drink the tears
    Wherwith their cheeks are wet.

6 A strife thou mak'st us *and a prey*
    To every neighbour foe,
Among themselves they §laugh, they §play,
    And §flouts at us they throw

---

* Gnorera.	† Gnashanta.
‡ Shalish.	§ Jilgnagu.

7 Return us, *and thy grace divine,*
   O God of Hosts *vouchsafe*
Cause thou thy face on us to shine,
   And then we shall be safe.

8 A Vine from Ægypt thou hast brought,
   Thy free love made it thine,
And drov'st out Nations *proud and haut,*
   To plant this *lovely* Vine.

9 Thou did'st prepare for it a place
   And root it deep and fast
That it *began to grow apace,*
   And fill'd the land *at last.*

10 With her *green* shade *that* cover'd *all,*
   The Hills were *over-spread*
Her Bows as *high as* Cedars tall
   Advanc'd their lofty head.

11 Her branches *on the western side*
   Down to the Sea she sent,
And *upward* to that river *wide*
   Her other branches *went.*

12 Why hast thou laid her Hedges low
   And brok'n down her Fence,
That all may pluck her, as they go,
   With rudest violence?

13 The *tusked* Boar out of the wood
   Up turns it by the roots,
While Beasts there brouze, and make their food
   Her Grapes and tender Shoots.

14 Return now, God of Hosts, look down
   From Heav'n, thy Seat divine,
Behold *us, but without a frown,*
   And visit this *thy* Vine.

15 Visit this Vine, which thy right hand
   Hath set, and planted *long,*
And the young branch, that for thy self
   Thou hast made firm and strong.

16 But now it is consum'd with fire,
   And cut *with Axes* down,
They perish at thy dreadfull ire,
   At thy rebuke and frown.

17 Upon the man of thy right hand
     Let thy *good* hand be *laid*,
   Upon the Son of Man, whom thou
     Strong for thyself hast made.
18 So shall we not go back from thee
     To wayes of sin and shame,
   Quick'n us thou, then *gladly* wee
     Shall call upon thy Name.
   Return us, *and thy grace divine*
     Lord God of Hosts *voutsafe*,
   Cause thou thy face on us to shine,
     And then we shall be safe.

¶ Psal. LXXXI

1 To God our strength sing loud, *and clear*,
     Sing loud to God *our King*,
   To Jacobs God, *that all may hear*
     Loud acclamations ring.
2 Prepare a Hymn, prepare a Song
     The Timbrel hither bring
   The *cheerfull* Psaltry bring along
     And Harp *with* pleasant *string*,
3 Blow, *as is wont*, in the new Moon
     With Trumpets *lofty sound*,
   Th' appointed time, the day wheron
     Our solemn Feast *comes round*.
4 This was a Statute *giv'n of old*
     For Israel *to observe*
   A Law of Jacobs God, *to hold*
     From whence they might not swerve.
5 This he a Testimony ordain'd
     In Joseph, *not to change*,
   When as he pass'd through Ægypt land;
     The Tongue I heard, was strange.
6 From burden, *and from slavish toyle*
     I set his shoulder free;
   His hands from pots, *and mirie soyle*
     Deliver'd were *by me*.

7 When trouble did thee sore assaile,
    On me then didst thou call,
And I to free thee *did not faile,*
    And led thee out of thrall.
I answer'd thee in *thunder deep
    With clouds encompass'd round;
I tri'd thee at the water *steep*
    Of Meriba *renown'd.*

8 Hear O my people, *heark'n well,*
    I testifie to thee
Thou antient stock of Israel,
    If thou wilt list to mee,

9 Through out the land of thy abode
    No alien God shall be
Nor shalt thou to a forein God
    In honour bend thy knee.

10 I am the Lord thy God which brought
    Thee out of Ægypt land
Ask large enough, and I, *besought,*
    Will grant thy full demand.

11 And yet my people would not *hear,*
    Nor hearken to my voice;
And Israel *whom I lov'd so dear*
    Mislik'd me for his choice.

12 Then did I leave them to their will
    And to their wandring mind;
Their own conceits they follow'd still
    Their own devises blind.

13 O that my people would *be wise*
    To serve me *all their daies,*
And O that Israel would *advise*
    To walk my *righteous* waies.

14 Then would I soon bring down their foes
    That now so proudly rise,
And turn my hand against *all those*
    That are their enemies.

15 Who hate the Lord should *then be fain*
    To bow to him and bend,
But *they, his People, should remain,*
    Their time should have no end.

* Be Sether ragnam.

16 And He would feed them *from the shock*
   With flowr of finest wheat,
And satisfie them from the rock
   With Honey *for their Meat.*

¶ Psal. LXXXII

1 GOD in the *great *assembly stands
   Of Kings and lordly States,
†Among the gods †on both his hands
   He judges and debates.
2 How long will ye ‡pervert the right
   With ‡judgment false and wrong
Favouring the wicked *by your might,*
   Who thence grow bold and strong?
3 §Regard the §weak and fatherless
   §Dispatch the §poor mans cause,
And ‖raise the man in deep distress
   By ‖just and equal Lawes.
4 Defend the poor and desolate,
   And rescue from the hands
Of wicked men the low estate
   Of him *that help demands.*
5 They know not nor will understand,
   In darkness they walk on,
The Earths foundations all are ¶mov'd
   And ¶out of order gon.
6 I said that ye were Gods, yea all
   The Sons of God most high
7 But ye shall die like men, and fall
   As other Princes *die.*
8 Rise God, **judge thou the earth *in might,*
   This *wicked* earth **redress,
For thou art he who shalt by right
   The Nations all possess.

* Bagnadath-el.   † Bekerev.
‡ Tishphetu gnavel.   § Shiphtu-**dal.**
‖ Hatzdiku.   ¶ Jimmotu.
              ** Shiphta.

¶ Psal. LXXXIII

1 BE not thou silent *now at length*
    O God hold not thy peace,
Sit not thou still O God of *strength*
    We cry and do not cease.

2 For lo thy *furious* foes *now* *swell
    And *storm outrageously,
And they that hate thee *proud and fell*
    Exalt their heads full hie.

3 Against thy people they †contrive
    ‡Their Plots and Counsels deep,
    §Them to ensnare they chiefly strive
‖Whom thou dost hide and keep.

4 Come let us cut them off say they,
    Till they no Nation be
That Israels name for ever may
    Be lost in memory.

5 For they consult ¶with all their might,
    And all as one in mind
Themselves against thee they unite
    And in firm union bind.

6 The tents of Edom, and the brood
    Of *scornful* Ishmael,
Moab, with them of Hagars blood
    That in the Desart dwell,

7 Gebal and Ammon *there conspire,*
    And *hateful* Amalec,
The Philistims, and they of Tyre
    Whose bounds the Sea doth check.

8 With them *great* Asshur also bands
    And doth confirm the knot,
All these have lent their armed hands
    To aid the Sons of Lot.

9 Do to them as to Midian *bold*
    That wasted all the Coast.
To Sisera, and as *is told*
    Thou didst to Jabins *hoast,*

---

* Jehemajun. † Jagnarimu. ‡ Sod.
§ Jithjagnatsu gnal. ‖ Tsephuneca. ¶ Lev jachdau.

When at the brook of Kishon *old*
    They were repulst and slain,
10 At Endor quite cut off, and rowl'd
    As dung upon the plain.

11 As Zeb and Oreb evil sped
    So let their Princes speed
As Zeba, and Zalmunna *bled*
    So let their Princes *bleed.*

12 *For they amidst their pride* have said
    By right now shall we seize
Gods houses, and *will now invade*
    *Their stately Palaces.

13 My God, oh make them as a wheel
    No quiet let them find,
Giddy and *restless* let *them reel*
    Like stubble from the wind.

14 As *when* an *aged* wood takes fire
    Which on a sudden straies,
The *greedy* flame runs hier and hier
    Till all the mountains blaze,

15 So with thy whirlwind them pursue,
    And with thy tempest chase;
16 †And till they †yield thee honour due,
    Lord fill with shame their face.

17 Asham'd and troubl'd let them be,
    Troubl'd and sham'd for ever,
Ever confounded, and so die
    With shame, *and scape it never.*

18 Then shall they know that thou whose name
    Jehova is alone,
Art the most high, *and thou the same*
    O're all the earth *art one.*

¶ Psal. LXXXIV

1 How lovely are thy dwellings fair!
    O Lord of Hoasts, how dear
The *pleasant* Tabernacles are!
    Where thou do'st dwell so near.

* Neoth Elohim bears both.   † They seek thy Name, *Heb.*

2 My Soul doth long and almost die
      Thy Courts O Lord to see,
   My heart and flesh aloud do crie,
      O living God, for thee.

3 There ev'n the Sparrow *freed from wrong*
      Hath found a house of *rest*,
   The Swallow there, to lay her young
      Hath built her *brooding* nest,
   Ev'n *by* thy Altars Lord of Hoasts
      They find their safe abode,
   And home they fly from round the Coasts
      Toward thee, My King, my God.

4 Happy, who in thy house reside
      Where thee they ever praise,

5 Happy, whose strength in thee doth bide,
      And in their hearts thy waies.

6 They pass through Baca's *thirstie* Vale,
      That dry and barren ground
   As through a fruitfull watry Dale
      Where Springs and Showrs abound.

7 They journey on from strength to strength
      With joy and gladsom cheer
   Till all before *our* God *at length*
      In Sion do appear.

8 Lord God of Hoasts hear *now* my praier
      O Jacobs God give ear,

9 Thou God our shield look on the face
      Of thy anointed *dear*.

10 For one day in thy Courts *to be*
      Is better, *and more blest*
   Then *in the joyes of Vanity*,
      A thousand daies *at best*.
   I in the temple of my God
      Had rather keep a dore,
   Then dwell in Tents, *and rich abode*
      With Sin *for evermore*.

11 For God the Lord both Sun and Shield
      Gives grace and glory *bright*,
   No good from them shall be with-held
      Whose waies are just and right.

12 Lord *God* of Hoasts *that raign'st on high,*
    That man is *truly* blest,
  Who *only* on thee doth relie,
  And in thee only rest.

¶ Psal. LXXXV

1 THY Land to favour graciously
    Thou hast not Lord been slack,
  Thou hast from *hard* Captivity
    Returned Jacob back.
2 Th' iniquity thou didst forgive
    That wrought thy people woe,
  And all their Sin, *that did thee grieve*
    Hast hid *where none shall know.*
3 Thine anger all thou hadst remov'd,
    And *calmly* didst return
  From thy *fierce wrath which we had prov'd
    Far worse then fire to burn.
4 God of our saving health and peace,
    Turn us, and us restore,
  Thine indignation cause to cease
    Toward us, *and chide no more.*
5 Wilt thou be angry without end,
    For ever angry thus
  Wilt thou thy frowning ire extend
    From age to age on us?
6 Wilt thou not †turn, and *hear our voice*
    And us again †revive,
  That so thy people may rejoyce
    By thee preserv'd alive.
7 Cause us to see thy goodness Lord,
    To us thy mercy shew
  Thy saving health to us afford
    And life in us renew.
8 *And now* what God the Lord will speak
    I will *go strait and* hear,

* Heb. The burning heat of thy **wrath.**
† Heb. Turn to quicken us.

For to his people he speaks peace
   And to his Saints *full dear*,
To his dear Saints he will speak peace,
   But let them never more
Return to folly, *but surcease*
   To trespass as before.

9 Surely to such as do him fear
   Salvation is at hand
And glory shall *ere long appear*
   To dwell within our Land.

10 Mercy and Truth *that long were miss'd*
   Now *joyfully* are met
Sweet Peace and Righteousness have kiss'd
   And hand in hand are set.

11 Truth from the earth *like to a flowr*
   Shall bud and blossom *then*,
And Justice from her heavenly bowr
   Look down *on mortal men.*

12 The Lord will also then bestow
   Whatever thing is good
Our Land shall forth in plenty throw
   Her fruits *to be our food.*

13 Before him Righteousness shall go
   His Royal Harbinger,
Then *will he come, and not be slow
   His footsteps cannot err.

¶ Psal. LXXXVI

1 THY *gracious* ear, O Lord, encline,
   O hear me *I thee pray*,
For I am poor, and almost pine
   With need, *and sad decay.*

2 Preserve my soul, for †I have trod
   Thy waies, and love the just,
Save thou thy servant O my God
   Who *still* in thee doth trust.

---

* Heb. He will set his steps to the way.
† Heb. I am good-loving, a doer of good and holy things.

3 Pitty me Lord for daily thee
    I call; 4 O make rejoyce
Thy Servants Soul; for Lord to thee
    I lift my soul *and voice*,

5 For thou art good, thou Lord art prone
    To pardon, thou to all
Art full of mercy, thou *alone*
    To them that on thee call.

6 Unto my supplication Lord
    Give ear, and to the crie
Of my *incessant* praiers afford
    Thy hearing graciously.

7 I in the day of my distress
    Will call on thee *for aid;*
For thou wilt *grant* me *free access*
    And answer, *what I pray'd.*

8 Like thee among the gods is none
    O Lord, nor any works
Of all that other gods have done
    Like to thy *glorious* works.

9 The Nations all whom thou hast made
    Shall come, *and all shall frame*
To bow them low before thee Lord,
    And glorifie thy name.

10 For great thou art, and wonders great
    By thy strong hand are done,
Thou *in thy everlasting Seat*
    Remainest God alone.

11 Teach me O Lord thy way *most right,*
    I in thy truth will bide,
To fear thy name my heart unite
    So shall it never slide

12 Thee will I praise O Lord my God
    Thee honour, and adore
With my whole heart, and blaze abroad
    Thy name for ever more.

13 For great thy mercy is toward me,
    And thou hast free'd my Soul
Eev'n from the lowest Hell set free
    From deepest darkness foul.

14 O God the proud against me rise
    And violent men are met
  To seek my life, and in their eyes
    No fear of thee have set.

15 But thou Lord art the God most mild
    Readiest thy grace to shew,
  Slow to be angry, and *art stil'd*
    Most mercifull, most true.

16 O turn to me *thy face at length,*
    And me have mercy on,
  Unto thy servant give thy strength,
    And save thy hand-maids Son.

17 Some sign of good to me afford,
    And let my foes *then* see
  And be asham'd, because thou Lord
    Do'st help and comfort me.

¶ Psal. LXXXVII

1 AMONG the holy Mountains *high*
    Is his foundation fast,
  There Seated in his Sanctuary,
    His Temple there is plac't.

2 Sions *fair* Gates the Lord loves more
    Then all the dwellings *faire*
  Of Jacobs *Land, though there be store,*
    And all within his care.

3 City of God, most glorious things
    Of thee *abroad* are spoke;

4 I mention Egypt, *where proud Kings*
    Did our forefathers yoke,
  I mention Babel to my friends,
    Philistia *full of scorn,*
  And Tyre with Ethiops *utmost ends,*
    Lo this man there was born:

5 But *twise that praise shall in our ear*
    Be said of Sion *last*
  This and this man was born in her,
    High God shall fix her fast.

6 The Lord shall write it in a Scrowle
    That ne're shall be out-worn
When he the Nations doth enrowle
    That this man there was born.
7 Both they who sing, and they who dance
    With sacred Songs are there,
In thee *fresh brooks, and soft streams glance*
    And all my fountains *clear.*

¶ Psal. LXXXVIII

1 LORD God that dost me save and keep,
    All day to thee I cry;
And all night long, before thee *weep*
    Before thee *prostrate lie.*
2 Into thy presence let my praier
    With sighs devout ascend
And to my cries, that *ceaseless are,*
    Thine ear with favour bend.
3 For cloy'd with woes and trouble store
    Surcharg'd my Soul doth lie,
My life *at deaths uncherful dore*
    Unto the grave draws nigh.
4 Reck'n'd I am with them that pass
    Down to the *dismal* pit
I am a *man, but weak alas
    And for that name unfit.
5 From life discharg'd and parted quite
    Among the dead *to sleep,*
And like the slain *in bloody fight*
    That in the grave lie *deep.*
Whom thou rememberest no more,
    Dost never more regard,
Them from thy hand deliver'd o're
    Deaths hideous house hath barr'd.
6 Thou in the lowest pit *profound*
    Hast set me *all forlorn,*
Where thickest darkness *hovers round,*
    In horrid deeps *to mourn.*

* Heb. A man without manly strength.

7 Thy wrath *from which no shelter saves*
  Full sore doth press on me;
  *Thou break'st upon me all thy waves,
   *And all thy waves break me.

8 Thou dost my friends from me estrange,
  And mak'st me odious,
  Me to them odious, *for they change*,
  And I here pent up thus.

9 Through sorrow, and affliction great
  Mine eye grows dim and dead,
  Lord all the day I thee entreat,
  My hands to thee I spread.

10 Wilt thou do wonders on the dead,
   Shall the deceas'd arise
   And praise thee *from their loathsom bed*
   With pale and hollow eyes?

11 Shall they thy loving kindness tell
   On whom the grave *hath hold*,
   Or they *who* in perdition *dwell*
   Thy faithfulness *unfold?*

12 In darkness can thy mighty *hand*
   Or wondrous acts be known,
   Thy justice in the *gloomy* land
   Of *dark* oblivion?

13 But I to thee O Lord do cry
   E're yet my life be spent,
   And *up to thee* my praier *doth hie*
   Each morn, and thee prevent.

14 Why wilt thou Lord my soul forsake,
   And hide thy face from me,

15 That am already bruis'd, and †shake
   With terror sent from thee;
   Bruz'd, and afflicted and *so low*
   As ready to expire,
   While I thy terrors undergo
   Astonish'd with thine ire.

16 Thy fierce wrath over me doth flow
   Thy threatnings cut me through.

* The Heb. bears both.
† Heb. Præ Concussione.

17 All day they round about me go,
　　Like waves they me persue.
18 Lover and friend thou hast remov'd
　　And sever'd from me far.
　　They *fly me now* whom I have lov'd,
　　And as in darkness are.

¶ Seneca, *Herc. Fur.* 922

There can be slaine
No sacrifice to God more acceptable
Then an unjust and wicked King.

¶ Psal. I. *Done into Verse*, 1653

BLESS'D is the man who hath not walk'd astray
In counsel of the wicked, and ith' way
Of sinners hath not stood, and in the seat
Of scorners hath not sate. But in the great
Jehovah's Law is ever his delight,
And in his Law he studies day and night.
He shall be as a tree which planted grows
By watry streams, and in his season knows
To yield his fruit, and his leaf shall not fall,
And what he takes in hand shall prosper all.
Not so the wicked, but as chaff which fann'd
The wind drives, so the wicked shall not stand
In judgment, or abide their tryal then,
Nor sinners in th' assembly of just men.
For the Lord knows th' upright way of the just,
And the way of bad men to ruine must.

¶ Psal. II. *Done* Aug. 8. 1653. *Terzetti*

WHY do the Gentiles tumult, and the Nations
　　Muse a vain thing, the Kings of th' earth upstand
With power, and Princes in their Congregations
Lay deep their plots together through each Land,
　　Against the Lord and his Messiah dear.
Let us break off, say they, by strength of hand

Their bonds, and cast from us, no more to wear,
    Their twisted cords : he who in Heaven doth dwell
    Shall laugh, the Lord shall scoff them, then severe
Speak to them in his wrath, and in his fell
    And fierce ire trouble them ; but I saith hee
    Anointed have my King (though ye rebell)
On Sion my holi' hill. A firm decree
    I will declare ; the Lord to me hath say'd
    Thou art my Son I have begotten thee
This day ; ask of me, and the grant is made ;
    As thy possession I on thee bestow
    Th' Heathen, and as thy conquest to be sway'd
Earths utmost bounds : them shalt thou bring full low
    With Iron Scepter bruis'd, and them disperse
    Like to a potters vessel shiver'd so.
And now be wise at length ye Kings averse
    Be taught ye Judges of the earth ; with fear
    Jehovah serve, and let your joy converse
With trembling ; kiss the Son least he appear
    In anger and ye perish in the way
    If once his wrath take fire like fuel sere.
Happy all those who have in him their stay.

¶ Psal. III. Aug. 9. 1653

When he fled from Absalom

LORD how many are my foes
      How many those
    That in arms against me rise
      Many are they
That of my life distrustfully thus say,
No help for him in God there lies.
But thou Lord art my shield my glory,
      Thee through my story
    Th' exalter of my head I count
      Aloud I cry'd
Unto Jehovah, he full soon reply'd
And heard me from his holy mount.

I lay and slept, I wak'd again,
> For my sustain
> Was the Lord. Of many millions
> > The populous rout
I fear not though incamping round about
They pitch against me their Pavillions.
Rise Lord, save me my God for thou
> > Hast smote ere now
> On the cheek-bone all my foes,
> > Of men abhor'd
Hast broke the teeth. This help was from the Lord;
Thy blessing on thy people flows.

¶ Psal. IV. *Aug.* 10. 1653

ANSWER me when I call
God of my righteousness
In straights and in distress
Thou didst me disinthrall
And set at large; now spare,
> Now pity me, and hear my earnest prai'r.
Great ones how long will ye
My glory have in scorn
How long be thus forborn
Still to love vanity,
To love, to seek, to prize
> Things false and vain and nothing else but lies?
Yet know the Lord hath chose
Chose to himself a part
The good and meek of heart
(For whom to chuse he knows)
Jehovah from on high
> Will hear my voyce what time to him I crie.
Be aw'd, and do not sin,
Speak to your hearts alone,
Upon your beds, each one,
And be at peace within.
Offer the offerings just
> Of righteousness and in Jehovah trust.

Many there be that say
Who yet will shew us good?
Talking like this worlds brood;
But Lord, thus let me pray,
On us lift up the light
    Lift up the favour of thy count'nance bright.
Into my heart more joy
And gladness thou hast put
Then when a year of glut
Their stores doth over-cloy
And from their plenteous grounds
    With vast increase their corn and wine abounds
In peace at once will I
Both lay me down and sleep
For thou alone dost keep
Me safe where ere I lie
As in a rocky Cell
    Thou Lord alone in safety mak'st me dwell.

¶ Psal. V. *Aug.* 12. 1653

JEHOVAH to my words give ear
    My meditation waigh
The voyce of my complaining hear
My King and God for unto thee I pray.
    Jehovah thou my early voyce
        Shalt in the morning hear
    Ith' morning I to thee with choyce
Will rank my Prayers, and watch till thou appear.
    For thou art not a God that takes
        In wickedness delight
    Evil with thee no biding makes
Fools or mad men stand not within thy sight.
    All workers of iniquity
        Thou hat'st; and them unblest
    Thou wilt destroy that speak a ly
The bloodi' and guileful man God doth detest.
    But I will in thy mercies dear
        Thy numerous mercies go
    Into thy house; I in thy fear

Will towards thy holy temple worship low
    Lord lead me in thy righteousness
      Lead me because of those
    That do observe if I transgress,
Set thy wayes right before, where my step goes.
    For in his faltring mouth unstable
      No word is firm or sooth
    Their inside, troubles miserable;
An open grave their throat, their tongue they smooth.
    God, find them guilty, let them fall
      By their own counsels quell'd;
    Push them in their rebellions all
Still on; for against thee they have rebell'd;
    Then all who trust in thee shall bring
      Their joy, while thou from blame
    Defend'st them, they shall ever sing
And shall triumph in thee, who love thy name.
    For thou Jehovah wilt be found
      To bless the just man still,
    As with a shield thou wilt surround
Him with thy lasting favour and good will.

¶ Psal. VI. *Aug.* 13. 1653

LORD in thine anger do not reprehend me
    Nor in thy hot displeasure me correct;
Pity me Lord for I am much deject
    Am very weak and faint; heal and amend me,
For all my bones, that even with anguish ake,
    Are troubled, yea my soul is troubled sore
And thou O Lord how long? turn Lord, restore
    My soul, O save me for thy goodness sake
For in death no remembrance is of thee;
    Who in the grave can celebrate thy praise?
Wearied I am with sighing out my dayes,
    Nightly my Couch I make a kind of Sea;
My Bed I water with my tears; mine Eie
    Through grief consumes, is waxen old and dark
Ith' mid'st of all mine enemies that mark.
    Depart all ye that work iniquitie.

Depart from me, for the voice of my weeping
    The Lord hath heard, the Lord hath heard my prai'r
My supplication with acceptance fair
    The Lord will own, and have me in his keeping.
Mine enemies shall all be blank and dash't
    With much confusion; then grow red with shame,
They shall return in hast the way they came
    And in a moment shall be quite abash't.

¶ Psal. VII. *Aug.* 14. 1653

Upon the words of Chush *the* Benjamite *against him*

LORD my God to thee I flie
Save me and secure me under
Thy protection while I crie
Least as a Lion (and no wonder)
He hast to tear my Soul asunder
Tearing and no rescue nigh.

Lord my God if I have thought
Or done this, if wickedness
Be in my hands, if I have wrought
Ill to him that meant me peace,
Or to him have render'd less,
And not fre'd my foe for naught;

Let th' enemy pursue my soul
And overtake it, let him tread
My life down to the earth and roul
In the dust my glory dead,
In the dust and there out spread
Lodge it with dishonour foul.

Rise Jehovah in thine ire
Rouze thy self amidst the rage
Of my foes that urge like fire;
And wake for me, their furi' asswage;
Judgment here thou didst ingage
And command which I desire.

So th' assemblies of each Nation
Will surround thee, seeking right,

Thence to thy glorious habitation
Return on high and in their sight.
Jehovah judgeth most upright
All people from the worlds foundation.

Judge me Lord, be judge in this
According to my righteousness
And the innocence which is
Upon me : cause at length to cease
Of evil men the wickedness
And their power that do amiss.

But the just establish fast,
Since thou art the just God that tries
Hearts and reins. On God is cast
My defence, and in him lies
In him who both just and wise
Saves th' upright of Heart at last.

God is a just Judge and severe,
And God is every day offended ;
If th' unjust will not forbear,
His Sword he whets, his Bow hath bended
Already, and for him intended
The tools of death, that waits him near.

(His arrows purposely made he
For them that persecute.) Behold
He travels big with vanitie,
Trouble he hath conceav'd of old
As in a womb, and from that mould
Hath at length brought forth a Lie.

He dig'd a pit, and delv'd it deep,
And fell into the pit he made,
His mischief that due course doth keep,
Turns on his head, and his ill trade
Of violence will undelay'd
Fall on his crown with ruine steep.

Then will I Jehovah's praise
According to his justice raise
And sing the Name and Deitie
Of Jehovah the most high.

❡ Psal. VIII. *Aug.* 14. 1653

O JEHOVAH our Lord how wondrous great
 And glorious is thy name through all the earth?
So as above the Heavens thy praise to set
 Out of the tender mouths of latest bearth,

Out of the mouths of babes and sucklings thou
 Hast founded strength because of all thy foes
To stint th' enemy, and slack th' avengers brow
 That bends his rage thy providence to oppose.

When I behold thy Heavens, thy Fingers art,
 The Moon and Starrs which thou so bright hast set,
In the pure firmament, then saith my heart,
 O what is man that thou remembrest yet,

And think'st upon him; or of man begot
 That him thou visit'st and of him art found;
Scarce to be less then Gods, thou mad'st his lot,
 With honour and with state thou hast him crown'd.

O're the works of thy hand thou mad'st him Lord,
 Thou hast put all under his lordly feet,
All Flocks, and Herds, by thy commanding word,
 All beasts that in the field or forrest meet.

Fowl of the Heavens, and Fish that through the wet
 Sea-paths in shoals do slide. And know no dearth.
O Jehovah our Lord how wondrous great
 And glorious is thy name through all the earth.

❡ The Fifth Ode of *Horace*. Lib. I

Quis multa gracilis te puer in Rosa, *Rendred almost word for word without Rhyme according to the Latin Measure, as near as the Language will permit.*

Horatius ex Pyrrhae illecebris tanquam e naufragio enataverat, cujus amore irretitos affirmat esse miseros.

 WHAT slender Youth bedew'd with liquid odours
 Courts thee on Roses in some pleasant Cave,

Pyrrha for whom bindst thou
    In wreaths thy golden Hair,
Plain in thy neatness; O how oft shall he
On Faith and changed Gods complain: and Seas
    Rough with black winds and storms
    Unwonted shall admire:
Who now enjoyes thee credulous, all Gold,
Who alwayes vacant, alwayes amiable
    Hopes thee; of flattering gales
    Unmindfull. Hapless they
To whom thou untry'd seem'st fair. Me in my vow'd
Picture the sacred wall declares t' have hung
    My dank and dropping weeds
    To the stern God of Sea.

¶ *Geoffrey* of *Monmouth*

Consultation had, *Brutus* taking with him *Gerion* his Diviner, and twelv of the ancientest, with wonted Ceremonies before the inward shrine of the Goddess, in Verse, as it seems the manner was, utters his request,

    Goddess of Shades, and Huntress, who at will
    Walk'st on the rowling Sphear, and through the deep,
    On thy third Reigne the Earth look now, and tell
    What Land, what Seat of rest thou bidst me seek,
    What certain Seat, where I may worship thee
    For aye, with Temples vow'd, and Virgin quires.

To whom sleeping before the Altar, *Diana* in a Vision
        that night thus answer'd,

    Brutus far to the West, in th' Ocean wide
    Beyond the Realm of *Gaul*, a Land there lies,
    Sea-girt it lies, where Giants dwelt of old,
    Now void, it fitts thy People; thether bend
    Thy course, there shalt thou find a lasting seat,
    There to thy Sons another *Troy* shall rise,
    And *Kings* be born of thee, whose dreaded might
    Shall aw the World, and Conquer Nations bold.

Latin,
Greek, and Italian
Poems

꙳

Latin, Greek and Italian Poems

¶ Elegia prima

ad *Carolum Diodatum*

TANDEM, chare, tuæ mihi pervenere tabellæ,
  Pertulit et voces nuncia charta tuas,
Pertulit occiduâ Devæ Cestrensis ab orâ
  Vergivium prono quà petit amne salum.
Multùm crede juvat terras aluisse remotas
  Pectus amans nostri, tamque fidele caput,
Quòdque mihi lepidum tellus longinqua sodalem
  Debet, at unde brevi reddere jussa velit.
Me tenet urbs refluâ quam Thamesis alluit undâ,
  Meque nec invitum patria dulcis habet.
Jam nec arundiferum mihi cura revisere Camum,
  Nec dudum vetiti me laris angit amor.
Nuda nec arva placent, umbrasque negantia molles,
  Quàm male Phœbicolis convenit ille locus!
Nec duri libet usque minas perferre Magistri
  Cæteraque ingenio non subeunda meo.
Si sit hoc exilium patrios adiisse penates,
  Et vacuum curis otia grata sequi,
Non ego vel profugi nomen, sortemve recuso,
  Lætus et exilii conditione fruor.
O utinam vates nunquam graviora tulisset
  Ille Tomitano flebilis exul agro ;
Non tunc Ionio quicquam cessisset Homero
  Neve foret victo laus tibi prima Maro.
Tempora nam licet hîc placidis dare libera Musis,
  Et totum rapiunt me mea vita libri.
Excipit hinc fessum sinuosi pompa theatri,
  Et vocat ad plausus garrula scena suos.
Seu catus auditur senior, seu prodigus hæres,
  Seu procus, aut positâ casside miles adest,

Sive decennali fœcundus lite patronus
    Detonat inculto barbara verba foro,
Sæpe vafer gnato succurrit servus amanti,
    Et nasum rigidi fallit ubique patris;
Sæpe novos illic virgo mirata calores
    Quid sit amor nescit, dum quoque nescit, amat.
Sive cruentatum furiosa Tragœdia sceptrum
    Quassat, et effusis crinibus ora rotat,
Et dolet, et specto, juvat et spectasse dolendo,
    Interdum et lacrymis dulcis amaror inest:
Seu puer infelix indelibata reliquit
    Gaudia, et abrupto flendus amore cadit,
Seu ferus è tenebris iterat Styga criminis ultor
    Conscia funereo pectora torre movens,
Seu mæret Pelopeia domus, seu nobilis Ili,
    Aut luit incestos aula Creontis avos.
Sed neque sub tecto semper nec in urbe latemus,
    Irrita nec nobis tempora veris eunt.
Nos quoque lucus habet vicinâ consitus ulmo
    Atque suburbani nobilis umbra loci.
Sæpius hic blandas spirantia sydera flammas
    Virgineos videas præteriisse choros.
Ah quoties dignæ stupui miracula formæ
    Quæ possit senium vel reparare Jovis;
Ah quoties vidi superantia lumina gemmas,
    Atque faces quotquot volvit uterque polus;
Collaque bis vivi Pelopis quæ brachia vincant,
    Quæque fluit puro nectare tincta Via,
Et decus eximium frontis, tremulosque capillos,
    Aurea quæ fallax retia tendit Amor.
Pellacesque genas, ad quas hyacinthina sordet
    Purpura, et ipse tui floris, Adoni, rubor.
Cedite laudatæ toties Heroides olim,
    Et quæcunque vagum cepit amica Jovem.
Cedite Achæmeniæ turritâ fronte puellæ,
    Et quot Susa colunt, Memnoniamque Ninon.
Vos etiam Danaæ fasces submittite Nymphæ,
    Et vos Iliacæ, Romuleæque nurus.
Nec Pompeianas Tarpëia Musa columnas
    Jactet, et Ausoniis plena theatra stolis.

Gloria virginibus debetur prima Britannis,
    Extera sat tibi sit fœmina posse sequi.
Tuque urbs Dardaniis Londinum structa colonis
    Turrigerum latè conspicienda caput,
Tu nimium felix intra tua mœnia claudis
    Quicquid formosi pendulus orbis habet.
Non tibi tot cælo scintillant astra sereno
    Endymioneæ turba ministra deæ,
Quot tibi conspicuæ formáque auróque puellæ
    Per medias radiant turba videnda vias.
Creditur huc geminis venisse invecta columbis
    Alma pharetrigero milite cincta Venus,
Huic Cnidon, et riguas Simoentis flumine valles,
    Huic Paphon, et roseam posthabitura Cypron.
Ast ego, dum pueri sinit indulgentia cæci,
    Mœnia quàm subitò linquere fausta paro;
Et vitare procul malefidæ infamia Circes
    Atria, divini molyos usus ope.
Stat quoque juncosas Cami remeare paludes,
    Atque iterum raucæ murmur adire Scholæ.
Interea fidi parvum cape munus amici,
    Paucaque in alternos verba coacta modos.

ANNO ÆTATIS 17

¶ Elegia tertia

In obitum Præsulis Wintoniensis

Mœstus eram, et tacitus nullo comitante sedebam,
    Hærebantque animo tristia plura meo,
Protinus en subiit funestæ cladis Imago
    Fecit in Angliaco quam Libitina solo;
Dum procerum ingressa est splendentes marmore turres
    Dira sepulchrali Mors metuenda face;
Pulsavitque auro gravidos et jaspide muros,
    Nec metuit satrapum sternere falce greges.
Tunc memini clarique ducis, fratrisque verendi
    Intempestivis ossa cremata rogis.

Et memini Heroum quos vidit ad æthera raptos,
    Flevit et amissos Belgia tota duces.
At te præcipuè luxi dignissime Præsul,
    Wintoniæque olim gloria magna tuæ;
Delicui fletu, et tristi sic ore querebar,
    Mors fera Tartareo diva secunda Jovi,
Nonne satis quod sylva tuas persentiat iras,
    Et quod in herbosos jus tibi detur agros,
Quodque afflata tuo marcescant lilia tabo,
    Et crocus, et pulchræ Cypridi sacra rosa,
Nec sinis ut semper fluvio contermina quercus
    Miretur lapsus prætereuntis aquæ?
Et tibi succumbit liquido quæ plurima cœlo
    Evehitur pennis quamlibet augur avis,
Et quæ mille nigris errant animalia sylvis,
    Et quod alunt mutum Proteos antra pecus,
Invida, tanta tibi cum sit concessa potestas,
    Quid juvat humanâ tingere cæde manus?
Nobileque in pectus certas acuisse sagittas,
    Semideamque animam sede fugâsse suâ?
Talia dum lacrymans alto sub pectore volvo,
    Roscidus occiduis Hesperus exit aquis,
Et Tartessiaco submerserat æquore currum
    Phœbus, ab Eöo littore mensus iter.
Nec mora, membra cavo posui refovenda cubili,
    Condiderant oculos noxque soporque meos.
Cum mihi visus eram lato spatiarier agro,
    Heu nequit ingenium visa referre meum.
Illic puniceâ radiabant omnia luce,
    Ut matutino cum juga sole rubent.
Ac veluti cum pandit opes Thaumantia proles,
    Vestitu nituit multicolore solum.
Non dea tam variis ornavit floribus hortos
    Alcinoi, Zephyro Chloris amata levi.
Flumina vernantes lambunt argentea campos,
    Ditior Hesperio flavet arena Tago.
Serpit odoriferas per opes levis aura Favoni,
    Aura sub innumeris humida nata rosis.
Talis in extremis terræ Gangetidis oris
    Luciferi regis fingitur esse domus.

Ipse racemiferis dum densas vitibus umbras
    Et pellucentes miror ubique locos,
Ecce mihi subito Præsul Wintonius astat,
    Sydereum nitido fulsit in ore jubar;
Vestis ad auratos defluxit candida talos,
    Infula divinum cinxerat alba caput.
Dumque senex tali incedit venerandus amictu,
    Intremuit læto florea terra sono.
Agmina gemmatis plaudunt cælestia pennis,
    Pura triumphali personat æthra tubâ.
Quisque novum amplexu comitem cantuque salutat,
    Hosque aliquis placido misit ab ore sonos;
Nate veni, et patrii felix cape gaudia regni,
    Semper ab hinc duro, nate, labore vaca.
Dixit, et aligeræ tetigerunt nablia turmæ,
    At mihi cum tenebris aurea pulsa quies.
Flebam turbatos Cephaleiâ pellice somnos,
    Talia contingant somnia sæpe mihi.

ANNO ÆTATIS 17

¶ In obitum Præsulis Eliensis

Adhuc madentes rore squalebant genæ,
    Et sicca nondum lumina;
Adhuc liquentis imbre turgebant salis,
    Quem nuper effudi pius,
Dum mœsta charo justa persolvi rogo
    Wintoniensis Præsulis.
Cum centilinguis Fama (proh semper mali
    Cladisque vera nuntia)
Spargit per urbes divitis Britanniæ,
    Populosque Neptuno satos,
Cessisse morti, et ferreis sororibus
    Te generis humani decus,
Qui rex sacrorum illâ fuisti in insulâ
    Quæ nomen Anguillæ tenet.
Tunc inquietum pectus irâ protinus
    Ebulliebat fervidâ

Tumulis potentem sæpe devovens deam:
　　Nec vota Naso in Ibida
Concepit alto diriora pectore,
　　Graiusque vates parciùs
Turpem Lycambis execratus est dolum,
　　Sponsamque Neobolen suam.
At ecce diras ipse dum fundo graves,
　　Et imprecor Neci necem,
Audisse tales videor attonitus sonos
　　Leni, sub aurâ, flamine:
Cæcos furores pone, pone vitream
　　Bilemque et irritas minas,
Quid temerè violas non nocenda numina,
　　Subitoque ad iras percita.
Non est, ut arbitraris elusus miser,
　　Mors atra Noctis filia,
Erebóve patre creta, sive Erinnye,
　　Vastóve nata sub Chao:
Ast illa cælo missa stellato, Dei
　　Messes ubique colligit;
Animasque mole carneâ reconditas
　　In lucem et auras evocat:
Ut cum fugaces excitant Horæ diem
　　Themidos Jovisque filiæ;
Et sempiterni ducit ad vultus Patris;
　　At justa raptat impios
Sub regna furvi luctuosa Tartari,
　　Sedesque subterraneas
Hanc ut vocantem lætus audivi, citò
　　Fœdum reliqui carcerem,
Volatilesque faustus inter milites
　　Ad astra sublimis feror:
Vates ut olim raptus ad cœlum senex
　　Auriga currus ignei,
Non me Boötis terruere lucidi
　　Sarraca tarda frigore, aut
Formidolosi Scorpionis brachia,
　　Non ensis Orion tuus.
Prætervolavi fulgidi solis globum,
　　Longéque sub pedibus deam

Vidi triformem, dum coercebat suos
    Frænis dracones aureis.
Erraticorum syderum per ordines,
    Per lacteas vehor plagas,
Velocitatem sæpe miratus novam,
    Donec nitentes ad fores
Ventum est Olympi, et regiam crystallinam, et
    Stratum smaragdis Atrium.
Sed hic tacebo, nam quis effari queat
    Oriundus humano patre
Amœnitates illius loci, mihi
    Sat est in æternum frui.

ANNO ÆTATIS **17**

¶ Elegia secunda

In obitum Præconis Academici Cantabrigiensis

TE, qui conspicuus baculo fulgente solebas
    Palladium toties ore ciere gregem,
Ultima præconum præconem te quoque sæva
    Mors rapit, officio nec favet ipsa suo.
Candidiora licet fuerint tibi tempora plumis
    Sub quibus accipimus delituisse Jovem,
O dignus tamen Hæmonio juvenescere succo,
    Dignus in Æsonios vivere posse dies,
Dignus quem Stygiis medicâ revocaret ab undis
    Arte Coronides, sæpe rogante dea.
Tu si jussus eras acies accire togatas,
    Et celer à Phoebo nuntius ire tuo,
Talis in Iliacâ stabat Cyllenius aula
    Alipes, æthereâ missus ab arce Patris.
Talis et Eurybates ante ora furentis Achillei
    Rettulit Atridæ jussa severa ducis.
Magna sepulchrorum regina, satelles Averni
    Sæva nimis Musis, Palladi sæva nimis,
Quin illos rapias qui pondus inutile terræ,
    Turba quidem est telis ista petenda tuis.

Vestibus hunc igitur pullis Academia luge,
  Et madeant lachrymis nigra feretra tuis.
Fundat et ipsa modos querebunda Elegëia tristes,
  Personet et totis nænia mœsta scholis.

ANNO ÆTATIS 16

¶ In obitum Procancellarii medici

PARERE Fati discite legibus,
Manusque Parcæ jam date supplices,
    Qui pendulum telluris orbem
      Iäpeti colitis nepotes.
Vos si relicto mors vaga Tænaro
Semel vocârit flebilis, heu moræ
    Tentantur incassùm dolique;
      Per tenebras Stygis ire certum est.
Si destinatam pellere dextera
Mortem valeret, non ferus Hercules
    Nessi venenatus cruore
      Æmathiâ jacuisset Œtâ.
Nec fraude turpi Palladis invidæ
Vidisset occisum Ilion Hectora, aut
    Quem larva Pelidis peremit
      Ense Locro, Jove lacrymante.
Si triste fatum verba Hecatëia
Fugare possint, Telegoni parens
    Vixisset infamis, potentique
      Ægiali soror usa virgâ.
Numenque trinum fallere si queant
Artes medentûm, ignotaque gramina,
    Non gnarus herbarum Machaon
      Eurypyli cecidisset hastâ.
Læsisset et nec te Philyreie
Sagitta echidnæ perlita sanguine,
    Nec tela te fulmenque avitum
      Cæse puer genitricis alvo.
Tuque O alumno major Apolline,
Gentis togatæ cui regimen datum,

Frondosa quem nunc Cirrha luget,
　Et mediis Helicon in undis,
　　Jam præfuisses Palladio gregi
Lætus, superstes, nec sine gloria,
　Nec puppe lustrasses Charontis
　　Horribiles barathri recessus.
At fila rupit Persephone tua
Irata, cum te viderit artibus
　Succoque pollenti tot atris
　　Faucibus eripuisse Mortis.
Colende Præses, membra precor tua
Molli quiescant cespite, et ex tuo
　Crescant rosæ, calthæque busto,
　　Purpureoque hyacinthus ore.
Sit mite de te judicium Æaci,
Subrideatque Ætnæa Proserpina,
　Interque felices perennis
　　Elysio spatiere campo.

ANNO ÆTATIS 17

¶ In quintum Novembris

JAM pius extremâ veniens Iäcobus ab arcto
Teucrigenas populos, latéque patentia regna
Albionum tenuit, jamque inviolabile fœdus
Sceptra Caledoniis conjunxerat Anglica Scotis:
Pacificusque novo felix divesque sedebat
In solio, occultique doli securus et hostis:
Cum ferus ignifluo regnans Acheronte tyrannus,
Eumenidum pater, æthereo vagus exul Olympo,
Forte per immensum terrarum erraverat orbem,
Dinumerans sceleris socios, vernasque fideles,
Participes regni post funera mœsta futuros.
Hic tempestates medio ciet aëre diras,
Illic unanimes odium struit inter amicos,
Armat et invictas in mutua viscera gentes;
Regnaque olivifera vertit florentia pace,
Et quoscunque videt puræ virtutis amantes,

Hos cupit adjicere imperio, fraudumque magister
Tentat inaccessum sceleri corrumpere pectus,
Insidiasque locat tacitas, cassesque latentes
Tendit, ut incautos rapiat, seu Caspia Tigris
Insequitur trepidam deserta per avia prædam
Nocte sub illuni, et somno nictantibus astris.
Talibus infestat populos Summanus et urbes
Cinctus cæruleæ fumanti turbine flammæ.
Jamque fluentisonis albentia rupibus arva
Apparent, et terra Deo dilecta marino,
Cui nomen dederat quondam Neptunia proles
Amphitryoniaden qui non dubitavit atrocem
Æquore tranato furiali poscere bello,
Ante expugnatæ crudelia sæcula Troiæ.
  At simul hanc opibusque et festâ pace beatam
Aspicit, et pingues donis Cerealibus agros,
Quodque magis doluit, venerantem numina veri
Sancta Dei populum, tandem suspiria rupit
Tartareos ignes et luridum olentia sulphur,
Qualia Trinacriâ trux ab Jove clausus in Ætna
Efflat tabifico monstrosus ab ore Tiphœus.
Ignescunt oculi, stridetque adamantinus ordo
Dentis, ut armorum fragor, ictaque cuspide cuspis;
Atque pererrato solum hoc lacrymabile mundo
Inveni, dixit, gens haec mihi sola rebellis,
Contemtrixque jugi, nostrâque potentior arte.
Illa tamen, mea si quicquam tentamina possunt,
Non feret hoc impune diu, non ibit inulta,
Hactenus; et piceis liquido natat aëre pennis;
Quà volat, adversi præcursant agmine venti,
Densantur nubes, et crebra tonitrua fulgent.
  Jamque pruinosas velox superaverat Alpes,
Et tenet Ausoniæ fines, à parte sinistrâ
Nimbifer Appenninus erat, priscique Sabini,
Dextra veneficiis infamis Hetruria, nec non
Te furtiva Tibris Thetidi videt oscula dantem;
Hinc Mavortigenæ consistit in arce Quirini.
Reddiderant dubiam jam sera crepuscula lucem,
Cum circumgreditur totam Tricoronifer urbem,
Panificosque Deos portat, scapulisque virorum

Evehitur, præeunt submisso poplite reges,
Et mendicantum series longissima fratrum;
Cereaque in manibus gestant funalia cæci,
Cimmeriis nati in tenebris, vitamque trahentes.
Templa dein multis subeunt lucentia tædis
(Vesper erat sacer iste Petro) fremitusque canentum
Sæpe tholos implet vacuos, et inane locorum.
Qualiter exululat Bromius, Bromiique caterva,
Orgia cantantes in Echionio Aracyntho,
Dum tremit attonitus vitreis Asopus in undis,
Et procul ipse cavâ responsat rupe Cithæron.

   His igitur tandem solenni more peractis,
Nox senis amplexus Erebi taciturna reliquit,
Præcipitesque impellit equos stimulante flagello,
Captum oculis Typhlonta, Melanchætemque ferocem,
Atque Acherontæo prognatam patre Siopen
Torpidam, et hirsutis horrentem Phrica capillis.
Interéa regum domitor, Phlegetontius hæres,
Ingreditur thalamos (neque enim secretus adulter
Producit steriles molli sine pellice noctes);
At vix compositos somnus claudebat ocellos,
Cum niger umbrarum dominus, rectorque silentum,
Prædatorque hominum falsâ sub imagine tectus
Astitit, assumptis micuerunt tempora canis,
Barba sinus promissa tegit, cineracea longo
Syrmate verrit humum vestis, pendetque cucullus
Vertice de raso, et ne quicquam desit ad artes,
Cannabeo lumbos constrinxit fune salaces,
Tarda fenestratis figens vestigia calceis.
Talis uti fama est, vastâ Franciscus eremo
Tetra vagabatur solus per lustra ferarum,
Sylvestrique tulit genti pia verba salutis
Impius, atque lupos domuit, Libycosque leones.

   Subdolus at tali Serpens velatus amictu,
Solvit in has fallax ora execrantia voces;
Dormis nate? Etiamne tuos sopor opprimit artus
Immemor O fidei, pecorumque oblite tuorum,
Dum cathedram venerande tuam, diademaque triplex
Ridet Hyperboreo gens barbara nata sub axe,
Dumque pharetrati spernunt tua jura Britanni.

Surge, age, surge piger, Latius quem Cæsar adorat,
Cui reserata patet convexi janua cæli,
Turgentes animos, et fastus frange procaces,
Sacrilegique sciant, tua quid maledictio possit,
Et quid Apostolicæ possit custodia clavis ;
Et memor Hesperiæ disjectam ulciscere classem,
Mersaque Iberorum lato vexilla profundo,
Sanctorumque cruci tot corpora fixa probrosæ,
Thermodoontéa nuper regnante puella.
At tu si tenero mavis torpescere lecto
Crescentesque negas hosti contundere vires,
Tyrrhenum implebit numeroso milite pontum,
Signaque Aventino ponet fulgentia colle :
Relliquias veterum franget, flammisque cremabit,
Sacraque calcabit pedibus tua colla profanis,
Cujus gaudebant soleis dare basia reges.
Nec tamen hunc bellis et aperto Marte lacesses ;
Irritus ille labor, tu callidus utere fraude,
Quælibet hæreticis disponere retia fas est ;
Jamque ad consilium extremis rex magnus ab oris
Patricios vocat, et procerum de stirpe creatos,
Grandævosque patres trabeâ, canisque verendos ;
Hos tu membratim poteris conspergere in auras,
Atque dare in cineres, nitrati pulveris igne
Ædibus injecto, quà convenere, sub imis.
Protinus ipse igitur quoscumque habet Anglia fidos
Propositi, factique mone, quisquámne tuorum
Audebit summi non jussa facessere Papæ?
Perculsosque metu subito, casumque stupentes
Invadat vel Gallus atrox, vel sævus Iberus.
Sæcula sic illic tandem Mariana redibunt,
Tuque in belligeros iterum dominaberis Anglos.
Et nequid timeas, divos divasque secundas
Accipe, quotque tuis celebrantur numina fastis.
Dixit et adscitos ponens malefidus amictus,
Fugit ad infandam, regnum illætabile, Lethen.

    Jam rosea Eoas pandens Tithonia portas
Vestit inauratas redeunti lumine terras ;
Mæstaque adhuc nigri deplorans funera nati
Irrigat ambrosiis montana cacumina guttis ;

Cum somnos pepulit stellatæ janitor aulæ
Nocturnos visus, et somnia grata revolvens.
   Est locus æternâ septus caligine noctis
Vasta ruinosi quondam fundamina tecti,
Nunc torvi spelunca Phoni, Prodotæque bilinguis
Effera quos uno peperit Discordia partu.
Hic inter cæmenta jacent præruptaque saxa,
Ossa inhumata virûm, et trajecta cadavera ferro ;
Hic Dolus intortis semper sedet ater ocellis,
Jurgiaque, et stimulis armata Calumnia fauces,
Et Furor, atque viæ moriendi mille videntur,
Et Timor, exanguisque locum circumvolat Horror,
Perpetuoque leves per muta silentia Manes,
Exululant, tellus et sanguine conscia stagnat.
Ipsi etiam pavidi latitant penetralibus antri
Et Phonos, et Prodotes, nulloque sequente per antrum
Antrum horrens, scopulosum, atrum feralibus umbris
Diffugiunt sontes, et retrò lumina vortunt,
Hos pugiles Romæ per sæcula longa fideles
Evocat antistes Babylonius, atque ita fatur :
Finibus occiduis circumfusum incolit æquor
Gens exosa mihi, prudens Natura negavit
Indignam penitùs nostro conjungere mundo :
Illuc, sic jubeo, celeri contendite gressu,
Tartareoque leves difflentur pulvere in auras
Et rex et pariter satrapæ, scelerata propago
Et quotquot fidei caluere cupidine veræ
Consilii socios adhibete, operisque ministros.
Finierat, rigidi cupidè paruere gemelli.
   Interea longo flectens curvamine cœlos
Despicit æthereâ dominus qui fulgurat arce,
Vanaque perversæ ridet conamina turbæ,
Atque sui causam populi volet ipse tueri.
   Esse ferunt spatium, quà distat ab Aside terra
Fertilis Europe, et spectat Mareotidas undas ;
Hic turris posita est Titanidos ardua Famæ
Ærea, lata, sonans, rutilis vicinior astris
Quàm superimpositum vel Athos vel Pelion Ossæ.
Mille fores aditusque patent, totidemque fenestræ,
Amplaque per tenues translucent atria muros ;

Excitat hic varios plebs agglomerata susurros;
Qualiter instrepitant circum mulctralia bombis
Agmina muscarum, aut texto per ovilia junco,
Dum Canis æstivum cœli petit ardua culmen.
Ipsa quidem summâ sedet ultrix matris in arce,
Auribus innumeris cinctum caput eminet olli,
Queis sonitum exiguum trahit, atque levissima captat
Murmura, ab extremis patuli confinibus orbis.
Nec tot Aristoride servator inique juvencæ
Isidos, immiti volvebas lumina vultu,
Lumina non unquam tacito nutantia somno,
Lumina subjectas late spectantia terras.
Istis illa solet loca luce carentia sæpe
Perlustrare, etiam radianti impervia soli;
Millenisque loquax auditaque visaque linguis
Cuilibet effundit temeraria, veráque mendax
Nunc minuit, modò confictis sermonibus auget.
Sed tamen a nostro meruisti carmine laudes
Fama, bonum quo non aliud veracius ullum,
Nobis digna cani, nec te memorasse pigebit
Carmine tam longo; servati scilicet Angli
Officiis vaga diva tuis, tibi reddimus æqua.
Te Deus æternos motu qui temperat ignes,
Fulmine præmisso alloquitur, terrâque tremente:
Fama siles? an te latet impia Papistarum
Conjurata cohors in meque meosque Britannos,
Et nova sceptrigero cædes meditata Iäcobo?
Nec plura, illa statim sensit mandata Tonantis,
Et satis antè fugax stridentes induit alas,
Induit et variis exilia corpora plumis;
Dextra tubam gestat Temesæo ex ære sonoram.
Nec mora, jam pennis cedentes remigat auras,
Atque parum est cursu celeres prævertere nubes,
Jam ventos, jam solis equos post terga reliquit:
Et primò Angliacas solito de more per urbes
Ambiguas voces, incertaque murmura spargit,
Mox arguta dolos, et detestabile vulgat
Proditionis opus, nec non facta horrida dictu
Authoresque addit sceleris, nec garrula cæcis
Insidiis loca structa silet; stupuere relatis,

Et pariter juvenes, pariter tremuere puellæ,
Effætique senes pariter, tantæque ruinæ
Sensus ad ætatem subitò penetraverat omnem.
Attamen interea populi miserescit ab alto
Æthereus pater, et crudelibus obstitit ausis
Papicolûm; capti pœnas raptantur ad acres;
At pia thura Deo, et grati solvuntur honores;
Compita læta focis genialibus omnia fumant;
Turba choros juvenilis agit: Quintoque Novembris
Nulla Dies toto occurrit celebratior anno.

¶ *In Proditionem Bombardicam*

CUM simul in regem nuper satrapasque Britannos
    Ausus es infandum perfide Fauxe nefas,
Fallor? an et mitis voluisti ex parte videri,
    Et pensare malâ cum pietate scelus?
Scilicet hos alti missurus ad atria cæli,
    Sulphureo curru flammivolisque rotis.
Qualiter ille feris caput inviolabile Parcis
    Liquit Iördanios turbine raptus agros.

¶ *In eandem*

SICCINE tentasti cælo donâsse Iäcobum
    Quae septemgemino Bellua monte lates?
Ni meliora tuum poterit dare munera numen,
    Parce precor donis insidiosa tuis.
Ille quidem sine te consortia serus adivit
    Astra, nec inferni pulveris usus ope.
Sic potiùs fœdos in cælum pelle cucullos,
    Et quot habet brutos Roma profana Deos.
Namque hac aut aliâ nisi quemque adjuveris arte,
    Crede mihi cæli vix bene scandet iter.

¶ *In eandem*

PURGATOREM animæ derisit Iäcobus ignem,
    Et sine quo superûm non adeunda domus.

Frenduit hoc trinâ monstrum Latiale coronâ
  Movit et horrificùm cornua dena minax.
Et Nec inultus, ait, temnes mea sacra Britanne,
  Supplicium spretâ relligione dabis.
Et si stelligeras unquam penetraveris arces,
  Non nisi per flammas triste patebit iter.
O quàm funesto cecinisti proxima vero,
  Verbaque ponderibus vix caritura suis!
Nam prope Tartareo sublime rotatus ab igni
  Ibat ad æthereas umbra perusta plagas.

¶ *In eandem*

QUEM modò Roma suis devoverat impia diris,
  Et Styge damnârat Tænarioque sinu,
Hunc vice mutatâ jam tollere gestit ad astra,
  Et cupit ad superos evehere usque Deos.

¶ *In inventorem Bombardæ*

IAPETIONIDEM laudavit cæca vetustas,
  Qui tulit ætheream solis ab axe facem;
At mihi major erit, qui lurida creditur arma,
  Et trifidum fulmen surripuisse Jovi.

ANNO ÆTATIS 18

¶ Elegia quarta

*Ad Thomam Junium præceptorem suum apud mercatores
Anglicos Hamburgæ agentes Pastoris munere fungentem*

CURRE per immensum subitò mea littera pontum,
  I, pete Teutonicos læve per æquor agros;
Segnes rumpe moras, et nil, precor, obstet eunti,
  Et festinantis nil remoretur iter.
Ipse ego Sicanio frænantem carcere ventos
  Æolon, et virides sollicitabo Deos,

Cæruleamque suis comitatam Dorída Nymphis,
    Ut tibi dent placidam per sua regna viam.
At tu, si poteris, celeres tibi sume jugales,
    Vecta quibus Colchis fugit ab ore viri,
Aut queis Triptolemus Scythicas devenit in oras
    Gratus Eleusinâ missus ab urbe puer.
Atque ubi Germanas flavere videbis arenas
    Ditis ad Hamburgæ mœnia flecte gradum,
Dicitur occiso quæ ducere nomen ab Hamâ,
    Cimbrica quem fertur clava dedisse neci,
Vivit ibi antiquæ clarus pietatis honore
    Præsul Christicolas pascere doctus oves ;
Ille quidem est animæ plusquam pars altera nostræ,
    Dimidio vitæ vivere cogor ego.
Hei mihi quot pelagi, quot montes interjecti
    Me faciunt aliâ parte carere mei!
Charior ille mihi quam tu, doctissime Graium,
    Cliniadi, pronepos qui Telamonis erat.
Quámque Stagirites generoso magnus alumno,
    Quem peperit Libyco Chaonis alma Jovi.
Qualis Amyntorides, qualis Philyrëius Heros
    Myrmidonum regi, talis et ille mihi.
Primus ego Aonios illo præeunte recessus
    Lustrabam, et bifidi sacra vireta jugi,
Pieriosque hausi latices, Clioque favente,
    Castalio sparsi læta ter ora mero.
Flammeus at signum ter viderat arietis Æthon
    Induxitque auro lanea terga novo,
Bisque novo terram sparsisti Chlori senilem
    Gramine, bisque tuas abstulit Auster opes :
Necdum ejus licuit mihi lumina pascere vultu,
    Aut linguæ dulces aure bibisse sonos.
Vade igitur, cursuque Eurum præverte sonorum,
    Quàm sit opus monitis res docet, ipsa vides.
Invenies dulci cum conjuge forte sedentem,
    Mulcentem gremio pignora chara suo,
Forsitan aut veterum prælarga volumina Patrum
    Versantem, aut veri biblia sacra Dei.
Cælestive animas saturantem rore tenellas,
    Grande salutiferæ religionis opus.

Utque solet, multam, sit dicere cura salutem,
   Dicere quam decuit, si modo adesset, herum.
Hæc quoque paulum oculos in humum defixa **modestos,**
   Verba verecundo sis memor ore loqui :
Hæc tibi, si teneris vacat inter prælia Musis
   Mittit ab Angliaco littore fida manus.
Accipe sinceram, quamvis sit sera, salutem ;
   Fiat et hoc ipso gratior illa tibi.
Sera quidem, sed vera fuit, quam casta recepit
   Icaris a lento Penelopeia viro.
Ast ego quid volui manifestum tollere crimen,
   Ipse quod ex omni parte levare nequit?
Arguitur tardus meritò, noxamque fatetur,
   Et pudet officium deseruisse suum.
Tu modò da veniam fasso, veniamque roganti,
   Crimina diminui, quæ patuere, solent.
Non ferus in pavidos rictus diducit hiantes,
   Vulnifico pronos nec rapit ungue leo.
Sæpe sarissiferi crudelia pectora Thracis
   Supplicis ad mœstas delicuere preces,
Extensæque manus avertunt fulminis ictus,
   Placat et iratos hostia parva Deos.
Jamque diu scripsisse tibi fuit impetus illi,
   Neve moras ultra ducere passus Amor.
Nam vaga Fama refert, heu nuntia vera malorum!
   In tibi finitimis bella tumere locis.
Teque tuàmque urbem truculento milite cingi,
   Et jam Saxonicos arma parasse duces.
Te circum latè campos populatur Enyo,
   Et sata carne virûm jam cruor arva rigat.
Germanisque suum concessit Thracia Martem,
   Illuc Odrysios Mars pater egit equos,
Perpetuóque comans jam deflorescit oliva,
   Fugit et ærisonam Diva perosa tubam,
Fugit, io! terris, et jam non ultima Virgo
   Creditur ad superas justa volasse domos.
Te tamen intereà belli circumsonat horror,
   Vivis et igncto solus inópsque solo ;
Et, tibi quam patrii non exhibuere penates
   Sede peregrinâ quæris egenus opem.

Patria dura parens, et saxis sævior albis
    Spumea quæ pulsat littoris unda tui,
Siccine te decet innocuos exponere fætus;
    Siccine in externam ferrea cogis humum,
Et sinis ut terris quærant alimenta remotis
    Quos tibi prospiciens miserat ipse Deus,
Et qui læta ferunt de cælo nuntia, quique
    Quæ via post cineres ducat ad astra, docent?
Digna quidem Stygiis quæ vivas clausa tenebris,
    Æternâque animæ digna perire fame!
Haud aliter vates terræ Thesbitidis olim
    Pressit inassueto devia tesqua pede,
Desertasque Arabum salebras, dum regis Achabi
    Effugit atque tuas, Sidoni dira, manus.
Talis et horrisono laceratus membra flagello,
    Paulus ab Æmathiâ pellitur urbe Cilix.
Piscosæque ipsum Gergessæ civis Iesum
    Finibus ingratus jussit abire suis.
At tu sume animos, nec spes cadat anxia curis,
    Nec tua concutiat decolor ossa metus.
Sis etenim quamvis fulgentibus obsitus armis,
    Intententque tibi millia tela necem,
At nullis vel inerme latus violabitur armis,
    Deque tuo cuspis nulla cruore bibet.
Namque eris ipse Dei radiante sub ægide tutus,
    Ille tibi custos, et pugil ille tibi;
Ille Sionææ qui tot sub mœnibus arcis
    Assyrios fudit nocte silente viros;
Inque fugam vertit quos in Samaritidas oras
    Misit ab antiquis prisca Damascus agris,
Terruit et densas pavido cum rege cohortes,
    Aere dum vacuo buccina clara sonat,
Cornea pulvereum dum verberat ungula campum,
    Currus arenosam dum quatit actus humum,
Auditurque hinnitus equorum ad bella ruentûm,
    Et strepitus ferri, murmuraque alta virûm.
Et tu (quod superest miseris) sperare memento,
    Et tua magnanimo pectore vince mala,
Nec dubites quandoque frui melioribus annis,
    Atque iterum patrios posse videre lares.

❡ Elegia septima

NONDUM blanda tuas leges Amathusia nôram,
  Et Paphio vacuum pectus ab igne fuit.
Sæpe cupidineas, puerilia tela, sagittas,
  Atque tuum sprevi maxime, numen, Amor.
Tu puer imbelles dixi transfige columbas,
  Conveniunt tenero mollia bella duci.
Aut de passeribus tumidos age, parve, triumphos,
  Hæc sunt militiæ digna trophæa tuæ:
In genus humanum quid inania dirigis arma?
  Non valet in fortes ista pharetra viros.
Non tulit hoc Cyprius, (neque enim Deus ullus ad iras
  Promptior) et duplici jam ferus igne calet.
Ver erat, et summæ radians per culmina villæ
  Attulerat primam lux tibi Maie diem:
At mihi adhuc refugam quærebant lumina noctem,
  Nec matutinum sustinuere jubar.
Astat Amor lecto, pictis Amor impiger alis,
  Prodidit astantem mota pharetra Deum:
Prodidit et facies, et dulce minantis ocelli,
  Et quicquid puero, dignum et Amore fuit.
Talis in æterno juvenis Sigeius Olympo
  Miscet amatori pocula plena Jovi;
Aut qui formosas pellexit ad oscula nymphas
  Thiodamantæus Naiade raptus Hylas.
Addideratque iras, sed et has decuisse putares,
  Addideratque truces, nec sine felle minas.
Et Miser exemplo sapuisses tutiùs, inquit,
  Nunc mea quid possit dextera testis eris.
Inter et expertos vires numerabere nostras,
  Et faciam vero per tua damna fidem.
Ipse ego si nescis strato Pythone superbum
  Edomui Phœbum, cessit et ille mihi;
Et quoties meminit Peneidos, ipse fatetur
  Certiùs et graviùs tela nocere mea.

Me nequit adductum curvare peritiùs arcum,
  Qui post terga solet vincere Parthus eques.
Cydoniusque mihi cedit venator, et ille
  Inscius uxori qui necis author erat.
Est etiam nobis ingens quoque victus Orion,
  Herculeæque manus, Herculeusque comes.
Jupiter ipse licet sua fulmina torqueat in me,
  Hærebunt lateri spicula nostra Jovis.
Cætera quæ dubitas meliùs mea tela docebunt,
  Et tua non leviter corda petenda mihi.
Nec te stulte tuæ poterunt defendere Musæ,
  Nec tibi Phœbæus porriget anguis opem.
Dixit, et aurato quatiens mucrone sagittam,
  Evolat in tepidos Cypridos ille sinus.
At mihi risuro tonuit ferus ore minaci,
  Et mihi de puero non metus ullus erat.
Et modò quà nostri spatiantur in urbe Quirites
  Et modò villarum proxima rura placent.
Turba frequens, faciéque simillima turba dearum
  Splendida per medias itque reditque vias.
Auctaque luce dies gemino fulgore coruscat,
  Fallor? an et radios hinc quoque Phœbus habet.
Hæc ego non fugi spectacula grata severus,
  Impetus et quò me fert juvenilis, agor.
Lumina luminibus malè providus obvia misi,
  Neve oculos potui continuisse meos.
Unam forte aliis supereminuisse notabam,
  Principium nostri lux erat illa mali.
Sic Venus optaret mortalibus ipsa videri,
  Sic regina Deûm conspicienda fuit.
Hanc memor objecit nobis malus ille Cupido,
  Solus et hos nobis texuit antè dolos.
Nec procul ipse vafer latuit, multæque sagittæ,
  Et facis a tergo grande pependit onus.
Nec mora, nunc ciliis hæsit, nunc virginis ori,
  Insilit hinc labiis, insidet inde genis :
Et quascunque agilis partes jaculator oberrat.
  Hei mihi, mille locis pectus inerme ferit.
Protinus insoliti subierunt corda furores,
  Uror amans intùs, flammaque totus eram.

Interea misero quæ jam mihi sola placebat,
  Ablata est oculis non reditura meis.
Ast ego progredior tacitè querebundus, et excors,
  Et dubius volui sæpe referre pedem.
Findor, et hæc remanet, sequitur pars altera votum,
  Raptaque tàm subitò gaudia flere juvat.
Sic dolet amissum proles Junonia cœlum,
  Inter Lemniacos præcipitata focos.
Talis et abreptum solem respexit, ad Orcum
  Vectus ab attonitis Amphiaraus equis.
Quid faciam infelix, et luctu victus, amores
  Nec licet inceptos ponere, neve sequi.
O utinam spectare semel mihi detur amatos
  Vultus, et coràm tristia verba loqui;
Forsitan et duro non est adamante creata,
  Forte nec ad nostras surdeat illa preces.
Crede mihi nullus sic infeliciter arsit,
  Ponar in exemplo primus et unus ego!
Parce precor teneri cum sis Deus ales amoris,
  Pugnent officio nec tua facta tuo.
Jam tuus O certè est mihi formidabilis arcus,
  Nate deâ, jaculis nec minus igne potens:
Et tua fumabunt nostris altaria donis,
  Solus et in superis tu mihi summus eris.
Deme meos tandem, vĕrùm nec deme, furores,
  Nescio cur, miser est suaviter omnis amans:
Tu modo da facilis, posthæc mea siqua futura est,
  Cuspis amaturos figat ut una duos.

Hæc ego mente olim lævâ, studioque supino
  Nequitiæ posui vana trophæa meæ.
Scilicet abreptum sic me malus impulit error,
  Indocilisque ætas prava magistra fuit.
Donec Socraticos umbrosa Academia rivos
  Præbuit, admissum dedocuitque jugum.
Protinus extinctis ex illo tempore flammis,
  Cincta rigent multo pectora nostra gelu.
Unde suis frigus metuit puer ipse sagittis,
  Et Diomedéam vim timet ipse Venus.

¶ Naturam non pati senium

HEU quàm perpetuis erroribus acta fatiscit
Avia mens hominum, tenebrisque immersa profundis
Oedipodioniam volvit sub pectore noctem!
Quæ vesana suis metiri facta deorum
Audet, et incisas leges adamante perenni
Assimilare suis, nulloque solubile sæclo
Consilium fati perituris alligat horis.

Ergóne marcescet sulcantibus obsita rugis
Naturæ facies, et rerum publica mater
Omniparum contracta uterum sterilescet ab ævo?
Et se fassa senem malè certis passibus ibit
Sidereum tremebunda caput? num tetra vetustas
Annorumque æterna fames, squalorque situsque
Sidera vexabunt? an et insatiabile Tempus
Esuriet Cælum, rapietque in viscera patrem?
Heu, potuitne suas imprudens Jupiter arces
Hoc contra munîsse nefas, et Temporis isto
Exemisse malo, gyrosque dedisse perennes?
Ergo erit ut quandoque sono dilapsa tremendo
Convexi tabulata ruant, atque obvius ictu
Stridat uterque polus, superâque ut Olympius aulâ
Decidat, horribilisque retectâ Gorgone Pallas.
Qualis in Ægæam proles Junonia Lemnon
Deturbata sacro cecidit de limine cæli.
Tu quoque Phœbe tui casus imitabere nati
Præcipiti curru, subitáque ferere ruinâ
Pronus, et extinctâ fumabit lampade Nereus,
Et dabit attonito feralia sibila ponto.
Tunc etiam aërei divulsis sedibus Hæmi
Dissultabit apex, imoque allisa barathro
Terrebunt Stygium dejecta Ceraunia Ditem
In superos quibus usus erat, fraternaque bella.

At Pater omnipotens fundati fortius astris
Consuluit rerum summæ, certoque peregit
Pondere fatorum lances, atque ordine summo
Singula perpetuum jussit servare tenorem.
Volvitur hinc lapsu mundi rota prima diurno;

Raptat et ambitos sociâ vertigine cælos.
Tardior haud solito Saturnus, et acer ut olim
Fulmineum rutilat cristatâ casside Mavors.
Floridus æternùm Phœbus juvenile coruscat,
Nec fovet effœtas loca per declivia terras
Devexo temone Deus ; sed semper amicâ
Luce potens eadem currit per signa rotarum,
Surgit odoratis pariter formosus ab Indis
Æthereum pecus albenti qui cogit Olympo
Mane vocans, et serus agens in pascua cœli,
Temporis et gemino dispertit regna colore.
Fulget, obitque vices alterno Delia cornu,
Cæruleumque ignem paribus complectitur ulnis.
Nec variant elementa fidem, solitóque fragore
Lurida perculsas jaculantur fulmina rupes.
Nec per inane furit leviori murmure Corus,
Stringit et armiferos æquali horrore Gelonos
Trux Aquilo, spiratque hyemem, nimbosque volutat.
Utque solet, Siculi diverberat ima Pelori
Rex maris, et raucâ circumstrepit æquora conchâ
Oceani Tubicen, nec vastâ mole minorem
Ægæona ferunt dorso Balearica cete.
Sed neque Terra tibi sæcli vigor ille vetusti
Priscus abest, servatque suum Narcissus odorem,
Et puer ille suum tenet, et puer ille, decorem
Phœbe tuusque, et Cypri, tuus, nec ditior olim
Terra datum sceleri celavit montibus aurum
Conscia, vel sub aquis gemmas. Sic denique in ævum
Ibit cunctarum series justissima rerum,
Donec flamma orbem populabitur ultima, latè
Circumplexa polos, et vasti culmina cæli ;
Ingentique rogo flagrabit machina mundi.

¶ *De Idea Platonica*
quemadmodum Aristoteles intellexit

DICITE sacrorum præsides nemorum deæ,
Tuque O noveni perbeata numinis
Memoria mater, quæque in immenso procul

Antro recumbis otiosa Æternitas,
Monumenta servans, et ratas leges Jovis,
Cælique fastos atque ephemeridas Deûm,
Quis ille primus cujus ex imagine
Natura sollers finxit humanum genus,
Æternus, incorruptus, æquævus polo,
Unusque et universus, exemplar Dei?
Haud ille Palladis gemellus innubæ
Interna proles insidet menti Jovis;
Sed quamlibet natura sit communior,
Tamen seorsùs extat ad morem unius,
Et, mira, certo stringitur spatio loci;
Seu sempiternus ille syderum comes
Cæli pererrat ordines decemplicis,
Citimúmve terris incolit Lunæ globum:
Sive inter animas corpus adituras sedens
Obliviosas torpet ad Lethes aquas:
Sive in remotâ forte terrarum plagâ
Incedit ingens hominis archetypus gigas,
Et diis tremendus erigit celsum caput
Atlante major portitore syderum.
Non cui profundum cæcitas lumen dedit
Dircæus augur vidit hunc alto sinu;
Non hunc silenti nocte Plëiones nepos
Vatum sagaci præpes ostendit choro;
Non hunc sacerdos novit Assyrius, licet
Longos vetusti commemoret atavos Nini,
Priscumque Belon, inclytumque Osiridem.
Non ille trino gloriosus nomine
Ter magnus Hermes (ut sit arcani sciens)
Talem reliquit Isidis cultoribus.
At tu perenne ruris Academi decus
(Hæc monstra si tu primus induxti scholis)
Jam jam pöetas urbis exules tuæ
Revocabis, ipse fabulator maximus,
Aut institutor ipse migrabis foras.

ANNO ÆTATIS 20

¶ Elegia quinta

In adventum veris

IN se perpetuo Tempus revolubile gyro
   Jam revocat Zephyros vere tepente novos!
Induiturque brevem Tellus reparata juventam,
   Jamque soluta gelu dulce virescit humus.
Fallor? an et nobis redeunt in carmina vires,
   Ingeniumque mihi munere veris adest?
Munere veris adest, iterumque vigescit ab illo
   (Quis putet) atque aliquod jam sibi poscit opus.
Castalis ante oculos, bifidumque cacumen oberrat,
   Et mihi Pyrenen somnia nocte ferunt,
Concitaque arcano fervent mihi pectora motu,
   Et furor, et sonitus me sacer intùs agit.
Delius ipse venit, video Penëide lauro
   Implicitos crines, Delius ipse venit.
Jam mihi mens liquidi raptatur in ardua cœli,
   Perque vagas nubes corpore liber eo.
Perque umbras, perque antra feror penetralia vatum,
   Et mihi fana patent interiora Deûm,
Intuiturque animus toto quid agatur Olympo,
   Nec fugiunt oculos Tartara cæca meos.
Quid tam grande sonat distento spiritus ore?
   Quid parit hæc rabies, quid sacer iste furor?
Ver mihi, quod dedit ingenium, cantabitur illo ;
   Profuerint isto reddita dona modo.
Jam Philomela tuos foliis adoperta novellis
   Instituis modulos, dum silet omne nemus.
Urbe ego, tu sylvâ simul incipiamus utrique,
   Et simul adventum veris uterque canat.
Veris, io! rediere vices, celebremus honores
   Veris, et hoc subeat Musa perennis opus.
Jam sol Æthiopas fugiens Tithoniaque arva,
   Flectit ad Arctöas aurea lora plagas.
Est breve noctis iter, brevis est mora noctis opacæ
   Horrida cum tenebris exulat illa suis.

Jamque Lycaonius plaustrum cæleste Boötes
    Non longâ sequitur fessus ut ante viâ,
Nunc etiam solitas circum Jovis atria toto
    Excubias agitant sydera rara polo.
Nam dolus et cædes, et vis cum nocte recessit,
    Neve Giganteum Dii timuere scelus.
Forte aliquis scopuli recubans in vertice pastor,
    Roscida cum primo sole rubescit humus,
Hac, ait, hac certè caruisti nocte puellâ
    Phœbe tuâ, celeres quæ retineret equos.
Læta suas repetit sylvas, pharetramque resumit
    Cynthia, Luciferas ut videt alta rotas,
Et tenues ponens radios gaudere videtur
    Officium fieri tam breve fratris ope.
Desere, Phœbus ait, thalamos Aurora seniles,
    Quid juvat effœto procubuisse toro?
Te manet Æolides viridi venator in herba,
    Surge, tuos ignes altus Hymettus habet.
Flava verecundo dea crimen in ore fatetur,
    Et matutinos ocyus urget equos.
Exuit invisam Tellus rediviva senectam,
    Et cupit amplexus Phœbe subire tuos ;
Et cupit, et digna est, quid enim formosius illâ,
    Pandit ut omniferos luxuriosa sinus,
Atque Arabum spirat messes, et ab ore venusto
    Mitia cum Paphiis fundit amoma rosis.
Ecce coronatur sacro frons ardua luco,
    Cingit ut Idæam pinea turris Opim ;
Et vario madidos intexit flore capillos,
    Floribus et visa est posse placere suis.
Floribus effusos ut erat redimita capillos
    Tænario placuit diva Sicana Deo.
Aspice Phœbe tibi faciles hortantur amores,
    Mellitasque movent flamina verna preces.
Cinnameâ Zephyrus leve plaudit odorifer alâ,
    Blanditiasque tibi ferre videntur aves.
Nec sine dote tuos temeraria quærit amores
    Terra, nec optatos poscit egena toros,
Alma salutiferum medicos tibi gramen in usus
    Præbet, et hinc titulos adjuvat ipsa tuos.

Quòd si te pretium, si te fulgentia tangunt
    Munera, (muneribus sæpe coemptus Amor)
Illa tibi ostentat quascunque sub æquore vasto,
    Et superinjectis montibus abdit opes.
Ah quoties cum tu clivoso fessus Olympo
    In vespertinas præcipitaris aquas,
Cur te, inquit, cursu languentem Phœbe diurno
    Hesperiis recipit Cærula mater aquis?
Quid tibi cum Tethy? Quid cum Tartesside lymphâ,
    Dia quid immundo perluis ora salo?
Frigora Phœbe meâ melius captabis in umbrâ,
    Huc ades, ardentes imbue rore comas.
Mollior egelidâ veniet tibi somnus in herbâ,
    Huc ades, et gremio lumina pone meo.
Quáque jaces circum mulcebit lene susurrans
    Aura per humentes corpora fusa rosas.
Nec me (crede mihi) terrent Semelëia fata,
    Nec Phäetonteo fumidus axis equo;
Cum tu Phœbe tuo sapientius uteris igni,
    Huc ades et gremio lumina pone meo.
Sic Tellus lasciva suos suspirat amores;
    Matris in exemplum cætera turba ruunt.
Nunc etenim toto currit vagus orbe Cupido,
    Languentesque fovet solis ab igne faces.
Insonuere novis lethalia cornua nervis,
    Triste micant ferro tela corusca novo.
Jamque vel invictam tentat superasse Dianam,
    Quæque sedet sacro Vesta pudica foco.
Ipsa senescentem reparat Venus annua formam,
    Atque iterum tepido creditur orta mari.
Marmoreas juvenes clamant Hymenæe per urbes,
    Litus io Hymen! et cava saxa sonant.
Cultior ille venit tunicâque decentior aptâ,
    Puniceum redolet vestis odora crocum.
Egrediturque frequens ad amœni gaudia veris
    Virgineos auro cincta puella sinus.
Votum est cuique suum, votum est tamen omnibus unum,
    Ut sibi quem cupiat, det Cytherea virum.
Nunc quoque septenâ modulatur arundine pastor,
    Et sua quæ jungat carmina Phyllis habet.

Navita nocturno placat sua sydera cantu,
 Delphinasque leves ad vada summa vocat.
Jupiter ipse alto cum conjuge ludit Olympo,
 Convocat et famulos ad sua festa Deos.
Nunc etiam Satyri cum sera crepuscula surgunt,
 Pervolitant celeri florea rura choro,
Sylvanusque suâ Cyparissi fronde revinctus,
 Semicaperque Deus, semideusque caper.
Quæque sub arboribus Dryades latuere vetustis
 Per juga, per solos expatiantur agros.
Per sata luxuriat fruticetaque Mænalius Pan,
 Vix Cybele mater, vix sibi tuta Ceres,
Atque aliquam cupidus prædatur Oreada Faunus,
 Consulit in trepidos dum sibi Nympha pedes,
Jamque latet, latitansque cupit male tecta videri,
 Et fugit, et fugiens pervelit ipsa capi.
Dii quoque non dubitant cælo præponere sylvas,
 Et sua quisque sibi numina lucus habet.
Et sua quisque diu sibi numina lucus habeto,
 Nec vos arboreâ dii precor ite domo.
Te referant miseris te Jupiter aurea terris
 Sæcla, quid ad nimbos aspera tela redis?
Tu saltem lentè rapidos age Phœbe jugales
 Quà potes, et sensim tempora veris eant.
Brumaque productas tardè ferat hispida noctes,
 Ingruat et nostro serior umbra polo.

¶ Elegia sexta

Ad Carolum Diodatum ruri commorantem

*Qui cum idibus Decemb. scripsisset, et sua carmina excusari pos-
tulasset si solito minus essent bona, quod inter lautitias quibus erat
ab amicis exceptus, haud satis felicem operam Musis dare se posse
affirmabat, hunc habuit responsum.*

Mitto tibi sanam non pleno ventre salutem,
 Quâ tu distento forte carere potes.
At tua quid nostram prolectat Musa camœnam,
 Nec sinit optatas posse sequi tenebras?
Carmine scire velis quàm te redamémque colámque,
 Crede mihi vix hoc carmine scire queas,

Nam neque noster amor modulis includitur arctis,
    Nec venit ad claudos integer ipse pedes.
Quàm bene solennes epulas, hilaremque Decembrim
    Festaque cœlifugam quæ coluere Deum,
Deliciasque refers, hyberni gaudia ruris,
    Haustaque per lepidos Gallica musta focos.
Quid quereris refugam vino dapibusque poesin?
    Carmen amat Bacchum, carmina Bacchus amat.
Nec puduit Phœbum virides gestasse corymbos,
    Atque hederam lauro præposuisse suæ.
Sæpius Aoniis clamavit collibus Euœ
    Mista Thyonêo turba novena choro.
Naso Corallæis mala carmina misit ab agris:
    Non illic epulæ non sata vitis erat.
Quid nisi vina, rosasque racemiferumque Lyæum
    Cantavit brevibus Tëia Musa modis?
Pindaricosque inflat numeros Teumesius Euan,
    Et redolet sumptum pagina quæque merum.
Dum gravis everso currus crepat axe supinus,
    Et volat Eléo pulvere fuscus eques.
Quadrimoque madens lyricen Romanus Iaccho
    Dulce canit Glyceran, flavicomamque Chloen.
Jam quoque lauta tibi generoso mensa paratu,
    Mentis alit vires, ingeniumque fovet.
Massica fœcundam despumant pocula venam,
    Fundis et ex ipso condita metra cado.
Addimus his artes, fusumque per intima Phœbum
    Corda, favent uni Bacchus, Apollo, Ceres.
Scilicet haud mirum tam dulcia carmina per te
    Numine composito tres peperisse Deos.
Nunc quoque Thressa tibi cælato barbitos auro
    Insonat argutâ molliter icta manu;
Auditurque chelys suspensa tapetia circum,
    Virgineos tremulâ quæ regat arte pedes.
Illa tuas saltem teneant spectacula Musas,
    Et revocent, quantum crapula pellit iners.
Crede mihi dum psallit ebur, comitataque plectrum
    Implet odoratos festa chorea tholos,
Percipies tacitum per pectora serpere Phœbum,
    Quale repentinus permeat ossa calor,

Perque puellares oculos digitumque sonantem
    Irruet in totos lapsa Thalia sinus.
Namque Elegía levis multorum cura deorum est,
    Et vocat ad numeros quemlibet illa suos;
Liber adest elegis, Eratoque, Ceresque, Venusque,
    Et cum purpureâ matre tenellus Amor.
Talibus inde licent convivia larga poetis,
    Sæpius et veteri commaduisse mero.
At qui bella refert, et adulto sub Jove cœlum,
    Heroasque pios, semideosque duces,
Et nunc sancta canit superum consulta deorum,
    Nunc latrata fero regna profunda cane,
Ille quidem parcè Samii pro more magistri
    Vivat, et innocuos præbeat herba cibos;
Stet prope fagineo pellucida lympha catillo,
    Sobriaque è puro pocula fonte bibat.
Additur huic scelerisque vacans, et casta juventus,
    Et rigidi mores, et sine labe manus.
Qualis veste nitens sacrâ, et lustralibus undis
    Surgis ad infensos augur iture Deos.
Hoc ritu vixisse ferunt post rapta sagacem
    Lumina Tiresian, Ogygiumque Linon,
Et lare devoto profugum Calchanta, senemque
    Orpheon edomitis sola per antra feris;
Sic dapis exiguus, sic rivi potor Homerus
    Dulichium vexit per freta longa virum,
Et per monstrificam Perseiæ Phœbados aulam,
    Et vada fœmineis insidiosa sonis,
Perque tuas rex ime domos, ubi sanguine nigro
    Dicitur umbrarum detinuisse greges.
Diis etenim sacer est vates, divûmque sacerdos,
    Spirat et occultum pectus, et ora Jovem.
At tu si quid agam, scitabere (si modò saltem
    Esse putas tanti noscere siquid agam)
Paciferum canimus cælesti semine regem,
    Faustaque sacratis sæcula pacta libris,
Vagitumque Dei, et stabulantem paupere tecto
    Qui suprema suo cum patre regna colit.
Stelliparumque polum, modulantesque æthere turmas,
    Et subitò elisos ad sua fana Deos.

Dona quidem dedimus Christi natalibus illa,
　Illa sub auroram lux mihi prima tulit.
Te quoque pressa manent patriis meditata cicutis,
　Tu mihi, cui recitem, judicis instar eris.

¶ Ad Patrem

Nunc mea Pierios cupiam per pectora fontes
Irriguas torquere vias, totumque per ora
Volvere laxatum gemino de vertice rivum;
Ut, tenues oblita sonos, audacibus alis
Surgat in officium venerandi Musa parentis.
Hoc utcunque tibi gratum pater optime carmen
Exiguum meditatur opus, nec novimus ipsi
Aptiùs à nobis quæ possint munera donis
Respondere tuis, quamvis nec maxima possint
Respondere tuis, nedum ut par gratia donis
Esse queat, vacuis quæ redditur arida verbis.
Sed tamen hæc nostros ostendit pagina census,
Et quod habemus opum chartâ numeravimus istâ,
Quæ mihi sunt nullæ, nisi quas dedit aurea Clio
Quas mihi semoto somni peperere sub antro,
Et nemoris laureta sacri Parnassides umbræ.
　Nec tu vatis opus divinum despice carmen,
Quo nihil æthereos ortus, et semina cæli,
Nil magis humanam commendat origine mentem,
Sancta Promethéæ retinens vestigia flammæ.
Carmen amant superi, tremebundaque Tartara carmen
Ima ciere valet, divosque ligare profundos,
Et triplici duros Manes adamante coercet.
Carmine sepositi retegunt arcana futuri
Phœbades, et tremulæ pallentes ora Sibyllæ;
Carmina sacrificus solennes pangit ad aras
Aurea seu sternit motantem cornua taurum;
Seu cùm fata sagax fumantibus abdita fibris
Consulit, et tepidis Parcam scrutatur in extis.
Nos etiam patrium tunc cum repetemus Olympum,
Æternæque moræ stabunt immobilis ævi,
Ibimus auratis per cæli templa coronis,
Dulcia suaviloquo sociantes carmina plectro,

Astra quibus, geminique poli convexa sonabunt.
Spiritus et rapidos qui circinat igneus orbes,
Nunc quoque sydereis intercinit ipse choreis
Immortale melos, et inenarrabile carmen;
Torrida dum rutilus compescit sibila serpens,
Demissoque ferox gladio mansuescit Orion;
Stellarum nec sentit onus Maurusius Atlas.
Carmina regales epulas ornare solebant,
Cum nondum luxus, vastæque immensa vorago
Nota gulæ, et modico spumabat cœna Lyæo.
Tum de more sedens festa ad convivia vates
Æsculeâ intonsos redimitus ab arbore crines,
Heroumque actus, imitandaque gesta canebat,
Et chaos, et positi latè fundamina mundi,
Reptantesque Deos, et alentes numina glandes,
Et nondum Ætneo quæsitum fulmen ab antro.
Denique quid vocis modulamen inane juvabit,
Verborum sensusque vacans, numerique loquacis?
Silvestres decet iste choros, non Orphea cantus,
Qui tenuit fluvios et quercubus addidit aures
Carmine, non citharâ, simulachraque functa canendo
Compulit in lacrymas; habet has à carmine laudes.

Nec tu perge precor sacras contemnere Musas,
Nec vanas inopesque puta, quarum ipse peritus
Munere, mille sonos numeros componis ad aptos,
Millibus et vocem modulis variare canoram
Doctus, Arionii meritò sis nominis hæres.
Nunc tibi quid mirum, si me genuisse poëtam
Contigerit, charo si tam propè sanguine juncti
Cognatas artes, studiumque affine sequamur:
Ipse volens Phœbus se dispertire duobus,
Altera dona mihi, dedit altera dona parenti,
Dividuumque Deum genitorque puerque tenemus.

Tu tamen ut simules teneras odisse camœnas,
Non odisse reor, neque enim, pater, ire jubebas
Quà via lata patet, quà pronior area lucri,
Certaque condendi fulget spes aurea nummi:
Nec rapis ad leges, malè custoditaque gentis
Jura, nec insulsis damnas clamoribus aures.
Sed magis excultam cupiens ditescere mentem,

R   M.

Me procul urbano strepitu, secessibus altis
Abductum Aoniæ jucunda per otia ripæ
Phœbæo lateri comitem sinis ire beatum.
Officium chari taceo commune parentis,
Me poscunt majora, tuo pater optime sumptu
Cùm mihi Romuleæ patuit facundia linguæ,
Et Latii veneres, et quæ Jovis ora decebant
Grandia magniloquis elata vocabula Graiis,
Addere suasisti quos jactat Gallia flores,
Et quam degeneri novus Italus ore loquelam
Fundit, barbaricos testatus voce tumultus,
Quæque Palæstinus loquitur mysteria vates.
Denique quicquid habet cœlum, subjectaque cœlo
Terra parens, terræque et cœlo interfluus aer,
Quicquid et unda tegit, pontique agitabile marmor,
Per te nosse licet, per te, si nosse libebit.
Dimotáque venit spectanda scientia nube,
Nudaque conspicuos inclinat ad oscula vultus,
Ni fugisse velim, ni sit libâsse molestum.
   I nunc, confer opes quisquis malesanus avitas
Austriaci gazas, Perüanaque regna præoptas.
Quæ potuit majora pater tribuisse, vel ipse
Jupiter, excepto, donâsset ut omnia, cœlo?
Non potiora dedit, quamvis et tuta fuissent,
Publica qui juveni commisit lumina nato
Atque Hyperionios currus, et fræna diei,
Et circum undantem radiata luce tiaram.
Ergo ego jam doctæ pars quamlibet ima catervæ
Victrices hederas inter, laurosque sedebo,
Jamque nec obscurus populo miscebor inerti,
Vitabuntque oculos vestigia nostra profanos.
Este procul vigiles curæ, procul este querelæ,
Invidiæque acies transverso tortilis hirquo,
Sæva nec anguiferos extende Calumnia rictus;
In me triste nihil fœdissima turba potestis,
Nec vestri sum juris ego; securaque tutus
Pectora, vipereo gradiar sublimis ab ictu.
   At tibi, chare pater, postquam non æqua merenti
Posse referre datur, nec dona rependere factis,
Sit memorâsse satis, repetitaque munera grato

Percensere animo, fidæque reponere menti.
   Et vos, O nostri, juvenilia carmina, lusus,
Si modo perpetuos sperare audebitis annos,
Et domini superesse rogo, lucemque tueri,
Nec spisso rapient oblivia nigra sub Orco,
Forsitan has laudes, decantatumque parentis
Nomen, ad exemplum, sero servabitis ævo.

¶ *Ad Leonoram Romæ canentem*

ANGELUS unicuique suus (sic credite gentes)
   Obtigit æthereis ales ab ordinibus.
Quid mirum? Leonora tibi si gloria major,
   Nam tua præsentem vox sonat ipsa Deum.
Aut Deus, aut vacui certè mens tertia cœli
   Per tua secretò guttura serpit agens;
Serpit agens, facilisque docet mortalia corda
   Sensim immortali assuescere posse sono.
Quòd si cuncta quidem Deus est, per cunctaque fusus,
   In te unâ loquitur, cætera mutus habet.

¶ *Ad eandem*

ALTERA Torquatum cepit Leonora Poëtam,
   Cujus ab insano cessit amore furens.
Ah miser ille tuo quantò feliciùs ævo
   Perditus, et propter te Leonora foret!
Et te Pieriâ sensisset voce canentem
   Aurea maternæ fila movere lyræ,
Quamvis Dircæo torsisset lumina Pentheo
   Sævior, aut totus desipuisset iners,
Tu tamen errantes cæcâ vertigine sensus
   Voce eadem poteras composuisse tuâ;
Et poteras ægro spirans sub corde quietem
   Flexanimo cantu restituisse sibi.

¶ *Ad eandem*

CREDULA quid liquidam Sirena Neapoli jactas,
   Claraque Parthenopes fana Achelöiados,

Littoreamque tuâ defunctam Naiada ripâ
   Corpora Chalcidico sacra dedisse rogo?
Illa quidem vivitque, et amœnâ Tibridis undâ
   Mutavit rauci murmura Pausilipi.
Illic Romulidûm studiis ornata secundis,
   Atque homines cantu detinet atque Deos.

¶ *Ad Salsillum*
poetam Romanum ægrotantem

SCAZONTES

O MUSA gressum quæ volens trahis claudum,
Vulcanioque tarda gaudes incessu,
Nec sentis illud in loco minus gratum,
Quàm cùm decentes flava Dëiope suras
Alternat aureum ante Junonis lectum,
Adesdum et hæc s'is verba pauca Salsillo
Refer, camœna nostra cui tantum est cordi,
Quamque ille magnis prætulit immeritò divis.
Hæc ergo alumnus ille Londini Milto,
Diebus hisce qui suum linquens nidum
Polique tractum, (pessimus ubi ventorum,
Insanientis impotensque pulmonis
Pernix anhela sub Jove exercet flabra)
Venit feraces Itali soli ad glebas,
Visum superbâ cognitas urbes famâ
Virosque doctæque indolem juventutis,
Tibi optat idem hic fausta multa Salsille,
Habitumque fesso corpori penitùs sanum;
Cui nunc profunda bilis infestat renes,
Præcordiisque fixa damnosùm spirat.
Nec id pepercit impia quòd tu Romano
Tam cultus ore Lesbium condis melos.
O dulce divûm munus, O salus Hebes
Germana! Tuque Phœbe morborum terror
Pythone cæso, sive tu magis Pæan
Libenter audis, hic tuus sacerdos est.
Querceta Fauni, vosque rore vinoso
Colles benigni, mitis Euandri sedes,

Siquid salubre vallibus frondet vestris,
Levamen ægro ferte certatim vati.
Sic ille charis redditus rursùm Musis
Vicina dulci prata mulcebit cantu.
Ipse inter atros emirabitur lucos
Numa, ubi beatum degit otium æternum,
Suam reclivis semper Ægeriam spectans.
Tumidusque et ipse Tibris hinc delinitus
Spei favebit annuæ colonorum:
Nec in sepulchris ibit obsessum reges
Nimiùm sinistro laxus irruens loro:
Sed fræna melius temperabit undarum,
Adusque curvi salsa regna Protumni.

¶ *Mansus*

Joannes Baptista Mansus Marchio Villensis vir ingenii laude, tum literarum studio, nec non et bellica virtute apud Italos clarus in primis est. Ad quem Torquati Tassi dialogus extat de Amicitia scriptus; erat enim Tassi amicissimus; ab quo etiam inter Campaniæ principes celebratur, in illo poemate cui titulus Gerusalemme conquistata, lib. 20

> Fra cavalier magnanimi, e cortesi
> Risplende il Manso————

Is authorem Neapoli commorantem summa benevolentia prosecutus est, multaque ei detulit humanitatis officia. Ad hunc itaque hospes ille antequam ab ea urbe discederet, ut ne ingratum se ostenderet, hoc carmen misit.

Hæc quoque Manse tuæ meditantur carmina laudi
Pierides, tibi Manse choro notissime Phœbi,
Quandoquidem ille alium haud æquo est dignatus honore,
Post Galli cineres, et Mecænatis Hetrusci.
Tu quoque si nostræ tantùm valet aura Camœnæ,
Victrices hederas inter, laurosque sedebis.
Te pridem magno felix concordia Tasso
Junxit, et æternis inscripsit nomina chartis,
Mox tibi dulciloquum non inscia Musa Marinum
Tradidit, ille tuum dici se gaudet alumnum,
Dum canit Assyrios divûm prolixus amores;
Mollis et Ausonias stupefecit carmine nymphas.
Ille itidem moriens tibi soli debita vates
Ossa tibi soli, supremaque vota reliquit.
Nec manes pietas tua chara fefellit amici,

Vidimus arridentem operoso ex ære poetam.
Nec satis hoc visum est in utrumque, et nec pia cessant
Officia in tumulo, cupis integros rapere Orco,
Quà potes, atque avidas Parcarum eludere leges:
Amborum genus, et variâ sub sorte peractam
Describis vitam, moresque, et dona Minervæ;
Æmulus illius Mycalen qui natus ad altam
Rettulit Æolii vitam facundus Homeri.
Ergo ego te Cliûs et magni nomina Phœbi
Manse pater, jubeo longum salvere per ævum
Missus Hyperboreo juvenis peregrinus ab axe.
Nec tu longinquam bonus aspernabere Musam,
Quæ nuper gelidâ vix enutrita sub Arcto
Imprudens Italas ausa est volitare per urbes.
Nos etiam in nostro modulantes flumine cygnos
Credimus obscuras noctis sensisse per umbras,
Quà Thamesis late puris argenteus urnis
Oceani glaucos perfundit gurgite crines.
Quin et in has quondam pervenit Tityrus oras.
Sed neque nos genus incultum, nec inutile Phœbo,
Quà plaga septeno mundi sulcata Trione
Brumalem patitur longâ sub nocte Boöten.
Nos etiam colimus Phœbum, nos munera Phœbo
Flaventes spicas, et lutea mala canistris,
Halantemque crocum (perhibet nisi vana vetustas)
Misimus, et lectas Druidum de gente choreas.
(Gens Druides antiqua sacris operata deorum
Heroum laudes imitandaque gesta canebant)
Hinc quoties festo cingunt altaria cantu
Delo in herbosâ Graiæ de more puellæ
Carminibus lætis memorant Corineïda Loxo,
Fatidicamque Upin, cum flavicomâ Hecaërge
Nuda Caledonio variatas pectora fuco.
Fortunate senex, ergo quacunque per orbem
Torquati decus, et nomen celebrabitur ingens,
Claraque perpetui succrescet fama Marini,
Tu quoque in ora frequens venies plausumque virorum,
Et parili carpes iter immortale volatu.
Dicetur tum sponte tuos habitasse penates
Cynthius, et famulas venisse ad limina Musas:

At non sponte domum tamen idem, et regis adivit
Rura Pheretiadæ cœlo fugitivus Apollo;
Ille licet magnum Alciden susceperat hospes;
Tantùm ubi clamosos placuit vitare bubulcos,
Nobile mansueti cessit Chironis in antrum,
Irriguos inter saltus frondosaque tecta
Peneium prope rivum: ibi sæpe sub ilice nigrâ
Ad citharæ strepitum blandâ prece victus amici
Exilii duros lenibat voce labores.
Tum neque ripa suo, barathro nec fixa sub imo,
Saxa stetere loco, nutat Trachinia rupes,
Nec sentit solitas, immania pondera, silvas,
Emotæque suis properant de collibus orni,
Mulcenturque novo maculosi carmine lynces.
Diis dilecte senex, te Jupiter æquus oportet
Nascentem, et miti lustrarit lumine Phœbus,
Atlantisque nepos; neque enim nisi charus ab ortu
Diis superis poterit magno favisse poetae.
Hinc longæva tibi lento sub flore senectus
Vernat, et Æsonios lucratur vivida fusos,
Nondum deciduos servans tibi frontis honores,
Ingeniumque vigens, et adultum mentis acumen.
O mihi si mea sors talem concedat amicum
Phœbæos decorâsse viros qui tam bene norit,
Si quando indigenas revocabo in carmina reges,
Arturumque etiam sub terris bella moventem;
Aut dicam invictæ sociali fœdere mensæ,
Magnanimos Heroas, et (O modo spiritus adsit)
Frangam Saxonicas Britonum sub Marte phalanges.
Tandem ubi non tacitæ permensus tempora vitæ,
Annorumque satur cineri sua jura relinquam,
Ille mihi lecto madidis astaret ocellis,
Astanti sat erit si dicam sim tibi curæ;
Ille meos artus liventi morte solutos
Curaret parvâ componi molliter urnâ.
Forsitan et nostros ducat de marmore vultus,
Nectens aut Paphiâ myrti aut Parnasside lauri
Fronde comas, at ego securâ pace quiescam.
Tum quoque, si qua fides, si præmia certa bonorum,
Ipse ego cælicolûm semotus in æthera divûm,

Quò labor et mens pura vehunt, atque ignea virtus
Secreti hæc aliquâ mundi de parte videbo
(Quantum fata sinunt) et totâ mente serenùm
Ridens purpureo suffundar lumine vultus
Et simul æthereo plaudam mihi lætus Olympo.

¶ Epitaphium Damonis

ARGUMENTUM

Thyrsis et Damon ejusdem viciniæ Pastores, eadem studia
sequuti a pueritiâ amici erant, ut qui plurimùm. Thyrsis
animi causâ profectus peregrè de obitu Damonis nuncium
accepit. Domum postea reversus, et rem ita esse comperto,
se, suamque solitudinem hoc carmine deplorat. Damonis
autem sub personâ hîc intelligitur Carolus Deodatus ex
urbe Hetruriæ Luca paterno genere oriundus, cætera Anglus;
ingenio, doctrina, clarissimisque cæteris virtutibus, dum
viveret, juvenis egregius.

HIMERIDES nymphæ (nam vos et Daphnin et Hylan,
Et plorata diu meministis fata Bionis)
Dicite Sicelicum Thamesina per oppida carmen:
Quas miser effudit voces, quæ murmura Thyrsis,
Et quibus assiduis exercuit antra querelis,
Fluminaque, fontesque vagos, nemorumque recessus,
Dum sibi præreptum queritur Damona, neque altam
Luctibus exemit noctem loca sola pererrans.
Et jam bis viridi surgebat culmus arista,
Et totidem flavas numerabant horrea messes,
Ex quo summa dies tulerat Damona sub umbras,
Nec dum aderat Thyrsis; pastorem scilicet illum
Dulcis amor Musæ Thusca retinebat in urbe.
Ast ubi mens expleta domum, pecorisque relicti
Cura vocat, simul assuetâ sedítque sub ulmo,
Tum vero amissum tum denique sentit amicum,
Cœpit et immensum sic exonerare dolorem.
    Ite domum impasti, domino jam non vacat, agni.
Hei mihi! quæ terris, quæ dicam numina cœlo,
Postquam te immiti rapuerunt funere Damon;

Siccine nos linquis, tua sic sine nomine virtus
Ibit, et obscuris numero sociabitur umbris?
At non ille, animas virgâ qui dividit aureâ,
Ista velit, dignumque tui te ducat in agmen,
Ignavumque procul pecus arceat omne silentum.
    Ite domum impasti, domino jam non vacat, agni.
Quicquid erit, certè nisi me lupus antè videbit,
Indeplorato non comminuere sepulchro,
Constabitque tuus tibi honos, longúmque vigebit
Inter pastores: Illi tibi vota secundo
Solvere post Daphnin, post Daphnin dicere laudes
Gaudebunt, dum rura Pales, dum Faunus amabit:
Si quid id est, priscamque fidem coluisse, piúmque,
Palladiásque artes, sociúmque habuisse canorum.
    Ite domum impasti, domino jam non vacat, agni.
Hæc tibi certa manent, tibi erunt hæc præmia Damon;
At mihi quid tandem fiet modò? quis mihi fidus
Hærebit lateri comes, ut tu sæpe solebas
Frigoribus duris, et per loca fœta pruinis,
Aut rapido sub sole, siti morientibus herbis?
Sive opus in magnos fuit eminùs ire leones
Aut avidos terrere lupos præsepibus altis;
Quis fando sopire diem, cantuque solebit?
    Ite domum impasti, domino jam non vacat, agni.
Pectora cui credam? quis me lenire docebit
Mordaces curas, quis longam fallere noctem
Dulcibus alloquiis, grato cùm sibilat igni
Molle pyrum, et nucibus strepitat focus, at malus auster
Miscet cuncta foris, et desuper intonat ulmo.
    Ite domum impasti, domino jam non vacat, agni.
Aut æstate, dies medio dum vertitur axe,
Cum Pan æsculeâ somnum capit abditus umbrâ,
Et repetunt sub aquis sibi nota sedilia nymphæ.
Pastoresque latent, stertit sub sepe colonus,
Quis mihi blanditiásque tuas, quis tum mihi risus,
Cecropiosque sales referet, cultosque lepores?
    Ite domum impasti, domino jam non vacat, agni.
At jam solus agros, jam pascua solus oberro,
Sicubi ramosæ densantur vallibus umbræ,
His serum expecto, supra caput imber et Eurus

Triste sonant, fractæque agitata crepuscula silvæ.
> Ite domum impasti, domino jam non vacat, agni.
Heu quam culta mihi priùs arva procacibus herbis
Involvuntur, et ipsa situ seges alta fatiscit!
Innuba neglecto marcescit et uva racemo,
Nec myrteta juvant; ovium quoque tædet, at illæ
Moerent, inque suum convertunt ora magistrum.
> Ite domum impasti, domino jam non vacat, agni.
Tityrus ad corylos vocat, Alphesibœus ad ornos,
Ad salices Ægon, ad flumina pulcher Amyntas,
Hîc gelidi fontes, hîc illita gramina musco,
Hîc Zephyri, hîc placidas interstrepit arbutus undas;
Ista canunt surdo, frutices ego nactus abibam.
> Ite domum impasti, domino jam non vacat, agni.
Mopsus ad hæc, nam me redeuntem forte notârat
(Et callebat avium linguas, et sydera Mopsus)
Thyrsi quid hoc? dixit, quæ te coquit improba bilis?
Aut te perdit amor, aut te malè fascinat astrum,
Saturni grave sæpe fuit pastoribus astrum,
Intimaque obliquo figit præcordia plumbo.
> Ite domum impasti, domino jam non vacat, agni.
Mirantur nymphæ, et quid te Thyrsi futurum est?
Quid tibi vis? aiunt, non hæc solet esse juventæ
Nubila frons, oculique truces, vultusque severi,
Illa choros, lususque leves, et semper amorem
Jure petit, bis ille miser qui serus amavit.
> Ite domum impasti, domino jam non vacat, agni.
Venit Hyas, Dryopéque, et filia Baucidis Ægle
Docta modos, citharæque sciens, sed perdita fastu,
Venit Idumanii Chloris vicina fluenti;
Nil me blanditiæ, nil me solantia verba,
Nil me, si quid adest, movet, aut spes ulla futuri.
> Ite domum impasti, domino jam non vacat, agni.
Hei mihi quam similes ludunt per prata juvenci,
Omnes unanimi secum sibi lege sodales,
Nec magis hunc alio quisquam secernit amicum
De grege, sic densi veniunt ad pabula thoes,
Inque vicem hirsuti paribus junguntur onagri;
Lex eadem pelagi, deserto in littore Proteus
Agmina Phocarum numerat, vilisque volucrum

Passer habet semper quicum sit, et omnia circum
Farra libens volitet, serò sua tecta revisens,
Quem si fors letho objecit, seu milvus adunco
Fata tulit rostro, seu stravit arundine fossor,
Protinus ille alium socio petit inde volatu.
Nos durum genus, et diris exercita fatis
Gens homines aliena animis, et pectore discors,
Vix sibi quisque parem de millibus invenit unum,
Aut si sors dederit tandem non aspera votis,
Illum inopina dies quâ non speraveris horâ
Surripit, æternum linquens in sæcula damnum.

    Ite domum impasti, domino jam non vacat, agni.
Heu quis me ignotas traxit vagus error in oras
Ire per aëreas rupes, Alpemque nivosam!
Ecquid erat tanti Romam vidisse sepultam?
Quamvis illa foret, qualem dum viseret olim,
Tityrus ipse suas et oves et rura reliquit;
Ut te tam dulci possem caruisse sodale,
Possem tot maria alta, tot interponere montes,
Tot sylvas, tot saxa tibi, fluviosque sonantes.
Ah certè extremùm licuisset tangere dextram,
Et bene compositos placidè morientis ocellos,
Et dixisse vale, nostri memor ibis ad astra.

    Ite domum impasti, domino jam non vacat, agni.
Quamquam etiam vestri nunquam meminisse pigebit
Pastores Thusci, Musis operata juventus,
Hic Charis, atque Lepos; et Thuscus tu quoque Damon,
Antiquâ genus unde petis Lucumonis ab urbe.
O ego quantus eram, gelidi cum stratus ad Arni
Murmura, populeumque nemus, quà mollior herba,
Carpere nunc violas, nunc summas carpere myrtos,
Et potui Lycidæ certantem audire Menalcam.
Ipse etiam tentare ausus sum, nec puto multùm
Displicui, nam sunt et apud me munera vestra
Fiscellæ, calathique et cerea vincla cicutæ,
Quin et nostra suas docuerunt nomina fagos
Et Datis, et Francinus, erant et vocibus ambo
Et studiis noti, Lydorum sanguinis ambo.

    Ite domum impasti, domino jam non vacat, agni.
Hæc mihi tum læto dictabat roscida luna,

Dum solus teneros claudebam cratibus hœdos.
Ah quoties dixi, cùm te cinis ater habebat,
Nunc canit, aut lepori nunc tendit retia Damon,
Vimina nunc texit, varios sibi quod sit in usus ;
Et quæ tum facili sperabam mente futura
Arripui voto levis, et præsentia finxi,
Heus bone numquid agis? nisi te quid forte retardat
Imus? et argutâ paulùm recubamus in umbra,
Aut ad aquas Colni, aut ubi jugera Cassibelauni?
Tu mihi percurres medicos, tua gramina, succos,
Helleborúmque, humilésque crocos, foliúmque hyacinthi,
Quasque habet ista palus herbas, artesque medentûm,
Ah pereant herbæ, pereant artesque medentûm
Gramina, postquam ipsi nil profecere magistro.
Ipse etiam, nam nescio quid mihi grande sonabat
Fistula, ab undecimâ jam lux est altera nocte,
Et tum forte novis admôram labra cicutis,
Dissiluere tamen rupta compage, nec ultra
Ferre graves potuere sonos, dubito quoque ne sim
Turgidulus, tamen et referam, vos cedite silvæ.
   Ite domum impasti, domino jam non vacat, agni.
Ipse ego Dardanias Rutupina per æquora puppes
Dicam, et Pandrasidos regnum vetus Inogeniæ,
Brennúmque Arviragúmque duces, priscúmque Belinum,
Et tandem Armoricos Britonum sub lege colonos ;
Tum gravidam Arturo fatali fraude Iögernen
Mendaces vultus, assumptáque Gorlöis arma,
Merlini dolus. O mihi tum si vita supersit,
Tu procul annosa pendebis fistula pinu
Multùm oblita mihi, aut patriis mutata camœnis
Brittonicum strides, quid enim? omnia non licet uni
Non sperâsse uni licet omnia, mi satis ampla
Merces, et mihi grande decus (sim ignotus in ævum
Tum licet, externo penitúsque inglorius orbi)
Si me flava comas legat Usa, et potor Alauni,
Vorticibúsque frequens Abra, et nemus omne Treantæ,
Et Thamesis meus ante omnes, et fusca metallis
Tamara, et extremis me discant Orcades undis.
   Ite domum impasti, domino jam non vacat, agni.
Hæc tibi servabam lentâ sub cortice lauri,

Hæc et plura simul, tum quæ mihi pocula Mansus,
Mansus Chalcidicæ non ultima gloria ripæ
Bina dedit, mirum artis opus, mirandus et ipse,
Et circùm gemino cælaverat argumento:
In medio rubri maris unda, et odoriferum ver
Littora longa Arabum, et sudantes balsama silvæ,
Has inter Phœnix divina avis, unica terris
Cæruleùm fulgens diversicoloribus alis
Auroram vitreis surgentem respicit undis.
Parte alia polus omnipatens, et magnus Olympus;
Quis putet? hic quoque Amor, pictæque in nube pharetræ,
Arma corusca faces, et spicula tincta pyropo;
Nec tenues animas, pectúsque ignobile vulgi
Hinc ferit, at circùm flammantia lumina torquens
Semper in erectum spargit sua tela per orbes
Impiger, et pronos nunquam collimat ad ictus,
Hinc mentes ardere sacræ, formæque deorum.
   Tu quoque in his, nec me fallit spes lubrica Damon,
Tu quoque in his certè es, nam quò tua dulcis abiret
Sanctáque simplicitas, nam quò tua candida virtus?
Nec te Lethæo fas quæsivisse sub orco,
Nec tibi conveniunt lacrymæ, nec flebimus ultrà,
Ite procul lacrymæ, purum colit æthera Damon,
Æthera purus habet, pluvium pede reppulit arcum;
Heroúmque animas inter, divósque perennes,
Æthereos haurit latices et gaudia potat
Ore sacro. Quin tu cœli post jura recepta
Dexter ades, placidúsque fave quicúnque vocaris,
Seu tu noster eris Damon, sive æquior audis
Diodotus, quo te divino nomine cuncti
Cœlicolæ nôrint, sylvísque vocabere Damon.
Quòd tibi purpureus pudor, et sine labe juventus
Grata fuit, quòd nulla tori libata voluptas,
En etiam tibi virginei servantur honores;
Ipse caput nitidum cinctus rutilante corona,
Lætáque frondentis gestans umbracula palmæ
Æternùm perages immortales hymenæos;
Cantus ubi, choreisque furit lyra mista beatis,
Festa Sionæo bacchantur et Orgia Thyrso.

JAN. 23. 1646

¶ Ad *Joannem Rousium*

Oxoniensis Academiæ Bibliothecarium

De libro Poematum amisso, quem ille sibi denuo mitti postulabat ut cum aliis nostris in Bibliotheca publica reponeret, Ode.

Strophe 1

GEMELLE cultu simplici gaudens liber,
Fronde licet geminâ,
Munditiéque nitens non operosâ,
Quam manus attulit
Juvenilis olim,
Sedula tamen haud nimii Poetæ;
Dum vagus Ausonias nunc per umbras
Nunc Britannica per vireta lusit
Insons populi, barbitóque devius
Indulsit patrio, mox itidem pectine Daunio
Longinquum intonuit melos
Vicinis, et humum vix tetigit pede;

Antistrophe

Quis te, parve liber, quis te fratribus
Subduxit reliquis dolo?
Cum tu missus ab urbe,
Docto jugiter obsecrante amico,
Illustre tendebas iter
Thamesis ad incunabula
Cærulei patris,
Fontes ubi limpidi
Aonidum, thyasusque sacer
Orbi notus per immensos
Temporum lapsus redeunte cœlo,
Celeberque futurus in ævum;

Strophe 2

Modó quis deus, aut editus deo
Pristinam gentis miseratus indolem

(Si satis noxas luimus priores
Mollique luxu degener otium)
Tollat nefandos civium tumultus,
Almaque revocet studia sanctus
Et relegatas sine sede Musas
Jam penè totis finibus Angligenûm;
Immundasque volucres
Unguibus imminentes
Figat Apollineâ pharetrâ,
Phinéamque abigat pestem procul amne Pegaséo.

Antistrophe

Quin tu, libelle, nuntii licet malâ
Fide, vel oscitantiâ
Semel erraveris agmine fratrum,
Seu quis te teneat specus,
Seu qua te latebra, forsan unde vili
Callo teréris institoris insulsi,
Lætare felix, en iterum tibi
Spes nova fulget posse profundam
Fugere Lethen, vehique Superam
In Jovis aulam remige pennâ;

Strophe 3

Nam te Roüsius sui
Optat peculî, numeróque justo
Sibi pollicitum queritur abesse,
Rogatque venias ille cujus inclyta
Sunt data virûm monumenta curæ:
Téque adytis etiam sacris
Voluit reponi quibus et ipse præsidet
Æternorum operum custos fidelis,
Quæstorque gazæ nobilioris,
Quàm cui præfuit Iön
Clarus Erechtheides
Opulenta dei per templa parentis
Fulvosque tripodas, donaque Delphica
Iön Actæa genitus Creusâ.

Antistrophe

Ergo tu visere lucos
Musarum ibis amœnos,
Diamque Phœbi rursus ibis in domum
Oxoniâ quam valle colit
Delo posthabitâ,
Bifidóque Parnassi jugo :
Ibis honestus,
Postquam egregiam tu quoque sortem
Nactus abis, dextri prece sollicitatus amici.
Illic legéris inter alta nomina
Authorum, Graiæ simul et Latinæ
Antiqua gentis lumina, et verum decus.

Epodos

Vos tandem haud vacui mei labores,
Quicquid hoc sterile fudit ingenium,
Jam serò placidam sperare jubeo
Perfunctam invidiâ requiem, sedesque beatas
Quas bonus Hermes
Et tutela dabit solers Roüsi,
Quò neque lingua procax vulgi penetrabit, atque longè
Turba legentum prava facesset ;
At ultimi nepotes,
Et cordatior ætas
Judicia rebus æquiora forsitan
Adhibebit integro sinu.
Tum livore sepulto,
Si quid meremur sana posteritas sciet
Roüsio favente.

Ode tribus constat Strophis, totidémque Antistrophis unâ demum
epodo clausis, quas, tametsi omnes nec versuum numero, nec certis
ubique colis exactè respondeant, ita tamen secuimus, commodè legendi
potius, quam ad antiquos concinendi modos rationem spectantes.
Alioquin hoc genus rectiùs fortasse dici monostrophicum debuerat.
Metra partim sunt κατὰ σχέσιν, partim ἀπολελυμένα. Phaleucia quæ
sunt, spondæum tertio loco bis admittunt, quod idem in secundo
loco Catullus ad libitum fecit.

¶ *Apologus de Rustico et Hero*

RUSTICUS ex malo sapidissima poma quotannis
    Legit, et urbano lecta dedit domino :
Hic incredibili fructûs dulcedine captus
    Malum ipsam in proprias transtulit areolas.
Hactenus illa ferax, sed longo debilis ævo,
    Mota solo assueto, protinùs aret iners.
Quod tandem ut patuit domino, spe lusus inani,
    Damnavit celeres in sua damna manus.
Atque ait, Heu quantò satius fuit illa coloni
    (Parva licet) grato dona tulisse animo !
Possem ego avaritiam frœnare, gulamque voracem :
    Nunc periere mihi et fœtus et ipsa parens.

¶ *In Salmasii Hundredam*

QUIS expedivit Salmasio suam Hundredam,
Picámque docuit verba nostra conari?
Magister artis venter, ac Iacobei
Centum exulantis viscera marsupii regis.
Quod si dolosi spes refulserit nummi
Ipse, Antichristi modo qui primatum Papæ
Minatus uno est dissipare sufflatu,
Cantabit ultrò Cardinalitium *melos.*

¶ *In Salmasium*

GAUDETE scombri, et quicquid est piscium salo,
Qui frigida hyeme incolitis algentes freta !
Vestrum misertus ille Salmasius eques
Bonus, amicire nuditatem cogitat ;
Chartæque largus, apparat papyrinos
Vobis cucullos, præferentes Claudii
Insignia, nomenque et decus, Salmasii,
Gestetis ut per omne cetarium forum
Equitis clientes, scriniis mungentium
Cubito virorum, et capsulis gratissimos.

¶ *Philosophus ad regem quendam qui eum*
ignotum et insontem inter reos forte captum inscius
damnaverat τὴν ἐπὶ θανάτῳ πορευόμενος, *hæc subito*
misit

Ὦ ἄνα εἰ ὀλέσῃς με τὸν ἔννομον, οὐδέ τιν' ἀνδρῶν
Δεινὸν ὅλως δράσαντα, σοφώτατον ἴσθι κάρηνον
Ῥηιδίως ἀφέλοιο, τόδ' ὕστερον αὖθι νοήσεις,
Μαψιδίως δ' ἄρ' ἔπειτα τεὸν πρὸς θυμὸν ὀδυρῇ,
Τοιόνδ' ἐκ πόλεος περιώνυμον ἄλκαρ ὀλέσσας.

¶ In Effigiei ejus Sculptorem

Ἀμαθεῖ γεγράφθαι χειρὶ τήνδε μὲν εἰκόνα
Φαίης τάχ' ἄν, πρὸς εἶδος αὐτοφυὲς βλέπων·
Τὸν δ' ἐκτυπωτὸν οὐκ ἐπιγνόντες, φίλοι,
Γελᾶτε φαύλου δυσμίμημα ζωγράφου.

¶ "Donna leggiadra . . ."

Donna leggiadra il cui bel nome honora
   L'herbosa val di Rheno, e il nobil varco,
   Ben è colui d'ogni valore scarco
   Qual tuo spirto gentil non innamora,
Che dolcemente mostra si di fuora
   De suoi atti soavi giamai parco,
   E i don', che son d'amor saette ed arco,
   La onde l' alta tua virtù s'infiora.
Quando tu vaga parli, o lieta canti
   Che mover possa duro alpestre legno,
   Guardi ciascun a gli occhi, ed a gli orecchi
L'entrata, chi di te si truova indegno ;
   Gratia sola di sù gli vaglia, inanti
   Che'l disio amoroso al cuor s'invecchi.

¶ "Qual in colle . . ."

Qual in colle aspro, al imbrunir di sera
   L'avezza giovinetta pastorella
   Va bagnando l'herbetta strana e bella
   Che mal si spande a disusata spera

Fuor di sua natia alma primavera,
 Cosi Amor meco insù la lingua snella
 Desta il fior novo di strania favella,
 Mentre io di te, vezzosamente altera,
Canto, dal mio buon popol non inteso
 E'l bel Tamigi cangio col bel Arno.
 Amor lo volse, ed io a l'altrui peso
Seppi ch' Amor cosa mai volse indarno.
 Deh! foss' il mio cuor lento e'l duro seno
 A chi pianta dal ciel si buon terreno.

CANZONE

❡ "Ridonsi donne..."

RIDONSI donne e giovani amorosi
M' accostandosi attorno, e perche scrivi,
Perche tu scrivi in lingua ignota e strana
Verseggiando d'amor, e come t'osi?
Dinne, se la tua speme sia mai vana,
E de pensieri lo miglior t' arrivi;
Cosi mi van burlando, altri rivi
Altri lidi t' aspettan, ed altre onde
Nelle cui verdi sponde
Spuntati ad hor, ad hor a la tua chioma
L'immortal guiderdon d'eterne frondi
Perche alle spalle tue soverchia soma?
 Canzon dirotti, e tu per me rispondi
Dice mia Donna, e'l suo dir, è il mio cuore
Questa è lingua di cui si vanta Amore.

❡ "Diodati, e te'l dirò..."

DIODATI, e te'l dirò con maraviglia,
 Quel ritroso io ch'amor spreggiar soléa
 E de suoi lacci spesso mi ridéa
 Gia caddi, ov'huom dabben talhor s'impiglia.
Ne treccie d'oro, ne guancia vermiglia
 M' abbaglian sì, ma sotto nova idea
 Pellegrina bellezza che'l cuor bea,
 Portamenti alti honesti, e nelle ciglia

Quel sereno fulgor d' amabil nero,
 Parole adorne di lingua piu d'una,
 E'l cantar che di mezzo l'hemispero
Traviar ben può la faticosa Luna,
  E degli occhi suoi auventa si gran fuoco
  Che l'incerar gli orecchi mi fia poco.

¶ "Per certo i bei . . ."

PER certo i bei vostr'occhi Donna mia
 Esser non puo che non fian lo mio sole
 Si mi percuoton forte, come ei suole
Per l'arene di Libia chi s'invia,
Mentre un caldo vapor (ne senti pria)
 Da quel lato si spinge ove mi duole,
 Che forse amanti nelle lor parole
Chiaman sospir; io non so che si sia:
Parte rinchiusa, e turbida si cela
 Scosso mi il petto, e poi n'uscendo poco
 Quivi d' attorno o s'agghiaccia, o s'ingiela;
Ma quanto a gli occhi giunge a trovar loco
 Tutte le notti a me suol far piovose
 Finche mia Alba rivien colma di rose.

¶ "Giovane piano . . ."

GIOVANE piano, e semplicetto amante
 Poi che fuggir me stesso in dubbio sono,
 Madonna a voi del mio cuor l'humil dono
Farò divoto; io certo a prove tante
L'hebbi fedele, intrepido, costante,
 De pensieri leggiadro, accorto, e buono;
 Quando rugge il gran mondo, e scocca il tuono,
S'arma di se, e d' intero diamante,
Tanto del forse, e d' invidia sicuro,
 Di timori, e speranze al popol use
 Quanto d'ingegno, e d' alto valor vago,
E di cetra sonora, e delle muse:
 Sol troverete in tal parte men duro
 Ove amor mise l'insanabil ago.

English Prose

English Prose

❦❦

¶ Of *Reformation*
touching Church Discipline in *England*

... Amongst many secondary, and accessory causes that
support Monarchy, these are not of least reckning, though
common to all other States: the love of the Subjects, the multitude, and valor of the people, and store of treasure. In all
these things hath the Kingdome bin of late sore weak'nd, and
chiefly by the Prelates. First let any man consider, that if any
Prince shall suffer under him a commission of autority to be
exerciz'd, till all the Land grone, and cry out, as against a
whippe of Scorpions, whether this be not likely to lessen, and
keel the affections of the Subject. Next what numbers of
faithfull, and freeborn Englishmen, and good Christians have
bin constrain'd to forsake their dearest home, their friends,
and kindred, whom nothing but the wide Ocean, and the
savage deserts of *America* could hide and shelter from the
fury of the Bishops. O Sir, if we could but see the shape of
our deare Mother *England*, as Poets are wont to give a personal form to what they please, how would she appeare, think
ye, but in a mourning weed, with ashes upon her head, and
teares abundantly flowing from her eyes, to behold so many of
her children expos'd at once, and thrust from things of dearest
necessity, because their conscience could not assent to things
which the Bishops thought *indifferent*. What more binding
then Conscience? what more free then *indifferency?* cruel then
must that *indifferency* needs be, that shall violate the strict
necessity of Conscience, merciles, and inhumane that free
choyse, and liberty that shall break asunder the bonds of Religion. Let the Astrologer be dismay'd at the portentous blaze
of comets, and impressions in the aire as foretelling troubles
and changes to states: I shall beleeve there cannot be a more
ill-boding signe to a Nation (*God* turne the Omen from us)
then when the Inhabitants, to avoid insufferable grievances at
home, are inforc'd by heaps to forsake their native Country.
Now wheras the only remedy, and amends against the depopu-

lation, and thinnesse of a Land within, is the borrow'd strength of firme alliance from without, these priestly Policies of theirs having thus exhausted our domestick forces, have gone the way also to leave us as naked of our firmest, and faithfullest neighbours abroad, by disparaging, and alienating from us all Protestant Princes, and Common-wealths, who are not ignorant that our Prelats, and as many as they can infect, account them no better then a sort of sacrilegious, and puritanical Rebels, preferring the *Spaniard* our deadly enemy before them, and set all orthodox writers at nought in comparison of the Jesuits, who are indeed the onely corrupters of youth, and good learning; and I have heard many wise, and learned men in *Italy* say as much. . . .

. . . The emulation that under the old Law was in the King toward the *Preist*, is now so come about in the Gospell, that all the danger is to be fear'd from the *Preist* to the *King*. Whilst the *Preists Office* in the Law was set out with an exteriour lustre of Pomp and glory, Kings were ambitious to be *Preists;* now *Preists* not perceiving the heavenly brightnesse, and inward splendor of their more glorious *Evangelick Ministery* with as great ambition affect to be Kings; as in all their courses is easie to be observ'd. Their eyes ever imminent upon worldly matters, their desires ever thirsting after worldly employments, in stead of diligent and fervent studie in the Bible, they covet to be expert in Canons, and Decretals, which may inable them to judge, and interpose in temporall Causes, however pretended *Ecclesiasticall*. Doe they not hord up *Pelfe*, seeke to bee potent in *secular Strength*, in *State Affaires*, in *Lands*, *Lordships*, and *Demeanes*, to *sway* and carry all before them in *high Courts*, and *Privie Counsels*, to bring into their grasp, the *high*, and *principall Offices* of the Kingdom? have they not been bold of late to check the *Common Law*, to slight and brave the indiminishable Majestie of our highest Court the Law-giving and Sacred *Parliament?* Doe they not plainly labour to exempt *Churchmen* from the *Magistrate?* Yea, so presumptuously as to question, and menace *Officers* that represent the *Kings Person* for using their Authority against drunken *Preists?* The cause of protecting *murderous Clergie-men* was the first heart-burning that swel'd up the audacious *Becket* to the pestilent, and odious vexation of *Henry* the second. Nay more, have not some of their devoted Schollers begun, I need not say to nibble, but openly to argue against the Kings *Supremacie?* is not the Cheife of them accus'd out of his owne Booke, and his *late Canons* to affect a certaine unquestionable *Patriarchat,* independent and unsubordinate to the Crowne? . . .

. . . Having fitted us only for peace, and that a servile peace, by lessening our numbers, dreining our estates, enfeebling our bodies, cowing our free spirits by those wayes as you have heard, their impotent actions cannot sustaine themselves the least moment, unlesse they rouze us up to a *Warre* fit for *Cain* to be the Leader of; an abhorred, a cursed, a Fraternall *Warre.* ENGLAND and SCOTLAND dearest Brothers both in *Nature,* and in CHRIST must be set to wade in one anothers blood; and IRELAND our free Denizon upon the back of us both, as occasion should serve: a piece of Service that the *Pope* and all his Factors have beene compassing to doe ever since the *Reformation.*

But ever-blessed be he, and ever glorifi'd that from his high watch-Tower in the Heav'ns discerning the crooked wayes of perverse, and cruell men, hath hitherto maim'd, and infatuated all their damnable inventions, and deluded their great Wizzards with a delusion fit for fooles and children; had GOD beene so minded hee could have sent a Spirit of *Mutiny* amongst us, as hee did betweene *Abimilech* and the *Sechemites,* to have made our Funerals and slaine heaps more in number then the miserable surviving remnant, but he, when wee least deserv'd, sent out a gentle gale, and message of peace from the wings of those his Cherubins, that fanne his Mercy-seat. Nor shall the *wisdome,* the *moderation,* the *Christian Pietie,* the *Constancy* of our Nobility and Commons of *England* be ever forgotten, whose calme, and temperat connivence could sit still, and smile out the stormy bluster of men more audacious, and precipitant, then of solid and deep reach, till their own fury had run it selfe out of breath, assailing, by rash and heady *approches,* the impregnable situation of our Liberty and safety, that laught such weake enginry to scorne, such poore drifts to make a *Nationall Warre* of a *Surplice Brabble,* a *Tippetscuffle,* and ingage the unattainted Honour of *English* Knighthood, to unfurle the streaming *Red Crosse*, or to reare the horrid *Standard* of those fatall guly Dragons for so unworthy a purpose, as to force upon their *Fellow-Subjects*, that which themselves are weary of, the *Skeleton* of a *Masse-Booke*. . . .

. . . But is this all? No, this Ecclesiasticall Supremacy draws to it the power to excommunicate Kings; and then followes the worst that can be imagin'd. Doe they hope to avoyd this by keeping *Prelates* that have so often don it? Not to exemplifie the malapert insolence of our owne *Bishops* in this kind towards our Kings: I shall turn back to the *Primitive*, and pure times, which the objecters would have the rule of reformation to us.

Not an assembly, but one *Bishop* alone, Saint AMBROSE of *Millan*, held *Theodosius* the most Christian Emperor under excommunication above eight moneths together, drove him from the Church in the presence of his Nobles, which the good Emperor bore with heroick *humility*, and never ceas't by prayers, and teares, till he was absolv'd, for which coming to the Bishop with *Supplication* into the *Salutatory*, some out Porch of the Church, he was charg'd by him of tyrannicall madnes against GOD, for comming into holy ground. At last upon conditions absolv'd, and after great *humiliation* approaching to the Altar to offer (as those thrise pure times then thought meet) he had scarse withdrawne his hand, and stood awhile, when a bold Arch-deacon comes in the Bishops name, and chaces him from within the railes telling him peremptorily that the place wherein he stood, was for none but the *Priests* to enter, or to touch: and this is another peece of pure *Primitive Divinity*. Thinke yee then our Bishops will forgoe the power of excommunication on whomsoever? No certainly, unlesse to compasse sinister ends, and then revoke when they see their time. And yet this most mild, though withall dredfull, and inviolable Prerogative of *Christs* diadem excommunication servs for nothing with them, but to prog, and pandar for fees, or to display their pride and sharpen their revenge, debarring men the protection of the Law, and I remember not whether in some cases it bereave not men all right to their worldly goods, and Inheritances besides the deniall of Christian buriall. But in the Evangelical, and reformed use of this sacred censure, no such prostitution, no

such *Iscariotical* drifts are to be doubted, as that *Spirituall*
doom, and sentence, should invade worldly possession, which
is the rightfull lot and portion, even of the wickedest men, as
frankly bestow'd upon them by the al-dispensing bounty, as
rain, and *Sun-shine*. No, no, it seekes not to bereave or destroy the body, it seekes to saue the Soule by humbling the
body, not by Imprisonment, or pecuniary mulct, much lesse
by stripes or bonds, or disinheritance, but by Fatherly admonishment, and Christian rebuke, to cast it into godly sorrow, whose end is joy, and ingenuous bashfulnesse to sin: if
that can not be wrought, then as a tender Mother takes her
Child and holds it over the pit with scarring words that it may
learne to feare, where danger is, so doth excommunication as
deerly, and as freely without money, use her wholsome and
saving terrors, she is instant, she beseeches, by all the deere,
and sweet promises of SALVATION she entices and woos, by
all the threatnings, and thunders of the *Law*, and rejected *Goss-
pel* she charges, and adjures; this is all her Armory, her muni-
tion, her Artillery, then she awaites with long-sufferance, and
yet ardent zeale. In briefe, there is no act in all the errand of
Gods Ministers to man-kind, wherein passes more loverlike
contestation betweene CHRIST and the Soule of a regenerate
man lapsing, then before, and in, and after the sentence of
Excommunication. As for the fogging proctorage of money,
with such an eye as strooke *Gehezi* with Leprosy, and *Simon
Magus* with a curse, so does she looke, and so threaten her
fiery whip against that banking den of theeves that dare thus
baffle, and buy and sell the awfull, and majestick wrincles of
her brow. He that is rightly and apostolically sped with her
invisible arrow, if he can be at peace in his Soule, and not
smel within him the brimstone of Hell, may have faire leave to
tell all his baggs over undiminish't of the least farding, may
eat his dainties, drinke his wine, use his delights, enjoy his
Lands, and liberties, not the least skin rais'd, not the least
haire misplac't for all that excommunication has done: much
more may a King injoy his rights, and Prerogatives unde-
flowr'd, untouch'd, and be as absolute, and compleat a King,
as all his royalties and revenu's can make him. . . .

. . . Let us not be so overcredulous, unlesse GOD hath
blinded us, as to trust our deer Soules into the hands of men

that beg so devoutly for the pride, and gluttony of their owne backs, and bellies, that sue and sollicite so eagerly, not for the saving of Soules, the consideration of which can have heer no place at all, but for their Bishopricks, Deaneries, Prebends, and Chanonies; how can these men not be corrupt, whose very cause is the bribe of their own pleading; whose mouths cannot open without the strong breath, and loud stench of avarice, Simony, and Sacrilege, embezling the treasury of the Church on painted, and guilded walles of Temples wherein God hath testified to have no delight, warming their Palace Kitchins, and from thence their unctuous, and epicurean paunches, with the almes of the blind, the lame, the impotent, the aged, the orfan, the widow, for with these the treasury of CHRIST ought to be, here must be his jewels bestow'd, his rich Cabinet must be emptied heer; as the constant martyr Saint *Laurence* taught the *Roman Prætor*. Sir would you know what the remonstrance of these men would have, what their Petition imply's? They intreate us that we would not be weary of those insupportable greevances that our shoulders have hitherto crackt under, they beseech us that we would think'em fit to be our Justices of peace, our Lords, our highest officers of State, though they come furnish't with no more experience then they learnt betweene the *Cook*, and the *manciple*, or more profoundly at the Colledge *audit*, or the *regent house*, or to come to their deepest insight, at their *Patrons Table;* they would request us to indure still the russling of their Silken Cassocks, and that we would burst our *mid-riffes* rather then laugh to see them under Sayl in all their Lawn, and Sarcenet, their shrouds, and tackle, with a *geometricall rhomboides* upon their heads: they would bear us in hand that we must of duty still appear before them once a year in *Jerusalem* like good circumcizd *males*, and *Females* to be taxt by the poul, to be scons't our head money, our tuppences in their Chaunlerly Shop-book of *Easter*. They pray us that it would please us to let them still hale us, and worrey us with their band-dogs, and Pursivants; and that it would please the *Parliament* that they may yet have the whipping, fleecing, and fleaing of us in their diabolical Courts to tear the flesh from our bones, and into our wide wounds instead of balm, to power in the oil of Tartar, vitriol, and mercury; Surely a right reasonable, innocent, and soft-hearted Petition. O the relenting bowels of the Fathers. Can this bee granted them unlesse GOD have smitten us with frensie from above, and with a dazling giddinesse at noon day? Should not those men rather be heard that come to plead against their owne preferments, their worldly advantages, their owne abundance; for honour, and obedience to *Gods word*, the conversion of Soules, the *Christian peace* of the Land, and *union* of the reformed *Catholick Church*, the *un-appropriating*, and *unmonopolizing* the rewards of *learning* and *industry*, from the greasie clutch of ignorance, and high feeding. We have tri'd already, and miserably felt what *ambition, worldly glory* and *immoderat wealth* can do, what the boistrous and contradictional hand of a temporall, earthly, and corporeall Spiritualty can availe to the edifying of Christs holy *Church;* were it such a desperate hazard to put to the venture the universall Votes of *Christs* Congregation, the fellowly and friendly yoke of a teaching and laborious Minis-tery, the Pastorlike and Apostolick imitation of meeke and unlordly Discipline, the gentle and benevolent mediocritie of Church-maintenance, without the ignoble Hucsterage of pidling *Tithes?* Were it such an incurable mischiefe to make a little triall, what all this would doe to the flourishing and growing up of *Christs* mysticall body? As rather to use every poore shift, and if that serve not, to threaten uproare and combustion, and shake the brand of Civill Discord?

O Sir, I doe now feele my selfe inwrapt on the sodaine into those mazes and *Labyrinths* of dreadfull and hideous thoughts, that which way to get out, or which way to end I know not, unlesse I turne mine eyes, and with your help lift up my hands to that Eternall and Propitious *Throne*, where nothing is readier then *grace* and *refuge* to the distresses of mortall Suppliants: and it were a shame to leave these serious thoughts lesse piously then the Heathen were wont to con-clude their graver discourses.

Thou therefore that sits't in light and glory unapprochable, *Parent of Angels* and *Men!* next thee I implore Omnipotent King, Redeemer of that lost remnant whose nature thou didst assume, ineffable and everlasting *Love!* And thou the third subsistence of Divine Infinitude, *illumining Spirit*, the joy and solace of created *Things!* one *Tri-personall* GODHEAD! looke upon this thy poore and almost spent, and expiring *Church*, leave her not thus a prey to these importunate *Wolves*, that wait and thinke long till they devoure thy tender *Flock*, these wilde *Boares* that have broke into thy *Vineyard*, and left the print of thir polluting hoofs on the Soules of thy Servants. O let them not bring about their damned *designes* that stand now at the entrance of the bottomlesse pit expecting the Watch-word to open and let out those dreadfull *Locusts* and *Scorpions*, to *re-involve* us in that pitchy *Cloud* of infernall darknes, where we shall never more see the *Sunne* of thy *Truth* againe, never hope for the cheerfull dawne, never more heare the *Bird* of *Morning* sing. Be mov'd with pitty at the afflicted state of this our shaken *Monarchy*, that now lies labouring under her throwes, and struggling against the grudges of more dreaded Calamities.

O thou that after the impetuous rage of five bloody Inundations, and the succeeding Sword of intestine *Warre*, soaking the Land in her owne gore, didst pitty the sad and ceasles revolution of our swift and thick-comming sorrowes when wee were quite breathlesse, of thy *free grace* didst motion *Peace*, and termes of Cov'nant with us, and having first welnigh freed us from *Antichristian* thraldome, didst build up this *Britannick Empire* to a glorious and enviable heighth with all her Daughter Ilands about her, stay us in this felicitie, let not the obstinacy of our halfe Obedience and will-Worship bring forth that *Viper* of *Sedition*, that for these Foure-score Yeares hath been breeding to eat through the entrals of our *Peace;* but let her cast her Abortive Spawne without the danger of this travailling and throbbing *Kingdome.* That we may still remember in our *solemne Thanksgivings*, how for us the *Northren Ocean* even to the frozen *Thule* was scatter'd with the proud Ship-wracks of the *Spanish Armado*, and the very maw of Hell ransack't, and made to give up her conceal'd destruction, ere shee could vent it in that horrible and damned blast.

O how much more glorious will those former Deliverances appeare, when we shall know them not onely to have sav'd us from greatest miseries past, but to have reserv'd us for greatest happinesse to come. Hitherto thou hast but freed us, and that not fully, from the unjust and Tyrannous Claime of thy Foes, now unite us intirely, and appropriate us to thy selfe, tie us everlastingly in willing Homage to the *Prerogative* of thy eternall *Throne*.

And now wee knowe, O thou our most certain hope and defence, that thine enemies have been consulting all the Sorceries of the *great whore*, and have joyn'd their Plots with that sad Intelligencing Tyrant that mischiefes the World with his Mines of *Ophir*, and lies thirsting to revenge his Navall ruines that have larded our Seas; but let them all take Counsell together, and let it come to nought, let them Decree, and doe thou Cancell it, let them gather themselves, and bee scatter'd, let them embattell themselves and bee broken, let them imbattell, and be broken, for thou art with us.

Then amidst the *Hymns*, and *Halleluiahs* of *Saints* some one may perhaps bee heard offering at high *strains* in new and lofty *Measures* to sing and celebrate thy *divine Mercies*, and *marvelous Judgements* in this Land throughout all AGES; whereby this great and Warlike Nation instructed and inur'd to the fervent and continuall practice of *Truth* and *Righteousnesse*, and casting farre from her the *rags* of her old *vices* may presse on hard to that *high* and *happy* emulation to be found the *soberest*, *wisest*, and *most Christian People* at that day when thou the Eternall and shortly-expected King shalt open the Clouds to judge the severall Kingdomes of the World, and distributing *Nationall Honours* and *Rewards* to Religious and just *Common-wealths*, shall put an end to all Earthly *Tyrannies*, proclaiming thy universal and milde *Monarchy* through Heaven and Earth. Where they undoubtedly that by their *Labours*, *Counsels*, and *Prayers* have been earnest for the *Common good of Religion* and their *Countrey*, shall receive, above the inferiour *Orders* of the *Blessed*, the *Regall* addition of *Principalities*, *Legions*, and *Thrones* into their glorious Titles, and in supereminence of *beatifick Vision* progressing the *datelesse* and *irrevoluble* Circle of *Eternity* shall clasp inseparable Hands with *joy*, and *blisse* in over measure for ever.

But they contrary that by the impairing and diminution of the true *Faith*, the distresses and servitude of their *Countrey* aspire to high *Dignity*, *Rule* and *Promotion* here, after a shamefull end in this *Life* (which *God* grant them) shall be thrown downe eternally into the *darkest* and *deepest Gulfe* of HELL, where under the *despightfull controule*, the trample and spurne of all the other *Damned*, that in the anguish of their *Torture* shall have no other ease then to exercise a *Raving* and *Bestiall Tyranny* over them as their *Slaves* and *Negro's*, they shall remaine in that plight for ever, the *basest*, the *lowermost*, the *most dejected*, most *underfoot* and *downe-trodden Vassals* of *Perdition*.

¶ Animadversions upon The *Remonstrants*
Defence against SMECTYMNUUS

Remon. They cannot name any man in this Nation that ever contradicted *Episcopacie*, till this present Age.

Answ. What an over-worne and bedrid Argument is this, the last refuge ever of old falshood, and therefore a good signe I trust that your Castle cannot hold out long. This was the plea of *Iudaisme*, and Idolatry against *Christ* and his *Apostles*, of *Papacie* against Reformation: and perhaps to the frailty of flesh and blood in a man destitute of better enlight'ning, may for some while bee pardonable; for what ha's fleshly apprehension other to subsist by then Succession, Custome, and Visibility, which onely hold if in his weaknesse and blindnesse he be loath to lose, who can blame? but in a *Protestant* Nation that should have throwne off these tatter'd Rudiments long agoe, after the many strivings of Gods Spirit, and our four-score yeares vexation of him in this our wildernesse since Reformation began, to urge these rotten Principles, and twit us with the present age, which is to us an age of ages wherein God is manifestly come downe among us, to doe some remarkable good to our Church or state, is as if a man should taxe the renovating and re-ingendring Spirit of God with innovation, and that new creature for an upstart noveltie; yea the new Ierusalem, which without your admired linke of succession descends from Heaven, could not scape some such like censure. If you require a further answer, it will not misbecome a Christian to bee either more magnanimous, or more devout then *Scipio* was, who in stead of other answer to the frivolous accusations of *Petilius* the *Tribune; This day Romans* (saith he) *I fought with* Hanibal *prosperously; let us all goe and thank the gods that gave us so great a victory:* in like manner will we now say, not caring otherwise to answer this un-Protestant-like Objection: in this Age, *Brittains* God hath reform'd his Church after many hundred yeers of *Popish* corruption; in this Age hee hath freed us from the intolerable yoke of *Prelats*, and *Papall* Discipline; in this age he hath renewed our *Protestation* against all those yet remaining dregs of superstition: Let us all goe every true protested *Brittaine* throughout the 3. *Kingdoms*, and render thanks to God the Father of light, and fountaine of heavenly grace, and to his son CHRIST our Lord; leaving this *Remonstrant* and his adherents to their owne designes, and let us recount even here without delay the patience and long suffering that God hath us'd towards our blindnesse and hardnes time after time. For he being equally neere to his whole Creation of Mankind, and of free power to turn his benefick and fatherly regard to what Region or Kingdome he pleases, hath yet ever had this Iland under the speciall indulgent eye of his providence: and pitying us the first of all other Nations, after he had decreed to purifie and renew his Church that lay wallowing in Idolatrous pollutions, sent first to us a healing messenger to touch softly our sores, and carry a gentle hand over our wounds: he knockt once and twice and came againe, opening our drousie eye-lids leasurely by that glimmering light which *Wicklef*, and his followers dispers't, and still taking off by degrees the inveterat scales from our nigh perist sight, purg'd also our deaf eares, and prepar'd them to attend his second warning trumpet in our Grandsires dayes. How else could they have beene able to have receiv'd the sudden assault of his reforming Spirit warring against humane Principles, and carnall sense, the pride of flesh that still cry'd up Antiquity, Custome, Canons, Councels and Lawes, and cry'd down the truth for noveltie, schisme, profanenesse and Sacriledge: when as we that have liv'd so long in abundant light, besides the sunny reflection of all the neighbouring Churches, have yet our hearts rivetted with those old opinions, and so obstructed and benumm'd with the same fleshly reasonings, which in our forefathers soone melted and gave way, against the morning beam of *Reformation*. If God had left undone this whole worke so contrary to flesh and blood, till these times, how should wee have yeelded to his heavenly call, had we beene taken, as they were, in the starknes of our ignorance, that yet after all these spirituall preparatives, and purgations have our earthly apprehensions so clamm'd and furr'd with the old levin. O if we freeze at noone after their earely thaw, let us feare lest the Sunne for ever hide himselfe, and turne his orient steps from our ingratefull Horizon justly condemn'd to be eternally benighted. Which dreadful judgement O thou the ever-begotten light, and perfect Image of the Father intercede may never come upon us, as we trust thou hast; for thou hast open'd our difficult and sad times, and given us an unexpected breathing after our long oppressions; thou hast done justice upon those that tyranniz'd over us, while some men waver'd, and admir'd a vaine shadow of wisedome in a tongue nothing slow to utter guile, though thou hast taught us to admire onely that which is good, and to count that onely praise-worthy which is grounded upon thy divine Precepts. Thou hast discover'd the plots, and frustrated the hopes of all the wicked in the Land; and put to shame the persecutors of thy Church; thou hast made our false *Prophets* to be found a lie in the sight of all the people, and chac'd them with sudden confusion and amazement before the redoubled brightnesse of thy descending cloud that now covers thy Tabernacle. Who is there that cannot trace thee now in thy beamy walke through the midst of thy Sanctuary, amidst those golden *candlesticks*, which have long suffer'd a dimnesse amongst us through the violence of those that had seiz'd them, and were more taken with the mention of their gold then of their starry light; teaching the doctrine of *Balaam* to cast a stumbling-block before thy servants, commanding them to eat things sacrifiz'd to Idols, and forcing them to fornication. Come therefore O thou that hast the seven starres in thy right hand, appoint thy chosen *Preists* according to their Orders, and courses of old, to minister before thee, and duely to dresse and powre out the consecrated oyle into thy holy and ever-burning lamps; thou hast sent out the spirit of prayer upon thy servants over all the Land to

this effect, and stirr'd up their vowes as the sound of many
waters about thy Throne. Every one can say that now certainly thou hast visited this land, and hast not forgotten the
utmost corners of the earth, in a time when men had thought
that thou wast gone up from us to the farthest end of the
Heavens, and hadst left to doe marvellously among the sons
of these last Ages. O perfect, and accomplish thy glorious
acts; for men may leave their works unfinisht, but thou art a
God, thy nature is perfection; shouldst thou bring us thus
far onward from *Egypt* to destroy us in this Wildernesse
though wee deserve; yet thy great name would suffer in the
rejoycing of thine enemies, and the deluded hope of all thy
servants. When thou hast settl'd peace in the Church, and
righteous judgement in the Kingdome, then shall all thy
Saints addresse their voyces of joy, and triumph to thee,
standing on the shoare of that red Sea into which our enemies
had almost driven us. And he that now for haste snatches up
a plain ungarnish't present as a thanke-offering to thee, which
could not bee deferr'd in regard of thy so many late deliverances wrought for us one upon another, may then perhaps
take up a Harp, and sing thee an elaborate Song to Generations. In that day it shall no more bee said as in scorne, this
or that was never held so till this present Age, when men have
better learnt that the times and seasons passe along under thy
feet, to goe and come at thy bidding, and as thou didst dig-
nifie our fathers dayes with many revelations above all the
fore-going ages, since thou tookst the flesh; so thou canst
vouchsafe to us (though unworthy) as large a portion of thy
spirit as thou pleasest; for who shall prejudice thy all-govern-
ing will? seeing the power of thy grace is not past away with
the primitive times, as fond and faithlesse men imagine,
but thy Kingdome is now at hand, and thou standing at the
dore. Come forth out of thy Royall Chambers, O Prince
of all the Kings of the earth, put on the visible roabes
of thy imperiall Majesty, take up that unlimited Scepter
which thy Almighty Father hath bequeath'd thee; for now
the voice of thy Bride calls thee, and all creatures sigh to bee
renew'd. . . .

¶ The Reason of Church-Governement

THE first and greatest reason of Church-government, we may securely with the assent of many on the adverse part, affirme to be, because we finde it so ordain'd and set out to us by the appointment of God in the Scriptures; but whether this be Presbyteriall, or Prelaticall, it cannot be brought to the scanning, untill I have said what is meet to some who do not think it for the ease of their inconsequent opinions, to grant that Church discipline is platform'd in the Bible, but that it is left to the discretion of men. To this conceit of theirs I answer, that it is both unsound and untrue. For there is not that thing in the world of more grave and urgent importance throughout the whole life of man, then is discipline. What need I instance? He that hath read with judgement, of Nations and Common-wealths, of Cities and Camps, of peace and warre, sea and land, will readily agree that the flourishing and decaying of all civill societies, all the moments and turnings of humane occasions are mov'd to and fro as upon the axle of discipline. So that whatsoever power or sway in mortall things weaker men have attributed to fortune, I durst with more confidence (the honour of divine providence ever sav'd) ascribe either to the vigor, or the slacknesse of discipline. Nor is there any sociable perfection in this life civill or sacred that can be above discipline, but she is that which with her musicall cords preserves and holds all the parts thereof together. Hence in those perfect armies of *Cyrus* in *Xenophon*, and *Scipio* in the Roman stories, the excellence of military skill was esteem'd, not by the not needing, but by the readiest submitting to the edicts of their commander. And certainly discipline is not only the removall of disorder, but if any visible shape can be given to divine things, the very visible shape and image of vertue, whereby she is not only seene in the regular gestures and motions of her heavenly paces as she walkes, but also makes the harmony of her voice audible to mortall eares. Yea the Angels themselves, in whom no disorder is fear'd, as the Apostle that saw them in his rapture describes, are distinguisht and quaterniond into their celestiall Princedomes, and Satrapies, according as God himselfe hath writ his imperiall decrees through the great provinces of heav'n. The state also of the blessed in Paradise, though never so perfect, is not therefore left without discipline, whose golden survaying reed marks out and measures every quarter and circuit of new Jerusalem. Yet it is not to be conceiv'd that those eternall effluences of sanctity and love in the glorified Saints should by this meanes be confin'd and cloy'd with repetition of that which is prescrib'd, but that our happinesse may orbe it selfe into a thousand vagancies of glory and delight, and with a kinde of eccentricall equation be as it were an invariable Planet of joy and felicity, how much lesse can we believe that God would leave his fraile and feeble, though not lesse beloved Church here below to the perpetuall stumble of conjecture and disturbance in this our darke voyage without the card and compasse of Discipline. Which is so hard to be of mans making, that we may see even in the guidance of a civill state to worldly happinesse, it is not for every learned, or every wise man, though many of them consult in common, to invent or frame a discipline, but if it be at all the worke of man, it must be of such a one as is a true knower of himselfe, and himselfe in whom contemplation and practice, wit, prudence, fortitude, and eloquence must be rarely met, both to comprehend the hidden causes of things, and span in his thoughts all the various effects that passion or complexion can worke in mans nature; and hereto must his hand be at defiance with gaine, and his heart in all vertues heroick. So far is it from the kenne of these wretched projectors of ours that bescraull their Pamflets every day with new formes of government for our Church. And therefore all the ancient lawgivers were either truly inspir'd as *Moses*, or were such men as with authority anough might give it out to be so, as *Minos*, *Lycurgus*, *Numa*, because they wisely forethought that men would never quietly submit to such a discipline as had not more of Gods hand in it then mans. To come within the narrownesse of houshold government, observation will shew us many deepe counsellers of state and judges to demean themselves incorruptly in the setl'd course of affaires, and many worthy Preachers upright in their lives, powerfull in their audience; but look upon either of these men where they are left to their own disciplining at home,

and you shall soone perceive for all their single knowledge
and uprightnesse, how deficient they are in the regulating of
their own family; not only in what may concerne the vertuous and decent composure of their minds in their severall
places, but that which is of a lower and easier performance,
the right possessing of the outward vessell, their body, in
health or sicknesse, rest or labour, diet, or abstinence, whereby to render it more pliant to the soule, and usefull to the
Common-wealth: which if men were but as good to discipline
themselves, as some are to tutor their Horses and Hawks, it
could not be so grosse in most housholds. . . .

. . . It was not the prevention of schisme, but it was schisme
it selfe, and the hatefull thirst of Lording in the Church that
first bestow'd a being upon Prelaty; this was the true cause,
but the pretence is stil the same. The Prelates, as they would
have it thought, are the only mawls of schisme. Forsooth if
they be put downe, a deluge of innumerable sects will follow;
we shall be all Brownists, Familists, Anabaptists. For the
word Puritan seemes to be quasht, and all that heretofore
were counted such, are now Brownists. And thus doe they
raise an evill report upon the expected reforming grace that
God hath bid us hope for, like those faithlesse spies, whose
carcasses shall perish in the wildernesse of their owne confused ignorance, and never taste the good of reformation.
Doe they keep away schisme? if to bring a num and chil'
stupidity of soul, an unactive blindnesse of minde upon the
people by their leaden doctrine, or no doctrine at all, if to
persecute all knowing and zealous Christians by the violence
of their courts, be to keep away schisme, they keep away
schisme indeed; and by this kind of discipline all *Italy* and
Spaine is as purely and politickly kept from schisme as *England* hath beene by them. With as good a plea might the
dead palsie boast to a man, tis I that free you from stitches
and paines, and the troublesome feeling of cold and heat, of
wounds and strokes; if I were gone, all these would molest
you. The Winter might as well vaunt it selfe against the
Spring, I destroy all noysome and rank weeds, I keepe downe
all pestilent vapours. Yes and all wholesome herbs, and all
fresh dews, by your violent and hidebound frost; but when
the gentle west winds shall open the fruitfull bosome of the

earth thus over-girded by your imprisonment, then the flowers put forth and spring, and then the Sunne shall scatter the mists, and the manuring hand of the Tiller shall root up all that burdens the soile without thank to your bondage. But farre worse then any frozen captivity is the bondage of Prelates, for that other, if it keep down any thing which is good, within the earth, so doth it likewise that which is ill, but these let out freely the ill, and keep down the good, or else keepe downe the lesser ill, and let out the greatest. Be asham'd at last to tell the Parlament ye curbe Schismaticks, when as they know ye cherish and side with Papists, and are now as it were one party with them, and tis said they helpe to petition for ye.   Can we believe that your government strains in good earnest at the petty gnats of schisme, when as we see it makes nothing to swallow the Camel heresie of *Rome;* but that indeed your throats are of the right Pharisaical straine. Where are those schismaticks with whom the Prelats hold such hot skirmish? shew us your acts, those glorious annals which your Courts of loathed memory lately deceas'd have left us? those schismaticks I doubt me wil be found the most of them such as whose only schisme was to have spoke the truth against your high abominations and cruelties in the Church; this is the schisme ye hate most, the removall of your criminous Hierarchy. A politick government of yours, and of a pleasant conceit, set up to remove those as a pretended schisme, that would remove you as a palpable heresie in government. If the schisme would pardon ye that, she might go jagg'd in as many cuts and slashes as she pleas'd for you. As for the rending of the Church, we have many reasons to thinke it is not that which ye labour to prevent so much as the rending of your pontificall sleeves: that schisme would be the sorest schisme to you, that would be Brownisme and Anabaptisme indeed. If we go downe, say you, as if *Adrians* wall were broke, a flood of sects will rush in. What sects? What are their opinions? give us the Inventory; it will appeare both by your former prosecutions and your present instances, that they are only such to speake of as are offended with your lawlesse government, your ceremonies, your Liturgy, an extract of the Masse book translated. But that they should be contemners of publick prayer, and Churches us'd without superstition, I trust God will manifest it ere long to be as false a slander, as your former slanders against the Scots. Noise it till ye be hoarse; that a rabble of Sects will come in, it will be answer'd ye, no rabble sir Priest, but a unanimous multitude of good Protestants will then joyne to the Church, which now because of you stand separated. This will be the dreadfull consequence of your removall. As for those terrible names of Sectaries and Schismaticks which ye have got together, we know your manner of fight, when the quiver of your arguments which is ever thin, and weakly stor'd, after the first brunt is quite empty, your course is to betake ye to your other quiver of slander, wherein lyes your best archery. And whom ye could not move by sophisticall arguing, them you thinke to confute by scandalous misnaming. Thereby inciting the blinder sort of people to mislike and deride sound doctrine and good christianity under two or three vile and hatefull terms, But if we could easily indure and dissolve your doubtiest reasons in argument, we shall more easily beare the worst of your unreasonablenesse in calumny and false report. Especially being foretold by Christ, that if he our Master were by your predecessors call'd Samaritan and Belzebub, we must not think it strange if his best Disciples in the reformation, as at first by those of your tribe they were call'd Lollards and Hussites, so now by you be term'd Puritans, and Brownists. But my hope is that the people of England will not suffer themselves to be juggl'd thus out of their faith and religion by a mist of names cast before their eyes, but will search wisely by the Scriptures, and look quite through this fraudulent aspersion of a disgracefull name into the things themselves: knowing that the Primitive Christians in their times were accounted such as are now call'd Familists and Adamites, or worse. And many on the Prelatick side like the Church of *Sardis* have a name to live, and yet are dead; to be Protestants, and are indeed Papists in most of their principles. Thus perswaded, this your old fallacy wee shall soone unmask, and quickly apprehend how you prevent schisme, and who are your schismaticks. . . .

. . . How happy were it for this frail, and as it may be truly call'd, mortall life of man, since all earthly things which have the name of good and convenient in our daily use, are withall so cumbersome and full of trouble if knowledge yet which is the best and lightsomest possession of the mind, were as the common saying is, no burden, and that what it wanted of being a load to any part of the body, it did not with a heavie advantage overlay upon the spirit. For not to speak of that knowledge that rests in the contemplation of naturall causes and dimensions, which must needs be a lower wisdom, as the object is low, certain it is that he who hath obtain'd in more then the scantest measure to know any thing distinctly of God, and of his true worship, and what is infallibly good and happy in the state of mans life, what in it selfe evil and miserable, though vulgarly not so esteem'd, he that hath obtain'd to know this, the only high valuable wisdom indeed, remembring also that God even to a strictnesse requires the improvment of these his entrusted gifts, cannot but sustain a sorer burden of mind, and more pressing then any support-able toil, or waight, which the body can labour under; how and in what manner he shall dispose and employ those summes of knowledge and illumination, which God hath sent him into this world to trade with. And that which aggravats the burden more, is, that having receiv'd amongst his allotted parcels certain pretious truths of such an orient lustre as no Diamond can equall, which never the lesse he has in charge to put off at any cheap rate, yea for nothing to them that will, the grate Marchants of this world fearing that this cours would soon discover, and disgrace the fals glitter of their deceitfull wares wherewith they abuse the people, like poor Indians with beads and glasses, practize by all means how they may suppresse the venting of such rarities and such a cheapnes as would undoe them, and turn their trash upon their hands. Therefore by gratifying the corrupt desires of men in fleshly doctrines, they stirre them up to persecute with hatred and contempt all those that seek to bear themselves uprightly in this their spiritual factory: which they foreseeing, though they cannot but testify of Truth and the excellence of that heavenly traffick which they bring, against what opposition, or danger soever, yet needs must it sit heavily upon their spirits, that being in Gods prime intention and their own, selected heralds of peace, and dispensers of treasure inestim-able without price to them that have no pence, they finde in the discharge of their commission that they are made the greatest variance and offence, a very sword and fire both in house and City over the whole earth. This is that which the sad Prophet *Jeremiah* laments, *Wo is me my mother, that thou hast born me a man of strife, and contention.* And although divine inspiration must certainly have been sweet to those ancient profets, yet the irksomnesse of that truth which they brought was so unpleasant to them, that every where they call it a burden. Yea that mysterious book of Revelation which the great Evangelist was bid to eat, as it had been some eye-brightning electuary of knowledge, and foresight, though it were sweet in his mouth, and in the learning, it was bitter in his belly; bitter in the denouncing. Nor was this hid from the wise Poet *Sophocles*, who in that place of his Tragedy where *Tiresias* is call'd to resolve K. *Edipus* in a matter which he knew would be grievous, brings him in bemoaning his lot, that he knew more then other men. For surely to every good and peaceable man it must in nature needs be a hatefull thing to be the displeaser, and molester of thousands; much better would it like him doubtlesse to be the messenger of gladnes and contentment, which is his chief intended busines, to all mankind, but that they resist and oppose their own true happinesse. But when God commands to take the trumpet and blow a dolorous or a jarring blast, it lies not in mans will what he shall say, or what he shall conceal. If he shall think to be silent, as *Jeremiah* did, because of the reproach and derision he met with daily, and *all his familiar friends watcht for his halting* to be reveng'd on him for speaking the truth, he would be forc't to confesse as he confest, *his word was in my heart as a burning fire shut up in my bones I was weary with forbearing, and could not stay.* Which might teach these times not suddenly to condemn all things that are sharply spoken, or vehemently written, as proceeding out of stomach, virulence and ill nature, but to consider rather that if the Prelats have leav to say the worst that can be said, and doe the worst that can be don, while they strive to keep to themselves to their great pleasure and commodity those things which they ought to render up, no man can be justly offended with him that shall endeavour to impart and bestow without any gain to himselfe those sharp, but saving words which would be a terror, and a torment in him to keep back. For me I have determin'd to lay up as the best treasure, and solace of a good old age, if God voutsafe it me, the honest liberty of free speech from my youth, where I shall think it available in so dear a concernment as the Churches good. For if I be either by disposition, or what other cause too inquisitive, or suspitious of my self and mine own doings, who can help it? but this I foresee, that should the Church be brought under heavy oppression, and God have given me ability the while to reason against that man that should be the author of so foul a deed, or should she by blessing from above on the industry and courage of faithfull men change this her distracted estate into better daies without the lest furtherance or contribution of those few talents which God at that present had lent me, I foresee what stories I should heare within my selfe, all my life after, of discourage and reproach. Timorous and ingratefull, the Church of God is now again at the foot of her insulting enemies: and thou bewailst, what matters it for thee or thy bewailing? when time was, thou couldst not find a syllable of all that thou hadst read, or studied, to utter in her behalfe. Yet ease and leasure was given thee for thy retired thoughts out of the sweat of other men. Thou hadst the diligence, the parts, the language of a man, if a vain subject were to be adorn'd or beautifi'd, but when the cause of God and his Church was to be pleaded, for which purpose that tongue was given thee which thou hast, God listen'd if he could heare thy voice among his zealous servants, but thou wert domb as a beast; from hence forward be that which thine own brutish silence hath made thee. Or else I should have heard on the other eare, slothfull, and ever to be set light by, the Church hath now overcom her late distresses after the unwearied labours of many her true servants that stood up in her defence; thou also wouldst take upon thee to share amongst them of their joy: but wherefore thou? where canst thou shew any word or deed of thine which might have hasten'd her peace; what ever thou dost now talke, or write, or look is the almes of other mens active prudence and zeale. Dare not now to say, or doe any thing better then thy former sloth and infancy, of if thou darst, thou dost impudently to make a thrifty purchase of boldnesse to thy selfe

out of the painfull merits of other men: what before was thy
sin, is now thy duty to be, abject, and worthlesse. These and
such like lessons as these, I know would have been my
Matins duly, and my Even-song. But now by this litle diligence, mark what a privilege I have gain'd; with good men
and Saints to clame my right of lamenting the tribulations of
the Church, if she should suffer, when others that have ventur'd nothing for her sake, have not the honour to be admitted mourners. But if she lift up her drooping head and
prosper, among those that have something more then wisht
her welfare, I have my charter and freehold of rejoycing to
me and my heires. Concerning therefore this wayward subject against prelaty, the touching whereof is so distastfull and
disquietous to a number of men, as by what hath been said
I may deserve of charitable readers to be credited, that neither
envy nor gall hath enterd me upon this controversy, but the
enforcement of conscience only, and a preventive fear least
the omitting of this duty should be against me when I would
store up to my self the good provision of peacefull hours. So
lest it should be still imputed to me, as I have found it hath
bin, that some self-pleasing humor of vain-glory hath incited me to contest with men of high estimation, now while
green yeers are upon my head, from this needlesse surmisall I
shall hope to disswade the intelligent and equal auditor, if I
can but say successfully that which in this exigent behoovs
me, although I would be heard only, if it might be, by the
elegant and learned reader, to whom principally for a while I
shal beg leav I may addresse my selfe. To him it will be no
new thing though I tell him that if I hunted after praise by the
ostentation of wit and learning, I should not write thus out of
mine own season, when I have neither yet compleated to my
minde the full circle of my private studies, although I complain not of any insufficiency to the matter in hand, or were
I ready to my wishes, it were a folly to commit any thing
elaborately compos'd to the carelesse and interrupted listening of these tumultuous times. Next if I were wise only to
mine own ends, I would certainly take such a subject as of it
self might catch applause, whereas this hath all the disadvantages on the contrary, and such a subject as the publish-
ing whereof might be delayd at pleasure, and time enough to

pencill it over with all the curious touches of art, even to the
perfection of a faultlesse picture, whenas in this argument the
not deferring is of great moment to the good speeding, that
if solidity have leisure to doe her office, art cannot have
much. Lastly, I should not chuse this manner of writing
wherin knowing my self inferior to my self, led by the genial
power of nature to another task, I have the use, as I may
account it, but of my left hand. And though I shall be foolish
in saying more to this purpose, yet since it will be such a folly
as wisest men going about to commit, have only confest and so
committed, I may trust with more reason, because with more
folly to have courteous pardon. For although a Poet soaring
in the high region of his fancies with his garland and singing
robes about him might without apology speak more of himself then I mean to do, yet for me sitting here below in the
cool element of prose, a mortall thing among many readers
of no Empyreall conceit, to venture and divulge unusual
things of my selfe, I shall petition to the gentler sort, it may
not be envy to me. I must say therefore that after I had from
my first yeeres by the ceaselesse diligence and care of my
father, whom God recompence, bin exercis'd to the tongues,
and some sciences, as my age would suffer, by sundry masters
and teachers both at home and at the schools, it was found
that whether ought was impos'd me by them that had the
overlooking, or betak'n to of mine own choise in English, or
other tongue, prosing or versing, but chiefly this latter, the
stile by certain vital signes it had, was likely to live. But
much latelier in the privat Academies of *Italy*, whither I was
favor'd to resort, perceiving that some trifles which I had in
memory, compos'd at under twenty or thereabout (for the
manner is that every one must give some proof of his wit and
reading there) met with acceptance above what was lookt for,
and other things which I had shifted in scarcity of books and
conveniences to patch up amongst them, were receiv'd with
written Encomiums, which the Italian is not forward to
bestow on men of this side the *Alps*, I began thus farre to
assent both to them and divers of my friends here at home,
and not lesse to an inward prompting which now grew daily
upon me, that by labour and intent study (which I take to be
my portion in this life) joyn'd with the strong propensity of

nature, I might perhaps leave something so written to after-times, as they should not willingly let it die. These thoughts at once possess me, and these other. That if I were certain to write as men buy Leases, for three lives and downward, there ought no regard be sooner had, then to Gods glory by the honour and instruction of my country. For which cause, and not only for that I knew it would be hard to arrive at the second rank among the Latines, I apply'd my selfe to that resolution which *Ariosto* follow'd against the perswasions of *Bembo*, to fix all the industry and art I could unite to the adorning of my native tongue; not to make verbal curiosities the end, that were a toylsom vanity, but to be an interpreter and relater of the best and sagest things among mine own Citizens throughout this Iland in the mother dialect. That what the greatest and choycest wits of *Athens*, *Rome*, or modern *Italy*, and those Hebrews of old did for their country, I in my proportion with this over and above of being a Christian, might doe for mine: not caring to be once nam'd abroad, though perhaps I could attaine to that, but content with these British Ilands as my world, whose fortune hath hitherto bin, that if the Athenians, as some say, made their small deeds great and renowned by their eloquent writers, *England* hath had her noble atchievments made small by the unskilfull handling of monks and mechanicks.

Time servs not now, and perhaps I might seem too profuse to give any certain account of what the mind at home in the spacious circuits of her musing hath liberty to propose to her self, though of highest hope, and hardest attempting, whether that Epick form whereof the two poems of *Homer*, and those other two of *Virgil* and *Tasso* are a diffuse, and the book of *Job* a brief model: or whether the rules of *Aristotle* herein are strictly to be kept, or nature to be follow'd, which in them that know art, and use judgement is no transgression, but an inriching of art. And lastly what K. or Knight before the conquest might be chosen in whom to lay the pattern of a Christian *Heroe*. And as *Tasso* gave to a Prince of *Italy* his chois whether he would command him to write of *Godfreys* expedition against the infidels, or *Belisarius* against the Gothes, or *Charlemain* against the Lombards; if to the instinct of nature and the imboldning of art ought may be trusted, and that there be nothing advers in our climat, or the fate of this age, it haply would be no rashnesse from an equal diligence and inclination to present the like offer in our own ancient stories. Or whether those Dramatick constitutions, wherein *Sophocles* and *Euripides* raigne shall be found more doctrinal and exemplary to a Nation, the Scripture also affords us a divine pastoral Drama in the Song of *Salomon* consisting of two persons and a double *Chorus*, as *Origen* rightly judges. And the Apocalyps of Saint *John* is the majestick image of a high and stately Tragedy, shutting up and intermingling her solemn Scenes and Acts with a seven-fold *Chorus* of halleluja's and harping symphonies: and this my opinion the grave autority of *Pareus* commenting that booke is sufficient to confirm. Or if occasion shall lead to imitat those magnifick Odes and Hymns wherein *Pindarus* and *Callimachus* are in most things worthy, some others in their frame judicious, in their matter most an end faulty: But those frequent songs throughout the law and prophets beyond all these, not in their divine argument alone, but in the very critical art of composition may be easily made appear over all the kinds of Lyrick poesy, to be incomparable. These abilities, wheresoever they be found, are the inspired guift of God rarely bestow'd, but yet to some (though most abuse) in every Nation: and are of power beside the office of a pulpit, to inbreed and cherish in a great people the seeds of vertu, and publick civility, to allay the perturbations of the mind, and set the affections in right tune, to celebrate in glorious and lofty Hymns the throne and equipage of Gods Almightinesse, and what he works, and what he suffers to be wrought with high providence in his Church, to sing the victorious agonies of Martyrs and Saints, the deeds and triumphs of just and pious Nations doing valiantly through faith against the enemies of Christ, to deplore the general relapses of Kingdoms and States from justice and Gods true worship. Lastly, whatsoever in religion is holy and sublime, in vertu amiable, or grave, whatsoever hath passion or admiration in all the changes of that which is call'd fortune from without, or the wily suttleties and refluxes of mans thoughts from within, all these things with a solid and treatable smoothnesse to paint out and describe. Teaching over the whole book of sanctity and vertu through all the instances of example with such delight to those especially of soft and delicious temper who will not so much as look upon Truth herselfe, unlesse they see her elegantly drest, that whereas the paths of honesty and good life appear now rugged and difficult, though they be indeed easy and pleasant, they would then appeare to all men both easy and pleasant though they were rugged and difficult indeed. And what a benefit this would be to our youth and gentry, may be soon guest by what we know of the corruption and bane which they suck in dayly from the writings and interludes of libidinous and ignorant Poetasters, who having scars ever heard of that which is the main consistence of a true poem, the choys of such persons as they ought to introduce, and what is morall and decent to each one, doe for the most part lap up vitious principles in sweet pils to be swallow'd down, and make the tast of vertuous documents harsh and sowr. But because the spirit of man cannot demean it selfe lively in this body without some recreating intermission of labour, and serious things, it were happy for the Common wealth, if our Magistrates, as in those famous governments of old, would take into their care, not only the deciding of our contentious Law cases and brauls, but the managing of our publick sports, and festival pastimes, that they might be, not such as were autoriz'd a while since, the provocations of drunkennesse and lust, but such as may inure and harden our bodies by martial exercises to all warlike skil and performance, and may civilize, adorn and make discreet our minds by the learned and affable meeting of frequent Academies, and the procurement of wise and artfull recitations sweetned with eloquent and gracefull inticements to the love and practice of justice, temperance and fortitude, instructing and bettering the Nation at all opportunities, that the call of wisdom and vertu may be heard every where, as *Salomon* saith, *She crieth without, she uttereth her voice in the streets, in the top of high places, in the chief concours, and in the openings of the Gates.* Whether this may not be not only in Pulpits, but after another persuasive method, at set and solemn Paneguries, in Theaters, porches, or what other place, or way may win most upon the people to receiv at once both recreation, and instruction, let them in autority consult. The thing which I had to say, and those intentions which have liv'd within me ever since I could conceiv my self any thing worth to my Countrie, I return to crave excuse that urgent reason hath pluckt from me by an abortive and foredated discovery. And the accomplishment of them lies not but in a power above mans to promise; but that none hath by more studious ways endeavour'd, and with more unwearied spirit that none shall, that I dare almost averre of my self, as farre as life and free leasure will extend, and that the Land had once infranchis'd her self from this impertinent yoke of prelaty, under whose inquisitorius and tyrannical duncery no free and splendid wit can flourish. Neither doe I think it shame to covnant with any knowing reader, that for some few yeers yet I may go on trust with him toward the payment of what I am now indebted, as being a work not to be rays'd from the heat of youth, or the vapours of wine, like that which flows at wast from the pen of some vulgar Amorist, or the trencher fury of a riming parasite, nor to be obtain'd by the invocation of Dame Memory and her Siren daughters, but by devout prayer to that eternall Spirit who can enrich with all utterance and knowledge, and sends out his Seraphim with the hallow'd fire of his Altar to touch and purify the lips of whom he pleases: to this must be added industrious and select reading, steddy observation, insight into all seemly and generous arts and affaires, till which in some measure be compast, at mine own peril and cost I refuse not to sustain this expectation from as many as are not loath to hazard so much credulity upon the best pledges that I can give them. Although it nothing content me to have disclos'd thus much before hand, but that I trust hereby to make it manifest with what small willingnesse I endure to interrupt the pursuit of no lesse hopes then these, and leave a calme and pleasing solitarynes fed with cherful and confident thoughts, to imbark in a troubl'd sea of noises and hoars disputes, put from beholding the bright countenance of truth in the quiet and still air of delightfull studies to come into the dim reflexion of hollow antiquities sold by the seeming bulk, and there be fain to club quotations with men whose learning and beleif lies in marginal stuffings, who when they have like good sumpters laid ye down their hors load of citations and fathers at your dore, with a rapsody of who and who were Bishops here or there, ye may take off their packsaddles, their days work is don, and episcopacy, as they think, stoutly vindicated. Let any gentle apprehension that can distinguish learned pains from unlearned drudgery, imagin what pleasure or profoundnesse can be in this, or what honour to deal against such adversaries. But were it the meanest under-service, if God by his Secretary conscience injoyn it, it were sad for me if I should draw back, for me especially, now when all men offer their aid to help ease and lighten the difficult labours of the Church, to whose service by the intentions of my parents and friends I was destin'd of a child, and in mine own resolutions, till comming to some maturity of yeers and perceaving what tyranny had invaded the Church, that he who would take Orders must subscribe slave, and take an oath withall, which unlesse he took with a conscience that would retch, he must either strait perjure, or split his faith, I thought it better to preferre a blamelesse silence before the sacred office of speaking bought, and begun with servitude and forswearing. Howsoever thus Church-outed by the Prelats, hence may appear the right I have to meddle in these matters, as before the necessity and constraint appear'd. . . .

. . . It was thought of old in Philosophy, that shame or to call it better, the reverence of our elders, our brethren, and friends was the greatest incitement to vertuous deeds and the greatest dissuasion from unworthy attempts that might be. Hence we may read in the Iliad where *Hector* being wisht to retire from the battel, many of his forces being routed, makes answer that he durst not for shame, lest the Trojan Knights and Dames should think he did ignobly. And certain it is that wheras Terror is thought such a great stickler in a Commonwealth, honourable shame is a farre greater, and has more reason. For where shame is there is fear, but where fear is there is not presently shame. And if any thing may be done to inbreed in us this generous and Christianly reverence one of another, the very Nurs and Guardian of piety and vertue, it can not sooner be then by such a discipline in the Church, as may use us to have in aw the assemblies of the faithful, and to count it a thing most grievous, next to the grieving of Gods Spirit, to offend those whom he hath put in autority, as a healing superintendence over our lives and behaviours, both to our own happines and that we may not give offence to good men, who without amends by us made, dare not against Gods command hold communion with us in holy things. And this will be accompanied with a religious dred of being outcast from the company of Saints, and from the fatherly protection of God in his Church, to consort with the devil and his angels. But there is yet a more ingenuous and noble degree of honest shame, or call it if you will an esteem, whereby men bear an inward reverence toward their own persons. And if the love of God as a fire sent from Heaven to be ever kept alive upon the altar of our hearts, be the first principle of all godly and vertuous actions in men, this pious and just honouring of our selves is the second, and may be thought as the radical moisture and fountain head, whence every laudable and worthy enterprize issues forth. And although I have giv'n it the name of a liquid thing, yet it is not incontinent to bound it self, as humid things are, but hath in it a most restraining and powerfull abstinence to start back, and glob it self upward from the mixture of any ungenerous and unbeseeming motion, or any soile wherewith it may peril to stain it self. Something I confesse it is to be asham'd of evil doing in the presence of any, and to reverence the opinion and the countenance of a good man rather then a bad, fearing most in his sight to offend, goes so farre as almost to be vertuous; yet this is but still the feare of infamy, and many such, when they find themselves alone, saving their reputation will compound with other scruples, and come to a close treaty with their dearer vices in secret. But he that holds himself in reverence and due esteem, both for the dignity of Gods image upon him, and for the price of his redemption, which he thinks is visibly markt upon his forehead, accounts himselfe both a fit person to do the noblest and godliest deeds, and much better worth then to deject and defile, with such a debasement and such a pollution as sin is, himselfe so highly ransom'd and enobl'd to a new friendship and filiall relation with God. Nor can he fear so much the offence and reproach of others, as he dreads and would blush at the reflection of his own severe and modest eye upon himselfe, if it should see him doing or imagining that which is sinfull though in the

deepest secrecy. How shall a man know to do himselfe this
right, how to performe this honourable duty of estimation
and respect towards his own soul and body? which way will
leade him best to this hill top of sanctity and goodnesse
above which there is no higher ascent but to the love of God
which from this self-pious regard cannot be assunder? no
better way doubtlesse then to let him duly understand that as
he is call'd by the high calling of God to be holy and pure, so
is he by the same appointment ordain'd, and by the Churches
call admitted to such offices of discipline in the Church to
which his owne spirituall gifts by the example of Apostolick
institution have autoriz'd him. For we have learnt that the
scornfull terme of Laick, the consecrating of Temples, car-
pets, and table-clothes, the railing in of a repugnant and con-
tradictive Mount Sinai in the Gospell, as if the touch of a lay
Christian who is never the lesse Gods living temple, could
profane dead judaisms, the exclusion of Christs people from
the offices of holy discipline through the pride of a usurping
Clergy, causes the rest to have an unworthy and abject
opinion of themselves; to approach to holy duties with a
slavish fear, and to unholy doings with a familiar boldnesse.
For seeing such a wide and terrible distance between religious things and themselves, and that in respect of a woodden
table and the perimeter of holy ground about it, a flagon pot,
and a linnen corporal, the Priest esteems their lay-ships unhallow'd and unclean, they fear religion with such a fear as
loves not, and think the purity of the Gospell too pure for
them, and that any uncleannesse is more sutable to their un-
consecrated estate. But when every good Christian throughly
acquainted with all those glorious privileges of sanctification
and adoption which render him more sacred then any dedicated altar or element, shall be restor'd to his right in the
Church, and not excluded from such place of spirituall
government as his Christian abilities and his approved good
life in the eye and testimony of the Church shall preferre
him to, this and nothing sooner will open his eyes to a wise
and true valuation of himselfe, which is so requisite and
high a point of Christianity, and will stirre him up to walk
worthy the honourable and grave imployment wherewith
God and the Church hath dignifi'd him: not fearing lest he

should meet with some outward holy thing in religion which his lay touch or presence might profane, but lest something unholy from within his own heart should dishonour and profane in himselfe that Priestly unction and Clergy-right whereto Christ hath entitl'd him. Then would the congregation of the Lord soone recover the true likenesse and visage of what she is indeed, a holy generation, a royall Priesthood, a Saintly communion, the houshold and City of God. And this I hold to be another considerable reason why the functions of Church-government ought to be free and open to any Christian man though never so laick, if his capacity, his faith, and prudent demeanour commend him. And this the Apostles warrant us to do. But the Prelats object that this will bring profanenesse into the Church, to whom may be reply'd, that none have brought that in more then their own irreligious courses; nor more driven holinesse out of living into livelesse things. For whereas God who hath cleans'd every beast and creeping worme, would not suffer S. *Peter* to call them common or unclean, the Prelat Bishops in their printed orders hung up in Churches have proclaim'd the best of creatures, mankind, so unpurifi'd and contagious, that for him to lay his hat, or his garment upon the Chancell table they have defin'd it no lesse hainous in expresse words then to profane the Table of the Lord. And thus have they by their Canaanitish doctrine (for that which was to the Jew but jewish is to the Christian no better then Canaanitish) thus have they made common and unclean, thus have they made profane that nature which God hath not only cleans'd, but Christ also hath assum'd. And now that the equity and just reason is so perspicuous, why in Ecclesiastick censure the assistance should be added of such, as whom not the vile odour of gaine and fees (forbid it God and blow it with a whirlewinde out of our land) but charity, neighbourhood, and duty to Church-government hath call'd together, where could a wiseman wish a more equall, gratuitous, and meek examination of any offence that he might happen to commit against Christianity then here? would he preferre those proud simoniacall Courts? Thus therefore the Minister assisted attends his heavenly and spirituall, cure. Where we shall see him both in the course of his proceeding, and first in the excellence of his end from the magistrate farre different, and not more different then excelling. His end is to recover all that is of man both soul and body to an everlasting health: and yet as for worldly happinesse, which is the proper sphere wherein the magistrate cannot but confine his motion without a hideous exorbitancy from law, so little aims the Minister, as his intended scope, to procure the much prosperity of this life, that oft-times he may have cause to wish much of it away, as a diet puffing up the soul with a slimy fleshinesse, and weakning her principall organick parts. Two heads of evill he has to cope with, ignorance and malice. Against the former he provides the daily Manna of incorruptible doctrine, not at those set meales only in publick, but as oft as he shall know that each infirmity, or constitution requires. Against the latter with all the branches thereof, not medling with that restraining and styptick surgery which the law uses, not indeed against the malady but against the eruptions, and outermost effects thereof. He on the contrary beginning at the prime causes and roots of the disease sends in those two divine ingredients of most cleansing power to the soul, Admonition and Reproof, besides which two there is no drug or antidote that can reach to purge the mind, and without which all other experiments are but vain, unlesse by accident. And he that will not let these passe into him, though he be the greatest King, as *Plato* affirms, must be thought to remaine impure within, and unknowing of those things wherein his purenesse and his knowledge should most appear. As soon therefore as it may be discern'd that the Christian patient by feeding otherwhere on meats not allowable, but of evill juice, hath disorder'd his diet, and spread an ill humour through his vains immediatly disposing to a sicknesse, the minister as being much neerer both in eye and duty, then the magistrate, speeds him betimes to overtake that diffus'd malignance with some gentle potion of admonishment; or if ought be obstructed, puts in his opening and discussive confections. This not succeeding after once or twice or oftner, in the presence of two or three his faithfull brethren appointed thereto he advises him to be more carefull of his dearest health, and what it is that he so rashly hath let down in to the divine vessel of his soul Gods temple. If this obtaine not, he then with

the counsell of more assistants who are inform'd of what diligence hath been already us'd, with more speedy remedies
layes neerer siege to the entrenched causes of his distemper,
not sparing such fervent and well aim'd reproofs as may best
give him to see the dangerous estate wherein he is. To this
also his brethren and friends intreat, exhort, adjure, and all
these endeavours, as there is hope left, are more or lesse
repeated. But if, neither the regard of himselfe, nor the reverence of his Elders and friends prevaile with him, to leave his
vitious appetite, then as the time urges, such engines of terror God hath given into the hand of his minister as to search
the tenderest angles of the heart: one while he shakes his
stubbornnesse with racking convulsions nigh dispaire, other
whiles with deadly corrosives he gripes the very roots of his
faulty liver to bring him to life through the entry of death.
Hereto the whole Church beseech him, beg of him, deplore
him, pray for him. After all this perform'd with what patience
and attendance is possible, and no relenting on his part, having done the utmost of their cure, in the name of God and of
the Church they dissolve their fellowship with him, and holding forth the dreadfull sponge of excommunion pronounce
him wip't out of the list of Gods inheritance, and in the custody of Satan till he repent. Which horrid sentence though it
touch neither life, nor limme, nor any worldly possession, yet
has it such a penetrating force, that swifter then any chimicall
sulphur, or that lightning which harms not the skin, and
rifles the entrals, it scorches the inmost soul. Yet even this
terrible denouncement is left to the Church for no other
cause but to be as a rough and vehement cleansing medcin,
where the malady is obdurat; a mortifying to life, a kind of
saving by undoing. . . .

¶ An Apology against a Pamphlet
call'd A Modest Confutation of the Animadversions
upon the Remonstrant against SMECTYMNUUS

IF, Readers, to that same great difficulty of well doing what
we certainly know, were not added in most men as great a
carelessenes of knowing what they, and others ought to do,

we had bin long ere this, no doubt but all of us much farther on our way to some degree of peace and happinesse in this king-dome. But since our sinfull neglect of practising that which we know to be undoubtedly true and good, hath brought forth among us, through Gods just anger so great a difficulty now to know that which otherwise might be soone learnt, and hath divided us by a controversie of great importance in-deed, but of no hard solution, which is the more our punish-ment, I resolv'd (of what small moment soever I might be thought) to stand on that side where I saw both the plain autority of Scripture leading, and the reason of justice and equity perswading; with this opinion which esteemes it more unlike a Christian to be a cold neuter in the cause of the Church, then the law of *Solon* made it punishable after a sedition in the State. And because I observe that feare and dull disposition, lukewarmenesse and sloth are not seldomer wont to cloak themselves under the affected name of moder-ation, then true and lively zeale is customably dispareg'd with the terme of indiscretion, bitternesse, and choler, I could not to my thinking honor a good cause more from the heart, then by defending it earnestly, as oft as I could judge it to behoove me, notwithstanding any false name that could be invented to wrong, or undervalue an honest meaning. Wherein although I have not doubted to single forth more then once, such of them as were thought the chiefe and most nominated opposers on the other side, whom no man else undertooke: if I have done well either to be confident of the truth, whose force is best seene against the ablest resistance, or to be jealous and tender of the hurt that might be done among the weaker by the intrapping autority of great names titl'd to false opinions, or that it be lawfull to attribute some-what to guifts of Gods imparting, which I boast not, but thankfully acknowledge, and feare also lest at my certaine account they be reckon'd to me many rather then few, or if lastly it be but justice not to defraud of due esteeme the wearisome labours and studious watchings, wherein I have spent and tir'd out almost a whole youth, I shall not distrust to be acquitted of presumption. Knowing that if heretofore all ages have receav'd with favour and good acceptance the earliest industry of him that hath beene hopefull, it were but hard measure now, if the freedome of any timely spirit should be opprest meerely by the big and blunted fame of his elder adversary; and that his sufficiency must be now sentenc't, not by pondering the reason he shewes, but by calculating the yeares he brings. However, as my purpose is not, nor hath beene formerly, to looke on my adversary abroad, through the deceaving glasse of other mens great opinion of him, but at home, where I may finde him in the proper light of his owne worth, so now against the rancor of an evill tongue, from which I never thought so absurdly, as that I of all men should be exempt, I must be forc't to proceed from the unfained and diligent inquiry of mine owne conscience at home (for better way I know not, Readers) to give a more true account of my selfe abroad then this modest Confuter, as he calls himselfe, hath given of me. Albeit that in doing this I shall be sensible of two things which to me will be nothing pleasant; the one is, that not unlikely I shall be thought too much a party in mine owne cause, and therein to see least; the other, that I shall be put unwillingly to molest the publick view with the vindication of a private name; as if it were worth the while that the people should care whether such a one were thus, or thus. Yet those I intreat who have found the leasure to reade that name, however of small repute, unworthily defam'd, would be so good and so patient as to heare the same person not unneedfully defended. I will not deny but that the best apology against false accusers is silence and sufferance, and honest deeds set against dishonest words. And that I could at this time most easily, and securely, with the least losse of reputation use no other defence, I need not despaire to win beliefe. Whether I consider both the foolish contriving, and ridiculous aiming of these his slanderous bolts, shot so wide of any suspicion to be fastn'd on me, that I have oft with inward contentment perceav'd my friends congratulating themselves in my innocence, and my enemies asham'd of their partners folly. Or whether I look at these present times wherein most men now scarce permitted the liberty to think over their owne concernments have remov'd the seat of their thoughts more outward to the expectation of publick events. Or whether the examples of men, either noble or religious, who have sat downe lately with a meeke silence and sufferance under many libellous endorsements, may be a rule to others, I might well appease my self to put up any reproaches in such an honourable society of fellow-sufferers using no other defence. And were it that slander would be content to make an end where it first fixes, and not seek to cast out the like infamy upon each thing that hath but any relation to the person traduc't, I should have pleaded against this Confuter by no other advocates, then those which I first commended, Silence, and Sufferance, and speaking deeds against faltering words. But when I discern'd his intent was not so much to smite at me, as through me to render odious the truth which I had written, and to staine with ignominy that Evangelick doctrine which opposes the tradition of Prelaty, I conceav'd my selfe to be now not as mine own person, but as a member incorporate into that truth whereof I was perswaded, and whereof I had declar'd openly to be a partaker. Whereupon I thought it my duty, if not to my selfe, yet to the religious cause I had in hand, not to leave on my garment the least spot, or blemish in good name so long as God should give me to say that which might wipe it off. Lest those disgraces which I ought to suffer, if it so befall me, for my religion, through my default religion be made liable to suffer for me. And, whether it might not something reflect upon those reverent men whose friend I may be thought in writing the Animadversions, was not my last care to consider, if I should rest under these reproaches having the same common adversary with them, it might be counted small credit for their cause to have found such an assistant, as this babler hath devis'd me. What other thing in his book there is of dispute, or question, in answering thereto I doubt not to be justifi'd; except there be who will condemne me to have wasted time in throwing downe that which could not keepe it selfe up. As for others who notwithstanding what I can allege have yet decreed to mis-interpret the intents of my reply, I suppose they would have found as many causes to have mis-conceav'd the reasons of my silence.

To beginne therefore an Apology for those animadversions which I writ against the Remonstrant in defence of *Smectymnus,* since the Preface, which was purposely set before them, is not thought apologeticall anough; it will be best to acquaint ye, Readers, before other things, what the meaning was to write them in that manner which I did. For I do not look to be askt wherefore I writ the book, it being no difficulty to answer that I did it to those ends which the best men propose to themselves when they write. But wherfore in that manner neglecting the maine bulk of all that specious antiquity, which might stunne children, but not men, I chose rather to observe some kinde of military advantages to await him at his forragings, at his watrings, and when ever he felt himselfe secure to solace his veine in derision of his more serious opponents. And here let me have pardon, Readers, if the remembrance of that which he hath licenc't himselfe to utter contemptuously of those reverend men provoke me to doe that over againe which some expect I should excuse as too freely done; since I have two provocations, his latest insulting in his short answer, and their finall patience. I had no fear but that the authors of *Smectymnus* to all the shew of solidity which the Remonstrant could bring, were prepar'd both with skill and purpose to returne a suffizing answer, and were able anough to lay the dust and pudder in antiquity, which he and his, out of stratagem, are wont to raise; but when I saw his weake arguments headed with sharpe taunts, and that his designe was, if he could not refute them, yet at least with quips and snapping adagies to vapour them out, which they bent only upon the businesse were minded to let passe, by how much I saw them taking little thought for their own injuries, I must confesse I took it as my part the lesse to endure that my respected friends through their own unnecessary patience should thus lye at the mercy of a coy flurting stile; to be girded with frumps and curtall gibes, by one who makes sentences by the Statute, as if all above three inches long were confiscat. To me it seem'd an indignity, that whom his whole wisdome could not move from their place, them his impetuous folly should presume to ride over. And if I were more warme then was meet in any passage of that booke, which yet I do not yeild, I might use therein the patronage of no worse an author then *Gregory Nyssen*, who mentioning his sharpnesse against *Eunomius* in the defence of his brother *Basil*, holds himselfe irreprovable in that it *was not for himselfe, but in the cause of his brother; and in such cases,* saith he, *perhaps it is worthier pardon to be angry, then to be cooler*. And whereas this Confuter taxes the whole discourse of levity, I shall shew ye, Readers, wheresoever it shall be objected in particular that I have answer'd with as little lightnesse as the Remonstrant hath given example. I have not beene so light as the palme of a Bishop which is the lightest thing in the world when he brings out his book of Ordination: For then contrary to that which is wont in releasing out of prison, any one that will pay his fees is layd hands on. Another reason, it would not be amisse though the Remonstrant were told, wherefore he was in that unusuall manner beleaguer'd; and this was it, to pluck out of the heads of his admirers the conceit that all who are not Prelaticall, are grosse-headed, thick witted, illiterat, shallow. Can nothing then but Episcopacy teach men to speak good English, to pick and order a set of words judiciously? Must we learne from Canons and quaint Sermonings interlin'd with barbarous Latin to illumin a period, to wreath an Enthymema with maistrous dexterity? I rather encline, as I have heard it observ'd, that a Jesuits Italian when he writes, is ever naught, though he be borne and bred a *Florentine*, so to thinke that from like causes we may go neere to observe the same in the stile of a Prelat. For doubtlesse that indeed according to art is most eloquent, which returnes and approaches neerest to nature from whence it came; and they expresse nature best, who in their lives least wander from her safe leading, which may be call'd regenerate reason. So that how he should be truly eloquent who is not withall a good man, I see not. Never the lesse as oft as is to be dealt with men who pride themselves in their supposed art, to leave them unexcusable wherin they will not be better'd there be of those that esteeme Prelaty a figment, who yet can pipe, if they can dance, nor will be unfurnisht to shew that what the Prelats admire and have not, others have and admire not. The knowledge whereof, and not of that only, but of what the Scripture teacheth us how we ought to withstand the perverters of the Gospell were those other motives which gave the animadversions no leave to remit a continuall vehemence throughout the book. For as in teaching, doubtlesse the Spirit of meeknesse is most powerfull, so are the meeke only fit persons to be taught: as for the proud, the obstinate, and false Doctors of mens devices, be taught they will not; but discover'd and laid open they must be. For how can they admit of teaching who have the condemnation of God already upon them for refusing divine instruction; that is, to be *fill'd with their own devices*, as in the Proverbs we may reade; therefore we may safely imitate the method that God uses; *with the froward to be froward, and to throw scorne upon the scorner*, whom if any thing, nothing else will heale. And if *the righteous shall laugh at the destruction of the ungodly*, they may also laugh at their pertinacious and incurable obstinacy, and at the same time be mov'd with detestation of their seducing malice, who imploy all their wits to defend a Prelaty usurpt, and to deprave that just government, which pride and ambition partly by fine fetches and pretences, partly by force, hath shoulder'd out of the Church. And against such kind of deceavers openly and earnestly to protest, lest any one should be inquisitive wherefore this or that man is forwarder then others, let him know that this office goes not by age, or youth, but to whomsoever God shall give apparently the will, the Spirit, and the utterance. Ye have heard the reasons for which I thought not my selfe exempted from associating with good men in their labours toward the Churches wellfare: to which if any one brought opposition, I brought my best resistance. If in requitall of this and for that I have not been negligent toward the reputation of my friends, I have gain'd a name bestuck, or as I may say, bedeckt with the reproaches and reviles of this modest Confuter, it shall be to me neither strange, nor unwelcome; as that which could not come in a better time.

Having render'd an account, what induc't me to write those animadversions in that manner as I writ them, I come now to see what the confutation hath to say against them; but so as the confuter shall hear first what I have to say against his confutation. And because he pretends to be a great conjector at other men by their writings, I will not faile to give ye, Readers, a present taste of him from his own title; hung out like a toling signe-post to call passengers, not simply *a confutation* but *a modest confutation* with a laudatory of it selfe obtruded in the very first word. Whereas a modest title should only informe the buyer what the book containes without furder insinuation, this officious epithet so hastily assuming the modesty which others are to judge of by reading, not the author to anticipate to himself by forestalling, is a strong presumption that his modesty set there to sale in the frontispice, is not much addicted to blush. A surer signe of his lost shame he could not have given, then seeking thus unseasonably to prepossesse men of his modesty. And seeing he hath neither kept his word in the sequel, nor omitted any kinde of boldnesse in slandering, tis manifest his purpose was only to rub the forehead of his title with this word *modest*, that he might not want colour to be the more impudent throughout his whole confutation. Next what can equally savour of injustice, and plaine arrogance, as to prejudice and forecondemne his adversary in the title for *slanderous and scurrilous*, and as the Remonstrants fashion is, for *frivolous, tedious, and false*, not staying till the Reader can hear him prov'd so in the following discourse; which is one cause of a suspicion that in setting forth this pamplet the Remonstrant was not unconsulted with; thus his first addresse was *an humble Remonstrance by a dutifull son of the Church*, almost as if he had said her white-boy. His next was *a defence* (a wonder how it scapt some praising adjunct) *against the frivolous and false exceptions of Smectymnus*, sitting in the chaire of his Title page upon his poore cast adversaries both as a Judge and Party, and that before the jury of Readers can be impannell'd. His last was *A short answer to a tedious vindication;* so little can he suffer a man to measure either with his eye or judgement, what is short or what tedious without his preoccupying direction: and from hence is begotten this *modest confutation against a slanderous and scurrilous libell*. I conceave, Readers, much may be guest at the man and his book, what depth there is, by the framing of his title, which being in this Remonstrant so rash, and unadvised as ye see, I conceit him to be neere a kin to him who set forth a Passion Sermon with a formall Dedicatory in great letters to our Saviour. Although I know that all we do ought to begin and end to his praise and glory, yet to inscribe him in a void place with flourishes, as a man in complement uses to trick up the name of some Esquire, Gentleman, or Lord Paramont at Common Law, to be his book-patron with the appendant form of a ceremonious presentment, wil ever appeare among the judicious to be but an insuls and frigid affectation. As no lesse was that before his book against the Brownists to write a Letter to a prosopopœa a certain rhetoriz'd woman whom he calls mother, and complains of some that laid whoredome to her charge; and certainly had he folded his Epistle with a superscription to be deliver'd to that female figure by any Post or Carrier who were not a Ubiquitary, it had beene a most miraculous greeting. We finde the Primitive Doctors as oft as they writ to Churches, speaking to them as to a number of faithfull brethren and sons, and not to make a cloudy transmigration of sexes in such a familiar way of writing as an Epistle ought to be, leaving the track of common adresse, to runne up, and tread the aire in metaphoricall compellations, and many fond utterances better let alone. But I step againe to this emblazoner of his Title page (whether it be the same man or no I leave it in the midst) and here I finde him pronouncing without reprieve those animadversions to be *a slanderous and scurrilous libell*. To which I, Readers, that they are neither slanderous, nor scurrilous, will answer in what place of his book he shall be found with reason, and not inke only in his mouth. Nor can it be a libell more then his owne, which is both namelesse, and full of slanders, and if in this that it freely speaks of things amisse in religion, but establisht by act of State, I see not how *Wickleffe* and *Luther*, with all the first Martyrs, and reformers, could avoid the imputation of libelling. I never thought the humane frailty of erring in cases of religion infamy to a State, no more then to a Councell; it had therefore beene neither civill, nor Christianly, to derogate the honour of the State for that cause, especially when I saw the Parlament it selfe piously and magnanimously bent to supply and reforme the defects and oversights of their forefathers, which to the godly and repentant ages of the Jewes were often matter of humble confessing and bewailing, not of confident asserting and maintaining. Of the State therefore I found good reason to speak all honourable things, and to joyne in petition with good men that petition'd: but against the Prelats who were the only seducers and mis-leaders of the State to constitute the government of the Church not rightly, me thought I had not vehemence anough. And thus, Readers, by the example which hee hath set mee I have given yee two or three notes of him out of his Title page; by which his firstlings feare not to guesse boldly at his whole lumpe, for that guesse will not faile ye; and although I tell him keen truth, yet he may beare with me, since I am like to chafe him into some good knowledge, and others, I trust, shall not mis-spend their leasure. For this my aime is, if I am forc't to be unpleasing to him whose fault it is, I shall not forget at the same time to be usefull in some thing to the stander by.

As therefore he began in the Title, so in the next leafe he makes it his first businesse to tamper with his Reader by syco-phanting and misnaming the worke of his adversary. He calls it *a mime thrust forth upon the stage to make up the breaches of those solemne Scenes betweene the Prelats and the Smectymnuans.* Wherein while he is so overgreedy to fix a name of ill sound upon another, note how stupid he is to expose himselfe, or his own friends to the same ignominy; likening those grave controversies to a piece of Stagery, or Scene-worke where his owne Remonstrant whether in Buskin or Sock must of all right be counted the chiefe Player, be it boasting *Thraso*, or *Davus that troubles all things*, or one who can shift into any shape, I meddle not; let him explicate who hath resembl'd the whole argument to a Comedy, for *Tragicall*, he sayes, *were too ominous*. Nor yet doth he tell us what a Mime is, whereof we have no pattern from ancient writers except some fragments, which containe many acute and wise sentences. And this we know in *Laertius*, that the Mimes of *Sophron* were of such reckning with *Plato*, as to take them nightly to read on and after make them his pillow. *Scaliger* describes a Mime to be a Poem imitating any action to stirre up laughter. But this being neither Poem, nor yet ridiculous, how is it but abusively taxt to be a Mime. For if every book which may by chance excite to laugh here and there, must be term'd thus, then may the Dialogues of *Plato*, who for those his writings hath obtain'd the surname of Divine, be esteem'd as they are by that detractor in *Athenæus*, no better then *Mimes*. Because there is scarce one of them, especially wherein some notable Sophister lies sweating and

turmoyling under the inevitable, and mercilesse dilemma's of
Socrates, but that hee who reads, were it *Saturne* himselfe,
would be often rob'd of more then a smile. And whereas he
tels us that *Scurrilous Mime was a personated grim lowring
foole*, his foolish language unwittingly writes foole upon his
owne friend, for he who was there *personated*, was only the
Remonstrant; the author is ever distinguisht from the person
he introduces. But in an ill houre hath his unfortunate rashnesse stumbl'd upon the mention of miming. That hee might
at length cease, which he hath not yet since he stept in, to
gall and hurt him whom hee would aide. Could he not beware, could he not bethink him, was he so uncircumspect, as
not to foresee, that no sooner would that word *Mime* be set
eye on in the paper, but it would bring to minde that wretched
pilgrimage over *Minshews* Dictionary call'd *Mundus alter et
idem*, the idlest and the paltriest Mime that ever mounted
upon banke. Let him ask *the Author of those toothlesse
Satyrs* who was the maker, or rather the anticreator of that
universall foolery, who he was, who like that other principle
of the *Maniches* the *Arch evill one*, when he had look't upon
all that he had made and mapt out, could say no other but
contrary to the Divine Mouth, that it was all very foolish.
That grave and noble invention which the greatest and sublimest wits in sundry ages, *Plato in Critias*, and our two
famous countreymen, the one in his *Utopia*, the other in his
new Atlantis chose, I may not say as a feild, but as a mighty
Continent wherein to display the largenesse of their spirits by
teaching this our world better and exacter things, then were
yet known, or us'd, this petty prevaricator of *America*, the
zanie of *Columbus*, (for so he must be till his worlds end)
having rambl'd over the huge topography of his own vain
thoughts, no marvell, if he brought us home nothing but a
meer tankard drollery, a venereous parjetory for a stewes.
Certainly he that could indure with a sober pen to sit and
devise laws for drunkards to carouse by, I doubt me whether
the very sobernesse of such a one like an unlicour'd *Silenus*,
were not stark drunk. Let him go now and brand another
man injuriously with the name of *Mime*, being himselfe the
loosest and most extravagant *Mime*, that hath been heard of;
whom no lesse then almost halfe the world could serve for

T   M.

stage roome to play the *Mime* in. And let him advise againe with Sir *Francis Bacon* whom he cites to confute others, what it is to *turn the sinnes of Christendome into a mimicall mockery, to rip up the saddest vices with a laughing countenance*, especially where neither reproofe nor better teaching is adjoynd. Nor is my meaning, Readers, to shift off a blame from my selfe, by charging the like upon my accuser, but shall only desire, that sentence may be respited, till I can come to some instance, whereto I may give answer.

Thus having spent his first onset not in confuting, but in a reasonlesse defaming of the book, the method of his malice hurries him to attempt the like against the Author: not by proofes and testimonies, but *having no certaine notice of me*, as he professes, *furder then what he gathers from the animadversions*, blunders at me for the rest, and flings out stray crimes at a venture, which he could never, though he be a Serpent, suck from any thing that I have written; but from his own stufft magazin, and hoard of slanderous inventions, over and above that which he converted to venome in the drawing. To me Readers, it happens as a singular contentment, and let it be to good men no slight satisfaction, that the slanderer here confesses, he has *no furder notice of mee then his owne conjecture.* Although it had been honest to have inquir'd, before he utter'd such infamous words, and I am credibly inform'd he did inquire, but finding small comfort from the intelligence which he receav'd, whereon to ground the falsities which he had provided, thought it his likeliest course under a pretended ignorance to let drive at randome, lest he should lose his odde ends which from some penurious Book of Characters he had been culling out and would faine apply. Not caring to burden me with those vices, whereof, among whom my conversation hath been, I have been ever least suspected; perhaps not without some suttlety to cast me into envie, by bringing on me a necessity to enter into mine own praises. In which argument I know every wise man is more unwillingly drawne to speak, then the most repining eare can be averse to heare. Neverthelesse since I dare not wish to passe this life unpersecuted of slanderous tongues, for God hath told us that to be generally prais'd is wofull, I shall relye on his promise to free the innocent from causelesse aspersions: whereof nothing sooner can assure me, then if I shall feele him now assisting me in the just vindication of my selfe, which yet I could deferre, it being more meet that to those other matters of publick debatement in this book I should give attendance first, but that I feare it would but harme the truth, for me to reason in her behalfe, so long as I should suffer my honest estimation to lye unpurg'd from these insolent suspicions. And if I shall be large, or unwonted in justifying my selfe to those who know me not, for else it would be needlesse, let them consider, that a short slander will oft times reach farder then a long apology: and that he who will do justly to all men, must begin from knowing how, if it so happen, to be not unjust to him selfe. I must be thought, if this libeller (for now he shewes himselfe to be so) can finde beliefe, after an inordinat and riotous youth spent at *the University*, to have bin at length *vomited out thence.* For which commodious lye, that he may be incourag'd in the trade another time, I thank him; for it hath given me an apt occasion to acknowledge publickly with all gratefull minde, that more then ordinary favour and respect which I found above any of my equals at the hands of those curteous and learned men, the Fellowes of that Colledge wherein I spent some yeares: who at my parting, after I had taken two degrees, as the manner is, signifi'd many wayes, how much better it would content them that I would stay; as by many Letters full of kindnesse and loving respect both before that time, and long after I was assur'd of their singular good affection towards me. Which being likewise propense to all such as were for their studious and civill life worthy of esteeme, I could not wrong their judgements, and upright intentions, so much as to think I had that regard from them for other cause then that I might be still encourag'd to proceed in the honest and laudable courses, of which they apprehended I had given good proofe. And to those ingenuous and friendly men who were ever the countnancers of vertuous and hopefull wits, I wish the best, and happiest things, that friends in absence wish one to another. As for the common approbation or dislike of that place, as now it is, that I should esteeme or disesteeme my selfe or any other the more for that, too simple and too credulous is the Confuter, if he thinke to obtaine with me, or any right discerner. Of small practize were that Physitian who could not judge by what both she or her sister, hath of long time vomited, that the worser stuffe she strongly keeps in her stomack, but the better she is ever kecking at, and is queasie. She vomits now out of sicknesse, but ere it be well with her, she must vomit by strong physick. In the meane while that *Suburb sinke*, as this rude Scavinger calls it, and more then scurrilously taunts it with the *plague*, having a worse plague, in his middle entraile, that suburb wherein I dwell, shall be in my account a more honourable place then his University. Which as in the time of her better health, and mine owne younger judgement I never greatly admir'd, so now much lesse. But he followes me to the City, still usurping and forging beyond his book notice, which only he affirmes to have had; *and where my morning haunts are he wisses not*. Tis wonder, that being so rare an Alchymist of slander, he could not extract that, as well as the University vomit, and the Suburb sinke which his art could distill so cunningly, but because his Limbeck failes him, to give him and envie the more vexation, Ile tell him. Those morning haunts are where they should be, at home, not sleeping, or concocting the surfets of an irregular feast, but up, and stirring, in winter often ere the sound of any bell awake men to labour, or to devotion; in Summer as oft with the Bird that first rouses, or not much tardier, to reade good Authors, or cause them to bee read, till the attention bee weary, or memory have its full fraught. Then with usefull and generous labours preserving the bodies health, and hardinesse; to render lightsome, cleare, and not lumpish obedience to the minde, to the cause of religion, and our Countries liberty, when it shall require firme hearts in sound bodies to stand and cover their stations, rather then to see the ruine of our Protestation, and the inforcement of a slavish life. These are the morning practises; proceed now to the afternoone; *in Playhouses*, he sayes, *and the Bordelloes*. Your intelligence, unfaithfull Spie of Canaan? he gives in his evidence, that *there he hath trac't me*. Take him at his word Readers, but let him bring good sureties, ere ye dismisse him, that while he pretended to dogge others, he did not turne in for his owne pleasure; for so much in effect he concludes against himselfe,

not contented to be caught in every other gin, but he must
be such a novice, as to be still hamper'd in his owne hempe.
In the Animadversions, saith he, I finde the mention of old
clokes, fals beards, night-walkers, and salt lotion; therefore
the Animadverter haunts Playhouses and Bordelloes; for if
hee did not, how could hee speake of such gear? Now that
he may know what it is to be a childe, and yet to meddle
with edg'd tooles, I turne his *Antistrephon* upon his owne
head; the Confuter knowes that these things are the furniture of Playhouses and Bordelloes, therefore by the same
reason the *Confuter himselfe hath beene trac't in those places.*
Was it such a dissolute speech telling of some Politicians who
were wont to eavesdroppe in disguises, to say they were often
lyable to a night-walking cudgeller, or the emptying of a
Urinall? What if I had writ as your friend the author of the
aforesaid *Mime, Mundus alter et idem,* to have bin ravisht like
some young *Cephalus* or *Hylas,* by a troope of camping
Huswives in *Viraginia,* and that he was there forc't to sweare
himselfe an uxurious varlet, then after a long servitude to
have come into *Aphrodisia* that pleasant Countrey that gave
such a sweet smell to his nostrils among the shamelesse
Courtezans of *Desvergonia?* surely he would have then concluded me as constant at the Bordello, as the gally-slave at
his Oare. But since there is such necessity to the hear-say of a
Tire, a Periwig, or a Vizard, that Playes must have bin seene,
what difficulty was there in that? when in the Colleges so
many of the young Divines, and those in next aptitude to
Divinity have bin seene so oft upon the Stage writhing and
unboning their Clergie limmes to all the antick and dishonest
gestures of Trinculo's, Buffons, and Bawds; prostituting the
shame of that ministery which either they had, or were nigh
having, to the eyes of Courtiers and Court-Ladies, with their
Groomes and *Madamoisellaes.* There while they acted, and
overacted, among other young scholars, I was a spectator;
they thought themselves gallant men, and I thought them
fools, they made sport, and I laught, they mispronounc't and
I mislik't, and to make up the *atticisme,* they were out, and I
hist. Judge now whether so many good text men were not
sufficient to instruct me of false beards and vizards without
more expositors; and how can this Confuter take the face to

object to me the seeing of that which his reverent Prelats allow, and incite their young disciples to act. For if it be unlawfull to sit and behold a mercenary Comedian personating that which is least unseemely for a hireling to doe, how much more blamefull is it to indure the sight of as vile things acted by persons either enter'd, or presently to enter into the ministery, and how much more foule and ignominious for them to be the actors.

But because as well by this upraiding to me the Bordello's, as by other suspicious glancings in his book he would seem privily to point me out to his Readers, as one whose custome of life were not honest, but licentious; I shall intreat to be born with though I digresse; and in a way not often trod acquaint ye with the summe of my thoughts in this matter through the course of my yeares and studies. Although I am not ignorant how hazardous it will be to do this under the nose of the envious, as it were in skirmish to change the compact order, and instead of outward actions to bring inmost thoughts into front. And I must tell ye Readers, that by this sort of men I have bin already bitten at; yet shall they not for me know how slightly they are esteem'd, unless they have so much learning as to reade what in Greek ᾿Απειροκαλία is, which together with envie is the common disease of those who censure books that are not for their reading. With me it fares now, as with him whose outward garment hath bin injur'd and ill bedighted; for having no other shift, what helpe but to turn the inside outwards, especially if the lining be of the same, or, as it is sometimes, much better. So if my name and outward demeanour be not evident anough to defend me, I must make tryall, if the discovery of my inmost thoughts can. Wherein of two purposes both honest, and both sincere, the one perhaps I shall not misse; although I faile to gaine beliefe with others of being such as my perpetuall thoughts shall heere disclose me, I may yet not faile of successe in perswading some, to be such really themselves, as they cannot believe me to be more then what I fain. I had my time Readers, as others have, who have good learning bestow'd upon them, to be sent to those places, where the opinion was it might be soonest attain'd: and as the manner is, was not unstudied in those authors which are most commended; whereof some

were grave Orators and Historians; whose matter me thought
I lov'd indeed, but as my age then was, so I understood
them; others were the smooth Elegiack Poets, whereof the
Schooles are not scarce. Whom both for the pleasing sound
of their numerous writing, which in imitation I found most
easie; and most agreeable to natures part in me, and for
their matter which what it is, there be few who know not, I
was so allur'd to read, that no recreation came to me better
welcome. For that it was then those years with me which are
excus'd though they be least severe, I may be sav'd the labour
to remember ye. Whence having observ'd them to account it
the chiefe glory of their wit, in that they were ablest to judge,
to praise, and by that could esteeme themselves worthiest to
love those high perfections which under one or other name
they took to celebrate, I thought with my selfe by every instinct and presage of nature which is not wont to be false, that
what imboldn'd them to this task might with such diligence
as they us'd imbolden me, and that what judgement, wit, or
elegance was my share, would herein best appeare, and best
value it selfe, by how much more wisely, and with more love
of vertue I should choose (let rude eares be absent) the object
of not unlike praises. For albeit these thoughts to some will
seeme vertuous and commendable, to others only pardonable,
to a third sort perhaps idle, yet the mentioning of them now
will end in serious. Nor blame it Readers, in those yeares to
propose to themselves such a reward, as the noblest dispositions above other things in this life have sometimes preferr'd.
Whereof not to be sensible, when good and faire in one person meet, argues both a grosse and shallow judgement, and
withall an ungentle, and swainish brest. For by the firme
setling of these perswasions I became, to my best memory, so
much a proficient, that if I found those authors any where
speaking unworthy things of themselves; or unchaste of
those names which before they had extoll'd, this effect it
wrought with me, from that time forward their art I still
applauded, but the men I deplor'd; and above them all preferr'd the two famous renowners of *Beatrice* and *Laura* who
never write but honour of them to whom they devote their
verse, displaying sublime and pure thoughts, without transgression. And long it was not after, when I was confirm'd in

this opinion, that he who would not be frustrate of his hope to write well hereafter in laudable things, ought him selfe to bee a true Poem, that is, a composition, and patterne of the best and honourablest things; not presuming to sing high praises of heroick men, or famous Cities, unlesse he have in himselfe the experience and the practice of all that which is praise-worthy. These reasonings, together with a certain nicenesse of nature, an honest haughtinesse, and self-esteem either of what I was, or what I might be, (which let envie call pride) and lastly that modesty, whereof though not in the Title page yet here I may be excus'd to make some beseeming profession, all these uniting the supply of their natural aide together, kept me still above those low descents of minde, beneath which he must deject and plunge himself, that can agree to salable and unlawfull prostitutions. Next, (for heare me out now Readers) that I may tell ye whether my younger feet wander'd; I betook me among those lofty Fables and Romances, which recount in solemne canto's the deeds of Knighthood founded by our victorious Kings; and from hence had in renowne over all Christendome. There I read it in the oath of every Knight, that he should defend to the expence of his best blood, or of his life, if it so befell him, the honour and chastity of Virgin or Matron. From whence even then I learnt what a noble vertue chastity sure must be, to the defence of which so many worthies by such a deare adventure of themselves had sworne. And if I found in the story afterward any of them by word or deed breaking that oath, I judg'd it the same fault of the Poet, as that which is attributed to *Homer;* to have written undecent things of the gods. Only this my minde gave me that every free and gentle spirit without that oath ought to be borne a Knight, nor needed to expect the guilt spurre, or the laying of a sword upon his shoulder to stirre him up both by his counsell, and his arme to secure and protect the weaknesse of any attempted chastity. So that even those books which to many others have bin the fuell of wantonnesse and loose living, I cannot thinke how unlesse by divine indulgence prov'd to me so many incitements as you have heard, to the love and stedfast observation of that vertue which abhorres the society of Bordello's. Thus from the Laureat fraternity of Poets, riper yeares, and the ceaselesse round of study and reading led me to the shady spaces of philosophy, but chiefly to the divine volumes of *Plato*, and his equall *Xenophon*. Where if I should tell ye what I learnt, of chastity and love, I meane that which is truly so, whose charming cup is only vertue which she bears in her hand to those who are worthy. The rest are cheated with a thick intoxicating potion which a certaine Sorceresse the abuser of loves name carries about; and how the first and chiefest office of love, begins and ends in the soule, producing those happy twins of her divine generation knowledge and vertue, with such abstracted sublimities as these, it might be worth your listning, Readers, as I may one day hope to have ye in a still time, when there shall be no chiding; not in these noises, the adversary as ye know, barking at the doore; or searching for me at the Burdello's where it may be he has lost himselfe, and raps up without pitty the sage and rheumatick old *Prelatesse* with all her young *Corinthian Laity* to inquire for such a one. Last of all not in time, but as perfection is last, that care was ever had of me, with my earliest capacity not to be negligently train'd in the precepts of Christian Religion: This that I have hitherto related, hath bin to shew, that though Christianity had bin but slightly taught me, yet a certain reserv'dnesse of naturall disposition, and morall discipline learnt out of the noblest Philosophy was anough to keep me in disdain of farre lesse incontinences then this of the Burdello. But having had the doctrine of holy Scripture unfolding those chaste and high mysteries with timeliest care infus'd, that *the body is for the Lord and the Lord for the body*, thus also I argu'd to my selfe; that if unchastity in a woman whom Saint *Paul* termes the glory of man, be such a scandall and dishonour, then certainly in a man who is both the image and glory of God, it must, though commonly not so thought, be much more deflouring and dishonourable. In that he sins both against his owne body which is the perfeter sex, and his own glory which is in the woman, and that which is worst, against the image and glory of God which is in himselfe. Nor did I slumber over that place expressing such high rewards of ever accompanying the Lambe, with those celestiall songs to others inapprehensible, but not to those who were not defil'd with women, which doubtlesse meanes fornication: For mariage must not be call'd a defilement. Thus large I have purposely bin, that if I have bin justly taxt with this crime, it may come upon me after all this my confession, with a tenne-fold shame. But if I have hitherto deserv'd no such opprobrious word, or suspicion, I may hereby ingage my selfe now openly to the faithfull observation of what I have profest. I go on to shew you the unbridl'd impudence of this loose rayler, who having once begun his race regards not how farre he flyes out beyond all truth and shame; who from the single notice of the animadversions, as he protests, will undertake to tell ye the very cloaths I weare, though he be much mistaken in my wardrobe. And like a son of Belial without the hire of *Jesabel* charges me *of blaspheming God and the King*, as ordinarily as he imagines *me to drink Sack and sweare*, meerely because this was a shred in his common place-book, and seem'd to come off roundly, as if he were some Empirick of false accusations to try his poysons upon me whether they would work or no. Whom what should I endeavour to refute more, whenas that book which is his only testimony returnes the lye upon him; not giving him the least hint of the author to be either a swearer, or a Sack drinker. And for the readers if they can believe me, principally for those reasons which I have alleg'd, to be of life and purpose neither dishonest, nor unchaste, they will be easily induc't to thinke me sober both of wine, and of word; but if I have bin already successelesse in perswading them, all that I can furder say will be but vaine; and it will be better thrift to save two tedious labours, mine of excusing, and theirs of needlesse hearing.

Proceeding furder I am met with a whole ging of words and phrases not mine, for he hath maim'd them, and like a slye depraver mangl'd them in this his wicked Limbo, worse then the ghost of *Deiphobus* appear'd to his friend *Æneas*. Here I scarce know them, and he that would, let him repaire to the place in that booke where I set them. For certainly this tormenter of semicolons is as good at dismembring and slitting sentences, as his grave Fathers the Prelates have bin at stigmatizing and slitting noses. By such handy craft as this what might he not traduce? Only that odour which being his own must needs offend his sense of smelling, since he will needs

bestow his foot among us, and not allow us to think he
weares a Sock, I shall endeavour it may be offencelesse to
other mens eares. The Remonstrant having to do with grave
and reverend men his adversaries, thought it became him to
tell them in scorne, that *the Bishops foot had beene in their
book and confuted it*, which when I saw him arrogate, to have
done that with his heeles that surpast the best consideration
of his head, to spurn a confutation among respected men, I
question'd not the lawfulnesse of moving his jollity to bethink him, what odor a Sock would have in such a painfull
businesse. And this may have chanc't to touch him more
neerly then I was aware; for indeed a Bishops foot that hath
all his toes maugre the gout, and a linnen Sock over it, is the
aptest embleme of the Prelate himselfe. Who being a pluralist, may under one Surplice which is also linnen, hide foure
benefices besides the metropolitan toe, and sends a fouler
stench to heaven, then that which this young queasinesse
reches at. And this is the immediate reason here why our
inrag'd Confuter, that he may be as perfet an hypocrite as
Caiaphas, ere he be a High Priest, cries out, *horrid blasphemy!* and like a recreant Jew calls for *stones*. I beseech ye
friends, ere the brick-bats flye, resolve me and your selves, is
it blasphemy, or any whit disagreeing from Christian meek-
nesse, when as Christ himselfe speaking of unsavory traditions, scruples not to name the Dunghill and the Jakes, for
me to answer a slovenly wincer of a confutation, that, if he
would needs put his foot to such a sweaty service, the odour
of his Sock was like to be neither musk, nor benjamin?
Thus did that foolish Monk in a barbarous Declamation
accuse *Petrarch* of blasphemy for dispraising the French
wines. But this which followes is plaine bedlam stuffe, this
is the *Demoniack legion* indeed, which the Remonstrant
feard had been against him, and now he may see is for him.
You that love Christ, saith he, *and know this miscreant wretch,
stone him to death, lest you smart for his impunity*. What
thinks the Remonstrant? does he like that such words as
these should come out of his shop, out of his Trojan horse?
to give the watch word like *a Guisian of Paris* to a mutiny or
massacre; to proclame a *Crusada* against his fellow Christian
now in this troublous and divided time of the Kingdome? if

he do, I shall say that to be the Remonstrant is no better then to be a Jesuit. And that if he and his accomplices could do as the rebels have done in *Ireland* to the Protestants, they would do in *England* the same to them that would no Prelats. For a more seditious and Butcherly Speech no Cell of *Loyola* could have belch't against one who in all his writing spake not, that any mans skin should be rais'd. And yet this cursing *Shimei* a hurler of stones, as well as a rayler, wants not the face instantly to make as though he *despair'd of victory unlesse a modest defence would get it him.* Did I erre at all, Readers, to foretell ye, when first I met with this title, that the epithet of modest there, was a certaine red portending signe, that he meant ere long to be most tempestuously bold, and shamelesse? Neverthelesse *he dares not say but there may be hid in his nature as much venomous Atheisme and profanation,* as he thinks, *hath broke out at his adversaries lips, but he hath not the soare running upon him,* as he would intimate *I have.* Now trust me not, Readers, if I be not already weary of pluming and footing this Seagull, so open he lies to strokes; and never offers at another, but brings home the dorre upon himselfe. For if the sore be running upon me, in all judgement I have scapt the disease, but he who hath as much infection hid in him, as he hath voluntarily confest, and cannot expell it, because hee is dull, for venomous Atheisme were no treasure to be kept within him else, let him take the part hee hath chosen, which must needs follow, to swell and burst with his owne inward venome.

Sect. 1.] But marke, Readers, there is a kind of justice observ'd among them that do evill, but this man loves injustice in the very order of his malice. For having all this while abus'd the good name of his adversary with all manner of licence in revenge of his Remonstrant, if they be not both one person, or as I am told, Father and Son, yet after all this he calls for satisfaction, when as he himselfe hath already taken the utmost farding. *Violence hath been done,* says he, *to the person of a holy, and religious Prelat.* To which, something in effect to what S. *Paul* answer'd of *Ananias*, I answer, *I wist not brethren that he was a holy and religious* Prelat; for evill is written of those who would be Prelats. And finding him thus in disguise without his superscription or *Phylactery* either of *holy* or *Prelat*, it were no sinne to serve him as *Longchamp* Bishop of *Elie* was serv'd in his disguise at *Dover:* He hath begun the measure namelesse, and when he pleases we may all appeare as we are. And let him be then what he will, he shall be to me so as I finde him principl'd. For neither must Prelat or Arch-Prelat hope to exempt himselfe from being reckon'd as one of the vulgar; which is for him only to hope whom true wisdome and the contempt of vulgar opinions exempts, it being taught us in the Psalmes that he who is in honour and understandeth not is as the beasts that perish. And now first *the manner of handling that cause* which I undertook, he thinks *is suspicious*, as if the wisest, and the best words were not ever to some or other suspicious. But where is the offence, the disagreement from Christian meek-nesse, or the precept of *Salomon* in answering folly? when the Remonstrant talks of *froth and scum*, I tell him there is none, and bid him *spare his Ladle:* when he brings in the messe with *Keale, Beef, and Brewesse*, what stomack in *England* could forbeare to call for flanks and briskets? Capon and whitebroth having beene likely sometimes in the same roome with Christ and his Apostles, why does it trouble him that it should be now *in the same leafe*, especially, where the discourse is not continu'd but interrupt? And let him tell me, is he wont to say grace, doth he not then name holiest names over the steame of costliest superfluities? Does he judge it foolish or dishonest to write that among religious things, which when he talks of religious things he can devoutly chew? is he afraid to name Christ where those things are written in the same leafe whom he fears not to name while the same things are in his mouth? Doth not Christ himselfe teach the highest things by the similitude *of old bottles and patcht cloaths?* Doth he not illustrate best things by things most evill? his own *comming* to be *as a thiefe in the night*, and the righteous mans *wisdome to that of an unjust Steward?* He might therefore have done better to have kept in *his canting beggars and heathen Altar* to sacrifice his thredbare criticisme of *Bomolochus* to an unseasonable Goddesse fit for him call'd Importunity, and have reserv'd his Greek derivation till he lecture to his fresh men, for here his itching pedantry is but flouted.

But to the end that nothing may be omitted which may furder satisfie any conscionable man, who notwithstanding what I could explaine before the animadversions, remains yet unsatisfi'd concerning that way of writing which I there defended, but this confuter whom it pinches, utterly disapproves, I shall assay once againe, and perhaps with more successe. If therefore the question were in oratory, whether a vehement vein throwing out indignation, or scorn upon an object that merits it, were among the aptest *Ideas* of speech to be allow'd, it were my work, and that an easie one to make it cleare both by the rules of best rhetoricians, and the famousest examples of the Greek and Roman Orations. But since the Religion of it is disputed, and not the art, I shall make use only of such reasons and autorities, as religion cannot except against. It will be harder to gainsay, then for me to evince that in the teaching of men diversly temper'd different wayes are to be try'd. The Baptist we know was a strict man remarkable for austerity and set order of life. Our Saviour who had all gifts in him was Lord to expresse his indoctrinating power in what sort him best seem'd; sometimes by a mild and familiar converse, sometimes with plaine and impartiall home-speaking regardlesse of those whom the auditors might think he should have had in more respect; otherwhiles with bitter and irefull rebukes if not teaching yet leaving excuselesse those his wilfull impugners. What was all in him, was divided among many others the teachers of his Church; some to be severe and ever of a sad gravity that they may win such, and check sometimes those who be of nature over-confident and jocond; others were sent more cheerefull, free, and still as it were at large, in the midst of an untrespassing honesty; that they who are so temper'd may have by whom they might be drawne to salvation, and they who are too scrupulous, and dejected of spirit might be often strengthn'd with wise consolations and revivings: no man being forc't wholly to dissolve that groundwork of nature which God created in him, the sanguine to empty out all his sociable livelinesse, the cholerick to expell quite the unsinning predominance of his anger; but that each radicall humour and passion wrought upon and corrected as it ought, might be made the proper mould and foundation of every mans peculiar guifts, and

vertues. Some also were indu'd with a staid moderation, and
soundnesse of argument to teach and convince the rationall
and sober-minded ; yet not therefore that to be thought the
only expedient course of teaching, for in times of opposition
when either against new heresies arising, or old corruptions to
be reform'd this coole unpassionate mildnesse of positive
wisdome is not anough to damp and astonish the proud resistance of carnall, and false Doctors, then (that I may have
leave to soare a while as the Poets use) then Zeale whose
substance is ethereal, arming in compleat diamond ascends
his fiery Chariot drawn with two blazing Meteors figur'd like
beasts, but of a higher breed then any the Zodiack yeilds,
resembling two of those four which *Ezechiel* and S. *John* saw,
the one visag'd like a Lion to expresse power, high autority
and indignation, the other of count'nance like a man to cast
derision and scorne upon perverse and fraudulent seducers ;
with these the invincible warriour Zeale shaking loosely the
slack reins drives over the heads of Scarlet Prelats, and such
as are insolent to maintaine traditions, brusing their stiffe
necks under his flaming wheels. Thus did the true Prophets
of old combat with the false ; thus Christ himselfe the fountaine of meeknesse found acrimony anough to be still galling
and vexing the Prelaticall Pharisees. But ye will say these had
immediat warrant from God to be thus bitter, and I say, so
much the plainer is it prov'd, that there may be a sanctifi'd
bitternesse against the enemies of truth. Yet that ye may not
think inspiration only the warrant thereof, but that it is as
any other vertue, or morall and generall observation, the
example of *Luther* may stand for all : whom God made choice
of before others to be of highest eminence and power in reforming the Church ; who not of revelation, but of judgement
writ so vehemently against the chiefe defenders of old un-
truths in the Romish Church, that his own friends and
favourers were many times offended with the fiercenesse of
his spirit ; yet he being cited before *Charles* the fifth to answer
for his books, and having divided them into three sorts,
whereof one was of those which he had sharply written, refus'd though upon deliberation giv'n him to retract or unsay
any word therein ; as we may reade in *Sleiden*. Yea he defends
his eagernesse, as being *of an ardent spirit, and one who could*

not write a dull stile; and affirm'd *hee thought it Gods will to have the inventions of men thus laid open, seeing that matters quietly handled, were quickly forgot.* And herewithall how usefull and available God had made this tart rhetorick in the Churches cause, he often found by his owne experience. For when he betook himselfe to lenity and moderation, as they call it, he reapt nothing but contempt both from *Cajetan* and *Erasmus,* from *Cocleus,* from *Ecchius* and others, insomuch that blaming his friends who had so counsel'd him, he resolv'd never to runne into the like error; if at other times he seeme to excuse his vehemence, as more then what was meet, I have not examin'd through his works to know how farre he gave way to his owne fervent minde; it shall suffice me to looke to mine own. And this I shall easily averre though it may seeme a hard saying, that the Spirit of God who is purity it selfe, when he would reprove any fault severely, or but relate things done or said with indignation by others, abstains not from some words not civill at other times to be spok'n. Omitting that place in Numbers at the killing of *Zimri and Cosbi* done by *Phineas* in the heighth of zeal, related as the Rabbines expound, not without an obscene word, we may finde in Deuteronomy and three of the Prophets, where God denouncing bitterly the punishments of Idolaters, tels them in a terme immodest to be utter'd in coole blood, that their wives shall be defil'd openly. But these, they will say were honest words in that age when they were spok'n. Which is more then any Rabbin can prove, and certainly had God been so minded, he could have pickt such words, as should never have come into abuse. What will they say to this. *David* going against *Nabal,* in the very same breath when he had but just before nam'd the *name of God,* he vowes not *to leave any alive of Nabals house that pisseth against the wall.* But this was unadvisedly spoke, you will answer, and set downe to aggravate his infirmity. Turne then to the first of Kings where God himselfe uses the phrase; *I will cut off from Jeroboam him that pisseth against the wall.* Which had it beene an unseemely speech in the heat of an earnest expression, then we must conclude that *Jonathan, or Onkelos the Targumists* were of cleaner language then he that made the tongue; for they render it as briefly, *I will cut off all who are at yeares of discretion,* that is to say so much discretion as to hide naked-nesse. Whereas God who is the author both of purity and eloquence, chose this phrase as fittest in that vehement character wherein he spake. Otherwise that plaine word might have easily bin forborne. Which the *Masoreths* and Rabbinicall *Scholiasts* not well attending, have often us'd to blurre the margent with *Keri,* instead of *Ketiv,* and gave us this insuls rule out of their *Talmud, That all words which in the Law are writ obscenely, must be chang'd to more civill words.* Fools who would teach men to read more decently then God thought good to write. And thus I take it to be manifest, that indignation against men and their actions notoriously bad, hath leave and autority oft times to utter such words and phrases as in common talke were not so mannerly to use. That ye may know, not only as the Historian speaks, *that all those things for which men plough, build, or saile, obey vertue,* but that all words and whatsoever may be spoken shall at some time in an unwonted manner wait upon her purposes.

Now that the confutant may also know as he desires, what force of teaching there is sometimes in laughter, I shall returne him in short, that laughter being one way of answering *A Foole according to his folly,* teaches two sorts of persons, first the Foole himselfe *not to be wise in his own conceit;* as *Salomon* affirms, which is certainly a great document, to make an unwise man know himselfe. Next, it teaches the hearers, in as much as scorne is one of those punishments which belong to men carnally wise, which is oft in Scripture declar'd; for when such are punisht *the simple are thereby made wise,* if *Salomons* rule be true. And I would ask, to what end *Eliah* mockt the false Prophets? was it to shew his wit, or to fulfill his humour? doubtlesse we cannot imagine that great servant of God had any other end in all which he there did, but to teach and instruct the poore misledde people. And we may frequently reade, that many of the Martyrs in the midst of their troubles, were not sparing to deride and scoffe their superstitious persecutors. Now may the confutant advise againe with Sir *Francis Bacon* whether *Eliah* and the Martyrs did well to turne religion into a Comedy, or Satir; *to rip up the wounds* of Idolatry and Superstition *with a laughing countenance.* So that for pious gravity his author here is matcht and overmatcht, and for wit and morality in one that followes.

> ——*laughing to teach the truth*
> *What hinders? as some teachers give to Boyes*
> *Junkets and knacks, that they may learne apace.*

Thus *Flaccus* in his first Satir, and in his tenth

> ——*Jesting decides great things*
> *Stronglier, and better oft then earnest can.*

I could urge the same out of *Cicero,* and *Seneca,* but he may content him with this. And hence forward, if he can learne, may know as well what are the bounds, and objects of laughter and vehement reproofe, as he hath knowne hitherto how to deserve them both. But lest some may haply think, or thus expostulat with me after all this debatement, who made you the busie Almoner to deale about this dole of laughter and reprehension which no man thanks your bounty for? To the urbanity of that man I should answer much after this sort: That I, friend objecter, having read of heathen Philosophers, some to have taught, that whosoever would but use his eare to listen, might heare the voice of his guiding *Genius* ever before him, calling and as it were pointing to that way which is his part to follow; others, as the Stoicks, to account reason, which they call the *Hegemonicon,* to be the common *Mercury* conducting without error those that give themselves obediently to be led accordingly, having read this, I could not esteeme so poorly of the faith which I professe, that God had left nothing to those who had forsaken all other doctrines for his, to be an inward witnesse, and warrant of what they have to do, as that they should need to measure themselves by other mens measures how to give scope, or limit to their proper actions; for that were to make us the most at a stand, the most uncertaine and accidentall wanderers in our doings, of all religions in the world. So that the question ere while mov'd who he is that spends thus the benevolence of laughter and reproofe so liberally upon such men as the Prelats, may returne with a more just demand, who he is not of place and knowledge never so mean, under whose contempt and jerk these men are not deservedly falne? neither can religion receive any wound by disgrace thrown upon the Prelats, since religion and they surely were never in such amity. They rather are the men who have wounded religion, and their stripes must heale her. I might also tell them, what *Electra* in *Sophocles*, a wise Virgin answer'd her wicked Mother who thought her selfe too violently reprov'd by her the daughter.

> *Tis you that say it, not I, you do the deeds,*
> *And your ungodly deeds finde me the words.*

If therefore the Remonstrant complaine of libels, it is because he feels them to be right aim'd. For I ask againe as before in the animadversions, how long is it since he hath dis-relisht libels? we never heard the least mutter of his voice against them while they flew abroad without controul or check defaming the Scots and Puritans. And yet he can remember of none but *Lysimachus Nicanor*, and *that he mislikt and censur'd*. No more but of one can the Remonstrant remember? What if I put him in minde of one more? What if of one more whereof the Remonstrant in many likelyhoods may be thought the author? Did he never see a Pamphlet intitl'd after his own fashion, *A survey of that foolish, seditious, scandalous, profane libell the Protestation protested?* The child doth not more expresly refigure the visage of his Father, then that book resembles the stile of the Remonstrant, in those idioms of speech, wherein he seemes most to delight: and in the seventeenth Page three lines together taken out of the Remonstrance word for word, not as a citation, but as an author borrowes from himselfe. Who ever it be, he may as justly be said to have libell'd, as he against whom he writes: there ye shall finde another man then here is made shew of, there he bites as fast as this whines. *Vinegar in the inke* is there *the antidote of Vipers*. *Laughing* in a religious controversie is there *a thrifty physick to expell his melancholy*. In the meane time the testimony of Sir *Francis Bacon* was not misalledg'd, complaining that libels on the Bishops part were utter'd openly; and if he hop't the Prelats *had no intelligence with the libellours*, he delivers it but as his favourable opinion. But had he contradicted himselfe, how could I assoil him here, more then a little before, where I know not how by entangling himselfe, he leaves an aspersion upon *Job*, which by any else I never heard laid to his charge. For having affirm'd that *there is no greater confusion then the confounding of jest and earnest*, presently he brings the example of *Job glancing at conceits of mirth, when he sate among the people with the gravity of a Judge upon him*. If jest and earnest be such a confusion, then were the people much wiser then *Job*, for *he smil'd, and they believ'd him not*. To defend Libels, which is that whereof I am next accus'd, was farre from my purpose. I had not so little share in good name, as to give another that advantage against my selfe. The summe of what I said, was that a more free permission of writing at some times might be profitable, in such a question especially wherein the Magistrates are not fully resolv'd; and both sides have equall liberty to write, as now they have. Not as when the Prelats bore sway, in whose time the bookes of some men were confuted, when they who should have answer'd were in close prison, deny'd the use of pen or paper. And the *Divine right of Episcopacy* was then valiantly asserted, when he who would have bin respondent, must have bethought himselfe withall how he could refute the *Clink*, or the *Gate-house*. If now therefore they be persu'd with bad words, who persecuted others with bad deeds, it is a way to lessen tumult rather then to encrease it; when as anger thus freely vented spends it selfe, ere it break out into action, though *Machiavell* whom he cites, or any *Machiavillian* Priest think the contrary.

Sect. 3.] Now Readers I bring ye to his third Section; wherein very cautiously, and no more then needs, lest I should take him for some Chaplaine at hand, some Squire of the body to his Prelat, one that serves not at the Altar only, but at the Court cup board, he will bestow on us a pretty modell of himselfe; and sobs me out halfe a dozen tizicall mottoes where ever he had them, hopping short in the measure of convulsion fits; in which labour the agony of his wit, having scapt narrowly, instead of well siz'd periods, he greets us with a quantity of thum-ring posies. *He has a fortune therefore good, because he is content with it.* This is a piece of sapience not worth the brain of a fruit-trencher; as if content were the measure of what is good or bad in the guift of fortune. For by this rule a bad man may have a good fortune, because he may be oft times content with it for many reasons which have no affinity with vertue, as love of ease, want of spirit to use more, and the like. *And therefore content*, he sayes, *because it neither goes before, nor comes behinde his merit*. Belike then if his fortune should go before his merit, he would not be content, but resigne, if we believe him, which I do the lesse, because he implyes that if it came behinde his merit, he would be content as little. Wheras if a wise mans content should depend upon such a *Therefore*, because his fortune came not behinde his merit, how many wise men could have content in this world? In his next pithy symbol I dare not board him, for he passes all *the seven wise Masters of Greece*, attributing to himselfe that which on my life *Salomon* durst not; *to have affections so equally temper'd that they neither too hastily adhere to the truth, before it be fully examin'd, nor too lazily afterward*. Which unlesse he only were exempted out of the corrupt masse of *Adam*, borne without sinne originall, and living without actuall, is impossible. Had *Salomon* (for it behoves me to instance in the wisest, dealing with such a transcendent Sage as this) had *Salomon* affections so equally temper'd, as *not adhering too lazily to the truth*, when God warn'd him of his halting in idolatry? do we reade that he repented hastily? did not his affections lead him hastily from an examin'd truth, how much more would they lead him slowly to it? Yet this man beyond a *Stoick apathy* sees truth as in a rapture, and cleaves to it. Not as through the dim glasse of his affections which in this frail mansion of flesh are ever unequally temper'd, pushing forward to error, and keeping back from truth oft times the best of men. But how farre this boaster is from knowing himselfe, let his *Preface* speake. Something I thought it was that made him so quick-sighted to gather such strange things out of the Animadversions, whereof the least conception could not be drawne from thence, of *Suburb sinks*, sometimes *out of wit and cloaths*, sometimes *in new Serge, drinking Sack, and swearing*, now I know it was this equall temper of his affections that gave him to see clearer then any fenell rub'd Serpent. Lastly, he has resolv'd *that neither person nor cause shall improper him*. I may mistake his meaning, for the word ye heare is *improper*. But whether if not a person, yet a good Personage, or Impropriation bought out for him would not *improper* him, because there may be a quirk in the word, I leave it for a Canonist to resolve.

Sect. 4.] And thus ends this Section, or rather dissection of himselfe, short ye will say both in breath, and extent, as in our own praises it ought to be, unlesse wherein a good name hath bin wrongfully attainted. Right, but if ye looke at what he ascribes to himselfe, *that temper of his affections* which cannot any where be but in Paradise, all the judicious *Panegyricks* in any language extant are not halfe so prolixe. And that well appears in his next removall. For what with putting his fancy to the tiptoe in this description of himselfe, and what with adventuring presently to stand upon his own legs without the crutches of his margent, which is the sluce most commonly, that feeds the drouth of his text, he comes so lazily on in a Similie, with his *arme full of weeds*, and demeanes himselfe in the dull expression so like a dough kneaded thing, that he has not spirit anough left him so farre to look to his *Syntaxis*, as to avoide nonsense. For it must be understood there that *the stranger*, and not *he who brings the bundle* would be *deceav'd in censuring the field*, which this hip-shot *Grammarian* cannot set into right frame of construction, neither here in the similitude, nor in the following *reddition* thereof, which being to this purpose, that *the faults of the best pickt out, and presented in gross, seem monstrous, this* saith he, *you have done, in pinning on his sleeve the faults of others;* as if to pick out his owne faults, and to pin the faults of others upon him, were to do the same thing. To answer therefore how I have cull'd out the evill actions of the Remonstrant from his vertues, I am acquitted by the dexterity and conveiance of his nonsense, loosing that for which he brought his parable. But what of other mens faults I have pinn'd upon his sleeve, let him shew. For whether he were the man who term'd the Martyrs *Foxian* confessors, it matters not; he that shall step up before others to defend a Church-government, which wants almost no circumstance, but only a name to be a plaine Popedome, a government which changes the fatherly and everteaching discipline of Christ into that Lordly and uninstructing jurisdiction which properly makes the Pope Antichrist, makes himselfe an

accessory to all the evill committed by those, who are arm'd
to do mischiefe by that undue government; which they by
their wicked deeds, do with a kinde of passive and unwitting
obedience to God, destroy. But he by plausible words and
traditions against the Scripture obstinately seeks to maintaine. They by their owne wickednesse ruining their owne
unjust autority make roome for good to succeed. But he by a
shew of good upholding the evill which in them undoes it
selfe, hinders the good which they by accident let in. Their
manifest crimes serve to bring forth an ensuing good and
hasten a remedy against themselves, and his seeming good
tends to reinforce their selfe-punishing crimes and his owne,
by doing his best to delay all redresse. Shall not all the
mischiefe which other men do, be layd to his charge, if
they doe it by that unchurchlike power which he defends?
Christ saith, *he that is not with me is against me, and he that
gathers not with me scatters.* In what degree of enmity to
Christ shall wee place that man then, who so is with him, as
that it makes more against him, and so gathers with him,
that it scatters more from him? shall it availe that man to say
he honours the Martyrs memory and treads in their steps?
No; the Pharisees confest as much of the holy Prophets. Let
him and such as he when they are in their best actions even
at their prayers looke to heare that which the Pharisees
heard from *John* the *Baptist* when they least expected, when
they rather lookt for praise from him. *Generation of Vipers
who hath warn'd ye to flee from the wrath to come?* Now that
ye have started back from the purity of Scripture which is the
only rule of reformation, to the old vomit of your traditions,
now that ye have either troubl'd or leven'd the people of God,
and the doctrine of the Gospell with scandalous ceremonies
and masse-borrow'd Liturgies, doe ye turne the use of that
truth which ye professe, to countenance that falshood which
ye gaine by? We also reverence the Martyrs but relye only
upon the Scriptures. And why we ought not to relye upon
the Martyrs I shall be content with such reasons as my confuter himselfe affords me; who is I must needs say for him
in that point as officious an adversary as I would wish to
any man. For *first*, saith he *there may be a Martyr in a wrong
cause, and as couragious in suffering as the best: sometimes in a*

*good cause with a forward ambition displeasing to God. Other-
whiles they that story of them out of blind zeale, or malice may
write many things of them untruly.* If this be so, as ye heare
his owne confession, with what safety can the Remonstrant
rely upon the Martyrs as *Patrons of his cause*, when as any of
those who are alleg'd for the approvers of our Liturgy or
Prelaty might have bin though not in a wrong cause Martyrs,
yet whether not vainly ambitious of that honour, or whether
not misreported, or misunderstood, in those their opinions
God only knowes. The testimony of what we believe in
religion must be such as the conscience may rest on to be infallible, and incorruptible, which is only the word of God.

Sect. 5.] His fifth Section finds it selfe agriev'd that the
Remonstrant should be taxt with the illegall proceedings of
the high Commission, and oath *Ex officio;* And first *whether
they were illegall or no, tis more then he knowes.* See this
malevolent Fox! that tyranny which the whole Kingdome
cry'd out against as stung with Adders, and Scorpions, that
tyranny which the Parlament in compassion of the Church
and Commonwealth hath dissolv'd, and fetch't up by the
roots, for which it hath receav'd the publick thanks and blessings of thousands this obscure thorn-eater of malice and detraction, as well as of *Quodlibets* and *Sophisms* knowes not
whether it were illegall or not. Evill, evill, would be your reward ye worthies of the Parlament, if this Sophister and his
accomplices had the censuring, or the sounding forth of your
labours. And that the Remonstrant cannot wash his hands
of all the cruelties exercis'd by the Prelats, is past doubting.
They scourg'd the confessors of the Gospell, and he held the
scourgers garments. They executed their rage, and he, if he
did nothing else, defended the government with the oath that
did it, and the ceremonies which were the cause of it: does he
think to be counted guiltlesse?

Sect. 6.] In the following Section I must foretell ye,
Readers, the doings will be rough and dangerous, the bating
of a *Satir*. And if the work seeme more triviall or boistrous
then for this discourse, let the Remonstrant thank the folly of
this confuter, who could not let a private word passe, but he
must make all this blaze of it. I had said that because the
Remonstrant was so much offended with those who were

tart against the Prelats, sure he lov'd toothlesse Satirs, which
I took were as improper as a toothed Sleekstone. This
Champion from behind the Arras cries out that those toothlesse Satyrs were of the Remonstrants making; and armes
himselfe here tooth and naile and *horne* to boot, to supply
the want of teeth, or rather of gumms in the Satirs. And for
an onset tels me that the simily of a Sleekstone *shewes I can
be as bold with a Prelat as familiar with a Laundresse.* But
does it not argue rather the lascivious promptnesse of his own
fancy, who from the harmelesse mention of a Sleekstone
could neigh out the remembrance of his old conversation
among the *Viraginian* trollops? For me, if he move me, I
shall claime his owne oath, the oath *Ex officio* against any
Priest or Prelat in the kingdome to have ever as much hated
such pranks as the best and chastest of them all. That
exception which I made against toothlesse Satirs the Confuter hopes I had from the *Satirist*, but is farre deceav'd:
neither had I ever read the hobbling *distick* which he means.
For this good hap I had from a carefull education to be
inur'd and season'd betimes with the best and elegantest
authors of the learned tongues, and thereto brought an eare
that could measure a just cadence, and scan without articu-
lating; rather nice and humorous in what was tolerable,
then patient to read every drawling versifier. Whence light-
ing upon this title of *toothlesse Satirs*, I will not conceale ye
what I thought, Readers, that sure this must be some sucking
Satir, who might have done better to have us'd his corall, and
made an end of breeding, ere he took upon him to weild a
Satirs whip. But when I heard him talk of *scouring the rusted
swords of elvish Knights*, doe not blame me, if I chang'd my
thought, and concluded him some desperate Cutler. But
why *his scornefull muse could never abide with tragick shoos
her ankles for to hide*, the pace of the verse told me that her
maukin knuckles were never shapen to that royall buskin.
And turning by chance to the sixth Satyr of his Second book I
was confirmed; where having begun loftily *in heavens universall Alphabet* he fals downe to that wretched poorenesse and
frigidity as to talke of *Bridge street in heav'n, and the Ostler
of heav'n*, and there wanting other matter to catch him a
heat, (for certaine he was in the frozen *Zone* miserably be-

numm'd) with thoughts lower then any Beadle betakes him to whip the signe posts of *Cambridge* Alehouses, the ordinary subject of freshmens tales, and in a straine as pittifull. Which for him who would be counted *the first English Satyr*, to abase himselfe to, who might have learnt better among the Latin, and Italian Satyrists, and in our own tongue from the *vision and Creed of Pierce plowman*, besides others before him, manifested a presumptuous undertaking with weak, and un-examin'd shoulders. For a Satyr as it was borne out of a *Tragedy*, so ought to resemble his parentage, to strike high, and adventure dangerously at the most eminent vices among the greatest persons, and not to creepe into every blinde Taphouse that fears a Constable more then a Satyr. But that such a Poem should be toothlesse I still affirme it to be a bull, taking away the essence of that which it calls it selfe. For if it bite neither the persons nor the vices, how is it a Satyr, and if it bite either, how is it toothlesse, so that toothlesse Satyrs are as much as if he had said toothlesse teeth. What we should do therefore with this learned Comment upon *teeth* and *horns* which hath brought this confutant into his *Pedantick* kingdome of *Cornucopia*, to reward him for glossing upon *hornes* even to the *Hebrew root*, I know not unlesse we should commend him to be Lecturer in East-cheap upon S. *Lukes* day, when they send their tribute to that famous hav'n by Detford. But we are not like to scape him so. For now the worme of *Criticisme* works in him, he will tell us the deriva-tion of *German rutters, of meat, and of ink*, which doubtlesse rightly apply'd with some gall in it may prove good to heale this tetter of *Pedagoguisme* that bespreads him, with such a *tenasmus* of originating, that if he be an Arminian and deny originall sinne, all the *etymologies* of his book shall witnesse that his brain is not meanly tainted with that infection.

Sect. 7.] His seventh section labours to cavill out the flawes which were found in the Remonstrants logick; who having layd downe for a generall proposition, that *civill polity is variable and arbitrary*, from whence was inferr'd logically upon him that he had concluded the polity of England to be arbitrary, for generall includes particular, here his defendant is not asham'd to confesse that the Remonstrants proposi-tion was sophisticall *by a fallacy call'd ad plures interroga-*

tiones which sounds to me somewhat strange that a Remonstrant of that pretended sincerity should bring deceitfull and
double dealing propositions to the Parlament. The truth is he
had let slip a shrewd passage ere he was aware, not thinking
the conclusion would turne upon him with such a terrible
edge, and not knowing how to winde out of the briars, he or
his substitute seems more willing to lay the integrity of his
Logick to pawn, and grant a fallacy in his owne *Major* where
none is, then be forc't to uphold the inference. For that
distinction *of possible and lawfull* is ridiculous to be sought
for in that proposition; no man doubting that it is possible
to change the forme of civill polity; and that it is held lawfull by that *Major*, the word *arbitrary* implyes. Nor will this
helpe him, to deny that it is arbitrary *at any time or by any
undertakers* (which are two limitations invented by him since)
for when it stands as he will have it now by his second edition
*civill polity is variable but not at any time or by any under-
takers*, it will result upon him, belike then at some time, and
by some undertakers it may. And so he goes on mincing the
matter, till he meets with something in Sir *Francis Bacon*,
then he takes heart againe and holds his *Major* at large. But
by and by as soon as the shadow of Sir *Francis* hath left him,
he fals off again warping and warping till he come to contradict
himselfe in diameter : and denies flatly that it is *either variable
or arbitrary, being once settl'd*. Which third shift is no lesse
a piece of laughter. For before the polity was settl'd how
could it be variable when as it was no polity at all, but either an
Anarchy or a *Tyranny*. That limitation therefore *of after setling*
is a meere *tautology*. So that in fine his former assertion is
now recanted *and civill polity is neither variable nor arbitrary*.

Sect. 8.] What ever else may perswade me that this confutation was not made without some assistance or advice of the
Remonstrant, yet in this eighth Section that his hand was not
greatly intermixt, I can easily believe. For it begins with this
surmise, that *not having to accuse the Remonstrant to the
King, I do it to the Parlament*, which conceit of the man
cleanly shoves the King out of the Parlament, and makes two
bodies of one. Whereas the Remonstrant in the Epistle to his
last *short answer, gives his supposall that they cannot be
sever'd in the rights of their severall concernments*. Mark,

Readers, if they cannot be sever'd in what is severall (which casts a Buls eye to go yoke with the toothlesse Satyrs) how should they be sever'd in their common concernments, the wellfare of the land, by due accusation of such as are the common grievances, among which I took the Remonstrant to be one. And therefore if I accus'd him to the Parlament, it was the same as to accuse him to the King. Next he casts it into the dish of I know not whom that *they flatter some of the House and libell others whose consciences made them vote contrary to some proceedings.* Those some proceedings can be understood of nothing else but the *Deputies* execution. And can this private concocter of malecontent, at the very instant when he pretends to extoll the Parlament, afford thus to blurre over, rather then to mention that publick triumph of their justice and constancy so high, so glorious, so reviving to the fainted Common-wealth with such a suspicious and murmuring expression as to call it *some proceedings?* and yet immediately hee falls to glozing, as if hee were the only man that rejoyc't at these times. But I shall discover to ye Readers, that this his praising of them is as full of nonsense and Scholastick foppery, as his meaning he himselfe discovers to be full of close malignity. His first *Encomium* is *that the Sun looks not upon a braver nobler convocation then is that of King, Peers, and Commons.* One thing I beg of ye Readers, as ye beare any zeale to learning, to elegance, and that which is call'd *Decorum* in the writing of praise, especially on such a noble argument, ye would not be offended, though I rate this cloister'd Lubber according to his deserts. Where didst thou learne to be so agueish, so pusillanimous, thou lozel Bachelour of Art, as against all custome and use of speech to terme the high and sovran Court of Parlament, a Convocation? was this the flower of all thy *Synonyma's* and voluminous *Papers* whose best *folios* are predestin'd to no better end then to make winding sheets in Lent for Pilchers? Could'st thou presume thus with one word speaking to clap as it were under hatches the King with all his Peeres and Gentry into square Caps, and Monkish hoods? How well dost thou now appeare to be a Chip of the old block that could finde *Bridge-street and Alehouses in heav'n;* why didst thou not to be his perfect imitator, liken the King to the Vice-chancellour and the Lords

to the Doctors. Neither is this an indignity only but a reproach, to call that inviolable residence of justice and liberty,
by such an odious name as now a *Convocation* is become;
which would be nothing injur'd, though it were stil'd the
house of bondage, whereout so many cruell tasks, so many
unjust burdens, have been laden upon the brused consciences
of so many Christians throughout the land. But which of
those worthy deeds, whereof we and our posterity must confesse this Parlament to have done so many and so noble,
which of those memorable acts comes first into his praises?
none of all, not one. What will he then praise them for? not
for any thing doing, but for deferring to do, for deferring to
chastise his leud and insolent *compriests*. Not that they have
deferr'd all, but that he hopes they will remit what is yet
behind. For the rest of his oratory that followes, so just is it
in the language of stall epistle non sense, that if he who made
it can understand it, I deny not but that he may deserve
for his pains a cast Doublet. When a man would looke he
should vent something of his owne, as ever in a set speech
the manner is with him that knowes any thing, he, lest we
should not take notice anough of his barren stupidity, declares it by Alphabet, and referres us to odde remnants in
his topicks. Nor yet content with the wonted room of his
margent, but he must cut out large docks and creeks into his
text to unlade the foolish frigate of his unseasonable autorities,
not wherewith to praise the Parlament, but to tell them what
he would have them do. What else there is, he jumbles
together in such a lost construction, as no man either letter'd,
or unletter'd will be able to piece up. I shall spare to tran-
scribe him, but if I do him wrong, let me be so dealt with.

Now although it be a digression from the ensuing matter,
yet because it shall not be said I am apter to blame others then
to make triall my selfe, and that I may after this harsh discord touch upon a smoother string, awhile to entertaine my
self and him that list, with some more pleasing fit, and not
the lest to testifie the gratitude which I owe to those publick
benefactors of their country, for the share I enjoy in the common peace and good by their incessant labours, I shall be so
troublesome to this declamer for once, as to shew him what
he might have better said in their praise. Wherein I must

mention only some few things of many, for more then that to a digression may not be granted. Although certainly their actions are worthy not thus to be spoken of by the way, yet if hereafter it befall me to attempt something more answerable to their great merits, I perceave how hopelesse it will be to reach the heigth of their prayses at the accomplishment of that expectation that weights upon their noble deeds, the unfinishing whereof already surpasses what others before them have left enacted with their utmost performance through many ages. And to the end we may be confident that what they do, proceeds neither from uncertaine opinion, nor sudden counsels, but from mature wisdome, deliberat vertue, and deere affection to the publick good, I shall begin at that which made them likeliest in the eyes of good men to effect those things for the recovery of decay'd religion and the Commonwealth, which they who were best minded had long wisht for, but few, as the times then were desperat, had the courage to hope for. First therefore the most of them being either of ancient and high Nobility, or at least of knowne and well reputed ancestry, which is a great advantage towards vertue one way, but in respect of welth, ease, and flattery, which accompanies a nice and tender education, is as much a hindrance another way, the good which lay before them they took, in imitating the worthiest of their progenitors, and the evill which assaulted their younger yeares by the temptation of riches, high birth, and that usuall bringing up, perhaps too favourable and too remisse, through the strength of an inbred goodnesse, and with the helpe of divine grace, that had markt them out for no meane purposes, they nobly overcame. Yet had they a greater danger to cope with; for being train'd up in the knowledge of learning, and sent to those places, which were intended to be the seed plots of piety and the Liberall Arts, but were become the nurseries of superstition, and empty speculation, as they were prosperous against those vices which grow upon youth out of idlenesse and superfluity, so were they happy in working off the harmes of their abused studies and labours; correcting by the clearnesse of their owne judgement the errors of their mis-instruction, and were as *David* was, wiser then their teachers. And although their lot fell into such times, and to be bred in such places, where if they chanc't to be taught any thing good, or of their own accord had learn't it, they might see that presently untaught them by the custome and ill example of their elders, so farre in all probability was their youth from being misled by the single power of example, as their riper years were knowne to be unmov'd with the baits of preferment, and undaunted for any discouragement and terror which appear'd often to those that lov'd religion, and their native liberty. Which two things God hath inseparably knit together, and hath disclos'd to us that they who seek to corrupt our religion are the same that would inthrall our civill liberty. Thus in the midst of all disadvantages and disrespects (some also at last not without imprisonment and open disgraces in the cause of their countrey) having given proofe of themselves to be better made and fram'd by nature to the love and practise of vertue, then others under the holiest precepts and best examples have been headstrong and prone to vice, and having in all the trialls of a firme ingrafted honesty not oftner buckl'd in the conflict, then giv'n every opposition the foile, this moreover was added by favour from heav'n, as an ornament and happinesse to their vertue, that it should be neither obscure in the opinion of men, nor eclipst for want of matter equall to illustrat it selfe; God and man consenting in joynt approbation to choose them out as worthiest above others to be both the great reformers of the Church, and the restorers of the Common-wealth. Nor did they deceave that expectation which with the eyes and desires of their countrey was fixt upon them; for no sooner did the force of so much united excellence meet in one globe of brightnesse and efficacy, but encountring the dazl'd resistance of tyranny, they gave not over, though their enemies were strong and suttle, till they had laid her groveling upon the fatall block. With one stroke winning againe our lost liberties and Charters, which our forefathers after so many battels could scarce maintaine. And meeting next, as I may so resemble, with the second life of tyranny (for she was growne an ambiguous monster, and to be slaine in two shapes) guarded with superstition which hath no small power to captivate the minds of men otherwise most wise, they neither were taken with her miter'd hypocrisie, nor terrifi'd with the push of her

bestiall hornes, but breaking them immediately forc't her to
unbend the pontifical brow, and recoile. Which repulse only,
given to the Prelats (that we may imagine how happy their
removall would be) was the producement of such glorious
effects and consequences in the Church, that if I should compare them with those exploits of highest fame in Poems and
Panegyricks of old, I am certaine it would but diminish and
impaire their worth, who are now my argument. For those
ancient worthies deliver'd men from such tyrants as were
content to inforce only an outward obedience, letting the
minde be as free as it could. But these have freed us from a
doctrine of tyranny that offer'd violence and corruption even
to the inward persuasion. They set at liberty Nations and
Cities of men good and bad mixt together: but these opening
the prisons and dungeons cal'd out of darknesse and bonds,
the elect Martyrs and witnesses of their Redeemer. They restor'd the body to ease and wealth; but these the oppres
conscience to that freedome which is the chiefe prerogative of
the Gospell; taking off those cruell burdens impos'd not by
necessity, as other tyrants are wont for the safeguard of their
lives, but laid upon our necks by the strange wilfulnesse and
wantonnesse of a needlesse and jolly persecuter call'd Indif
ference. Lastly, some of those ancient deliverers have had
immortall praises for preserving their citizens from a famine
of corne. But these by this only repulse of an unholy *hier
archy* almost in a moment replenisht with saving knowledge
their countrey nigh famisht for want of that which should
feed their souls. All this being done while two armies in the
field stood gazing on, the one in reverence of such noblenesse
quietly gave back, and dislodg'd; the other spight of the
unrulinesse, and doubted fidelity in some regiments, wa
either perswaded or compell'd to disband and retire
home. With such a majesty had their wisdome begirt it
selfe, that whereas others had levied warre to subdue a
nation that sought for peace, they sitting here in peace could
so many miles extend the force of their single words as to
overawe the dissolute stoutnesse of an armed power secretl
stirr'd up and almost hir'd against them. And having by
solemne protestation vow'd themselves and the kingdom
anew to God and his service, and by a prudent foresight

above what their Fathers thought on, prevented the dissolution and frustrating of their designes by an untimely breaking up, notwithstanding all the treasonous plots against them, all the rumours either of rebellion, or invasion, they have not bin yet brought to change their constant resolution, ever to think fearlesly of their owne safeties, and hopefully of the Common-wealth. Which hath gain'd them such an admiration from all good men, that now they heare it as their ord'nary surname, to be saluted the Fathers of their countrey; and sit as gods among daily Petitions and publick thanks flowing in upon them. Which doth so little yet exalt them in their own thoughts, that with all gentle affability and curteous acceptance they both receave and returne that tribute of thanks which is tender'd them; testifying their zeale and desire to spend themselves as it were peice-meale upon the grievances and wrongs of their distressed Nation. Insomuch that the meanest artizans and labourers, at other times also women, and often the younger sort of servants assembling with their complaints, and that sometimes in a lesse humble guise then for petitioners, have gone with confidence, that eituher their meannesse would be rejected, nor their simplicity contemn'd, nor yet their urgency distasted either by the dignity, wisdome, or moderation of that supreme Senate; nor did they depart unsatisfi'd. And indeed, if we consider the generall concourse of suppliants, the free and ready admittance, the willing and speedy redresse in what is possible, it will not seeme much otherwise, then as if some divine commission from heav'n were descended to take into hearing and commiseration the long remedilesse afflictions of this kingdome; were it not that none more then themselves labour to remove and divert such thoughts, lest men should place too much confidence in their persons, still referring us and our prayers to him that can grant all, and appointing the monthly return of publick fasts and supplications. Therefore the more they seeke to humble themselves, the more does God by manifest signes and testimonies visibly honour their proceedings; and sets them as the mediators of this his cov'nant which he offers us to renew. Wicked men daily conspire their hurt, and it comes to nothing, rebellion rages in our Irish Province, but with miraculous and losselesse victories of few against

u   **M.**

many is daily discomfited and broken; if we neglect not this early pledge of Gods inclining towards us, by the slacknesse of our needfull aids. And whereas at other times we count it ample honour when God voutsafes to make man the instrument and subordinate worker of his gracious will, such acceptation have their prayers found with him, that to them he hath bin pleas'd to make himselfe the agent, and immediat performer of their desires; dissolving their difficulties when they are thought inexplicable, cutting out wayes for them where no passage could be seene; as who is there so regardlesse of Divine providence, that from late occurrences will not confesse. If therefore it be so high a grace when men are preferr'd to be but the inferior officers of good things from God, what is it when God himselfe condescends, and workes with his owne hands to fulfill the requests of men; which I leave with them as the greatest praise that can belong to humane nature. Not that we should think they are at the end of their glorious progresse, but that they will go on to follow his Almighty leading, who seems to have thus cov'-nanted with them, that if the will and the endeavour shall be theirs, the performance and the perfeting shall be his. Whence only it is that I have not fear'd, though many wise men have miscarried in praising great designes before the utmost event, because I see who is their assistant, who their confederat, who hath ingag'd his omnipotent arme, to support and crowne with successe their faith, their fortitude, their just and magnanimous actions, till he have brought to passe all that expected good which his servants trust is in his thoughts to bring upon this land in the full and perfet reformation of his Church.

Thus farre I have digrest, Readers, from my former subject; but into such a path, as I doubt not ye will agree with me, to be much fairer and more delightfull then the rode way I was in. And how to break off suddenly into those jarring notes, which this Confuter hath set me, I must be wary, unlesse I can provide against offending the eare, as some Musicians are wont skilfully to fall out of one key into another without breach of harmony. By good luck therefore his ninth Section is spent in mournfull elegy, certaine passionat soliloquies, and two whole pages of interrogatories that praise the Remonstrant even to the sonetting of *his fresh cheeks, quick eyes, round tongue, agil hand, and nimble invention.*

In his tenth Section he will needs erect figures, and tell fortunes. *I am no Bishop,* he sayes, *I was never borne to it;* let me tell therefore this wizzard since he calculats so right, that he may know there be in the world, and I among those who nothing admire his Idol a Bishoprick, and hold that it wants so much to be a blessing, as that I rather deeme it the meerest, the falsest, the most unfortunate guift of fortune. And were the punishment and mīsery of being a Prelat Bishop terminated only in the person, and did not extend to the affliction of the whole Diocesse, if I would wish any thing in bitternesse of soule to mine enemy, I would wish him the biggest and the fattest Bishoprick. But hee proceeds; and the familiar belike informs him, that *a rich Widow, or a Lecture, or both, would content me;* whereby I perceave him to be more ignorant in his art of divining then any Gipsy. For this I cannot omit without ingratitude to that providence above, who hath ever bred me up in plenty, although my life hath not bin unexpensive in learning, and voyaging about, so long as it shall please him to lend mee what he hath hitherto thought good, which is anough to serve me in all honest and liberall occasions, and something over besides. I were unthankfull to that highest bounty, if I should make my selfe so poore, as to sollicite needily any such kinde of *rich hopes* as this Fortune-teller dreams of. And that he may furder learne how his Astrology is wide all the houses of heav'n in spelling mariages, I care not if I tell him thus much profestly, though it be to the losing of my *rich hopes,* as he calls them, that I think with them who both in prudence and elegance of spirit would choose a virgin of mean fortunes honestly bred, before the wealthiest widow. The feind therefore that told our *Chaldean* the contrary was a lying feind. His next venome he utters against a prayer which he found in the animadversions, angry it seems to finde any prayers but in the Service Book. He dislikes it, and I therefore like it the better. *It was theatricall,* he sayes. And yet it consisted most of Scripture language: it had no *Rubrick* to be sung in an antick Coape upon the Stage of a High Altar. *It was big-mouth'd* he sayes; no marvell; if it were fram'd as the voice of three Kingdomes:

neither was it a prayer so much as a hymne in prose frequent both in the Prophets, and in humane authors; therefore the stile was greater then for an ordinary prayer: *It was an astounding prayer.* I thank him for that confession, so it was intended to astound and to astonish the guilty Prelats; and this Confuter confesses that with him it wrought that effect. But in that which followes, he does not play the Soothsayer but the diabolick slanderer of prayers. *It was made,* he sayes, *not so much to please God, or to benefit the weale publick* (how dares the Viper judge that) *but to intimate,* saith he, *your good abilities, to her that is your rich hopes, your Maronilla.* How hard it is when a man meets with a Foole to keepe his tongue from folly. That were miserable indeed to be a Courter of *Maronilla,* and withall of such a haplesse invention, as that no way should be left me to present my meaning but to make my selfe a canting Probationer of orisons. The Remonstrant when he was as young as I could

> *Toothlesse*   *Teach each hollow Grove to sound his love*
> *Satyrs,*   *Wearying eccho with one changelesse word.*

And so he well might, and all his auditory besides with his *teach each.*

> *Toothlesse*   *Whether so me list my lovely thoughts to sing,*
> *Satyrs,*   *Come dance ye nimble dryads by my side,*
>   *Whiles I report my fortunes or my loves.*

Delicious! he had that whole bevie at command whether in morrice or at May pole. Whilest I, by this figure-caster must be imagin'd in such distresse as to sue to *Maronilla,* and yet left so impoverisht of what to say, as to turne my Liturgy into my Ladies Psalter. Believe it graduat, I am not altogether so rustick, and nothing so irreligious, but as farre distant from a Lecturer, as the meerest Laick, for any consecrating hand of a Prelat that shall ever touch me. Yet I shall not decline the more for that, to speak my opinion in the controversie next mov'd. *Whether the people may be allow'd for competent judges of a ministers ability.* For how else can be fulfill'd that which God hath promis'd, to power out such abundance of knowledge upon all sorts of men in the times of the Gospell? how should the people examine the doctrine which is taught them, as Christ and his Apostles continually bid them do? how should they *discerne and beware of false Prophets, and try every spirit*, if they must be thought unfit to judge of the ministers abilities: the Apostles ever labour'd to perswade the Christian flock that they *were call'd in Christ to all perfectnesse of spirituall knowledge, and full assurance of understanding in the mystery of God*. But the non-resident and plurality-gaping Prelats the gulphs and whirle pools of benefices, but the dry pits of all sound doctrine, that they may the better preach what they list to their sheep, are still possessing them that they are sheep indeed, without judgement, without understanding, *the very beasts of Mount Sinai*, as this Confuter calls them; which words of theirs may serve to condemne them out of their owne mouths; and to shew the grosse contrarieties that are in their opinions. For while none thinke the people so void of knowledge as the Prelats think them, none are so backward and malignant as they to bestow knowledge upon them; both by suppressing the frequency of Sermons, and the printed explanations of the English bible. No marvell if the people turne beasts, when their Teachers themselves as *Isaiah* calls them, *Are dumbe and greedy dogs that can never have anough, ignorant, blind, and cannot understand, who while they all look their own way every one for his gaine from his quarter*, how many parts of the land are fed with windy ceremonies instead of sincere milke; and while one Prelat enjoyes the nourishment and right of twenty Ministers, how many waste places are left as darke as *Galile of the Gentiles, sitting in the region and shadow of death;* without preaching Minister, without light. So little care they of beasts to make them men, that by their sorcerous doctrine of formalities they take the way to transforme them out of Christian men into *Judaizing* beasts. Had they but taught the land, or suffer'd it to be taught, as Christ would it should have bin, in all plenteous dispensation of the word, then the poore mechanick might have so accustom'd his eare to good teaching, as to have discern'd betweene faithfull teachers and false. But now with a most inhumane cruelty they who have put out the peoples eyes reproach them of their blindnesse. Just as the Pharisees their true Fathers were wont; who could not indure that the people should be thought competent judges of Christs doctrine, although we know they judg'd farre better then those great Rabbies. Yet *this people*, said they, *that knowes not the law is accurst.* We need not the autority of *Pliny* brought to tell us, the people cannot judge of a minister. Yet that hurts not. For as none can judge of a Painter, or Statuary but he who is an Artist, that is, either in the *Practick* or the *Theory*, which is often separated from the practick, and judges learnedly without it, so none can judge of a Christian teacher, but he who hath, either the practize, or the knowledge of Christian religion, though not so artfully digested in him. And who almost of the meanest Christians hath not heard the Scriptures often read from his childhood, besides so many Sermons and Lectures more in number then any student hath heard in Philosophy, whereby he may easily attaine to know when he is wisely taught and when weakly. Whereof three wayes I remember are set downe in Scripture. The one is to reade often that best of books written to this purpose, that not the wise only but the simple and ignorant may learne by them; the other way to know of a minister, is by the life he leads, whereof the meanest understanding may be apprehensive. The last way to judge aright in this point is when he who judges, lives a Christian life himselfe. Which of these three will the Confuter affirme to exceed the capacity of a plaine artizan? And what reason then is there left wherefore he should be deny'd his voice in the election of his minister, as not thought a competent discerner? It is but arrogance therefore, and the pride of a *metaphysicall* fume, to thinke that *the mutinous rabble* (for so he calls the Christian congregation) *would be so mistaken in a Clerk of the University* that were to be their minister. I doubt me those Clerks that think so are more mistaken in themselves, and what with truanting and debaushery, what with false grounds and the weaknesse of naturall faculties in many of them (it being a maxim in some men to send the simplest of their sonnes thither) perhaps there would be found among them as many unsolid and corrupted judgements both in doctrine and life, as in any other two Corporations of like bignesse. This is undoubted that if any Carpenter Smith, or Weaver, were such a bungler in his trade, as the greater number of them are in their profession, he would starve for any custome. And should he

exercise his manifacture, as little as they do their talents, he
would forget his art: and should he mistake his tooles as they
do theirs, he would marre all the worke he took in hand.
How few among them that know to write, or speak in a pure
stile, much lesse to distinguish the *idea's*, and various kinds
of stile: in Latine barbarous, and oft not without *solecisms*,
declaiming in rugged and miscellaneous geare blown together
by the foure winds, and in their choice preferring the gay
rankensse of *Apuleius*, *Arnobius*, or any moderne fustianist,
before the native *Latinisms* of *Cicero*. In the Greek tongue
most of them unletter'd, or unenter'd to any sound proficiency
in those *Attick* maisters of morall wisdome and eloquence.
In the Hebrew text, which is so necessary to be understood
except it be some few of them, their lips are utterly uncircumcis'd. No lesse are they out of the way in philosophy;
pestring their heads with the saplesse dotages of old *Paris*
and *Salamanca*. And that which is the main point, in their
Sermons affecting the comments and postils of Friers and
Jesuits, but scorning and slighting the reformed writers. In
so much that the better sort among them will confesse it a
rare matter to heare a true edifying Sermon in either of their
great Churches; and that such as are most humm'd and applauded there, would scarce be suffer'd the second hearing in
a grave congregation of pious Christians. Is there cause why
these men should overween, and be so queasie of the rude
multitude, lest their deepe worth should be undervalu'd for
want of fit umpires? No my *matriculated confutant* there will
not want in any congregation of this Island, that hath not
beene altogether famisht, or wholly perverted with Prelatish
leven, there will not want divers plaine and solid men, that
have learnt by the experience of a good conscience, what it is
to be well taught, who will soone look through and through
both the lofty nakednesse of your *Latinizing* Barbarian, and
the finicall goosery of your neat Sermon-actor. And so I
leave you and your fellow *starres*, as you terme them, *of
either horizon*, meaning I suppose either *hemisphere*, unlesse
you will be ridiculous in your astronomy. For the rationall
horizon in heav'n is but one, and the sensible horizons in earth
are innumerable; so that your allusion was as erroneous as
your starres. But that you did well to prognosticat them

all at lowest in the horizon, that is either seeming bigger then they are through the mist and vapour which they raise, or else sinking, and wasted to the snuffe in their westerne socket.

Sect. 11.] His eleventh Section intends I know not what unlesse to clog us with the residue of his phlegmatick sloth, discussing with a heavie pulse the *expedience of set formes:* which no question but to some, and for some time may be permitted, and perhaps there may be usefully set forth by the Church a common *directory* of publick prayer, especially in the administration of the Sacraments. But that it should therefore be inforc't where both minister and people professe to have no need, but to be scandaliz'd by it, that, I hope, every sensible Christian will deny. And the reasons of such deniall the confuter himselfe, as his bounty still is to his adversary, will give us out of his affirmation. First saith he, *God in his providence hath chosen some to teach others and pray for others, as ministers and Pastors.* Whence I gather, that however the faculty of others may be, yet that they whom God hath set apart to his ministery, are by him endu'd with an ability of prayer; because their office is to pray for others. And not to be the lip-working deacons of other mens appointed words. Nor is it easily credible that he who can preach well should be unable to pray well; when as it is indeed the same ability to speak affirmatively, or doctrinally, and only by changing the mood to speak prayingly. In vaine therefore do they pretend to want utterance in prayer, who can finde utterance to preach. And if prayer be the guift of the Spirit, why do they admit those to the Ministery, who want a maine guift of their function, and prescribe guifted men to use that which is the remedy of another mans want; setting them their tasks to read, whom the Spirit of God stands ready to assist in his ordinance with the guift of free conceptions. What if it be granted to the infirmity of some Ministers (though such seeme rather to be halfe ministers) to help themselves with a set forme, shall it therefore be urg'd upon the plenteous graces of others? and let it be granted to some people while they are babes in Christian guifts, were it not better to take it away soone after, as we do loitering books, and *interlineary* translations from children; to stirre up and exercise that portion of the spirit which is in them, and not impose it upon congregations who not only deny to need it, but as a thing troublesome and offensive refuse it. Another reason which he brings for liturgie, is *the preserving of order, unity, and piety,* and the same shall be my reason against Liturgy. For I Readers, shall alwayes be of this opinion, that obedience to the Spirit of God, rather then to the faire seeming pretences of men, is the best and most dutifull order that a Christian can observe. If the Spirit of God manifest the guift of prayer in his Minister, what more seemely order in the congregation, then to go along with that man in our devoutest affections? for him to abridge himselfe by reading, and to forestall himselfe in those petitions, which he must either omit, or vainly repeat, when he comes into the Pulpit under a shew of order, is the greatest disorder. Nor is unity lesse broken, especially by our Liturgy, though this author would almost bring the Communion of Saints to a Communion of Liturgicall words. For what other reformed Church holds communion with us by our liturgy, and does not rather dislike it? and among our selves who knowes it not to have bin a perpetuall cause of disunion. Lastly, it hinders piety rather then sets it forward, being more apt to weaken the spirituall faculties, if the people be not wean'd from it in due time; as the daily powring in of hot waters quenches the naturall heat. For not only the body, and the mind, but also the improvement of Gods Spirit is quickn'd by using. Whereas they who will ever adhere to liturgy, bring themselves in the end to such a passe by overmuch leaning as to loose even the legs of their devotion. These inconveniences and dangers follow the compelling of set formes: but that the toleration of the English Liturgy now in use, is more dangerous then the compelling of any other which the reformed Churches use, these reasons following may evince. To contend that it is fantasticall, if not senselesse in some places, were a copious argument, especially in the *Responsories.* For such alternations as are there us'd must be by severall persons; but the Minister and the people cannot so sever their interests, as to sustaine severall persons; he being the only mouth of the whole body which he presents. And if the people pray he being silent, or they ask one thing and he another, it either changes the property, making the Priest the people, and

the people the Priest by turnes, or else makes two persons
and two bodies representative where there should be but one.
Which if it be nought else, must needs be a strange quaint-
nesse in ordinary prayer. The like, or worse may be said of
the *Litany*, wherein neither Priest nor people speak any intire
sense of themselves throughout the whole I know not what to
name it; only by the timely contribution of their parted
stakes, closing up as it were the *schisme* of a slic't prayer, they
pray not in vaine, for by this means they keep life betweene
them in a piece of gasping sense, and keep downe the sawci-
nesse of a continuall rebounding nonsense. And hence it is
that as it hath been farre from the imitation of any warranted
prayer, so we all know it hath bin obvious to be the pattern of
many a Jig. And he who hath but read in good books of
devotion and no more, cannot be so either of eare or judgement unpractiz'd to distinguish what is grave, *patheticall*,
devout, and what not, but will presently perceave this Liturgy
all over in conception leane and dry, of affections empty and
unmoving, of passion, or any height whereto the soule might
soar upon the wings of zeale, destitute and barren: besides
errors, *tautologies*, impertinences, as those thanks in the
womans Churching for her delivery from Sunburning and
Moonblasting, as if she had bin travailing not in her bed, but
in the deserts of *Arabia*. So that while some men cease not to
admire the incomparable frame of our Liturgy, I cannot but
admire as fast what they think is become of judgement, and
tast in other men, that they can hope to be heard without
laughter, And if this were all, perhaps it were a complyable
matter. But when we remember this our liturgy where we
found it, whence we had it, and yet where we left it, still serving to all the abominations of the Antichristian temple, it
may be wonder'd how we can demurre whether it should be
done away or no, and not rather feare we have highly
offended in using it so long. It hath indeed bin pretended to
be more ancient then the Masse, but so little prov'd that
whereas other corrupt Liturgies have had withall such a seeming antiquity, as that their publishers have ventur'd to ascribe
them with their worst corruptions either to S. *Peter*, S. *James*,
S. *Mark*, or at least to *Chrysostome*, or *Basil*, ours hath bin
never able to find either age, or author allowable, on whom

to father those things therein which are least offensive,
except the two Creeds, for *Te Deum* has a smach in it of
Limbus Patrum. As if Christ had not *open'd the kingdome of
heaven* before he had *overcome the sharpnesse of death*. So
that having receav'd it from the Papall Church as an originall
creature, for ought can be shewn to the contrary, form'd and
fashion'd by work maisters ill to be trusted, we may be assur'd that if God loathe the best of an Idolaters prayer, much
more the conceited fangle of his prayer. This Confuter himselfe confesses that a community of the same set forme in
prayers, is that which *makes Church and Church truly one;*
we then using a Liturgy farre more like to the Masse-book
then to any Protestant set forme, by his owne words must
have more communion with the *Romish Church*, then with
any of the reformed. How can we then not partake with them
the curse and vengeance of their superstition, to whom we
come so neere in the same set forme and dresse of our
devotion? do we thinke to sift the matter finer then we are
sure God in his jealousie will? who detested both the gold and
the spoile of Idolatrous Cities, and forbid the eating of things
offer'd to Idols. Are we stronger then he, to brook that which
his heart cannot brook? It is not surely because we think that
praiers are no where to be had but at *Rome;* that were a
foule scorne and indignity cast upon all the reformed
Churches, and our own; if we imagine that all the godly
Ministers of England are not able to new mould a better and
more pious Liturgy then this which was conceav'd and in-
fanted by an idolatrous Mother: how basely were that to
esteeme of Gods Spirit, and all the holy blessings and priviledges of a true Church above a false? Heark ye Prelats, is
this your glorious Mother of England, who when as Christ
hath taught her to pray, thinks it not anough unlesse she adde
thereto the teaching of Antichrist? How can we believe ye
would refuse to take the stipend of Rome, when ye shame not
to live upon the almes-basket of her prayers? will ye perswade
us that ye can curse Rome from your hearts when none but
Rome must teach ye to pray? *Abraham* disdain'd to take so
much as a thred or a shoo latchet from the King of *Sodome*,
though no foe of his, but a wicked King, and shall we receave our prayers at the bounty of our more wicked enemies?

whose guifts are no guifts, but the instruments of our bane? Alas that the Spirit of God should blow as an uncertaine wind, should so mistake his inspiring, to misbestow his guifts promis'd only to the elect, that the idolatrous shoulde finde words acceptable to present God with and abound to their neighbours, while the true professors of the Gospell can find nothing of their own worth the constituting, wherewith to worship God in publick. Consider if this be to magnifie the Church of England, and not rather to display her naked-nesse to all the world. Like therefore as the retaining of this Romish Liturgy is a provocation to God, and a dishonour to our Church, so is it by those ceremonies, those purifyings and offrings at the Altar, a pollution and disturbance to the Gos-pell it selfe; and a kinde of driving us with the foolish *Gala-tians* to another gospell. For that which the Apostles taught hath freed us in religion from the *ordinances of men*, and com-mands that *burdens be not laid* upon the redeemed of Christ, though the formalist will say, what no decency in Gods wor-ship? Certainly Readers, the worship of God singly in it selfe, the very act of prayer and thanksgiving with those free and unimpos'd expressions which from a sincere heart un-bidden come into the outward gesture, is the greatest decency that can be imagin'd. Which to dresse up and garnish with a devis'd bravery abolisht in the law, and disclam'd by the Gospell addes nothing but a deformed uglinesse. And hath ever afforded a colourable pretense to bring in all those traditions and carnalities that are so killing to the power and vertue of the Gospell. What was that which made the Jewes figur'd under the names of *Aholah* and *Aholibah* go a whoor-ing after all the heathens inventions, but that they saw a religion gorgeously attir'd and desirable to the eye? What was all, that the false Doctors of the Primitive Church, and ever since have done, but *to make a faire shew in the flesh*, as S. *Pauls* words are? If we have indeed given a bill of divorce to Popery and superstition, why do we not say as to a divors't wife; those things which are yours take them all with you, and they shall sweepe after you? Why were not we thus wise at our parting from Rome? Ah like a crafty adulteresse she forgot not all her smooth looks and inticing words at her parting; yet keep these letters, these tokens, and these few ornaments; I am not all so greedy of what is mine, let them preserve with you the memory of what I am? No, but of what I was, once faire and lovely in your eyes. Thus did those tender hearted reformers dotingly suffer themselves to be overcome with harlots language. And she like a witch, but with a contrary policy did not take something of theirs that she might still have power to bewitch them, but for the same intent left something of her own behind her. And that her whoorish cunning should prevaile to work upon us her deceitfull ends, though it be sad to speak, yet such is our blindnesse, that we deserve. For we are deepe in dotage. We cry out *Sacrilege and misdevotion* against those who in zeale have demolish't the dens and cages of her uncleane wallowings. We stand for a Popish Liturgy as for the ark of our Cov'nant. And so little does it appeare our prayers are from the heart, that multitudes of us declare, they know not how to pray but by rote. Yet they can learnedly invent a prayer of their own to the Parlament, that they may still ignorantly read the prayers of other men to God. They object that if wee must forsake all that is Rome's, we must bid adieu to our Creed; and I had thought our Creed had bin of the Apostles; for so it beares title. But if it be hers let her take it. We can want no Creed, so long as we want not the Scriptures. We magnifie those who in reforming our Church have inconsiderately and blamefully permitted the old leven to remaine and soure our whole lumpe. But *they were Martyrs;* True and he that looks well into the book of Gods providence, if he read there that God for this their negligence and halting, brought all that following persecution upon this Church, and on themselves, perhaps will be found at the last day not to have read amisse.

Sect. 12.] But now, Readers, we have the Port within sight; his last Section which is no deepe one, remains only to be foarded, and then the wisht shoare. And here first it pleases him much, that he hath discri'd me, as he conceaves, to be unread in the Counsels. Concerning which matter it will not be unnecessary to shape him this answer; That some years I had spent in the stories of those Greek and Roman exploits, wherein I found many things both nobly done, and worthily spoken: when comming in the method of time to that age wherein the Church had obtain'd a Christian Emperor, I so prepar'd my selfe as being now to read examples of wisdome and goodnesse among those who were foremost in the Church, not else where to be parallell'd: But to the amazement of what I expected, Readers, I found it all quite contrary; excepting in some very few, nothing but ambition, corruption, contention, combustion: in so much that I could not but love the Historian *Socrates*, who in the proem to his fifth book professes, *He was faine to intermixe affaires of State, for that it would be else an extreame annoyance to heare in a continu'd discourse the endlesse brabbles and counterplottings of the Bishops.* Finding therefore the most of their actions in single to be weak, and yet turbulent, full of strife and yet flat of spirit, and the summe of their best councels there collected, to be most commonly in questions either triviall and vaine, or else of short, and easie decision without that great bustle which they made, I concluded that if their single ambition and ignorance was such, then certainly united in a Councell it would be much more; and if the compendious recitall of what they there did was so tedious and unprofitable, then surely to sit out the whole extent of their tattle in a dozen volumes, would be a losse of time irrecoverable. Besides that which I had read of S. *Martin*, who for his last sixteene yeares could never be perswaded to be at any Councell of the Bishops. And *Gregory Nazianzen* betook him to the same resolution affirming to *Procopius, that of any Councell, or meeting of Bishops he never saw good end; nor any remedy thereby of evill in the Church, but rather an increase. For,* saith he, *their contentions and desire of Lording no tongue is able to expresse.* I have not therefore I confesse read more of the Councels save here and there, I should be sorry to have bin such a prodigall of my time: but that which is better, I can assure this Confuter; I have read into them all. And if I want any thing yet, I shall reply something toward that which in the defence of *Muræna* was answer'd by *Cicero to Sulpitius* the Lawyer. If ye provoke me (for at no hand else will I undertake such a frivolous labour) I will in three months be an expert councelist. For be not deceav'd, Readers, by men that would overawe your eares with big names and huge Tomes that contradict and repeal one another, because they can cramme a margent with citations. Do but winnow their chaffe from their wheat, ye shall see their great heape shrink and wax thin past beliefe. From hence he passes to enquire wherefore I should blame the vices of the Prelats only, seeing the inferiour Clergy is knowne to be as faulty. To which let him heare in briefe; that those Priests whose vices have been notorious, are all Prelaticall, which argues both the impiety of that opinion, and the wicked remisnesse of that government. We hear not of any which are call'd *Nonconformists* that have been accus'd for scandalous living; but are known to be pious, or at least sober men. Which is a great good argument, that they are in the truth and Prelats in the error. He would be resolv'd next *What the corruptions of the Universities concerne the Prelats?* and to that let him take this, That the Remonstrant having spok'n as if learning would decay with the removall of Prelats, I shew'd him that while books were extant, and in print, learning could not readily be at a worse passe in the Universities then it was now under their government. Then he seeks to justifie the pernicious Sermons of the Clergy, as if they upheld soveranty, when as all Christian soveranty is by law, and to no other end but to the maintenance of the common good. But their doctrine was plainly the dissolution of law which only sets up sov'ranty, and the erecting of an arbitrary sway according to privat will, to which they would enjoyne a slavish obedience without law; which is the known definition of a tyrant, and a tyranniz'd people. A little beneath he denies that great riches in the Church are the baits of pride and ambition: of which error to undeceave him, I shall allege a reputed divine autority, as ancient as *Constantine*, which his love to antiquity must not except against; and to adde the more weight, he shall learne it rather in the words of our old Poet *Gower* then in mine, that he may see it is no new opinion, but a truth deliver'd of old by a voice from heav'n, and ratify'd by long experience.

> *This Constantine which heal hath found*
> *Within Rome anon let found*
> *Two Churches which he did make*
> *For Peter and for Pauls sake:*
> *Of whom he had a vision,*
> *And yafe therto possession*

Of Lordship and of worlds good;
But how so that his will was good
Toward the Pope and his Franchise
Yet hath it proved otherwise
To see the working of the deed,
For in Chronick thus I read
Anon as he hath made the yeft
A voice was heard on high the left
Of which all Rome was adrad
And said this day venim is shad
In holy Church, of temporall
That medleth with the spirituall
And how it stant in that degree
Yet may a man the sooth see.
God amend it whan he will
I can thereto none other skill.

But there were beasts of prey, saith he, before wealth was
bestow'd on the Church. What though? because the Vulturs
had then but small pickings; shall we therefore go and fling
them a full gorge? if they for lucre use to creepe into the
Church undiscernably, the more wisdome will it be so to provide that no revennu there may exceed the golden mean.
For so, good Pastors will be content, as having need of no
more, and knowing withall the precept and example of Christ
and his Apostles, and also will be lesse tempted to ambition.
The bad will have but small matter whereon to set their mischiefe a work. And the worst and sutlest heads will not come
at all, when they shall see the crop nothing answerable to
their capacious greedinesse. For small temptations allure but
dribling offendors; but a great purchase will call such as both
are most able of themselves, and will be most inabl'd hereby
to compasse dangerous projects. But saith he, *A widows*
house will tempt as well as a Bishops Palace. Acutely spok'n.
Because neither we, nor the Prelats can abolish widows
houses which are but an occasion taken of evill without
the Church, therefore we shall set up within the Church a
Lottery of such prizes as are the direct inviting causes of
avarice and ambition, both unnecessary and harmefull to be
propos'd, and most easie, most convenient, and needfull to be

remov'd. *Yea but they are in a wise dispencers hand.* Let
them be in whose hand they will, they are most apt to blind,
to puffe up and pervert the most seeming good. And how
they have bin kept from Vultures, what ever the dispencers
care hath bin, we have learnt by our miseries. But this which
comes next in view, I know not what good vein, or humor
took him, when he let drop into his paper. *I that was ere
while the ignorant, the loyterer, on the sudden by his permission am now granted to know something.* And that *such
a volley of expressions* he hath met withall, *as he would never
desire to have them better cloth'd.* For me, Readers, although
I cannot say that I am utterly untrain'd in those rules which
best Rhetoricians have giv'n, or unacquainted with those
examples which the prime authors of eloquence have written
in any learn'd tongu, yet true eloquence I find to be none, but
the serious and hearty love of truth: And that whose mind so
ever is fully possest with a fervent desire to know good things,
and with the dearest charity to infuse the knowledge of them
into others, when such a man would speak, his words (by
what I can expresse) like so many nimble and airy servitors
trip about him at command, and in well order'd files, as he
would wish, fall aptly into their own places. But now to the
remainder of our discours. Christ refus'd great riches, and
large honours at the Devils hand. But why, saith he, *as they
were tender'd by him from whom it was a sin to receave them.*
Timely remember'd : why is it not therefore as much a sin to
receave a Liturgy of the masses giving, were it for nothing
else but for the giver? *But he could make no use of such a high
estate,* quoth the Confuter; opportunely. For why then
should the servant take upon him to use those things which
his master had unfitted himselfe to use, that hee might teach
his ministers to follow his steps in the same ministery. But
they were offer'd him to a bad end. So they prove to the Prelats; who after their preferment most usually change the
teaching labour of the word, into the unteaching ease of
Lordship over consciences, and purses. But hee proceeds,
God entic't the Israelites with the promise of Canaan. Did not
the Prelats bring as slavish mindes with them, as the Jewes
brought out of Egypt, they had left out that instance. Besides that it was then the time, when as the best of them, as

Saint *Paul* saith, *was shut up unto the faith under the Law* their School-maister, who was forc't to intice them as children with childish enticements. But the Gospell is our manhood, and the ministery should bee the manhood of the Gospell, not to looke after, much lesse so basely to plead for earthly rewards. *But God incited* the wisest man *Salomon with these means.* Ah Confuter of thy selfe, this example hath undone thee, *Salomon* askt an understanding heart, which the Prelats have little care to ask. He askt no riches which is their chiefe care: therefore was the prayer of *Salomon* pleasing to God: hee gave him wisdome at his request, and riches without asking: as now hee gives the Prelats riches at their seeking, and no wisdome because of their perverse asking. But hee gives not over yet, *Moses had an eye to the reward.* To what reward, thou man that looks't with *Balaams* eyes, to what reward had the faith of *Moses* an eye to? He that had forsaken all the greatnesse of *Egypt*, and chose a troublesome journey in his old age through the Wildernesse, and yet arriv'd not at his journies end His faithfull eyes were fixt upon that incorruptible reward, promis'd to *Abraham* and his seed in the *Messiah*, hee sought a heav'nly reward which could make him happy, and never hurt him, and to such a reward every good man may have a respect. But the Prelats are eager of such rewards as cannot make them happy, but can only make them worse. *Jacob* a Prince borne, vow'd, that if God would *but give him bread to eat and raiment to put on, then the Lord should be his God.* But the Prelats of meane birth, and oft times of lowest, making shew as if they were call'd to the spirituall and humble ministery of the Gospell, yet murmur, and thinke it a hard service, unlesse contrary to the tenour of their profession, they may eat the bread and weare the honours of Princes. So much more covetous and base they are then *Simon Magus*, for he proffer'd a reward to be admitted to that work, which they will not be meanly hir'd to. But saith he, *Are not the Clergy members of Christ, why should ont each member thrive alike?* Carnall textman! As if worldly thriving were one of the priviledges wee have by being in Christ, and were not a providence oft times extended more liberally to the Infidell then to the Christian. Therefore must the Ministers of Christ not be over rich or great in the world, because their calling is spirituall, not secular; because they have a speciall warfare, which is not to be intangl'd with many impediments: because their Maister Christ gave them this precept, and set them this example, told them this was the mystery of his comming, by meane things and persons to subdue mighty ones: and lastly because a middle estate is most proper to the office of teaching. Whereas higher dignity teaches farre lesse, and blindes the teacher. Nay, saith the Confuter, fetching his last indeavour, *The Prelats will be very loath to let go their Baronies, and votes in Parlament*, and calls it *Gods cause*, with an unsufferable impudence. *Not that they love the honours and the means*, good men and generous, *but that they would not have their countrey made guilty of such a sacrilege and injustice.* A worthy Patriot for his owne corrupt ends! That which hee imputes as sacrilege to his countrey, is the only way left them to purge that abominable sacrilege out of the land, which none but the Prelats are guilty of. Who for the discharge of one single duty receave and keepe that which might bee anough to satisfie the labours of many painefull Ministers better deserving then themselves. Who possiesse huge Benefices for lazie performances, great promotions, only for the execution of a cruell disgospelling jurisdiction. Who ingrosse many pluralities under a *non-resident* andslubbring dispatch of soules. Who let hundreds of parishes famish in one *Diocesse*, while they the Prelats are mute, and yet injoy that wealth that would furnish all those darke places with able supply, and yet they eat, and yet they live at the rate of Earles, and yet hoard up. They who chase away all the faithfull Shepheards of the flocke, and bring in a dearth of spirituall food, robbing thereby the Church of her dearest treasure, and sending heards of souls starvling to Hell, while they feast and riot upon the labours of hireling Curats, consuming and purloyning even that which by their foundation is allow'd, and left to the poore, and to reparations of the Church. These are they who have bound the land with the sinne of Sacrilege, from which mortall ingagement wee shall never be free, till wee have totally remov'd with one labour as one individuall thing Prelaty and Sacrilege. And herein will the King be a true defender of the Faith, not by paring or lessning, but by distributing in due proportion the maintenance of the Church, that all parts of the Land may equally partake the plentifull and diligent preaching of the faith, the scandall of Ceremonies thrown out, that delude and circumvent the faith. And the usurpation of Prelats laid levell, who are in words the Fathers, but in their deeds the oppugners of the faith. This is that which will best confirme him in that glorious title. Thus yee have heard, Readers, how many shifts and wiles the Prelats have invented to save their ill got booty. And if it be true, as in Scripture it is foretold, that pride and covetousnesse are the sure markes of those false Prophets which are to come, then boldly conclude these to bee as great seducers, as any of the latter times. For betweene this and the judgement day, doe not look for any arch deceavers who in spight of reformation will use more craft, or lesse shame to defend their love of the world, and their ambition, then these Prelats have done. And if yee thinke that soundnesse of reason, or what force of argument soever, will bring them to an ingenuous silence, yee think that which will never be. But if ye take that course which *Erasmus* was wont to say *Luther* tooke against the Pope and Monks, if yee denounce warre against their Miters and their bellies, ye shall soon discerne that *Turbant* of pride which they weare upon their heads to be no *helmet of salvation*, but the meere mettle and horn-work of Papall jurisdiction; and that they have also this guift, like a certaine kinde of some that are possest, to have their voice in their bellies, which being well drain'd and taken downe, their great Oracle, which is only there, will soone be dumbe, and the *Divine right of Episcopacy* forthwith expiring, will put us no more to trouble with tedious antiquities and disputes.

¶ The Doctrine and Discipline of Divorce

To the Parlament of *ENGLAND*, with the Assembly

If it were seriously askt, and it would be no untimely question, Renowned Parlament, select Assembly, who of all Teachers and Maisters that have ever taught hath drawn the most Disciples after him, both in Religion, and in manners, it might bee not untruly answer'd, Custome. Though vertue be commended for the most perswasive in her Theory; *and Conscience in the plain demonstration of the spirit, finds most evincing, yet whether it be the secret of divine will, or the originall blindnesse we are born in, so it happ'ns for the most part, that Custome still is silently receiv'd for the best instructer. Except it be, because her method is so glib and easie, in some manner like to that vision of Ezekiel, rowling up her sudden book of implicit knowledge, for him that will, to take and swallow down at pleasure; which proving but of bad nourishment in the concoction, as it was heedlesse in the devouring, puffs up unhealthily, a certaine big face of pretended learning, mistaken among credulous men, for the wholesome habit of soundnesse and good constitution; but is indeed no other, then that swoln visage of counterfeit knowledge and literature, which not onely in private marrs our education, but also in publick is the common climer into every chaire, where either Religion is preach't, or Law reported: filling each estate of life and profession, with abject and servil principles; depressing the high and Heaven-born spirit of Man, far beneath the condition wherin either God created him, or sin hath sunke him. To persue the Allegory, Custome being but a meer face, as Eccho is a meere voice, rests not in her unaccomplishment, untill by secret inclination, she accorporat her selfe with error, who being a blind and Serpentine body without a head, willingly accepts what he wants, and supplies what her incompleatnesse went seeking. Hence it is, that Error supports Custome, Custome count'nances Error. And these two between them would persecute and chase away all truth and solid wisdome out of humane life, were it not that God, rather then man, once in many ages, cals together the prudent and Religious counsels of Men, deputed to represse the encroachments, and to work off the inveterate blots and obscurities wrought upon our minds by the suttle insinuating of Error and Custome: Who with the numerous and vulgar train of their followers, make it their chief designe to envie and cry-down the industry of free reasoning, under the terms of humor, and innovation; as if the womb of teeming Truth were to be clos'd up, if she presume to bring forth ought, that sorts not with their unchew'd notions and suppositions. Against which notorious injury and abuse of mans free soule to testifie and oppose the utmost that study and true labour can attaine, heretofore the incitement of men reputed grave hath led me among others;*

*and now the duty and the right of an instructed Christian cals
me through the chance of good or evill report, to be the sole
advocate of a discount'nanc't truth: a high enterprise Lords and
Commons, a high enterprise and a hard and such as every
seventh Son of a seventh Son does not venture on. Nor have I
amidst the clamor of so much envie and impertinence, whether
to appeal, but to the concourse of so much piety and wisdom
heer assembl'd. Bringing in my hands an ancient and most
necessary, most charitable, and yet most injur'd Statute of*
Moses: *not repeal'd ever by him who only had the authority,
but thrown aside with much inconsiderat neglect, under the
rubbish of Canonicall ignorance: as once the whole law was by
some such like conveyance in* Josiahs *time. And hee who shall
indeavour the amendment of any old neglected grievance in
Church or State, or in the daily course of life, if he be gifted
with abilities of mind that may raise him to so high an undertaking, I grant he hath already much wherof not to repent him;
yet let me arreed him, not to be the foreman of any mis-
judg'd opinion, unless his resolutions be firmly seated in a
square and constant mind, not conscious to it self of any deserved blame, and regardles of ungrounded suspicions. For
this let him be sure he shall be boorded presently by the ruder
sort, but not by discreet and well nurtur'd men, with a thousand
idle descants and surmises. Who when they cannot confute the
least joynt or sinew of any passage in the book; yet God forbid
that truth should be truth because they have a boistrous conceit of some pretences in the Writer. But were they not more
busie and inquisitive then the Apostle commends, they would
hear him at least,* rejoycing, so the truth be preacht, whether
of envie or other pretence whatsoever: *For Truth is as impossible to be soil'd by any outward touch, as the Sun beam.
Though this ill hap wait on her nativity, that shee never comes
into the world, but like a Bastard, to the ignominy of him that
brought her forth: till Time the Midwife rather then the
mother of Truth, have washt and salted the Infant, declar'd her
legitimat, and Churcht the father of his young* Minerva, *from
the needlesse causes of his purgation. Your selves can best
witnesse this, worthy Patriots, and better will, no doubt, hereafter: for who among ye of the formost that have travail'd in
her behalfe to the good of Church, or State, hath not been often*

traduc't to be the agent of his own by-ends, under pretext of Reformation. So much the more I shall not be unjust to hope, that however Infamy, or Envy may work in other men to do her fretfull will against this discourse, yet that the experience of your own uprightnesse mis-interpreted, will put ye in mind to give it free audience and generous construction. What though the brood of Belial, the draffe of men, to whom no liberty is pleasing, but unbridl'd and vagabond lust without pale or partition, will laugh broad perhaps, to see so great a strength of Scripture mustering up in favour, as they suppose, of their debausheries; they will know better, when they shall hence lerne, that honest liberty is the greatest foe to dishonest licence. And what though others out of a waterish and queasy conscience because ever crasy and never yet sound, will rail and fancy to themselves, that injury and licence is the best of this Book? Did not the distemper of their own stomacks affect them with a dizzy megrim, they would soon tie up their tongues, and discern themselves like that Assyrian blasphemer all this while reproaching not man but the Almighty, the holy one of Israel, *whom they doe not deny to have belawgiv'n his own sacred people with this very allowance, which they now call injury and licence, and dare cry shame on, and will doe yet a while, till they get a little cordiall sobriety to settle their qualming zeale. But this question concerns not us perhaps: Indeed mans disposition though prone to search after vain curiosities, yet when points of difficulty are to be discusst, appertaining to the removal of unreasonable wrong and burden from the perplext life of our brother, it is incredible how cold, how dull, and farre from all fellow feeling we are, without the spurre of self-concernment. Yet if the wisdome, the justice, the purity of God be to be cleer'd from foulest imputations which are not yet avoided, if charity be not to be degraded and trodd'n down under a civil Ordinance, if Matrimony be not to be advanc't like that exalted perdition, writt'n of to the* Thessalonians, above all that is called God, *or goodnesse, nay, against them both, then I dare affirm there will be found in the Contents of this Booke, that which may concern us all. You it concerns chiefly, Worthies in Parlament, on whom as on our deliverers, all our grievances and cares, by the merit of your eminence and fortitude are devolv'd: Me it concerns next, having with much labour and faithfull diligence first found out, or at least with a fearlesse and communicative candor first publisht to the manifest good of Christendome, that which calling to witnesse every thing mortall and immortall, I beleeve unfainedly to be true. Let not other men thinke their conscience bound to search continually after truth, to pray for enlightning from above, to publish what they think they have so obtain'd, and debar me from conceiving my self ty'd by the same duties. Yee have now, doubtlesse by the favour and appointment of God, ye have now in your hands a great and populous Nation to Reform; from what corruption, what blindnes in Religion yee know well; in what a degenerat and fal'n spirit from the apprehension of native liberty, and true manlines, I am sure ye find: with what unbounded licence rushing to whordoms and adulteries needs not long enquiry: insomuch that the fears which men have of too strict a discipline, perhaps exceed the hopes that can bee in others, of ever introducing it with any great successe. What if I should tell ye now of dispensations and indulgences, to give a little the rains, to let them play and nibble with the bait a while; a people as hard of heart as that Egyptian Colony that went to Canaan. This is the common doctrine that adulterous and injurious divorces were not conniv'd only, but with eye open allow'd of old for hardnesse of heart. But that opinion, I trust, by then this following argument hath been well read, will be left for one of the mysteries of an indulgent Antichrist, to farm out incest by, and those his other tributary pollutions. What middle way can be tak'n then, may some interrupt, if we must neither turn to the right nor to the left, and that the people hate to be reform'd: Mark then, Judges and Lawgivers, and ye whose Office it is to be our teachers, for I will utter now a doctrine, if ever any other, though neglected or not understood, yet of great and powerfull importance to the governing of mankind. He who wisely would restrain the reasonable Soul of man within due bounds, must first himself know perfectly, how far the territory and dominion extends of just and honest liberty. As little must he offer to bind that which God hath loos'n'd, as to loos'n that which he hath bound. The ignorance and mistake of this high point, hath heapt up one huge half of all the misery that hath bin since* Adam. *In the Gospel we shall read a supercilious crew of masters, whose holinesse, or rather whose evil*

*eye, grieving that God should be so facil to man, was to set
straiter limits to obedience, then God had set; to inslave the
dignity of man, to put a garrison upon his neck of empty and
overdignifi'd precepts: And we shall read our Saviour never
more greev'd and troubl'd, then to meet with such a peevish
madnesse among men against their owne freedome. How can
we expect him to be lesse offended with us, when much of the
same folly shall be found yet remaining where it lest ought, to
the perishing of thousands. The greatest burden in the world
is superstition; not only of Ceremonies in the Church, but of
imaginary and scarcrow sins at home. What greater weakning, what more suttle stratagem against our Christian warfare,
when besides the grosse body of real transgressions to encounter; wee shall be terrifi'd by a vain and shadowy menacing of
faults that are not: When things indifferent shall be set to over-
front us, under the banners of sin, what wonder if wee be routed,
and by this art of our Adversary, fall into the subjection of
worst and deadliest offences. The superstition of the Papist
is,* touch not, taste not, *when* God *bids both: and ours is,*
part not, separat not, *when God and charity both permits and
commands.* Let all your things be done with charity, *saith St.*
Paul: *and his Master saith,* She is the fulfilling of the Law.
*Yet now a civil, an indifferent, a sometime disswaded Law of
mariage, must be forc't upon us to fulfill, not onely without
charity, but against her. No place in Heav'n or Earth, except
Hell, where charity may not enter: yet mariage the Ordinance
of our solace and contentment, the remedy of our lonelinesse
will not admit now either of charity or mercy to come in and
mediate or pacifie the fiercenes of this gentle Ordinance, the
unremedied lonelinesse of this remedy. Advise yee well, supreme Senat, if charity be thus excluded and expulst, how yee
will defend the untainted honour of your own actions and proceedings: He who marries, intends as little to conspire his
own ruine, as he that swears Allegiance: and as a whole people
is in proportion to an ill Government, so is one man to an ill
mariage. If they against any authority, Covnant, or Statute, may
by the soveraign edict of charity, save not only their lives, but
honest liberties from unworthy bondage, as well may he against
any private Covnant, which hee never enter'd to his mischief,
redeem himself from unsupportable disturbances to honest*

peace, and just contentment: And much the rather, for that to resist the highest Magistrat though tyrannizing, God never gave us expresse allowance, only he gave us reason, charity, nature and good example to bear us out; but in this economicall misfortune, thus to demean our selves, besides the warrant of those foure great directors, which doth as justly belong hither, we have an expresse law of God, and such a law, as wherof our Saviour with a solemn threat forbid the abrogating. For no effect of tyranny can sit more heavy on the Commonwealth, then this houshold unhappines on the family. And farewell all hope of true Reformation in the state, while such an evil as this lies undiscern'd or unregarded in the house. On the redresse wherof depends, not only the spiritfull and orderly life of our grown men, but the willing, and carefull education of our children. Let this therfore be new examin'd, this tenure and free-hold of mankind, this native and domestick Charter giv'n us by a greater Lord then that Saxon *King the Confessor. Let the statutes of God be turn'd over, be scann'd a new, and consider'd; not altogether by the narrow intellectuals of quotationists and common placers, but (as was the ancient right of Counsels) by men of what liberall profession soever, of eminent spirit and breeding joyn'd with a diffuse and various knowledge of divine and human things; able to ballance and define good and evil, right and wrong throughout every state of life; able to shew us the waies of the Lord, strait and faithfull as they are, not full of cranks and contradictions, and pit falling dispenses, but with divine insight and benignity measur'd out to the proportion of each mind and spirit, each temper and disposition, created so different each from other, and yet by the skill of wise conducting, all to become uniform in vertue. To expedite these knots were worthy a learned and memorable Synod; while our enemies expect to see the expectation of the Church tir'd out with dependencies and independencies how they will compound, and in what Calends. Doubt not, worthy Senators, to vindicate the sacred honour and judgement of* Moses *your predecessor, from the shallow commenting of Scholasticks and Canonists. Doubt not after him to reach out your steddy hands to the mis-inform'd and wearied life of man; to restore this his lost heritage into the houshold state; wherwith be sure that peace and love, the best subsistence of a Christian family will return home from*

*whence they are now banisht; places of prostitution will be lesse
haunted, the neighbors bed lesse attempted, the yoke of prudent and manly discipline will be generally submitted to, sober
and well order'd living will soon spring up in the Commonwealth. Ye have an author great beyond exception,* Moses;
*and one yet greater, he who hedg'd in from abolishing, every
smallest jot and tittle of precious equity contain'd in that Law,
with a more accurat and lasting Masoreth, then either the
Synagogue of* Ezra, *or the* Galilean *School at* Tiberias *hath
left us. Whatever else ye can enact, will scarce concern a third
part of the Brittish name: but the benefit and good of this your
magnanimous example, will easily spread far beyond the banks
of* Tweed *and the* Norman *Iles. It would not be the first, or
second time, since our ancient* Druides, *by whom this Iland was
the Cathedral of Philosophy to* France, *left off their pagan rites,
that England hath had this honour vouchsaft from Heav'n, to
give out reformation to the World. Who was it but our English*
Constantine, *that baptiz'd the Roman Empire? who but the*
Northumbrian Willibrode, *and* Winifride *of* Devon *with their
followers, were the first Apostles of* Germany? *who but* Alcuin
and Wicklef *our Country men open'd the eyes of* Europe, *the
one in arts, the other in Religion. Let not England, forget her
precedence of teaching nations how to live.*

*Know, Worthies, know and exercise the privilege of your
honour'd Country. A greater title I heer bring ye, then is either
in the power or in the policy of* Rome *to give her Monarchs;
this glorious act will stile ye the defenders of Charity. Nor is
this yet the highest inscription that wil adorn so religious and so
holy a defence as this; behold heer the pure and sacred Law
of God, and his yet purer and more sacred name offring themselves to you first, of all Christian reformers to be acquitted
from the long suffer'd ungodly attribute of patronizing Adultery. Deferre not to wipe off instantly these imputative blurrs
and stains cast by rude fancies upon the throne and beauty it
self of inviolable holines: lest some other people more devout
and wise then wee, bereav us this offer'd immortal glory, our
wonted prerogative, of being the first asserters in every great
vindication. For me, as farre as my part leads me, I have already my greatest gain, assurance and inward satisfaction to
have don in this nothing unworthy of an honest life, and studies*

*wel employ'd. With what event among the wise and right under-
standing handfull of men, I am secure. But how among the
drove of Custom and Prejudice this will be relisht, by such
whose capacity, since their youth run ahead into the easie creek
of a System or a Medulla, sayls there at will under the blown
physiognomy of their unlabour'd rudiments, for them, what
their tast will be, I have also surety sufficient, from the entire
league that hath bin ever between formal ignorance and grave
obstinacie. Yet when I remember the little that our Saviour
could prevail about this doctrine of Charity against the crabbed
textuists of his time, I make no wonder, but rest confident that
who so preferrs either Matrimony, or other Ordinance before
the good of man and the plain exigence of Charity, let him
professe Papist, or Protestant, or what he will, he is no better
then a Pharise, And understands not the Gospel: whom as a
misinterpreter of Christ I openly protest against; and provoke
him to the triall of this truth before all the world: and let him
bethink him withall how he will soder up the shifting flaws of his
ungirt permissions, his venial and unvenial dispences, wherwith
the Law of God pardoning and unpardoning hath bin shamefully branded, for want of heed in glossing, to have eluded and
baffl'd out all Faith and chastity from the mariagebed of that
holy seed, with politick and judiciall adulteries. I seek not to
seduce the simple and illiterat; my errand is to find out the
choicest and the learnedest, who have this high gift of wisdom
to answer solidly, or to be convinc't. I crave it from the piety,
the learning and the prudence which is hous'd in this place. It
might perhaps more fitly have bin writt'n in another tongue;
and I had don so, but that the esteem I have of my Countries
judgement, and the love I bear to my native language to serv it
first with what I endeavour, made me speak it thus, ere I assay
the verdit of outlandish readers. And perhaps also heer I might
have ended nameles, but that the addresse of these lines
chiefly to the Parlament of England might have seem'd ingratefull not to acknowledge by whose Religious care, unwearied watchfulnes, couragious and heroick resolutions, I
enjoy the peace and studious leisure to remain,*

The Honourer and Attendant of their

Noble worth and vertues,

JOHN MILTON.

MANY men, whether it be their fate, or fond opinion, easily perswade themselves, if God would but be pleas'd a while to withdraw his just punishments from us, and to restrain what power either the devill, or any earthly enemy hath to work us woe, that then mans nature would find immediate rest and releasement from all evils. But verily they who think so, if they be such as have a mind large enough to take into their thoughts a generall survey of humane things, would soon prove themselves in that opinion farre deceiv'd. For though it were granted us by divine indulgence to be exempt from all that can be harmfull to us from without, yet the perversnesse of our folly is so bent, that we should never lin hammering out of our owne hearts, as it were out of a flint, the seeds and sparkles of new misery to our selves, till all were in a blaze againe. And no marvell if out of our own hearts, for they are evill; but ee'n out of those things which God meant us, either for a principall good, or a pure contentment, we are still hatching and contriving upon our selves matter of con-tinuall sorrow and perplexitie. What greater good to man then that revealed rule, whereby God vouchsafes to shew us how he would be worshipt? And yet that not rightly under-stood, became the cause that once a famous man in *Israel* could not but oblige his conscience to be the sacrificer, or if not, the jaylor of his innocent and only daughter. And was the cause ofttimes that Armies of valiant men have given up their throats to a heathenish enemy on the Sabbath day: fondly thinking their defensive resistance to be as then a work unlawfull. What thing more instituted to the solace and delight of man then marriage? and yet the mis-interpret-ing of some Scripture directed mainly against the abusers of the Law for divorce giv'n by *Moses*, hath chang'd the blessing of matrimony not seldome into a familiar and co-inhabiting mischiefe; at least into a drooping and disconsolate houshold captivity, without refuge or redemption. So ungovern'd and so wild a race doth superstition run us from one extreme of abused liberty into the other of unmercifull restraint. For although God in the first ordaining of marriage, taught us to what end he did it, in words expresly implying the apt and cheerfull conversation of man with woman, to comfort and refresh him against the evill of solitary life, not mentioning the purpose of generation till afterwards, as being but a secondary end in dignity, though not in necessity; yet now, if any two be but once handed in the Church, and have tasted in any sort the nuptiall bed, let them find themselves never so mistak'n in their dispositions through any error, concealment, or misadventure, that through their different tempers, thoughts, and constitutions, they can neither be to one another a remedy against lonelines, nor live in any union or contentment all their dayes, yet they shall, so they be but found suitably weapon'd to the least possibility of sensuall injoyment, be made, spight of *antipathy* to fadge together, and combine as they may to their unspeakable wearisomnes and despaire of all sociable delight in the ordinance which God establisht to that very end. What a calamity is this, and as the Wise-man if he were alive, would sigh out in his owne phrase, what a *sore evill is this under the Sunne!* All which we can referre justly to no other author then the Canon Law and her adherents, not consulting with charitie, the interpreter and guide of our faith, but resting in the meere element of the Text; doubtles by the policy of the devill to make that gracious ordinance become unsupportable, that what with men not daring to venture upon wedlock, and what with men wearied out of it, all inordinate licence might abound. It was for many ages that mariage lay in disgrace with most of the ancient Doctors, as a work of the flesh, almost a defilement, wholly deny'd to Priests, and the second time disswaded to all, as he that reads *Tertullian* or *Jerom* may see at large. Afterwards it was thought so Sacramentall, that no adultery or desertion could dissolve it; and this is the sence of our Canon Courts in *England* to this day, but in no other reformed Church els: yet there remains in them also a burden on it as heavie as the other two were disgracefull or superstitious, and of as much iniquity, crossing a Law not onely writt'n by *Moses*, but character'd in us by nature, of more antiquity and deeper ground then marriage it selfe; which Law is to force nothing against the faultles proprieties of nature: yet that this may be colourably done, our Saviours words touching divorce, are as it were congeal'd into a stony rigor, inconsistent both with his doctrine and his office, and that which he preacht onely to the conscience, is by Canonicall tyranny snatcht into the compulsive censure of a judiciall Court; where Laws are impos'd even against the venerable and secret power of natures impression, to love what ever cause be found to loath. Which is a hainous barbarisme both against the honour of mariage, the dignity of man and his soule, the goodnes of Christianitie, and all the humane respects of civilitie. . . .

. . . This therefore shall be the task and period of this discourse to prove, first that other reasons of divorce besides adultery, were by the Law of *Moses*, and are yet to be allow'd by the Christian Magistrate as a peece of justice, and that the words of Christ are not hereby contraried. Next, that to prohibit absolutely any divorce whatsoever except those which *Moses* excepted, is against the reason of Law, as in due place I shall shew out of *Fagius* with many additions. He therefore who by adventuring shall be so happy as with successe to light the way of such an expedient liberty and truth as this, shall restore the much wrong'd and over-sorrow'd state of matrimony, not onely to those mercifull and life-giving remedies of *Moses*, but, as much as may be, to that serene and blisfull condition it was in at the beginning; and shall deserv of all apprehensive men (considering the troubles and distempers which for want of this insight have bin so oft in Kingdomes, in States and Families) shall deserve to be reckon'd among the publick benefactors of civill and humane life; above the inventors of wine and oyle; for this is a far dearer, far nobler, and more desireable cherishing to mans life, unworthily expos'd to sadness and mistake, which he shall vindicate. Not that licence and levety and unconsented breach of faith should herein be countenanc't, but that some conscionable and tender pitty might be had of those who have unwarily in a thing they never practiz'd before, made themselves the bondmen of a luckles and helples matrimony. In which Argument he whose courage can serve him to give the first on-set, must look for two severall oppositions: the one from them who having sworn themselves to long custome and the letter of the Text, will not out of the road: the other from those whose grosse and vulgar apprehensions conceit but low of matrimoniall purposes, and in the work of male and female think they have all. Neverthelesse, it shall be here sought by due wayes to be made appeare, that those words of God in the institution, promising a meet help against lonelines; and those words of Christ, *That his yoke is easie and his burden light,* were not spoken in vain; for if the knot of marriage may in no case be dissolv'd but for adultery, all the burd'ns and services of the Law are not so intolerable. This onely is desir'd of them who are minded to judge hardly of thus maintaining, that they would be still and heare all out, nor thinke it equall to answer deliberate reason with sudden heat and noise; remembring this, that many truths now of reverend esteem and credit, had their birth and beginning once from singular and private thoughts; while the most of men were otherwise possest; and had the fate at first to be generally exploded and exclaim'd on by many violent opposers; yet I may erre perhaps in soothing my selfe that this present truth reviv'd, will deserve on all hands to be not sinisterly receiv'd, in that it undertakes the cure of an inveterate disease crept into the best part of humane societie: and to doe this with no smarting corrosive, but with a smooth and pleasing lesson, which receiv'd hath the vertue to soften and dispell rooted and knotty sorrowes: and without inchantment if that be fear'd, or spell us'd, hath regard at once both to serious pitty, and upright honesty; that tends to the redeeming and restoring of none but such as are the object of compassion, having in an ill houre hamper'd themselves to the utter dispatch of all their most beloved comforts and repose for this lives term. But if we shall obstinately dislike this new overture of unexpected ease and recovery, what remains but to deplore the frowardnes of our hopeles condition, which neither can endure the estate we are in, nor admit of remedy either sharp or sweet. Sharp we our selves distast; and sweet, under whose hands we are, is scrupl'd and suspected as too lushious. In such a posture Christ found the *Jews,* who were neither won with the austerity of *John the Baptist,* and thought it too much licence to follow freely the charming pipe of him who sounded and proclaim'd liberty and reliefe to all distresses: yet Truth in some age or other will find her witnes, and shall be justify'd at last by her own children.

To remove therefore if it be possible, this great and sad oppression which through the strictnes of a literall interpreting hath invaded and disturb'd the dearest and most peaceable estate of houshould society, to the over-burdening, if not the over-whelming of many Christians better worth then to be so deserted of the Churches considerate care, this position shall be laid down, first proving, then answering what may be objected either from Scripture or light of reason.

That indisposition, unfitnes, or contrariety of mind, arising from a cause in nature unchangeable, hindring and ever likely to hinder the main benefits of conjugall society, which are solace and peace, is a greater reason of divorce then naturall frigidity, especially if there be no children, and that there be mutuall consent....

... For all sence and equity reclaims that any Law or Cov'-nant how solemne or strait soever, either between God and man, or man and man, though of Gods joyning, should bind against a prime and principall scope of its own institution, and of both or either party cov'nanting; neither can it be of force to ingage a blameles creature to his owne perpetuall sorrow, mistak'n for his expected solace, without suffering charity to step in and doe a confest good work of parting those whom nothing holds together, but this of Gods joyning, falsly suppos'd against the expresse end of his own ordinance. And what his chiefe end was of creating woman to be joyn'd with man, his own instituting words declare, and are infallible to informe us what is mariage and what is no mariage: unlesse we can think them set there to no purpose: *It is not good,* saith he, *that man should be alone; I will make him a help meet for him.* From which words so plain, lesse cannot be concluded, nor is by any learned Interpreter, then that in Gods intention a meet and happy conversation is the chiefest and the noblest end of mariage: for we find here no expression so necessarily implying carnall knowledge, as this prevention of lonelines to the mind and spirit of man. To this, *Fagius, Calvin, Pareus, Rivetus,* as willingly and largely assent as can be wisht. And indeed it is a greater blessing from God, more worthy so excellent a creature as man is, and a higher end to honour and sanctifie the league of marriage, whenas the solace and satisfaction of the mind is regarded and provided for before the sensitive pleasing of the body. And with all generous persons maried thus it is; that where the mind and person pleases aptly, there some unaccomplishment of the bodies delight may

X   M.

be better born with, then when the mind hangs off in an un-
closing disproportion, though the body be as it ought; for
there all corporall delight will soone become unsavoury and
contemptible. And the solitarines of man, which God had
namely and principally order'd to prevent by mariage, hath
no remedy, but lies under a worse condition then the lone-
liest single life; for in single life the absence and remotenes of
a helper might inure him to expect his own comforts out of
himselfe, or to seek with hope; but here the continuall sight
of his deluded thoughts without cure, must needs be to him,
if especially his complexion incline him to melancholy, a
daily trouble and pain of losse in som degree like that which
Reprobats feele. Lest therefore so noble a creature as man
should be shut up incurably under a worse evill by an easie
mistake in that ordinance which God gave him to remedy a
lesse evill, reaping to himselfe sorrow while he went to rid
away solitarines, it cannot avoid to be concluded, that if the
woman be naturally so of disposition, as will not help to remove, but help to increase that same God forbidd'n lonelines
which will in time draw on with it a generall discomfort and
dejection of mind, not beseeming either Christian profession
or morall conversation, unprofitable and dangerous to the
Common-wealth, when the houshold estate, out of which
must flourish forth the vigor and spirit of all publick enter-
prizes is so ill contented and procur'd at home, and cannot
be supported; such a mariage can be no mariage whereto
the most honest end is wanting. . . .

. . . How vaine therefore is it, and how preposterous in the
Canon Law to have made such carefull provision against the
impediment of carnall performance, and to have had no care
about the unconversing inability of mind, so defective to the
purest and most sacred end of matrimony: and that the vessell of voluptuous enjoyment must be made good on him
that has taken it upon trust without any caution, when as the
mind from whence must flow the acts of peace and love, a
farre more pretious mixture then the quintessence of an
excrement, though it be found never so deficient and unable
to performe the best duty of marriage in a cheerfull and agreeable conversation, shall be thought good anough, however
flat and melancholious it be, and must serve, though to the

eternall disturbance and languishing of him that complains him. Yet wisdom and charity waighing Gods owne institution, would think that the pining of a sad spirit wedded to lonelines should deserve to be free'd, aswell as the impatience of a sensuall desire so providently reliev'd. Tis read to us in the Liturgy, that *we must not marry to satisfie the fleshly appetite, like brute beasts that have no understanding;* but the Canon so runs, as if it dreamt of no other matter then such an appetite to be satisfy'd; for if it happen that nature hath stopt or extinguisht the veins of sensuality, that mariage is annull'd. But though all the faculties of the understanding and conversing part after triall appeare to be so ill and so aversly met through natures unalterable working, as that neither peace, nor any sociable contentment can follow, 'tis as nothing, the contract shall stand as firme as ever, betide what will. What is this, but secretly to instruct us, that however many grave reasons are pretended to the maried life, yet that nothing indeed is thought worth regard therein, but the prescrib'd satisfaction of an irrationall heat; which cannot be but ignominious to the state of mariage, dishonourable to the undervalu'd soule of man, and even to Christian Doctrine it selfe. While it seems more mov'd at the disappointing of an impetuous nerve, then at the ingenuous grievance of a mind unreasonably yoakt; and to place more of mariage in the channell of concupiscence, then in the pure influence of peace and love, whereof the soules lawfull contentment is the one onely fountain.

But some are ready to object, that the disposition ought seriously to be consider'd before. But let them know again, that for all the warinesse can be us'd, it may yet befall a discreet man to be mistak'n in his choice, and we have plenty of examples. The sobrest and best govern'd men are least practiz'd in these affairs; and who knowes not that the bashfull muteness of a virgin may oft-times hide all the unliveliness and naturall sloth which is really unfit for conversation; nor is there that freedom of accesse granted or presum'd, as may suffice to à perfect discerning till too late: and where any disposition is suspected, what more usuall then the perswasion of friends, that acquaintance, as it increases, will amend all. And lastly, it is not strange though many who have spent their youth chastly, are in some things not so quick-sighted, while they hast so eagerly to light the nuptiall torch; nor is it therefore that for a modest error a man should forfeit so great a happines, and no charritable means to release him. Since they who have liv'd most loosely by reason of their bold accustoming, prove most succesfull in their matches, because their wild affections unsetling at will, have been as so many divorces to teach them experience. When as the sober man honouring the appearance of modesty, and hoping well of every sociall vertue under that veile, may easily chance to meet, if not with a body impenetrable, yet often with a mind to all other due conversation inaccessible, and to all the more estimable and superior purposes of matrimony uselesse and almost liveles: and what a solace, what a fit helpe such a consort would be through the whole life of a man, is lesse pain to conjecture then to have experience. . . .

. . . This pure and more inbred desire of joyning to it selfe in conjugall fellowship a fit conversing soul (which desire is properly call'd love) *is stronger then death*, as the spouse of Christ thought, *many waters cannot quench it, neither can the floods drown it*. This is that rationall burning that mariage is to remedy, not to be allay'd with fasting, nor with any penance to be subdu'd, which how can he asswage who by mishap hath met the most unmeetest and unsutable mind? Who hath the power to struggle with an intelligible flame, not in paradice to be resisted, become now more ardent by being fail'd of what in reason it lookt for; and even then most unquencht, when the importunity of a provender burning is well anough appeas'd; and yet the soule hath obtained nothing of what it justly desires. Certainly such a one forbidd'n to divorce, is in effect forbidd'n to marry, and compell'd to greater difficulties then in a single life; for if there be not a more human burning which mariage must satisfie, or els may be dissolv'd, then that of copulation, mariage cannot be honourable for the meet reducing and terminating lust between two: seeing many beasts in voluntary and chosen couples, live together as unadulterously, and are as truly maried in that respect. But all ingenuous men will see that the dignity and blessing of mariage is plac't rather in the mutuall enjoyment of that which the wanting soul needfully

seeks, then of that which the plenteous body would joyfully
give away. Hence it is that *Plato* in his festival discourse
brings in *Socrates* relating what he fain'd to have learnt
from the Prophetesse *Diotima*, how *Love* was the sonne of
Penury, begot of *Plenty* in the garden of *Jupiter*. Which
divinely sorts with that which in effect *Moses* tells us, that
Love was the son of *Lonelines*, begot in Paradice by that
sociable and helpfull aptitude which God implanted between man and woman toward each other. The same also is
that burning mention'd by S. *Paul*, whereof mariage ought to
be the remedy; the Flesh hath other mutuall and easie curbs
which are in the power of any temperate man. When therefore this originall and sinles *Penury* or *Lonelines* of the soul
cannot lay it selfe downe by the side of such a meet and acceptable union as God ordain'd in marriage, at least in some
proportion, it cannot conceive and bring forth *Love*, but remains utterly unmarried under a formall wedlock and still
burnes in the proper meaning of S. *Paul*. Then enters *Hate*,
not that Hate that sins, but that which onely is naturall dis-
satisfaction and the turning aside from a mistaken object : if
that mistake have done injury, it fails not to dismisse with
recompence; for to retain still, and not be able to love, is to
heap up more injury. Thence this wise and pious Law of
dismission now defended took beginning: He therefore who
lacking of his due in the most native and humane end of
mariage, thinks it better to part then to live sadly and injuriously to that cheerfull covnant (for not to be belov'd and yet
retain'd is the greatest injury to a gentle spirit) he I say who
therefore seeks to part, is one who highly honours the maried
life and would not stain it : and the reasons which now move
him to divorce, are equall to the best of those that could first
warrant him to marry; for, as was plainly shewn, both the
hate which now diverts him and the lonelinesse which leads
him still powerfully to seeke a fit help, hath not the least grain
of a sin in it, if he be worthy to understand himselfe. . . .

. . . Fourthly, Mariage is a cov'nant the very beeing
whereof consists, not in a forc't cohabitation, and counterfet performance of duties, but in unfained love and peace.
And of matrimoniall love no doubt but that was chiefly
meant, which by the ancient Sages was thus parabl'd, That

Love, if he be not twin-born, yet hath a brother wondrous like him, call'd *Anteros:* whom while he seeks all about, his chance is to meet with many fals and faining Desires that wander singly up and down in her likenes. By them in their borrow'd garb, Love though not wholly blind, as Poets wrong him, yet having but one eye, as being born an Archer aiming, and that eye not the quickest in this dark region here below, which is not Loves proper sphere, partly out of the simplicity, and credulity which is native to him, often de-ceiv'd, imbraces and consorts him with these obvious and suborned striplings, as if they were his Mothers own Sons, for so he thinks them, while they suttly keepe themselves most on his blind side. But after a while, as his manner is, when soaring up into the high Tower of his *Apogæum*, above the shadow of the earth, he darts out the direct rayes of his then most piercing eyesight upon the impostures, and trim disguises that were us'd with him, and discerns that this is not his genuin brother, as he imagin'd, he has no longer the power to hold fellowship with such a personall mate. For strait his arrows loose their golden heads, and shed their purple feathers, his silk'n breades untwine, and slip their knots, and that originall and firie vertue giv'n him by Fate, all on a sudden goes out and leaves him undeifi'd and des-poil'd of all his force: till finding *Anteros* at last, he kindles and repairs the almost faded ammunition of his Deity by the reflection of a co-equal and *homogeneal* fire. Thus mine author sung it to me; and by the leave of those who would be counted the only grave ones; this is no meer amatorious novel (though to be wise and skilful in these matters, men heretofore of greatest name in vertue, have esteemed it one of the highest arks that human contemplation circling up-wards, can make from the globy sea whereon she stands) but this is a deep and serious verity, shewing us that Love in mariage cannot live nor subsist unlesse it be mutual; and where love cannot be, there can be left of wedlock nothing, but the empty husk of an outside matrimony; as undelightfull and unpleasing to God, as any other kind of hypocrisie. So farre is his command from tying men to the observance of duties which there is no help for, but they must be dissembl'd. If *Salomons* advice be not over frolick, *Live joyfully*, saith he, *with the wife whom thou lovest, all thy dayes, for that is thy portion.* How then, where we finde it impossible to rejoyce or to love, can we obey this precept? how miserably do we defraud our selves of that comfortable portion which God gives us, by striving vainly to glue an error together which God and nature will not joyn; adding but more vexation and violence to that blisfull society by our importunate superstition, that will not hearken to St. *Paul*, 1 *Cor*. 7. who speaking of mariage and divorce, determines plain enough in generall, that God therein *hath call'd us to peace* and not *to bondage*. Yea God himself commands in his Law more then once, and by his Prophet *Malachy*, as *Calvin* and the best translations read, that *he who hates let him divorce;* that is he who cannot love: hence is it that the Rabbins and *Maimonides* famous among the rest in a Book of his set forth by *Buxtorsius*, tells us, that *Divorce was permitted by* Moses *to preserve peace in mariage, and quiet in the family.* Surely the Jewes had their saving peace about them, aswell as we, yet care was tak'n that this wholsom provision for houshould peace should also be allow'd them; and must this be deny'd to Christians? O perversnes! that the Law should be made more provident of peacemaking then the Gospel! that the Gospel should be put to beg a most necessary help of mercy from the Law, but must not have it: and that to grind in the mill of an undelighted and servil copulation, must be the only forc't work of a Christian mariage, oft times with such a yokefellow, from whom both love and peace, both nature and Religion mourns to be separated. I cannot therefore be so diffident, as not securely to conclude, that he who can receive nothing of the most important helps in mariage, being thereby disinabl'd to return that duty which is his, with a cleare and hearty countnance; and thus continues to grieve whom he would not, and is no lesse griev'd, that man ought even for loves sake and peace to move Divorce upon good and liberall conditions to the divorc't. And it is a lesse breach of wedlock to part with wise and quiet consent betimes, then still to soile and profane that mystery of joy and union with a polluting sadnesse and perpetuall distemper; for it is not the outward continuing of mariage that keepes whole that cov'nant, but whosoever does most according to peace and love, whether in mariage or in divorce, he it is that breaks mariage least; it being so often written, that *Love onely is the fullfilling of every Commandement*.

Fifthly, as those Priests of old were not to be long in sorrow, or if they were, they could not rightly execute their function; so every true Christian in a higher order of Priesthood is a person dedicate to joy and peace, offering himselfe a lively sacrifice of praise and thanksgiving, and there is no Christian duty that is not to be season'd and set off with cheerefulnes; which in a thousand outward and intermitting crosses may yet be done well, as in this vale of tears, but in such a bosome affliction as this, crushing the very foundation of his inmost nature when he shall be forc't to love against a possibility, and to use a dissimulation against his soule in the perpetuall and ceaseles duties of a husband doubtles his whole duty of serving God must needs be blurr'd and tainted with a sad unpreparednesse and dejection of spirit, wherein God has no delight. Who sees not therfore how much more Christianity it would be to break by divorce that which is more broken by undue and forcible keeping, rather then *to cover the Altar of the Lord with continuall teares so that he regardeth not the offering any more*, rather then that the whole worship of a Christian mans life should languish and fade away beneath the weight of an immesurable griefe and discouragement. And because some think the childr'n of a second matrimony succeeding a divorce would not be a holy seed, it hinder'd not the Jews from being so, and why should we not think them more holy then the off-spring of a former ill-twisted wedlock, begott'n only out of a bestiall necessitie without any true love or contentment, or joy to their parents, so that in some sense we may call them the *children of wrath* and anguish, which will as little conduce to their sanctifying, as if they had been bastards; for nothing more then disturbance of mind suspends us from approaching to God. Such a disturbance especially as both assaults our faith and trust in Gods providence, and ends, if there be not a miracle of vertue on either side, not onely in bitternes and wrath, the canker of devotion, but in a desperate and vitious carelesnes; when he sees himself without fault of his, train'd by a deceitfull bait into a snare of misery, betrai'd by an alluring ordinance, and

then made the thrall of heavines and discomfort by an undivorcing Law of God, as he erroneously thinks, but of mans
iniquitie, as the truth is; for that God preferres the free and
cheerfull worship of a Christian, before the grievous and
exacted observance of an unhappy marriage, besides that the
generall maximes of Religion assure us, will be more manifest by drawing a parallell argument from the ground of
divorcing an Idolatresse, which was, lest he should alienate
his heart from the true worship of God: and what difference
is there whether she pervert him to superstition by her inticing sorcery, or disinable him in the whole service of God
through the disturbance of her unhelpfull and unfit society;
and so drive him at last through murmuring and despair to
thoughts of Atheisme; neither doth it lessen the cause of
separating in that the one willingly allures him from the
faith, the other perhaps unwillingly drives him; for in the
account of God it comes all to one that the wife looses him a
servant; and therfore by all the united force of the *Deca-
logue* she ought to be disbanded, unlesse we must set marriage above God and charity, which is a doctrine of devils no
lesse then forbidding to marry....

... The sixt place declares this prohibition to be as re-
spectlesse of humane nature as it is of religion, and therefore
is not of God. He teaches that an unlawfull mariage may be
lawfully divorc't. And that those who having throughly discern'd each others disposition which oft-times cannot be till
after matrimony, shall then find a powerful reluctance and
recoile of nature on either side blasting all the content of their
mutuall society, that such persons are not lawfully maried (to
use the Apostles words) *Say I these things as a man, or saith
not the Law also the same? for it is writt'n,* Deut. 22. *Thou
shalt not sowe thy vineyard with divers seeds, lest thou defile
both. Thou shalt not plow with an Ox and an Asse together,*
and the like. I follow the pattern of S. *Pauls* reasoning;
Doth God care for Asses and Oxen, how ill they yoke together,
*or is it not said altogether for our sakes? for our sakes no doubt
this is writt'n.* Yea the Apostle himself in the forecited 2
Cor. 6. 14. alludes from that place of *Deut.* to forbid mis-
yoking mariage; as by the Greek word is evident, though he
instance but in one example of mis-matching with an Infidell:

yet next to that what can be a fouler incongruitie, a greater violence to the reverend secret of nature, then to force a mixture of minds that cannot unite, and to sowe the furrow of mans nativity with seed of two incoherent and uncombining dispositions; which act being kindly and voluntarie, as it ought, the Apostle in the language he wrote call'd *Eunoia*, and the Latines *Benevolence*, intimating the originall thereof to be in the understanding and the will: if not, surely there is nothing which might more properly be call'd a malevolence rather; and is the most injurious and unnaturall tribute that can be extorted from a person endew'd with reason, to be made pay out the best substance of his body, and of his soul too, as some think, when either for just and powerfull causes he cannot like, or from unequall causes finds not recompence. And that there is a hidden efficacie of love and hatred in man as wel as in other kinds, not morall, but naturall, which though not alwayes in the choyce, yet in the successe of mariage will ever be most predominant, besides daily experience, the author of *Ecclesiasticus*, whose wisedom hath set him next the Bible, acknowledges, 13. 16. *A man*, saith he, *will cleave to his like*. But what might be the cause, whether each ones alotted *Genius* or proper Starre, or whether the supernall influence of Schemes and angular aspects or this elementall *Crasis* here below, whether all these joyntly or singly meeting friendly, or unfriendly in either party, I dare not, with the men I am likest to clash, appear so much a Philosopher as to conjecture. The ancient proverb in *Homer* lesse obstruse entitles this work of leading each like person to his like, peculiarly to God himself: which is plain anough also by his naming of a meet or like help in the first espousall instituted; and that every woman is meet for every man, none so absurd as to affirm. Seeing then there is indeed a two-fold Seminary or stock in nature, from whence are deriv'd the issues of love and hatred distinctly flowing through the whole masse of created things, and that Gods doing ever is to bring the due likenesses and harmonies of his works together, except when out of two contraries met to their own destruction, he moulds a third existence, and that it is error, or some evil Angel which either blindly or maliciously hath drawn together in two persons ill imbarkt in wedlock the sleeping discords and enmities of nature lull'd on purpose with some false bait, that they may wake to agony and strife, later then prevention could have wisht, if from the bent of just and honest intentions beginning what was begun, and so continuing, all that is equall, all that is fair and possible hath been tri'd, and no accommodation likely to succeed what folly is it still to stand combating and battering against invincible causes and effects, with evill upon evill, till either the best of our dayes be linger'd out, or ended with some speeding sorrow. The wise *Ecclesiasticus* advises rather, 37. 27. *My sonne, prove thy soule in thy life, see what is evill for it, and give not that unto it.* Reason he had to say so; for if the noysomnesse or disfigurement of body can soon destroy the sympathy of mind to wedlock duties, much more wil the annoyance and trouble of mind infuse it self into all the faculties and acts of the body, to render them invalid, unkindly, and even unholy against the fundamentall law book of nature, which *Moses* never thwarts, but reverences: therefore he commands us to force nothing against sympathy or naturall order, no not upon the most abject creatures; to shew that such an indignitie cannot be offer'd to man without an impious crime. And certainly those divine meditating words of finding out a meet and like help to man, have in them a consideration of more then the indefinite likenesse of womanhood; nor are they to be made waste paper on, for the dulnesse of Canon divinity: no nor those other allegorick precepts of beneficence fetcht out of the closet of nature to teach us goodnes and compassion in not compelling together unmatchable societies, or if they meet through mischance, by all consequence to dis-joyn them, as God and nature signifies and lectures to us not only by those recited decrees, but ev'n by the first and last of all his visible works; when by his divorcing command the world first rose out of Chaos, nor can be renewed again out of confusion but by the separating of unmeet consorts.

Seventhly, The Canon Law and Divines consent, that if either party be found contriving against anothers life, they may be sever'd by divorce; for a sin against the life of mariage, is greater then a sin against the bed: the one destroys, the other but defiles: The same may be said touching those persons who being of a pensive nature and cours of life, have sum'd up all their solace in that free and lightsome conversation which God and man intends in mariage: wherof when they see themselves depriv'd by meeting an unsociable consort, they oft-times resent one anothers mistake so deeply, that long it is not ere griefe end one of them. When therfore this danger is foreseen, that the life is in perill by living together, what matter is it whether helples grief, or wilfull practice be the cause; This is certain, that the preservation of life is more worth then the compulsory keeping of mariage; and it is no lesse then crueltie to force a man to remain in that state as the solace of his life, which he and his friends know will be either the undoing or the disheartning of his life. And what is life without the vigor and spiritfull exercise of life? how can it be usefull either to private or publick employment? shall it therfore be quite dejected, though never so valuable, and left to moulder away in heavines for the superstitious and impossible performance of an ill-driv'n bargain? Nothing more inviolable then vows made to God, yet we read in *Numbers* that if a wife had made such a vow, the meer will and authoritie of her husband might break it; how much more may he break the error of his own bonds with an unfit and mistak'n wife, to the saving of his welfare, his life, yea his faith and vertue from the hazard of over-strong temptations; for if man be Lord of the Sabbath, to the curing of a Fevor, can he be lesse then Lord of mariage in such important causes as these? . . .

. . . What covnant more contracted with God, and lesse in mans power, then the vow which hath once past his lips? yet if it be found rash, if offensive, if unfruitfull either to Gods glory or the good of man, our doctrine forces not error and unwillingnes irksomly to keep it, but counsels wisdome and better thoughts boldly to break it; therfore to enjoyn the indissoluble keeping of a mariage found unfit against the good of man both soul and body, as hath bin evidenc't is to make an idol of mariage, to advance it above the worship of God and the good of man, to make it a transcendent command, above both the second and the first Table, which is a most prodigious doctrine.

Next, wheras they cite out of the *Proverbs*, that it is the *Covnant of God*, and therfore more then human, that consequence is manifestly false: for so the covnant which *Zedechiah* made with the Infidell King of *Babel*, is call'd the *Covnant of God*. Ezek. 17. 19. which would be strange to heare counted more then a human covnant. So every covnant between man and man, bound by oath, may be calld the covnant of God, because God therin is attested. So of mariage he is the authour and the witnes; yet hence will not follow any divine astriction more then what is subordinate to the glory of God and the main good of either party; for as the glory of God and their esteemed fitnesse one for the other was the motive which led them both at first to think without other revelation that God had joyned them together, So when it shall be found by their apparent unfitnesse, that their continuing to be man and wife is against the glory of God and their mutuall happinesse, it may assure them that God never joynd them; who hath reveal'd his gracious will not to set the ordinance above the man for whom it was ordain'd: not to canonize mariage either as a tyrannesse or a goddesse over the enfranchiz'd life and soul of man: for wherin can God delight, wherin be worshipt, wherin be glorify'd by the forcible continuing of an improper and ill-yoking couple? He that lov'd not to see the disparity of severall cattell at the plow, cannot be pleas'd with any vast unmeetnesse in mariage. Where can be the peace and love which must invite God to such a house, may it not be feared that the not divorcing of such a helplesse disagreement, will be the divorcing of God finally from such a place? But it is a triall of our patience they say: I grant it: but which of *Jobs* afflictions were sent him with that law, that he might not use means to remove any of them if he could? And what if it subvert our patience and our faith too? Who shall answer for the perishing of all those souls perishing by stubborn expositions of particular and inferior precepts against the generall and supreme rule of charity? They dare not affirm that mariage is either a Sacrament, or a mystery, though all those sacred things give place to man, and yet they invest it with such an awfull sanctity, and give it such adamantine chains to bind with, as if it were to be worshipt like some Indian deity, when it can conferre no blessing upon us, but works more and more to our misery. To such teachers the saying of S. *Peter* at the Councell of

Jerusalem will do well to be apply'd: *Why tempt ye God to put a yoke upon the necks* of Christian men, which neither the *Jews*, Gods ancient people, *nor we are able to bear:* and nothing but unwary expounding hath brought upon us.

To these considerations this also may be added as no improbable conjecture; seeing that sort of men who follow *Anabaptism, Familism, Antinomianism,* and other fanatick dreams, (if we understand them not amisse) be such most commonly as are by nature addicted to Religion, of life also not debausht, and that their opinions having full swinge, do end in satisfaction of the flesh, it may be come with reason into the thoughts of a wise man, whether all this proceed not partly, if not chiefly, from the restraint of some lawfull liberty, which ought to be giv'n men, and is deny'd them. As by Physick we learn in menstruous bodies, where natures current hath been stopt, that the suffocation and upward forcing of some lower part, affects the head and inward sense with dotage and idle fancies. And on the other hand, whether the rest of vulgar men not so religiously professing do not give themselves much the more to whoredom and adulteries, loving the corrupt and venial discipline of clergie Courts, but hating to hear of perfect reformation: when as they foresee that then fornication shall be austerely censur'd, adultery punisht, and mariage the appointed refuge of nature, though it hap to be never so incongruous and displeasing, must yet of force be worn out, when it can be to no other purpose but of strife and hatred, a thing odious to God. This may be worth the study of skilfull men in Theology, and the reason of things: and lastly to examine whether some undue and ill grounded strictnesse upon the blamelesse nature of man, be not the cause in those places where already reformation is, that the discipline of the Church so often and so unavoidably brok'n, is brought into contempt and derision. And if it be thus, let those who are still bent to hold this obstinate *literality,* so prepare themselves as to share in the account for all these transgressions, when it shall be demanded at the last day by one who will scan and sift things with more then a literall wisdom of equity; for if these reasons be duly ponder'd, and that the Gospel is more jealous of laying on excessive burdens then ever the Law was, lest the soul of a

Christian which is inestimable, should be over-tempted and cast away, considering also that many properties of nature, which the power of regeneration it self never alters, may cause dislike of conversing even between the most sanctify'd, which continually grating in harsh tune together, may breed some jarre and discord, and that end in rancor and strife, a thing so opposite both to mariage and to Christianity, it would perhaps be lesse scandall to divorce a naturall disparity, then to link violently together an unchristian dissention, committing two ensnared souls inevitably to kindle one another, not with the fire of love, but with a hatred *inconcileable*, who were they dissevered, would be straight friends in any other relation. But if an alphabeticall servility must be still urged, it may so fall out, that the true Church may unwittingly use as much cruelty in forbidding to divorce, as the Church of Antichrist doth wilfully in forbidding to marry. . . .

. . . For this is a solid rule, that every command giv'n with a reason, binds our obedience no otherwise then that reason holds. Of this sort was that command in *Eden; Therefore shall a man cleave to his wife, and they shall be one flesh:* which we see is no absolute command, but with an inference, *Therefore:* the reason then must be first consider'd, that our obedience be not mis-obedience. The first is, for it is not single, because the wife is to the husband *flesh of his flesh,* as in the verse going before. But this reason cannot be sufficient of it self; for why then should he for his wife leave his father and mother, with whom he is farre *more flesh of flesh and bone of bone,* as being made of their substance. And besides it can be but a sorry and ignoble society of life, whose unseperable injunction depends meerly upon flesh and bones. Therefore we must look higher, since Christ himself recalls us to the beginning, and we shall finde that the primitive reason of never divorcing, was that sacred and not vain promise of God to remedy mans lonelines by *making him a meet help for him,* though not now in perfection, as at first; yet still in proportion as things now are. And this is repeated vers. 20. when all other creatures were fitly associated and brought to *Adam,* as if the divine power had bin in some care and deep thought, because *there was not yet found a help meet for man.* And can we so slightly depresse the all-wise purpose of a deliberating God, as if his consultation had produc't no other good for man but to joyn him with an accidentall companion of propagation, which his sudden word had already made for every beast? nay a farre lesse good to man it will be found, if she must at all aventures be fasten'd upon him individually. And therefore even plain sense and equity, and, which is above them both, the all-interpreting voice of Charity her selfe cries loud that this primitive reason, this consulted promise of God *to make a meet help*, is the onely cause that gives authority to this command of not divorcing, to be a command. And it might be further added, that if the true definition of a wife were askt in good earnest, this clause being *a meet help* would shew it selfe so necessary, and so essential in that demonstrative argument, that it might be logically concluded: therefore she who naturally and perpetually is no meet help, can be no wife; which cleerly takes away the difficulty of dismissing such a one. If this be not thought anough, I answer yet furder, that mariage, unlesse it mean a fit and tolerable mariage, is not inseparable neither by nature nor institution. Not by nature for then those Mosaick divorces had bin against nature, if separable and inseparable be contraries, as who doubts they be: and what is against nature is against Law, if soundest Philosophy abuse us not: by this reckning *Moses* should be most unmosaick, that is, most illegall, not to say most unnaturall. Nor is it inseparable by the first institution: for then no second institution in the same Law for so many causes could dissolve it: it being most unworthy a human (as *Plato's* judgment is in the fourth book of his *Lawes*) much more a divine Law-giver to write two several decrees upon the same thing. But what would *Plato* have deem'd if the one of these were good, the other evill to be done? Lastly, suppose it bee inseparable by institution, yet in competition with higher things, as religion and charity in mainest matters, and when the chiefe end is frustrate for which it was ordain'd, as hath been shown, if still it must remain inseparable, it holds a strange and lawlesse propriety from all other works of God under heaven. From these many considerations we may safely gather, that so much of the first institution as our Saviour mentions, for he mentions not all, was but to quell and put to non-plus the tempting Pharises; and to lay open their ignorance and shallow understanding of the Scriptures. For, saith he, *have ye not read that he which made them at the beginning, made them male and female, and said, for this cause shall a man cleave to his wife?* which these blind usurpers of *Moses* chair could not gainsay: as if this single respect of male and female were sufficient against a thousand inconveniences and mischiefes, to clogge a rationall creature to his endlesse sorrow unrelinquishably, under the guilefull superscription of his intended solace and comfort. What if they had thus answer'd, Master, if thou mean to make wedlock as inseparable as it was from the beginning, let it be made also a fit society, as God meant it, which we shall soone understand it ought to be, if thou recite the whole reason of the law. Doubtlesse our Saviour had applauded their just answer. For then they had expounded this command of Paradise, even as *Moses* himselfe expounds it by his lawes of divorce, that is, with due and wise regard had to the premises and reasons of the first command, according to which, without unclean and temporizing permissions he instructs us in this imperfect state what we may lawfully doe about divorce.

But if it be thought that the Disciples offended at the rigour of Christs answer, could yet obtain no mitigation of the former sentence pronounc't to the Pharises, it may be fully answer'd, that our Saviour continues the same reply to his Disciples, as men leaven'd with the same customary licence, which the Pharises maintain'd, and displeas'd at the removing of a traditionall abuse whereto they had so long not unwillingly bin us'd: it was no time then to contend with their slow and prejudicial belief, in a thing wherein an ordinary measure of light in Scripture, with some attention might afterwards informe them well anough. And yet ere Christ had finisht this argument, they might have pickt out of his own concluding words, an answer more to their minds, and in effect the same with that which hath been all this while entreating audience. *All men*, said he, *cannot receive this saying save they to whom it is given, he that is able to receive it let him receive it*. What saying is this which is left to a mans choice to receive or not receive? What but the married life. Was our Saviour so mild and favourable to the weaknesse of a single man, and is he turn'd on the sudden so rigorous and inexorable to the distresses and extremities of an ill wedded man? Did hee so graciously give leave to change the better single life for the worse maried life? Did he open so to us this hazardous and accidentall doore of mariage to shut upon us like the gate of death without retracting or returning, without permitting to change the worst, most insupportable, most unchristian mischance of mariage for all the mischiefes and sorrowes that can ensue, being an ordinance which was especially giv'n as a cordial and exhilarating cup of solace the better to beare our other crosses and afflictions? questionlesse this were a hardheartednesse of undivorcing, worse then that in the Jewes which they say extorted the allowance from *Moses*, and is utterly dissonant from all the doctrine of our Saviour. After these considerations therefore to take a law out of Paradise giv'n in time of originall perfection, and to take it barely without those just and equall inferences and reasons which mainly establish it, nor so much as admitting those needfull and safe allowances wherewith *Moses* himselfe interprets it to the faln condition of man, argues nothing in us but rashnesse and contempt of those meanes that God left us in his pure and chast Law, without which it will not be possible for us to performe the strict imposition of this command: or if we strive beyond our strength, we shall strive to obay it otherwise then God commands it. And lamented experience daily teaches the bitter and vain fruits of this our presumption, forcing men in a thing wherein we are not able to judge either of their strength, or of their sufferance. Whom neither one vice or other by naturall addiction, but onely marriage ruins, which doubtlesse is not the fault of that ordinance, for God gave it as a blessing, nor alwayes, of mans mis-choosing; it being an error above wisdom to prevent, as examples of wisest men so mistaken manifest: it is the fault therefore of a perverse opinion that will have it continu'd in despite of nature and reason, when indeed it was never truly joyn'd. All those expositers upon the fifth of *Mathew* confesse the Law of *Moses* to be the Law of the Lord, wherein no addition or diminution hath place; yet comming to the point of divorce, as if they fear'd not to be call'd least in the kingdom of heav'n, any slight evasion will content them to reconcil those contradictions which they make between Christ and *Moses*, between Christ and Christ. . . .

. . . And that we may learn better how to value a grave and prudent Law of *Moses*, and how unadvisedly we smatter with our lips, when we talk of Christs abolishing any judicial Law of his great Father, except in some circumstances which are judaical rather then judicial, and need no abolishing, but cease of themselves, I say again that this recited law of *Moses* contains a cause of divorce greater beyond compare then that for adultery; and who so cannot so conceive it, errs and wrongs exceedingly a law of deep wisdome, for want of well fadoming. For let him mark no man urges the just divorcing of adultery, as it is a sin, but as it is an injury to mariage; and though it be but once committed and that without malice, whether through importunity or opportunity, the Gospel does not therefore disswade him who would therefore divorce; but that natural hatred whenever it arises, is a greater evil in mariage, then the accident of adultery, a greater defrauding, a greater injustice, and yet not blameable, he who understands not after all this representing, I doubt his will like a hard spleen draws faster then his understanding can well sanguifie. Nor did that man ever know or feel what it is to love truly, nor ever yet comprehend in his thoughts what the true intent of mariage is. And this also will be somewhat above his reach, but yet no lesse a truth for lack of his perspective, that as no man apprehends what vice is so well as he who is truly vertuous, no man knows hell like him who converses most in heav'n, so there is none that can estimate the evil and the affliction of a natural hatred in matrimony, un lesse he have a soul gentle anough and spacious anough to contemplate what is true love.

And the reason why men so disesteem this wise-judging Law of God, and count hate, or *the not finding of favour*, as it is there term'd, a humorous a dishonest and slight cause of divorce, is because themselves apprehend so little reason of what true concord is: for if they did, they would be juster in their ballancing between natural hatred and casuall adultery; this being but a transient injury, and soone amended, I mean as to the party against whom the trespasse is: but that other

being an unspeakable and unremitting sorrow and offence
whereof no amends can be made, no cure, no ceasing but by
divorce, which like a divine touch in one moment heals all;
and like the word of God, in one instant hushes outragious
tempests into a sudden stilnesse and peacefull calm. Yet all
this so great a good of Gods own enlarging to us, is by the
hard rains of them that sit us, wholly diverted and imbezzl'd
from us. Maligners of mankind! But who hath taught you to
mangle thus, and make more gashes in the miseries of a
blamelesse creature, with the leaden daggers of your literall
decrees, to whose ease you cannot adde the tittle of one small
atome, but by letting alone your unwholesome Surgery. . . .

. . . Thus at length wee see both by this and by other places,
that there is scarce any one saying in the Gospel, but must
bee read with limitations and distinctions, to bee rightly understood; for Christ gives no full comments or continued discourses, but as *Demetrius* the Rhetoritian phrases it, speakes
oft in monosyllables, like a maister, scattering the heavenly
grain of his doctrine like pearl heere and there, which requires a skilfull and laborious gatherer; who must compare
the words he findes, with other precepts, with the end of
every ordinance, and with the generall *analogie* of Evangeli-
call doctrine: otherwise many particular sayings would bee
but strange repugnant riddles; and the Church would offend
in granting divorce for frigidity, which is not here accepted
with adultery, but by them added. And this was it undoubtedly which gave reason to S. *Paul* of his own authority,
as hee professes, and without command from the Lord, to
enlarge the seeming construction of those places in the Gospell, by adding a case wherein a person deserted, which is
somthing lesse then divorc't, may lawfully marry again. And
having declar'd his opinion in one case, he leaves a furder
liberty for Christian prudence to determine in cases of like
importance; using words so plain as are not to be shifted off,
that a brother or a sister is not under bondage in such cases,
adding also, that *God hath call'd us to peace* in mariage.

Now if it be plain that a Christian may be brought into
unworthy *bondage*, and his religious *peace* not only interrupted now and then, but perpetually and finally hinderd in
wedlock by mis-yoking with a diversity of nature as well as of

religion the reasons of S. *Paul* cannot be made speciall to that one case of infidelity, but are of equal moment to a divorce, where ever Christian liberty and peace are without fault equally obstructed. That the ordinance which God gave to our comfort, may not be pinn'd upon us to our undeserved thraldom, to be coop't up as it were in mockery of wedlock, to a perpetual betrothed lonelines and discontent, if nothing worse ensue. There being nought els of mariage left between such, but a displeasing and forc't remedy against the sting of a bruit desire; which fleshly accustoming without the souls union and commixture of intellectual delight, as it is rather a soiling then a fulfilling of mariage-rites, so is it anough to imbase the mettle of a generous spirit, and sinks him to a low and vulgar pitch of endeavour in all his actions, or, which is wors, leaves him in a dispairing plight of abject and hardn'd thoughts: which condition rather then a good man should fall into, a man usefull in the service of God and mankind, Christ himself hath taught us to dispence with the most sacred ordinance of his worship: even for a bodily healing to dispence with that holy and speculative rest of Sabbath, much more then with the erroneous observance of an ill-knotted mariage, for the sustaining of an overcharg'd faith and perseverance. . . .

And though bad causes would take licence by this pretext, if that cannot be remedied, upon their conscience be it, who shall so doe. This was that hardnes of heart, and abuse of a good law which *Moses* was content to suffer, rather then good men should not have it at all to use needfully. And he who to run after one lost sheep, left ninety nine of his own flock at randome in the Wildernes, would little perplex his thought for the obduring of nine hunder'd and ninety such as will dayly take worse liberties, whether they have permission or not. To conclude, as without charity God hath giv'n no commandment to men, so without it, neither can men rightly beleeve any commandment giv'n. For every act of true faith, as well that whereby we beleeve the law, as that whereby wee endeavour the law, is wrought in us by charity: according to that in the divine hymne of St. *Paul*, 1 *Cor.* 13. *Charity beleeveth all things:* not as if she were so credulous, which is the exposition hitherto current, for that were a trivial praise, but to teach us that charity is the high governesse of our belief, and that we cannot safely assent to any precept writt'n in the Bible, but as charity commends it to us. Which agrees with that of the same Apostle to the *Ephes.* 4. 14. 15. where he tels us that the way to get a sure undoubted knowledge of things, is to hold that for truth which accords most with charity. Whose unerring guidance and conduct having follow'd as a loadstarre with all diligence and fidelity in this question, I trust, through the help of that illuminating Spirit which hath favour'd me, to have don no every daies work: in asserting after many ages the words of Christ with other Scriptures of great concernment from burdensom and remorsles obscurity, tangl'd with manifold repugnances, to their native lustre and consent between each other: hereby also dissolving tedious and *Gordian* difficulties, which have hitherto molested the Church of God, and are now decided not with the sword of *Alexander*, but with the immaculate hands of charity, to the unspeakable good of Christendome. And let the extreme literalist sit down now and revolve whether this in all necessity be not the due result of our Saviours words or if he persist to be otherwise opinion'd, let him well advise, lest thinking to gripe fast the Gospel, he be found in stead with the canon law in his fist: whose boisterous edicts tyrannizing the blessed ordinance of mariage into the quality of a most unnatural and unchristianly yoke, have giv'n the flesh this advantage to hate it, and turn aside, oft times unwillingly, to all dissolute uncleannesse, even till punishment it self is weary, and overcome by the incredible frequency of trading lust, and uncontroull'd adulteries. Yet men whose Creed is custome, I doubt not but will be still endeavouring to hide the sloth of their own timerous capacities with this pretext, that for all this tis better to endure with patience and silence this affliction which God hath sent. And I agree tis true; if this be exhorted and not enjoyn'd but withall, it will be wisely don to be as sure as may be, that what mans iniquity hath laid on, be not imputed to God's sending, least under the colour of an affected patience we detaine our selves at the gulphs mouth of many hideous temptations, not to be withstood without proper gifts, which, as *Perkins* well notes, God gives not ordinarily, no not to most earnest prayers. Therefore we pray, *Lead us not into temptation*, a vain prayer, if having led ourselves thither, we love to stay in that perilous condition. God sends remedies, as well as evills; under which he who lies and groans, that may lawfully acquit himselfe, is accessory to his own ruin: nor will it excuse him, though he suffer through a sluggish fearfulnes to search throughly what is lawfull, for feare of disquieting of a secure falsity of an old opinion. Who doubts not but that it may be piously said, to him who would dismisse frigidity, bear your trial, take it, as if God would have you live this life of continence: if he exhort this, I hear him as an Angell, though he speak without warrant: but if he would compell me, I know him for Satan. To him who divorces an adulteresse, Piety might say; Pardon her; you may shew much mercy, you may win a soul: yet the law both of God and man leaves it freely to him. For God loves not to plow out the heart of our endeavours with over-hard tasks. God delights not to make a drudge of vertue, whose actions must be all elective and unconstraind. Forc't vertue is as a bolt overshot, it goes neither forward nor backward, and does no good as it stands. Seeing therefore that neither Scripture nor reason hath laid this unjust austerity upon divorce, we may resolve that nothing else hath wrought it, but that letter-bound servility of the Canon Doctors, supposing mariage to be a Sacrament, and out of the art they have to lay unnecessary burdens upon all men, to make a fair shew in the fleshly observance of matrimony, though peace and love with all other conjugall respects fare never so ill. And indeed the Papists who are the strictest forbidders of divorce, are the easiest libertines to admit of grossest uncleannesse; as if they had a designe by making wedlock a supportlesse yoke, to violate it most, under colour of preserving it most inviolable: and withall delighting, as their mystery is, to make men the day-labourers of their own afflictions, as if there were such a scarcity of miseries from abroad, that we should be made to melt our choycest home blessings, and coin them into crosses, for want whereby to hold commerce with patience. If any therefore who shall hap to read this discourse, hath been through misadventure ill ingag'd in this contracted evill here complain'd of, and finds the fits and workings of a high impatience frequently upon him, of all those wild words which men in misery think to ease themselves by uttering, let him not op'n his lips against the providence of heav'n, or tax the wayes of God and his divine truth: for they are equall, easie, and not burdensome; nor do they ever crosse the just and reasonable desires of men, nor involve this our portion of mortall life, into a necessity of sadnesse and malecontent, by laws commanding over the unreducible *antipathies* of nature sooner or later found: but allow us to remedy and shake off those evils into which human error hath led us through the midst of our best intentions; and to support our incident extremities by that authentick precept of soveran charity; whose grand commission is to doe and to dispose over all the ordinances of God to man; that love and truth may advance each other to everlasting. While we literally superstitious through customary faintnesse of heart, not venturing to pierce with our free thoughts into the full latitude of nature and religion, abandon our selves to serve under the tyranny of usurpt opinions, suffering those ordinances which were allotted to our solace and reviving, to trample over us and hale us into a multitude of sorrowes which God never meant us. And where he set us in a fair allowance of way, with honest liberty and prudence to our guard, we never leave subtilizing and casuisting till we have straitn'd and par'd that liberal path into a rasors edge to walk on, between a precipice of unnecessary mischief on either side: and starting at every false Alarum, we do not know which way to set a foot forward with manly confidence and Christian resolution, through the confused ringing in our eares of *panick* scruples and amazements.

Another act of papall encroachment it was, to pluck the power and arbitrement of divorce from the master of the family, into whose hands God and the law of all Nations had put it, and Christ so left it, preaching onely to the conscience, and not authorizing a judiciall Court to tosse about and divulge the unaccountable and secret reasons of disaffection between man and wife, as a thing most improperly answerable to any such kind of triall. But the Popes of *Rome* perceiving the great revenue and high authority it would give them ev'n over Princes, to have the judging and deciding of such a main con-

sequence in the life of man as was divorce, wrought so upon
the superstition of those ages, as to divest them of that right
which God from the beginning had entrusted to the husband:
by which means they subjected that ancient and naturally
domestick prerogative to an externall and unbefitting Judicature. For although differences in divorce about Dowries,
Jointures, and the like, besides the punishing of adultery,
ought not to passe without referring, if need be, to the Magistrate, yet that the absolute and final hindring of divorce cannot belong to any civil or earthly power, against the will and
consent of both parties, or of the husband alone, some
reasons will be here urg'd as shall not need to decline the
touch. But first I shall recite what hath bin already yeilded
by others in favour of this opinion. *Grotius* and many more
agree that notwithstanding what Christ spake therin to the
conscience, the Magistrate is not therby enjoyn'd ought
against the preservation of civil peace, of equity, and of convenience. Among these *Fagius* is most remarkable, and gives
the same liberty of pronouncing divorce to the Christian
Magistrate, as the Mosaick had. *For whatever* saith he,
*Christ spake to the regenerate, the Judge hath to deal with the
vulgar: if therfore any through hardnesse of heart will not be a
tolerable wife or husband, it will be lawfull as well now as of old
to passe the bill of divorce, not by privat, but by publicke authority. Nor doth man separate them then, but God by his law of
divorce giv'n by Moses. What can hinder the Magistrate from
so doing, to whose government all outward things are subject,
to separate and remove from perpetual vexation and no small
danger, those bodies whose minds are already separate: it being
his office to procure peaceable and convenient living in the
Common-wealth; and being as certain also, that they so necessarily separated cannot all receive a single life.* And this I
observe that our divines do generally condemn separation
of bed and board, without the liberty of second choice; if
that therfore in some cases be most purely necessary, as who
so blockish to deny, then is this also as needfull. Thus farre
by others is already well stept, to inform us that divorce is
not a matter of Law but of Charity: if there remain a fur-
long yet to end the question, these following reasons may
serve to gain it with any apprehension not too unlearned, or

too wayward. First because ofttimes the causes of seeking divorce reside so deeply in the radical and innocent affections of nature, as is not within the diocese of Law to tamper with. Other relations may aptly anough be held together by a civil and vertuous love. But the duties of man and wife are such as are chiefly conversant in that love, which is most ancient and meerly naturall; whose two prime statutes are to joyn it self to that which is good and acceptable and friendly; and to turn aside and depart from what is disagreeable, displeasing and unlike: of the two this latter is the strongest, and most equall to be regarded: for although a man may often be unjust in seeking that which he loves, yet he can never be unjust or blamable in retiring from his endles trouble and distast, whenas his tarrying can redound to no true content on either side. Hate is of all things the mightiest divider, nay, is division it self. To couple hatred therfore, though wedlock try all her golden links, and borrow to her aid all the iron manacles and fetters of Law, it does but seek to twist a rope of sand, which was a task, they say, that pos'd the divell. And that sluggish feind in hell *Ocnus*, whom the Poems tell of, brought his idle cordage to as good effect, which never serv'd to bind with, but to feed the Asse that stood at his elbow. And that the restrictive Law against divorce, attains as little to bind any thing truly in a disjoynted mariage, or to keep it bound, but serves only to feed the ignorance, and definitive impertinence of a doltish Canon, were no absurd allusion. To hinder therfore those deep and serious regresses of nature in a reasonable soul parting from that mistak'n help which he justly seeks in a person created for him, recollecting himself from an unmeet help which was never meant, and to detain him by compulsion in such an unpredestin'd misery as this, is in diameter against both nature and institution: but to interpose a jurisdictive power upon the inward and irremediable disposition of man, to command love and sympathy, to forbid dislike against the guiltles instinct of nature, is not within the Province of any Law to reach, and were indeed an uncommodious rudenesse, not a just power: for that Law may bandy with nature, and traverse her sage motions, was an error in *Callicles* the Rhetorician, whom *Socrates* from high principles confutes in *Plato's Gorgias*. If therfore divorce may be so naturall, and that Law and Nature are not to go contrary, then to forbid divorce compulsively, is not onely against nature, but against law.

Next it must be remember'd that all law is for some good that may be frequently attain'd without the admixture of a worse inconvenience; and therfore many grosse faults, as ingratitude and the like, which are too far within the soul, to be cur'd by constraint of law, are left only to be wrought on by conscience and perswasion. Which made *Aristotle* in the 10th of his *Ethicks* to *Nichomachus*, aim at a kind of division of law into private or perswasive, and publick or compulsive. Hence it is that the law forbidding divorce, never attains to any good end of such prohibition, but rather multiplies evil. For if natures resistlesse sway in love or hate be once compell'd, it grows carelesse of it self, vitious, uselesse to friends, unserviceable and spiritlesse to the Commonwealth. Which *Moses* rightly foresaw, and all wise Lawgivers that ever knew man, what kind of creature he was. The Parliament also and Clergy of England were not ignorant of this, when they consented that *Harry* the eighth might put away his Queen *Anne* of *Cleve*, whom he could not like after he had been wedded halfe a yeere; unlesse it were that contrary to the proverb, they made a necessity of that which might have been a vertue in them to doe. For even the freedome and eminence of mans creation gives him to be a Law in this matter to himselfe, being the head of the other Sex which was made for him: whom therefore though he ought not to injure, yet neither should he be forc't to retain in society to his own overthrow, nor to heare any judge therin above himself. It being also an unseemly affront to the sequestr'd and vail'd modesty of that sex, to have her unpleasingnesse and other concealments bandied up and down, and aggravated in open Court by those hir'd masters of tongue-fence. Such uncomely exigences it befell no lesse a Majesty then *Henry* the eighth to be reduc't to; who finding just reason in his conscience to forgoe his brothers wife, after many indignities of being deluded, and made a boy of by those his two Cardinall Judges, was constrain'd at last for want of other proof that she had been carnally known by Prince *Arthur*, ev'n to uncover the nakednesse of that vertuous Lady, and to recite openly the obscene evidence of his brothers Chamberlain. Yet it pleas'd God to make him see all the tyranny of *Rome*, by discovering this which they exercis'd over divorce; and to make him the beginner of a reformation to this whole Kingdome by first asserting into his *familiary* power the right of just divorce. Tis true, an adultresse cannot be sham'd anough by any publick proceeding: but that woman whose honour is not appeach't, is lesse injur'd by a silent dismission, being otherwise not illiberally dealt with, then to endure a clamouring debate of utterlesse things, in a busines of that civill secrecy and difficult discerning, as not to be over-much question'd by neerest friends. Which drew that answer from the greatest and worthiest *Roman* of his time *Paulus Emilius*, being demanded why he would put away his wife for no visible reason, *This Shoo*, said he, and held it out on his foot, *is a neat shoo, a new shoo, and yet none of you know where it wrings me:* much lesse by the unfamiliar cognisance of a fee'd gamester can such a private difference be examin'd, neither ought it.

Again, if Law aim at the firm establishment and preservation of matrimonial faith, wee know that cannot thrive under violent means, but is the more violated. It is not when two unfortunately met are by the Canon forc't to draw in that yoke an unmercifull dayes work of sorrow till death unharnesse 'em, that then the Law keeps mariage most unviolated and unbrok'n: but when the Law takes order that mariage be acountant and responsible to perform that society, whether it be religious, civill, or corporal, which may be conscionably requir'd and claim'd therin, or else to be dissolv'd if it cannot be undergone: This is to make mariage most indissoluble, by making it a just and equall dealer, a performer of those due helps which instituted the covnant, being otherwise a most unjust contract, and no more to be maintain'd under tuition of law, then the vilest fraud, or cheat, or theft that may be committed. But because this is such a secret kind of fraud or theft, as cannot be discern'd by law, but only by the plaintife himself, therfore to divorce was never counted a politicall or civill offence neither to *Jew* nor *Gentile*, nor by any judiciall intendment of Christ, further then could be discern'd to transgresse the allowance of *Moses*, which was of necessity so large, that it doth all one as if it sent back the matter undeterminable at law, and intractable by rough dealing, to have instructions and admonitions bestow'd about it by them whose spirituall office is to adjure and to denounce, and so left to the conscience. The Law can onely appoint the just and equall conditions of divorce, and is to look how it is an injury to the divorc't, which in truth it can be none, as a meer separation; for if she consent, wherin has the Law to right her? or consent not; then is it either just, and so deservd; or if unjust, such in all likelihood was the divorcer, and to part from an unjust man is a happinesse, and no injury to be lamented. But suppose it be an injury, the law is not able to amend it, unles she think it other then a miserable redress to return back from whence she was expelled, or but intreated to be gone, or else to live apart still maried without mariage, a maried widow. Last, if it be to chast'n the divorcer, what Law punishes a deed which is not morall, but natural, a deed which cannot certainly be found to be an injury, or how can it be punisht by prohibiting the divorce, but that the innocent must equally partake both in the shame and in the smart. So that which way soever we look the Law can to no rationall purpose forbid divorce, it can only take care that the conditions of divorce be not injurious. Thus then we see the trial of law how impertinent it is to this question of divorce, how helplesse next, and then how hurtfull. . . .

. . . Let not therfore the frailty of man goe on thus inventing needlesse troubles to it self, to groan under the false imagination of a strictnes never impos'd from above; enjoyning that for duty which is an impossible and vain supererogating. *Be not righteous overmuch*, is the counsell of *Ecclesiastes, why shouldst thou destroy thy selfe?* Let us not be thus over-curious to strain at *atoms*, and yet to stop every vent and cranny of permissive liberty, lest nature wanting those needfull pores, and breathing places which God hath not debarr'd our weaknesse, either suddenly break out into some wide rupture of open vice, and frantick heresie, or else inwardly fester with repining and blasphemous thoughts, under an unreasonable and fruitlesse rigor of unwarranted law. Against which evills nothing can more beseem the religion of the Church, or the wisedom of the State, then to consider timely and provide. And in so doing, let them not doubt but they shall vindicate the misreputed honour of God and his great Lawgiver, by suffering him to give his own laws according to the condition of mans nature best known to him, without the unsufferable imputation of dispencing legally with many ages of ratify'd adultery. They shall recover the misattended words of Christ to the sincerity of their true sense from manifold contradictions, and shall open them with the key of charity. Many helpless Christians they shall raise from the depth of sadnes and distresse, utterly unfitted, as they are, to serve God or man: many they shall reclaime from obscure and giddy sects, many regain from dissolute and brutish licence, many from desperate hardnes, if ever that were justly pleaded. They shall set free many daughters of *Israel*, not wanting much of her sad plight *whom Satan had bound eighteen years*. Man they shall restore to his just dignity, and prerogative in nature, preferring the souls free peace before the promiscuous draining of a carnall rage. Mariage from a perilous hazard and snare, they shall reduce to bee a more certain hav'n and retirement of happy society; when they shall judge according to God and *Moses*, and how not then according to Christ? when they shall judge it more wisdom and goodnes to break that covnant seemingly and keep it really, then by compulsion of law to keep it seemingly, and by compulsion of blameles nature to break it really, at least if it were ever truly joyn'd. The vigor of discipline they may then turne with better successe upon the prostitute loosenes of the times, when men finding in themselves the infirmities of former ages, shall not be constrain'd above the gift of God in them, to unprofitable and impossible observances never requir'd from the civilest, the wisest, the holiest Nations, whose other excellencies in morall vertue they never yet could equall. Last of all, to those whose mind still is to maintain textuall restriction, whereof the bare sound cannot consist sometimes with humanity, much lesse with charity, I would ever answer by putting them in remembrance of a command above all commands, which they seem to have forgot, and who spake it; in comparison whereof this which they so exalt, is but a petty and subordinate precept. *Let them goe* therefore with whom I am loath to couple them, yet they will needs run into the same blindnes with the Pharises, *let them goe therefore* and consider well what this lesson means, *I will have mercy and not sacrafice;* for on that *saying all the Law and Prophets depend,* much more the Gospel whose end and excellence is mercy and peace: Or if they cannot learn that, how will they heare this, which yet I shall not doubt to leave with them as a conclusion: That God the Sonne hath put all other things under his own feet; but his Commandements hee hath left all under the feet of Charity.

¶ Of Education

To Master *Samuel Hartlib.* Written above Twenty Years since.

Mr. *Hartlib,*

I AM long since perswaded, that to say, or do ought worth memory and imitation, no purpose or respect should sooner move us, then simply the love of God, and of mankind. Nevertheless to write now the reforming of Education, though it be one of the greatest and noblest designs that can be thought on, and for the want whereof this Nation perishes, I had not yet at this time been induc't, but by your earnest entreaties, and serious conjurements; as having my mind for the present half diverted in the pursuance of some other assertions, the knowledge and the use of which, cannot but be a great furtherance both to the enlargement of truth, and honest living, with much more peace. Nor should the laws of any private friendship have prevail'd with me to divide thus, or transpose my former thoughts, but that I see those aims, those actions which have won you with me the esteem of a person sent hither by some good providence from a far country to be the occasion and the incitement of great good to this Island. And, as I hear, you have obtain'd the same repute with men of most approved wisdom, and some of highest authority among us. Not to mention the learned correspondence which you hold in foreign parts, and the extraordinary pains and diligence which you have us'd in this matter both here, and beyond the Seas; either by the definite will of God so ruling, or the peculiar sway of nature, which also is Gods working. Neither can I think that so reputed, and so valu'd as you are, you would to the forfeit of your own discerning ability, impose upon me an unfit and over-ponderous argument, but that the satisfaction which you profess to have receiv'd from those incidental Discourses which we have wander'd into, hath prest and almost constrain'd you into a perswasion, that what you require from me in this point, I neither ought, nor can in conscience deferre beyond this time both of so much need at once, and so much opportunity to try what God hath determin'd. I will not resist therefore, whatever it is either of divine, or humane obligement that you lay upon me; but will forthwith set down in writing, as you request me, that voluntary *Idea*, which hath long in silence presented it self to me, of a better Education, in extent and comprehension far more large, and yet of time far shorter, and of attainment far more certain, then hath been yet in practice. Brief I shall endeavour to be; for that which I have to say, assuredly this Nation hath extream need should be done sooner then spoken. To tell you therefore what I have benefited herein among old renowned Authors, I shall spare; and to search what many modern *Janua's* and *Didactics* more than ever I shall read, have projected, my inclination leads me not. But if you can accept of these few observations which have flowr'd off, and are, as it were, the burnishing of many studious and contemplative years altogether spent in the search of religious and civil knowledge, and such as pleas'd you so well in the relating, I here give you them to dispose of.

The end then of Learning is to repair the ruines of our first Parents by regaining to know God aright, and out of that knowledge to love him, to imitate him, to be like him, as we may the neerest by possessing our souls of true vertue, which being united to the heavenly grace of faith makes up the highest perfection. But because our understanding cannot in this body found it self but on sensible things, nor arrive so clearly to the knowledge of God and things invisible, as by orderly conning over the visible and inferior creature, the same method is necessarily to be follow'd in all discreet teaching. And seeing every Nation affords not experience and tradition enough for all kind of Learning, therefore we are cheifly taught the Languages of those people who have at any time been most industrious after Wisdom; so that Language is but the Instrument conveying to us things usefull to be known. And though a Linguist should pride himself to have all the Tongues that *Babel* cleft the world into, yet, if he have not studied the solid things in them as well as the Words and Lexicons, he were nothing so much to be esteem'd a learned man, as any Yeoman or Tradesman competently wise in his Mother Dialect only. Hence appear the many mistakes which have made Learning generally so unpleasing and so unsuccessful; first we do amiss to spend seven or eight years meerly in scraping together so much miserable Latine and Greek, as might be learnt otherwise easily and delightfully in one year. And that which casts our proficiency therein so much behind, is our time lost partly in too oft idle vacancies given both to Schools and Universities, partly in a preposterous exaction, forcing the empty wits of Children to compose Theams, Verses and Orations, which are the acts of ripest judgment and the final work of a head fill'd by long reading and observing, with elegant maxims, and copious invention. These are not matters to be wrung from poor striplings, like blood out of the Nose, or the plucking of untimely fruit: besides the ill habit which they get of wretched barbarizing against the Latin and Greek *idiom*, with their untutor'd *Anglicisms*, odious to be read, yet not to be avoided without a well continu'd and judicious conversing among pure Authors digested, which they scarce taste, whereas, if after some preparatory grounds of speech by their certain forms got into memory, they were led to the praxis thereof in some chosen short book lesson'd throughly to them, they might then forthwith proceed to learn the substance of good things, and Arts in due order, which would bring the whole language quickly into their power. This I take to be the most rational and most profitable way of learning Languages, and whereby we may best hope to give account to God of our youth spent herein: And for the usual method of teaching Arts, I deem it to be an old errour of Universities not yet well recover'd from the Scholastick grossness of barbarous ages, that in stead of beginning with Arts most easie, and those be such as are most obvious to the sence, they present their young unmatriculated Novices at first comming with the most intellective abstractions of Logick and Metaphysicks: So that they having but newly left those Grammatick flats and shallows where they stuck unreasonably to learn a few words with lamentable construction, and now on the sudden transported under another climate to be tost and turmoil'd with their unballasted wits in fadomless and unquiet deeps of controversie, do for the most part grow into hatred and contempt of Learning, mockt and deluded all this while with ragged Notions and Babblements, while they expected worthy and delightful knowledge; till poverty or youthful years call them importunately their several wayes, and hasten them with the sway of friends either to an ambitious and mercenary, or ignorantly zealous Divinity; Some allur'd to the trade of Law, grounding their purposes not on the prudent and heavenly contemplation of justice and equity which was never taught them, but on the promising and pleasing thoughts of litigious terms, fat contentions, and flowing fees; others betake them to State affairs, with souls so unprincipl'd in vertue, and true generous breeding, that flattery, and Court shifts and tyrannou; Aphorisms appear to them the highest points of wisdom-instilling their barren hearts with a conscientious slavery, if, as I rather think, it be not fain'd. Others lastly of a more delicious and airie spirit, retire themselves knowing no better, to the enjoyments of ease and luxury, living out their daies in feast and jollity; which indeed is the wisest and safest course of all these, unless they were with more integrity undertaken. And these are the fruits * of mispending our prime youth at the Schools and Universities as we do, either in learning meer words or such things chiefly, as were better unlearnt.

I shall detain you no longer in the demonstration of what we should not do, but strait conduct ye to a hill side, where I will point ye out the right path of a vertuous and noble Education; laborious indeed at the first ascent, but else so smooth, so green, so full of goodly prospect, and melodious sounds on every side, that the Harp of *Orpheus* was not more charming.

*1644 version: "And these are the errours, and these are the fruits..."

I doubt not but ye shall have more adoe to drive our dullest and laziest youth, our stocks and stubbs from the infinite desire of such a happy nurture, then we have now to hale and drag our choisest and hopefullest Wits to that asinine feast of sow-thistles and brambles which is commonly set before them, as all the food and entertainment of their tenderest and most docible age. I call therefore a compleat and generous Education that which fits a man to perform justly, skilfully and magnanimously all the offices both private and publick of Peace and War. And how all this may be done between twelve, and one and twenty, less time then is now bestow'd in pure trifling at Grammar and *Sophistry*, is to be thus order'd.

First to find out a spatious house and ground about it fit for an *Academy*, and big enough to lodge a hundred and fifty persons, whereof twenty or thereabout may be attendants, all under the government of one, who shall be thought of desert sufficient, and ability either to do all, or wisely to direct, and oversee it done. This place should be at once both School and University, not needing a remove to any other house of Schollership, except it be some peculiar Colledge of Law, or Physick, where they mean to be practitioners; but as for those general studies which take up all our time from *Lilly* to the commencing, as they term it, Master of Art, it should be absolute. After this pattern, as many Edifices may be converted to this use, as shall be needful in every City throughout this Land, which would tend much to the encrease of Learning and Civility every where. This number, less or more thus collected, to the convenience of a foot Company, or interchangeably two Troops of Cavalry, should divide their daies work into three parts, as it lies orderly. Their Studies, their Exercise, and their Diet.

For their Studies, First they should begin with the chief and necessary rules of some good Grammar, either that now us'd, or any better: and while this is doing, their speech is to be fashion'd to a distinct and clear pronunciation, as near as may be to the *Italian*, especially in the Vowels. For we *Englishmen* being far Northerly, do not open our mouths in the cold air, wide enough to grace a Southern Tongue; but are observ'd by all other Nations to speak exceeding close and inward: So that to smatter Latine with an English mouth, is as ill a hearing as Law-French. Next to make them expert in the usefullest points of Grammar, and withall to season them, and win them early to the love of vertue and true labour, ere any flattering seducement, or vain principle seise them wandering, some easie and delightful Book of Education would be read to them; whereof the Greeks have store, as *Cebes, Plutarch*, and other Socratic discourses. But in Latin we have none of classic authority extant, except the two or three first Books of *Quintilian*, and some select pieces elsewhere. But here the main skill and groundwork will be, to temper them such Lectures and Explanations upon every opportunity, as may lead and draw them in willing obedience, enflam'd with the study of Learning, and the admiration of Vertue; stirr'd up with high hopes of living to be brave men, and worthy Patriots, dear to God, and famous to all ages. That they may despise and scorn all their childish, and ill-taught qualities, to delight in manly, and liberal Exercises: which he who hath the Art, and proper Eloquence to catch them with, what with mild and effectual perswasions, and what with the intimation of some fear, if need be, but chiefly by his own example, might in a short space gain them to an incredible diligence and courage: infusing into their young brests such an ingenuous and noble ardor, as would not fail to make many of them renowned and matchless men. At the same time, some other hour of the day, might be taught them the rules of Arithmetick, and soon after the Elements of Geometry even playing, as the old manner was. After evening repast, till bed-time their thoughts will be best taken up in the easie grounds of Religion, and the story of Scripture. The next step would be to the Authors of *Agriculture, Cato, Varro*, and *Columella*, for the matter is most easie, and if the language be difficult, so much the better, it is not a difficulty above their years. And here will be an occasion of inciting and inabling them hereafter to improve the tillage of their Country, to recover the bad Soil, and to remedy the waste that is made of good: for this was one of *Hercules* praises. Ere half these Authors be read (which will soon be with plying hard, and daily) they cannot chuse but be masters of any ordinary prose. So that it will be then seasonable for them to learn in any modern Author, the use of the Globes, and all the Maps; first with the old names, and then with the new: or they might be then capable to read any compendious method of natural Philosophy. And at the same time might be entring into the Greek tongue, after the same manner as was before prescrib'd in the Latin; whereby the difficulties of Grammar being soon overcome, all the Historical Physiology of *Aristotle* and *Theophrastus* are open before them, and as I may say, under contribution. The like access will be to *Vitruvius*, to *Seneca's* natural questions, to *Mela, Celsus, Pliny,* or *Solinus*. And having thus past the principles of *Arithmetick, Geometry, Astronomy,* and *Geography* with a general compact of Physicks, they may descend in *Mathematicks* to the instrumental science of *Trigonometry*, and from thence to Fortification, Architecture, Enginry, or Navigation. And in natural Philosophy they may proceed leisurely from the History of Meteors, Minerals, plants and living Creatures as far as Anatomy. Then also in course might be read to them out of some not tedious Writer the Institution of Physick; that they may know the tempers, the humours, the seasons, and how to manage a crudity: which he who can wisely and timely do, is not only a great Physitian to himself, and to his friends, but also may at some time or other, save an Army by this frugal and expenseless means only; and not let the healthy and stout bodies of young men rot away under him for want of this discipline; which is a great pity, and no less a shame to the Commander. To set forward all these proceedings in Nature and Mathematicks, what hinders, but that they may procure, as oft as shal be needful, the helpful experiences of Hunters, Fowlers, Fishermen, Shepherds, Gardeners, Apothecaries; and in the other sciences, Architects, Engineers, Mariners, Anatomists; who doubtless would be ready some for reward, and some to favour such a hopeful Seminary. And this will give them such a real tincture of natural knowledge, as they shall never forget, but daily augment with delight. Then also those Poets which are now counted most hard, will be both facil and pleasant, *Orpheus, Hesiod, Theocritus, Aratus, Nicander, Oppian, Dionysius,* and in Latin *Lucretius, Manilius,* and the rural part of *Virgil*.

By this time, years and good general precepts will have furnisht them more distinctly with that act of reason which in *Ethics* is called *Proairesis:* that they may with some judgement contemplate upon moral good and evil. Then will be requir'd a special reinforcement of constant and sound endoctrinating to set them right and firm, instructing them more amply in the knowledge of Vertue and the hatred of Vice: while their young and pliant affections are led through all the moral works of *Plato, Xenophon, Cicero, Plutarch, Laertius,* and those *Locrian* remnants; but still to be reduc't in their nightward studies wherewith they close the dayes work, under the determinate sentence of *David* or *Salomon,* or the Evanges and Apostolic Scriptures. Being perfect in the knowledge of personal duty, they may then begin the study of Economics. And either now, or before this, they may have easily learnt at any odd hour the *Italian* Tongue. And soon after, but with wariness and good antidote, it would be wholsome enough to let them taste some choice Comedies, Greek, Latin, or *Italian:* Those Tragedies also that treat of Houshold matters, as *Trachiniæ, Alcestis,* and the like. The next remove must be to the study of *Politicks;* to know the beginning, end, and reasons of Political Societies; that they may not in a dangerous fit of the Common-wealth be such poor, shaken, uncertain Reeds, of such a tottering Conscience, as many of our great Counsellors have lately shewn themselves, but stedfast pillars of the State. After this they are to dive into the grounds of Law, and legal Justice; deliver'd first, and with best warrant by *Moses;* and as far as humane prudence can be trusted, in those extoll'd remains of Grecian Lawgivers, *Licurgus, Solon, Zaleucus, Charondas,* and thence to all the Roman *Edicts* and Tables with their *Justinian;* and so down to the *Saxon* and common Laws of *England,* and the Statutes. Sundayes also and every evening may be now understandingly spent in the highest matters of *Theology,* and Church History ancient and modern: and ere this time the Hebrew Tongue at a set hour might have been gain'd, that the Scriptures may be now read in their own original; whereto it would be no impossibility to add the *Chaldey,* and the *Syrian* Dialect. When all these employments are well conquer'd, then will the choice Histories,

Heroic Poems, and *Attic* Tragedies of stateliest and most regal argument, with all the famous Political Orations offer themselves; which if they were not only read; but some of them got by memory, and solemnly pronounc't with right accent, and grace, as might be taught, would endue them even with the spirit and vigor of *Demosthenes* or *Cicero, Euripides,* or *Sophocles.* And now lastly will be the time to read with them those organic arts which inable men to discourse and write perspicuously, elegantly, and according to the fittest stile of lofty, mean, or lowly. Logic therefore so much as is useful, is to be referr'd to this due place with all her well couch't Heads and Topics, untill it be time to open her contracted palm into a gracefull and ornate Rhetorick taught out of the rule of *Plato, Aristotle, Phalereus, Cicero, Hermogenes, Longinus.* To which Poetry would be made subsequent, or indeed rather precedent, as being less suttle and fine, but more simple, sensuous and passionate. I mean not here the prosody of a verse, which they could not but have hit on before among the rudiments of Grammar; but that sublime Art which in *Aristotles Poetics,* in *Horace,* and the *Italian* Commentaries of *Castelvetro, Tasso, Mazzoni,* and others, teaches what the laws are of a true *Epic* Poem, what of a *Dramatic,* what of a *Lyric,* what Decorum is, which is the grand master-piece to observe. This would make them soon perceive what despicable creatures our common Rimers and Play-writers be, and shew them, what religious, what glorious and magnificent use might be made of Poetry both in divine and humane things. From hence and not till now will be the right season of forming them to be able Writers and Composers in every excellent matter, when they shall be thus fraught with an universal insight into things. Or whether they be to speak in Parliament or Counsel, honour and attention would be waiting on their lips. There would then also appear in Pulpits other Visages, other gestures, and stuff otherwise wrought then what we now sit under, oft times to as great a trial of our patience as any other that they preach to us. These are the Studies wherein our noble and our gentle Youth ought to bestow their time in a disciplinary way from twelve to one and twenty; unless they rely more upon their ancestors dead, then upon themselves living. In which methodical course it is so suppos'd they must proceed by the steddy pace of learning onward, as at convenient times for memories sake to retire back into the middle ward, and sometimes into the rear of what they have been taught, untill they have confirm'd, and solidly united the whole body of their perfeted knowledge, like the last embattelling of a Roman Legion. Now will be worth the seeing what Exercises and Recreations may best agree, and become these Studies.

Their Exercise

The course of Study hitherto briefly describ'd, is, what I can guess by reading, likest to those ancient and famous Schools of *Pythagoras, Plato, Isocrates, Aristotle* and such others, out of which were bred up such a number of renowned Philosophers, Orators, Historians, Poets and Princes all over *Greece, Italy,* and *Asia,* besides the flourishing Studies of *Cyrene* and *Alexandria.* But herein it shall exceed them, and supply a defect as great as that which *Plato* noted in the Common-wealth of *Sparta;* whereas that City train'd up their Youth most for War, and these in their Academies and *Lycæum,* all for the Gown, this institution of breeding which I here delineate, shall be equally good both for Peace and War. Therefore about an hour and a half ere they eat at Noon should be allow'd them for exercise and due rest afterwards: But the time for this may be enlarg'd at pleasure, according as their rising in the morning shall be early. The Exercise which I commend first, is the exact use of their Weapon, to guard and to strike safely with edge, or point; this will keep them healthy, nimble, strong, and well in breath, is also the likeliest means to make them grow large and tall, and to inspire them with a gallant and fearless courage, which being temper'd with seasonable Lectures and Precepts to them of true Fortitude and Patience, will turn into a native and heroick valour, and make them hate the cowardise of doing wrong. They must be also practiz'd in all the Locks and Gripes of Wrastling, wherein English men were wont to excell, as need may often be in fight to tugg or grapple, and to close. And this perhaps will be enough, wherein to prove and heat their single strength. The interim of unsweating themselves regularly, and convenient rest before meat may both

with profit and delight be taken up in recreating and composing their travail'd spirits with the solemn and divine harmonies of Musick heard or learnt; either while the skilful
Organist plies his grave and fancied descant, in lofty fugues,
or the whole Symphony with artful and unimaginable touches
adorn and grace the well studied chords of some choice Composer; sometimes the Lute, or soft Organ stop waiting on
elegant Voices either to Religious, martial, or civil Ditties;
which if wise men and Prophets be not extreamly out, have
a great power over dispositions and manners, to smooth and
make them gentle from rustick harshness and distemper'd
passions. The like also would not be unexpedient after Meat
to assist and cherish Nature in her first concoction, and send
their minds back to study in good tune and satisfaction.
Where having follow'd it close under vigilant eyes till about
two hours before supper, they are by a sudden alarum or
watch word, to be call'd out to their military motions, under
skie or covert, according to the season, as was the Roman
wont; first on foot, then as their age permits, on Horseback,
to all the Art of Cavalry; That having in sport, but with much
exactness, and daily muster, serv'd out the rudiments of their
Souldiership in all the skill of Embattelling, Marching, Encamping, Fortifying, Besieging and Battering, with all the
helps of ancient and modern stratagems, *Tacticks* and warlike
maxims, they may as it were out of a long War come forth
renowned and perfect Commanders in the service of their
Country. They would not then, if they were trusted with fair
and hopeful armies, suffer them for want of just and wise
discipline to shed away from about them like sick feathers,
though they be never so oft suppli'd: they would not suffer
their empty and unrecrutible Colonels of twenty men in a
Company to quaff out, or convey into secret hoards, the
wages of a delusive list, and a miserable remnant: yet in the
mean while to be over-master'd with a score or two of drunkards, the only souldery left about them, or else to comply
with all rapines and violences. No certainly, if they knew
ought of that knowledge that belongs to good men or good
Governours, they would not suffer these things. But to return to our own institute, besides these constant exercises at
home, there is another opportunity of gaining experience to

be won from pleasure it self abroad; In those vernal seasons of the year, when the air is calm and pleasant, it were an injury and sullenness against nature not to go out, and see her riches, and partake in her rejoycing with Heaven and Earth. I should not therefore be a perswader to them of studying much then, after two or three year that they have well laid their grounds, but to ride out in Companies with prudent and staid Guides, to all the quarters of the Land: learning and observing all places of strength, all commodities of building and of soil, for Towns and Tillage, Harbours and Ports for Trade. Sometimes taking Sea as far as to our Navy, to learn there also what they can in the practical knowledge of sailing and of Sea-fight. These ways would try all their peculiar gifts of Nature, and if there were any secret excellence among them, would fetch it out, and give it fair opportunities to advance it self by, which could not but mightily redound to the good of this Nation, and bring into fashion again those old admired Vertues and Excellencies, with far more advantage now in this purity of Christian knowledge. Nor shall we then need the *Monsieurs* of *Paris* to take our hopefull Youth into their slight and prodigal custodies and send them over back again transform'd into Mimicks, Apes and Kicshoes. But if they desire to see other Countries at three or four and twenty years of age, not to learn Principles but to enlarge Experience, and make wise observation, they will by that time be such as shall deserve the regard and honour of all men where they pass, and the society and friendship of those in all places who are best and most eminent. And perhaps then other Nations will be glad to visit us for their Breeding, or else to imitate us in their own Country.

Now lastly for their Diet there cannot be much to say, save only that it would be best in the same House; for much time else would be lost abroad, and many ill habits got; and that it should be plain, healthful, and moderate I suppose is out of controversie. Thus Mr. *Hartlib*, you have a general view in writing, as your desire was, of that which at several times I had discourst with you concerning the best and Noblest way of Education; not beginning as some have done from the Cradle, which yet might be worth many considerations, if brevity had not been my scope, many other circumstances also I could have mention'd, but this to such as have the worth in them to make trial, for light and direction may be enough. Only I believe that this is not a Bow for every man to shoot in that counts himself a Teacher; but will require sinews almost equal to those which *Homer* gave *Ulysses;* yet I am withall perswaded that it may prove much more easie in the assay, then it now seems at distance, and much more illustrious: howbeit not more difficult then I imagine, and that imagination presents me with nothing but very happy and very possible according to best wishes; if God have so decreed, and this age have spirit and capacity enough to apprehend.

¶ Areopagitica

A Speech for the Liberty of UNLICENC'D PRINTING

To the Parlament of England

Τουλεύθερον δ' ἐκεῖνο. τίς θέλει πόλει
Χρηστόν τι βούλευμ' εἰς μέσον φέρειν ἔχων;
Καὶ ταῦθ' ὁ χρῄζων λαμπρός ἐσθ', ὁ μὴ θέλων
Σιγᾷ. τί τούτων ἔστ' ἰσαίτερον πόλει;

Euripid. Hicetid.

This is true Liberty, when free-born men
Having to advise the public may speak free,
Which he who can, and will, deserv's high praise,
Who neither can nor will, may hold his peace;
What can be juster in a State then this?

Euripid. Hicetid.

THEY who to States and Governours of the Commonwealth direct their Speech, High Court of Parlament, or wanting such accesse in a private condition, write that which they foresee may advance the publick good; I suppose them as at the beginning of no meane endeavour, not a little alter'd and mov'd inwardly in their mindes: Some with doubt of what will be the successe, others with feare of what will be the censure; some with hope, others with confidence of what they have to speake. And me perhaps each of these dispositions, as the subject was whereon I enter'd, may have at other times variously affected; and likely might in these formost expressions now also disclose which of them sway'd most, but that the very attempt of this addresse thus made, and the thought of whom it hath recourse to, hath got the power within me to a passion, farre more welcome then incidentall to a Preface. Which though I stay not to confesse ere any aske, I shall be blamelesse, if it be no other, then the joy and gratulation which it brings to all who wish and promote their Countries liberty; whereof this whole Discourse propos'd will be a certaine testimony, if not a Trophey. For this is not the liberty which wee can hope, that no grievance ever should arise in the Commonwealth, that let no man in this World expect; but when complaints are freely heard, deeply consider'd, and speedily reform'd, then is the utmost bound of civill liberty attain'd, that wise men looke for. To which if I now manifest by the very sound of this which I shall utter, that wee are already in good part arriv'd, and yet from such a steepe disadvantage of tyranny and superstition grounded into our principles as was beyond the manhood of a *Roman* recovery, it will bee attributed first, as is most due, to the strong assistance of God our deliverer, next to your faithfull guidance and undaunted Wisdome, Lords and Commons of *England*. Neither is it in Gods esteeme the diminution of his glory, when honourable things are spoken of good men and worthy Magistrates; which if I now first should begin to doe, after so fair a progresse of your laudable deeds, and such a long obligement upon the whole Realme to your indefatigable vertues, I might be justly reckn'd among the tardiest, and the unwillingest of them that praise yee. Neverthelesse there being three principall things, without which all praising is but Courtship and flattery, First, when that only is prais'd which is solidly worth praise: next when greatest likelihoods are brought that such things are truly and really in those persons to whom they are ascrib'd, the other, when he who praises, by shewing that such his actuall perswasion is of whom he writes, can demonstrate that he flatters not; the former two of these I have heretofore endeavour'd, rescuing the employment from him who went about to impaire your

merits with a triviall and malignant *Encomium;* the latter as
belonging chiefly to mine owne acquittall, that whom I so
extoll'd I did not flatter, hath been reserv'd opportunely to
this occasion. For he who freely magnifies what hath been
nobly done, and fears not to declare as freely what might be
done better, gives ye the best cov'nant of his fidelity; and that
his loyalest affection and his hope waits on your proceedings.
His highest praising is not flattery, and his plainest advice is a
kinde of praising; for though I should affirme and hold by
argument, that it would fare better with truth, with learning,
and the Commonwealth, if one of your publisht Orders which
I should name, were call'd in, yet at the same time it could
not but much redound to the lustre of your milde and equall
Government, when as private persons are hereby animated to
thinke ye better pleas'd with publick advice, then other
statists have been delighted heretofore with publicke flattery.
And men will then see what difference there is between the
magnanimity of a trienniall Parlament, and that jealous
hautinesse of Prelates and cabin Counsellours that usurpt of
late, when as they shall observe yee in the midd'st of your
Victories and successes more gently brooking writt'n exceptions against a voted Order, then other Courts, which had
produc't nothing worth memory but the weake ostentation of
wealth, would have endur'd the least signifi'd dislike at any
sudden Proclamation. If I should thus farre presume upon
the meek demeanour of your civill and gentle greatnesse,
Lords and Commons, as what your publisht Order hath
directly said, that to gainsay, I might defend my selfe with
ease, if any should accuse me of being new or insolent, did
they but know how much better I find ye esteem it to imitate the old and elegant humanity of Greece, then the bar-
barick pride of a *Hunnish* and *Norwegian* statelines. And out
of those ages, to whose polite wisdom and letters we ow that
we are not yet *Gothes* and *Jutlanders*, I could name him who
from his private house wrote that discourse to the Parlament
of *Athens*, that perswades them to change the forme of
Democraty which was then establisht. Such honour was done
in those dayes to men who profest the study of wisdome and
eloquence, not only in their own Country, but in other Lands,
that Cities and Siniories heard them gladly, and with great

respect, if they had ought in publick to admonish the State. Thus did *Dion Prusæus* a stranger and a privat Orator counsell the *Rhodians* against a former Edict: and I abound with other like examples, which to set heer would be superfluous. But if from the industry of a life wholly dedicated to studious labours, and those naturall endowments haply not the worst for two and fifty degrees of northern latitude, so much must be derogated, as to count me not equall to any of those who had this priviledge, I would obtain to be thought not so inferior, as your selves are superior to the most of them who receiv'd their counsell: and how farre you excell them, be assur'd, Lords and Commons, there can no greater testimony appear, then when your prudent spirit acknowledges and obeyes the voice of reason from what quarter soever it be heard speaking; and renders ye as willing to repeal any Act of your own setting forth, as any set forth by your Predecessors.

If ye be thus resolv'd, as it were injury to thinke ye were not, I know not what should withhold me from presenting ye with a fit instance wherein to shew both that love of truth which ye eminently professe, and that uprightnesse of your judgement which is not wont to be partiall to your selves; by judging over again that Order which ye have ordain'd *to regulate Printing. That no Book, pamphlet, or paper shall be henceforth Printed, unlesse the same be first approv'd and licenc't by such,* or at least one of such as shall be thereto appointed. For that part which preserves justly every mans Copy to himselfe, or provides for the poor, I touch not, only wish they be not made pretenses to abuse and persecute honest and painfull Men, who offend not in either of these particulars. But that other clause of Licencing Books, which we thought had dy'd with his brother *quadragesimal* and *matrimonial* when the Prelats expir'd, I shall now attend with such a Homily, as shall lay before ye, first the inventors of it to bee those whom ye will be loath to own; next what is to be thought in generall of reading, what ever sort the Books be; and that this Order avails nothing to the suppressing of scandalous, seditious, and libellous Books, which were mainly intended to be supprest. Last, that it will be primely to the discouragement of all learning, and the stop of Truth, not only by disexercising and blunting our abilities in what we know

already, but by hindring and cropping the discovery that might
bee yet further made both in religious and civill Wisdome.

I deny not, but that it is of greatest concernment in the
Church and Commonwealth, to have a vigilant eye how
Bookes demeane themselves, as well as men; and thereafter
to confine, imprison, and do sharpest justice on them as
malefactors: For Books are not absolutely dead things, but
doe contain a potencie of life in them to be as active as that
soule was whose progeny they are; nay they do preserve as in
a violl the purest efficacie and extraction of that living intellect that bred them. I know they are as lively, and as vigor-
ously productive, as those fabulous Dragons teeth; and being
sown up and down, may chance to spring up armed men.
And yet on the other hand unlesse warinesse be us'd, as good
almost kill a Man as kill a good Book; who kills a Man kills
a reasonable creature, Gods Image; but hee who destroyes a
good Booke, kills reason it selfe, kills the Image of God, as it
were in the eye. Many a man lives a burden to the Earth; but
a good Booke is the pretious life-blood of a master spirit,
imbalm'd and treasur'd up on purpose to a life beyond life.
'Tis true, no age can restore a life, whereof perhaps there is no
great losse; and revolutions of ages doe not oft recover the
losse of a rejected truth, for the want of which whole Nations
fare the worse. We should be wary therefore what persecution we raise against the living labours of publick men, how
we spill that season'd life of man preserv'd and stor'd up in
Books; since we see a kinde of homicide may be thus committed, sometimes a martyrdome, and if it extend to the whole
impression, a kinde of massacre, whereof the execution ends
not in the slaying of an elementall life, but strikes at that
ethereall and fift essence, the breath of reason it selfe, slaies
an immortality rather then a life. But lest I should be condemn'd of introducing licence, while I oppose Licencing, I refuse not the paines to be so much Historicall, as will serve
to shew what hath been done by ancient and famous Commonwealths, against this disorder, till the very time that this
project of licencing crept out of the *Inquisition*, was catcht up
by our Prelates, and hath caught some of our Presbyters.

In *Athens* where Books and Wits were ever busier then in
any other part of *Greece*, I finde but only two sorts of writings

which the Magistrate car'd to take notice of; those either
blasphemous and Atheisticall, or Libellous, Thus the Books
of *Protagoras* were by the Judges of *Areopagus* commanded
to be burnt, and himselfe banisht the territory for a discourse begun with his confessing not to know *whether there
were gods, or whether not:* And against defaming, it was decreed that none should be traduc'd by name, as was the manner of *Vetus Comœdia*, whereby we may guesse how they censur'd libelling: And this course was quick enough, as *Cicero*
writes, to quell both the desperate wits of other Atheists, and
the open way of defaming, as the event shew'd. Of other
sects and opinions though tending to voluptuousnesse, and
the denying of divine providence they tooke no heed. Therefore we do not read that either *Epicurus*, or that libertine
school of *Cyrene*, or what the *Cynick* impudence utter'd, was
ever question'd by the Laws. Neither is it recorded that the
writings of those old Comedians were supprest, though the
acting of them were forbid; and that *Plato* commended the
reading of *Aristophanes* the loosest of them all, to his royall
scholler *Dionysius*, is commonly known, and may be excus'd,
if holy *Chrysostome*, as is reported, nightly studied so much
the same Author and had the art to cleanse a scurrilous vehemence into the stile of a rousing Sermon. That other leading
City of *Greece*, *Lacedæmon*, considering that *Lycurgus* their
Law-giver was so addicted to elegant learning, as to have
been the first that brought out of *Ionia* the scatter'd workes of
Homer, and sent the Poet *Thales* from *Creet* to prepare and
mollifie the *Spartan* surlinesse with his smooth songs and
odes, the better to plant among them law and civility, it is to
be wonder'd how muselesse and unbookish they were, mind-
ing nought but the feats of Warre. There needed no licencing
of Books among them for they dislik'd all, but their owne
Laconick Apothegms, and took a slight occasion to chase
Archilochus out of their City, perhaps for composing in a
higher straine then their owne souldierly ballats and roundels
could reach to: Or if it were for his broad verses, they were
not therein so cautious, but they were as dissolute in their
promiscuous conversing; whence *Euripides* affirmes in
Andromache, that their women were all unchaste. Thus much
may give us light after what sort Bookes were prohibited

among the Greeks. The Romans also for many ages train'd
up only to a military roughnes, resembling most the *Lace-
dæmonian* guise, knew of learning little but what their twelve
Tables, and the *Pontifick* College with their *Augurs* and
Flamins taught them in Religion and Law, so unacquainted
with other learning, that when *Carneades* and *Critolaus*, with
the *Stoick Diogenes* comming Embassadors to *Rome*, tooke
thereby occasion to give the City a tast of their Philosophy,
they were suspected for seducers by no lesse a man than *Cato*
the Censor, who mov'd it in the Senat to dismisse them
speedily, and to banish all such *Attick* bablers out of *Italy*.
But *Scipio* and others of the noblest Senators withstood him
and his old *Sabin* austerity; honour'd and admir'd the men;
and the Censor himself at last in his old age fell to the study
of that whereof before hee was so scrupulous. And yet at the
same time *Nævius* and *Plautus* the first Latine comedians had
fill'd the City with all the borrow'd Scenes of *Menander* and
Philemon. Then began to be consider'd there also what was
to be don to libellous books and Authors; for *Nævius* was
quickly cast into prison for his unbridl'd pen, and releas'd by
the *Tribunes* upon his recantation: We read also that libels
were burnt, and the makers punisht by *Augustus*. The like
severity no doubt was us'd if ought were impiously writt'n
against their esteemed gods. Except in these two points, how
the world went in Books, the Magistrat kept no reckoning.
And therefore *Lucretius* without impeachment versifies his
Epicurism to *Memmius*, and had the honour to be set forth
the second time by *Cicero* so great a father of the Commonwealth; although himselfe disputes against that opinion in his
own writings. Nor was the Satyricall sharpnesse, or naked
plainnes of *Lucilius*, or *Catullus*, or *Flaccus*, by any order
prohibited. And for matters of State, the story of *Titus
Livius*, though it extoll'd that part which *Pompey* held, was
not therefore supprest by *Octavius Cæsar* of the other Faction. But that *Naso* was by him banisht in his old age, for the
wanton Poems of his youth, was but a meer covert of State
over some secret cause: and besides, the Books were neither
banisht nor call'd in. From hence we shall meet with little
else but tyranny in the Roman Empire, that we may not marvell, if not so often bad, as good Books were silenc't. I shall

therefore deem to have bin large anough in producing what among the ancients was punishable to write, save only which, all other arguments were free to treat on.

By this time the Emperors were become Christians, whose discipline in this point I doe not finde to have bin more severe then what was formerly in practice. The Books of those whom they took to be grand Hereticks were examin'd, refuted, and condemn'd in the generall Councels; and not till then were prohibited, or burnt by autority of the Emperor. As for the writings of Heathen authors, unlesse they were plaine invectives against Christianity, as those of *Porphyrius* and *Proclus*, they met with no interdict that can be cited, till about the year 400, in a *Carthaginian* Councel, wherein Bishops themselves were forbid to read the Books of Gentiles, but Heresies they might read: while others long before them on the contrary scrupl'd more the Books of Hereticks, then of Gentiles. And that the primitive Councels and Bishops were wont only to declare what Books were not commendable, passing no furder, but leaving it to each ones conscience to read or to lay by, till after the yeare 800, is observ'd already by *Padre Paolo* the great unmasker of the *Trentine* Councel. After which time the Popes of *Rome* engrossing what they pleas'd of Politicall rule into their owne hands, extended their dominion over mens eyes, as they had before over their judgements, burning and prohibiting to be read, what they fansied not; yet sparing in their censures, and the Books not many which they so dealt with: till *Martin* the 5. by his Bull not only prohibited, but was the first that excommunicated the reading of hereticall Books; for about that time *Wicklef* and *Husse* growing terrible, were they who first drove the Papall Court to a stricter policy of prohibiting. Which cours *Leo* the 10, and his successors follow'd, untill the Councell of Trent, and the Spanish Inquisition engendring together brought forth, or perfeted those Catalogues, and expurging Indexes that rake through the entralls of many an old good Author, with a violation wors then any could be offer'd to his tomb. Nor did they stay in matters Hereticall, but any subject that was not to their palat, they either condemn'd in a prohibition, or had it strait into the new Purgatory of an Index. To fill up the measure of encroachment, their last invention was to ordain that no Book, pamphlet, or paper should be Printed (as if S. *Peter* had bequeath'd them the keys of the Presse also out of Paradise) unlesse it were approv'd and licenc't under the hand of 2 or 3 glutton Friers. For example:

> Let the Chancellor *Cini* be pleas'd to see if in this present work be contain'd ought that may withstand the Printing,
> *Vincent Rabatta* Vicar of *Florence.*

> I have seen this present work, and finde nothing athwart the Catholick faith and good manners: In witnesse whereof I have given, etc.
> *Nicolò Cini* Chancellor of *Florence.*

> Attending the precedent relation, it is allow'd that this present work of *Davanzati* may be Printed,
> *Vincent Rabatta, etc.*

> It may be Printed, *July* 15.
> Friar *Simon Mompei d'Amelia* Chancellor of the holy office in *Florence.*

Sure they have a conceit, if he of the bottomlesse pit had not long since broke prison, that this quadruple exorcism would barre him down. I feare their next designe will be to get into their custody the licencing of that which they say* *Claudius* intended, but went not through with. Voutsafe to see another of their forms the Roman stamp:

> *Imprimatur*, If it seem good to the reverend Master of the holy Palace,
> *Belcastro* Vicegerent.
> *Imprimatur*
> Friar *Nicolò Rodolphi* Master of the holy Palace.

Sometimes 5 *Imprimaturs* are seen together dialogue-wise in the Piatza of one Title page, complementing and ducking each to other with their shav'n reverences, whether the Author, who stands by in perplexity at the foot of his Epistle, shall to the Presse or to the spunge. These are the pretty responsories,

---

* Quo veniam daret flatum crepitumque ventris in convivio emittendi. Sueton. in Claudio.

these are the deare Antiphonies that so bewitcht of late our Prelats, and their Chaplaines with the goodly Eccho they made; and besotted us to the gay imitation of a lordly *Imprimatur*, one from Lambeth house, another from the West end of *Pauls;* so apishly Romanizing, that the word of command still was set downe in Latine; as if the learned Grammaticall pen that wrote it, would cast no ink without Latine: or perhaps, as they thought, because no vulgar tongue was worthy to expresse the pure conceit of an *Imprimatur;* but rather, as I hope, for that our English, the language of men ever famous, and formost in the atchievements of liberty, will not easily finde servile letters anow to spell such a dictatorie presumption. And thus ye have the Inventors and the originall of Book-licencing ript up, and drawn as lineally as any pedigree. We have it not, that can be heard of, from any ancient State, or politie, or Church, nor by any Statute left us by our Ancestors elder or later; nor from the moderne custom of any reformed Citty, or Church abroad; but from the most Antichristian Councel, and the most tyrannous Inquisition that ever inquir'd. Till then Books were ever as freely admitted into the World as any other birth; the issue of the brain was no more stifl'd then the issue of the womb: no envious *Juno* sate cros-leg'd over the nativity of any mans intellectuall off-spring; but if it prov'd a Monster, who denies, but that it was justly burnt, or sunk into the Sea. But that a Book in wors condition then a peccant soul, should be to stand before a Jury ere it be borne to the World, and undergo yet in darknesse the judgement of *Radamanth* and his Collegues, ere it can passe the ferry backward into light, was never heard before, till that mysterious iniquity provokt and troubl'd at the first entrance of Reformation, sought out new limbo's and new hells wherein they might include our Books also within the number of their damned. And this was the rare morsell so officiously snatcht up, and so ilfavourdly imitated by our inquisiturient Bishops, and the attendant minorities their Chaplains. That ye like not now these most certain Authors of this licencing order, and that all sinister intention was farre distant from your thoughts, when ye were importun'd the passing it, all men who know the integrity of your actions, and how ye honour Truth, will clear yee readily.

But some will say, What though the Inventors were bad, the thing for all that may be good? It may so; yet if that thing be no such deep invention, but obvious, and easie for any man to light on, and yet best and wisest Commonwealths through all ages, and occasions have forborne to use it, and falsest seducers, and oppressors of men were the first who tooke it up, and to no other purpose but to obstruct and hinder the first approach of Reformation; I am of those who beleeve, it will be a harder alchymy then *Lullius* ever knew, to sublimat any good use out of such an invention. Yet this only is what I request to gain from this reason, that it may be held a dangerous and suspicious fruit, as certainly it deserves, for the tree that bore it, untill I can dissect one by one the properties it has. But I have first to finish, as was propounded, what is to be thought in generall of reading Books, what ever sort they be, and whether be more the benefit, or the harm that thence proceeds?

Not to insist upon the examples of *Moses*, *Daniel* and *Paul*, who were skilfull in all the learning of the Ægyptians, Caldeans, and Greeks, which could not probably be without reading their Books of all sorts, in *Paul* especially, who thought it no defilement to insert into holy Scripture the sentences of three Greek Poets, and one of them a Tragedian, the question was, notwithstanding sometimes controverted among the Primitive Doctors, but with great odds on that side which affirm'd it both lawfull and profitable, as was then evidently perceiv'd, when *Julian* the Apostat, and suttlest enemy to our faith, made a decree forbidding Christians the study of heathen learning: for, said he, they wound us with our own weapons, and with our owne arts and sciences they overcome us. And indeed the Christians were put so to their shifts by this crafty means, and so much in danger to decline into all ignorance, that the two *Apollinarii* were fain as a man may say, to coin all the seven liberall Sciences out of the Bible, reducing it into divers forms of Orations, Poems, Dialogues, ev'n to the calculating of a new Christian Grammar. But saith the Historian *Socrates*, The providence of God provided better then the industry of *Apollinarius* and his son, by taking away that illiterat law with the life of him who devis'd it. So great an injury they then held it to be depriv'd of

Hellenick learning; and thought it a persecution more under-
mining, and secretly decaying the Church, then the open
cruelty of *Decius* or *Dioclesian*. And perhaps it was the same
politick drift that the Divell whipt St. *Jerom* in a lenten dream,
for reading *Cicero;* or else it was a fantasm bred by the feaver
which had then seis'd him. For had an Angel bin his dis-
cipliner, unlesse it were for dwelling too much upon Cicero-
nianisms, and had chastiz'd the reading, not the vanity, it had
bin plainly partiall; first to correct him for grave *Cicero*, and
not for scurrill *Plautus* whom he confesses to have bin reading not long before; next to correct him only, and let so
many more ancient Fathers wax old in those pleasant and
florid studies without the lash of such a tutoring apparition;
insomuch that *Basil* teaches how some good use may be
made of *Margites* a sportfull Poem, not now extant, writ by
Homer; and why not then of *Morgante* an Italian Romanze
much to the same purpose. But if it be agreed we shall be
try'd by visions, there is a vision recorded by *Eusebius* far
ancienter then this tale of *Jerom* to the Nun *Eustochium*, and
besides has nothing of a feavor in it. *Dionysius Alexandrinus*
was about the year 240, a person of great name in the Church
for piety and learning, who had wont to avail himself much
against hereticks by being conversant in their Books; untill a
certain Presbyter laid it scrupulously to his conscience, how
he durst venture himselfe among those defiling volumes.
The worthy man loath to give offence fell into a new debate
with himselfe what was to be thought; when suddenly a
vision sent from God, it is his own Epistle that so averrs it,
confirm'd him in these words: Read any books what ever
come to thy hands, for thou art sufficient both to judge aright,
and to examine each matter. To this revelation he assented
the sooner, as he confesses, because it was answerable to
that of the Apostle to the Thessalonians, Prove all things,
hold fast that which is good. And he might have added another remarkable saying of the same Author; To the pure all
things are pure, not only meats and drinks, but all kinde of
knowledge whether of good or evill; the knowledge cannot
defile, nor consequently the books, if the will and conscience
be not defil'd. For books are as meats and viands are; some
of good, some of evill substance; and yet God in that un-

apocryphall vision, said without exception, Rise, *Peter*, kill and eat, leaving the choice to each mans discretion. Wholesome meats to a vitiated stomack differ little or nothing from unwholesome; and best books to a naughty mind are not unappliable to occasions of evill. Bad meats will scarce breed good nourishment in the healthiest concoction; but herein the difference is of bad books, that they to a discreet and judicious Reader serve in many respects to discover, to confute, to forewarn, and to illustrate. Wherof what better witnes can ye expect I should produce, then one of your own now sitting in Parlament, the chief of learned men reputed in this Land, Mr. *Selden*, whose volume of naturall and national laws proves, not only by great autorities brought together, but by exquisite reasons and theorems almost mathematically demonstrative, that all opinions, yea errors, known, read, and collated, are of main service and assistance toward the speedy attainment of what is truest. I conceive therefore, that when God did enlarge the universall diet of mans body, saving ever the rules of temperance, he then also, as before, left arbitrary the dyeting and repasting of our minds; as wherein every mature man might have to exercise his owne leading capacity. How great a vertue is temperance, how much of moment through the whole life of man? yet God committs the managing so great a trust, without particular Law or prescription, wholly to the demeanour of every grown man. And therefore when he himself tabl'd the Jews from heaven, that Omer which was every mans daily portion of Manna, is computed to have bin more then might have well suffic'd the heartiest feeder thrice as many meals. For those actions which enter into a man, rather then issue out of him, and therefore defile not, God uses not to captivat under a perpetuall childhood of prescription, but trusts him with the gift of reason to be his own chooser; there were but little work left for preaching, if law and compulsion should grow so fast upon those things which hertofore were govern'd only by exhortation. *Salomon* informs us that much reading is a wearines to the flesh; but neither he, nor other inspir'd author tells us that such, or such reading is unlawfull: yet certainly had God thought good to limit us herein, it had bin much more expedient to have told us what was unlawfull, then what was wearisome. As for the burning of those Ephesian books by St. *Pauls* converts, 'tis reply'd the books were magick, the Syriack so renders them. It was a privat act, a voluntary act, and leaves us to a voluntary imitation: the men in remorse burnt those books which were their own; the Magistrat by this example is not appointed: these men practiz'd the books, another might perhaps have read them in some sort usefully. Good and evill we know in the field of this World grow up together almost inseparably; and the knowledge of good is so involv'd and interwoven with the knowledge of evill, and in so many cunning resemblances hardly to be discern'd, that those confused seeds which were impos'd on *Psyche* as an incessant labour to cull out, and sort asunder, were not more intermixt. It was from out the rinde of one apple tasted, that the knowledge of good and evill as two twins cleaving together leapt forth into the World. And perhaps this is that doom which *Adam* fell into of knowing good and evill, that is to say of knowing good by evill. As therefore the state of man now is; what wisdome can there be to choose, what continence to forbeare without the knowledge of evill? He that can apprehend and consider vice with all her baits and seeming pleasures, and yet abstain, and yet distinguish, and yet prefer that which is truly better, he is the true wayfaring Christian. I cannot praise a fugitive and cloister'd vertue, unexercis'd and unbreath'd, that never sallies out and sees her adversary, but slinks out of the race, where that immortall garland is to be run for, not without dust and heat. Assuredly we bring not innocence into the world, we bring impurity much rather: that which purifies us is triall, and triall is by what is contrary. That vertue therefore which is but a youngling in the contemplation of evill, and knows not the utmost that vice promises to her followers, and rejects it, is but a blank vertue, not a pure; her whitenesse is but an excrementall whitenesse; Which was the reason why our sage and serious Poet *Spencer*, whom I dare be known to think a better teacher then *Scotus* or *Aquinas*, describing true temperance under the person of *Guion*, brings him in with his palmer through the cave of Mammon, and the bowr of earthly blisse that he might see and know, and yet abstain. Since therefore the knowledge

and survay of vice is in this world so necessary to the constituting of human vertue, and the scanning of error to the
confirmation of truth, how can we more safely, and with
lesse danger scout into the regions of sin and falsity then by
reading all manner of tractats, and hearing all manner of
reason? And this is the benefit which may be had of books
promiscuously read. But of the harm that may result hence
three kinds are usually reckn'd. First, is fear'd the infection that may spread; but then all human learning and controversie in religious points must remove out of the world, yea
the Bible it selfe; for that oftimes relates blasphemy not
nicely, it describes the carnall sense of wicked men not un-
elegantly, it brings in holiest men passionately murmuring
against providence through all the arguments of *Epicurus:* in
other great disputes it answers dubiously and darkly to the
common reader: And ask a Talmudist what ails the modesty
of his marginall Keri, that *Moses* and all the Prophets cannot
perswade him to pronounce the textuall Chetiv. For these
causes we all know the Bible it selfe put by the Papist into the
first rank of prohibited books. The ancientest Fathers must
be next remov'd, as *Clement* of *Alexandria,* and that *Eusebian* book of Evangelick preparation, transmitting our ears
through a hoard of heathenish obscenities to receive the Gospel. Who finds not that *Irenæus, Epiphanius, Jerom,* and
others discover more heresies then they well confute, and that
oft for heresie which is the truer opinion. Nor boots it to say
for these, and all the heathen Writers of greatest infection, if
it must be thought so, with whom is bound up the life of
human learning, that they writ in an unknown tongue, so
long as we are sure those languages are known as well to the
worst of men, who are both most able, and most diligent to
instill the poison they suck, first into the Courts of Princes,
acquainting them with the choicest delights, and criticisms of
sin. As perhaps did that *Petronius* whom *Nero* call'd his
Arbiter, the Master of his revels; and that notorious ribald
of *Arezzo,* dreaded, and yet dear to the Italian Courtiers. I
name not him for posterities sake, whom *Harry* the 8. nam'd
in merriment his Vicar of hell. By which compendious way
all the contagion that foreine books can infuse, will finde a
passage to the people farre easier and shorter then an Indian

voyage, though it could be sail'd either by the North of *Cataio* Eastward, or of *Canada* Westward, while our Spanish licencing gags the English Presse never so severely. But on the other side that infection which is from books of controversie in Religion, is more doubtfull and dangerous to the learned, then to the ignorant; and yet those books must be permitted untoucht by the licencer. It will be hard to instance where any ignorant man hath bin ever seduc't by Papisticall book in English, unlesse it were commended and expounded to him by some of that Clergy: and indeed all such tractats whether false or true are as the Prophesie of *Isaiah* was to the *Eunuch*, not to be *understood without a guide*. But of our Priests and Doctors how many have bin corrupted by studying the comments of Jesuits and *Sorbonists*, and how fast they could transfuse that corruption into the people, our experience is both late and sad. It is not forgot, since the acute and distinct *Arminius* was perverted meerly by the perusing of a namelesse discours writt'n at *Delf*, which at first he took in hand to confute. Seeing therefore that those books, and those in great abundance which are likeliest to taint both life and doctrine, cannot be supprest without the fall of learning, and of all ability in disputation, and that these books of either sort are most and soonest catching to the learned, from whom to the common people what ever is hereticall or dissolute may quickly be convey'd, and that evill manners are as perfectly learnt without books a thousand other ways which cannot be stopt, and evill doctrine not with books can propagate, except a teacher guide, which he might also doe without writing, and so beyond prohibiting, I am not able to unfold, how this cautelous enterprise of licencing can be exempted from the number of vain and impossible attempts. And he who were pleasantly dispos'd, could not well avoid to lik'n it to the exploit of that gallant man who thought to pound up the crows by shutting his Parkgate. Besides another inconvenience, if learned men be the first receivers out of books, and dispredders both of vice and error, how shall the licencers themselves be confided in, unlesse we can conferr upon them, or they assume to themselves above all others in the Land, the grace of infallibility, and uncorruptednesse? And again, if it be true, that a wise man like a good refiner can gather gold out of the drossiest volume, and that a fool will be a fool with the best book, yea or without book, there is no reason that we should deprive a wise man of any advantage to his wisdome, while we seek to restrain from a fool, that which being restrain'd will be no hindrance to his folly. For if there should be so much exactnesse always us'd to keep that from him which is unfit for his reading, we should in the judgement of *Aristotle* not only, but of *Salomon*, and of our Saviour, not voutsafe him good precepts, and by consequence not willingly admit him to good books; as being certain that a wise man will make better use of an idle pamphlet, then a fool will do of sacred Scripture. 'Tis next alleg'd we must not expose our selves to temptations without necessity, and next to that, not imploy our time in vain things. To both these objections one answer will serve, out of the grounds already laid, that to all men such books are not temptations, nor vanities; but usefull drugs and materialls wherewith to temper and compose effective and strong med'cins, which mans life cannot want. The rest, as children and childish men, who have not the art to qualifie and prepare these working mineralls, well may be exhorted to forbear, but hinder'd forcibly they cannot be by all the licencing that Sainted Inquisition could ever yet contrive; which is what I promis'd to deliver next, That this order of licencing conduces nothing to the end for which it was fram'd; and hath almost prevented me by being clear already while thus much hath bin explaining. See the ingenuity of Truth, who when she gets a free and willing hand, opens her self faster, then the pace of method and discours can overtake her. It was the task which I began with, To shew that no Nation, or well instituted State, if they valu'd books at all, did ever use this way of licencing; and it might be answer'd, that this is a piece of prudence lately discover'd. To which I return, that as it was a thing slight and obvious to think on, so if it had bin difficult to finde out, there wanted not among them long since, who suggested such a cours; which they not following, leave us a pattern of their judgement, that it was not the not knowing, but the not approving, which was the cause of their not using it. *Plato*, a man of high autority indeed, but least of all for his Commonwealth, in the book of his laws, which no City ever yet receiv'd, fed his fancie with making many edicts to his ayrie Burgomasters, which they who otherwise admire him, wish had bin rather buried and excus'd in the *genial* cups of an *Academick* night-sitting. By which laws he seems to tolerat no kind of learning, but by unalterable decree, consisting most of practicall traditions, to the attainment whereof a Library of smaller bulk then his own dialogues would be abundant. And there also enacts that no Poet should so much as read to any privat man, what he had writt'n, untill the Judges and Law-keepers had seen it, and allow'd it: But that *Plato* meant this Law peculiarly to that Commonwealth which he had imagin'd, and to no other, is evident. Why was he not else a Law-giver to himself, but a transgressor, and to be expell'd by his own Magistrats; both for the wanton epigrams and dialogues which he made, and his perpetuall reading of *Sophron Mimus*, and *Aristophanes*, books of grossest infamy, and also for commending the latter of them though he were the malicious libeller of his chief friends, to be read by the Tyrant *Dionysius*, who had little need of such trash to spend his time on? But that he knew this licencing of Poems had reference and dependence to many other proviso's there set down in his fancied republic, which in this world could have no place: and so neither he himself, nor any Magistrat, or City ever imitated that cours, which tak'n apart from those other collaterall injunctions must needs be vain and fruitlesse. For if they fell upon one kind of strictnesse, unlesse their care were equall to regulat all other things of like aptnes to corrupt the mind, that single endeavour they knew would be but a fond labour; to shut and fortifie one gate against corruption, and be necessitated to leave others round about wide open. If we think to regulat Printing, thereby to rectifie manners, we must regulat all recreations and pastimes, all that is delightfull to man. No musick must be heard, no song be set or sung, but what is grave and *Dorick*. There must be licencing dancers, that no gesture, motion, or deportment be taught our youth but what by their allowance shall be thought honest; for such *Plato* was provided of; It will ask more then the work of twenty licencers to examin all the lutes, the violins, and the ghittarrs in every house; they must not be suffer'd to prattle as they

doe, but must be licenc'd what they may say. And who shall
silence all the airs and madrigalls, that whisper softnes in
chambers? The Windows also, and the *Balcone's* must be
thought on, there are shrewd books, with dangerous Frontis-
pieces set to sale; who shall prohibit them, shall twenty
licencers? The villages also must have their visitors to enquire
what lectures the bagpipe, and the rebbeck reads ev'n to the
ballatry, and the gammuth of every *municipal* fidler, for these
are the Countrymans *Arcadia's* and his *Monte Mayors*. Next,
what more Nationall corruption, for which England hears ill
abroad, then houshold gluttony; who shall be the rectors of
our daily rioting? and what shall be done to inhibit the multitudes that frequent those houses where drunk'nes is sold and
harbour'd? Our garments also should be referr'd to the licencing of some more sober work-masters to see them cut
into a lesse wanton garb. Who shall regulat all the mixt conversation of our youth, male and female together, as is the
fashion of this Country, who shall still appoint what shall be
discours'd, what presum'd, and no furder? Lastly, who shall
forbid and separat all idle resort, all evill company? These
things will be, and must be; but how they shall be lest hurtfull, how lest enticing, herein consists the grave and governing wisdom of a State. To sequester out of the world into
Atlantick and *Eutopian* polities, which never can be drawn
into use, will not mend our condition; but to ordain wisely as
in this world of evill, in the midd'st whereof God hath plac't
us unavoidably. Nor is it *Plato's* licencing of books will doe
this, which necessarily pulls along with it so many other
kinds of licencing, as will make us all both ridiculous and
weary, and yet frustrat; but those unwritt'n, or at least un-
constraining laws of vertuous education, religious and civill
nurture, which *Plato* there mentions, as the bonds and liga-
ments of the Commonwealth, the pillars and the sustainers
of every writt'n Statute; these they be which will bear chief
sway in such matters as these, when all licencing will be easily
eluded. Impunity and remissenes, for certain are the bane of
a Commonwealth, but here the great art lyes to discern in
what the law is to bid restraint and punishment, and in what
things perswasion only is to work. If every action which is
good, or evill in man at ripe years, were to be under pittance,

and prescription, and compulsion, what were vertue but a
name, what praise could be then due to well-doing, what
grammercy to be sober, just or continent? many there be that
complain of divin Providence for suffering *Adam* to transgresse, foolish tongues! when God gave him reason, he gave
him freedom to choose, for reason is but choosing; he had
bin else a meer artificiall *Adam*, such an *Adam* as he is in the
motions. We our selves esteem not of that obedience, or love,
or gift, which is of force: God therefore left him free, set before him a provoking object, ever almost in his eyes herein
consisted his merit, herein the right of his reward, the praise
of his abstinence. Wherefore did he creat passions within us,
pleasures round about us, but that these rightly temper'd are
the very ingredients of vertu? They are not skilfull consider-
ers of human things, who imagin to remove sin by removing
the matter of sin; for, besides that it is a huge heap increasing
under the very act of diminishing, though some part of it
may for a time be withdrawn from some persons, it cannot
from all, in such a universall thing as books are; and when
this is done, yet the sin remains entire. Though ye take
from a covetous man all his treasure, he has yet one jewell
left, ye cannot bereave him of his covetousnesse. Banish
all objects of lust, shut up all youth into the severest discipline that can be exercis'd in any hermitage, ye cannot
make them chaste, that came not thither so: such great care
and wisdom is requir'd to the right managing of this point.
Suppose we could expell sin by this means; look how much
we thus expell of sin, so much we expell of vertue: for the
matter of them both is the same; remove that, and ye remove
them both alike. This justifies the high providence of God,
who though he command us temperance, justice, continence,
yet powrs out before us ev'n to a profusenes all desirable
things, and gives us minds that can wander beyond all limit
and satiety. Why should we then affect a rigor contrary to
the manner of God and of nature, by abridging or scanting
those means, which books freely permitted are, both to the
triall of vertue, and the exercise of truth. It would be better
done to learn that the law must needs be frivolous which
goes to restrain things, uncertainly and yet equally working to
good, and to evill. And were I the chooser, a dram of well-

doing should be preferr'd before many times as much the
forcible hindrance of evill-doing. For God sure esteems the
growth and compleating of one vertuous person, more then
the restraint of ten vitious. And albeit what ever thing we
hear or see, sitting, walking, travelling, or conversing may be
fitly call'd our book, and is of the same effect that writings
are, yet grant the thing to be prohibited were only books, it
appears that this order hitherto is far insufficient to the end
which it intends. Do we not see, not once or oftner, but weekly that continu'd Court-libell against the Parlament and City,
Printed, as the wet sheets can witnes, and dispers't among us,
for all that licencing can doe? yet this is the prime service a
man would think, wherein this order should give proof of it
self. If it were executed, you'l say. But certain, if execution
be remisse or blindfold now, and in this particular, what will
it be hereafter, and in other books. If then the order shall not
be vain and frustrat, behold a new labour, Lords and Commons, ye must repeal and proscribe all scandalous and unlicenc't books already printed and divulg'd; after ye have
drawn them up into a list, that all may know which are condemn'd, and which not; and ordain that no forrein books be
deliver'd out of custody, till they have bin read over. This
office will require the whole time of not a few overseers, and
those no vulgar men. There be also books which are partly
usefull and excellent, partly culpable and pernicious; this
work will ask as many more officials, to make expurgations,
and expunctions, that the Commonwealth of learning be not
damnify'd. In fine, when the multitude of books encrease
upon their hands, ye must be fain to catalogue all those
Printers who are found frequently offending, and forbidd the
importation of their whole suspected *typography*. In a word,
that this your order may be exact, and not deficient, ye must
reform it perfectly according to the model of *Trent* and *Sevil*,
which I know ye abhorre to doe. Yet though ye should con-
discend to this, which God forbid, the order still would be
but fruitlesse and defective to that end whereto ye meant it.
If to prevent sects and schisms, who is so unread or so uncat-
echis'd in story, that hath not heard of many sects refusing
books as a hindrance, and preserving their doctrine unmixt
for many ages, only by unwritt'n traditions. The Christian

faith, for that was once a schism, is not unknown to have spread all over *Asia*, ere any Gospel or Epistle was seen in writing. If the amendment of manners be aym'd at, look into Italy and Spain, whether those places be one scruple the better, the honester, the wiser, the chaster, since all the inquisitionall rigor that hath bin executed upon books.

Another reason, whereby to make it plain that this order will misse the end it seeks, consider by the quality which ought to be in every licencer. It cannot be deny'd but that he who is made judge to sit upon the birth, or death of books whether they may be wafted into this world, or not, had need to be a man above the common measure, both studious, learned, and judicious; there may be else no mean mistakes in the censure of what is passable or not; which is also no mean injury. If he be of such worth as behoovs him, there cannot be a more tedious and unpleasing Journey-work, a greater losse of time levied upon his head, then to be made the perpetuall reader of unchosen books and pamphlets, oftimes huge volumes. There is no book that is acceptable unlesse at certain seasons; but to be enjoyn'd the reading of that at all times, and in a hand scars legible, whereof three pages would not down at any time in the fairest Print, is an imposition which I cannot beleeve how he that values time, and his own studies, or is but of a sensible nostrill should be able to endure. In this one thing I crave leave of the present licencers to be pardon'd for so thinking: who doubtlesse took this office up, looking on it through their obedience to the Parlament, whose command perhaps made all things seem easie and unlaborious to them; but that this short triall hath wearied them out already, their own expressions and excuses to them who make so many journeys to sollicit their licence, are testimony anough. Seing therefore those who now possesse the imployment, by all evident signs wish themselves well ridd of it, and that no man of worth, none that is not a plain unthrift of his own hours is ever likely to succeed them, except he mean to put himself to the salary of a Presse-corrector, we may easily foresee what kind of licencers we are to expect hereafter, either ignorant, imperious, and remisse, or basely pecuniary. This is what I had to shew wherein this order cannot conduce to that end, whereof it bears the intention.

I lastly proceed from the no good it can do, to the manifest hurt it causes, in being first the greatest discouragement and affront, that can be offer'd to learning and to learned men. It was the complaint and lamentation of Prelats, upon every least breath of a motion to remove pluralities, and distribute more equally Church revenu's, that then all learning would be for ever dasht and discourag'd. But as for that opinion, I never found cause to think that the tenth part of learning stood or fell with the Clergy: nor could I ever but hold it for a sordid and unworthy speech of any Churchman who had a competency left him. If therefore ye be loath to dishearten utterly and discontent, not the mercenary crew of false pretenders to learning, but the free and ingenuous sort of such as evidently were born to study, and love lerning for it self, not for lucre, or any other end, but the service of God and of truth, and perhaps that lasting fame and perpetuity of praise which God and good men have consented shall be the reward of those whose publisht labours advance the good of mankind, then know, that so far to distrust the judgement and the honesty of one who hath but a common repute in learning, and never yet offended, as not to count him fit to print his mind without a tutor and examiner, lest he should drop a scism, or something of corruption, is the greatest displeasure and indignity to a free and knowing spirit that can be put upon him. What advantage is it to be a man over it is to be a boy at school, if we have only scapt the ferular, to come under the fescu of an *Imprimatur?* if serious and elaborat writings, as if they were no more then the theam of a Grammar lad under his Pedagogue must not be utter'd without the cursory eyes of a temporizing and extemporizing licencer. He who is not trusted with his own actions, his drift not being known to be evill, and standing to the hazard of law and penalty, has no great argument to think himself reputed in the Commonwealth wherin he was born, for other then a fool or a foreiner. When a man writes to the world, he summons up all his reason and deliberation to assist him; he searches, meditats, is industrious, and likely consults and conferrs with his judicious friends; after all which done he takes himself to be inform'd in what he writes, as well as any that writ before him; if in this the most consummat act of his

z   M.

fidelity and ripenesse, no years, no industry, no former proof of his abilities can bring him to that state of maturity, as not to be still mistrusted and suspected, unlesse he carry all his considerat diligence, all his midnight watchings, and expence of *Palladian* oyl, to the hasty view of an unleasur'd licencer, perhaps much his younger, perhaps far his inferiour in judgement, perhaps one who never knew the labour of book-writing, and if he be not repulst, or slighted, must appear in Print like a punie with his guardian, and his censors hand on the back of his title to be his bayl and surety, that he is no idiot, or seducer, it cannot be but a dishonor and deroga-tion to the author, to the book, to the priviledge and dignity of Learning. And what if the author shall be one so copious of fancie, as to have many things well worth the adding, come into his mind after licencing, while the book is yet under the Presse, which not seldom happ'ns to the best and diligentest writers; and that perhaps a dozen times in one book. The Printer dares not go beyond his licenc't copy; so often then must the author trudge to his leav-giver, that those his new insertions may be viewd; and many a jaunt will be made, ere that licencer, for it must be the same man, can either be found, or found at leisure; mean while either the Presse must stand still, which is no small damage, or the author loose his accuratest thoughts, and send the book forth wors then he had made it, which to a diligent writer is the greatest melan-choly and vexation that can befall. And how can a man teach with autority, which is the life of teaching, how can he be a Doctor in his book as he ought to be, or else had better be silent, whenas all he teaches, all he delivers, is but under the tuition, under the correction of his patriarchal licencer to blot or alter what precisely accords not with the hidebound humor which he calls his judgement. When every acute reader upon the first sight of a pedantick licence, will be ready with these like words to ding the book a coits distance from him, I hate a pupil teacher, I endure not an instructer that comes to me under the wardship of an overseeing fist. I know nothing of the licencer, but that I have his own hand here for his arro-gance; who shall warrant me his judgement? The State, Sir, replies the Stationer, but has a quick return, The State shall be my governours, but not my criticks; they may be mistak'n in the choice of a licencer, as easily as this licencer may be mistak'n in an author: This is some common stuffe; and he might adde from Sir *Francis Bacon,* That *such authoriz'd books are but the language of the times.* For though a licencer should happ'n to be judicious more then ordnary, which will be a great jeopardy of the next succession, yet his very office, and his commission enjoyns him to let passe nothing but what is vulgarly receiv'd already. Nay, which is more lamentable, if the work of any deceased author, though never so famous in his life time, and even to this day, come to their hands for licence to be Printed, or Reprinted, if there be found in his book one sentence of a ventrous edge, utter'd in the height of zeal, and who knows whether it might not be the dictat of a divine Spirit, yet not suiting with every low decrepit humor of their own, though it were *Knox* himself, the Reformer of a Kingdom that spake it, they will not pardon him their dash: the sense of that great man shall to all posterity be lost, for the fearfulnesse, or the presumptuous rashnesse of a perfunctory licencer. And to what an author this violence hath bin lately done, and in what book of greatest consequence to be faithfully publisht, I could now instance, but shall forbear till a more convenient season. Yet if these things be not resented seriously and timely by them who have the remedy in their power, but that such iron moulds as these shall have autority to knaw out the choisest periods of exquisitest books, and to commit such a treacherous fraud against the orphan remainders of worthiest men after death, the more sorrow will belong to that haples race of men, whose misfortune it is to have understanding. Henceforth let no man care to learn, or care to be more then worldly wise; for certainly in higher matters to be ignorant and slothfull, to be a common stedfast dunce will be the only pleasant life, and only in request.

And as it is a particular disesteem of every knowing person alive, and most injurious to the writt'n labours and monuments of the dead, so to me it seems an undervaluing and vilifying of the whole Nation. I cannot set so light by all the invention, the art, the wit, the grave and solid judgement which is in England, as that it can be comprehended in any twenty capacities how good soever, much lesse that it should not passe except their superintendence be over it, except it be sifted and strain'd with their strainers, that it should be uncurrant without their manuall stamp. Truth and understanding are not such wares as to be monopoliz'd and traded in by tickets and statutes, and standards. We must not think to make a staple commodity of all the knowledge in the Land, to mark and licence it like our broad cloth, and our wooll packs. What is it but a servitude like that impos'd by the Philistims, not to be allow'd the sharpning of our own axes and coulters, but we must repair from all quarters to twenty licencing forges. Had any one writt'n and divulg'd erroneous things and scandalous to honest life, misusing and forfeiting the esteem had of his reason among men, if after conviction this only censure were adjudg'd him, that he should never henceforth write, but what were first examin'd by an appointed officer, whose hand should be annext to passe his credit for him, that now he might be safely read, it could not be apprehended lesse then a disgracefull punishment. Whence to include the whole Nation, and those that never yet thus offended, under such a diffident and suspectfull prohibition, may plainly be understood what a disparagement it is. So much the more, when as dettors and delinquents may walk abroad without a keeper, but unoffensive books must not stirre forth without a visible jaylor in thir title. Nor is it to the common people lesse then a reproach; for if we be so jealous over them, as that we dare not trust them with an English pamphlet, what doe we but censure them for a giddy, vitious, and ungrounded people; in such a sick and weak estate of faith and discretion, as to be able to take nothing down but through the pipe of a licencer. That this is care or love of them, we cannot pretend, whenas in those Popish places where the Laity are most hated and dispis'd the same strictnes is us'd over them. Wisdom we cannot call it, because it stops but one breach of licence, nor that neither; whenas those corruptions which it seeks to prevent, break in faster at other dores which cannot be shut.

And in conclusion it reflects to the disrepute of our Ministers also, of whose labours we should hope better, and of the proficiencie which thir flock reaps by them, then that after all this light of the Gospel which is, and is to be, and all this continuall preaching, they should be still frequented with such an unprincipl'd, unedify'd, and laick rabble, as that the whiffe of every new pamphlet should stagger them out of thir catechism, and Christian walking. This may have much reason to discourage the Ministers when such a low conceit is had of all their exhortations, and the benefiting of their hearers, as that they are not thought fit to be turn'd loose to three sheets of paper without a licencer, that all the Sermons, all the Lectures preacht, printed, vented in such numbers, and such volumes, as have now wellnigh made all other books unsalable, should not be armor anough against one single *enchiridion*, without the castle St. *Angelo* of an *Imprimatur*.

And lest som should perswade ye, Lords and Commons, that these arguments of lerned mens discouragement at this your order, are meer flourishes, and not reall, I could recount what I have seen and heard in other Countries, where this kind of inquisition tyrannizes; when I have sat among their lerned men, for that honor I had, and bin counted happy to be born in such a place of *Philosophic* freedom, as they suppos'd England was, while themselvs did nothing but bemoan the servil condition into which lerning amongst them was brought; that this was it which had dampt the glory of Italian wits; that nothing had bin there writt'n now these many years but flattery and fustian. There it was that I found and visited the famous *Galileo* grown old, a prisner to the Inquisition, for thinking in Astronomy otherwise then the Franciscan and Dominican licencers thought. And though I knew that England then was groaning loudest under the Prelaticall yoak, neverthelesse I took it as a pledge of future happines, that other Nations were so perswaded of her liberty. Yet was it beyond my hope that those Worthies were then breathing in her air, who should be her leaders to such a deliverance, as shall never be forgott'n by any revolution of time that this world hath to finish. When that was once begun, it was as little in my fear, that what words of complaint I heard among lerned men of other parts utter'd against the Inquisition, the same I should hear by as lerned men at home utterd in time of Parlament against an order of licencing; and that so generally, that when I had disclos'd my self a companion of their discontent, I might say, if without envy, that he whom an honest *quæstorship* had indear'd to the *Sicilians*, was not more by them importun'd against *Verres*, then the favourable opinion which I had among many who honour ye, and are known and respected by ye, loaded me with entreaties and perswasions, that I would not despair to lay together that which just reason should bring into my mind, toward the removal of an undeserved thraldom upon lerning. That this is not therefore the disburdning of a particular fancie, but the common grievance of all those who had prepar'd their minds and studies above the vulgar pitch to advance truth in others, and from others to entertain it, thus much may satisfie. And in their name I shall for neither friend nor foe conceal what the generall murmur is; that if it come to inquisitioning again, and licencing, and that we are so timorous of our selvs, and so suspicious of all men, as to fear each book, and the shaking of every leaf, before we know what the contents are, if some who but of late were little better then silenc't from preaching, shall come now to silence us from reading, except what they please, it cannot be guest what is intended by som but a second tyranny over learning: and will soon put it out of controversie that Bishops and Presbyters are the same to us both name and thing. That those evills of Prelaty which before from five or six and twenty Sees were distributivly charg'd upon the whole people, will now light wholly upon learning, is not obscure to us: whenas now the Pastor of a small unlearned Parish, on the sudden shall be exalted Archbishop over a large dioces of books, and yet not remove, but keep his other cure too, a mysticall pluralist. He who but of late cry'd down the sole ordination of every novice Batchelor of Art, and deny'd sole jurisdiction over the simplest Parishioner, shall now at home in his privat chair assume both these over worthiest and excellentest books and ablest authors that write them. This is not, Yee Covnants and Protestations that we have made, this is not to put down Prelaty, this is but to chop an Episcopacy, this is but to translate the Palace *Metropolitan* from one kind of dominion into another, this is but an old canonicall slight of *commuting* our penance. To startle thus betimes at a meer unlicenc't pamphlet will after a while be afraid of every conventicle, and a while after will make a conventicle of every Christian meeting. But I am certain that a State govern'd by the rules of justice and fortitude, or a Church built and founded upon the rock of faith and true knowledge, cannot be so pusillanimous. While things are yet not constituted in Religion, that freedom of writing should be restrain'd by a discipline imitated from the Prelats, and learnt by them from the Inquisition to shut us up all again into the brest of a licencer, must needs give cause of doubt and discouragement to all learned and religious men. Who cannot but discern the finenes of this politic drift, and who are the contrivers; that while Bishops were to be baited down, then all Presses might be open; it was the peoples birthright and priviledge in time of Parlament, it was the breaking forth of light. But now the Bishops abrogated and voided out of the Church, as if our Reformation sought no more, but to make room for others into their seats under another name, the Episcopall arts begin to bud again, the cruse of truth must run no more oyle, liberty of Printing must be enthrall'd again under a Prelaticall commission of twenty, the privilege of the people nullify'd, and which is wors, the freedom of learning must groan again, and to her old fetters; all this the Parlament yet sitting. Although their own late arguments and defences against the Prelats might remember them that this obstructing violence meets for the most part with an event utterly opposite to the end which it drives at: instead of suppressing sects and schisms, it raises them and invests them with a reputation: *The punishing of wits enhaunces their autority*, saith the Vicount St. *Albans, and a forbidd'n writing is thought to be a certain spark of truth that flies up in the faces of them who seeke to tread it out.* This order therefore may prove a nursing mother to sects, but I shall easily shew how it will be a step-dame to Truth: and first by disinabling us to the maintenance of what is known already.

Well knows he who uses to consider, that our faith and knowledge thrives by exercise, as well as our limbs and complexion. Truth is compar'd in Scripture to a streaming fountain; if her waters flow not in a perpetuall progression, they sick'n into a muddy pool of conformity and tradition. A man may be a heretick in the truth; and if he beleeve things only because his Pastor sayes so, or the Assembly so determins, without knowing other reason, though his belief be true, yet the very truth he holds, becomes his heresie. There is not any burden that som would gladlier post off to another, then the charge and care of their Religion. There be, who knows not that there be of Protestants and professors who live and dye in as arrant an implicit faith, as any lay Papist of Loretto. A wealthy man addicted to his pleasure and to his profits, finds Religion to be a traffick so entangl'd, and of so many piddling accounts, that of all mysteries he cannot skill to keep a stock going upon that trade. What should he doe? fain he would have the name to be religious, fain he would bear up with his neighbours in that. What does he therefore, but resolvs to give over toyling, and to find himself out som factor, to whose care and credit he may commit the whole managing of his religious affairs; som Divine of note and estimation that must be. To him he adheres, resigns the whole ware-house of his religion, with all the locks and keyes into his custody; and indeed makes the very person of that man his religion; esteems his associating with him a sufficient evidence and commendatory of his own piety. So that a man may say his religion is now no more within himself, but is becom a dividuall movable, and goes and comes neer him, according as that good man frequents the house. He entertains him, gives him gifts, feasts him, lodges him; his religion comes home at night, praies, is liberally supt, and sumptuously laid to sleep, rises, is saluted, and after the malmsey, or some well spic't bruage, and better breakfasted then he whose morning appetite would have gladly fed on green figs between *Bethany* and *Jerusalem*, his Religion walks abroad at eight, and leavs his kind entertainer in the shop trading all day without his religion.

Another sort there be who when they hear that all things shall be order'd, all things regulated and setl'd; nothing writt'n but what passes through the custom-house of certain Publicans that have the tunaging and the poundaging of all free spok'n truth, will strait give themselvs up into your hands, mak'em, and cut'em out what religion ye please; there be delights, there be recreations, and jolly pastimes that will fetch the day about from sun to sun, and rock the tedious year as in a delightfull dream. What need they torture their heads with that which others have tak'n so strictly, and so unalterably into their own pourveying. These are the fruits which a dull ease and cessation of our knowledge will bring forth among the people. How goodly, and how to be wisht were such an obedient unanimity as this, what a fine conformity would it starch us all into? doubtles a stanch and solid peece of framework, as any January could freeze together.

Nor much better will be the consequence ev'n among the Clergy themselvs; it is no new thing never heard of before, for a *parochiall* Minister, who has his reward, and is at his *Hercules* pillars in a warm benefice, to be easily inclinable, if he have nothing else that may rouse up his studies, to finish his circuit in an English concordance and a *topic folio*, the gatherings and savings of a sober graduatship, a *Harmony* and a *Catena*, treading the constant round of certain common doctrinall heads, attended with their uses, motives, marks and means, out of which as out of an alphabet or sol fa by forming and transforming, joyning and dis-joyning variously a little book-craft, and two hours meditation might furnish him unspeakably to the performance of more then a weekly charge of sermoning: not to reck'n up the infinit helps of interlinearies, breviaries, *synopses*, and other loitering gear. But as for the multitude of Sermons ready printed and pil'd up, on every text that is not difficult, our London trading St. *Thomas* in his vestry, and adde to boot St. *Martin*, and St. *Hugh*, have not within their hallow'd limits more vendible ware of all sorts ready made: so that penury he never need fear of Pulpit provision, having where so plenteously to refresh his magazin. But if his rear and flanks be not impal'd, if his back dore be not secur'd by the rigid licencer, but that a bold book may now and then issue forth, and give the assault to some of his old collections in their trenches, it will concern him then to keep waking, to stand in watch, to set good guards and sentinells about his receiv'd opinions, to walk the round and counter-round with his fellow inspectors, fearing lest any of his flock be seduc't, who also then would be better instructed, better exercis'd and disciplin'd. And God send that the fear of this diligence which must then be us'd, doe not make us affect the lazines of a licencing Church.

For if we be sure we are in the right, and doe not hold the truth guiltily, which becomes not, if we our selves condemn not our own weak and frivolous teaching, and the people for an untaught and irreligious gadding rout, what can be more fair, then when a man judicious, learned, and of a conscience, for ought we know, as good as theirs that taught us what we know, shall not privily from house to house, which is more dangerous, but openly by writing publish to the world what his opinion is, what his reasons, and wherefore that which is now thought cannot be sound. Christ urg'd it as wherewith to justifie himself, that he preacht in publick; yet writing is more publick then preaching; and more easie to refutation, if need be, there being so many whose businesse and profession meerly it is, to be the champions of Truth; which if they neglect, what can be imputed but their sloth, or unability?

Thus much we are hinder'd and dis-inur'd by this cours of licencing toward the true knowledge of what we seem to know. For how much it hurts and hinders the licencers themselves in the calling of their Ministery, more then any secular employment, if they will discharge that office as they ought, so that of necessity they must neglect either the one duty or the other, I insist not, because it is a particular, but leave it to their own conscience, how they will decide it there.

There is yet behind of what I purpos'd to lay open, the incredible losse, and detriment that this plot of licencing puts us to, more then if som enemy at sea should stop up all our hav'ns and ports, and creeks, it hinders and retards the importation of our richest Marchandize, Truth: nay it was first establisht and put in practice by Antichristian malice and mystery on set purpose to extinguish, if it were possible, the light of Reformation, and to settle falshood; little differing from that policie wherewith the Turk upholds his *Alcoran*, by the prohibition of Printing. 'Tis not deny'd, but gladly confest, we are to send our thanks and vows to heav'n, louder then most of Nations, for that great measure of truth which we enjoy, especially in those main points between us and the Pope, with his appertinences the Prelats: but he who thinks we are to pitch our tent here, and have attain'd the utmost prospect of reformation, that the mortall glasse wherein we contemplate, can shew us, till we come to *beatific* vision, that man by this very opinion declares, that he is yet farre short of Truth.

Truth indeed came once into the world with her divine Master, and was a perfect shape most glorious to look on: but when he ascended, and his Apostles after him were laid asleep, then strait arose a wicked race of deceivers, who as that story goes of the *Ægyptian Typhon* with his conspirators, how they dealt with the good *Osiris*, took the Virgin Truth, hewd her lovely form into a thousand peeces, and scatter'd them to the four winds. From that time ever since, the sad friends of Truth, such as durst appear, imitating the carefull search that *Isis* made for the mangl'd body of *Osiris*, went up and down gathering up limb by limb still as they could find them. We have not yet found them all, Lords and Commons, nor ever shall doe, till her Masters second comming; he shall bring together every joynt and member, and shall mould them into an immortall feature of lovelines and perfection. Suffer not these licencing prohibitions to stand at every place of opportunity forbidding and disturbing them that continue seeking, that continue to do our obsequies to the torn body of our martyr'd Saint. We boast our light; but if we look not wisely on the Sun it self, it smites us into darknes. Who can discern those planets that are oft *Combust*, and those stars of brightest magnitude that rise and set with the Sun, untill the opposite motion of their orbs bring them to such a place in the firmament, where they may be seen evning or morning. The light which we have gain'd, was giv'n us, not to be ever staring on, but by it to discover onward things more remote from our knowledge. It is not the unfrocking of a Priest, the unmitring of a Bishop, and the removing him from off the *Presbyterian* shoulders that will make us a happy Nation, no, if other things as great in the Church, and in the rule of life both economicall and politicall be not lookt into and reform'd, we have lookt so long upon the blaze that *Zuinglius* and *Calvin* hath beacon'd up to us, that we are stark blind. There be who perpetually complain of schisms and sects, and make it such a calamity that any man dissents from their maxims. 'Tis their own pride and ignorance which causes the disturbing, who neither will hear with meeknes, nor can convince, yet all must be supprest which is not found in their *Syntagma*. They are the troublers, they are the dividers of unity, who neglect and permit not others to unite those dissever'd peeces which are yet wanting to the body of Truth. To be still searching what we know not, by what we know, still closing up truth to truth as we find it (for all her body is *homogeneal*, and proportionall) this is the golden rule in *Theology* as well as in Arithmetick, and makes up the best harmony in a Church; not the forc't and outward union of cold, and neutrall, and inwardly divided minds.

Lords and Commons of England, consider what Nation it is wherof ye are, and wherof ye are the governours: a Nation not slow and dull, but of a quick, ingenious, and piercing spirit, acute to invent, suttle and sinewy to discours, not beneath the reach of any point the highest that human capacity can soar to. Therefore the studies of learning in her deepest Sciences have bin so ancient, and so eminent among us, that Writers of good antiquity, and ablest judgement have bin perswaded that ev'n the school of *Pythagoras* and the *Persian* wisdom took beginning from the old Philosophy of this Iland. And that wise and civill Roman, *Julius Agricola*, who govern'd once here for *Cæsar*, preferr'd the naturall wits of Britain, before the labour'd studies of the French. Nor is it for nothing that the grave and frugal *Transilvanian* sends out yearly from as farre as the mountanous borders of *Russia*, and beyond the *Hercynian* wildernes, not their youth, but their stay'd men, to learn our language, and our *theologic* arts. Yet that which is above all this, the favour and the love of heav'n we have great argument to think in a peculiar manner propitious and propending towards us. Why else was this Nation chos'n before any other, that out of her as out of *Sion* should be proclam'd and sounded forth the first tidings and trumpet of Reformation to all *Europ*. And had it not bin the obstinat perversnes of our Prelats against the divine and admirable spirit of *Wicklef*, to suppresse him as a schismatic and *innovator*, perhaps neither the *Bohemian Husse* and *Jerom*, no nor the name of *Luther*, or of *Calvin* had bin ever known: the glory of reforming all our neighbours had bin compleatly ours. But now, as our obdurat Clergy have with violence demean'd the matter, we are become hitherto the latest and the backwardest Schollers, of whom God offer'd to have made us the teachers. Now once again by all concurrence of signs, and by the generall instinct of holy and devout men, as they daily and solemnly expresse their thoughts, God is decreeing to begin some new and great period in his Church, ev'n to the reforming of Reformation it self: what does he then but reveal Himself to his servants, and as his manner is, first to his English-men; I say as his manner is, first to us, though we mark not the method of his counsels, and are unworthy. Behold now this vast City; a City of refuge, the mansion house of liberty, encompast and surrounded with his protection; the shop of warre hath not there more anvils and hammers waking, to fashion out the plates and instruments of armed Justice in defence of beleaguer'd Truth, then there be pens and heads there, sitting by their studious lamps, musing, searching, revolving new notions and idea's wherwith to present, as with their homage and their fealty the approaching Reformation: others as fast reading, trying all things, assenting to the force of reason and convincement. What could a man require more from a Nation so pliant and so prone to seek after knowledge. What wants there to such a towardly and pregnant soile, but wise and faithfull labourers, to make a knowing people, a Nation of Prophets, of Sages, and of Worthies. We reck'n more then five months yet to harvest; there need not be five weeks, had we but eyes to lift up, the fields are white already. Where there is much desire to learn, there of necessity will be much arguing, much writing, many opinions; for opinion in good men is but knowledge in the making. Under these fantastic terrors of sect and schism, we wrong the earnest and zealous thirst after knowledge and understanding which God hath stirr'd up in this City. What some lament of, we rather should rejoyce at, should rather praise this pious forwardnes among men, to reassume the ill deputed care of their Religion into their own hands again. A little generous prudence, a little forbearance of one another, and som grain of charity might win all these diligences to joyn, and unite into one generall and brotherly search after Truth; could we but forgoe this Prelaticall tradition of crowding free consciences and Christian liberties into canons and precepts of men. I doubt not, if some great and worthy stranger should come among us, wise to discern the mould and temper of a people, and how to govern it, observing the high hopes and aims, the diligent alacrity of our extended thoughts and reasonings in the pursuance of truth and freedom, but that he would cry out as *Pirrhus* did, admiring the Roman docility and courage, if such were my *Epirots*, I would not despair the greatest design that could be attempted to make a Church or Kingdom happy. Yet these are the men cry'd out against for schismaticks and sectaries; as if, while the Temple of the Lord was building, some cutting, some squaring the marble, others hewing the cedars, there should be a sort of irrationall men who could not consider there must be many schisms and many dissections made in the quarry and in the timber, ere the house of God can be built. And when every stone is laid artfully together, it cannot be united into a continuity, it can but be contiguous in this world; neither can every peece of the building be of one form; nay rather the perfection consists in this, that out of many moderat varieties and brotherly dissimilitudes that are not vastly disproportionall arises the goodly and the gracefull symmetry that commends the whole pile and structure. Let us therefore be more considerat builders, more wise in spirituall architecture, when great reformation is expected. For now the time seems come, wherein *Moses* the great Prophet may sit in heav'n rejoycing to see that memorable and glorious wish of his fulfill'd, when not only our sev'nty Elders, but all the Lords people are become Prophets. No marvell then though some men, and some good men too perhaps, but young in goodnesse, as *Joshua* then was, envy them. They fret, and out of their own weaknes are in agony, lest these divisions and subdivisions will undoe us. The adversarie again applauds, and waits the hour, when they have brancht themselves out, saith he, small anough into parties and partitions, then will be our time. Fool! he sees not the firm root out of which we all grow, though into branches: nor will beware untill he see our small divided maniples cutting through at every angle of his ill united and unweildy brigade. And that we are to hope better of all these supposed sects and schisms, and that we shall not need that solicitude honest perhaps though over timorous of them that vex in this behalf, but shall laugh in the end, at those malicious applauders of our differences, I have these reasons to perswade me.

First, when a City shall be as it were besieg'd and blockt about, her navigable river infested, inrodes and incursions round, defiance and battell oft rumor'd to be marching up ev'n to her walls, and suburb trenches, that then the people, or the greater part, more then at other times, wholly tak'n up with the study of highest and most important matters to be reform'd, should be disputing, reasoning, reading, inventing, discoursing, ev'n to a rarity, and admiration, things not before discourst or writt'n of, argues first a singular good will, contentednesse and confidence in your prudent foresight, and safe government, Lords and Commons; and from thence derives it self to a gallant bravery and well grounded contempt of their enemies, as if there were no small number of as great spirits among us, as his was, who when Rome was nigh besieg'd by *Hannibal*, being in the City, bought that peece of ground at no cheap rate, whereon *Hannibal* himself encampt his own regiment. Next it is a lively and cherfull presage of our happy successe and victory. For as in a body, when the blood is fresh, the spirits pure and vigorous, not only to vital, but to rationall faculties, and those in the acutest, and the pertest operations of wit and suttlety, it argues in what good plight and constitution the body is, so when the cherfulnesse of the people is so sprightly up, as that it has, not only wherewith to guard well its own freedom and safety, but to spare, and to bestow upon the solidest and sublimest points of controversie, and new invention, it betok'ns us not degenerated, nor drooping to a fatall decay, but casting off the old and wrincl'd skin of corruption to outlive these pangs and wax young again, entring the glorious waies of Truth and prosperous vertue destin'd to become great and honourable in these latter ages. Methinks I see in my mind a noble and puissant Nation rousing herself like a strong man after sleep, and shaking her invincible locks: Methinks I see her as an Eagle muing her mighty youth, and kindling her undazl'd eyes at the full midday beam; purging and unscaling her long abused sight at the fountain it self of heav'nly radiance; while the whole noise of timorous and flocking birds, with those also that love the twilight, flutter about, amaz'd at what she means, and in their envious gabble would prognosticat a year of sects and schisms.

What should ye doe then, should ye suppresse all this flowry crop of knowledge and new light sprung up and yet springing daily in this City, should ye set an *Oligarchy* of twenty ingrossers over it, to bring a famin upon our minds again, when we shall know nothing but what is measur'd to us by their bushel? Beleeve it, Lords and Commons, they who counsell ye to such a suppressing doe as good as bid ye suppresse your selves; and I will soon shew how. If it be desir'd to know the immediat cause of all this free writing and free speaking, there cannot be assign'd a truer then your own mild and free and human government; it is the liberty, Lords and Commons, which your own valorous and happy counsels have purchast us, liberty which is the nurse of all great wits; this is that which hath rarify'd and enlightn'd our spirits like the influence of heav'n; this is that which hath enfranchis'd, enlarg'd and lifted up our apprehensions degrees above themselves. Ye cannot make us now lesse capable, lesse knowing, lesse eagerly pursuing of the truth, unlesse ye first make your selves, that made us so, lesse the lovers, lesse the founders of our true liberty. We can grow ignorant again, brutish, formall, and slavish, as ye found us; but you then must first become that which ye cannot be, oppressive, arbitrary, and tyrannous, as they were from whom ye have free'd us. That our hearts are now more capacious, our thoughts more erected to the search and expectation of greatest and exactest things, is the issue of your owne vertu propagated in us; ye cannot suppresse that unlesse ye reinforce an abrogated and mercilesse law, that fathers may dispatch at will their own children. And who shall then sticke closest to ye, and excite others? not he who takes up armes for cote and conduct and his four nobles of Danegelt. Although I dispraise not the defence of just immunities, yet love my peace better, if that were all. Give me the liberty to know, to utter, and to argue freely according to conscience, above all liberties.

What would be best advis'd then, if it be found so hurtfull and so unequall to suppresse opinions for the newnes, or the

unsutablenes to a customary acceptance, will not be my task
to say; I only shall repeat what I have learnt from one of
your own honourable number, a right noble and pious Lord,
who had he not sacrific'd his life and fortunes to the Church
and Commonwealth, we had not now mist and bewayl'd a
worthy and undoubted patron of this argument. Ye know
him I am sure; yet I for honours sake, and may it be eternall
to him, shall name him, the Lord *Brook*. He writing of Episcopacy, and by the way treating of sects and schisms, left Ye
his vote, or rather now the last words of his dying charge,
which I know will ever be of dear and honour'd regard with
Ye, so full of meeknes and breathing charity, that next to his
last testament, who bequeath'd love and peace to his Disciples, I cannot call to mind where I have read or heard words
more mild and peacefull. He there exhorts us to hear with
patience and humility those, however they be miscall'd, that
desire to live purely, in such a use of Gods Ordinances, as the
best guidance of their conscience gives them, and to tolerat
them, though in some disconformity to our selves. The book
it self will tell us more at large being publisht to the world,
and dedicated to the Parlament by him who both for his life
and for his death deserves, that what advice he left be not laid
by without perusall.

And now the time in speciall is, by priviledge to write and
speak what may help to the furder discussing of matters in
agitation. The Temple of *Janus* with his two *controversal*
faces might now not unsignificantly be set open. And though
all the windes of doctrin were let loose to play upon the earth,
so Truth be in the field, we do injuriously by licencing and
prohibiting to misdoubt her strength. Let her and Falshood
grapple; who ever knew Truth put to the wors, in a free and
open encounter. Her confuting is the best and surest suppressing. He who hears what praying there is for light and
clearer knowledge to be sent down among us, would think
of other matters to be constituted beyond the discipline of
Geneva, fram'd and fabric't already to our hands. Yet when
the new light which we beg for shines in upon us, there be
who envy, and oppose, if it come not first in at their case-
ments. What a collusion is this, whenas we are exhorted by
the wise man to use diligence, *to seek for wisdom as for hidd'n*

treasures early and late, that another order shall enjoyn us to know nothing but by statute. When a man hath bin labouring the hardest labour in the deep mines of knowledge, hath furnisht out his findings in all their equipage, drawn forth his reasons as it were a battell raung'd, scatter'd and defeated all objections in his way, calls out his adversary into the plain, offers him the advantage of wind and sun, if he please; only that he may try the matter by dint of argument, for his opponents then to sculk, to lay ambushments, to keep a narrow bridge of licencing where the challenger should passe, though it be valour anough in souldiership, is but weaknes and cowardise in the wars of Truth. For who knows not that Truth is strong next to the Almighty; she needs no policies, nor stratagems, nor licencings to make her victorious, those are the shifts and the defences that error uses against her power: give her but room, and do not bind her when she sleeps, for then she speaks not true, as the old *Proteus* did, who spake oracles only when he was caught and bound, but then rather she turns herself into all shapes, except her own, and perhaps tunes her voice according to the time, as *Micaiah* did before *Ahab*, untill she be adjur'd into her own likenes. Yet is it not impossible that she may have more shapes then one. What else is all that rank of things indifferent, wherein Truth may be on this side, or on the other, without being unlike her self. What but a vain shadow else is the abolition of *those ordinances, that hand writing nayl'd to the crosse*, what great purchase is this Christian liberty which *Paul* so often boasts of. His doctrine is, that he who eats or eats not, regards a day, or regards it not, may doe either to the Lord. How many other things might be tolerated in peace, and left to conscience, had we but charity, and were it not the chief strong hold of our hypocrisie to be ever judging one another. I fear yet this iron yoke of outward conformity hath left a slavish print upon our necks; the ghost of a linnen decency yet haunts us. We stumble and are impatient at the least dividing of one visible congregation from another, though it be not in fundamentalls; and through our forwardnes to suppresse, and our backwardnes to recover any enthrall'd peece of truth out of the gripe of custom, we care not to keep truth separated from truth, which is the fiercest rent and disunion of all. We doe not see that while we still affect by all means a rigid externall formality, we may as soon fall again into a grosse conforming stupidity, a stark and dead congealment of *wood and hay and stubble* forc't and frozen together, which is more to the sudden degenerating of a Church then many *subdichotomies* of petty schisms. Not that I can think well of every light separation, or that all in a Church is to be expected *gold and silver and pretious stones:* it is not possible for man to sever the wheat from the tares, the good fish from the other frie; that must be the Angels Ministery at the end of mortall things. Yet if all cannot be of one mind, as who looks they should be? this doubtles is more wholsome, more prudent, and more Christian that many be tolerated, rather then all compell'd. I mean not tolerated Popery, and open superstition, which as it extirpats all religious and civill supremacies, so it self should be extirpat, provided first that all charitable and compassionat means be us'd to win and regain the weak and the misled: that also which is impious or evil absolutely either against faith or maners no law can possibly permit, that intends not to unlaw it self: but those neighboring differences, or rather indifferences, are what I speak of, whether in some point of doctrine or of discipline, which though they may be many, yet need not interrupt *the unity of Spirit*, if we could but find among us *the bond of peace*. In the mean while if any one would write, and bring his helpfull hand to the slow-moving Reformation which we labour under, if Truth have spok'n to him before others, or but seem'd at least to speak, who hath so bejesuited us that we should trouble that man with asking licence to doe so worthy a deed? and not consider this, that if it come to prohibiting, there is not ought more likely to be prohibited then truth it self; whose first appearance to our eyes blear'd and dimm'd with prejudice and custom, is more unsightly and unplausible then many errors, ev'n as the person is of many a great man slight and contemptible to see to. And what doe they tell us vainly of new opinions, when this very opinion of theirs, that none must be heard, but whom they like, is the worst and newest opinion of all others; and is the chief cause why sects and schisms doe so much abound, and true knowledge is kept at distance from us; besides yet a greater danger which is in it.

For when God shakes a Kingdome with strong and health-full commotions to a generall reforming, 'tis not untrue that many sectaries and false teachers are then busiest in seduc-ing; but yet more true it is, that God then raises to his own work men of rare abilities, and more then common industry not only to look back and revise what hath bin taught hereto-fore, but to gain furder and goe on, some new enlightn'd steps in the discovery of truth. For such is the order of Gods en-lightning his Church, to dispense and deal out by degrees his beam, so as our earthly eyes may best sustain it. Neither is God appointed and confin'd, where and out of what place these his chosen shall be first heard to speak; for he sees not as man sees, chooses not as man chooses, lest we should de-vote our selves again to set places, and assemblies, and out-ward callings of men; planting our faith one while in the old Convocation house, and another while in the Chappell at Westminster; when all the faith and religion that shall be there canoniz'd, is not sufficient without plain convincement, and the charity of patient instruction to supple the least bruise of conscience, to edifie the meanest Christian, who de-sires to walk in the Spirit, and not in the letter of human trust, for all the number of voices that can be there made; no though *Harry* the 7. himself there, with all his leige tombs about him, should lend them voices from the dead, to swell their number. And if the men be erroneous who appear to be the leading schismaticks, what witholds us but our sloth, our self-will, and distrust in the right cause, that we doe not give them gentle meetings and gentle dismissions, that we debate not and examin the matter throughly with liberall and fre-quent audience; if not for their sakes, yet for our own? seeing no man who hath tasted learning, but will confesse the many waies of profiting by those who not contented with stale receits are able to manage, and set forth new positions to the world. And were they but as the dust and cinders of our feet, so long as in that notion they may yet serve to polish and brighten the armoury of Truth, ev'n for that respect they were not utterly to be cast away. But if they be of those whom God hath fitted for the speciall use of these times with eminent and ample gifts, and those perhaps neither among the Priests, nor among the Pharisees, and we in the hast of a precipitant zeal shall make no distinction, but resolve to stop their mouths, because we fear they come with new and dangerous opinions, as we commonly forejudge them ere we understand them, no lesse then woe to us, while thinking thus to defend the Gospel, we are found the persecutors.

There have bin not a few since the beginning of this Parlament, both of the Presbytery and others who by their unlicenc't books to the contempt of an *Imprimatur* first broke that triple ice clung about our hearts, and taught the people to see day: I hope that none of those were the perswaders to renew upon us this bondage which they themselves have wrought so much good by contemning. But if neither the check that *Moses* gave to young *Joshua,* nor the countermand which our Saviour gave to young *John,* who was so ready to prohibit those whom he thought unlicenc't, be not anough to admonish our Elders how unacceptable to God their testy mood of prohibiting is, if neither their own remembrance what evill hath abounded in the Church by this lett of licencing, and what good they themselves have begun by transgressing it, be not anough, but that they will perswade, and execute the most *Dominican* part of the Inquisition over us, and are already with one foot in the stirrup so active at suppressing, it would be no unequall distribution in the first place to suppresse the suppressors themselves; whom the change of their condition hath puft up, more then their late experience of harder times hath made wise.

And as for regulating the Presse, let no man think to have the honour of advising ye better then your selves have done in that Order publisht next before this, that no book be Printed, unlesse the Printers and the Authors name, or at least the Printers be register'd. Those which otherwise come forth, if they be found mischievous and libellous, the fire and the executioner will be the timeliest and the most effectuall remedy, that mans prevention can use. For this *authentic* Spanish policy of licencing books, if I have said ought, will prove the most unlicenc't book it self within a short while; and was the immediat image of a Star-chamber decree to that purpose made in those very times when that Court did the rest of those her pious works, for which she is now fall'n from

the Starres with *Lucifer*. Whereby ye may guesse what kinde
of State prudence, what love of the people, what care of
Religion, or good manners there was at the contriving, although with singular hypocrisie it pretended to bind books
to their good behaviour. And how it got the upper hand of
your precedent Order so well constituted before, if we may
beleeve those men whose profession gives them cause to enquire most, it may be doubted there was in it the fraud of
some old *patentees* and *monopolizers* in the trade of book-
selling; who under pretence of the poor in their Company not
to be defrauded, and the just retaining of each man his severall copy, which God forbid should be gainsaid, brought
divers glosing colours to the House, which were indeed but
colours, and serving to no end except it be to exercise a su-
periority over their neighbours, men who doe not therefore
labour in an honest profession to which learning is indetted,
that they should be made other mens vassalls. Another end is
thought was aym'd at by some of them in procuring by petition this Order, that having power in their hands, malignant
books might the easier scape abroad, as the event shews.
But of these *Sophisms* and *Elenchs* of marchandize I skill not:
This I know, that errors in a good government and in a bad
are equally almost incident; for what Magistrate may not be
mis-inform'd, and much the sooner, if liberty of Printing be
reduc't into the power of a few? But to redresse willingly and
speedily what hath bin err'd, and in highest autority to esteem
a plain advertisement more then others have done a sumptuous bribe, is a vertue (honour'd Lords and Commons) answerable to Your highest actions, and whereof none can
participat but greatest and wisest men.

¶ Tetrachordon

. . . [*For man to be alone.*] Som would have the sense heerof
to be in respect of procreation only: and *Austin* contests that
manly friendship in all other regards had bin a more becom-
ming solace for *Adam*, then to spend so many secret years in
an empty world with one woman. But our Writers deservedly reject this crabbed opinion; and defend that there is a

peculiar comfort in the maried state besides the genial bed, which no other society affords. No mortall nature can endure either in the actions of Religion, or study of wisdome, without somtime slacking the cords of intense thought and labour: which lest we should think faulty, God himself conceals us not his own recreations before the world was built; *I was,* saith the eternall wisdome, *dayly his delight, playing alwayes before him.* And to him indeed wisdom is as a high towr of pleasure, but to us a steep hill, and we toyling ever about the bottom: he executes with ease the exploits of his omnipotence, as easie as with us it is to will: but no worthy enterprise can be don by us without continuall plodding and wearisomnes to our faint and sensitive abilities. We cannot therefore alwayes be contemplative, or pragmaticall abroad, but have need of som delightfull intermissions, wherin the enlarg'd soul may leav off a while her severe schooling; and like a glad youth in wandring vacancy, may keep her hollidaies to joy and harmles pastime: which as she cannot well doe without company, so in no company so well as where the different sexe in most resembling unlikenes, and most unlike resemblance cannot but please best and be pleas'd in the aptitude of that variety. Wherof lest we should be too timorous, in the aw that our flat sages would form us and dresse us, wisest *Salomon* among his gravest Proverbs countenances a kinde of ravishment and erring fondnes in the entertainment of wedded leisures; and in the Song of Songs, which is generally beleev'd, even in the jolliest expressions to figure the spousals of the Church with Christ, sings of a thousand raptures between those two lovely ones farre on the hither side of carnall enjoyment. . . .

. . . [*What therefore God hath joyned, let no man put asunder.*] But heare the christian prudence lies to consider what God hath joyn'd; shall wee say that God hath joyn'd error, fraud, unfitnesse, wrath, contention, perpetuall lonelinesse, perpetuall discord; what ever lust, or wine, or witchery, threate, or inticement, avarice or ambition hath joyn'd together, faithfull with unfaithfull, christian with antichristian, hate with hate, or hate with love, shall we say this is Gods joyning? . . .

¶ Colasterion

... I have now don that, which for many causes I might
have thought, could not likely have bin my fortune, to bee
put to this under-work of scowring and unrubbishing the low
and sordid ignorance of such a presumptuous lozel. Yet
Hercules had the labour once impos'd upon him to carry
dung out of the *Augean* stable. At any hand I would bee
ridd of him: for I had rather, since the life of man is likn'd to
a Scene, that all my entrances and *exits* might mixe with such
persons only, whose worth erects them and their actions to a
grave and *tragic* deportment, and not to have to doe with
Clowns and Vices. But if a man cannot peaceably walk into
the world, but must bee infested, somtimes at his face, with
dorrs and horsflies, somtimes beneath, with bauling whip-
pets, and shin-barkers, and these to bee set on by plot and
consultation with a *Junto* of Clergy men and Licencers, commended also and rejoyc't in by those whose partiality cannot
yet forgoe old papisticall principles, have I not cause to bee
in such a manner defensive, as may procure mee freedom to
pass more unmolested heerafter by these incumbrances, not
so much regarded for themselvs, as for those who incite
them. And what defence can properly bee us'd in such a despicable encounter as this, but either the flap or the spurn? If
they can afford mee none but a ridiculous adversary, the
blame belongs not to mee, though the whole Dispute bee
strew'd and scatter'd with ridiculous. And if hee have such
an ambition to know no better who are his mates, but among
those needy thoughts, which though his two faculties of
Serving-man and Solliciter, should compound into one mon-
grel, would bee but thin and meager, if in this penury of Soul
hee can bee possible to have the lustiness to think of fame, let
him but send mee how hee calls himself, and I may chance not
fail to endorse him on the back-side of posterity, not a *golden*, but a brazen Asse. Since my fate extorts from mee a
talent of sport, which I had thought to hide in a napkin, hee
shall bee my *Batrachomuomachia*, my *Bavius*, my *Calandrino*,
the common adagy of ignorance and over-weening. Nay perhaps, as the provocation may bee, I may bee driv'n to curle

up this gliding prose into a rough *Sotadic*, that shall rime him into such a condition, as instead of judging good Books to bee burnt by the executioner, hee shall be readier to be his own hangman. Thus much to this *Nuisance*.

But as for the Subject it self which I have writt, and now defend, according as the opposition beares, if any man equal to the matter shall think it appertains him to take in hand this controversy, either excepting against ought writt'n, or perswaded hee can shew better how this question of such moment to bee throughly known may receav a true determination, not leaning on the old and rott'n suggestions wheron it yet leanes, if his intents bee sincere to the public, and shall carry him on without bitternes to the opinion, or to the person dissenting, let him not, I entreate him, guess by the handling, which meritoriously hath bin bestowd on this object of contempt and laughter, that I account it any displeasure don mee to bee contradicted in Print: but as it leads to the attainment of any thing more true, shall esteem it a benefit; and shall know how to return his civility and faire Argument in such a sort, as hee shall confess that to doe so is my choise, and to have don thus was my chance.

¶ The Tenure of Kings and Magistrates

... For Divines, if ye observe them, have thir postures, and thir motions no less expertly, and with no less variety then they that practice feats in the Artillery-ground. Sometimes they seem furiously to march on, and presently march counter; by and by they stand, and then retreat; or if need be can face about, or wheele in a whole body, with that cunning and dexterity as is almost unperceavable; to winde themselves by shifting ground into places of more advantage. And Providence onely must be the drumm, Providence the word of command, that calls them from above, but always to som larger Benefice, or acts them into such or such figures, and promotions. At thir turnes and doublings no men readier; to the right, or to the left; for it is thir turnes which they serve cheifly; heerin only singular; that with them there is no certain hand right or left; but as thir own commodity thinks best to call it. But if there come a truth to be defended, which to them, and thir interest of this world seemes not so profitable, strait these nimble motionists can finde no eev'n leggs to stand upon: and are no more of use to reformation throughly performd, and not superficially, or to the advancement of Truth (which among mortal men is alwaies in her progress) then if on a sudden they were strook maime, and crippl'd. Which the better to conceale, or the more to countnance by a general conformity to thir own limping, they would have *Scripture*, they would have *reason* also made to halt with them for company; and would putt us off with impotent conclusions, lame and shorter then the premises. In this posture they seem to stand with great zeale and confidence on the wall of *Sion;* but like *Jebusites*, not like *Israelites*, or *Levites:* blinde also as well as lame, they discern not *David* from *Adonibezec:* but cry him up for the Lords anointed, whose thumbs and great toes not long before they had cut off upon thir Pulpit cushions. . . .

¶ The readie and easie Way to establish a free Commonwealth

. . . After our Liberty and Religion thus prosperously fought for, gain'd, and many Years possess'd, except in those unhappy Interruptions, which God hath remov'd; now that nothing remains, but in all reason the certain hopes of a speedy and immediat Settlement for ever in a firm and free Commonwealth, for this extoll'd and magnifi'd Nation, regardless both of Honour won, or Deliverances voutsaf't from Heaven, to fall back, or rather to creep back so poorly, as it seems the multitude would, to thir once abjur'd and detested Thraldom of Kingship, to be our selves the slanderers of our own just and religious Deeds, though don by som to covetous and ambitious Ends, yet not therfore to be stain'd with thir Infamy, or they to asperse the Integrity of others; and yet these now by revolting from the Conscience of Deeds well done, both in Church and State, to throw away and forsake, or rather to betray a just and noble Cause for the mixture of bad Men who have ill manag'd and abus'd it, (which had our

Fathers done heretofore, and on the same pretence deserted true Religion, what had long ere this become of our Gospel, and all Protestant Reformation so much intermixt with the Avarice and Ambition of som Reformers?) and by thus relapsing, to verify all the bitter Predictions of our triumphing Enemies, who will now think they wisely discern'd and justly censur'd both us and all our Actions as rash, rebellious, hypocritical and impious, not only argues a strange degenerate Contagion suddenly spread among us, fitted and prepar'd for new Slavery, but will render us a Scorn and Derision to all our Neighbours. And what will they at best say of us, and of the whole *English* Name, but scoffingly, as of that foolish Builder mention'd by our Saviour, who began to build a Tower, and was not able to finish it? Where is this goodly Tower of a Commonwealth, which the *English* boasted they would build to overshadow Kings, and be another *Rome* in the West? The Foundation indeed they laid gallantly, but fell into a wors Confusion, not of Tongues, but of Factions, than those at the Tower of *Babel;* and have left no Memorial of thir Work behind them remaining, but in the common Laughter of *Europe.* Which must needs redound the more to our shame, if we but look on our Neighbours the *United Provinces,* to us inferior in all outward Advantages; who notwithstanding, in the midst of greater Difficulties, couragiously, wisely, constantly went through with the same Work, and are settl'd in all the happy enjoyments of a potent and flourishing Republic to this day.

Besides this, if we return to Kingship, and soon repent, as undoubtedly we shall, when we begin to find the old incroachments coming on by little and little upon our Consciences, which must necessarily proceed from King and Bishop united inseparably in one Interest, we may be forc'd perhaps to fight over again all that we have fought, and spend, over again all that we have spent, but are never like to attain thus far as we are now advanc'd to the recovery of our Freedom, never to have it in possession as we now have it, never to be vouchsaft hereafter the like Mercies and signal Assistances from Heaven in our Cause: if by our ingrateful backsliding we make these fruitless, flying now to regal Concessions from his divine condescensions, and gracious answers to our once importuning Prayers against the Tyranny which we then groan'd under; making vain and viler than dirt, the Blood of so many thousand faithful and valiant *English* men, who left us in this Liberty bought with thir Lives; losing by a strange after-game of Folly, all the battels we have won, together with all *Scotland* as to our Conquest, hereby lost, which never any of our Kings could conquer, all the Treasure we have spent, not that corruptible Treasure only, but that far more precious of all our late miraculous Deliverances; treading back again with lost labour, all our happy steps in the progress of Reformation, and most pitifully depriving our selves the instant fruition of that free Government which we have so dearly purchas'd, a free Commonwealth, not only held by wisest men in all Ages the noblest, the manliest, the equallest, the justest Government, the most agreeable to all due Liberty and proportion'd Equality, both Human, Civil, and Christian, most cherishing to Vertue and true Religion, but also (I may say it with greatest probability) plainly commended, or rather enjoin'd by our Saviour himself, to all Christians, not without remarkable disallowance, and the brand of *Gentilism* upon Kingship. God in much displeasure gave a King to the Israelites, and imputed it a sin to them that they sought one: but *Christ* apparently forbids his Disciples to admit of any such heathenish Government; *The Kings of the Gentiles,* saith he, *exercise Lordship over them;* and they that *exercise Authority upon them are call'd Benefactors: but ye shall not be so; but he that is greatest among you, let him be as the younger; and he that is chief, as he that serveth.* The occasion of these his words was the ambitious desire of *Zebede's* two Sons, to be exalted above thir Brethren in his Kingdom, which they thought was to be ere long upon Earth. That he speaks of Civil Government, is manifest by the former part of the Comparison, which infers the other part to be always in the same kind. And what Government comes nearer to this precept of Christ, than a free Commonwealth; wherin they who are greatest, are perpetual Servants and drudges to the public at thir own cost and charges, neglect thir own Affairs, yet are not elevated above thir Brethren; live soberly in thir Families, walk the Streets as other men, may be spoken to freely, familiarly, friendly, without Adoration? Wheras a

King must be ador'd like a Demigod, with a dissolute and haughty Court about him, of vast expence and Luxury, Masks and Revels, to the debauching of our prime Gentry both Male and Female; not in thir pastimes only, but in earnest, by the loos imployments of Court-service, which will be then thought honorable. There will be a Queen of no less charge; in most likelihood Outlandish and a Papist, besides a Queen-mother such already; together with both thir Courts and numerous Train: then a Royal issue, and ere long severally their sumptuous Courts; to the multiplying of a servil Crew, not of Servants only, but of Nobility and Gentry, bred up then to the hopes not of Publick, but of Court-Offices, to be Stewards, Chamberlains, Ushers, Grooms, even of the Close Stool; and the lower thir minds debas'd with Court-opinions, contrary to all Vertue and Reformation, the haughtier will be thir Pride and Profuseness, We may well remember this not long since at home; or need but look at present into the *French* Court, where Enticements and Preferments daily draw away and pervert the Protestant Nobility. As to the burden of expence, to our cost we shall soon know it; for any good to us deserving to be term'd no better than the vast and lavish price of our subjection, and thir Debauchery, which we are now so greedily cheapning, and would so fain be paying most inconsideratly to a single Person; who for any thing wherin the public really needs him, will have little els to do, but to bestow the eating and drinking of excessive Dainties, to set a pompous face upon the superficial actings of State, to pageant himself up and down in Progress among the perpetual bowing and cringings of an abject People, on either side deifying and adoring him for nothing done that can deserve it. For what can he more than another man? who even in the expression of a late Court-poet, sits only like a great Cypher set to no purpose before a long row of other significant Figures. Nay, it is well and happy for the People if thir King be but a Cypher, being oft times a Mischief, a Pest, a scourge of the Nation, and which is wors, not to be remov'd, not to be controul'd, much less accus'd or brought to punishment, without the danger of a common ruin, without the shaking and almost subversion of the whole Land: wheras in a free Commonwealth, any Governor or chief Counselor offending, may be remov'd and punish'd without the least Commotion. Certainly then that People must needs be mad or strangely infatuated, that build the chief hope of thir common happiness or safety on a single Person; who if he happen to be good, can do no more than another man; if to be bad, hath in his hands to do more evil without check, then millions of other men. The happiness of a Nation must needs be firmest and certainest in a full and free Council of thir own electing, where no single Person, but Reason only sways. And what madness is it for them who might manage nobly thir own Affairs themselves, sluggishly and weakly to devolve all on a single Person; and more like Boys under Age than Men, to commit all to his patronage and disposal, who neither can perform what he undertakes, and yet for undertaking it, though royally paid, will not be thir Servant, but thir Lord? How unmanly must it needs be, to count such a one the breath of our Nostrils, to hang all our felicity on him, all our safety, our well-being, for which if we were aught els but Sluggards or Babies, we need depend on none but God and our own Counsels, our own active Vertue and Industry. *Go to the Ant, thou sluggard,* saith *Solomon; consider her ways, and be wise; which having no Prince, Ruler, or Lord, provides her Meat in the Summer, and gathers her food in the Harvest:* which evidently shews us, that they who think the Nation undon without a King, though they look grave or haughty, have not so much true Spirit and Understanding in them as a Pismire: neither are these diligent Creatures hence concluded to live in lawless anarchy, or that commended, but are set the examples to imprudent and ungovern'd men, of a frugal and self-governing Democraty or Commonwealth; safer and more thriving in the joint Providence and Counsel of many industrious equals, than under the single domination of one imperious Lord. It may be well wonder'd that any Nation stiling themselves free, can suffer any man to pretend Hereditary right over them as thir Lord; when as by acknowledging that Right, they conclude themselves his Servants and his Vassals, and so renounce thir own freedom. Which how a People and thir Leaders especially can do, who have fought so gloriously for Liberty; how they can change thir noble Words and Actions, heretofore so becoming the majesty of a free People, into the base necessity of Court-flatteries and Prostrations, is not only strange and admirable, but lamentable to think on. That a Nation should be so valorous and courageous to win thir Liberty in the Field, and when they have won it, should be so heartless and unwise in thir Councils, as not to know how to use it, value it, what to do with it, or with themselves; but after ten or twelve years prosperous War and contestation with Tyranny, basely and besottedly to run thir Necks again into the Yoke which they have broken, and prostrate all the fruits of thir Victory for naught at the feet of the vanquish'd, besides our loss of Glory, and such an example as Kings or Tyrants never yet had the like to boast of, will be an ignominy if it befal us, that never yet befel any Nation possess'd of thir Liberty; worthy indeed themselves, whatsoever they be, to be for ever slaves; but that part of the Nation which consents not with them, as I perswade me, of a great number, far worthier than by their means to be brought into the same Bondage. Considering these things so plain, so rational, I cannot but yet furder admire on the other side, how any man who hath the true principles of Justice and Religion in him, can presume or take upon him to be a King and Lord over his Brethren, whom he cannot but know whether as Men or Christians, to be for the most part every way equal or superior to himself: how he can display with such Vanity and Ostentation his regal splendor so supereminently above other Mortal men; or being a Christian, can assume such extraordinary Honour and Worship to himself, while the Kingdom of Christ our common King and Lord, is hid to this World, and such *gentilish* imitation forbid in express words by himself to all his Disciples. . . .

. . . But admit, that Monarchy of it self may be convenient to som Nations; yet to us who have thrown it out, receiv'd back again, it cannot but prove pernicious. For Kings to com, never forgetting thir former Ejection, will be sure to fortify and arm themselves sufficiently for the future against all such Attempts hereafter from the People: who shall be then so narrowly watch'd and kept so low, that though they would never so fain, and at the same rate of thir Blood and Treasure, they never shall be able to regain what they now have purchas'd and may enioy, or to free themselves from any

Yoke impos'd upon them: nor will they dare to go about it; utterly disheartn'd for the future, if these thir highest Attempts prove unsuccessful; which will be the Triumph of all Tyrants herafter over any People that shall resist Oppression; and thir Song will then be, to others, how sped the rebellious English? to our Posterity, how sped the Rebels your Fathers? . . .

. . . Yet neither shall we obtain or buy at an easy rate this new gilded Yoke which thus transports us: a new royal Revenue must be found, a new Episcopal; for those are individual: both which being wholy dissipated or bought by privat Persons, or assign'd for Service don, and especially to the Army, cannot be recovered without a general Detriment and Confusion to Mens Estates, or a heavy Imposition on all Mens Purses; Benefit to none, but to the worst and ignoblest sort of Men, whose hope is to be either the Ministers of Court, Riot and Excess, or the Gainers by it: But not to speak more of Losses and extraordinary Levies on our Estates, what will then be the Revenges and Offences remember'd and return'd, not only by the chief Person, but by all his Adherents; Accounts and Reparations that will be requir'd, Suits, Inditements, Inquiries, Discoveries, Complaints, Informations, who knows against whom or how many, though perhaps Neuters, if not to utmost Infliction, yet to Imprisonment, Fines, Banishment, or Molestation; if not these, yet disfavor, discountenance, disregard and contempt on all but the known Royalist or whom he favors, will be plenteous: nor let the new royaliz'd Presbyterians perswade themselves that thir old doings, though now recanted, will be forgotten; whatever Conditions be contriv'd or trusted on. Will they not beleeve this; nor remember the Pacification how it was kept to the *Scots;* how other solemn Promises many a time to us? Let them but now read the diabolical forerunning Libels, the Faces, the Gestures that now appeer foremost and briskest in all public places, as the Harbingers of those that are in expectation to raign over us; let them but hear the Insolencies, the Menaces, the Insultings of our newly animated common Enemies crept lately out of thir Holes, thir Hell, I might say, by the Language of thir infernal Pamphlets, the Spue of every Drunkard, every Ribald; nameless, yet not for want of Licence, but for very shame of thir own vile Persons, not daring to name themselves, while they traduce others by name; and give us to foresee, that they intend to second thir wicked Words, if ever they have Power, with more wicked Deeds. Let our zealous Backsliders forethink now with themselves, how thir Necks yok'd with these Tigers of *Bacchus*, these new Fanatics of not the preaching but the sweating-tub, inspir'd with nothing holier than the Venereal Pox, can draw one way under Monarchy to the establishing of Church Disciplin with these new-disgorg'd Atheisms: yet shall they not have the honor to yoke with these, but shall be yok'd under them; these shall plow on thir backs. And do they among them who are so forward to bring in the single Person, think to be by him trusted or long regarded? So trusted they shall be and so regarded, as by Kings are wont reconcil'd Enemies; neglected and soon after discarded, if not prosecuted for old Traytors; the first Inciters, Beginners, and more than to the third part actors of all that follow'd. . . .

. . . The whole freedom of Man consists either in Spiritual or Civil Liberty. As for Spiritual, who can be at rest, who can enjoy any thing in this World with contentment, who hath not liberty to serve God, and to save his own Soul, according to the best Light which God hath planted in him to that purpose, by the reading of his reveal'd Will, and the guidance of his Holy Spirit? That this is best pleasing to God, and that the whole Protestant Church allows no supream Judg or Rule in Matters of Religion, but the Scriptures; and these to be interpreted by the Scriptures themselves, which necessarily infers Liberty of Conscience; I have heretofore prov'd at large in another Treatise; and might yet furder by the public Declarations, Confessions and Admonitions of whole Churches and States, obvious in all Histories since the Reformation.

This Liberty of Conscience, which above all other things ought to be to all Men dearest and most precious, no Government more inclinable not to favor only, but to protect, than a Free Commonwealth; as being most magnanimous, most fearless and confident of its own fair Proceedings. Wheras Kingship, though looking big, yet indeed most pusillanimous, full of Fears, full of Jealousies, startl'd at every Ombrage, as it hath been observ'd of old to have ever suspected most, and mistrusted them who were in most esteem for Vertue and Generosity of Mind; so it is now known to have most in doubt and suspicion, them who are most reputed to be religious. Queen *Elizabeth*, though her self accounted so good a Protestant, so moderate, so confident of her Subjects Love, would never give way so much as to Presbyterian Reformation in this Land, though once and again besought, as *Camden* relates, but imprison'd and persecuted the very Proposers therof; alleging it as her Mind and Maxim unalterable, that such Reformation would diminish Regal Authority. What Liberty of Conscience can we then expect of others, far wors principl'd from the Cradle, train'd up and govern'd by *Popish* and *Spanish* Counsels, and on such depending hitherto for subsistence? Especially what can this last Parlament expect, who having reviv'd lately and publish'd the Cov'nant, have reingag'd themselves, never to readmit Episcopacy? Which no Son of *Charles* returning, but will most certainly bring back with him, if he regard the last and strictest Charge of his Father, *to persevere in, not the Doctrin only, but Government of the Church of* England; *not to neglect the speedy and effectual suppressing of Errors and Schisms;* among which he accounted Presbytery one of the chief. Or if, notwithstanding that Charge of his Father, he submit to the Cov'nant, how will he keep Faith to us, with Disobedience to him; or regard that Faith given, which must be founded on the breach of that last and solemnest paternal Charge, and the Reluctance, I may say the Antipathy, which is in all Kings against Presbyterian and Independent Discipline? For they hear the Gospel speaking much of Liberty; a word which Monarchy and her Bishops both fear and hate, but a Free Commonwealth both favors and promotes; and not the word only, but the thing it self. But let our Governors beware in time, lest thir hard measure to Liberty of Conscience be found the Rock wheron they shipwrack themselves, as others have don before them in the cours wherin God was directing thir Steerage to a Free Commonwealth; and the abandoning of all those whom they call *Sectaries*, for the detected Falshood and Ambition of som, be a wilful rejection of thir own chief Strength and Interest in the freedom of all Protestant Religion, under what abusive Name soever calumniated.

The other part of our Freedom consists in the Civil Rights and Advancements of every Person according to his Merit: the enjoyment of those never more certain, and the access to these never more open, than in a Free Commonwealth. Both which, in my Opinion, may be best and soonest obtain'd, if every County in the Land were made a kind of subordinate Commonalty or Commonwealth, and one chief Town or more, according as the Shire is in Circuit, made Cities, if they be not so call'd already; where the Nobility and chief Gentry, from a proportionable compass of Territory annex'd to each City, may build Houses or Palaces befitting thir Quality, may bear part in the Government, make thir own Judicial Laws, or use these that are, and execute them by thir own elected Judicatures and Judges without Appeal, in all things of Civil Government between Man and Man: so they shall have Justice in thir own hands, Law executed fully and finally in thir own Counties and Precincts, long wish'd and spoken of, but never yet obtain'd; they shall have none then to blame but themselves, if it be not well administer'd; and fewer Laws to expect or fear from the supreme Autority; or to those that shall be made, of any great concernment to Public Liberty, they may, without much trouble in these Commonalties, or in more General Assemblies call'd to thir Cities from the whole Territory on such occasion, declare and publish thir assent or dissent by Deputies, within a time limited, sent to the Grand Council; yet so as this thir Judgment declar'd, shall submit to the greater number of other Counties or Commonalties, and not avail them to any exemption of themselves, or refusal of Agreement with the rest, as it may in any of the *United Provinces*, being Sovran within it self, oft-times to the great disadvantage of that Union. In these Imployments they may much better than they do now, exercise and fit themselves till thir Lot fall to be chosen into the Grand Council, according as thir Worth and Merit shall be taken notice of by the People. As for Controversies that shall happen between Men of several Counties, they may repair, as they do now, to the Capital City, or any other more commodious, indifferent Place, and equal Judges. And this I find to have been practis'd in the old *Athenian* Commonwealth, reputed the first and ancientest place of Civility in all

Greece: that they had in thir several Cities, a Peculiar; in *Athens*, a common Government; and thir Right, as it befel them, to the Administration of both. They should have here also Schools and Academies at thir own choice, wherin thir Children may be bred up in thir own sight to all Learning and noble Education; not in Grammar only, but in all Liberal Arts and Exercises. This would soon spread much more Knowledg and Civility, yea, Religion, through all parts of the Land, by communicating the natural heat of Government and Culture more distributively to all extreme parts, which now lie num and neglected, would soon make the whole Nation more industrious, more ingenuous at home; more potent, more honourable abroad. To this a Free Commonwealth will easily assent; (nay, the Parlament hath had already som such thing in design) for of all Governments a Commonwealth aims most to make the People flourishing, vertuous, noble and high-spirited. Monarchs will never permit; whose Aim is to make the People wealthy indeed perhaps, and well fleec't, for thir own shearing, and the supply of Regal Prodigality; but otherwise softest, basest, vitiousest, servilest, easiest to be kept under; and not only in Fleece, but in Mind also sheepishest; and will have all the Benches of Judicature annex'd to the Throne, as a Gift of Royal Grace, that we have Justice don us; whenas nothing can be more essential to the freedom of a People, than to have the administration of Justice, and all Publick Ornaments, in thir own Election, and within thir own Bounds, without long travelling or depending on remote Places to obtain thir Right, or any Civil Accomplishment; so it be not supreme, but subordinate to the general Power and Union of the whole Republic. In which happy firmness, as in the Particular above-mention'd, we shall also far exceed the *United Provinces,* by having, not as they (to the retarding and distracting oft-times of thir Counsels or urgentest occasions) many Sov'ranties united in one Commonwealth, but many Commonwealths under one united and entrusted Sov'ranty. And when we have our Forces by Sea and Land, either of a faithful Army, or a setl'd Militia, in our own hands, to the firm establishing of a Free Commonwealth, public Accounts under our own inspection, general Laws and Taxes, with thir Causes in our own

Domestic Suffrages, Judicial Laws, Offices and Ornaments at home in our own ordering and administration, all distinction of Lords and Commoners, that may any way divide or sever the Public Interest, remov'd, what can a perpetual Senat have then, wherin to grow corrupt, wherin to encroach upon us, or usurp? or if they do, wherin to be formidable? Yet if all this avail not to remove the Fear or Envy of a perpetual Sitting, it may be easily provided, to change a third part of them yearly, or every two or three Years, as was above-mention'd; or that it be at those times in the Peoples choice, whether they will change them, or renew thir Power, as they shall find cause.

I have no more to say at present: few words will save us, well consider'd; few and easy things, now seasonably don. But if the People be so affected, as to prostitute Religion and Liberty to the vain and groundless apprehension, that nothing but Kingship can restore Trade, not remembring the frequent Plagues and Pestilences that then wasted this City, such as through God's Mercy we never have felt since; and that Trade flourishes no where more than in the Free Commonwealths of *Italy*, *Germany* and the *Low Countries*, before thir eyes at this day: yet if Trade be grown so craving and importunate through the profuse living of Tradesmen, that nothing can support it, but the luxurious Expences of a Nation upon Trifles or Superfluities; so as if the People generally should betake themselves to Frugality, it might prove a dangerous matter, lest Tradesmen should mutiny for want of Trading; and that therfore we must forgo and set to sale Religion, Liberty, Honor, Safety, all Concernments Divine or Human, to keep up Trading. If, lastly, after all this Light among us, the same Reason shall pass for current, to put our Necks again under Kingship, as was made use of by the *Jews* to return back to *Egypt*, and to the worship of thir Idol Queen, because they falsly imagin'd that they then liv'd in more plenty and prosperity; our Condition is not sound but rotten, both in Religion and all Civil Prudence; and will bring us soon, the way we are marching, to those Calamities which attend always and unavoidably on Luxury, all national Judgments under Forein or Domestic Slavery:

So far we shall be from mending our condition by monarchizing our Government, whatever new Conceit now possesses us. However with all hazard I have ventur'd what I thought my Duty to speak in season, and to forewarn my Country in time; wherin I doubt not but there be many wise Men in all Places and Degrees, but am sorry the Effects of Wisdom are so little seen among us. Many Circumstances and Particulars I could have added in those things wherof I have spoken; but a few main Matters now put speedily in execution, will suffice to recover us, and set all right: And ther will want at no time who are good at Circumstances; but Men who set thir Minds on main Matters, and sufficiently urge them, in these most difficult times I find not many. What I have spoken, is the Language of that which is not call'd amiss *The good Old Cause:* if it seem strange to any, it will not seem more strange, I hope, than convincing to Backsliders. Thus much I should perhaps have said, though I were sure *I* should have spoken only to Trees and Stones; and had none to cry to, but with the Prophet, *O Earth, Earth, Earth!* to tell the very Soil it self, what her perverse Inhabitants are deaf to. Nay, though what I have spoke, should happ'n (which Thou suffer not, who didst create Mankind free; nor Thou next, who didst redeem us from being Servants of Men!) to be the last words of our expiring Liberty. But I trust I shall have spoken Perswasion to abundance of sensible and ingenuous Men; to som perhaps whom God may raise of these Stones to become Children of reviving Liberty; and may reclaim, though they seem now chusing them a Captain back for *Egypt,* to bethink themselves a little, and consider whither they are rushing; to exhort this Torrent also of the People, not to be so impetuous, but to keep thir due Channel; and at length recovering and uniting thir better Resolutions, now that they see already how open and unbounded the insolence and rage is of our common Enemies, to stay these ruinous Proceedings, justly and timely fearing to what a Precipice of Destruction the deluge of this epidemic Madness would hurry us, through the general defection of a misguided and abus'd Multitude.

¶ The History of Britain

... I am now to write of what befell the *Britans* from *fifty and three years before the Birth of our Saviour*, when first the *Romans* came in, till the decay and ceasing of that Empire; a story of much truth, and for the first hundred years and somwhat more, collected without much labour. So many and so prudent were the Writers, which those two, the civilest, and the wisest of *European Nations*, both *Italy* and *Greece*, afforded to the actions of that Puissant Citty. For worthy deeds are not often destitute of worthy relaters: as by a certain Fate great Acts and great Eloquence have most commonly gon hand in hand, equalling and honouring each other in the same Ages. 'Tis true that in obscurest times, by shallow and unskilfull Writers, the indistinct noise of many Battels, and devastations, of many Kingdoms over-run and lost, hath come to our Eares. For what wonder, if in all Ages, Ambition and the love of rapine hath stirr'd up greedy and violent men to bold attempts in wasting and ruining Warrs, which to posterity have left the work of Wild Beasts and Destroyers, rather then the Deeds and Monuments of men and Conquerours. But he whose just and true valour uses the necessity of Warr and Dominion, not to destroy but to prevent destruction, to bring in liberty against Tyrants, Law and Civility among barbarous Nations, knowing that when he Conquers all things else, he cannot Conquer *Time*, or *Detraction*, wisely conscious of this his want, as well as of his worth not to be forgott'n or conceal'd, honours and hath recourse to the aid of Eloquence, his freindliest and best supply; by whose immortal Record his noble deeds, which else were transitory, becoming fixt and durable against the force of Yeares and Generations, he fails not to continue through all Posterity, over *Envy*, *Death*, and *Time*, also victorious. ...

... But at *Cæsars* coming hither, such likeliest were the *Britans*, as the Writers of those times,* and thir own actions represent them; in courage and warlike readiness to take advantage by ambush or sudden onset, not inferiour to the *Romans*, nor *Cassibelan* to *Cæsar*, in Weapons, Armes, and

* *Dion. Mela. Cæsar.*

the skill of Encamping, Embattailing, Fortifying, over-match't; thir Weapons were a short Speare and light Target, a Sword also by thir side, thir fight sometimes in Chariots phang'd at the Axle with Iron Sithes, thir bodies most part naked, only painted with woad in sundrie figures to seeme terrible* as they thought, but poursu'd by Enemies, not nice of thir painting to run into Bogs, worse then *wild Irish* up to the Neck, and there to stay many daies holding a certain mor-sel in thir mouths no bigger then a bean, to suffice hunger;† but that receit, and the temperance it taught, is long since unknown among us: thir Towns and strong holds‡ were spaces of ground fenc't about with a Ditch and great Trees fell'd overthwart each other, thir buildings within were thatch't Houses for themselves and thir Cattell: in peace the Upland Inhabitants besides hunting tended thir flocks and heards, but with little skill of Countrie affaires;§ the makeing of Cheese they commonly knew not, Woole or Flax they spun not, gard'ning and planting many of them knew not; clothing they had none, but what the skins of Beasts afforded them,‖ and that not alwaies; yet gallantrie they had,¶ painting thir own skins with severall Portratures of Beast, Bird, or Flower, *a Vanitie which hath not yet left us, remov'd only from the skin to the skirt behung now with as many colour'd Ribands and gewgawes;* towards the Sea side they till'd the ground and liv'd much after the manner of *Gaules* thir Neighbours, or first Planters:** thir money was brazen pieces or Iron Rings, thir best Merchandise Tin, the rest trifles of Glass, Ivorie and such like,†† yet Gemms and Pearles they had, saith *Mela*, in some Rivers: thir Ships of light timber wickerd with Oysier be-tweene, and coverd over with Leather, serv'd not therefore to tranceport them farr, and thir commodities were fetch't away by Foren Merchants: thir dealing, *saith Diodorus*, plaine and simple without fraude; thir civil Government under many Princes and States,‡‡ not confederate or consulting in common, but mistrustfull, and oft-times warring one with the other, which gave them up one by one an easie Conquest to the *Romans:* thir Religion was governd by a sort of Priests

---

* *Herodian.*   † *Dion.*   ‡ *Cæsar. Strabo.*
§ *Dion. Strabo.*   ‖ *Herodian.*   ¶ *Solinus.*   ** *Cæsar.*
†† *Tacitus, Diodor. Strabo, Lucan.*   ‡‡ *Tacitus. Mela.*

or Magicians call'd *Druides* from the Greek name of an *Oke*, which Tree they had in greate reverence, and the *Missleto* especially growing theron; *Plinie* writes them skill'd in Magic no less then those of *Persia:* by thir abstaining from a Hen, a Hare, and a Goose, from Fish also, *saith Dion,* and thir opinion of the Soules passing after Death into other Bodies,* they may be thought to have studied *Pythagoras;* yet Philosophers I cannot call them, reported men factious and ambitious, contending somtimes about the archpriesthood not without civil Warr† and slaughter; nor restrein'd they the people under them from a lew'd adulterous and incestuous life, ten or twelve men absurdly against nature, possessing one woman as thir common Wife, though of neerest Kin, Mother, Daughter, or Sister; Progenitors not to be glori'd in. . . .

. . . *Suetonius* adding to his Legion other old Officers, and Souldiers thereabout, which gatherd to him, were neer upon ten thousand; and purposing with those not to deferr Battel, had chos'n a place narrow, and not to be overwing'd, on his rear a Wood; being well inform'd that his Enemies were all in Front on a plain unapt for ambush: the Legionaries stood thic in order, impal'd with light armed; the Horse on either Wing. The *Britans* in Companies and Squadrons were every where shouting and swarming, such a multitude as at other time never; no less reckon'd then 200 and 30 thousand, so feirce and confident of Victorie, that thir Wives also came in Waggons to sit and behold the sport, as they made full account of killing *Romans:* a folly doubtless for the serious *Romans* to smile at, as a sure tok'n of prospering that day: a Woeman also was thir Commander in Chief. For *Boadicea* and her Daughters ride about in a Chariot, telling the tall Champions as a great encouragement, that with the *Britans* it was usual for Woemen to be thir Leaders. A deal of other fondness they put into her mouth, not worth recital; how she was lash'd, how her Daughters were handl'd, things worthier silence, retirment, and a Vail, then for a Woeman to repeat, as don to hir own person, or to hear repeated before an host of men. *The Greek Historian*‡ setts her in the field on a high heap of Turves, in a loose-bodied Gown declaming, a Spear in her

* *Cæsar.*   † *Cæsar.*   ‡ *Dion.*

hand, a Hare in her bosome, which after a long circumlocu-
tion she was to let slip among them for lucks sake, then
praying to *Andate the British Goddess*, to talk again as fondly as before. And this they do out of a vanity, hoping to em-
bellish and set out thir Historie with the strangeness of our
manners, not careing in the mean while to brand us with the
rankest note of Barbarism, as if in *Britain* Woemen were Men,
and Men Woemen. I affect not set speeches in a Historie, unless known for certain to have bin so spok'n in effect as they
are writ'n, nor then, unless worth rehearsal; and to invent
such, though eloquently, as some Historians have done, is an
abuse of posteritie, raising, in them that read, other conceptions of those times and persons then were true. Much less
therefore do I purpose heer or elsewhere to Copie out tedious
Orations without decorum, though in thir Authors compos'd
ready to my hand. Hitherto what we have heard of *Cassibelan*,
Togadumnus, *Venusius*, and *Caractacus* hath bin full of
magnanimitie, soberness, and martial skill: but the truth is,
that in this Battel, and whole business, the *Britans* never more
plainly manifested themselves to be right *Barbarians;* no rule,
no foresight, no forecast, experience or estimation, either of
themselves or of thir Enemies; such confusion, such impotence, as seem'd likest not to a Warr, but to the wild hurrey
of a distracted Woeman, with as mad a Crew at her heeles.
Therefore *Suetonius* contemning thir unruly noises, and fierce
looks, heart'ns his men but to stand close a while, and strike
manfully this headless rabble that stood neerest, the rest
would be a purchase, rather then a toil. And so it fell
out; for the Legion, when they saw thir time, bursting out like
a violent wedge, quickly broke and dissipated what oppos'd
them; all else held only out thir necks to the slayer, for thir
own Carts and Waggons were so plac'd by themselves, as left
them but little room to escape between. The *Roman* slew all;
men, women, and the very drawing Horses lay heap'd along
the Field in a gory mixture of slaughter. About fowrscore
thousand *Britans* are said to have bin slain on the place; of
the Enemy scarse 400 and not many more wounded. *Boadicea* poysond her self, or, as others say, sick'n'd and dy'd.
*She was of Stature big and tall, of visage grim and stern

* *Dion.*

harsh of voice, her hair of bright colour flowing down to her hipps; she wore a plighted Garment of divers colours, with a great gold'n Chain; button'd over all a thick robe. *Gildas* calls her the craftie lioness, and leaves an ill fame upon her doeings. *Dion* sets down otherwise the order of this fight, and that the field was not won without much difficultie, nor without intention of the *Britans* to give another Battel, had not the Death of *Boadicea* come betweene. . . .

. . . For *Britan*, to speak a truth not oft'n spok'n, as it is a Land fruitfull enough of men stout and courageous in warr, soe it is naturally not over-fertill of men able to govern justly and prudently in peace, trusting onely in thir Motherwit; who consider not justly, that civility, prudence, love of the Publick good, more then of money or vaine honour, are to this soile in a manner outlandish; grow not here, but in mindes well implanted with solid and elaborat breeding, too impolitic els and rude, if not headstrong and intractable to the industry and vertue either of executing or understanding true Civill Goverment. Valiant indeed, and prosperous to win a field; but to know the end and reason of winning, unjudicious, and unwise: in good or bad succes, alike unteachable. For the Sun, which wee want, ripens wits as well as fruits; and as Wine and Oil are imported to us from abroad, soe must ripe understanding, and many Civill Vertues, be imported into our mindes from Foren Writings, and Examples of best Ages; we shall els miscarry still, and com short in the attempts of any great enterprize. . . .

. . . Thus much through all the South was troubl'd in Religion [A.D. 617], as much were the North parts disquieted through Ambition. For *Ethelfrid* of *Bernicia*, as was touch't before, having thrown *Edwin* out of *Deira*, and join'd that Kingdome to his own, not content to have bereav'd him of his right, whose known vertues and high parts gave cause of suspition to his Enemies, sends Messengers to demand him of *Redwald* King of *East-Angles;* under whose protection, after many years wandring obscurely through all the Iland, he had plac'd his safety. *Redwald*, though having promis'd all defence to *Edwin* as to his suppliant, yet tempted with continual and large offers of gold, and not contemning the puissance of *Ethelfrid*, yeilded at length, either to dispatch him,

or to give him into thir hands:* but earnestly exhorted by
his Wife, not to betray the Faith and inviolable Law of Hos-
pitality and refuge giv'n, preferrs his first promise as the
more Religious, nor only refuses to deliver him; but since War
was thereupon denounc't, determins to be beforehand with
the danger; and with a sudden Army rais'd, surprises *Ethelfrid*, little dreaming an invasion, and in a fight near to the
East-side of the River *Idle*, on the *Mercian* border, now
Nottinghamshire, slaies him,† dissipating easily those few
Forces which he had got to march out over-hastily with him;
who yet as a testimony of his Fortune, not his Valour to be
blam'd, slew first with his own hands, *Reiner* the Kings Son
His two Sons *Oswald*, and *Oswi*, by *Acca*, *Edwins* Sister,
escap'd into *Scotland*. By this Victory, *Redwald* became so
far superior to the other *Saxon* Kings, that *Beda* reck'ns him
the next after *Ella* and *Ethelbert;* who besides this Conquest
of the North, had likewise all on the hitherside *Humber* at
his obedience. He had formerly in *Kent* receav'd Baptism,‡
but coming home and perswaded by his Wife, who still it
seems, was his Chief Counseller to good or bad alike, re-
laps'd into his old Religion; yet not willing to forgoe his
new, thought it not the worst way, lest perhaps he might err
in either, for more assurance to keep them both; and in the
same Temple erected one Altar to Christ, another to his
Idols. But *Edwin*, as with more deliberation he undertook,
and with more sincerity retain'd the Christian profession, so
also in power and extent of dominion far exceeded all before
him; subdueing all, saith *Beda*, English or British, eev'n to
the Iles, then call'd *Mevanian*, *Anglesey*, and *Man;* setl'd in
his Kingdome by *Redwald*, he sought in mariage *Edelburga*,
whom others call *Tate*, the Daughter of *Ethelbert*. To whose
Embassadors, *Eadbald* her Brother made answer, that to
wed thir Daughter to a Pagan, was not the Christian Law.
Edwin repli'd, that to her Religion he would be no hindrance,
which with her whole Houshold she might freely exercise.
And moreover, that if examin'd it were found the better, he
would imbrace it. These ingenuous offers, op'ning so fair a
way to the advancement of truth, are accepted [A.D. 625], and
Paulinus as a spiritual Guardian sent along with the Virgin.

* *Malmsb* l. 1, c. 3.   † *Camden*.   ‡ *Bed.* .2. c. 15.

He being to that purpose made Bishop by *Justus*, omitted no occasion to plant the Gospel in those parts, but with small success, till the next year [A.D. 626], *Cuichelm*, at that time one of the two *West-Saxon* Kings, envious of the greatness which he saw *Edwin* growing up to, sent privily *Eumerus* a hir'd Sword-man to assassin him; who under pretence of doing a message from his Master, with a poison'd Weapon, stabs at *Edwin*, conferring with him in his House, by the River *Derwent* in *Yorkeshire*, on an Easter-day; which *Lilla* one of the Kings Attendants, at the instant perceaving, with a loyalty that stood not then to deliberate, abandon'd his whole body to the blow; which notwithstanding made passage through to the Kings Person, with a wound not to be slighted. The murderer encompass'd now with Swords, and desperate, fore-revenges his own fall with the Death of another, whom his Poinard reach'd home. *Paulinus* omitting no opportunity to win the King from misbeleef, obtain'd at length this promise from him; that if Christ, whom he so magnifi'd, would give him to recover of his wound, and victory of his Enemies who had thus assaulted him, he would then become Christian, in pledge whereof he gave his young Daughter *Eanfled* to be bred up in Religion; who with 12 others of his Family, on the day of *Pentecost* was baptiz'd. And by that time well recover'd of his wound; to punish the Authors of so foul a fact, he went with an Army against the *West-Saxons:* whom having quell'd by War, and of such as had conspir'd against him, put some to Death, others pardon'd, he return'd home victorious, and from that time worship'd no more his Idols, yet ventur'd not rashly into Baptism, but first took care to be instructed rightly, what he learnt, examining and still considering with himself and others, whom he held wisest; though *Boniface* the Pope, by large Letters of exhortation, both to him and his Queen, was not wanting to quicken his beleef. But while he still deferr'd, and his deferring might seem now to have past the maturity of wisedome to a faulty lingring, *Paulinus* by Revelation, as was beleev'd, coming to the knowledge of a secret, which befell him strangly in the time of his troubles, on a certain day went in boldly to him, and laying his right hand on the head of the King, ask'd him if he rememberd what that sign meant; the King trembling, and in a maze riseing up, strait fell at his Feet. Behold, saith *Paulinus*, raising him from the ground; God hath deliver'd you from your Enemies, and giv'n you the Kingdome, as you desir'd: perform now what long since you promis'd him, to receave his Doctrine which I now bring you, and the Faith, which if you accept, shall to your temporal felicity, add Eternal. The promise claim'd of him by *Paulinus*, how and wherefore made, though savouring much of Legend, is thus related. *Redwald*, as we heard before, dazl'd with the gold of *Ethelfrid*, or by his threatning overaw'd, having promis'd to yeild up *Edwin*, one of his faithfull Companions, of which he had some few with him in the Court of *Redwald*, that never shrunk from his adversity, about the first howr of night comes in hast to his Chamber, and calling him forth for better secrecy, reveles to him his danger, offers him his aid to make escape; but that course not approv'd, as seeming dishonourable without more manifest cause to begin distrust towards one who had so long bin his only refuge, the friend departs. *Edwin* left alone without the Palace Gate, full of sadness and perplext thoughts, discerns about the dead of night, a man neither by countnance nor by habit to him known, approaching towards him. Who after salutation, ask'd him why at this howr, when all others were at rest, he alone so sadly sat waking on a cold Stone? *Edwin* not a little misdoubting who he might be, ask'd him again, what his sitting within dores, or without, concern'd him to know? To whom he again, think not that who thou art, or why sitting heer, or what danger hangs over thee, is to me unknown: But what would you promise to that man, who ever would befriend you out of all these troubles, and perswade *Redwald* to the like? All that I am able, answer'd *Edwin*. And he, what if the same man should promise to make you greater then any English King hath bin before you? I should not doubt, quoth *Edwin*, to be answerably gratefull. And what if to all this he would inform you, said the other, in a way to happiness, beyond what any of your Ancestors hath known? would you hark'n to his Counsel? *Edwin* without stopping promis'd he would. And the other laying his right hand on *Edwins* head, when this sign, saith he, shall next befall thee, remember this time of night, and this discourse, to perform what thou hast

promis'd, and with these words disappeering, left *Edwin*
much reviv'd, but not less fill'd with wonder, who this unknown should be. When suddenly the friend who had bin gon
all this while to list'n furder what was like to be decree'd of
Edwin, comes back and joyfully bids him rise to his repose,
for that the Kings mind, though for a while drawn aside, was
now fully resolv'd not only not to betray him, but to defend
him against all Enemies, as he had promis'd. This was said to
be the cause why *Edwin* admonish't by the Bishop of a sign
which had befaln him so strangely, and as he thought so
secretly, arose to him with that reverence and amazement, as
to one sent from Heav'n, to claim that promise of him which
he perceav'd well was due to a Divine power, that had assisted
him in his troubles. To *Paulinus* therefore he makes answer,
that the Christian Beleef he himself ought by promise, and
intended to receave; but would conferr first with his Cheif
Peers and Counsellers, that if they likewise could be won, all
at once might be baptiz'd. They therfore being ask'd in
Counsel what thir opinion was concerning this new Doctrine,
and well perceaving which way the King enclin'd, every one
thereafter shap'd his reply. The Cheif-Preist speaking first,
discover'd an old grudge he had against his Gods, for advancing others in the Kings Favour above him thir Cheif
Preist: another hiding his Court-compliance with a grave
sentence, commended the choise of certain before uncertain,
upon due examination; to like purpose answer'd all the rest
of his Sages, none op'nly dissenting from what was likely to
be the Kings Creed: wheras the preaching of *Paulinus* could
work no such effect upon them, toiling till that time without
success. Whereupon *Edwin* renouncing Heathenism, became Christian: and the Pagan Preist, offring himself freely
to demolish the Altars of his former Gods, made some amends for his teaching to adore them. . . .

. . . Thus representing the state of things in this Iland,
Beda surceas'd to write. Out of whom cheifly hath bin
gatherd, since the *Saxons* arrival, such as hath bin deliverd, a
scatterd story pickt out heer and there, with some trouble
and tedious work from among his many Legends of Visions
and Miracles; toward the latter end so bare of civill matters,
as what can be thence collected may seem a Calendar rather

then a History, tak'n up for the most part with succession of Kings, and computation of years, yet those hard to be reconcil'd with the *Saxon Annals*. Thir actions we read of, were most commonly Wars, but for what cause wag'd, or by what Councells carried on, no care was had to let us know: wherby thir strength and violence we understand, of thir wisedom, reason, or justice, little or nothing, the rest superstition and monastical affectation; Kings one after another leaving thir Kingly Charge, to run thir heads fondly into a Monks Cowle: which leaves us uncertain, whether *Beda* was wanting to his matter, or his matter to him. Yet from hence to the *Danish* Invasion it will be worse with us, destitute of *Beda*. Left only to obscure and blockish Chronicles; whom *Malmsbury*, and *Huntingdon*, (for neither they then we had better Authors of those times) ambitious to adorn the History, make no scruple oft-times, I doubt to interline with conjectures and surmises of thir own: them rather then imitate, I shall choose to represent the truth naked, though as lean as a plain Journal. Yet *William* of *Malmsbury* must be acknowledg'd, both for stile and judgment, to be by far the best Writer of them all: but what labour is to be endur'd turning over Volumes of Rubbish in the rest, *Florence* of *Worster*, *Huntingdon*, *Simeon* of *Durham*, *Hoveden*, *Mathew* of *Westminster*, and many others of obscurer note, with all thir monachisms, is a penance to think. Yet these are our only Registers, transcribers one after another for the most part, and somtimes worthy enough for the things they register. This travail rather then not know at once what may be known of our antient story, sifted from Fables and impertinences, I voluntarily undergo; and to save others, if they please the like unpleasing labour; except those who take pleasure to be all thir life time, rakeing in the Foundations of old Abbies and Cathedrals. . . .

Appendix

ENGLISH VERSIONS OF THE LATIN, GREEK,
AND ITALIAN POEMS

Appendix

FROM THE LATIN

¶ To Charles Diodati

LATE though thy Letter, friend, the Herald sheet
    Brought me thy tones complete—
Brought thine own tones from Deva's western shore,
    Where Chester's stream doth pour
Her hurrying flood into Vergivian brine.   *Lat.* 5
    Trust me, it helps to know
Far Countries bred the Heart that loves me so—
    That faithful mind withal—
Distance yet owes that charming Friend of mine—
    Soon render'd, on recall!
I in this City, which the Thames doth lave
    With brimm'd refluctuant wave,   10
In my dear native home contented dwell,
    Nor reedy Camus' spell,
Nor love of "Rooms" late interdict, doth fret:
    Bare treeless fields, that want
All softening shadows mild, can ne'er enchant
    Muse-votaries, nor yet
Joy I to abide the austere Master's threat   15
    (And more, my mind brooks not!)
If, at my Father's hearth, blithe leisure spent
    Care-free, be banishment,
An outlaw's name and fate I'll not despise,   20
    But to be "banish'd" prize!
Had Tomis' Bard exil'd, who liv'd forlorn
    No heavier trials borne,
His songs had match'd Ionian Homer's lays
    And vanquish'd Virgil's bays!
Here may I dedicate whene'er I chuse,
    Free hours to the quiet Muse: 25

Each book I live by, all my mind inspires;
    Me overply'd, then draws
The rounded theatre's pomp, and all my applause
    The rattling stage requires:
Now gray Rogue—spendthrift Heir—now Suitor sighs—   30
    Now (in Civilian guise)
Soldier—now Counsel, flown with ten-year case,
    In court devoid of grace
Thunders his Norman jargon of the laws:
    Now sly Slave's aidance, lent
To amorous Son, puts hard Sire off the scent,
    Or Maids, new fires that prove,   35
Of love naught knowing, yet—unknowing—love.
    Next, phrenzied Tragedy sways
Her gory wand: wild-hair'd, with rolling eyes,
    I watch her agonize;
For somehow, though my gaze begetteth grief,
    Yet gazing gives relief;
Some bitter sweetness oft my tear allays: 40
    As when, in piteous wise
Yon ill-starr'd youth, his love-dream shatter'd, dies
    Ere tasted Hymen's bliss;
Or when from forth night's shades (the Styx recrost)
    Some dread, avenging ghost
Sounds with death-torch the depth of sin's abyss
    In guilty hearts that lies:
Or Troy's illustrious Line, or Pelops', weep,   45
    Or Kreon's House that met
Of her incestuous sires the monstrous debt.
    Not always home I keep,
Nor City-pent; nor lost for me the flow
    Of Mays that come and go!
A park invites, where elms close-neighb'ring grow,
    And grove's suburban shade   50
Renown'd; where thou shalt mark thee, maid by maid,
    Glide past the virgin quires.
Star-like they shine, forth-breathing softest fires:
    Alas, how oft some charm
I've marvel'd at, that might (as me appears)
    Make Jove forget his years!

Alas, how oft have I seen eyes whose light   55
    Surpass'd the diamond bright,
Or what clear lamps the wheeling Poles convey;
    Necks, too, whose ivory white
Might well outgrace a twice-liv'd Pelops' arm
    (Or ev'n that heavenly "Way",
Which with translucent nectar tinged doth flow)—
    Captiving curve of brow;
Soft-waving locks (the golden-tangled net   60
    That wily Love doth set)—
Allure of cheeks that Hyacinthus' glow
    To tarnish'd turn, and pale
The sheen, Adonis, of thy flower's vermeil!
    Now (tho' oft-sung) give place
Ye demi-goddesses! all Shapes of Love
    That lur'd that gadding Jove:
Tower'd heads of the House of Persia's ancient race;   65
    Dwellers in Susa old,
And Nineveh, great Memnon's Orient Hold!
    Your haughty "Colours" ground,
Greek nymphs and Trojan maids!—and Roman, too:
    Let not with boast undue
Your Bard of that Tarpeian Rock o'erpraise
    His "Pompey's Portico",
Or "stoles Ausonian" that his theatres throng: 70
    The supreme bays belong
To Britain's daughters! Ye outland damsels, thank
    If next to these ye rank!
And London—thou whom Trojan hands did raise—
    Whom crowns, conspicuous far,
That fame of Towers which thy adorning are,
    Rejoice that naught's to show
Of beauty in this pendulous orb below,   75
    But what thy walls surround!
Nor shine more sparkling stars in Heav'n's serene
    About Endymion's Queen
(Ministrant bevies) than, with gold bedight
    And beauty's lovely light,
Those maids that all thy thoroughfares make bright.   80
    Hither came Venus fair

Erstwhile ('tis held), drawn by her yoked pair
    Of doves, while momently
About her flew her quiver'd soldiery;
    For this, from Cnidos turn'd,
And those fair-water'd vales of Simois,
    Ev'n Paphos she—for this—
Ev'n her own spring of Cyprian roses spurn'd!   85
    But while it yet befalls
Cupid is mild, to leave these lucky walls
    (And flee false Circe's halls
Unprais'd!) I mean, holpen by medicine
    Of Moly, plant divine.
'Tis set: to roam o'er Camus' rushy fen
Once more; to face the hoarse School's roar again!   90

Meanwhile, this tribute slight from friend confest
Accept—few words in verse altern comprest.

                      (W. S.)

AT THE AGE OF SEVENTEEN

¶ On the Death of the Bishop of Winchester

DEJECT and dumb, companionless I sate;
And while great woes innumerous smote my breast,
Appear'd the Fantasm of that fatal Pest
Which in this Land Death's goddess wrought of late,
When Death himself with funeral torch of dread
Enter'd our barons' marble-glistering Halls,   *Lat.* 5
And smote their gold and jasper-laden walls,
And with bold sickle struck our nobles dead
On heaps. That Duke I then remembered
Fam'd, with his great ally, whose bones were burn'd
On pyres untimely; I remember'd, too,   10
The heroes that all Belgia from her view
Saw rapt when she for her lost leaders mourn'd.

Yet thee, most noble prelate—thee in chief,
Of thine own Winchester the glory late—   15
I wail'd, and melting into tears of grief,

I sadly thus deplor'd:
O cruel Death, whom next in power we rate
    To Tartarus' dread Lord,
Is't not enow, that at thine anger's blast
    Our Woods must take alarm?
    That in thy danger grows
Each Herb of the field—that Lillies at thy breath
Must shrivel, and the Crocus, and the Rose   20
    (Hallow'd to Venus' charm)
Must wither and decay for thee, O Death?—
    Thee, who forbidden hast
The oak confining with the Stream, for aye
To gaze the clear smooth-sliding watery flow;
    To whom all Fowls that fly,
    (Our wing'd Diviners of the liquid sky)
    Must one and all succumb;
And myriad Beasts that in the dark woods stray,   25
    And Proteus' sea-calves dumb
    That of his caves subsist.
O envious Goddess, wherefore dost thou list—
Thou, with such powers endu'd—thy hands to dye
With human blood? this noble breast to ply
With thy keen shafts unerring, and to chase
As now, this heav'n-born Spirit from his place?

    While, much revolving thus, some tears I shed,   30
From western Ocean dewy Hesperus rose,
And Phoebus that from our far eastern shore
    His course had measur'd o'er,
Had sunk his chariot in the Atlantick wave.   35
    Then in my hollow bed
    Reclin'd, I sought repose,
Till night and sleep begun mine eyes to close:
    Meseemeth that I have
Stray'd hence afar into a fair wide Field,
Whereof no skill, alack! doth me bested
    To tell the things reveal'd.
There the broad champain shines with purple ray,
As hills flush roseate with the dawn of day;   40
And as when all her wealth bright Iris shows,

The ground in many-colour'd livery glows.
Not Flora with more mingled hues and quaint—
Flora, with whom light Zephyr loves to play—
The Gardens of Alcinoüs did paint!
Streams, molten silver, lave those vernant leas,   45
 Whose sands flash costlier gold
Than far-fam'd Tagus' banks Hesperian hold;
Through treasuries of odorous opulence glides
Mild-whispering Favonius, western Breeze
 Whose humid breath abides
Beneath soft leaves of rose innumerous born.
Such was the Palace of the Lord of Morn   50
('Tis fabled) on the extreme Ganges' strand.
 But while I, wonder-strook
At those deep shadows cast by the clustering Vines
 And luminous levels, look,
Clear, on a sudden, in my ken doth stand
The mitr'd Dead! Lo, with what starry light
His glorious visage shines!   55
Sky-robes of downward flow with dazzling white
To his golden sandals sweep. A snowy band
Encompasseth that hallow'd head of his.
While cometh in such habiliment as this
The Venerable Sire, with joyous sound
 Thrills all the flowery ground!
The heavenly host clap all their jewell'd wings,
The loud uplifted Trump of Victory sings   60
In the clear air, as each his new compeer
Salutes with song and close imbracements dear;
While One with peaceful lips doth thus proceed:
Come, Son, partake of happiness always
In this thy Father's Kingdom, and be freed
Henceforth, of all thy long laborious days.

 He spake; and angel bands, on wing upborne,   65
Touch'd their bright harps. But with the night was sped
My golden peace. Since then those dreams I mourn,
With Cephalus' false love, Aurora, fled.
Would that to me such dreams might oft return!

          (W. S.)

¶ On the Death of the Bishop of Ely

MOIST cheeks with weeping stain'd were mine;
Eyes still wet and swoln with brine,
Left by many a falling tear
Which duty shed beside the bier,
While the last sad rites I paid   *Lat.* 5
To Winchester's beloved shade:
When Fame, hundred-tongu'd (beshrew
Her for presage passing true
When she blabs of loss or woe!)
Through rich Britain's towns did go,
Where the sons of Neptune dwell,   10
Scattering the tidings fell
That thou wert by death subdu'd—
By Death and the Iron Sisterhood—
Thou, the glory of our race;
Thou who didst the mitre grace
In the Isle that did (they fame)
Borrow of her Eels her name!   15
Instantly, hot wrath opprest,
Surging high, my troubl'd breast
Till I oft had dedicate
To her tombs the Queen of Fate!
    Ne'er did Ovid's *Ibis* pour
Deeper, direr curse of yore:
Ne'er Archilochus invoke   20
More malisons for troth-plight broke
On Lycambes' perfidy,
And his daughter, false as he!
But while deep cursings fill'd my breath
Devoting Death himself to death,   25
Aw-strook, I heard strange sounds like these
Wafted on the gentle breeze:

    Cease this blind wrath, this glassy spleen,
These blustr'ings vain! Why hast thou been
O'er-rash to flout Celestial Powers
Safe from all assail of ours—   30

Gods o'er-rathe to anger wrought?
Death is not as thou hast thought
(O thou poor deluded wight!)
The sable daughter of old Night;
Nor Erebus', nor Fury's spawn,
Nor was ingender'd ere time's dawn
'Neath Chaos waste; but She from high
Sent down from out the starry sky,   35
The ripen'd sheaves of Jove doth bind,
And from this gross corporeal rind
The prison'd souls of men doth call
To light and airs Celestial;
As when the fleet Hours wake the Day,
Daughters of Jove and Themis they.   40
Before the Eternal Father's face
She cites the dead, but drives apace
The obdurate duly to his doom
In the sad Tartarean gloom
Of Pluto's subterranean Hall.
I with joy obey'd her call,
And with warriors wing'd did speed   45
From sordid fleshly fetters freed,
Jubilant to the starry sphere,
As of yore the aged seer
Rapt on fiery wheels did fly
(With his chariot) to the sky.   50
To me Boötes' wagon bright,
Slow'd with cold, brought no affright;
Not the ugly Scorpion's claws,
Not Orion's sword did cause
My flight to fail! Out-towering clean
The globed sun's resplendent sheen,   55
Far beneath my feet I see
The orb of triple Hecate
What time, as wont, with golden rein
She doth her dragon yoke refrain.
Past the planets rank'd I soar,
Past the Milky Torrent's shore,   60
Admiring oft my new-found rate
Of speed, till to the Olympian Gate

Of Pearl I come, and (rising sheer)
That Crystalline Palace clear,
With emerald y-paven court!—
But here must I to dumb resort;   65
For who of mortal sire begot
Could paint that ever-blissful spot?
Enow it is for me on high
To taste heav'n's joys eternally.   (W. S.)

AT THE AGE OF SEVENTEEN

¶ On the Death of the Cambridge
University Bedell

THOU whose glittering mace's sheen
Pallas' flocks did oft convene,
Spite thy Beadleship art now
By unpitying Death laid low—
(Thus, though "Last of Beadles" hight
His own office doth he slight!)
Though white locks thy temples crown'd,   *Lat.* 5
Snowier than the plumes renown'd
Under which Jove's self (they say)
On a time disguised lay.
Justly, juice Thessalian brew'd
Had procur'd thee youth renew'd,
Justly hadst thou reached the span
Of the years Æsonian;
Justly, Æsculapius' aid
(When so oft a goddess pray'd)   10
Thee had sav'd by Med'cine's skill
From the Stygian waters chill.
When thy Phoebus bade thee all
Ranks array'd in Gown to call—
Thee, his mission'd Herald fleet—
Then wouldst thou, with winged feet
Like Cyllenian Hermes stand
In Troy Hall at Jove's command,

Sent from Heavenly ramparts down;   15
So, for all Achilles' frown,
To him Eurybates addrest
Agamemnon's stern behest.
Then why, O mighty Queen of Graves
(Thou most submiss of Pluto's slaves),
Wilt serve the Muse so ruthlessly?
To Pallas' self so ruthless be?
Why not chuse with thee to dwell
Those who are clods insensible?
Surely such should be the crew   20
Whom thy darts should chief pursue!
Yet, Cambridge, now in garb severe
Mourn thy Dead—his sable bier
Drench with many a falling tear;
And let Elegy complain
In her sweetest saddest strain,
Till her sorrowing Dirge's woe
All thy farthest Schools o'erflow.
                                            (W. S.)

AT THE AGE OF SIXTEEN

¶ On the Death of the Vice-Chancellor,
a Physician

LEARN to Heav'n's decrees to bow,
And pay to Fate your suppliant vow,
Children of Iapetus,
In this round world pendulous
As inhabiters who dwell :   *Lat.* 5
If tear-bringing Death from Hell
Stray'd shall cite you once, what wile,
What demur, will him beguile?
Go ye must to Stygian gloom;
If to combat mortal doom
Man's right arm control'd the force,   10
Turbulent Alcides' corse
Ne'er had been in death laid low
On Emathian Œta's brow,

Poison'd by the Centaur's blood;
Ne'er false Pallas' envious mood
Basely brought all Troy to view
Hector dead: Sarpedon, too,   15
Whom Achilles' "shadow" slew,
Ne'er had fall'n by Locrian brand,
While Jove's self did weeping stand!
If Hecat's spells held Death at bay,
Would not Circe too this day,
Maugre all her infamy,
Dwell yet with Humanity?
And Medea in her hand   20
Brandish yet her potent wand?
Liv'd in herbs that men ignore,
Or in Medicine's skill a store
Of divine efficacy
To foil the Fatal Sisters Three,
Herb-renown'd Machaon ne'er
Had been smitten by the spear
Of Eurypylus, nor should
Cheiron else have been subdu'd
By the shaft anointed o'er   25
With the Hydra's venom'd gore;
Aesculapius, nor to thee
Had the dread artillery
Of thy grandsire spoken doom,
Son, who wast from mother's womb
Untimely ripp'd! And thou whose name
Dims thy master Phoebus' fame,   30
Thou (to whom was given to rule
Over all this Gowned School),
Thou whom our new Delphi now
Mourns with every leafy bough—
Mourneth our new Helicon
Mid her springs—wert living on,
And living wouldst thy days possess
In renown and happiness
O'er Pallas' Flock to bear the sway;
Nor hadst, wandering astray,   35
Fared in Charon's bark to this

Nook of Death's abhorr'd abyss.
But, alack, Persephone
Slit thy thin-spun life when she,
Mov'd with indignation, saw
How many did from Death's dark maw
Thy high skill to save conduce
With those herbs of virtuous juice! 40

Chancellor rever'd, I pray
That thy limbs in quiet may
'Neath our velvet sward repose,
And that from thy grave the rose
And the marigold may grow,
And, with mouth of Tyrian glow,
Hyacinthus' purple cup!
Then, at life's last summing up,
May just Æacus' decree 45
Such compassion show to fhee—
May Proserpin on thee smile
So, from her Sicilian isle,
That among the Blest on high
Where the Fields Elysian lie,
Thou mayst rove eternally. (W. S.)

AT THE AGE OF SEVENTEEN

¶ On the Fifth of November

SCARCE had devout James, come from farthest north,
Begun his reign over this Troyborn folk
And widespread empire of the Albions—
Scarce had the Bond Inviolable join'd
To Scots Caledonia England's sovranty, *Lat.* 5
And scarce had he, Peacemaker, ta'en his throne
In wealth and bliss (secure of foe, secure
Of secret guile), when that fierce tyrant, lord
Of Acheron, fiery torrent, and whom as sire
The Furies own, from Heav'n's Ethereal height
Outlaw'd and vagabond, earth's orb enorm
At random roam'd, the fellows of his crime

Tells o'er, and faithful Followers of his House; 10
Who after divers lamentable deaths
Shall of his Kingdom be participant.
Here in mid-air he kindles tempests dire,
There between friends, of mind unanimous,
Builds hate—for mutual strife arms Warlike Lands;
But those Peace-prosperous, where the olive thrives 15
Subverts, and all that unstain'd virtue love
He (Master of Frauds) fain to his realm would add,
Tempting all hearts to sin impervious.
More, with mute ambush, nets invisible,
He seeks to entrap unwary souls: as when
The Caspian tigress through the wilderness, 20
By moonless night, 'neath drowsily winking stars,
Tracks her scared prey; so stormy Midnight's Lord
Summanus, wreath'd with blue whirlwind of flame
And fume, corrupts whole peoples with their towns.
But now the whitening fields appear, begirt 25
With cliffs wave-echoing round—the country dear
To Neptune, designate of old by name
After his son, who swam the seas and dar'd
With hosting fierce to threat grim Hercules
Before that bitter time of ravaged Troy. 30

When Satan saw this land with feastful peace
And affluence bless'd, and all her fields o'er-teem'd
With Ceres' favours, and (which griev'd him more
Than all) a people worshipping the high
And holy spirit of the One True God—
Then vented he at last such bursting sighs, 35
Tartarean flames, and lurid sulphurous reek
Stench-breeding, as Typhoeus wont of old
(Portentous bulk, by Jove 'neath Etna pent)
Spew forth with noisome gape in Sicily;
His eyes blaze sparks, and like to clatter'd iron,
Or spear-point against spear-point harshly jarr'd,
His adamantine fangs, edge gnash'd on edge,
Grind: This wide world o'er-roam'd, most lamentable 40
One sight I found! This rebel folk alone
Contemptuous of my yoke, for all my wiles

Persist o'erstrong. But if my efforts aught
Avail, they shall not long enjoy exempt
My vengeance and requital : these declared,   45
On pitchy wings he swims the liquid air ;
And wheresoe'er he flies, the trouping winds
Precede his course contrarious, the dense clime
Thickening with glare of thunderbolts frequent.
Soon had he cross'd swift-wing'd the frosty Alp,
Holding the frontiers of Ausonia :
The stormy Appennine sinister lay
Extended, and that antique land Sabine ;   50
Upon his right hand stretcht Etruria, fam'd
For sorceries : thee, Tiber, too, he saw
Give Thetis stealthy kisses. These out-flown,
On Mars-born Romulus' citadel he lit.

Late twilight had renew'd her dubious gleam
Whenas the wearer of the Triple Crown,   55
Encompassing the City, bare aloft
His bread-made gods ; himself, the while, of men
Upshoulder'd high. Before him, supple-kneed,
Went kings, and (endless train) Friars Mendicant,
Wax tapers in their hands (stone-blind they wear
Their lives out, bred in dark Cimmerian night !).   60
The temple reach'd, fair-lit with cressets ranged
(Saint Peter's Eve it was), their thunderous hymns
Re-echoing fill'd the hollow domes and void
Inane : as when the Winegod Bromius howls,
Or Bromius' crew on Cadmean Aracynth,   65
Chaunting their phrenzied rites : with glassy wave
Of clear translucence shock'd Asopus trembles ;
Loud-bellowing Cithaeron, hollow rock, responds.

These rites, at length, in solemn sort perform'd :
Since silent Night had quit the aged arms
Of Erebus, and now with scourge of whip   70
Her chariot-team drave headlong—Typhlos "blind",
Wild "Black-mane" Melanchaetes, Siopë
The "Silent", of infernal sire begot,
And Phrix the "Shudderer", with rough-bristled mane !

Meanwhile, the king-subduer, heir to the realm
Of Phlegeton, his chamber gain'd (nor doth   75
This secret Paramour waste barren nights
Without fair mistress) but he scarce had clos'd
His eyes in peace, when the swart Lord of Shades,
King of the Silent Dead, whose prey is man,
Stood by the couch in lying shape disguis'd;
With counterfeited snows his temples gleam'd;   80
Covered his breast, a long beard pendulous;
With trail of skirt, his gown of ashen gray
Swept to the ground. To rearward of his crown
Smooth-shaven, hung the cowl; and, lest his arts
Should want of aught, a cord of hempen knot
His lusty loins begirt; his lagging feet   85
In openwork of window'd sandals clad.
Ev'n such (the fable runs) went Francis once
Alone in the untrodden wilderness
Among foul lairs of beasts, and though himself
Unsainted yet, unto the sylvan tribes
The saintly message of salvation gave,
And wolves—and e'en the Lybick lions—tam'd.

Mask'd in such garb's disguise, the Serpent sly   90
Insinuating from detestable lips,
Pour'd forth these accents low: Sleep'st thou, my son?—
Thou of the faith forgetful? Thou of thy flock
Oblivious—while thy throne and triple crown
Are scoff'd, O Holy Father, by a race
Barbaric, born beneath the northern skies;   95
For see, how Britain's bowmen spurn thy sway!
Come, rouse thee, rouse from sloth, who art ador'd
Of the Roman Caesar!—thou, for whom the Gates
Of vaulted heaven fly open! Break these spirits
Swelling with wanton pride, and teach them, thou—
These impious ones—what power thy malison hath, 100
O keeper of the Apostolick keys!
Forget not to avenge the shatter'd Fleet
Hesperian, and the Spaniard's ensigns whelm'd
In ocean's gulf, and bodies of the saints
On shameful gallows hang'd, in the late reign

2 B   M.

Of the Amazonian Virgin! But if Thou,
Drowsing on couch of down, wilt spare to crush   105
The waxing power of the foe, full soon will they,
With men-at-arms filling the Tyrrhene Sea
Plant their gay standards on the Aventine;
The reliques of your fathers will they break—
Yea, burn with fire, and soon with foot profane   110
Trample upon the sacred neck of him
Whose shoes ev'n princes once were fain to kiss!
Yet do not these unto the open field
Of war provoke, since fruitless were thy toil.
Spend all thy skill in guile; for is't not right
To stretch for hereticks what nets you will?   115
Lo, their great king now calls to Parliament,
From those far distant shores, his commoners, peers,
Temp'ral and spiritual, in robes of state,
With venerable white locks. These blow to the winds,
Limb-meal and all, into fine ashes blasted
With flame of nitrous powder, introduced   120
Beneath the Chambers where they did convene.
But now first warn whoever faithful be
In England of thy purpos'd deed; for which
Of all thy flock dare contravene thy hest?
Then, while the foe rootbound with sudden fear,   125
Stands stunn'd at this immense calamity,
Let fierce Frank, Spaniard fell, the land invade.
Thus shall the Marian age at last return,
Thou bend the warlike English to thy sway.
Then fear thou nought, but all thy Holy Men
And Women, and all the Powers whom ye extol   130
In solemn festival—propitious know.
Craftily he spake; then, doff'd his garb's disguise,
To joyless Lethe, realm abhorrent, fled.

Now, while the roseate Morn flings open wide
Heav'n's orient portals, and at light's return
Invests the earth with gold, Dawn weeping still   135
Her swart son Memnon and his grievous end:
(Wherefore bedews she with ambrosial tears
The mountain-tops), the Porter of the Gate

Roll'd back Night's pleasing shapes and dreams, and drave
Sleep from the doors of that star-powder'd Hall.

There is a place with everduring gloom
Of darkness wall'd, where huge foundations lie   140
Of massy architecture—ruins vast
Age-old, but now the den of Murder grim
And fork-tongu'd Treachery (both of Discord wild
Whelp'd at one birth): here amid rended rocks
And quarries hewn, inhumate bones of men
And sword-slain corpses lie; here blackmoor Guile   145
Sits ever rolling eyes askance, and Strife
And Calumny, whose jaws are barb'd with stings,
And Phrenzie and Death in thousand forms appear!
Here Fright, here blood-drain'd Horror, flap their wings
About that Spot; here, too, perpetually
The unessential Ghost through mute silence
Howls, and the conscious Earth clots, soak'd with gore!   150
Meanwhile, within the bowels of the Cave,
Her owners, Treachery and Murder, lurk
Shuddering, and—though with none pursuing them
Within that Cave, (Cave whose black Rocks appal,
Shagg'd with Death's shades)—with fearful looks revers'd,
Each his self way, the felon pair take flight.

Babylon's high priest these Roman ruffians hails   155
(Of agelong fealty prov'd), and straight bespeaks:
Far on the western confines of the globe
Dwells 'mid circumfluous seas a folk of me
Abhorr'd, and of wise Nature judg'd unfit
To be conjoin'd at all with world of ours:
Thither, I charge you, swiftly bend your course.   160
Them with Tartarean powder, race accurst
Into thin air both king and princes blow!
But whoso be with loyal ardour fir'd
For the true faith, as parties to your plot
And furtherers executant receive.
He spake; obeyed with warmth the twins severe!   165
But he who doth the slow-bow'd welkin bend
And lightens from his airy citadel,

Looks down, and smiling at the vain attempts
Of men perverse, will now himself protect
His people's cause.

There is a place ('tis said)
From Asia as from fertile Europe far,   170
Looking towards the Mareotick Lake:
Here Fame, the Titans' sister, situate hath
Her Tower exalted, brazen, echoing, broad;
And closelier neighbouring the starry fires
Than Athos or, on Ossa, Pelion piled.
Here stand a thousand gates and porches wide;   175
A thousand windows, and her spacious courts
Gleam through thin walls transpicuous. A throng
Thick-swarming here a confus'd murmur wakes,
Like cluster'd flies that round the milking-pails
Or reed-inwoven sheepcotes buzz and hum
When to the cope of heaven, in sultry hour   180
The Dog-star climbs. Here Fame as mistress sits
(Her Mother's veng'ress) on her pinnacle
Aloft; and all around her lifted head
Innumerous ears prick up, in sort to take
The least of sounds and catch the lightest breath
Whisper'd from the ends of this far-spreading earth;
Nor ever was, O Argus (thou who wert   185
The Heifer's unjust warden), thy harsh mask
Spangled with eyes more numerous—eyes that were
More wakeful than in silent sleep to drowse
(Eyes gazing far and wide all lands below):
With these, forsooth, she useth oft to search
Regions that lack our day—ev'n those that are
To the bright-beaming Sun impenetrable.   190
Thus, all of heard and seen with thousand tongues
Babbling, she poureth forth to whom you will,
O'er-rash; and now with false extenuates true,
Now with trickt speeches truth advantageth.
Yet thou, O Fame, hast of my song deserv'd
Praises for one good deed, than which was ne'er   195
Achiev'd aught worthier for my Muse to sing.
Nor shall I e'er repent to have sung thee, too,

In epic strain. We English, by thy means
Defended, render thee thanksgivings due,
O fickle goddess! For to thee did Jove,
Who rules the forces of the eternal fires—
His previous bolt dispatch'd, while Earth yet shook,   200
Address these words: And art thou silent, Fame?
Or hath that impious band of Papists who
Against me and my Britons have conspir'd,
Escap'd thee quite, with that unheard of slaughter
Plann'd for the sceptr'd James? Thus far he spake.
Fame heard forthwith the Thunderer's behest;
And, though so swift before, she now put on   205
Loud-buzzing wings—put on her slender form
To deck, new plumage pied—then in right hand
Her trump Calabrian bronze sonorous took,
And oar'd with spreaded vans the buxom air.
Nor was't enough that she should thus prevent
The flying clouds, but now outstript the winds
Themselves, and now the horses of the sun: 210
Dark sayings she through Englands' cities first
And obscure whisperings spreads (her wont), and then
With shrilling voice forth-publisheth the guile
And whole abhorrent plot of Treachery.
Nor deeds alone—dire deeds to tell!—reveals
But naming authors of the crime, holds not   215
Her peace—divulges ambush laid in nooks
Obscure! Aghast to hear such rumours, youths
And maidens too, and seniors worn with eld,
Gasp, and all ages to the heart at once
Are pierced with sense of universal Wrack!
Meanwhile the heav'nly Power Ethereal, mov'd   220
With pity for his people, hath frustrate
The Papists' savage and audacious acts:
They straight captiv'd, are hal'd to pains condign;
But unto God are thankful hymns of praise
And duteous incense paid. With genial fires
Of joy the cross-roads smoke; where thronging youth   225
Tumultuous dance—nor lives in all the year,
A day than Fifth November more renown'd!

                                        (W. S.)

¶ On the Gunpowder Plot

WHEN thou of late didst heinous wrong intend,
Perfidious Fawkes! 'gainst Britain's Chiefs and Throne,
Schemer, say true, was this not sure thine end?
Gentle to seem in part, thy crime to atone
With impious piety; despatching so
Thy victims swift to Heav'n's high courts sublime
In sulphurous car on whirling wheels aglow?
Even as that fam'd seer in antique time,
From savage Fates secure, who, whirlwind-borne,
Left Jordan's fields to seek the realms of morn.

(A. V.)

¶ On the same

GREAT Beast that 'mong the Seven Hills dost hide—
Did thine attempt by such a road ensue
To have offer'd James to Heav'n? If naught beside
Thy Beast-Head hath of better off'ring due,
Withhold, I pray, thy gifts of purpose fell.
Lo! full of years 'mid his star-fellows bright
Spurning thine aid our King hath soar'd to dwell,
Nor needs infernal dust to speed his flight.
Therefore, withhold; and to the Heav'ns amain
Send rather up thy hoods accurst and vile
And every brutish god whom Rome profane
Enshrines; for if by such or other guile
Thou help them not, trust well my word, they ne'er
Shall tread the steep path to Celestial air.

(A. V.)

¶ On the same

KING James made mock of purgatorial fire;
Which if foregone, th' abodes of those on high
No spirit of man receive: with gnashings dire
The Roman monster triple-crown'd gave cry,

Shaking his tenfold horns in horrid threat—
Briton, thou mayst not unaveng'd despise
That which We sacred hold. Shalt pay thy debt
For holy things disdain'd; so to the skies
If e'er thou enter in, those domes bestarr'd
By paths of mournful flame shall be achiev'd.
Oh, how nigh fun'ral truth, prophetic bard,
Thou sangst, how nigh the grave event conceiv'd
Thy words; for nether fires his shade almost
Upwhirl'd, consum'd, to join th' ethereal host.

(A. V.)

¶ On the same

WHOM, late, Rome impious vow'd to vengeance dread,
And unto Styx and Taenarus promisèd,
Him now toward starry spheres perverse doth she
Yearn to raise up 'mid Heav'n's high company.

(A. V.)

¶ On the Inventor of Gunpowder

OLD times—unwitting—sang Prometheus praise,
From Phœbus' coach who reft th'ethereal blaze;
Yet mightier far, meseems, who stole (they tell)
Own Jove's thrice-forkèd bolt and arms of Hell.

(A. V.)

AT THE AGE OF EIGHTEEN

¶ To Thomas Young

(His tutor: now performing the duties of "Pastor" to the English
Merchants of Hamburg.)

SPEED, letter, speed the measureless Ocean o'er!
　　Go seek the Land Almain
　　Across the smooth sea-floor:

Break off dull sloth and may
Nought check thy going, or thy haste delay!   *Lat.* 5
I, on my part, will Æolus invoke
(Where he, in Sicilian dungeon, doth refrain
The winds) the greenhair'd gods, and (azurn Queen)
    Doris, with all her train
      Of nymphs through their domain
    To grant thee passage fair.
But get thee, if thou canst, such fleet-wing'd yoke   10
As once from Jason's sight Medea bare,
Or young Triptolemus their happiness
Brought from Eleusis Scythia's shores to bless.
Then when Almannia's tawny sands appear,
To wealthy Hamburgh's walls thy footsteps steer—
    She (as her name doth show)   15
From murder'd Hama hath her title ta'en:
    (Whom Dansker mace laid low).
A prelate dwells there prais'd that doth exceed
In antique piety, Christ's flock to feed.
Of more than half my heart by him bereft,   20
Lo, I with this divided half am left!
Ah, look what seas, what mountains intervene
My other dearer self and me between!
Dearer to me than thou, O Socrates
(Most learn'd of Greeks), to Alcibiades
(The son of Clinias he, fam'd Ajax' breed)—
Than great Stagirite sage to Philip's heir   25
(The lofty-soul'd) whom erst Olympias bare
    Of Lybian Jove the seed!—
Than Phoenix, or than Cheiron, half-divine,
To stern Achilles' heart—is he to mine.
With him to guide my steps, I first assay'd
The Muses' secret bowers and hallow'd mount,   30
The Clov'n Parnassus' sward; Pieria's fount
Drain'd deep, and thrice my joyful brow allay'd,
While Clio smil'd, with Castaly's pure wine.

But flaming Aethon thrice the Ram had spy'd,
And thrice his fleecy back with gold had dy'd,
Twice thy new verdure, Flora, had o'er-spread   35

Old Earth, and twice had winds autumnal shed
    Thy wealth; nor might I feast
Mine eyes upon his countenance—mine ear
    Drink in his accents dear!
Go, vie in speed with the loud-roaring East;
So shall appear the strong necessity   40
    That my behests alledge.
Him shalt thou find by his sweet spouse to sit,
With children nurs'd on knee (love's darling pledge!)
Turning some early Father's volume vast,
    Or Book of Holy Writ,   45
On tender minds Celestial dew to shed
(Redemptive task of high sublimity!)
Next, give him greetings warm (as love once led),
Saying what would grace thy master, were he by.
Then, with thine eyelids something downward cast
And lips compos'd to shamefast gravity,   50
    Forget not thou my plea
To urge: These words (if the mild Muse mid foes
    Warring may interpose)
By faithful hand from England's shore were sent;
O'erdue, I sue: take greetings warmly meant—
If late, the warmer welcome may they have,   55
As was the kiss laggard Ulysses gave
O'erdue, but true, to chaste Penelope.

But how could I of this just charge be quit,
Which I the offender can no way condone?
Prov'd justly Loiterer—I that fault admit;
Asham'd, agree my duty all undone.   60
Then wilt thou not forgive, when I avow
My guilt (which, "own'd to", "half-aton'd" may grow):
Mild o'er scared victims will the lion pause,
    Nor part his yawning jaws;
Nor tear them prone with lacerating claws.
Oft, too, the Thracian bandite fierce, that bare   65
The Northern lance, would melt at suppliant's prayer,
And hands uplift avert the thunderstone—
    So too, might haply one
Slight offering, when the gods are wroth, atone.

Long purpos'd I to write, but now my will   70
(Love suffering not) would further loitering blame
        For in mine ear vague Fame
Hath nois'd, alack!—herald too sure of ill—
That in thy neighb'ring countries war doth flame;
That whilst a barbarous soldiery surround
Thee and thy city, Saxon chiefs have found   75
Arms; that Bellona devastates the plain
And gore bedews the corpse-sown fields like rain:
Since Thracia now to Germany concedes
The native God of Battles that she breeds,
And thitherward Mars drives his Thracian steeds.
The olive, that did hitherto upshoot,
        Now loseth flower and fruit;   80
And Peace, that loathes the brazen trump of War,
        Is fled from earth afar—
Is fled—ah, then, that "Justest Maid" who pass'd
Heav'nward, was not (as men misdeem'd) "the Last"!
But while war's horrors roaring round thee swell
        Thou dost unfriended dwell,
Poor, among strangers, seeking means to live—   85
Means thine own native country ne'er did give.

O Mother Land, inhospitable Home.
Sterner than are the white cliffs of thine Isle
        That break the seas in foam,
        Why ruthlessly exile
(O Iron-Heart!) sons that are void of guile   90
To seek in outland coasts the bread they lack:
        Sons by Jove's foresight sent
To bring from heav'n glad tidings of content,
And teach how leads, through death, the starward track?
Wert not in Stygian darkness rightly pent   95
To die of thy pin'd soul's eternal dearth?
Ev'n so the Thisbite Seer the wilds of earth
And rugged wastes of Araby must tread   100
With unaccustom'd foot, when Ahab's hand
He fled and thine Phenician Fury-queen!
Cilician Paul so, from Philippi bann'd,
Tortur'd and torn by shrieking scourges, bled

Whenas he forth was led;
Suffer'd so He who was of Life the Lord,
What time to leave their coasts it was implor'd
By those ingrateful fishers Gadarene.   105

Hope, then, and shun despair, though cares beset;
Nor let thy shuddering frame grow pale with fright.
What though thou be with glittering swords begirt,
And though a thousand darts destruction threat,
Yet none shall e'er thy side unharnest hurt,
Nor with thy spouting blood one blade be wet.   110
Jehovah's self, with fulgent buckler bright,
Shall 'neath his wings defend, and for thee fight:
Ev'n He who smote the Assyrian host at deep
     Midnight 'neath Sion's Keep,
Routed the army that Damascus hoar   115
From age-old fields did on Samaria pour;
Who the mass'd cohorts, with their fearful king,
With terrours whelm'd—clarions, that seem'd to sing
In empty air!—through rolling dust amain
Drum the reverberant hooves that trample the plain!
The desert sands their jumping chariots jar!   120
Their prancing horses neigh to meet the war
Mid clatter'd iron and deep-breath'd groans of pain!

Hope, then—for with the unluckiest Hope may dwell—
With that high courage all thy troubles quell,
     Nor hold incredible   125
That happier years are yet upstor'd for thee,
And thou once more thy native hearth shalt see.

                                                (W. S.)

¶ In My Nineteenth Year

MILD goddess of the Amathusian Shrine,
     Ere learnt love's laws of thee—
     Of Paphian fires heart-free—
     I scoff'd Love's darts as toys
     Befitting none but boys,
And scorn'd, O mightiest Love, thy power divine!

Go, child (I cried), go shoot thy turtles tame—   *Lat.* 5
Mild warfare should so young Commander need!
Go, boy, thy high triumphs o'er sparrows lead:
Worthy such warlike trophies were to suit
  Thy martial ardour's bruit;
But at mankind why those weak weapons aim?
Thy quiver the strength of man could n'er exceed.   10

  This Cupid could not brook
(Readier than he no god to anger took);
With double heat his cruel heart 'gan flame.

'Twas Spring, and o'er the farmhouse roofs the light
Streaming had usher'd in the first of May;   15
But still mine eyes sought the retreating Night,
Unable to sustain the blaze of Day.
Suddenly, with painted wings, my couch anigh
Stood tireless Love: whose softly threat'ning eye,
His quiver a-swing, his mien (with all that may
Adorn the boy, or Love) the god betray!   20
  So, in Heav'n's halls divine,
Young Trojan Ganymede full-mix'd the wine
I' the cup of amorous Jove; so Hylas, son
Of the Dryop King, rapt by a Naiad, won
The beauteous nymphs his kisses to receive.
But Cupid added wrath (you would believe   25
It well became him!): added, too, withal,
  Harsh threatenings mixt with gall.
Wretch! (quoth he) 'twould have cost thee far less pain
  From others' fate to learn;
  But now shalt thou in turn
Bear witness to the weight of my right hand,
  And be among the band
Enroll'd who of its powers expert, complain: 30
Thus to thy cost shall I much credit gain.
'Twas I myself (what if thou dost not know?)
  Who laid proud Phoebus low—
Elate, from Python conquest, yet to me
  He yielded victory!
On Daphne thinking, he will oft confess

My darts more sure, and of more deadliness,
Than his. The Parthian vanquishes by flight,   35
In drawing bow, yet ne'er can pass my sleight.
To me the Cretan hunter yields, and he
Who ambush'd Procris slew unweetingly;
Giant Orion was by me o'erthrown;
Hercules' Arm by me; by me the Friend
Of Hercules. Though Jove his thunderstone   40
Against me whirl, yet every shaft I send
    Shall pierce Jove's side to the bone.
If further doubts remain, my schooling dart
Shall teach thee rather (tho' to hit thy heart
    In no light mood I try);   45
For neither may thy Muses thee defend
Unwise, nor Phoebus' serpent succour bring!
He spake, his gold-barb'd arrow brandishing,
And to the warm bosom of Venus flew.
Yet, as those thunderous words at me he threw,
I all but laugh'd, nor fear o' the stripling knew.   50

    But now those quarters of the town delight
Where Londoners expatiate, and now
The neighb'ring country hamlets me invite.
A crowd, a radiant crowd, that seem to show
Like goddesses, are passing to and fro;
Who make the day with double splendour glow.   55
Am I deceived, or doth their borrow'd sheen
    Make Phoebus' self more bright?
I fled not sternly from that pleasant scene
Averse, but walk'd where bent of youth might lead,
Letting my eyes meet theirs with little heed—
Nor from their gaze might I withdraw mine own!   60
One that outshin'd them all, I there beheld
    (That first of days did I
Count the beginning of this malady!):
Venus return'd to earth, such charms had shown;
Or Juno, that as Queen of Heaven excell'd   65
    In grace unparallel'd.
This maid sly Cupid, heedful of his wrath,
    Cast fairly in my path;

By him alone that snare for me was plann'd.
Then lurk'd he to waylay me near the track,
    Full-quiver'd. At his back
There swung the burden of his mighty brand.
Next clung the rogue suddenly to each lid
Of the maiden's eyes; then to her mouth: now slid
Her very lips between; now shelt'ring hid   70
In a dimpled cheek: and thence where'er he stray'd
Wandering at large, the limber bowman made
A thousand wounds in my unguarded breast.
At once strange fevers new my heart infest;
    Love's fires through all my frame
Storm'd, and I grew one universal Flame.
But while I yet more sorrowful became,
She who alone could peace of mind restore,   75
Was rapt from vision—to be seen no more!

    Stunn'd—silent, sad, half-wishful of return—
      I go, but rent in twain—
      The body doth remain;
The soul to follow her desire doth yearn!
Joys rapt so rathe 'tis balm indeed to weep;   80
So Juno's son, hurl'd from the heavenly steep
'Mid Lemnian hearths, Olympus' loss did mourn;
    So, on the sinking sun
Amphiaraus look'd his last, when borne
To Hades by his startled steeds. Undone   85
And whelm'd in woe, which course shall I pursue?
    How hope the love begun
To fly, or follow? Ah, could I behold
For one brief moment her dear countenance—
Yea, hold converse in words (sad words, is true!)
Unless of stubborn adamantine mould,
She, to my prayers might not be deaf, perchance!   90
Sure none e'er wasted with unluckier fire,
Whose first (and sole) example be I known!
Then spare me, O winged god of soft desire,
    Nor let thy deeds be shown
Conflicting with thine office! Now, O son
Of Venus, now with terrours huge I see   95

Thy bow! O thou who dost in potency
Of bolts and burning brand alike agree,
Henceforth mine offerings shall smoke upon
Thine altars! Thou alone I vow for me
Ever supreme of all the gods shalt be!
Then lastly from this passion set me free—
Nay, free me not, since (though I know not why)   100
Some sweetness blends with lover's misery.
So prosper thou this single orison:
Whatever Fair be destin'd mine to be
One shaft may pierce both hearts, and make us one.

Epilogue

Vain trophies these of idleness that I
With care low-thoughted and perverse of mind,
Erected. 'Twas mine own delusion blind
    That drave my steps awry,
And youth, ungovern'd, evil schooling gave;
Till from her shady bowers the Academy   *Lat.* 5
Proffer'd cool streams of the Socratick wave,
And taught me to unlearn the yoke I tried;
At once, for aye, the flames of passion died!
Arm'd as with solid ice, my breast congeals.
Fear lest his shafts should freeze, young Cupid feels;
And lovely Venus dreads to find indeed   10
In me the vehemence of Diomede!

                              (W. S.)

¶ Nature Not Impaired by Time

AH, how self-wearied, droops man's wandering Mind,
By incessant errors torn, that wrap his breast
In palpable obscure: a night as blind
As that of Oedipus! Precipitant
Unwisdom drives her by her own deeds to test
The deeds of Heav'n; her own edicts to hold
Equal to laws of old
Engraven on unwasting adamant,   *Lat.* 5
Limiting Fate's plan—which Time's dissolve defies—
To her own volant hour that passing dies.

Shall Nature's face, then, drawn to spare and dry,
Gloom wrinkle-furrow'd? She of whom were born
All things, our general Mother—need to mourn   10
The wither'd womb of age? Confessing eld,
Shall she that went with starry head upheld,
Pace with slow steps irresolute, tremulously?
Shall foul antiquity, or famin'd maw
Of years eterne, with rust and draff they draw
Afflict the stars? Or shall insatiate Time
Greedily ingorging his own Sire sublime,   15
Devour whole Heav'n? Could Jove improvident
Have fortified his strongholds, to prevent
Such sacrilege, and, from Time's ravage freed,
Their courses everlasting have decreed?
Else, time shall be when Heav'n's high-storey'd floor
Must lapse, down-ruining with outrageous roar!
When, with that shock convuls'd, both poles withal   20
Will grate harsh thunder, and from his highbuilt Hall
Olympian Jove will fall—
With Pallas too, bearing her shield of dread
(That unmaskt horror of the Gorgon's head)
As once fell Vulcan, thrown
In headlong rout from heav'n's high grundsel down
To Lemnos! Then (O Phoebus) wilt thou vie   25
With thine own son, perdition—hurl'd from the sky
In swift careering chariot precipitously!
Then ocean, when thy lamp extinguish'd is,
Shall smoke, and from his wondering waves a hiss
Of sound sinister rise!
Then aëry Haemus' Top shall split, till flies
His firm-set base asunder—the whole Hill-chain
Acroceraunian missive flung amain
Clash justling in the bottomless abyss,   30
Affrighting Stygian Dis—
(Ev'n Dis, who had us'd them erst for warfare rude
'Gainst the high gods in that fraternal feud)!
    Nay, the Almighty Father, on the sum
Of things consulting, more securely bas'd
The constellations, and unerring plac'd   35
In poise the Scales of Fate adjusted plumb!

To move in supreme order thus, He taught
All things that are, each to perpetuate
Eternally his course predestinate:
Thus is the Prime Wheel of Creation brought
To turn in course diurnal and to steer
With link'd revolve each softly rolling sphere;
Thus Saturn's motion slacks not, nor less bright
Gleams with red glare malign, Mars' armed casque;   40
In fadeless bloom, too, doth young Phoebus burn—
No need his Chariot slope, for Earth to bask
Her vales o'er-teem'd, since he with friendly light
Through the same sphere-borne signs shall aye return!
Still riseth fair from odorous India's side,   45
The Star that on Olympus' snowy height
His skyey flocks doth shepherd, with the morn
Calling them home, but leading them at eve
To pasture in the skies (Time's realms receive
Hence the twin hues that Day from Night divide);
Still bright Diana's alternating horn
Waxes and wanes, her arms expanded wide   50
Encompassing the empyrean blue;
And still the Elements their pact keep true;
Still the red Lightning with accustom'd roar
Shatters the rocky shore.
Harsh-voiced as e'er, the wild North-west to-day
Tempests the void; with cold as keen the North—
The bitter North—scourgeth nigh-hand to flay
The harnest Scythian,
And rolls the clouds and breathes whole winter forth!   55
Still too the Sea-King cleaves Sicilian
Pelorus' foot; still, o'er wide waters, swell
The hollow roarings of his herald's shell.
Nor do the Balearick "Whales" now bear
Upon their backs Aegaeon's bulk, to spare
Of size enormous grown!
Nor is thy primal age's vigour flown,   60
O Earth,—his fragrance yet Narcissus keeps;—
Yet he whom Phoebus weeps,
And Venus' favourite comely are as aye!
Ne'er too did shamefast Earth more treasures hold—

Gems under sea, 'neath hills her baneful gold!   65
Thus changeless shall endure, most justly true
This Order of the World, time's end unto—
Then the Last Day's conflagrance Earth shall waste,
From Pole to pole, with Heav'ns huge vault embrac'd,
And all this Universal Frame entire
Flame, as on one stupendous funeral Pyre.   (W. S.)

¶ Plato's *Ideas*
(As Criticized by Aristotle)

DECLARE, O mighty Goddess Powers,
Presiding o'er the Sacred Bowers,
And thou (yclept Mnemosyne)
Blest Mother of the Deity
Ninefold, and thou who in some deep
Far Cave, reclin'd at ease, dost keep
Jove's Records and his fix'd Decrees,
Archives and high solemnities—   *Lat.* 5
(Thou who art hight "Eternity"!)
Declare, who First of All was he
Whom skilful Nature chose as Plan
And Pattern for the race of Man.
    Eterne—Unwasting—with the Skies
Coeval—and (by contraries)
One—Universal—he, 'tis said,
In God's similitude was made!   10
(Sure, Pallas Maid had ne'er such twin,
That dwelt unborn Jove's brain within)—
Whose general nature, shared with all,
Is special, individual!
While strange to say his separate place
Shrinks to one single spot of space!   15
Chance he may rove the ten-spher'd heights,
Companion of the Eternal Lights,
Or in yon orbed Moon abide
That sticks so close our Earth beside;
Or on forgetful Lethe's banks
Sit listlessly amid the ranks

Of souls that wait imbodiment—
Or whether (if 'tis rather meant!)
Some far sequester'd shore upon   20
Of this our World, he stalks alone,
Man's archetype, with Titan stride
And head upheav'd, as who defied
The gods—of more majestick size
Than Atlas, Shoulderer of the Skies!
　　Of none like him the Theban seer
Whose outward blindness made more clear
His mind's deep vision, e'er had sight   25
And none like him at dead of night
Did Hermes of the winged heel
To his sagacious seers reveal!
Of none like him was rumour least
E'er known to the Assyrian Priest
Who erst of antique Belus told,
And long descent of Ninus old,
And great Osiris, glorious name!   30
Nor yet, though triply crown'd with fame,
Did thrice-great Hermes, Mystick wise,
His like to Isis' priests devise.
Then thou, fam'd Star of Academe   35
Perennial, who wert first to dream
And, in thy Schools, such Marvels spread,
Wilt not now leave unrespited
Thy banish'd Bards, or (since art shown
Greatest of all the Fablers known)
Though Founder of thy State, be sent
Thyself, like them, to banishment!
　　　　　　　　　　　　　　　(W. S.)

AT THE AGE OF TWENTY

¶ On the Approach of Spring

Look, how revolving Time's perpetual round
Fresh zephyrs yet with glowing Spring renews:
Look how, her transient youth resum'd, the ground
From frost unfetter'd, wears her tenderest green!
Err I, or doth new strength inform my Muse,   *Lat.* 5
And are her powers refresh'd the gift of Spring?

'Tis by Spring's gift that she restor'd hath been.
Admire who will, some novel task she'd seek;
Since ever in mine eyes' imagining,
Float Castaly and Clov'n Parnassus' peak,   10
Whence nightly dreams to me Peirene bring.
Hot grows my heart, stirr'd by a force unseen,
And hallow'd sounds impel my raptur'd mind.
Apollo comes—Behold those locks entwin'd
With Daphnian bays—'tis Phoebus' self I see!
    Slipt now from the body free   15
My spirit, rapt to lofts of liquid sky,
Hovereth where the gadding clouds go by;
Anon, through caves of gloomy shade she hies
(The Bards' remote sequester'd sanctuaries),
    Till op'd each secret shrine
    Of Heav'n, I may divine
Whate'er shall hap in all her boundaries;—
Nor do blind Tartarus' gulfs escape mine eyes!

    From parted lips what loftier accents flow?
What birth portends this rapturous holy fire?
What but that Spring which did my mind inspire,
To her own bounty shall her praises owe?

O Philomel, who from thy close-rooft house   25
Of leaves fresh-budded, leadest trill on trill,
    When all the woods are still,
Let us begin—thou perch'd mid forest boughs;
    I city-pent—to sing
As one the charms of new-arrived Spring.
Hail! 'tis again Spring's turn! Her praise awake;   30
And may the Muse this task perennial make!
The sun, with golden reins turn'd northward, flees
The Ethiopians and Tithonus' leas:
Brief grows Night's path—brief pause of Darkness deep
What time mid horrid shades she dwells immur'd:—
The northern Wagoner which erst endur'd   35
The swink of lengthier course, the Wain pursues
Tireless; few grow the watchful fires that use
Their vigil round the courts of Jove to keep,

Since with retreat of Night
Murder and Guile and Rapine take their flight;   40
Nor do the Gods now fear the Giants' spite!

Haply, on lofty crag, some shepherd swain
Reclin'd, while blush Earth's dews with Break of Day,
Shall have to Phoebus said:
Phoebus, this night—this very night—didst lack
That maid of thine whose wont was to restrain
  Thy swift careering steeds.
How eagerly, with quiver at her back,   45
Cynthia her well-beloved woods to gain
  Upon her journey speeds,
Till she beholds, on high, Day's glistering wheels,
And as her fainter beams she quencheth, feels
Right glad (methinks) her part was done so soon
  By her twin-brother's boon!
Wilt thou not leave, Aurora (Phoebus cried),
  Thine aged bridegroom's bed?   50
On yon cold couch what boots it to recline?
Thy hunter, Cephalus, on the sward doth bide
Thy coming. Rouse thee, then! The soaring peak
Of Mount Hymettus holds that flame of thine.
The gold-hair'd goddess feels her bashful cheek
  Her conscious guilt betray,
And faster yet her matin chariot drives.   55
Soon, doff'd foul age's weeds, the Earth revives
And craves thy embrace, O Phoebus—craves what she
Deserves, for what yet lovelier couldst thou see,
When in voluptuous beauty to the air
Her all-prolific bosom she doth bare,
And spiced Sabean harvestings exhale
(Breathing mild balms whose scent impregns the gale)
  Her lovely lips betwixt,   60
With rare perfume of Paphian roses mixt?

Lo, as the towering pines round Ops do grow
On Ida's mount, yon sacred grove imbowers
Like to a diadem her lofty brow;
Anon, she plaits her dewy hair with flowers

Of every hue that may her lover move:—   65
(Proserpin so pleas'd Pluto when she ware
That loose train of her flower-inwoven hair!)
Hark, Phoebus, since thy bride doth willing prove,
    How every vernal air
Makes honey'd supplication for thy love!
Look how the West clappeth his musky wing,
Fragrant of cinnamon, and clapping sighs,
      While every bird that flies   70
To thee, methinks, doth salutation bring!

   No rash bride portionless is Earth that might
Crave courtings nor, of destitute, hath need
    For thine espousals' meed.
Kindly she offers virtuous herbs to suit
    Thy healing skill's repute.
If then this prize—her glittering gifts—thee move   75
    (For gifts may purchase love),
Know that for thee she keeps the wealth she hides
    Beneath huge ocean's tides,
Or piled mountains, height up-heav'd on height.
Ay me! when wearied of Olympus' crest   80
Up-toil'd, thou dip'st into the western deep,
How oft with thee she pleads: O Phoebus, why
O'er-ply'd with those oft journeyings through the sky,
Doth blue-hair'd Tethys thee to the bosom take
Of her Hesperian waters? What dost make
With that Sea-goddess, or the Atlantick wave?
Why in foul brine thy god-like features lave?   85
Far better wert allay them in my shade.
Hither, then, come; those flaming tresses steep
In drench of dew: in my cool grasses laid,
Slumber shall gentlier on thine eyelids rest.
Come, then, and lay thy splendours on my breast;
And where thou liest may whispering zephyrs creep
Caressingly about our limbs in sleep
Reclin'd, their dews the humid roses weep!   90
When thou thy fire more wisely governest,
How can the flaming fate of Semele,
Or Phaeton's hot-smoking axle-tree,

Hold any terrors yet in store for me?
Then come, and lay thy splendours on my breast.

While wanton Earth her mind doth sighing show, 95
Her general brood pursue their Parent's ways;
For vagabond Cupid now wide-ranging strays
Around the globe, and from the sun's bright blaze
Kindleth afresh his torches' bickering rays.
Newstrung, his deadly bow sings loud and shrill;
Flash his bright shafts new-barb'd, forecasting woe: 100
So seeketh he that Maid unconquer'd still,
       Diana's self to tame,
And Vesta goddess pure, in wonted seat
Of vigil by her holy altar flame.
Venus with Spring repairs her beauty's wane,
And seems fresh-ris'n from forth the warm sea-foam, 105
While youthful bands through marble cities roam
Uplifting loud the Hymenaean strain,
Till both the shore and hollow cliffs repeat
       Hail Hymen! in refrain.
See the god go in grace the more complete
Of festal garb, beseeming to the eye
And redolent of the purple saffron's dye,
While many a maid, with gold-encinctur'd breast, 110
Comes forth to taste the joys of glorious May!
Each prayeth and every prayer holds one request:
To win from Venus him she loves the best;
His sev'n-reed pipe the shepherd tunes amain,
And Phyllis finds a song to suit his lay.

Now chaunts the mariner his nightly song 115
That charms the stars; which when the dolphins hear,
Upleaping through the shoaling surf they peer.
On high Olympus Jove makes mirth, withal,
Himself to sport with Juno; at his call
Their household gods glad to the banquet throng.
While lated twilight grows, the Satyrs tread
In skimming dance by troups the flowery mead. 120
       Sylvanus, too, is near
(Who hath his brows with his own cypress twin'd):

Upward a god, and downward goat, combin'd.
The Dryads that 'neath aged trees lay hid,
Range wide the lonely fields and hills amid;
    On slopes of Maenalus
Arcadian Pan himself grown riotous,   125
Alike through meadow doth, and thicket, flee—
    Scarce Mother Cybele
From his pursuit, or Ceres safe may be!

Now seeketh, too, his prey an amorous Faun
To make some Oread: she to shroud doth fly,
Saving her fears; yet hidden, half-withdrawn
From view, half visible, courts discovery: 130
Flies—yet in flying doth her fear belie!

Now before Heav'n's own self the gods approve
Their woods, where kindly Powers haunt every grove
(So haunt they long!). Then from the woods you love,
Do not, ye gods, again I pray you, rove!
So may new Golden Ages call thee, Jove,   135
To earth once more; where men that wish thee, mourn:—
    Why needest thou return
Thy thunders' fell artillery to use?
At least, do not, O Phoebus, thou refuse
This train of bridals to prolong, but slow
The course of Spring that she may tardier go:
Less soon rude winter's long-drawn nights appal,   140
And later 'thwart our Pole the shadows fall!

                              (W. S.)

¶ To Charles Diodati

Who had, during his residence in the country, written to the author, begging him to excuse his verses if they were less good than usual, because, amid the festivities with which his friends had welcomed him, he was unable to give enough favourable attention to the Muses. This was the reply that he received:

FROM me, fed sparely, "health" to thee (since thou
Full-fed to surfeit, mayst to want it, prove)—
What needs thy Muse, then, mine to challenge now,
Keeping me from the shades of my desire?

From Song, wouldst all my fond devotion know? *Lat.* 5
    Trust me—all, no Song can say,
Nor can crampt measures thus confine my love—
    Love that, of gait entire
To halting feet will ne'er himself convey.
    How well dost thou portray
Those festal scenes to gay December dear; 10
Rites done to God, Heav'n's fugitive, joys that all
    The wintry landskip cheer—
Jest-loving firesides, boon with grapes of Gaul!
Why blame the Muse "from wine and banquet fled"?
Bacchus to Song, Song is to Bacchus wed;
    Nor e'er did Phoebus scorn
With ivy's emerald bunches to adorn 15
    His brows, nor ivy-crown
To exchange with Bacchus for his bays' renown.

How oft when on Aonian mountains went
The Muses Nine, mingled in mystic rout
Of wild Thyone's sort, they rais'd their shout
Evoe! whereas even my Ovid sent
From Danube's plain but wretched lays and lean,
    Since there no merriment
Of feast was heard, no vine had planted been. 20

What did the Muse—his Muse whom Teos bore—
    In her brief lyric line
    Sing but of rose and wine
And those close-clustering locks that Bacchus wore?
Nay, who but Bacchus of Teumessus' steep
    Could with such tones inspire
    The chords of Pindar's lyre,
Whose every page breathes of the cup drain'd deep?
When overturn'd with harsh-jarr'd grating groan, 25
    The ponderous chariot lies,
    And thence head-foremost flies
The driver, swart with dust Olympian, thrown!

Drench'd in the four-years-mellow'd vintaging,
Rome's lyric Bard would Chloe's sunbright hair,
    Or Glycera, sweetly sing.

So all rich, sumptuous fare
That decks thy board, impowereth the brain,   30
Cherisheth the wit: thy cup's true Massick glow
Foams mantling with the Muse's richest vein;
And as from cask thy builded numbers flow!
Added the arts and Phoebus—pour'd like wine
Into thy bosom's core—ev'n so combine
Apollo, Ceres, Bacchus: Lyre, Corn, Vine;   35
Whose natures all conjoin'd, 'twere no great odds
Should thy sweet strains proceed from three such gods.

    Next shall the harp Orphean thee enthrall
(Of gold y-wrought, soft-touch'd by tuneful hand),
Or where the tap'stry hangings round thee fall,
Virginals, at whose tremulous strings' command   40
    Trip the fair dancers' feet.
Long be thy Muse detain'd by pageants meet
As these, and may they back to memory bring
All, sullen Surfeit err'd in banishing!
    Then, while the ivory keys
    Leap, and the feastful throng
Consenting with the quill-beat's harmonies,
O'erflows those perfum'd halls with dance and song,
    Like unsuspected flame
    Thrilling through all thy frame   45
(Trust me!), the god through every sense thou'lt find
Creep, while from maidens' eyes and fingertips
Melodious, the Lyric goddess slips
Through every porch and inlet of thy mind.

    For know, that winged Elegy doth concern
Full many a god, and to her measures still
    Calls any wight she will.   50
To her come Bacchus, Erato, Ceres,
And Venus, and young Cupid, too, his turn
(The "rose-red" Mother's little son!) with these;
For bards who sing such scenes rich feasts we keep,
And season'd wines wherein to drench them deep.

    But who chaunts wars, and climes that brook control 55
Of full-grown Jove, or chiefs above the span

Of human, or devote Heroic soul,
Or the Eternal gods' Celestial Plan,
Or Hell's deep worlds aw'd by that baying Hound—
Austere as Samos' sage his life should be: 60
His harmless banquet herbs, and on the ground
Hard by, upfill'd from the wave translucent, stand
    His dish of beechen tree;
    The clear crystalline Spring
Alone his cup's abstemious plenishing.
To these add youth unstain'd and pure of sin,
Steel'd and unspotted both of heart and hand:
So risest thou, O holy Augur, dight
    In robes of glistering white, 65
With lustral waters' sluice, to enter in
Before the throne of anger'd Deity!
After this sort Tiresias liv'd (they write)—
Tiresias, wiser for his banish'd sight;
So Linos, bard of Thebes in time gone by;
    Seer Calchas thus unhom'd
Fled his doom'd hearth; so aged Orpheus roam'd 70
Who oft in desert cave the savage beast
Tam'd; and he, too, that liv'd on nature's least—
Brook-drinking Homer, who o'er ocean's strait
Ulysses led, and through the enchanted Gate—
False Circe's Halls—and where the shoals did ring
With nymph-like voices luring—yea, O King 75
Infernal, through thy courts!—to check the brood
Of ghosts, detain'd by the black-flowing blood!
For sure, to heav'n the Bard is dedicate,
    And is the gods' high-priest,
To breathe the hidden Jove from lips and breast.

    Still wouldst thou ask mine occupation now
(If soothly yet thou deem'st so slight a thing— 80
What task is mine—importeth thee to know),
The Peaceful Prince of heavenly Seed I sing,
And that propitious age which was foretold
    In Holy Books of old,—
    Whimperings Celestial
Of him, in lowly Stall,

Who with his Father now on high doth reign;—
Of Star Heav'n-teem'd; and squadron'd angels strain—   85
Of many an Idol sudden at his own fane
Ras'd flat! Upon the Day when Christ was born
Such was my gift, brought by first beams of morn.

Tun'd to my native reed, packt safely here
These verses wait for thee: which in thine ear   90
Repeated, thou shalt be my judge to hear.

(W. S.)

¶ To My Father

Now could I wish that the Pierian Source
Throughout my breast
In fertilizing streams should wind her course
And that the waters of the Cloven Crest
Their brimming flood betwixt my lips should pour;
That so my Muse, her slenderer lays forsworn,
On wing adventrous borne,
Father rever'd, to honour thee should soar!   *Lat.* 5
Light task, this little Song I meditate
(Howe'er it please); but offering none know I
That with thy bounties could more amply vie—
Bounties no gift, though costliest could repay!—
Much less dry thanks which vacuous words convey   10
To thy munificence were adequate!
Yet I display herein my whole estate;
Yon sheet doth all my wealth enumerate:
Resources which, at best compute, were nought—
Save what my golden Muse, what Clio gave,
Born of my dreams in some secluded cave,   15
Or from the shadows of Parnassus caught,
Where those deep groves of sacred laurel wave.
Yet song—divine Song—do not scorn (I plead)—
The Bard's set task, which most of all shows trace
Of birth Ethereous and Celestial seed—
Most, too, as heavenly sprung, man's mind doth grace
With hallow'd sparks from her Promethean reed!   20

Dear to the gods is Song—'twas Song that stirr'd
To her dark Tartarean gulfs strong-shuddering Hell,
Fast bound the Infernal Powers, and ev'n with chain
Of triple adamantine forge the herd
Of stubborn ghosts could quell!
In Song the votresses of Phoebus' fane
And pale-mouth'd Sybils tremblingly foretell   25
Secrets of distant ages held in store;
The Priest that doth at festal altars pray,
Composeth Song, whene'er he seeks to slay
Yon bull with gilded horn, astrive to gore!
Or sagely o'er the reeking flesh doth pore
Divine of things to be,
And reads from entrails warm the Fates' decree.
Ourselves, where stretch (regain'd our native Skies)   30
Those moveless ages of Eternity,
Shall progress the Celestial Sanctuaries,
Our brows begirt with golden circlets proud,
To soft-tongu'd quill-beat marrying dulcet Song,
Whose sound the stars and the round welkin bow'd
From pole to answering pole shall far prolong:
Ev'n now the fiery Cherub that in ring
Rounds their swift orbs, with starry quires doth sing 35
His interpos'd refrain:
The unexpressive, the immortal strain,
Which the bright-blazing Serpent glows to list,
His searing hisses whist!
Orion, softening, drops the sword he show'd;—
Atlas (the Moor!) less feels his starry load!   40

Time was when Song made princely banquets bright,
Ere luxury and the wide ingulfing maw
Of Gluttony attain'd their noted height.
Time was, with moderate cups their board was crown'd,
Whenas, at sumptuous feasts, the Bard by Law
Of custom sate, his unshorn tresses bound   45
With wreath of oak, and sang heroic feat—
Deeds to inflame the breast—or Chaos vast
(Wherein of this wide Universe were cast
The broad foundations), or of gods that crept

The ground—of Powers divine that acorns eat—
Of bolts unsought that still 'neath Etna slept.

Last, what avails mere warbling of the voice,   50
Devoid of words—sense—numbers eloquent?
Such chaunting may the woodland quires rejoice;
But not therewith had Orpheus been content,
Whose song—not lute alone—the rivers stay'd;
Who to the oaks gave ears; whose singing made
Melt into weeping each departed shade:
'Tis Song that unto him such praise hath lent.   55

The sacred Muses, then, disdain no more,
I pray; nor them for weak and vain decry:
Whose bounty with such skill thy mind did store
To wed a thousand notes with numbers apt
And modulate the voice melodious, lapt
In thousand warbled trills of harmony!—
Heir to Arion's fame shouldst justly be!   60
What marvel, then, if chance thou didst beget
A destin'd Bard in me,
And if, in such dear bond of kinship met,
As kinsmen we our tastes and talents share?
Phoebus, desiring thus himself to twin,
Giving thee gifts, yet some to me did spare.   65
Hence is it that as sire and son we win
Dividual lot in his divinity.
To hate my gentle Muse, though thou mayst feign,
Thou canst not hate her, Father, I maintain:
Since never hast thou bid me go where lies
The broad highway and easier field of gain—
And hopes of high-piled gold bedazzling draw,
Nor halest to the Bar, and Publick Law   70
(Sore-wrench'd, too oft!) nor with disgustful cries
Mine ears dost peal: but seeking only power
My mind well-stor'd with richer wealth to dower,
In deep retirement from the City's roar,
Lettest me thus in jocund leisure stride
At mine Apollo's side,   75
With benediction from the Muses' shore.

The old dear dues of sire to son pass'd by,
Things weightier call. When at thy charge the Store
Of Roman Eloquence had op'd her door,
And Latin graces, and (which might behove   80
The lips of very Jove)
Those vowell'd flights of Greek sublimity:
Unto all these, at thy persuasion, I
Added the flowers that are the brag of Gaul,
The speech that newborn Italy withal
Pours with perverted dialect in that tongue
Which still of raids barbarian testifies:—
All mysteries, too, the Hebrew harpist sung;   85
Last, all that Heav'n, or Mother Earth may bear,
Or 'twixt these interfus'd, the ambient air—
What wave and restless ocean's plain conceal:
Thou canst, and if I ask, thou wilt reveal.
Comes Science, fair to see to, her form divine
Disrob'd of cloud: thus bared, her glorious eyes   90
She inclines for kisses—'less my mind display
Disrelish (if their gust might prove malign.)
Go now, and heap you wealth, to match with mine,
Ye who prefer (of senseless fools the pride!)
Austria's ancestral wealth, or empire wide
Of Incas!—More, could sire to son assign   95
For finishing his gifts, save heav'n alone,
Were Jove the giver? Or had Phaethon
Gifts more choice-worthy from his Sire (had they
Only been safe!), who gave his youthful son
World-lights, Hyperion's car, the reins of Day,
The Diadem that shone
Redundant of his coruscating ray?   100

Hence I, although but least of the scholars' throng,
Shall sit 'mid ivy-crowns and laurels proud;
Nor mix obscure the idle rout among,
But may, from eyes profane, my footsteps shroud!
Begone, ye wakeful Cares! Hence, Murmurings!   105
Hence, thou wry goatish leer squint Envy flings!
Nor ope thy serpent jaws, fell Slander, here!
Me, brood most foul, ye have no power to harm!

Nor am within your jurisdiction's sphere;
But scap'd, with breast secure against alarm
Of viperous fangs, I on my way shall go
The more elate. Yet since I ne'er could know,
Dear Father, how for thy deserts I may
Make recompense, make deeds thy gifts repay—
May this suffice, that with good heed I keep
Thy listed Gifts in mind, character'd deep! 110

Epilogue

O Verses, pastime of my youthful days,
If ye dare hope eternally to live
And see the light, and thus your lord survive
(So dark Oblivion drive you not to dwell
In gloom Tartarean), haply will this praise
Of mine uptreasure well,
And that dear Parent's name which was so long
The burden of my song,
To unborn ages as Example tell.

(W. S.)

¶ To Leonora
Singing at Rome

EACH mortal hath—let mortals all avow—
An angel wing'd from Heav'nly ranks ordain'd
His head to guard: fair Leonora, thou
No marvel showst if loftier glory gain'd;
For thy sweet voice, unhelp'd, doth sure declare
God's self at hand. Or God, or if not he,
Some third mind, downsped from the vacuous air,
Glides through thy throat's suave channels secretly;
Secret inspires, and with smooth influence
By gradual steps doth hearts of human kind
To song o'erhuman tune. Yea, though th' immense
Of things be God, whose spirit unconfin'd
Throughout the whole be fus'd; yet he his will
By thy sole tongue proclaims, and else is still.

(A. V.)

¶ To the same

ANOTHER Leonore captiving cast
The poet Tasso from his mind's demesne,
Thro' frenzied love o'erborne. His dolours vast
In thine age, Leonore, had happier been,
For love of thee endur'd: that spirit opprest
Had heard thee, singing with Pierian strain,
Impel thy mother's lyre-strings, thus addrest,
To golden harmony; nor were't in vain
Though wilder than Dircean Pentheus he
His eyes had roll'd—or fall'n sans sense entire:
Thou in the blind whirl of his phantasy
Hadst known by song to calm him; so to inspire
By stirring song his harass'd heart that straight
Peace-breathing, shouldst him to himself translate.

(A. V.)

¶ To the same

WHAT vaunt is thine, by credulous tongues made known,
Naples! of Acheloüs' child, renown'd
Parthenope, Sea-Siren—for thine own
Enshrin'd; and on Chalcidean funeral-mound
Consum'd: that shore-nymph perish'd by thy strand?
She liveth still! from Pausilipo's roar
Translated, habiting that pleasant land
Wash'd by old Tiber's wave. Her evermore
All Romulus' sons applaud: her Siren strain
Doth mortal men and deathless gods enchain.

(A. V.)

¶ To Salzilli

MY Muse, who all agog to go,
Trailest thy limping progress slow,
As halt as Vulcan's, never dreaming
Such lame progress less beseeming
Than fair Deiopeia's neat
And shapely ankles, when she beat

2C   M.

Heav'n-floor with light alternate tread   *Lat.* 5
Before Queen Juno's Golden Bed!
Come, Muse, this message at my prayer
In few unto Salzilli bear:
That holding all too dear my song,
He doth the Great Immortals wrong!
Thus far saith Milton, London-nurst,
His home-nest quitted, where the Worst   10
Of Winds that sweep the region pole,
(Fell Eurus) powerless to control
His lungs' mad rage, neath naked sky
His panting gusts drives furiously.

Arriv'd yon rich Italian ground   15
To see proud Cities, far renown'd,
Sage Elders, Youth of learn'd report,
Ben'sons he prays of every sort
For thee, Friend, and, though worn with pain,
A body soon made whole again—
Though spleen so deep thy reins infest,
And breathe such suffering through thy breast,   20
As scarce thy noble spirit spares,
Whose Roman lips frame Lesbian airs!

Health, Hebe's Heav'n-sent sister dear,
And Phoebus (would'st thou rather hear
'All-Healer'?) who—the Python slain—   25
Of all Diseases art the bane,
Here is a Priest to serve your Fane!

Oakgroves of Faunus, Hills benign
With dews dissolving into wine,
And Seats of mild Evander old,
Bring every herb your vallies hold
Of virtuous leaf, and bid them vie   30
To heal your sick Bard's malady.
To his dear Muses once again
Restor'd, he'll charm the neighb'ring plain
With lays entrancing—till, maybe,
Ev'n Numa shall admire, where he
In darkness couch'd of forests deep
Eternal ease and bliss doth keep
While lov'd Egeria charms his eyes!   35

Then, what though tumid Tiber rise,
Assuaged by that enchanting strain
The farmers' hopes of garner'd grain
He'll timely prosper, nor loose-rein'd
Run to the leftward unrestrain'd
King's monuments to overthrow;
But with moist curb his billows' flow   40
Hereafter rule, with sterner sway,
Down to Portumnus' briny Bay!

(W. S.)

¶ To Manso

Giovanni Battista Manso, Marquis of Villa, is most highly celebrated among the Italians not only for his talents in the pursuit of
literature but also for military valour. It was to him that Torquato
Tasso's Dialogue on Friendship was addressed; for he was a very close
friend of Tasso, who celebrated him among the nobles of Campania in
his poem called *The Conquest of Jerusalem* (Bk. XX):

> Fra cavalier magnanimi, é cortesi
> Risplende il Manso——

He treated the author during his stay in Naples with the utmost
kindness, and showed him many marks of courtesy. His guest, therefore, to avoid the appearance of ingratitude, sent him this poem before
he left the city.

Now meditates new song Pieria's Muse
To praise thee, Manso, who among the quire
That Phoebus doth inspire,
Art famous. Worthier of such favour none
Hath the god reckon'd, since Etruria's son,
Maecenas, and the ash of Gallus' pyre!
Thou (if this breeze prevail, my Muse's plea!)   *Lat.* 5
Mid ivy-crowns and laurels proud shalt use
To sit. 'Tis long, mutual affinity
With mighty Tasso's join'd hath grav'n thy name
Upon the records of immortal fame.
Next, the sage Muse Marini dulcet-voiced
Trusted to thee; in thee he too rejoiced: 10
Foster-sire of the prolix song he pours
Of gods Assyrian and their soft amours—
Song that Italia's maids did much bemuse.
Dying, to thee alone his fated dust

He left, his latest vows alone to thee!
Nor didst thou fail the friend who placed his trust   15
In thy fond truth: Marini's features set
In labour'd bronzework smile at us. And yet
All's not enough; nor was thy high concern
For both these poets ended with the urn:
But since with all her power thy spirit did yearn
To snatch them twain unscath'd from Orcus' jaws
(Elusive of the Fatal Sisters' laws
Ravening, thou toldest of their birth, their course   20
Of life 'neath changeful stars, their natural force,
Their gifts of mind—rivalling the Carian who
Æolian Homer's life divinely drew.

    Hence, Manso, I who thee as sire revere,
In Clio's and great Phoebus' name present   25
Prayers for thy health through many a happy year.
Although, of years unripe, my steps I bent
From Hyperborean zone to sojourn here,
Thou of thy noble mind wilt ne'er refuse
For too remote, my Muse,
Which sparely nurtur'd 'neath the freezing Bear,
Hath fear'd not (overbold, perchance) to fly
Throughout the cities of thine Italy.

    We, too, have swans that on our River's breast   30
Ourselves through night's dark watches fluting seem
To have heard where Thames, drawing his silver stream
From urns crystalline, with effusion wide
Imbathes his sea-green locks in ocean's tide.
Nay, once these selfsame shores our "Tityrus" press'd!
No race barbarian we; nor are we thought   35
Unprofitable to the Muse, although
Our coasts that lie beneath the furrowing Plough
Wintry Boötes' livelong night endure.
Ourselves with orisons have Phoebus sought,
And golden, bearded ears to Phoebus brought,
With yellowing apples heap'd in baskets high,
And crocus breathing exhalation pure!
Nay more—unless, perchance, that bruit hath been   40

Nois'd something idly of antiquity—
'Twas we who sent those maiden quires elect
From out the Druid sect—
Those reverend Bards, who when as priests array'd
At rites of Britain's gods their vows they paid,
Would deeds to inflame the breast, and heroes, sing!
Hence, too, the Grecian maids, whenas they ring
Their altars round with festal carolling
(As they are wont to do, in Delos green!),   45
With joyous lays Loxo commemorate
(Corineus' child!), Upis, who sang of Fate,
And Hekaërge of the yellow hair:
'Twas Britain's woad that stain'd their bosoms bare!

And so, high-fortun'd Sire, in every clime
Where'er the fame of Tasso's vast renown   50
Shall be remember'd, and, to brilliance grown,
Marini's honours wax through dateless time,
Thou shalt enjoy, with them, an equal soar
And thine oft praise on lips of men shall roam,
Till one shall say: Apollo found a home,
Willing, with thee, and that the Muses came
As handmaids to thy door!
Less willing—fugitive from heav'n—the same
Apollo sought the abode and wide demesne   55
Of King Admetus (loath, though he before
The host of mighty Hercules had been),
Only, whene'er the god had fain be rid
The boist'rous herdsmen's clamourings, he went
Mild Chiron's cave illustrious to frequent,   60
Fair-water'd fields and green-roof'd woods amid;
Where by Peneius' wave, 'neath holm-oak shade,
To the lute's murmur, by the entreaty sway'd
Of his fond friend, he oft would soothe the long
Hard labours of his banishment with song.
Then reel'd the banks. Then the deep chasm's abyss   65
Downward to his nethermost boulders stirr'd; the brow
Of Œta nodded, and did somewhat miss
The burden of massy woods that wont to bow
His shoulders; from their native Hills uprent,

The mountain ashes quickly gliding came:
At those new notes grew spotted lynxes tame.

Heav'n-beloved Sire, O thou whose birth upon,   70
Jove's perfect justice, Hermes (Maia's child),
With Phoebus' gentle light must needs have shone;
For if high gods had not upon thee smil'd
From birth, how hadst thou gotten to thy ward
So excellent a Bard?
Hence, gently flowering, turns thine age to spring;
Hence, too, thy living years make marchandise   75
Of long life's thread on Æson's spindles wound,
Keeping unfall'n thy forehead's dignities;
Hence that ripe wit and mind mature and sound.
O, should my fortune e'er such patron bring—
So skill'd to adorn the sons of Phoebus found—
Should I recall, to grace the songs I sing,   80
Britain's old kings and Arthur marshalling wars
Ev'n in the World Beneath—should e'er I tell
Of the Table's Fellowship invincible:
Heroes great-soul'd—should I with Britain's Mars
(So but the Muse due inspiration give!)
The imbattl'd Saxon squares to havock rive—
Then, when my songful Life has fetch'd her round,   85
When ripe of years to Death I pay my dues,
He bending o'er my dying bed shall stand,
While tears his eyes suffuse,
Content if in his ear "Be true", I say!
In little urn then will he gently lay   90
My limbs, relax'd by Death's discolouring hand—
Ay, haply then will he of marble too
My living features hew,
And for my hair the Paphian myrtle braid,
Or leaves of laurel from Parnassus' glade;
But I shall rest, in dreamless slumber laid.

Then I too—if any faith the just requite   95
With treasure in heav'n uplaid—I who aspire,
With toil and mind unstain'd and virtue's fire,
To ascend, where all the Saints in bliss unite,

Shall view from regions veil'd to mortal sight
These rites fulfil'd (whate'er the fates allow),
And smiling then, with all my mind serene
And forehead glowing with Celestial sheen,
Shall in high heav'n sublime contentment know.

(W. S.)

¶ The Lament for Damon

SISTERS of Himera's Spring,
(Who Daphnis' hold, and Hylas' memory, dear
With Bion's many days deep-sorrow'd bier)—
By City'd Thames an air Sicilian sing!
Sing Thyrsis' loud laments, of heavy cheer,
Each moan of woe and every whisper'd tear;
Complaints he search'd, withal, each cavern'd nook, *Lat.* 5
Sequester'd grove, river and gadding brook,
Sorrowing for Damon reft him; nor would spare
Mid-night his griefs, but roam'd lone regions bare.
Twice with green ear the rising stalk 'gan swell,
The granges twice their golden harvests tell, 10
Since that predestin'd Morn
Unto the Shades below had Damon borne—
Nor Thyrsis come! True is, him overlong
In Tuscan city held soft charm of song.
But when a mind full furnish't and the thought 15
Of his neglected flock him homeward brought,
He then, when 'neath the accustom'd elm he sate
And felt as ne'er before his lost friend's fate,
'Gan thus unload his measureless sorrow's weight:
 Home, lambs, unfed; grief tasks your herdman now!

Ay me, what Powers frequenting earth shall I
Invoke, what Powers in Heav'n's sublime abode— 20
Powers that have rapt thy life so ruthlessly?
Canst quit me thus? Can thy clear spirit be fled
Unwept, to join the throng of the Obscure Dead?
Not so may Hermes make arbitrement,
But pointing rather with his golden rod

Which doth the Souls divide,
Thee to a troop judg'd not unworthy, guide,
Far from the songless herd ignoble pent.　25
　Home, lambs, unfed; grief tasks your herdman now!

　Yet know, whatever fate may hold in store—
Unless some wolf prevent my sight perchance
(With his dumb-striking glance).
Thou shalt not wholly moulder in the grave
Unwept, but high-establisht honour have,
To live upon the lips of every swain.　30
Unto thy favouring angel cheerly they
(From Daphnis next) their orisons will pay;
Cheerly to thee (thee next from Daphnis) raise
Their due concent of praise
So long as Pales with secure delight—
So long as Faunus our trim fields invite.
If booteth aught to have cherish'd gods of yore;
If aught, thy zeal for arts of Pallas' lore;
If booteth aught a songful friend to gain.　35
　Home, lambs, unfed; grief tasks your herdman now!

　Dead Shepherd, thine this meed, these sureties dear;
But what shall me at bitter end betide?
What faithful, fond compeer
Will cleave as thou (so closely!) to my side?
Or who (as oftest thou) with me will stay
In pitiless frosts where rime thick-teemed lies,
Or singeing noons when parch'd the green herb dies?　40
Who aid, maybe, when I
Must lions huge at range of spear assay,
Or scare the greedy wolves from sheepfolds high?
Who lull with speech, with song the lingering day?
　Home, lambs, unfed; grief tasks your herdman now!

　Who shall, henceforth, unlock my heart, or show　45
To swage the heavy wound of biting cares?
Who with commercings sweet
The livelong watches of the night shall cheat,
When hiss in the genial glow the juicy pears

And crackle of chestnuts all the hearthstone floods?
Without, the felon South to shreds doth blow
The world, while o'er the elm his thunder broods. 50
    Home, lambs, unfed; grief tasks your herdman now!

When summer hours on noonday axle glide;
When in the tall oaks' shade
Great Pan to rest is laid;
When seek their watery haunts the nymphs once more;
When swains lie close; 'neath hedge the plowmen snore—
Who shall thy graces lost to me restore, 55
Laugh, polish'd wit—salt, with old Attick vy'd?
    Home, lambs, unfed; grief tasks your herdman now!

Companionless, the fields, the farms, I rove
Companionless, and where the valley's bowers
With thickest-woven branchings dark the grove,
Wait night. O'erhead, the gale moans with the showers; 60
Thro' shuddering dusk the shipwrackt forest lowers.
    Home, lambs, unfed; grief tasks your herdman now!

Woe's me! what wanton growths my fields o'ertwine—
My late trim fields! How droops with mildew blast 65
My ripening corn! On the unwedded vine
Forlorn the clusters waste;
Nor please the myrtles—irks the shepherd's hook—
The mournful flock up to their master look.
    Home, lambs, unfed; grief tasks your herdman now!

Hark, to the hazels Tityrus' challenge rings!
Alphesibœus calls to mountain-ash— 70
Ægon to the willows—to the river-plash
Comely Amyntas: Here (they cry) are springs,
Cool springs, and mossy turf-enamellings.
Here breathes the West! here to smooth waters' flow
Arbutus interposes whisperings low—
Deaf to their pipings, the coverts gain'd, I go.
    Home, lambs, unfed; grief tasks your herdman now!

Here Mopsus, who had chanced my homing feet 75
To spy—he knew the speech of all that flies:

Mopsus, the star-gazer—What's this? (he cries),
Thyrsis, what wicked spleen thy veins doth heat?
Art lost for love? o'erlookt by baleful star?
Saturn brings oft mischance where shepherds are;
His slanting lead deep in their bosom lies.   80
   Home, lambs, unfed; grief tasks your herdman now!

Marvelling, the nymphs: What's coming to thee now?
Thyrsis, what lack'st? Is this youth's wonted gait—
Ire-darting eyes, crabb'd looks, and cloudy brow?
Nay! dance and dalliance, love's unwearying vow,   85
Are youth's! Twice luckless, who has lov'd o'erlate.
   Home, lambs, unfed; grief tasks your herdman now!

Came Hyas—Dryopé—came (whom Baucis bore)
Mistress of measures and the lutist's "art"
Aeglé—consum'd, alas! by pride of heart—
Came Chloris, habitant of Chelmer's shore: 90
Nought their soft words, kind pityings, solace me!
Nought recks me now that is, nor aught to be!
   Home, lambs, unfed; grief tasks your herdman now!

Alas! the well-matcht steers i' the field that sport,
All mutual friends by nature's bond unite;   95
Nor will the steer one friend from his herd-mates sort:
So to their feed come jackals troopingly;
Each hairy wild ass pairs in turn with each;
The tribes of ocean with that law comply,
For Proteus on his solitary beach
Counts o'er by companies his serried seals.   100
So, 'mong wing'd fowl, though deem'd of common rate,
The sparrow hath companion when he wheels
Blithe-wing'd o'er all the corn-fields, roosting late
If Death that partner smite,
By ditcher's reed, or hooked beak of kite,
He seeks with friendly swerve another mate.   105
We men, Fate-driv'n, endure a sterner life;
Minds all estrangement—hearts distract with strife.
·Scarce, haply, shalt thou find—

Ev'n out of thousands—one true kindred mind.
Or if late vows from Chance win smooth relief,
Some day, some hour unween'd of, shall betide   110
To snatch him from thy side,
Leaving thee agelong—nay, eternal grief!
   Home, lambs, unfed; grief tasks your herdman now!

Alas, what gadding folly drew me astray
To traverse shores I knew not of, and tread
Peaks hung aloft in heav'n, and Alpine snow?
Was there such need to see Rome's grave (although   115
Rome were as Tityrus saw her when he left
His flocks, his fields?)—to mourn of thee bereft
Who wast so pleasant, friend! How could I dream,
Twixt thee and me so many a deep to spread—
Woods, rocks—so many a range and roaring stream?   120
Ah, at the end I could have else compos'd
Thy dying eyes, thy hand in mine have clos'd,
That last farewell to say:
"Think of me still upon thy starward way!"
   Home, lambs, unfed; grief tasks your herdman now!

Yet never (be ye sure) shall I repine,   125
O Tuscan swains, for memories of you,
Dear Youths who offer at the Muses' Shrine.
Here "Grace" and "Wit" were, and (a Tuscan too)
Thou Damon, thou whose house her founder drew
From that old city of the Lucumo.
O, how transported was my mind, when I
Diffus'd beside cool Arno's whispering flow,
In poplar glade, where tenderer grass doth grow,   130
Could violets pluck—pluck myrtles as they bend—
Hear with Menalcas Lycidas contend!
I, too, dar'd try, nor all displeas'd your mood,
Methinks, for here your gifts beside me lie—
Baskets, and wax-bound pipes and wine-cups rare:—   135
Did not your beeches learn my name to bear,
Dati, Francini, Doctor-poets good
(Both famous, boasting both the Lydian blood)?
   Home, lambs, unfed; grief tasks your herdman now!

To all this, when I no grief did apprehend,   140
The dewy moon sung burden, by whose light
My kids in hurdled cotes alone I penn'd.
How oft, when blacken'd ash held all my friend,
Unto myself I said: Now Damon sings;
Now haply for a hare his nets he flings—
Now weaves him osiers for their several use.
Thus all I did, so sure of future muse,   145
My winged wishes came
To seize, and as of present time, did frame:
Ho, friend! not working, now? If nought thee stay,
Shall we go forth and for a while be laid
To rest, reclin'd 'neath the clear-singing shade
By Colne waters, or "lands" of Cassivellaun?
Thou shalt recount the virtuous juices drawn   150
From thy choice simples—humble saffron, or
Leafage of hyacinth and hellebore,
And herbs whereof that fen of thine hath store,
And all "Physicians' skill"!
Go, rot, ye "herbs"!—and rot—"Physicians' skill"!
Simples!—since ye could serve your lord so ill!
But I—(to reckon since the eleventh night
Is one more day), when some sublimer flight   155
My oat was sounding, scarce had laid my lip
To these new pipes, when they apart did slip,
Snapping their band; whereafter they no more
Their loftier tones could pour.
Ev'n now, misgives me lest, perchance, my lay
Presumptuously should soar.—   160
Nay, I will tell it! Woodland Songs, give way!
Home, lambs, unfed; grief tasks your herdman now!

Of Trojan ships that rode off Richboro's strand
I'd sing, and of this ancient royal Isle
Of Inogen, daughter of King Pandrasus;
Antique Belin, Dukes Bran, Arviragus;   165
Then, of new Britain in Armoric land;
Next, of Igraine, who was by fatal wile
Of Arthur's birth expectant, with the guile
Of that false Gorlois' looks and armour ta'en,

Merlin's untruth. O last, should life remain,
On yon old pine, my Reed, thou'lt hang again—
How much forgot—or for thy native Muse   170
The shrilling sound of Britain's war-pipe chuse.
But what? Too much for one all things to be,
Or hope—'twere guerdon great enough for me,
Fame great enough: henceforth unknown I'll bide,
Inglorious quite to all the world beside,
If fairhair'd Ouse, and all who Alan drink,   175
All Severn's whirlpools—Trent's tree-bosom'd brink—
Thou, chief, my Thames—and Tamar's ore-stain'd urn—
And utmost Orkney's waves of me may learn.
Home, lambs, unfed; grief tasks your herdman now!

These I for thee in baybark tough did store,—   180
These, and more too, with wine-cups twain beside
(The gift of Manso, Manso whom the shore
Of Naples boasteth her supremest pride)
Each wondrous—like their master—who had wrought
Both them about with train of linked thought,
Ingraven on either side in answering moods:
The Red Sea middest, and odour-breathing spring,   185
With those far coasts of Araby, and woods
A-sweat with tears of balm,
Where Phoenix, bird divine, with rainbow wing
(Earth's singular fowl), an azurn flame doth fling,
While rereward to her gaze the watery calm
Doth the glass'd image of the Dawnrise bring.
Then vast Olympus, on the reverse hand,   190
And uttermost-opening firmament expand.
What! Love's cloud-painted quivers here, on high—
That bright artillery—that burning brand—
Darts dipt i' the red-gold dye!
Hence wounds he not slight souls, the common cry,
But casting far abroad his blazing eyes,
Strews through the spheres his shafts in upward wise   195
Tireless, and aimeth ne'er a lowlier blow;
Whence, sacred minds and godlike shapes do glow.
Thou among these (nor doth some glib surmise
Delude me, Damon!) now most surely art;

For whither else should wend thy single heart   200
So heavenly mild—thy virtues' shining guise?
How wrong to have sought in that forgetful Deep
Thee whom no tears befit! No more I'll weep.
Begone, ye tears! He dwells in those pure skies—
He no less pure!—and doth our rainbow spurn;
And now, 'mid hero souls and gods eterne,   205
Quaffs immortality and joys his fill
With mouth new-purged of ill.
Do thou, when heard thou hast heav'n's each decree,
With lucky words, calm presence, favour me,
What name soever thou shouldst justlier hear—
Or Damon, or that sacred name that's dear
To all the saints, "Diodati". What though!   210
Still to our Woods wilt "Damon" be below!
Since thy bright honour and thy youth unstain'd
Have equal favour gain'd,
Since savour of fleshly lust thou ne'er didst know,
Behold the honours of virginity
Reserv'd for thee on high;—
Where that bright brow attir'd with flaming gold,   215
Broad umbrage of triumphal palm shalt hold,
And evermore as guest
Of the Celestial Marriage-feast partake;
There dance and song concent tempestuous make
With harpings of the Blest,
While Sion's Thyrsus Rod to phrenzie brings
His mystic Vintage rites and Banquetings.

London [1639-40].   (W. S.)

¶ To John Rouse

On a lost volume of my poems which he desired me to send him for
the second time, so that he might place it with my other works in the
Public Library.

This ode is composed of three strophes, and the same number of
antistrophes, closed finally with an epode; although they do not all
correspond either in the number of lines, or tally exactly everywhere,
colon to colon, I have divided them in this way with the object of their
being read to advantage, rather than with an eye to the observance of

the ancient methods of chaunting. In other respects this style of poem ought perhaps more strictly to be called monostrophic. The metres are partly κατὰ σχέσιν, partly ἀπολελυμένα. The Phalæcians which occur, twice admit a spondee in the third foot, just as Catullus did so in the second foot.

Strophe 1

My little Book, in single vesture gay
    (Though twin, and leav'd for two!)
Whose Neatness doth unstudy'd charms display,
    Transmitted long ago
By a young hand industrious, although
Not yet of a complete accomplish'd Bard,—
Who now upon his dallyings forth would set
Through Woods Italian, now on Britain's sward:
Aloof, he first indulged his native lute,
Then thundering forth, with "Daunian" Latin quill,
Outlandish songs, strange to his neighbours still—
On the firm ground scarce ever planted foot!

Antistrophe

Say, little Book, who was it by deceit
Thee from thy company of brethren rent
When—as my learned Friend did oft entreat—
    From forth this City sent—
Thou faredst on the way that Fame holds dear
To the cradle-streams of Thames (cerulean Sire);
Whence well the Muses' fountains crystal-clear,
Their hallowed Train initiate to inspire—
That Train throughout the world preeminent—
    Which, while the Heavenly Sphere
Returns through lapsing Ages vast, shall be
    Commemorated to Eternity!

Strophe 2

But now what God, what seed of heavenly Line,
Pitying the pristine genius of our race
(If our old faults are all aton'd, and base
Degen'rate slackness, grown to sloth supine),
These monstrous Civil Jars will terminate?
What Power restore our peaceful Arts, of late

From almost all the bounds of England sent
With the unhous'd Muses into banishment?
Who will with shafts from Phoebus' quiver pierce
This obscene winged Brood, of talons fierce
To rapine? Who this Phinean Plague will strive
Afar from Thames' Muse-haunted Stream to drive?

Antistrophe

Yet, little Book, though thou by perfidy,
    Or carrier's negligence
For once didst wander from thy brother's band,
In whatso den thou lurkedst privily,
Chaf'd haply by some tasteless huckster's hand,
Callous and coarse, rejoice in confidence,
    Since now once more for thee
Dawneth new hope, that thou may'st yet make shift
To 'scape the Lake Oblivious and be
Oar'd by thy wings, to Jove's high Courts uplift!

Strophe 3

Rejoice, since Rouse to own thee, so desires,
And, from the full tale promis'd, doth lament
Thine absence, and for thine arrive requires—
He to whom high memorials are lent
Of famous men, within that Sanctuary
    Would place thee, where
He doth himself preside devotedly
Warden of deathless Works—a Treasury
Of nobler worth than fam'd Erechtheus' heir
(Ion, whom Attick Maid Creusa bare)—
Had charge of: Ion, who i' the wealthy Shrine
    Of his great Sire divine
    Was Guardian of that Hoard
Where tripods brown, and Delphick Gifts were stor'd.

Antistrophe

So shalt thou go once more the Muses' Dale
Imbower'd to visit, and Apollo's Fane
    In that Oxonian vale

Which made the god disdain
His Delos and twin-clov'n Parnassus' chain;
High-honour'd shalt thou go, who didst obtain
　　This most transcendent fate—
　　(For which my clever Friend
　　Did such entreaties send)—
There to be read 'mong volumes of the Great
Illustrious, who to Rome and Hellas lent
Their antique Splendour and true Ornament!

Epode

Thus then, my Works, ye were not all in vain,
(Who pouring did from my lean wits proceed)
Now late, all envy spent, I bid ye rest
At Peace, in that Elysium of the Blest
Which Hermes' favour, and the jealous heed
Of Rouse shall give you; where
The coarse-tongu'd crowd profane may enter ne'er—
But readers of the lewder sort depart!
And when, perchance, our heirs hereafter born—
　　An age more whole of heart
　　And ripe of brain—
　　Herein shall bring to bear
　　An estimate more fair,
Then, thanks to Rouse, will (o'er the Tomb of Scorn)
A sane Age know if I should any praise retain!

(W. S.)

¶ Fable of the Peasant and his Landlord

A RUSTIC from his private apple-tree
The richest fruit pluck'd each year constantly,
And to his liege in town the off'ring sent.
Who, by the fruit's exquisite blandishment
Entic'd, the tree herself at length transferr'd
To his own plot. She, straightway, disinterr'd
From her accustom'd soil, and worn with years—
Fertile thus far, now parch'd—no longer bears

Her wonted load. When he the fact saw plain—
All greedy hopes play'd false, all tried in vain—
His quick-stretch'd hands, quick in their own despite,
The master curs'd, and thus bewail'd his plight:
Ah! how much more 'twere meet those gifts assign'd
Freely to me, though small, with grateful mind
To have ta'en, by a tenant's grace. Had I but reck'd
My greed to have curb'd and appetites unchecked!
Now perish'd all, naught to my ravenings left,
Of progeny and parent, both, bereft.
                                                          (A. V.)

¶ On the Hundreda of Salmasius

Who show'd Salmasius to prate
Of "hundreds", or that magpie taught
Our speech to attempt? Insatiate,
His paunch, of Art the Master, wrought
This deed: Jacobuses gave aid.
An hundred—purse's guts outroll'd
Of exil'd King. Lo! if display'd
There once be hope of trait'rous gold,
He who of late his threat flung down
To scatter wide the primacy
Of Antichrist in Papal crown
With one prodigious puff—e'en he
Will uncompell'd his words disown
And 'mid the Cardinals intone.
                                                          (A. V.)

¶ On Salmasius

Rejoice! ye mackerel, and whate'er
Of fishy form in briny deep
There be, that in your watery lair
Feel winter's frosts upon you creep.
Salmasius, kindly Knight, hath ta'en
Compassion on your nakedness,
And seeks to clothe ye: whence—amain
Preparing papery largess—

He makes for each a paper hood,
Arms, name, and honours blazoning wide
Of Claude Salmasius, his brood;
That 'mong the fish-stalls ye may ride
From end to end o' the market-place,
In your Knight-liege's livery
As henchmen deck'd: so may ye grace
With fair investment, sweet to see,
Baskets and barrels eke of those
That wipe on sleeve a dripping nose.

(A. V.)

FROM THE GREEK

¶ A philosopher, unknown and innocent,
chancing to be taken captive among criminals by a
certain King, and by him unawares condemned to
death, sent him these lines forthwith:

KING, if thou slay me who have ne'er transgress'd
'Gainst law nor fellow-man, know that this head,
Though sage, may easily at thy behest
Be lopp'd; yet shalt thou learn thyself misled
Hereafter, and shalt long lament in vain
So fam'd a champion of thy kingdom slain.

(A. V.)

¶ On the Engraver of his Likeness

A CLOWNISH hand this likeness grav'd, thou'lt cry,
If thou the true original espy.
Friends, much in doubt whose image doth appear,
The boorish limner mock that set it here.

(A. V.)

¶ Six Sonnets

I

O LADY fair, whose honoured name doth grace
Green vale and noble ford of Rheno's stream—
Of all worth void the man I surely deem
Whom thy fair soul enamoureth not apace,
When softly self-revealed in outer space
By actions sweet with which thy will doth teem,
And gifts—Love's bow and shafts in their esteem
Who tend the flowers one day shall crown thy race.
When thou dost lightsome talk or gladsome sing,—
A power to draw the hill-trees, rooted hard—
The doors of eyes and ears let that man keep,
Who knows himself unworthy thy regard.
Grace from above alone him help can bring,
That passion in his heart strike not too deep.

II

As in the twilight brown, on hillside bare,
Useth to go the little shepherd maid,
Watering some strange fair plant, poorly displayed,
Not thriving in unwonted soil and air,
Far from its native springtime's genial care;
So on my ready tongue hath Love assayed
Of a strange speech to wake new flower and blade,
While I of thee, in scorn so debonair,
Sing songs whose sense is to my people lost—
Yield the fair Thames, and the fair Arno gain.
Love willed it so, and I, at others' cost,
Already knew Love never willed in vain.
Ill would slow mind, hard heart reward the toil
Of him who plants from heaven so good a soil.

III

LADIES, and youths that in their favour bask,
With mocking smiles come round me: Prithee, why,
Why dost thou with an unknown language cope,
Love-riming? Whence the courage for the task?
Tell us—so never frustrate be thy hope,
And the best thoughts still to thy thinking fly!
Thus mocking they: Thee other streams, they cry,
Thee other shores, another sea demands,
Upon whose verdant strands
Are budding, every moment, for thy hair,
Immortal guerdon, leaves that will not die;
An over-burden on thy back why bear?—
Song, I will tell thee; thou for me reply:
My lady saith—and her word is my heart—
This is Love's mother-tongue, and fits his part.

IV

DIODATI—and I muse to tell the tale—
This stubborn I, that Love was wont despise,
And made a laughter of his snares, unwise,
Am fallen, where honest feet will sometimes fail.
Not golden tresses, not a cheek vermeil,
Bewitched me thus; but, in a new-world guise,
A beauty that the heart beatifies;
A mien where high-souled modesty I hail;
Eyes softly splendent with a darkness dear;
A speech that more than one tongue vassal hath;
A voice that in the middle hemisphere
Might make the tired moon wander from her path;
While from her eyes such potent flashes shoot,
That to stop hard my ears would little boot.

V

CERTES, my lady sweet, your blessed eyes—
It cannot be but that they are my sun;
As strong they smite me as he smites upon
The man whose way o'er Lybian desert lies,

The while a vapour hot doth me surprise,
From that side springing where my pain doth wonn;
Perchance accustomed lovers—I am none,
And know not—in their speech call such things sighs;
A part shut in, itself, sore vexed, conceals,
And shakes my bosom; part, undisciplined,
Breaks forth, and all about in ice congeals;
But that which to mine eyes the way doth find,
Makes all my nights in silent showers abound,
Until my dawn* returns, with roses crowned.

VI

A MODEST youth, in love a simpleton,
When to escape myself I seek and shift,
Lady, I of my heart the humble gift
Vow unto thee. In trials many a one,
True, brave, it has been, firm to things begun,
By gracious, prudent, worthy thoughts uplift.
When roars the great world, in the thunder-rift,
Its own self, armour adamant, it will don,
From chance and envy as securely barred,
From hopes and fears that still the crowd abuse,
As inward gifts and high worth coveting,
And the resounding lyre, and every Muse.
There only wilt thou find it not so hard
Where Love hath fixed his ever cureless sting.

(G. M.)

* Alba—I suspect a hint at the lady's name.—G. M.

Notes

Notes

❧❧

*The line-numbers are counted from the top of the page, and refer
only to the verses, irrespective of poem titles or prose interpolations*

ENGLISH POEMS

p. 4, l. 18. *On the Death of a fair Infant.* 'Spheare': According to
the Ptolemaic system, the universe consisted of eight
concentric spheres of space, to which two more were
afterwards added. These spheres—the first seven
carrrying the sun, moon, and planets; the eighth,
the fixed stars—revolved, at different speeds, round
the earth: moved by the outermost sphere, or
primum mobile. Prof. J. Burnet, in *The Greek
Strain in English Literature* (Eng. Assoc.) shows that
Milton erred in attributing to Pythagoras and Plato
the notion that the planets were fixed on spheres.

p. 6, l. 16. *At a Vacation Exercise.* 'wardrope' (wardrobe): a collection of fine words and phrases.

p. 8, l. 16. 'indented': having short, sharp turns.

p. 10, l. 28. *On the Morning of Christ's Nativity.* 'whist': hushed.

p. 11, l. 24. 'silly': innocent or simple.

p. 12, l. 16. 'unexpressive ': unutterable.

p. 15, l. 19. 'unshower'd Grass': because of the absence of rain
in Egypt.

p. 16, l. 12. 'youngest teemed': latest born.

p. 18, l. 1. *The Passion.* 'Quarry': squared block of stone.

p. 19, l. 17. *On Shakespear.* 1630. 'unvalu'd': invaluable.

p. 20, l. 14. *Another on the same.* 'sphear-metal': the most durable material in the composition of the spheres.

p. 21, l. 8. *An Epitaph on the Marchioness of Winchester.* 'Winchester': John Paulet, fifth Marquis.

p. 21, l. 9. 'Vicount(s)': Viscount Savage.

p. 21, l. 9. 'Earls heir': i.e. of Thos. Darcy, Earl Rivers.

p. 22, l. 26. 'Helicon': Cambridge University as the "Home of
the Muses".

p. 24, l. 5. *Arcades.* 'state' was used in the sense of a circular
canopy over a throne. It was also called a " heaven"

p. 25, l. 6. 'thwarting': refers to the supposed malign influence
of lightning on plants.

p. 25, l. 18. 'celestial Sirens': who sit upon the nine enfolded
spheres; an imagination contributed by Plato, in the
vision of Er (*Republic*), to the Pythagorean doctrine,

that "the Sun, the Moon, and the five planets then known, with the heaven of the fixed stars, formed a scale or octave, the intervals of which were numerically determined by the distances between the orbits" (Burnet): the "music of the spheres".

p. 27, l. 26. *Upon the Circumcision.* 'whilear': a little earlier.

p. 29, l. 7. *L'Allegro.* 'night-Raven': a "raven" only in the poets (Gk. νυκτικόραξ); identified (1936), by Sir D'Arcy Thompson, as the long-eared or horned owl.

p. 30, l. 10. 'Eglantine': some kind of "thorny" plant, probably a wild rose, or dog-rose; not sweet-briar as sometimes explained, because that has been already mentioned (l. 9).

p. 31, l. 16. 'rebecks': a kind of (Moorish) fiddle.

p. 31, l. 26. 'Friars Lanthorn': really Jack o' Lantern or Will-o'-the-wisp. Milton has invented this term with satirical intention.

p. 32, l. 8. 'Saffron robe': the marriage robe in ancient Rome was saffron coloured.

p. 32. l. 8. 'Taper': torch.

p. 32, l. 14. 'Sock': the light shoe typical of Roman Comedy (contrasted with the buskin, or high boot, of ancient Greek Tragedy).

p. 33, l. 14. *Il Penseroso.* 'Prince Memnon(s)': the comely son of Tithonus (half-brother of Priam), the founder of Susa; his sister was the beautiful Himera or Hemera.

p. 33, l. 15. 'starr'd': set in the heavens.

p. 33, l. 15. 'Ethiope Queen': Cassiopea. But it was the beauty of her daughter, Andromeda, not her own, that she set above that of the sea-nymphs.

p. 33, l. 25. 'woody Ida's': Mt. Ida in Crete.

p. 33, l. 31. 'stole': usually means a veil in Milton (as in Spenser).

p. 33, l. 31. 'Cipres Lawn': a kind of black filmy gauze; "lawn" and "cipres" are often, but not always, distinguished.

p. 35, l. 3. 'out-watch the Bear': sit up all night (the Bear does not set).

p. 35, l. 4. 'thrice great Hermes': so-called by the Greeks, who identified him with the Egyptian god Tahuti (or Thoth), the god of writing, and of all knowledge. Later he was regarded as the composer of the forty-two so-called "Hermetic" books (really written at Alexandria about the second to the fourth centuries A.D.); these came to be considered an encyclopædia of all knowledge, especially of magic; they have now been translated and published by the late W. Scott (*Hermetica*, 1924-1936.)

p. 35, l. 4. 'unsphear': to bring back from the (celestial) sphere or heaven.

p. 35, l. 16.   'tale of Troy divine': In Milton's proposed Epic of Britain, the legend of the descent of the Britons from the Trojan Brutus was to have taken a great place; hence the many references by Milton to Troy and the Trojans. It is fully dealt with in his *History of Britain.*

p. 35, l. 18.   'Buskind': see note, p. 32, l. 14.

p. 35, l. 26.   'Cambuscan': Genghis Khan (lit. Universal Lord); his two sons were Algarsife and Camball, and Canace was his daughter.

p. 35, l. 28.   'who had Canace': According to Chaucer, it was another Camball (Cambalo) that fought with Camball and Algarsife, to win "Canacee". For the "ring" and "glass", see Squyeres Tale, 124-157.

p. 36, l. 32.   'Cloysters pale': pale = shadowy. Cp. *P.L.* VII, 331, "studious walks and shades"; *Il Pens.* 121, "pale career of Night".

p. 36, l. 34.   'massy proof': of tried stability.

p. 37, l. 19.   *A Mask.* 'pin-fold': a pound for strayed animals.

p. 39, l. 11.   'Ounce': the lynx.

p. 40, l. 35.   'Cotytto': a Thracian goddess, worshipped with nocturnal orgies.

p. 41, l. 1.   'Hecat'': the moon-goddess.

p. 41, l. 17.   'trains': artifices.

p. 43, l. 1.   'siding': protecting.

p. 45, l. 5.   'swinkt': worn out with toil.

p. 45, l. 39.   'warranted': safe-guarded.

p. 46, l. 13.   'star of Arcady': Callisto, a nymph of Arcady, was changed into a she-bear by Zeus to deceive Hera—who, upon discovering this, had her slain by Artemis. She was then set among the stars by Zeus as Arctos (the Great Bear), her son, Arcas, becoming the Lesser Bear.

p. 46, l. 14.   'Tyrian Cynosure': "Tyrian" because it was the bright star in the Little Bear, by which the Phœnicians steered—the Greeks steering by the Great Bear.

p. 46, l. 31.   'over-exquisite': over particular.

p. 48, l. 40.   'brinded': brindled.

p. 50, l. 10.   'iron stakes': the swords. But the metaphor might well be from pointed stakes planted at the bottom of a medieval "wolf-pit".

p. 51, l. 15.   'stabl'd wolves': probably captive wolves in their "stalls", or dens.

p. 53, l. 40.   'Moly': the magical herb, producing forgetfulness, mentioned in Homer (*Od.* IV, 219-229).

p. 55, l. 7.   'Nepenthes': the care-dispelling drink of Homer.

p. 55, l. 40.   'budge Doctors': "fur-hooded" Masters, or graduates.

p. 57, l. 13.   'bolt': either to shoot off or to sift (as flour). Probably the latter.

p. 59, l. 24.   'urchin': as a mischievous elf.

p. 60, l. 14.   'Carpathian wisard': Proteus. (Carpathus was an island in the Mediterranean.)

p. 60, l. 36.   'Turkis': turquoise.

p. 63, l. 30.   'purfl'd scarf': scarf decorated with coloured borders.

p. 64, l. 1.   'Assyrian Queen': Ishtar, the Mesopotamian Venus, counterpart of the Roman Venus, as Tammuz is of Adonis.

p. 65, l. 17. *Lycidas.* 'Gray-fly': the gadfly or "breeze".

p. 66, l. 4.   'wisard': prophetic; applied to the "ancient, hallowed Dee" because it was thought to foretell by its encroachments, now on the soil of England, now of Wales, which of the two countries was to prosper at the expense of the other.

p. 66, l. 35.   'Mincius': (now *Mincio*) which joins the river Po near Mantua, and hence signifies Roman pastoral verse (like that of Virgil—the "Mantuan").

p. 67, l. 5.   'Hippotades': Æolus, god of winds (son of Hippotas).

p. 67, l. 33.   'scrannel': thin, meagre, harsh (a northern dialect word).

p. 67, l. 39.   'two-handed engine': Suggested solutions are:—

1. The two-edged sword of Rev. i, 16.
2. The sword of Michael.
3. The two houses of Parliament "destined to effect the much-needed Reform" (Masson).
4. The iron sceptre of Christ's anger (Tillyard).
5. The axe of Reformation.

The last two are prompted by passages in Milton's *Of Reformation touching Church Discipline in England;* the last, which is the most probable, deriving from "they" (the bishops) "feeling the ax of God's reformation hewing at the old and hollow trunk of papacy". Episcopacy was *under the axe* at the time when the pamphlet was written.

p. 68, l. 8.   'quaint': exquisite, choice, dainty.

p. 68, l. 11.   'rathe': early (an old positive form of *rather, rathest*).

p. 68, l. 29.   'fable of Bellerus': "Fabled Bellerus". *Bellerium* was the name given to the land's end by old geographers.

p. 68, l. 31.   'Bayona's hold': a stronghold on the Galician coast of Spain.

p. 68, l. 33.   'Dolphins': allusion to the Greek legend of Arion, who was cast overboard, but carried to safety on a dolphin's back.

p. 69, l. 5.   'unexpressive': unutterable.

p. 69, l. 21.   'blew': possibly blue was the colour of the "gown" at Christ's College in 1637 as in present times.

p. 69, l. 32. *Captain or Colonel...*   'Emathian Conqueror': Alexander.

p. 69, l. 35.   'sad Electra's Poet': Euripides. Plutarch tells the story that the Spartan general Lysander spared all but the walls of Athens after its capture, upon hearing one of the choruses from the *Electra* of Euripides (lines 167, etc.) sung by an Athenian.

p. 70, l. 16. *Daughter to that good Earl...*   'that good Earl': James Ley (1550-1629), first Earl of Marlborough; after holding various high legal appointments became Lord High Treasurer (1624); later, Lord President of the Council. His daughter ("honoured Margaret") and her husband were especial friends of Milton at this period.

p. 70, ll. 21-22.   'at Chæronea ... Old man eloquent': Isocrates, the Greek orator, who died upon hearing of Philip's victory over the Athenians at Chæronea, 338 B.C., the battle which extinguished the independence of the Greek city-states.

p. 70, l. 29. *A book was writ of late...*   'Tetrachordon': lit. "four-stringed" (Gk. τετράχορδος), was the title of Milton's pamphlet of 1645 on the "Four Chief Places in Scripture" relating to marriage and its dissolution.

p. 71, l. 4.   'Gordon': either George, Lord Gordon, eldest son of the Marquis of Huntly, or his brother Charles. Both were strong partisans of Montrose.

p. 71, l. 5.   'Galasp': probably George Gillespie, one of the Scottish Presbyterian representatives at Westminster—in any case, one of the chief Royalist officers under Montrose.

p. 71, l. 8.   'Sir John Cheek' (1514-1557): first holder of the Professorship of Greek at Cambridge; became tutor in Greek to Edward VI.

p. 71, l. 16. *On the same.*   'Latona's twin-born progenie': Apollo and Artemis. Ovid tells the story of the Lycean peasants who railed at Latona and were changed into frogs.

p. 71, l. 25. *To Mr. H. Lawes, on his Aires.*   'Harry': Henry Lawes ("Gentleman of the Chapel Royal" and a member of the King's "private musicke") was a great friend of Milton and had composed airs for his *Maske.*

p. 72, ll. 4-5.   'Dante ... Casella': Dante (*Purg.* II, 10) describes how, upon his meeting with his musician friend in Purgatory, he persuaded him to sing a passage from his own *Convito.*

p. 72, l. 13. *When Faith and Love* ... 'golden rod': allusion to the "golden reed", Rev. xxi, 15.

p. 72, l. 22. *On the new forcers of Conscience under the Long Parliament.* 'Liturgie': the liturgy (Prayer Book) was forbidden and Episcopacy abolished by Parliament in 1639.

p. 72, l. 27. 'classic': a Presbyterian term, referring to the Presbyterian council or synod (*classis*), the subdivision of a "province"—"province" corresponding to parish.

p. 72, l. 28. 'A.S.': Adam Steuart, a strong partisan of the Presbyterians, who used to sign his pamphlets with his initials.

p. 72, l. 28. 'Rotherford': Samuel Rutherford, Professor of Divinity at St. Andrews; one of the Presbyterian representatives at Westminster.

p. 72, l. 32. 'Edwards': a well-known Presbyterian preacher, author of a pamphlet called *Gangræna*, in which Milton was attacked.

p. 72, l. 32. 'Scotch what d'ye call': the Rev. Robert Baillie, Professor of Divinity at Glasgow University and later Principal; who had attacked Milton in a pamphlet called *A Dissuasive from the Errors of the Time* (1645).

p. 73, l. 1. 'packing': trickery.

p. 73, l. 1. 'Trent': the Council of.

p. 73, l. 4. 'bauk your Ears': spare your ears; with a reference to Prynne, the lawyer, who had been pilloried and had his ears cropped, by order of the Star Chamber. *Technical Note:* This poem is a *sonnetto codato*, or "tailed" sonnet.

p. 73, l. 8. *To my Lord Fairfax.* 'Fairfax': the third Lord Fairfax (1612-1671), who became Cromwell's C.-in-C.

p. 73, l. 15. 'to Imp': to graft a sound feather in place of a broken one (hawking term).

p. 74, l. 1. *To Sir Henry Vane.* 'Sir Henry Vane the Younger': (1612-1662) Governor of Massachusetts (1636-1637); became one of the chief enemies of the King in the Long Parliament, and was executed at the Restoration.

p. 74, l. 4. 'fierce Epirote': Pyrrhus.

p. 74, l. 4. 'the African': Hannibal.

p. 75, l. 8. *On the late Massacher in Piemont.* 'triple Tyrant': the Papacy with its triple crown.

p. 75, l. 11. *Lawrence of vertuous Father* ... 'vertuous Father': Henry Lawrence, who became Lord President of the Council.

p. 75, l. 25. *Cyriack, whose Grandsire* ... 'Cyriack': Cyriack Skinner, a lawyer, who had been one of Milton's pupils.

p. 75, l. 25.   'Grandsire': Sir E. Coke, the celebrated judge (1551-1634).

p. 75, l. 32.   'the Swede': Charles X, then at war with Russia and Poland.

p. 76, l. 18. *Methought I saw* . . .   'espoused Saint': Catherine Woodcock, Milton's second wife, who died in 1658, three months after marriage.

p. 85,   30. *Paradise Lost.* Book I. 'Tuscan Artist': Galileo, who, taking the idea of the telescope from Lippershey, the Dutch optician, improved upon it and applied it to astronomy, in 1609. He discovered the uneven character of the moon's surface, the satellites of Jupiter and Saturn, Saturn's ring, the "horns" of the crescent of Venus [a crescent when she is "in conjunction"], and that the galaxy was "powdered with stars": phenomena (except Saturn's ring) referred to in *Paradise Lost.*

p. 86, l. 9.   'Busiris': really the name of a Delta town, but here used as the name of the Pharaoh who was drowned in the Red Sea.

p. 88, l. 33.   'Asphaltick Pool': the Dead Sea.

p. 89, l. 7.   'uncompounded': elemental.

p. 90, l. 2.   'grunsel': (i.e. ground-sill) door-sill.

p. 90, l. 6.   'Azotus': Ashdod.

p. 90, l. 20.   'Osiris': husband of Isis and father of Horus; said to have introduced agriculture and the arts into Egypt and became the chief agricultural (and funeral) god; his emblems the shepherd's crook and the goatherd's lash. The bull-god Hapi (Apis) was one of his manifestations ("Theophanies").

p. 91, l. 18.   'middle Air': In late medieval theory there were three regions of the air—the middle one intensely cold, region of mist, rain, hail, and snow.

p. 92, l. 37.   'small infantry': of the Dwarfs (with play on "infantry") in their war with the Cranes.

p. 93, l. 5.   'Aspramont': near Nice; famous in medieval romance.

p. 93, l. 5.   'Montalban': a castle in Guienne; famous in medieval romance.

p. 93, l. 9.   'Fontarabbia': The rearguard of Charlemagne's army was defeated at Roncesvalles in 778; but this is about 40 miles from Fuentarabbia. Charles himself was not slain there; he died at Aix in 814.

p. 95, l. 36.   'Babel': the Great Tower of Babylon (from *Bab-ili,* lit. "Gate of God", in the native cuneiform script).

p. 95, l. 39.   'reprobate': a term in metallurgy for an alloy that shows itself to be adulterated when tested. So in Jer. vi, 30, "reprobate silver".

p. 96, l. 6.   'Bullion dross': scum of the boiling metal.

p. 96, l. 22.   'Serapis': the "Osirified" form of the bull-god Hapi, whose cult, Hellenized by Ptolemy I, became widespread throughout the Greek world. The chief Serapium was at Alexandria, the lesser at Memphis.

p. 97, l. 36.   'expatiate': walk about at large, or freely.

p. 99, l. 9.   Book II. 'success': event, or result, of an undertaking; here = failure.

p. 107, l. 15. 'determin'd': ended.

p. 108, l. 12. 'punie': late born, hence inferior.

p. 108, l. 36. 'Synod': assembly.

p. 110, l. 22. 'intend': occupy yourselves.

p. 112, l. 2.   'sounding Alchymie': trumpet made of resonant metal; "alchemy gold" was the name of an amalgam.

p. 113, l. 37. 'Serbonian Bog': (*Yam Suf*) parallel to coast of Lower Egypt. Darius II lost *part* of his army there during his Egyptian expedition.

p. 113, l. 38. 'Casius': summit of a hill-range N.E. of Egypt.

p. 114, l. 5.   'starve': to be benumbed with cold.

p. 115, l. 12. 'impal'd': surrounded with a paling.

p. 120, l. 7.   'buxom': soft, yielding.

p. 122, l. 12. 'Vannes': wings.

p. 122, l. 30. 'Arimaspian': one-eyed race of Scythia, who stole the gold of the Ural Mountains from its guardians, the gryphons, to adorn their hair.

p. 124, l. 23. 'justling Rocks': the Symplegades, at the mouth of the Black Sea, they ceased to move after the passage of the *Argo*.

p. 125, l. 4.   'brok'n': First Edition reading; Second Edition "brok'd".

p. 127, l. 2.   Book III. 'drop serene': *gutta serena* or "amaurosis" —alternatively suggested with "suffusion" (cataract) as a cause of Milton's blindness.

p. 137, l. 8.   'Imaus': not, here, the Himalayas, but the Bolor Range, between Turkestan and China.

p. 137, l. 13. 'Hydaspes': now the river Jelum (Punjab).

p. 137, l. 15. 'Sericana': country W.S.W. of China.

p. 138, l. 4.   'Sennaar': Plain of Shinar.

p. 138, l. 20. 'trepidation': a theory of the oscillation of the heavenly spheres to explain certain difficulties of the Ptolemaic system.

p. 138, l. 20. 'that first mov'd': the *primum mobile*. See note on "Spheare", p. 825.

p. 139, l. 3.   'Frontispice': pediment.

p. 139, l. 13. 'mysteriously': symbolically. This passage is reminiscent of the symbolical steps of Purgatory described by Dante (*Purg.* c, IX, 68-92).

p. 140, l. 13. 'Canopie': earth's shadow cast by the sun.

p. 140, l. 15. 'fleecie Starr': Aries.

p. 141, l. 22. 'Limbec': alembic.

p. 142, l. 20. 'succinct': girt up.

p. 144, l. 13. 'quintessence': fifth element, apart from the four; introduced both by Plato and Aristotle.

p. 148, l. 40. Book IV. 'Assyrian mount': Niphates.

p. 150, l. 2. 'fishie fume': from the burning heart and liver of a fish; prescribed by the angel Raphael for expelling Asmodeus (*Book of Tobit*, Apocrypha).

p. 152, l. 29. 'Nyseian Ile': The whole of this account of the Island of Nysa (whence the name of the wine god Dio-Nysus), in which it is described as "girt by the river Triton", and as the isle where Amalthea's "florid son" (Bacchus) grew up, hidden by the Lybian Jove (Ammon) from the jealous eyes of Rhea, is taken from Diodorus Siculus III, 67.

p. 152, l. 30. 'Cham': Ham.

p. 152, l. 39. 'Assyrian Garden': Eden.

p. 154, l. 23. 'Insinuating': progressing in curves.

p. 158, l. 1. 'individual': indivisible.

p. 158, l. 8. 'unreprov'd': blameless.

p. 160, l. 29. 'volubil': revolving.

p. 163, l. 32. 'Japhet': Iapetus, the Titan (father of Prometheus); held by the Greeks to have been, through Prometheus' son Deucalion, the ancestor of mankind.

p. 164, l. 38. 'golden shafts': Cupid had golden shafts to kindle, leaden to repel, love.

p. 169, l. 37. 'arreede': advise.

p. 170, l. 6. 'limitarie': of, or stationed on, the border line.

p. 170, l. 15. 'ported Spears': spears held aslope in both hands in front of the breast and crossing the left shoulder, in readiness for the charge.

p. 170, l. 38. 'sequel': revealed consequence.

p. 174, l. 33. 'God or Man': of superhuman or human beings.

p. 176, l. 17. Book V. 'quaternion': fourfold formation (air, earth, water, fire).

p. 177, l. 19. 'seaventimes-wedded Maid': Sara's seven husbands were destroyed by Asmodeus (*Book of Tobit*, Apocrypha).

p. 178, ll. 20-21. 'Cyclades ... Samos': Samos was not one of the Cyclades.

p. 178, l. 28. 'Phœnix': believed unique of its kind and "singular", nesting alone in a solitary tree. At the end of every five centuries it came from Arabia to Heliopolis [not Thebes] and, having immolated itself, rose from its own ashes; the only bird according to the Rabbis that did not eat the forbidden fruit, therefore immortal.

p. 178, l. 34. 'lineaments': outlines of the whole person.

p. 180, l. 21. 'moust': must.

p. 180, l. 21. 'meathes': meads.

p. 180, l. 25. 'unfum'd': undistilled.

2D   M

p. 186, l. 28.   'Tissues': fine cloths inwoven with gold or silver.

p. 192, l. 17.   'unsucceeded': without successor; everlasting.

p. 195, l. 10. Book VI. 'Obsequious': complaisant, or obedient.

p. 195, l. 19.   'in procinct': in readiness.

p. 196, l. 24.   'reluctant': struggling; forcing their way through.

p. 196, l. 35.   'obvious': lying in the way.

p. 197, l. 4.   'terrene': stretch of ground.

p. 197, l. 19.   'hosting': warlike encounter.

p. 197, l. 27.   'Idol': mock image; simulacrum.

p. 202, l. 40.   'opposition': two planets are "in opposition", or "opposite", when separated by 180°. This is said to be a "malign aspect" (astrol.).

p. 203, l. 15.   'griding': cutting with a grating or grinding sound.

p. 207, l. 7.   'ambient': enveloping.

p. 207, l. 40.   'adusted': burnt up; reduced by fire.

p. 218, l. 19. Book VII. 'Aleian Field': the plain in Asia Minor where Bellerophon fell to earth from the back of Pegasus.

p. 219, l. 7.   'Rhodope': mountain range between Thrace and Macedonia.

p. 226, l. 15.   'implicit': entangled, interwoven.

p. 227, l. 18.   'her' (horns): first edition, "his".

p. 227, l. 19.   'tincture': absorption.

p. 227, l. 20.   'peculiar': individual "property".

p. 228, l. 14.   'Sculles': shoals.

p. 228, l. 33.   'summ'd thir Penns': brought their wing-feathers to full growth (falcon.).

p. 229, l. 29.   'wonns': dwells.

p. 229, l. 39.   'Libbard': leopard.

p. 233, l. 12.   'Unison': solo.

p. 233, l. 32.   'Hyaline': the "glassy sea" of Rev. iv, 6.

p. 235, l. 8.   Book VIII. 'officiate': supply.

p. 235, l. 9.   'this punctual spot': this mere point.

p. 236, ll. 29-30. 'Eccentric ... Epicycle': devices of the old (Ptolemaic) astronomers for explaining anomalies in the (apparent) movements of the sun.

p. 237, l. 5.   'Officious': ministering.

p. 237, l. 40.   'rhomb': the great wheel (the Tenth Sphere or *Primum Mobile*). See note on "Spheare", p. 825.

p. 239, l. 21.   'impertinence'; irrelevance.

p. 240, l. 16.   'uncouth': unfamiliar and hazardous.

p. 244, l. 13.   'intense': strained, taut.

p. 250, l. 17.   'green Cape': Cape Verde.

p. 252, l. 9.   Book IX. 'the Greek': Ulysses.

p. 252, l. 25.   'Impresses': devices on a shield.

p. 252, l. 26.   'Base(s)': short skirt, worn by knights on horseback.

p. 252, l. 28.   'Sewer(s)': head-servant in charge of the dishes at a banquet.

p. 252, l. 28.   'Seneshals': house-stewards.

p. 253, l. 28.   'Mæotis': Sea of Azov.

p. 257, l. 8.   'Spring': thicket.

p. 262, l. 40.   'tedded': spread out for drying.

p. 264, l. 6.   'indented': with short sharp turns.

p. 264, l. 16.   'the God': Æsculapius, god of medicine, who travelled in serpent shape to Rome with the ambassadors who came to fetch him in time of plague.

p. 267, l. 14.   'Bearth': produce.

p. 270, l. 2.   'humane': human.

p. 276, l. 10.   'oblige': make guilty; liable to penalty.

p. 278, l. 18.   'Worm': serpent (in early English, snake or dragon).

p. 278, l. 38.   'brown': dusky.

p. 279, l. 11.   'Figtree': A misconception due originally to Pliny (*Nat. Hist.* XI, 5), who confuses the *banyan* tree of India, which has relatively small leaves, with the immense-leaved banana. Pliny compares the latter's leaves to the "shield of an Amazon". (In the West Indies small bananas are still called "figs".)

p. 289, l. 18. Book X. 'Feature': shape.

p. 289, l. 20.   'Sagacious': quick-scented.

p. 289, l. 29.   'Cronian Sea': the Arctic Ocean. "Kronian" after Saturn (Kronos).

p. 289, l. 30.   'imagin'd way': problematic "North-East Passage", here supposed to be choked with icebergs by two Arctic winds blowing in opposite directions.

p. 289, l. 31.   'Petsora': river in North-East Russia.

p. 290, l. 7.   'Susa': "Shushan the Palace" of the old Persian Kings; on the Choaspes.

p. 290, l. 12.   'Pontifical': bridge-building (with play on *Pontiff*).

p. 291, l. 7.   'Pontifice': bridge.

p. 291, l. 40.   'Quadrature': the Heavenly City is "four square" (Rev. xxi, 16).

p. 293, l. 6.   'Grand': grandees.

p. 293, l. 12.   'Sophi': (the Elect) title of a Persian dynasty.

p. 293, l. 14.   'Aladule': greater Armenia.

p. 293, l. 15.   'Tauris': Tabriz.

p. 294, l. 16.   'unoriginal': existing from the beginning.

p. 295, l. 12.   'supplanted': tripped up.

p. 295, l. 23.   'Amphisbæna': here a snake with head at each end; now used of a lizard with indistinguishable head and tail.

p. 295, l. 24.   'Hydrus': sea-snake.

p. 295, l. 24.   'Cerastes': horned serpent.

p. 295, l. 24.   'Ellops': a kind of serpent—originally, a fish—(from ἔλοψ, "mute").

p. 295, l. 25.   'Dipsas': snake whose bite caused fatal thirst.

p. 295, l. 27.   'Ophiusa': Iviza

p. 296, l. 38.   'purchase': quarry.

p. 297, l. 20.   'unhide-bound': with skin undistended by food.

p. 298, l. 38. 'Sextile, Square, and Trine': When two planets are in square, they are separated by 90°. There are five aspects in astrology: conjunction, when two planets or stars, are in one line; sextile, when they are distant from each other 60°; square, 90°; and trine, 120° (this aspect, not being "opposite", is "benign"). The first is called Synod by the Greeks; the second is the distance of one-sixth of the Zodiac; the third is when they form a quadrant; the fourth, a distance of one-third of the Zodiac; the fifth (opposition) is one-half. (Masson.)

p. 299, l. 13. 'Atlantick Sisters': the Pleiads.

p. 299, l. 13. 'Spartan Twins': Castor and Pollux (the constellations).

p. 299, l. 18. 'vernant': coming into verdure.

p. 299, l. 25. 'Estotiland': formerly the tract of country between Baffin's and Hudson's Bay.

p. 299, l. 27. 'Thyestean Banquet': at which Atreus served up the bodies of his brother Thyestes' murdered children. The sun was alleged to have shrunk back to avoid the sight; Milton represents the sun as *shocked* at "that tasted Fruit".

p. 299, l. 35. 'Norumbega': a tract of South-East Canada.

p. 304, l. 11. 'pretended': stretched or spread before (of a screen, or mask, as in Latin).

p. 309, l. 14. 'Tine': kindle (hence *tinder*).

p. 310, l. 6. Book XI. 'Prevenient': forestalling.

p. 310, l. 20. 'Dimentionless': non-material.

p. 311, l. 6. 'manuring': manœuvring, in older sense of cultivating the ground by "manual" labour.

p. 312, l. 24. 'defended': forbidden.

p. 315, l. 3. 'tour': tower; soaring flight (falcon.).

p. 316, l. 21. 'Sarra': Tyre.

p. 320, l. 6. 'Cambalu': Mongol for Peking.

p. 320, l. 8. 'Paquin': Peking.

p. 320, l. 10. 'golden Chersonese': Malay Peninsula.

p. 320, l. 16. 'Ercoco': Abyssinian port on the Red Sea.

p. 320, l. 17. 'Quiloa': an island and town off Zanzibar.

p. 320, l. 17. 'Melind': a seaport north of Zanzibar.

p. 320, l. 18. 'Sofala thought Ophir': One of the chief traditional sites of this mountain was the golden Chersonese (Malay Peninsula) with Mt. Ophir at Malacca. (True site probably in Southern Arabia.)

p. 320, l. 21. 'Almansor': Caliph of Baghdad, eighth century A.D.

p. 320, l. 21. 'Sus': Tunis.

p. 320, l. 22. 'Tremisen': one of the five North African "Barbary" states.

p. 320, l. 28. 'Geryons Sons': Spaniards (from the name of an early King of Spain, who is described as of monstrous—probably, deformed—shape).

p. 320, l. 32. 'Euphrasie and Rue': plants regarded as eye specifics.

p. 322, l. 17. 'Lazar-house': hospital.

p. 322, l. 25. 'Marasmus': the "wasting sickness"; consumption.

p. 324, l. 19. 'volant': quick, nimble (lit. flying); technically exact description of fugal music.

p. 324, l. 21. 'resonant': re-echoing or repeating itself.

p. 324, ll. 30-31. 'wrought Fusil': cast (from molten metal).

p. 331, l. 9. 'horned': rivers were called "horned" by the Romans from their divided branches, or channels.

p. 331, l. 13. 'Orcs': grampuses.

p. 331, l. 18. 'hull': drift.

p. 332, l. 4. 'listed': striped.

p. 334, l. 17. Book XII. 'gurge': whirlpool.

p. 337, l. 36. 'Botches': boils.

p. 338, l. 7. 'River-dragon': crocodile; used fig. of Pharaoh (cp. Ezek. xxix, 3).

p. 342, l. 4. 'Kings': Cyrus, Darius, Artaxerxes.

p. 342, ll. 12-13. 'seise the Scepter': when Aristobulus, son of the high priest John Hyrcanus, became king he was displaced by Pompey in favour of Antipater, father of Herod.

p. 343, l. 9. 'recure': recover.

p. 346, l. 36. 'of respiration': refreshing.

p. 349, l. 6. 'marish': marsh.

p. 349, l. 11. 'adust': burnt or scorched.

p. 350, l. 6. *Paradise Regain'd.* Book I. 'full summ'd': see note to p. 228, l. 33.

p. 358, l. 11. 'stubs': stumps.

p. 367, l. 15. Book II. 'Pellean Conquerour': Alexander.

p. 367, l. 18. 'sirnam'd of Africa': Scipio Africanus, the elder.

p. 371, l. 3. 'Gris-amber-steam'd': steamed with ambergris.

p. 371, l. 9. 'stately side-bord by the wine': "side-bord" in the earlier sense of a shelf, or shelves, at the side of the hall, upon which the drinking-cups were ranged. Special "side-bords", or "cupboards", of five tiers were reserved exclusively for Royalty, and "stately" seems to imply that this "side-bord", with its cups and wines, was a royal compliment to Christ.

p. 371, l. 19. 'Logres': the main part of England, east of the Severn—now the Midlands.

p. 375, ll. 25-26. Book III. 'young Pompey ... Pontic King': Pompey defeated Mithridates in his 44th year.

p. 377, l. 11. 'young African': Scipio Africanus, the elder.

p. 381, l. 37. 'Hecatompylos': ("City of the Hundred Gates") capital of Parthia, residence of the ancient Persian kings.

p. 382, l. 1. 'Nisibis': a once famous capital town of North-East Mesopotamia.

p. 382, l. 2. 'Artaxata': ancient capital of Armenia.

p. 382, l. 12.   'Sogdiana': a country now, roughly, inclusive of Turkestan and Bokhara.

p. 382, l. 19.   'Rhombs': ancient infantry diamond-shape formation.

p. 382, l. 26.   'Arachosia': now, roughly, Afghanistan.

p. 382, l. 27.   'Margiana': now the district of Merv.

p. 382, l. 27.   'Hyrcania(n)': a province of Parthia, between the Caspian and the Oxus.

p. 382, l. 28.   'Iberia(n)': a country lying between the Black Sea and the Caspian, as distinguished from the western Iberia (Spain and Portugal).

p. 382, l. 29.   'Atropatia': North Media.

p. 382, l. 30.   'Adiabene': district of Mosul, or Assyria Proper (Mosul, on bank of Tigris opposite to site of Nineveh).

p. 382, l. 31.   'Balsara('s)': Bassora.

p. 383, l. 8.   'Agrican': King of Tartary who for love of Angelica, daughter of Gallaphrone, King of Cathay (China), besieged Albracca with a colossal army.

p. 383, l. 9.   'as Romances tell': e.g. Boiardo's *Orlando Innamorato*.

p. 383, l. 10.   'Gallaphrone': see *Agrican* above.

p. 383, l. 12.   'Prowest': most courageous.

p. 383, l. 37.   'Hyrcanus': last but one of the Maccabees.

p. 384, l. 23.   'Plausible': deserving of applause.

p. 386, l. 38. Book IV. 'Parallax': magical device of atmospheric refraction.

p. 387, l. 24.   'turmes': companies of Roman cavalry.

p. 387, l. 29.   'Meroe': in Upper Nubia.

p. 387, l. 33.   'Taprobane': Ceylon.

p. 387, l. 37.   'Tauric': of Taurica; now the Crimea.

p. 388, l. 33.   'Cittron': citron wood from Mt. Atlas, more valued than gold.

p. 388, l. 33.   'Atlantic stone': probably from quarries near Mt. Atlas.

p. 388, l. 37.   'Myrrhine': some translucent material, either natural or artificial, of which costly vases were made.

p. 388, l. 38.   'studs': small knops or knobs.

p. 390, l. 39.   'Tetrarch(s)': Roman governor of fourth part of a province.

p. 391, l. 32.   'Idolisms': prejudices.

p. 391, l. 33.   'evinc't': conquered.

p. 391, l. 34.   'specular Mount': place of observation.

p. 392, l. 11.   'Stoa': a porch; here the famous painted Porch of Athens where Zeno, the Stoic, taught.

p. 392, l. 17.   'Melesigenes': Homer, so-called from the name of the river Meles, near Smyrna, one of the chief places to which his birth is assigned.

p. 394, l. 32.   'Statists': statesmen.

p. 400, l. 1.　'Antæus': cp. Pindar, Pyth. Ode, l. 114.

p. 401, l. 3.　'debel': conquer (lit. war down).

p. 407, l. 5.　*Samson Agonistes.* 'interlunar': between the old and new moon phases.

p. 407, l. 22.　'obnoxious': exposed to.

p. 408, l. 9.　Chalybean temper'd': wrought by the Chalybes, famous metal-workers of Asia Minor.

p. 411, l. 3.　'ambition': canvassing, or soliciting.

p. 412, l. 28.　'obstriction': obligation.

p. 412, l. 40.　'verdit': verdict.

p. 416, l. 9.　'Idolists': idolators.

p. 424, l. 3.　'extenuate': underrate.

p. 430, l. 16.　'Paranymph': friend of the bridegroom (or "best man"). From the Gk. of St. John, iii, 10.

p. 430, l. 35.　'cleaving mischief': allusion to the poisoned shirt of Hercules.

p. 431, l. 36.　'Emims': a giant race of Moab (proper plural, Emim).

p. 432, l. 3.　'listed': roped off for a combat.

p. 432, l. 37.　'vant-brass': armour for the forearm.

p. 434, l. 31.　'Politician': intriguing.

p. 438, l. 1.　'Antics': buffoons.

p. 445, l. 7.　'banks': benches.

p. 445, l. 16.　'Cataphract(s)': horse and man all clad in mail.

p. 447, l. 12.　'tame villatic Fowl': "farmyard" fowl (a phrase from Pliny).

p. 447, l. 16.　'self-begott'n bird': Phœnix. See note to p. 178, l. 28

p. 447, l. 17.　'embost': imbosked (buried in the woods). The phœnix was supposed to nest, however, on a solitary tree.

p. 447, l. 19.　'Holocaust': an offering burnt whole.

p. 447, l. 24.　'secular': living for ages.

p. 447, l. 30.　'Sons of Caphtor': Philistines.

p. 448, l. 32.　'acquist': acquisition.

NOTES TO THE TRANSLATIONS

p. 453. *Psalm CXIV.* A rendering into Greek, and not an original Greek poem; hence in the Translations section.

p. 454. Dante, *Inf.* XIX, 115. From *Of Reformation touching Church-Discipline in England*, 1641.

p. 454. Petrarch, *Son.* 107. From *Of Reformation touching Church-Discipline in England*, 1641.

p. 454. Ariosto, *Orl. Fur.* XXXIV, 79. From *Of Reformation touching Church-Discipline in England*, 1641. Recast from Sir John Harington's translation. See Mr. Gawsworth's Note, p. 853.

p. 455. Phrynichus, *Incert. Fab.* 5, 17. From *The Reason of Church-Government*, 1641.

p. 455. Horace, *Sat.* I, 1, 24. From *An Apology against a Pamphlet*, 1642.

p. 455. Horace, *Sat.* I, 10, 14. From *An Apology against a Pamphlet*, 1642.

p. 455. Sophocles, *Elec.* 624. From *An Apology against a Pamphlet*, 1642.

p. 455. Euripides, *Supp.* 438. From *Areopagitica*, 1644.

p. 455. Horace, *Ep.* I, 16, 40. From *Tetrachordon*, 1645.

p. 470. Seneca, *Herc. Fur.* 922. From *The Tenure of Kings and Magistrates*, 1649.

p. 477. *The Fifth Ode of Horace.* Lib. I. *Translation of Latin inscription at head:* Horace had escaped from the allurements of Pyrrha as one who was saved from shipwreck by swimming; he avers that they who are enchained by her love are wretched indeed.

p. 478. *Geoffrey of Monmouth.* From *The History of Britain*, 1670. Milton writes: "These Verses Originally Greek, were put in Latin, saith *Virunnius*, by *Gildas* a British Poet, and him to have liv'd under *Claudius.* Which granted true, adds much to the Antiquitie of this Fable; and indeed the Latin Verses are much better, then for the Age of *Geoffrey* ap-*Arthur*, unless perhaps *Joseph of Exeter*, the only smooth Poet of those times, befreinded him. . . ."

NOTES TO THE LATIN, GREEK, AND ITALIAN POEMS

p. 755, l. 5. *Elegia prima.* 'Vergivian brine': the Irish Sea.

p. 755, l. 15. ' "Rooms" late interdict': referring to his brief rustication.

p. 755, l. 25. 'Tomis' Bard exil'd: Ovid.

p. 756, l. 9. 'Norman jargon of the laws': cp. Cowper.

p. 756, l. 24. 'avenging ghost': Professor E. Bensly suggests as of Tantalus and Thyestes in plays of Seneca.

p. 757, l. 19. Nineveh . . . Memnon's . . . hold': Susa, not Nineveh. Milton corrected himself in *P.L.* X, 308.

p. 757, l. 23. 'Bard of that Tarpeian Rock': Ovid.

p. 757, l. 29. 'London . . . Trojan hands did raise': as in the Brutus legend.

p. 758, l. 19. *Elegia tertia.* 'fatal Pest': Plague of London.

p. 763, l. 19. *Elegia secunda.* 'juice Thessalian brew'd': by a "Thessalian" witch.

p. 763, l. 24. 'goddess pray'd': Athene is imagined to plead for the Bishop as Artemis pleaded for Hippolytus.

p. 764, l. 22. *In obitum Procancellarii medici*. 'Iapetus': Japhet.

p. 765, l. 5.   'shadow': Lat. *larva* (i.e. "spectre" of the dead), here used of Patroclus.

p. 765, ll. 32-34. 'our new Delphi . . . Helicon': Cambridge, as the "Home of the Muses".

p. 766, l. 26. *In quintum Novembris*. 'Bond Inviolable': the personal union of the Crowns in James I.

p. 767, ll. 20-21. 'Neptune . . . his son': "For Albion the sonne of Neptune was"—Spenser *F.Q.*, Bk. IV, c. xi, st. 16.

p. 767, l. 23.   'ravaged Troy': a reference to the Brutus legend.

p. 769, l. 3.   'secret Paramour': but Pius V was a man of strictly moral conduct and rigid discipline.

p. 769, l. 16.   'Francis': probably Francis of Assisi.

p. 769, l. 31.   'Roman Cæsar': Holy Roman Emperor.

p. 772, l. 6.   'Looking towards the Mareotick Lake': fig. "looking towards Africa". The lake, the Birket-el-Mariout, originally ran parallel to the Mediterranean, separated only by a ridge of sand, S.W. of the Canopic branch of the Nile in the north delta.

General Note. In a Latin letter of 21 April, 1647, to Carlo Dati, the Florentine noble, Milton writes that he feared his friend might be offended by the harshness of his references to the Pope in this poem, and accordingly refrained from sending it. He besought Dati to obtain for him "from the rest of our friends" the same freedom of speech which was permitted to Dante and Petrarch, as well as, "with amazing generosity", to himself personally when he was discussing religious matters in his "native manner" during his Italian visit.

p. 774, l. 8 *On the Gunpowder Plot*. 'that fam'd seer': Elijah.

p. 775, l. 15. *On the Inventor of Gunpowder*. 'Prometheus': Lat. *Iapetides;* P. being a son of Iapetus.

p. 776, l. 9. *Elegia quarta*. 'Fleet-wing'd yoke': a yoke of dragons.

p. 776, l. 27. 'Stagirite sage': Aristotle.

p. 776, l. 37. 'thrice': In his letter to Young of 26 March 1625, he excuses himself for not having written to Young for three years.

p. 777, ll. 22-25. There are four remarkable assonances in the Latin—*sinceram . . . sera . . . sera . . . vera*—which have been indicated in the rendering.

p. 778, l. 17. 'Justest Maid': Astraea (Ov. *Met.* 1, 149). Milton makes the same comment in his fourth Prolusion, asking whether she were indeed the "last"—Peace and Truth having abandoned the Earth.

p. 781, ll. 7-8. *Elegia septima*. 'Friend of Hercules': possibly Telamon.

p. 782, l. 22. 'Juno's son, hurl'd': Mulciber or Vulcan.

p. 784, ll. 24-25. *Naturam non pati senium.* 'Vie . . . perdition': "vie wisdom with his Parliament"—E'ικονοκλ. XI.

p. 785, l. 6. 'With link'd revolve': or "With intervolve"—*P.L.* V, 623.

p. 785, l. 32. 'herald's shell': Triton's.

p. 786, ll. 11-12. *De Ideâ Platonicâ.* 'Deity Ninefold': the Nine Muses, daughters of Memoria or Mnemosyne.

p. 787, l. 16. 'Assyrian Priest': Berosus, priest of Bel at Babylon, c. 350 B.C.

p. 787, l. 18. 'Ninus': legendary king, husband of Semiramis.

p. 787, l. 19. 'Osiris': legendary king of Egypt, husband of Isis.

p. 787, l. 21. 'Hermes': Egyptian Tahuti (Thoth); traditional author of the forty-two "Hermetic" books (so-called; really works of the Neo-Platonic School).

p. 787, l. 23. 'Star of Academe': Plato.

p. 788, l. 30. *Elegia quinta.* 'perennial': Milton's "quotannis" of the first (1645) Ed. of the minor poems was criticized by Salmasius (*Resp.* 5), and corrected by Milton to "perennis" in the second (1673) Ed.

p. 788, l. 31. 'sun . . . flees the Ethiopians': i.e. at the vernal equinox.

p. 793, l. 3. *Elegia sexta.* 'crampt measures': "of that style of writing . . . fast bound and fettered by definite feet and syllables." (Milton's letter to C. Diodati, Sept. 1637, translated by Phyllis B. Tillyard: *Milton. Private Correspondence and Academic Exercises*, C.U.P., 1932.)

p. 793, l. 19. 'Thyone('s)': mother of Bacchus.

p. 793, l. 21. 'Danube's plain': Tomis.

p. 793, l. 24. 'Muse whom Teos bore': Anacreon.

p. 794, l. 5. 'from cask': as "from the wood".

p. 794, l. 25. 'the god': Phœbus.

p. 795, l. 4. 'Samos' sage': Pythagoras.

p. 795, l. 35. 'Peaceful Prince': referring to his *Nativity Ode*.

p. 797, ll. 15-16. *Ad Patrem.* Tillyard (*Milton*, p. 78) describes this line as mature and perfect and beyond translation.

p. 797, l. 26. 'Serpent': Cowper translates "Huge Ophiuchus", but Serpens is a different constellation, of eleven stars, next to Ophiuchus, above Scorpio.

p. 797, l. 39. 'gods that crept': like the animal gods of Egypt.

p. 798, l. 35. 'In deep retirement': probably at Horton.

p. 799, l. 12. 'Hebrew harpist': in reference to his translation of the Psalms.

p. 800. *To Leonora, Singing at Rome.* Leonora Baroni was a very celebrated singer, whom Milton heard during his Italian tour at a concert in the palace of Cardinal Barberini.

p. 801, l. 1. *To the same.* 'Another Leonore': Leonora d'Este,
the sister of Tasso's patron, the Duke of Ferrara.
According to Manso's *Vita del Tasso*, Tasso was
infatuated also with two other young women named
Leonora, one of whom was in the service of the
Princess of Este. That Tasso's mental instability
was due to unrequited love, as Milton implies, is
romantic fiction.

p. 801, l. 7. 'thy mother's lyre-strings': Leonora's mother, the
beautiful Adriana Baroni, accompanied her on the
lyre.

p. 801, l. 17. *To the same.* 'Parthenope': Pliny and Virgil mention
that in early times Naples was called Parthenope
because the Siren of that name had been drowned
at sea and buried there.

p. 801. *Ad Salsillum.* "The original is written in a measure
called Scazon, which signifies limping; and the
measure is so denominated, because, though in
other respects Iambic, it terminates with a Spondee,
and has, consequently, a more tardy movement.
The reader will immediately see that this property
of the Latin verse cannot be imitated in English."
—Cowper.

p. 803, l. 24. *Mansus.* 'gods Assyrian . . . amours': Marini's poem
was *L'Adone;* about Venus and Adonis (their As-
syrian names are Ishtar and Tammuz).

p. 804, l. 12. 'the Carian': Herodotus.

p. 804, l. 13. 'Homer's life': not now attributed to Herodotus.

p. 804, l. 24. 'swans': Cp. Jonson's reference to Shakespeare as
the "sweet swan of Avon" and to his "flights upon
the banks of Thames". But Spenser was probably
even more prominently in Milton's mind.

p. 804, l. 29. ' our "Tityrus"' : Spenser's name for Chaucer.

p. 805, l. 1. 'Nois'd . . . of antiquity': *Herod.* IV, 35, etc.

p. 807, l. 6. *Epitaphium Damonis.* 'Himera': Himera in Sicily.

p. 807, l. 10. 'Thyrsis': Milton.

p. 808, l. 7. 'dumb-striking glance': referring to the Roman
superstition that if a wolf on meeting with a man
saw him first, the man would be struck dumb.

p. 808, l. 15. 'Pales': the rural god or goddess.

p. 810, l. 13. 'Came Hyas . . .': the names in this passage clearly
refer to persons of Milton's acquaintance.

p. 811, l. 22. 'Tuscan swains': Milton's Florentine friends.

p. 812, l. 14. 'Colne waters . . . Cassivellaun': The Colne flows
by the neighbourhood of St. Albans, and the site of
the Roman colony of Verulamium (once a British
capital of the late first century B.C.), Cassivel-
launus' stronghold, has been discovered a few miles
away, near Wheathamstead.

p. 812, l. 32. 'Trojan ships ... Richborough': legendary British history out of which Milton proposed to create an epic.

p. 812, l. 34. 'Inogenia': Imogen.

p. 813, l. 10. 'Severn's whirlpools': Lat., *Abra;* thought by some to mean the Humber.

Bibliographical Note.—Dr. Leicester Bradner in 1933 identified this poem, entered in the B.M. catalogue as *Damon,* as Milton's. No other copy has been found, so that it is apparently the unique first edition. (Ref. B.M. *Quarterly,* Vol. VII, No. 2.)

p. 815, l. 10. *Ad Joannem Rousium.* ' "Daunian" Latin': apparently "rustic" or "country" Latin (the book contained both English and Latin poems).

p. 815, l. 12. 'planted foot': Tillyard (*Milton*), "Almost trod on air."

p. 816, l. 5. 'Phinean Plague': Phineus, son of Agenor, was plagued by Harpies for cruelty to his sons. The "Harpies", in this case, were the Royalists then holding Oxford.

p. 818. *On the Hundreda of Salmasius:* 'In Salmasii Hundred-am', from Milton's *Defensio secunda. Salmasius:* Claude Saumaise, author of the *Defensio Regia pro Carolo* (1649), attacking the English as regicides, which was answered by Milton in his *Defensio prima;* a Professor at Leyden of Swiss birth; a scholar and anti-Papal controversialist of international reputation; discoverer of the Palatine Anthology.

p. 818, l. 12. 'Hundreds': satirizing Salmasius's *Defensio Regia pro Carolo* I (1649); seizing on his affectation of a wide-spread knowledge of English institutions as displayed in his pretentious Latinizing of such terms as aldermen, hundred (in the sense of the sub-division of a county, or shire, having its own Court), etc.: "Aldermanni," "Hundreda."

p. 818, l. 15. 'Jacobuses . . . An hundred': the alleged bribing of Salmasius by the English Royalists was no doubt a false charge.

p. 820, l. 2. *Donna Leggiadra . . .* 'Rheno's stream': one of the frontiers of Romagna; twice mentioned by Dante: *Inf.* XVIII, 61; *Purg.* XIV, 95.

ENGLISH PROSE

p. 537, l. 39. *Of Reformation touching Church-discipline .* 'Tip-pet-scuffle': a law-court wrangle.

p. 539, l. 27. 'banking': benching (selling on benches, or money-tables).

p 539, l. 28.   'bassle': mock.

p. 540, l. 33.   'poul': poll.

p. 540, l. 34.   'Chaunlerly': chandlerly.

p. 542, l. 34.   'maw of Hell': the cellars of the Houses of Parliament charged with gunpowder in readiness for the "damned blast".

p. 543, l. 7.   'great whore': Rome, the Miltonic Babylon.

p. 543, l. 16.   'new and lofty Measures': the organic verse of *Paradise Lost.*

p. 544, l. 10. *Animadversions upon the Remonstrants Defence . . .*   'Remonstrant': Joseph Hall, Bishop of Norwich, who had published *Episcopacy by Divine Right* in 1640, and *An Humble Remonstrance to the High Court of Parliament* in Jan. 1641.

p. 545, l. 1 *et seq.*   'then': than.

p. 545, l. 33 *et seq.*   'humane': human (spelt in both ways in the seventeenth century, with no distinction of meaning).

p. 557, l. 9. *The Reason of Church-Governement . . .*   'yet since it will be such a folly . . . courteous pardon': The wisest men, recognizing its semblance of folly, have proceeded with it none the less, only saving the face of its apparent foolishness with an apology: this shows that the folly *is* only a semblance and that in reality the act has value; therefore, in as far as my outward folly may seem to be the greater, my actual praiseworthiness is the more.   So that the "more folly" demands the readier "pardon". (A most involved passage.)

p. 557, l. 17.   'of no Empyreall conceit': in no exalted mood.

p. 560, l. 37.   'Paneguries': solemn assemblies.

p. 560, l. 40.   'The thing which I had to say . . . pluckt from me by an abortive and foredated discovery': my poetic and reformative message forced into unseasonable and premature divulgement.

p. 566, l. 35.   'discussive': breaking up; dispersing.

p. 567, title. *An Apology against a Pamphlet . . .*   'Smectymnuus': composed of the initials of five Puritan divines—Stephen Marshal, Edmund Calamy, Thomas Young, Matthew Newcomen, and William Spurstow—joint authors of *An Answer to a Book Entituled An Humble Remonstrance*, (1641) (i.e. Bishop Hall's tract, above).

p. 571, l. 30.   'frumps': flouts.

p. 571, l. 30.   'curtall': curtailed (sharp and short).

p. 574, l. 22.   'white-boy': mother's darling.

p. 574, l. 35.   'him who . . . Saviour': Bishop Hall ("To the only honour and glory of God, my dear and blessed Saviour," etc. Extant in his published works.).

p. 576, l. 23. 'Thraso': see note on "that detractor . . ." below.

p. 576, l. 23. 'Davus that troubles all things': the stock figure (in Terence) of the wily slave who betrays his master for gain.

p. 576, l. 38. 'that detractor in Athenæus': Athenæus says (VI, 58) that Thraso was a well-known flatterer of Hieronymus who became tyrant of Syracuse in 214 B.C., and (VI, 65) quotes a passage in Plato's *Phædo* hostile to flatterers; but no direct connection of Plato and Thraso is apparently to be found.

p. 577, l. 2. 'were it Saturne himselfe': Saturn, the mythical king who introduced agriculture and civilization in general into Italy, was regarded by some after his sudden disappearance as a god of the nether world.

p. 577, l. 15. 'Minshews Dictionary': *Minsheu (John) Ductor in Linguas: The Guide into the Tongues, with their Agreement and Consent one with another; as also their Etymologies, that is, the Reasons and Divinations of all, or the most Part of Wordes in these Eleuen Languages, viz.:*

1. English	*7. Spanish*
2. British or Welsh	*8. Portuguez*
3. Low Dutch	*9. Latine*
4. High Dutch	*10. Greeke*
5. French	*11. Hebrew, etc.*
6. Italian	

(1625).

p. 577, l. 15. 'Mundus alter et idem': *Mundus Alter et idem sive Terra Australis ante hoc semper incognita longis itineribus peregrini Academici nuperrime illustrata, Auth. Mercurio Britannico;* a burlesque romance by Bishop Hall, satirizing gluttony, drunkenness, and licentiousness.

p. 577, l. 17. 'banke': bench.

p. 577, l. 17. 'The Author of those toothlesse Satyrs': Bishop Hall.

p. 579, l. 16. 'vomited out thence': Milton's rustication from Cambridge (1626) was probably due to an outspoken difference with his tutor. He was allowed to return during the same term, and his tutor was changed.

p. 580, l. 7, 'Suburb sinke': Milton was living in Aldersgate Street.

p. 581, l. 37. 'the atticisme': the passage in general is imitated from Demosthenes' *De Corona* (315,10) in Reiske's *Oratores Attici*.

p. 582, l. 22. "Ἀπειροκαλία': lack of aesthetic appreciation.

p. 585, l. 17. 'Corinthian Laity': Corinth was notorious for its prostitutes.

p. 587, l. 38. 'Guisian of Paris': an adherent of the duc de Guise in the massacre of St. Bartholomew.

p. 588, l. 19. 'pluming and footing': plucking, and taking away the claws.

p. 588, l. 20. 'dorre': dore; bat (in the sense of battledore and shuttlecock).

p. 588, l. 37. 'Ananias': a slip for Caiaphas.

p. 589, l. 35. 'canting beggars ... Altar': "Such language you could scarce hear from the mouths of canting beggars at an heathen altar; much less was it looked for in a treatise of controversiall Theologie. . . ." (Bishop Hall and his son's *Modest Confutation*).

p. 589, l. 36. 'criticisme of Bomolochus': Hall's "critical"—or meticulously pedantic—marginal note, in which he shows that his "canting beggars at an heathen altar" (above) is an allusion to the primary signification of βωμολόχοι (buffoons). He quotes Aristotle's *Nic. Ethics*, 4, 8, which contains the word, and Magirus' comment, deriving -λόχοι from λέχομαι (lie). According to this, βωμολόχοι were originally beggars who lay about beside the altars (βωμόι) of the gods, soliciting alms from those who sacrificed, and meanwhile (hence "canting") cracking coarse jokes. (However, λέχομαι is a spurious form, and the source is probably λοχάω [lurk]).

p. 593, l. 7. 'Keri': "Read" (a marginal gloss).

p. 593, l. 7. 'Ketiv': (so) written.

p. 595, l. 16. 'Lysimachus Nicanor': the pen-name of John Corbet, a well-known contemporary anti-Presbyterian writer who had been expelled from the ministry, and also the title of a tract he published.

p. 596, l. 21. 'the Clink': prison in Clink Street, Southwark, in the Bishop of Winchester's liberty.

p. 596, l. 21. 'the Gate-house': prison in Westminster.

p. 596, l. 32. 'tizicall': consumptive.

p. 597, l. 38. 'fenell rub'd Serpent': According to Pliny (*Nat. Hist.* 8, 99), snakes shed their winter-begrimed skins, and shine like spring, by means of fennel juice. Prescribed for the eyes by old medical writers; perhaps tried by Milton himself when he experimented with his failing eyesight.

p. 598, l. 1. 'Personage, or Impropriation': ecclesiastical property converted to private use and profit.

p. 598, l. 14. 'margent': margin.

p. 598, l. 16. 'arme full of weeds ... stranger ... bundle': "He that shall weed a field of corn, bind the weeds up in sheaves, and present them at once to the eye of a stranger, that is ignorant how much good wheat the field bears, beside those weeds, may very well be

deceived in censuring that field; especially if he
which presents them hath put into the heap such
weeds as came from elsewhere. Thus it fares with
men, when the evill actions of the best are picked
and culled out from their virtues, and all presented
in grosse together to the eye or ear of him who is
otherwise ignorant of the persons whose vices or
faults they are." (*Modest Confutation.*)

p. 601, l. 17. 'Satirist': Bishop Hall.

p. 601, l. 23. 'nice and humorous': fastidious and humouring
(from a superior level).

p, 601, l. 34. 'maukin': morkin (diseased, scabrous).

p. 602, l. 14. 'bull': "Milton is the oldest author in whom we
have discovered the jocular substitution of *bull* for
blunder." Thus J. A. St. John in the *Bohn* edition
of Milton's prose works; but the O.E.D. shows
that other writers, notably Selden, had already used
bull in this sense.

p. 602, l. 23. 'Lecturer in East-cheap ... Detford': alludes to
proceedings at the annual *Horn Fair*, held on Oct.
18, and probably succeeding days. This was ori-
ginated by King John, who made the grant of a
fair to the inhabitants of Charlton; at first intended
for the sale of goods made of *horn*, it came to be
associated with horns on the head, and cuckolds.
There was an old saying, "All's fair at Horn Fair,"
which meant that any kind of practical joke was
allowed. The atmosphere was one of licentious
ribaldry. A procession of holiday-makers started
from Cuckold's Point (near Deptford, also called
Cuckold's *Haven*) and marched through Deptford
and adjoining townships. Another procession
paraded Eastcheap and its environs. "Tribute" pre-
sumably means the toll paid to the King on the sale
of goods in the Fair. In the Middle Ages on feast
days displays of learning were common in the
pulpits of Festival churches; hence the reference
to "lecturer". If the lecturing in this case took
place in a church, that church was almost certainly
St. Clement's in Clement's Lane; but, more probably, it took place in the open air.

p. 602, l. 30. 'tenasmus': constant desire to defecate.

p. 603, l. 8. 'Major': major premise (log.).

p. 604, l. 11. 'Deputies execution': the Earl of Strafford's execution, 1640.

p. 604, l. 29. 'lozel': good-for-nothing.

p. 605, l. 16. 'stall epistle non sense': open letters, or pamphlets,
on sale at street-stalls.

p. 611, l. 34. 'prayer': *Of Reformation touching Church-Discipline in England* (pp. 535-544), at the close.

p. 612, l. 11.   'Maronilla': an ugly but rich widow (Martial's *Epigrams*, Bk. I, No. 10.).

p. 615, l. 16.   'old Paris and Salamanca': medieval universities.

p. 619, l. 3.   'Limbus Patrum': borderland where the Fathers of the Church, saints, and martyrs awaited the resurrection.

p. 623, l. 35.   'heal': salvation.

p. 623, l. 40.   'yafe': gave.

p. 624, l. 7.   'yeft': gift.

p. 624, l. 10.   'venim': venom, poison.

p. 624, l. 10.   'shad': shed, poured.

p. 630, l. 5.   *The Doctrine and Discipline of Divorce.* 'seventh Son of a seventh Son': proverbially a seer or genius.

p. 630, l. 18.   'arreed': advise.

p. 635, l. 8.   'Masoreth': a corpus of Old Testament exposition.

p. 635, l. 13.   'Norman Iles': the Channel Islands.

p. 636, l. 5.   'Medulla': summary, compendium.

p. 636, l. 32.   'verdit': verdict.

p. 637, l. 12.   'lin': cease.

p. 639, l. 6.   'humane': human.

p. 646, l. 14.   'Apogæum': apogee.

p. 646, l. 19.   'personall': impersonated.

p. 659, l. 35.   'humorous': capricious.

p. 671, title.   *Of Education.* 'Hartlib': Samuel Hartlib, an educational reformer; nationality unknown.

p. 671, l. 20.   'some other assertions': his writings on divorce.

p. 672, l. 24.   'Janua's and Didactics': educational theorists or innovators.

p. 678, l. 10.   'Locrian remnants': Περὶ ψυχᾶς κόσμου καὶ φύσιος ("On the Soul of the World and Nature"), a treatise in the Doric dialect, attributed to Timæus of Locris (c. 390 B.C.).

p. 681, l. 31.   'unrecrutible Colonels': unable, or unwilling, to fill up the deficiency of men with recruits (passive form with active meaning).

p. 681, l. 33.   'a delusive list, and a miserable remnant': a bogus enumeration of what in reality was a "miserable remnant".

p. 683, l. 11.   'according to': accordance with.

p. 684, l. 40.   *Areopagitica.* 'him who went about': Bishop Hall, whose attack upon the Smectymnuans (see note to p. 567) had been rebutted by Milton.

p. 685, l. 19.   'cabin Counsellours': Cabinet Ministers (with special reference to the infamous Junto).

p. 685, l. 34.   'him who from his private house': Isocrates, author of the Λόγος Ἀρεοπαγιτικός, which advocated the restoration of the old democracy to Athens.

p. 685, l. 40.   'Siniories': lordly demesnes.

p. 686, l. 31.　'quadragesimal and matrimonial': refers to licences for non-observance of "fish-days" during Lent, and marriage licences.

p. 687, l. 31.　'fift essence': quintessence.

p. 691, l. 35.　'responsories': chanted responses.

p. 691, l. 35.　'Antiphonies': anthems.

p. 692, l. 4.　'Lambeth house': the residence of the Archbishop of Canterbury.

p. 692, l. 4.　'West end of Pauls': the residence of the Bishop of London.

p. 692, l. 30.　'mysterious iniquity': see Rev. xvii, 5. "Upon her forehead was a name written, *Mystery*, . . ."

p. 697, l. 17.　'marginall Keri': (Heb. *Keri* = "Read"); a gloss.

p. 697, l. 21.　'Clement of Alexandria': his Λόγος προτρεπτικὸς πρὸς τοὺς Ἑλλήνας (of the second century) admonishing the Greeks against the impurities of polytheism.

p. 697, l. 21.　'that Eusebian book': Eusebius' Εὐαγγελικῆς ἀποδείξεως προπαρασκευή (The Evangelical Preparation); of the third-fourth century.

p. 697, l. 33.　'criticisms': refinements, niceties.

p. 697, l. 35.　'ribald of Arezzo': Aretino (1492-1557), an outrageous satirist, who was sometimes bribed and sometimes flogged.

p. 697, l. 38.　'Vicar of hell': perhaps Wolsey; or Skelton, once tutor to Prince Harry, Rector of Diss, or Dis, in Norfolk (Dis being the name of the infernal regions as well as of its god). Yet the reason given by Milton for withholding the man's name—"for posterities sake"—seems a sinister phrase, suggesting in the context pernicious authorship, which is not ascribable either to Wolsey or to Skelton. Hales suggests that the phrase signifies merely that "some known descendants of Skelton or of Wolsey were living when Milton wrote".

p. 698, l. 2.　'Cataio': Cathay, a province of Tartary.

p. 701, l. 7.　'rebbeck': early form of the violin; first with two, later with three strings.

p. 701, l. 8.　'ballatry': balladry (collect. plur., as in "yeomanry").

p. 701, l. 8.　'gammuth': gamut.

p. 701, l. 9.　'Arcadia's': the Countess of Pembroke's *Arcadia* (1590), which was immensely popular in the seventeenth century.

p. 701, l. 9.　'Monte Mayors': Monte Mayor, Portuguese by birth, the popularity of whose pastoral romance, *Diana*, spread from Spain throughout Europe.

p. 703, l. 10.　'Court-libell': the *Mercurius Aulicus* (*Court Mercury*) a pioneer, virulent, Royalist, weekly paper (1642-1645).

p. 706, l. 34.   'coits' : quoits.
p. 709, l. 12.   'enchiridion' : hand-book (with word-play on its other signification of dagger).
p. 709, l. 12.   'castle St. Angelo' : once the papal fortress (then the Pope's prison).
p. 710, l. 1.   'he whom . . . quæstorship' : Cicero.
p. 710, l. 28.   'mysticall' : mysterious.
p. 710, l. 35.   'chop' : exchange.
p. 713, l. 14.   'Harmony' : hand-book attempting to reconcile incongruous Scriptural narrations.
p. 713, l. 15.   'Catena' : a list, or series ("chain"), of authorities.
p. 716, l. 3.   'Syntagma' : collection ; general hand-book, especially of systematized philosophical points.
p. 716, l. 27.   'Hercynian wildernes' : the mountainous forest regions (according to Cæsar) of southern and central Germany ; (according to Pliny and Tacitus) between the Thüringerwald and Carpathian Mountains.
p. 720, l. 34.   'four nobles of Danegelt' : periphrasis for ship-money.
p. 722, l. 25.   'those ordinances' : *Col.* II, 14, "Blotting out the handwriting of ordinances that was against us, which was contrary to us, and took it out of the way, nailing it to his cross."
p. 723, l. 4.   'wood and hay and stubble' : I Cor. iii, 12.
p. 723, l. 6.   'subdichotomies' : minor sub-divisions.
p. 728, l. 35.   *Colasterion.* 'Bavius' : mentioned in Horace's *Satires* as a bad poet.
p. 728, l. 35.   'Calandrino' : a character in Boccaccio ; a simpleton.
p. 729, l. 1.   'Sotadic' : effected in the sonnet beginning, "A Book was writ of late call'd *Tetrachordon.*" (Sotades, a coarse Greek poet.)
p. 729, l. 28. *The Tenure of Kings and Magistrates.* 'unperceavable' : inconceivable.
p. 730, l. 29. *The readie and easie Way to establish a free Commonwealth.* 'som' : the retrograde Presbyterians.
p. 740, l. 26.   'Ornaments' : official distinctions, dignities.

NOTE ON THE SONNETS TO FAIRFAX, CROMWELL, VANE, AND (SECOND ONE) TO CYRIACK SKINNER

These four sonnets were first published in Edward Philips' *Letters of State*, 1694. The Sonnet to Cromwell in Philips' version is defective in the fifth and sixth lines, which in the present edition have been made up from the Cambridge MS. For

"And on the neck of crowned Fortune proud
    Hast reard Gods Trophies and his work pursu'd,"

Philips has only

> "And Fought God's Battels, and his Work pursu'd."

The Cambridge MS. versions are as follows:

On yᵉ Lord Gen. Fairfax at yᵉ seige of Colchester

Fairfax, whose name in armes through Europe rings
    Filling each mouth with envy, or with praise,
    And all her jealous monarchs with amaze,
    And rumors loud, that daunt remotest kings,
Thy firm unshak'n vertue ever brings
    Victory home, though new rebellions raise
    Thir Hydra heads, and the fals North displaies
    Her brok'n league, to impe their serpent wings,
O yet a nobler task awaites thy hand;
    For what can Warr, but endless warr still breed,
    Till Truth, and Right from Violence be freed,
And Public Faith cleard from the shamefull brand
    Of Public Fraud. In vain doth Valour bleed
    While Avarice, and Rapine share the land.

Cromwell, our cheif of men, who through a cloud
    Not of warr onely, but detractions rude,
    Guided by faith and matchless Fortitude
    To peace and truth thy glorious way hast plough'd,
And on the neck of crowned Fortune proud
    Hast reard Gods Trophies and his work pursu'd,
    While Darwen stream with blood of Scotts imbru'd,
    And Dunbarr feild resounds thy praises loud,
And Worsters laureat wreath; yet much remaines
    To conquer still; peace hath her victories
    No less renownd then warr, new foes aries
Threatning to bind our soules with secular chaines:
    Helpe us to save free Conscience from the paw
    Of hireling wolves whose Gospell is their maw.

(Milton wrote, and deleted, the title: "To the Lord *Generall Cromwell May 1652* On the proposalls of certaine ministers at yᵉ Commtee for Propagation of the Gospell.")

To Sʳ Henry Vane the younger

Vane, young in yeares, but in sage counsell old,
    Then whome a better Senatour nere held
    The helme of Rome, when gownes not armes repelld
    The feirce Epeirot and the African bold,
Whether to settle peace or to unfold
    The drift of hollow states hard to be spelld,
    Then to advise how warr may best, upheld,
    Move by her two maine nerves, Iron and Gold

In all her equipage; besides to know
   Both spirituall powre and civill, what each meanes
   Thou hast learnt well, a praise which few have won
   What severs each thou hast learnt, which few hav don.
The bounds of either sword to thee we ow.
   Therfore on thy firme hand religion leanes
   In peace, and reck'ns thee her eldest son.

Cyriack, this three years day these eys, though clear
   To outward view, of blemish or of spot;
   Bereft of light thir seeing have forgot,
   Nor to thir idle orbs doth sight appear
Of Sun or Moon or Starre throughout the year,
   Or man or woman. Yet I argue not
   Against heavns hand or will, nor bate a jot
   Of heart or hope; but still bear up and steer
Right onward. What supports me dost thou ask?
   The conscience, Friend, to have lost them overply'd
   In libertyes defence, my noble task,
Of which all Europe talks from side to side.
   This thought might lead me through the worlds vain mask
   Content though blind, had I no better guide.

The following Note has been received from Mr. John Gawsworth:

UNAUTHENTICATED FRAGMENTS ATTRIBUTED TO MILTON BY MITFORD AND BEECHING

IN the Rev. John Mitford's text of *The Poetical Works of John Milton, Printed from the Original Editions*, the nine pieces that follow are included, some inaccurately recorded, in the section entitled "Miscellaneous Poems":

(I) Terence

In silence now, and with attention wait,
That ye may learn what th' Eunuch has to prate.

(II) Ovid

Abstain, as Manhood you esteem,
From *Salmacis* pernicious Stream:
If but one moment there you stay,
Too dear you'l for your Bathing pay,—
Depart nor Man nor Woman, but a Sight
Disgracing both, a loath'd Hermaphrodite.

(III) Horace

The Power that did create, can change the Scene
Of things; make mean of great, and great of mean;
The brightest Glory can eclipse with Night,
And place the most obscure in dazling Light.

(IV) Virgil

No *Eastern* Nation ever did adore
The Majesty of Soveraign Princes more.

(V) Homer

Glaucus, in *Lycia* we're ador'd like Gods:
What makes 'twixt us and others so great odds ?

(VI) Horace

All barb'rous People, and their Princes too,
   All Purple Tyrants honour you;
   The very wandring *Scythians* do.

Support the Pillar of the *Roman* State,
Lest all Men be involv'd in one Mans fate.
   Continue us in Wealth and Peace;
   Let Wars and Tumults ever cease.

(VII) Catullus

The worst of Poets, I my self declare,
By how much you the best of Patrons are.

(VIII) Epigram on *Salmasius's* Hundreda

Who taught *Salmasius,* that *French* chatt'ring Pye,
To aim at *English,* and HUNDREDA cry?
The starving Rascal, flusht with just a *Hundred*
English Jacobusses, HUNDREDA blunder'd.
An out-law'd King's last stock.—A hundred more,
Would make him pimp for th' Antichristian Whore;
And in *Rome's* praise employ his poyson'd Breath,
Who threatn'd once to stink the Pope to death.

(IX) Virgil

And *Brittains* interwove held up the Purple hangings.

In point of fact, these are not by Milton, though the original
Latin of (VIII), an epigram on Salmasius, is. They are translations
by Joseph Washington of Greek and Latin verses quoted by Milton in his *Pro Populo Anglicano Defensio,* 1650. They first appeared
in Washington's pioneer translation into English of that work, *A
Defence of the People of England,* 1692. Mitford strangely fails to
give, it may be noted, two further verses, quoted by Milton and
rendered by Washington:

Thou slavish knight of Cappadocia

and

Live under certain Fundamental Laws.

But, if Mitford's source was not Washington directly, and was
some early editor of Milton's Poetical Works, that editor may also
have failed to reproduce these two verses, and this might well
account for their omission from the Mitford text,

Proceeding further, Mitford, in his section entitled "Epigramma-
tum Liber", included, from *Pro Populo Anglicano Defensio Secunda*, 1654, the distich:

> *Galli*, ex concubitu gravidam te, *Pontia, Mori*,
> Quis bene moratam, morigeramque neget?

disregarding Milton's preceding phrase, "Unde aliquis, et lepidi
sanè, quisquis erat, ingenii, hoc distochon." And, in the same
section, he reprinted, from Toland's *Life of Milton*, 1698, the lines
Ad Christinam Suecorum Reginam, nomine Cromwelli,* though
Mary Marvell had published them in the posthumous edition of
Andrew Marvell's *Miscellaneous Poems*, 1681, certifying, under
date 15th October, 1680, "all these Poems, as also the other things
in this Book contained, are Printed according to the exact Copies
of my late dear Husband, under his own Hand-writing, being found
since his Death among his other Papers."

Canon Beeching's Oxford University Press text of the Poetical
Works is unsatisfactory in a kindred matter. He prints, without
any explanatory notes, "A Collection of Passages Translated in the
Prose Writings"; and among these passages are the two following
citations made by Milton in *Of Reformation touching Church-
Discipline in England*, 1641, from Ariosto, *Orlando Furioso*,
XXXIV, 72, lines 5-8 and XXXIV, 79, lines 5-8:

> And to be short, at last his guid him brings
> Into a goodly valley, where he sees
> A mighty mass of things strangely confus'd
> Things that on earth were lost or were abus'd.
>
> · · · · · ·
>
> Then past he to a flowry Mountain green,
> Which once smelt sweet, now stinks as odiously;
> This was that gift (if you the truth will have)
> That *Constantine* to good *Sylvestro* gave.

A collation of the first edition of *Of Reformation touching
Church-Discipline in England* reveals that Milton spelt "mass" as
"masse", "Mountain" as "Mountaine", "green" as "greene", the
second "he" as "hee", and placed commas after "strangely confus'd" and "were lost". These points are significant; for, when
Beeching's versions are restored to the form in which Milton
printed the lines, it is even more evident how very little Miltonic
modification there is here of two passages from Sir John Harington's *Orlando Furioso in English Heroical Verse* which, in the 1634
third revised edition, stand thus:

> But to be short, at last his guide him brings
> Unto a goodly valley, where he sees

---

* This epigram is not included in the present edition, though the
case against its Miltonic authorship—or, at any rate, part-authorship—
does not appear conclusive.—EDITOR.

A mighty masse of things straungely confus'd,
Things that on earth were lost, or were abus'd.

     .   .   .   .   .

Then by a faire green mountaine he did passe,
That once smelt sweet, but now it stinks perdye,
This was that gift (be't said without offence)
That *Constantine* gave *Silvester* long since.

I prefer to quote from this 1634 edition of Harington since it contains spellings approximating more closely to Milton's reproductions than do those of the first (1591) edition. The 1591 variants are "goodlie", "vallie", "confused", "abused", "fayre", and "mountain". Milton is known to have possessed a copy of Harington's *Ariosto* (see G. C. Williamson's *Milton Tercentenary: the Portraits . . . and Writings of J. Milton*, etc., Camb. 1908, p. 91, item 228), and, in fact, it was exhibited in Christ's College, Cambridge, during the celebrations there in 1908. But it is not recorded which edition the poet owned, though Mr. A. F. Scholfield has stated that the copy is "said to contain marginal notes in the handwriting of Milton".

Beeching (who appears completely ignorant of Harington's translation), furthermore, quotes both these passages as ˙rom Stanza 80 of *Orlando Furioso*, XXXIV. In this he has doubtless been misled by Masson, who including the second passage only,* also attributed it to Stanza 80.

The following Note has been received from Mr. W. Skeat:

THE METRE OF THE LATIN ELEGIES AND SYLVÆ

THE method which has been followed in these translations is necessarily to some extent novel. Milton's *Elegies* are composed entirely in the Elegiac metre, but a rendering of the whole book into alternate long and short lines would be intolerable. Only the first Elegy has, therefore, been (experimentally) so translated. The *Sylvæ* are in various metres (not Elegiacs), but mostly hexameters. There are two special reasons for employing the *Lycidas* metre (modelled on the "free musical paragraph", as it has been called, of the Italians) in these renderings. In the first place, Milton himself used it in a number of his shorter (and early) poems: in *On Time, Upon the Circumcision, At a solemn Musick*, and of course throughout *Lycidas;* also (at a very much later date) in the *Samson Agonistes* choruses. Secondly, it was in hexameters that he chose to veil his grief from the eyes of the crowd when he came to compose the *Epitaphium Damonis*.

---

    * I have followed Masson and printed the second passage only; for Milton's "And" for "But" and "Into" for "Unto" in the first passage seem insufficient modifications for including it among his poetical works.—EDITOR.

The Lycidaean metre has, therefore, been chosen for the renderings of Milton's own hexameters, the November verses being excepted, because they are obviously an attempt in the Epical style, and also the lines to Rouse, which being in irregular metre are rendered in an irregular metre also. But, at the same time, a lighter and more lyrical tone has been given to the renderings of the Elegies by introducing into them an increased number of half-lines, or "broken melodies", as they have been called, so as to preserve Milton's own metrical distinction between the two parts. *

Again, Milton's Latin verse is so condensed and his English so expansive, as to put a merely line-for-line rendering out of question; the translation must follow Milton's lead and reflect the most sensitive emotions of his subtly varying moods if the giving of the detailed content is the chief object in view. Of course, some readers may nevertheless prefer a line-for-line translation, requiring only the substantial drift of the original; for these, Cowper's translations will always be accessible.

As regards the diction, experiment shows that these Latin poems will not adapt themselves readily to an alien idiom. Renderings in any modern up-to-date idiom simply cease to be Miltonic, whereas (owing to Milton's not infrequent habit of using corresponding English and Latin word-forms and constructions) his own diction assists, and perhaps even sometimes suggests, the choice of the word actually required for the translation.

Since the Latin poems are mainly Milton's *Juvenilia*, no translations of them could be expected to do more than reflect in some measure Milton's more immature and youthful style. Belonging, moreover, mostly to his Cambridge period, they were often written to order (several being obituaries lamenting the deaths of Bishops, or of Academic functionaries, such as the Vice-Chancellor, or Esquire Bedell). Their most absorbing interest lies in the fact that we find ourselves here, so to speak, in Milton's workshop, and can trace in their progress the early workings and development of one of the world's mightiest intellects.

---

* This distinction is, of course, much more obvious in editions which follow Milton's own (non-chronological) arrangement of his Latin poems in two parts, than in the present edition.—EDITOR.

ENGLISH PROSE CONCORDANCE

OF REFORMATION . . .

p. 535. "Amongst many . . ." 1st Ed.: p. 56. Mitford:* III. 44.
p. 536. "The emulation . . ."   ,,   p. 65.   ,,   ,, 51.
p. 537. "Having fitted . . ."   ,,   p. 68.   ,,   ,, 53.
p. 538. "But is this . . ."   ,,   p. 80.   ,,   ,, 63.
p. 539. "Let us not . . ."   ,,   p. 83.   ,,   ,, 66.

    (First Ed.: 90 small quarto pages of text.)

ANIMADVERSIONS UPON THE REMONSTRANT'S DEFENCE . . .

p. 544. "*Remon.* They can-
       not . . ."   1st Ed.: p. 34.   Mitford: III. 218.

    (First Ed.: 68 small quarto pages of text.)

THE REASON OF CHURCH GOVERNEMENT . . .

p. 548. "The first and great-
       est . . ."   1st Ed.: p. 3.   Mitford: III. 97.
p. 550. "It was not . . ."   ,,   p. 22.   ,,   ,, 124.
p. 552. "How happy . . ."   ,,   p. 33.   ,,   ,, 138.
p. 562. "It was thought . . ."   ,,   p. 53.   ,,   ,, 165

    (First Ed.: 65 small quarto pages of text.)

AN APOLOGY AGAINST A PAMPHLET . . .

p. 567. Herein complete.   Mitford: III. 250.

    (First Ed.: 59 small quarto pages of text.)

THE DOCTRINE AND DISCIPLINE OF DIVORCE . . .

p. 628. Prefatory Letter.   2nd Ed.: p.(iii). Mitford: IV. 3.
p. 637. "Many men . . ."   ,,   p. 1.   ,,   ,, 14.
p. 639. "This therefore . . ."   ,,   p. 4.   ,,   ,, 18.
p. 641. "For all sence . . ."   ,,   p. 7.   ,,   ,, 23.
p. 642. "How vaine . . ."   ,,   p. 9.   ,,   ,, 25.
p. 644. "This pure . . ."   ,,   p. 12.   ,,   ,, 29.
p. 645. "Fourthly . . ."   ,,   p. 14.   ,,   ,, 32.
p. 649. "The sixt place . . ."   ,,   p. 24.   ,,   ,, 47.
p. 652. "What cov'nant . . ."   ,,   p. 28.   ,,   ,, 53.
p. 655. "For this is . . ."   ,,   p. 49.   ,,   ,, 83.
p. 659. "And that we . . ."   ,,   p. 65.   ,,   ,, 107.
p. 660. "Thus at length . . ."   ,,   p. 69.   ,,   ,, 113.
p. 669. "Let not therfore . . ."   ,,   p. 81.   ,,   ,, 130.

    (Second Ed.: 88 small quarto pages of text.)

    * *The Works of John Milton* . . . (Bickers) 1863.

OF EDUCATION . . .
p. 671. Herein complete.　　　　　　　　　　　Mitford: IV. 379.
　　(Reprint at the end of the Second Ed. of Milton's minor poems:
　　pages 95-117.)

AREOPAGITICA . . .
p. 683. Herein complete.　　　　　　　　　　　Mitford: IV. 395.
　　　　　　(First Ed.: 40 small quarto pages of text.)

TETRACHORDON . . .
p. 726. "For man to be . . ."　1st Ed.: p.　8.　Mitford: IV. 155.
p. 727. "What therefore . . ."　　　"　　p. 47.　　　"　　　　"　213.
　　　　　　(First Ed.: 104 small quarto pages of text.)

COLASTERION . . .
p. 728. "I have now . . ."　　　1st Ed.: p. 26.　Mitford: IV. 376.
　　　　　　(First Ed.: 27 small quarto pages of text.)

THE TENURE OF KINGS AND MAGISTRATES . . .
p. 729. "For Divines . . ."　　2nd Ed.: p. 57.　Mitford: IV. 499.
　　　　　　(Second Ed.: 60 small quarto pages of text.)

THE READIE AND EASIE WAY TO ESTABLISH A FREE
　　COMMONWEALTH . . .*
p. 730. "After our . . ."　　　　　　　　　　　Mitford: V　425.
p. 735. "But admit . . ."　　　　　　　　　　　　　"　　"　443.
p. 736. "Yet neither . . ."　　　　　　　　　　　　"　　"　444.
p. 737. "The whole free-
　　　　　dom . . ."　　　　　　　　　　　　　　　"　　"　447.

THE HISTORY OF BRITAIN . . .
p. 743. "I am now . . ."　　　　　1st Ed.: p. 31. Mitford: V.　28.
p. 743. "But at Cæsars . . ."　　　　"　　p. 47.　　"　　"　44.
p. 745. "Suetonius . . ."　　　　　　"　　p. 65.　　"　　"　60.
p. 747. "For Britan . . ."　　　2nd Ed. addition　"　　"　100.
p. 747. "Thus much . . ."　　　1st Ed. p. 146.　"　　"　146.
p. 751. "Thus representing . . ."　　"　　p. 172.　"　　"　171.
　　　　　　(First Ed.: 308 small quarto pages of text.)

* There is no copy of the Second—enlarged and otherwise modified
—Edition in the British Museum or Bodleian Libraries. A First Edition text is given, with the Second Edition variants, by Mr. E. M. Clark
in volume 51 of *Yale Studies in English*, 1915. The Second Edition
text, which he took from the copy in the library of Mr. W. A. White
of New York City, differs a good deal in spelling and the employment of capital letters from the Mitford version: in which the spelling, on the whole, is more modern and the capitals are much more
elaborately disposed. The latter circumstance appears to indicate
that Mitford printed from a more carefully prepared—and possibly
later—edition. His text has, accordingly, been adopted here.